Lecture Notes in Computer Science 2126

Edited by G. Goos, J. Hartmanis and J. van Leeuwen

Lecture Notes in Computer Science 2126
Edited by G. Goos, J. Hartmanis, and J. van Leeuwen

Springer
Berlin
Heidelberg
New York
Barcelona
Hong Kong
London
Milan
Paris
Singapore
Tokyo

Patrick Cousot (Ed.)

Static Analysis

8th International Symposium, SAS 2001
Paris, France, July 16-18, 2001
Proceedings

 Springer

Series Editors

Gerhard Goos, Karlsruhe University, Germany
Juris Hartmanis, Cornell University, NY, USA
Jan van Leeuwen, Utrecht University, The Netherlands

Volume Editors

Patrick Cousot
École Normale Supérieure, Département d'Informatique
45 rue d'Ulm, 75230 Paris Cedex 05, France
E-mail: Patrick.Cousot@ens.fr

Cataloging-in-Publication Data applied for

Die Deutsche Bibliothek - CIP-Einheitsaufnahme

Static analysis : 8th international symposium ; proceedings / SAS 2001,
Paris, France, July 16 - 18, 2001. Patrick Cousot (ed.). - Berlin ;
Heidelberg ; New York ; Barcelona ; Hong Kong ; London ; Milan ; Paris ;
Singapore ; Tokyo : Springer, 2001
 (Lecture notes in computer science ; Vol. 2126)
 ISBN 3-540-42314-1

CR Subject Classification (1998): D.1, D.2.8, D.3.2-3, F.3.1-2, F.4.2

ISSN 0302-9743
ISBN 3-540-42314-1 Springer-Verlag Berlin Heidelberg New York

Springer-Verlag Berlin Heidelberg New York
a member of BertelsmannSpringer Science+Business Media GmbH

http://www.springer.de

© Springer-Verlag Berlin Heidelberg 2001
Printed in Germany

Typesetting: Camera-ready by author, data conversion by Christian Grosche, Hamburg
Printed on acid-free paper   SPIN: 10839956   06/3142   5 4 3 2 1 0

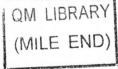

Preface

Static analysis is a research area aimed at developing principles and tools for verification and semantics-based manipulation of programs and high-performance implementation of programming languages. The series of Static Analysis Symposia is a forum for the presentation and discussion of advances in the area.

This volume contains the papers presented at the Eighth International Static Analysis Symposium (SAS 2001), which was held July 16–18, 2001 at the Sorbonne in Paris, France. Previous SAS symposia were held in Santa Barbara, CA, USA (LNCS 1824), Venice, Italy (LNCS 1694), Pisa, Italy (LNCS 1503), Paris, France (LNCS 1302), Aachen, Germany (LNCS 1145), Glasgow, UK (LNCS 983), Namur, Belgium (LNCS 864), following the international workshop WSA in Padova, Italy (LNCS 724), Bordeaux, France (Bigre Vol. 81-82) and JTASPEFL/WSA, Bordeaux, France (Bigre Vol. 74).

The program committee meeting was held at the École Normale Supérieure in Paris on March 31, 2001, and 21 papers were selected from 62 submissions. In addition to the contributed papers, this volume includes invited papers by Rustan LEINO and Martin RINARD. This volume also contains the abstracts of an invited talk by Fred SCHNEIDER and of the presentations by Bruno BLANCHET, Andrew GORDON, Andrew MYERS, and David WAGNER at an invited session on security.

May 2001   Patrick COUSOT

Program Committee

Patrick COUSOT (Chair)	École Normale Supérieure, Paris, France
Maurice BRUYNOOGHE	Katholieke Universiteit Leuven, Belgium
Gilberto FILÉ	Università degli Studi di Padova, Italy
Masami HAGIYA	University of Tokyo, Japan
Chris HANKIN	Imperial College, London, UK
Laurie HENDREN	McGill University, Montreal, Canada
Manuel HERMENEGILDO	Universidad Politécnica de Madrid, Spain
Neil D. JONES	DIKU, University of Copenhagen Denmark
James LARUS	Microsoft Research, Redmond, USA
Jens PALSBERG	Purdue University, USA
Shmuel SAGIV	Tel-Aviv University, Israel
David SANDS	Chalmers University of Technology and University of Göteborg, Sweden
David SCHMIDT	Kansas State University, USA
Mary Lou SOFFA	University of Pittsburgh , USA
Harald SØNDERGAARD	The University of Melbourne, Australia
Reinhard WILHELM	Universität des Saarlandes, Germany
Kwangkeun YI	KAIST, Taejon, Korea

General Chair

Radhia COUSOT	CNRS & École Polytechnique, Paris, France

Referees

Joonseon Ahn	Jungtaek Kim	Prakash Panangaden
Francisco Bueno	Naoki Kobayashi	Corina Pasareanu
Michele Bugliesi	Marc Langenbach	German Puebla
Daniel Cabeza	Peeter Laud	G. Ramalingam
Luca Cardelli	Julia Lawall	Francesco Ranzato
Manuel Carro	Michael Leuschel	Sukyoung Ryu
Livio Colussi	Pedro Lopez-Garcia	Ran Shaham
Agostino Cortesi	Henning Makholm	Joern Schneider
Jérôme Feret	Damien Massé	Alexander Serebrenik
Danny De Schreye	Laurent Mauborgne	Nikola Shilov
Nurit Dor	Antoine Miné	Zoltan Somogyi
Roberto Giacobazzi	Torben Mogensen	Vugranam C. Sreedhar
Michael Huth	Peter Môller Neergaard	Peter Stuckey
Gerda Janssens	David Monniaux	Martin Sulzmann
Daniel Kaestner	Laszlo Nemeth	Ulrich Ultes-Nitsche
Mahmut Kandemir	Flemming Nielson	Sofie Verbaeten

Sponsoring Institutions

The SAS 2001 conference was supported by the following organizations:
Centre National de la Recherche Scientifique (CNRS),
École Normale Supérieure,
École Polytechnique,
Ministère de la Recherche.

The SAS 2001 conference was organized in cooperation with the European Association for Programming Languages and Systems (EAPLS).

Table of Contents

Invited Paper

Data Structures

Pointer Analysis

Model Checking

Abstract Model Checking

Invited Talk

Mobility

Invited Session on Security

Analysis of Multithreaded Programs

Martin Rinard

Laboratory for Computer Science
Massachusetts Institute of Technology
Cambridge, MA 02139
rinard@lcs.mit.edu
http//:www.cag.lcs.mit.edu/~rinard

Abstract. The field of program analysis has focused primarily on sequential programming languages. But multithreading is becoming increasingly important, both as a program structuring mechanism and to support efficient parallel computations. This paper surveys research in analysis for multithreaded programs, focusing on ways to improve the efficiency of analyzing interactions between threads, to detect data races, and to ameliorate the impact of weak memory consistency models. We identify two distinct classes of multithreaded programs, activity management programs and parallel computing programs, and discuss how the structure of these kinds of programs leads to different solutions to these problems. Specifically, we conclude that augmented type systems are the most promising approach for activity management programs, while targeted program analyses are the most promising approach for parallel computing programs.

1 Introduction

Multithreading is a widely used structuring technique for modern software. Programmers use multiple threads of control for a variety of reasons: to build responsive servers that interact with multiple clients, to run computations in parallel on a multiprocessor for performance, and as a structuring mechanism for implementing rich user interfaces. In general, threads are useful whenever the software needs to manage a set of tasks with varying interaction latencies, exploit multiple physical resources, or execute largely independent tasks in response to multiple external events.

Developing analyses for multithreaded programs can be a challenging activity. The primary complication is characterizing the effect of the interactions between threads. The obvious approach of analyzing all interleavings of statements from parallel threads fails because of the resulting exponential analysis times. A central challenge is therefore developing efficient abstractions and analyses that capture the effect of each thread's actions on other parallel threads.

Researchers have identified several ways to use the results of analyzing multithreaded programs. Multithreading enables several new kinds of programming errors; the potential severity of these errors and difficulty of exposing them via

P. Cousot (Ed.): SAS 2001, LNCS 2126, pp. 1–19, 2001.

testing has inspired the development of analyses that detect these errors stat- ically. Most of the research in this area has focused on detecting data races (which occur when two threads access the same data without synchronization and one of the accesses is a write) and deadlocks (which occur when threads are permanently blocked waiting for resources). Researchers have also developed optimizations for multithreaded programs; some of these optimizations gener- alize existing optimizations for sequential programs while others are specific to multithreaded programs.

After surveying research in the analysis and optimization of multithreaded programs, we discuss the issues associated with detecting data races in more depth. We first identify two distinct classes of multithreaded programs, *activity management programs*, which use threads to manage a set of conceptually concurrent activities, and *parallel computing programs*, which use threads to ex- ecute computations in parallel for performance on a multiprocessor. For activity management programs, we conclude that the appropriate mechanism is an aug- mented type system that guarantees that the program is free of data races. Because such a type system would provide information about the potential in- teractions between parallel threads, it could also serve as a foundation for new, very precise analyses. For parallel computing programs, we conclude that the ap- propriate mechanism is a set of specialized analyses, each tailored for a specific concurrency and data usage pattern.

The remainder of the paper is structured as follows. Section 2 surveys uses of the analysis information while Section 3 discusses the analyses researchers have developed for multithreaded programs, focusing on ways to improve the efficiency of analyzing interactions between parallel threads. Sections 4 and 5 discuss data race detection for activity management programs and parallel com- puting programs, respectively. Section 6 presents several issues associated with the use of weak memory consistency models. We conclude in Section 7.

2   Analysis Uses

Researchers have proposed several uses for analysis information extracted from multithreaded programs. The first use is to enable optimizations, both gener- alizations of traditional compiler optimizations to multithreaded programs and optimizations that make sense only for multithreaded programs. The second use is to detect anomalies in the parallel execution such as data races or deadlock.

2.1   Optimization Uses

A problem with directly applying traditional compiler optimizations to multi- threaded programs is that the optimizations may reorder accesses to shared data in ways that may be observed by threads running concurrently with the trans- formed thread [72]. One approach is to generalize standard program representa- tions, analyses, and transformations to safely optimize multithreaded programs even in the presence of accesses to shared data [91, 87, 57, 62, 56, 64]. The presence of multithreading may also inspire optimizations with no obvious counterpart in the optimization of sequential programs. Examples include communication optimizations [59, 100], optimizing mutual exclusion synchronization [30, 31, 79, 3, 98, 11, 13, 21, 82], and optimizing barrier synchronization [96]. A more conservative approach is to ensure that the optimizations preserve the semantics of the original program by first identifying regions of the program that do not interact with other threads, then applying optimizations only within these regions. The analysis problem is determining which statements may interact with other threads and which may not. Escape analysis is an obvious analysis to use for this purpose — it recognizes data that is captured within the current thread and therefore inaccessible to other threads [11, 21, 98, 13, 82]. The programming model may also separate shared and private data [92, 89, 81, 58], in some cases the analysis may automatically infer when pointers point to private data [65]. More elaborate analyses may recognize actions (such as acquiring a mutual exclusion lock or obtaining the only existing reference to an object) that temporarily give the thread exclusive access to specific objects potentially accessed by multiple threads. A final approach is to expect the programmer to correctly synchronize the program, then enable traditional compiler optimizations within any region that does not contain an action (for example, a synchronization action or thread creation action) that is designed to mediate interactions between threads [78]. This approach has the advantage that it eliminates the need to perform a potentially expensive interthread analysis as a prerequisite for applying traditional optimizations to multithreaded programs. The (serious) disadvantage is that optimization may change the result that the program computes.

2.2   Data Race Detection

In an unsafe language like C, there are a number of program actions that are almost always the result of programmer error, regardless of the context in which they occur. Examples include array bounds violations and accessing memory after it has been deallocated. If the program engages in these actions, it can produce behavior that is very difficult to understand. Several well-known language design and implementation techniques (garbage collection, array bounds checks) can completely eliminate these kinds of errors. The cost is additional execution overhead and a loss of programmer control over aspects of the program's execution. The result was that, for many years, the dominant programming programming language (C) provided no protection at all against this class of errors.

For programs that use threads, an analogous error is a data race, which occurs when multiple threads access the same data without an intervening synchronization operation, and one of the accesses is a write. A data race is almost always the result of a programming error, with a common outcome being the corruption of the accessed data structures. The fact that data races may show up only intermittently due to different timings on different executions adds an extra layer of complexity not present for sequential programs. The most widely used multithreaded languages, Java, C, and C++ (augmented with a threads package), leave the programmer totally responsible for avoiding data races by correctly synchronizing the computation. The result is that many systems builders view the use of threads as an inherently unsafe programming practice [76].

Presented with this problem, researchers have developed a set of analyses for determining if a program may have a data race. Some analyses allow the programmer to declare an association between data and locks, then check that the program holds the lock whenever it accesses the corresponding data [94, 28]. Other analyses trace the control transfers associated with the use of synchronization constructs such as the post and wait constructs used in parallel dialects of Fortran [71, 18, 36, 17], the Ada rendezvous constructs [95, 99, 33, 70, 35], or the Java wait and notify constructs [73, 74]. The goal is to determine that the synchronization actions temporally separate conflicting accesses to shared data. In some cases it may be important to recognize that parallel tasks access disjoint regions of the same data structure. Researchers have developed many sophisticated techniques for extracting or verifying this kind of information. There are two broad categories: analyses that characterize the accessed regions of dense matrices [8, 53, 7, 50, 77, 9, 5, 38, 47, 84], and analyses that extract or verify reachability properties of linked data structures [60, 19, 51, 43, 85]. Although many of these analyses were originally developed for the automatic parallelization of sequential programs, the basic approaches should generalize to handle the appropriate kinds of multithreaded programs. Researchers have also developed dynamic race detection algorithms, which monitor a running program to detect races in that specific execution [32, 88, 20], but provide no guarantees about other executions.

Despite the sophistication of existing static techniques, the diversity and complexity of sharing patterns in multithreaded programs means that the static data race detection problem is still far from solved. In fact, as we discuss further in Section 4, we believe the ultimate solution for most programs will involve an augmented type system that eliminates the possibility of data races at the language level.

2.3   Deadlock Detection

Researchers have developed a variety of analyses for detecting potential deadlocks in Ada programs which use rendezvous synchronization [95, 99, 69, 29, 66, 34, 24, 16, 12]. A rendezvous takes place between a call statement in one thread and an accept statement in another. The analyses match corresponding calls and accepts to determine if every call will eventually participate in a rendezvous. If not, the program is considered to deadlock. We note that deadlock traditionally arises from circular waiting to acquire resources, and is a classic problem in multithreaded programs. In this context, programs typically use mutual exclusion synchronization rather than rendezvous synchronization. We expect that a deadlock detection analysis for programs that use mutual exclusion synchronization would obtain a partial order on the acquired resources and check that the program always respects this order. The order could be obtained from the programmer or extracted automatically from an analysis of the program.

3   Analysis Algorithms

We next discuss some of the issues that arise when applying standard approaches to analyze multithreaded programs. We focus on ways to improve the efficiency of analyzing interactions between different threads.

3.1   Dataflow Analysis for Multithreaded Programs

Dataflow analysis performs an abstract interpretation of the program to discover program invariants at each program point [55, 54, 26]. Conceptually, one can view these analyses as propagating information along control-flow paths, an approach that works reasonably well for sequential programs in part because each statement typically has few direct control-flow successors. The straightforward generalization of this approach to multithreaded programs would propagate information between statements of parallel threads [27, 22]. The issue is that the direct control-flow successors of a statement in one thread typically include most if not all of the statements in all parallel threads. Propagating information along all of these potential control-flow edges leads to an algorithm with intractable execution times. The driving question is how to reduce the number of paths that the analysis must explicitly consider.

Control-Flow Analysis. One approach is to analyze the program's use of synchronization constructs to discover regions of tasks that may not execute concurrently, then remove edges between these regions. The characteristics of the analysis depend on the specific synchronization constructs. Researchers have developed algorithms for programs that use the post and wait constructs used in parallel dialects of Fortran [18, 36, 17], for the Ada rendezvous constructs [95, 33, 70, 35], and for the Java wait and notify constructs [73, 74]. The basic idea behind these algorithms is to match each blocking action (such as a wait or accept) with its potential corresponding trigger actions (such as post or notify) from other threads. The analysis uses the information to determine that the statements before the trigger action must execute before the statements after the blocking action.

   In general, the algorithms for post and wait constructs are designed to work within parallel loops that access dense matrices. These programs use the post and wait constructs to ensure that a write to an array element in one parallel loop iteration precedes reads to that same element in other iterations. The techniques therefore focus on correlating the array accesses with the corresponding post and wait constructs that order them. The algorithms for the Ada rendezvous and Java wait and notify constructs tend to be most effective for programs in which the threads execute different code, enabling the analysis to distinguish between threads at the level of the code that each thread executes. We expect the algorithms to be less effective for server programs in which many threads execute the same code [61].

Coarsening the Analysis Granularity. Another way to reduce the analysis time is to collect adjacent instructions from threads into larger groups, then treat each group as a unit in the interthread analysis [97, 45, 23, 75]. The typical approach is to collect together instructions that do not interact with other threads; in this case the resulting coarsening of the analysis granularity does not affect the precision of the final analysis result. Because the relevant interactions usually take place at instructions from different threads that access the same data, the presence of references may significantly complicate the determination of which instructions may interact with other threads. One approach is to interleave a pointer analysis with the analysis that determines the instructions that may interact with other threads [23, 25], another approach would use the results of a previous efficient pointer analysis to find these instructions (candidate analyses include flow-insensitive analyses [93, 4] and analyses that do not analyze interleavings of instructions from different threads [83]).

Interference-Based Analyses. Interference-based analyses maximally coarsen the analysis granularity — they analyze each thread as a unit to compute a result that characterizes all potential interactions with other threads. The extracted analysis information then flows from the end of each thread to the beginning of all other parallel threads. For standard bitvector analyses such as live variables and reaching definitions, this approach somewhat surprisingly delivers an efficient algorithm with the same precision as an algorithm that explicitly analyzes all possible interleavings [57]. For more complicated analyses such as pointer analysis, existing algorithms based on this approach overestimate the effect of potential interactions between threads and lose precision [83, 86]. Finally, if the language semantics rules out the possibility of interactions between tasks, analyzing each task as a unit seems obviously the correct way to proceed [46].

3.2 Flow-Insensitive Analyses

Unlike dataflow analyses, flow-insensitive analyses produce the same result regardless of the order in which the statements appear in the program or the number of times that they are executed [93, 4, 37]. They therefore trivially extend to handle multithreaded programs. The analysis results can be used directly or as a foundation to enhance the effectiveness of more detailed flow-sensitive analyses.

3.3 Challenges

The primary challenge for analyzing multithreaded programs remains developing abstractions and analyses that precisely characterize interactions between threads. For explicit interactions that take place at synchronization constructs, the primary goal is to match interacting pairs of constructs. For implicit interactions that take place at memory locations accessed by multiple threads, the primary goal is to find instructions that access the same memory locations, then characterize the combined effect of the instructions. The use of dynamic memory allocation, object references, and arrays significantly complicates the analysis of these implicit interactions because they force the analysis to disambiguate the accesses to avoid analyzing interactions that never occur when the program runs. The problem is especially acute for programs that use references because interactions between instructions that access references may, in turn, affect the locations that other instructions access. One of the main challenges is therefore to develop efficient disambiguation analyses for multithreaded programs. We see several potential foundations for these analyses: an augmented type system (see Section 4), efficient interference-based or flow-insensitive pointer analyses, or exploiting structured control constructs such as parallel loops to confine the concurrency to a small part of the program and enable the use of very precise, detailed analyses.

Many existing analyses assume a very simple model of multithreaded execution characterized by the absence of one or more of dynamic object creation, dynamic thread creation, references to objects (including thread objects), and procedure or method calls. Given the pervasive use of these constructs in many multithreaded programs, an important challenge is to develop algorithms that can successfully analyze programs that use these constructs.

4   Data Race Freedom in Activity Management Programs

Given the problems associated with data races and the current inability of automated techniques to verify that a range of programs are free of data races, techniques that guarantee data race freedom are of interest. The primary issue that shapes the field is the reason for using multiple threads and the resulting data usage patterns of the program. In this section we focus on *activity management programs*, or programs that use threads to manage a set of conceptually parallel activities such as interacting with a remote client [10, 49]. Because of the loose connection between the computations of the threads, these programs typically use an unstructured form of concurrency in which each thread executes independently of its parent thread. These programs typically manipulate several different kinds of data with different synchronization requirements. To successfully verify data race freedom for these programs, the implementation must take these differences into account and use algorithms tailored for the properties that are relevant for each kind of data.

- **Private Data:** Data accessed by only a single thread.
- **Inherited Data:** Data created or initialized by a parent thread, then passed as a parameter to a child thread. Once the child threads starts its execution, the parent thread no longer accesses the data.
- **Migrating Data:** Data that is passed between parallel threads, often as part of producer/consumer relationships. Although multiple threads access migrating data, at each point in time there is a single thread that has conceptual ownership of the data and no other threads access the data until ownership changes.

- **Published Data:** Data that is initialized by a single thread, then distributed to multiple reader threads for read-only access.
- **Mutex Data:** Data that is potentially accessed and updated by multiple parallel threads, with the updates kept consistent with mutual exclusion synchronization.
- **Reader/Writer Data:** An extension of mutex data to support concurrent access by readers and exclusive access by writers.

Program actions temporally separate accesses from different threads and ensure data race freedom. For inherited data, the thread creation action separates the parent accesses from the child accesses. For mutex and reader/writer data, the lock acquire and release actions separate accesses from different threads. For published data, the action that makes a reference to the data accessible to multiple reader threads separates the writes of the initializing thread from the reads of the reader threads. For migrating data, the actions that transfer ownership of the data from one thread to the next separate the accesses. Mutex, published, and migrating data often work together to implement common communication patterns in multithreaded programs. For example, a shared queue usually contains mutex data (the queue header) and migrating data (the elements of the queue).

Given the diversity of the different kinds of data and the complexity of their access patterns, we believe it will be extremely difficult for any analysis to automatically reconstruct enough information to verify data race freedom in the full range of activity management programs. We therefore focus on language mechanisms that enable the programmer and the analysis to work together to establish that the program is free of data races.

4.1   Augmented Type Systems for Race-Free Programs

Many of the first researchers to write multithreaded programs were acutely aware of the possibility of data races, and developed languages that prevented the programmer from writing programs that contained them. The basic idea was to force each thread to acquire exclusive ownership of data before writing it, either by acquiring a lock on the data or by ensuring that the data is inaccessible to other threads. Concurrent Pascal, for example, carefully limits the use of references to ensure that the sharing between threads takes place only via data copied into and out of mutex data encapsulated in monitors [15]. In effect, the language uses copy operations to convert migrating, inherited, and published data into private data. Because these copy operations take place in the context of a synchronized update to mutex data, they execute atomically with respect to the threads sharing the data. It is possible to generalize this approach to handle a wider range of data structures, including linked data structures containing references [6].

Another approach is to provide an augmented type system that enables the programmer to explicitly identify shared data accessible to multiple threads [40, 41, 14]. Each piece of shared data is associated with a mutual exclusion lock and the type system enforces the constraint that the program holds the associated lock whenever it accesses the corresponding shared data. The type system may also support a variety of other kinds of data that can be safely accessed without synchronization; examples include private data accessible to only a single thread, constant data that is never modified once it has been initialized, and value data that may be copied into and out of shared data. It is also possible to use a linear type system to ensure the existence of at most one reference to a given piece of data, with the data owned by the thread that holds its reference [14]. In this scenario, the movements of inherited and migrating data between threads correspond to acquisitions and releases of the unique reference to the moving data.

In spirit, these type systems extend the basic safe monitor approach developed in the 1970s to work for modern languages with linked data structures. The key challenge is controlling the use of references to eliminate the possibility of inadvertently making unsynchronized data reachable to multiple threads concurrently. Note that the most general solution to this problem would be to track all references to inherited, migrating, or published data and verify that threads did not use these references to incorrectly access the data. The difficulty of solving this general problem inspired the variety of other, more constrained, solutions described above.

4.2   Future Directions in Augmented Type Systems

The next step is to use some combination of language design and program analysis to better understand the referencing behavior of the program and support a wider range of thread interaction patterns. We anticipate that the implementation will focus on inherited, migrating, and published data. We view the situation for mutex and read/write data as comparatively settled — current type systems or their relatively straightforward generalizations should be adequate for ensuring that mutex data is correctly synchronized. The implementation will therefore focus on extracting or verifying the following kinds of information:

- **Reachability:** We anticipate that the implementation will use reachability information to verify the correct use of private, migrating, and inherited data. Specifically, it will verify that private data is reachable only from the thread that initially created the data and that when an ownership change takes place for inherited or migrating data, the data is inaccessible to the previous owner.
- **Write Checking:** For published data, which is reachable to multiple threads, the implementation must verify that the data is never written once it becomes accessible to multiple threads. There are two key components: identifying the transition from writable to read only, and verifying the absence of writes after the transition.

  For read/write data, we anticipate that programmers will use locking constructs that enable reads to execute concurrently but serialize writes with respect to all other accesses. The implementation must verify that all reads are protected by a held read lock and all writes are protected by a held write lock.

4.3   Impact on Other Analyses

Because the augmented type information would enable the analysis to dramatically reduce the number of potential interthread interactions that it must consider, we expect it to enable researchers to develop quite precise and practical analyses that extract or verify detailed properties of the shared data. We anticipate an approach that divides the program into atomic regions that access only shared or private data, then analyzes the program at the granularity of these regions. The analysis would analyze sequential interactions between regions from the same thread and some subset of the interleaved interactions between regions from different threads that access the same data, obtaining a result valid for all interleavings that might occur when the program runs. In effect, the analysis would view each region as an operation on shared or private data. Potentially extracted or verified properties include representation invariants for shared data, monotonicity properties of operations on shared data, and recognition of sets of commuting operations on shared data.

4.4   Adoption Prospects

For activity management programs, we anticipate that it will be both technically feasible and valuable to develop an expressive augmented type system that guarantees data race freedom. The key question is whether such a type system would be accepted in practice. Factors that would influence its acceptance include how widespread multithreaded programming becomes, the ability of programmers to develop programs without data races in the absences of such a type system, the consequences of the data races programmers leave in the code, how well the extended type system supports the full range of thread interaction patterns, and whether programmers perceive the extended information as a burden or a benefit. One potential approach might separate the extended type information from the rest of program, enabling programmers to use the standard type system for sequential programs and the extended system for multithreaded programs. Another approach might provide standard defaults that work for most cases, with the programmer adjusting the defaults only when necessary. We note that over time, sequential languages have moved towards providing more safety guarantees, which argues for acceptance of increased safety in multithreaded languages.

5   Data Race Freedom in Parallel Computing Programs

Parallel computing programs use threads to subdivide a single computational task into multiple parallel subtasks for execution on a multiprocessor. Unlike activity management programs, parallel computing programs often execute a sequence of steps, with the concurrency exploited within but not between steps.

The structure therefore closely corresponds to the structure one would use for a sequential program that performed the same computation. Because different steps may use the same piece of data in different ways, it is crucial for the implementation to identify the threads in different phases and treat each phase separately. The difficulty of identifying parallel phases depends on the specific concurrency generation constructs. If the program uses long-lived threads that persist across steps but periodically synchronize at a barrier, reconstructing the structure is a challenging analysis problem [2]. If the program uses structured control constructs such as parallel loops or recursively generates parallel computations in a divide and conquer fashion [42], the parallel phases are obvious from the syntactic structure of the program.

Parallel computing programs use many of the same kinds of data as activity management programs. An additional complication is the fact that the parallel tasks often access disjoint parts of the same data structure. Over the years researchers have developed many sophisticated techniques for extracting or verifying this kind of information, both for programs that access dense matrices [8, 53, 7, 50, 77, 9, 5, 38, 47, 84] and for programs that manipulate linked data structures [60, 19, 51, 43, 85]. Parallel computing programs may also use reductions and commuting operations, in which case it may be important to generalize algorithms from the field of automatic parallelization to verify that the program executes deterministically [39, 44, 48, 80]. In general, the programmer can reasonably develop programs with quite sophisticated access patterns and data structures, with the data race freedom of the program depending on the detailed properties of the data structures and the algorithms that manipulate them. It therefore seems unlikely that a general approach would be able to verify data race freedom for the full range of parallel computing programs.

Because of the close correspondence between the parallel and sequential versions of the program, it is often useful to view the threading constructs in parallel computing programs as annotations that express the programmer's expectations about the lack of dependences between parts of the program rather than as constructs that must generate parallel computation to preserve the semantics of the program. In this context, the analysis problem would be framed as a sequential program analysis that determines whether the identified parts of the program lack dependences. An advantage of this approach is that it eliminates the need to analyze interactions between parallel threads.

In general, we view guaranteed data race freedom as both less feasible and potentially less important for parallel computing programs than for activity management programs. It is less feasible because it may depend on very detailed properties of arbitrarily sophisticated array access patterns or linked data structures. It is potentially less important because the parallelism tends to be confined within single parallel algorithms rather than operating across the entire execution of the program. While the algorithms in parallel computing programs may have very complicated internal structure, the fact that the potential interactions can be localized significantly increases the programmer's ability to avoid inadvertent data races. Somewhat paradoxically, these properties raise the value of automatic program analysis algorithms that can verify the data race freedom of parallel computing programs. There is room for a suite of targeted analyses, each of which is designed to analyze programs that access a certain kind of data in a certain way. The ability to confine the concurrency within a small part of the program makes it feasible to use very detailed, precise analyses.

6   Weak Memory Consistency Models

For a variety of performance reasons, many implementations of multithreaded languages have a weak memory consistency model that allows the implementation to change the order in which writes from one thread are observed in parallel threads [1, 78]. Moreover, standard weak consistency models enable executions in which different threads observe different orders for the same sequence of writes from a parallel thread. Weak consistency models are often considered to be counterintuitive because they break the abstraction of a single memory accessed by sequentially executing threads [52].

One might wonder how programmers are expected to successfully develop programs in languages with weak memory consistency models. Conceptually, weak consistency models do not reorder writes across synchronization operations. So the intention is that programmers will write properly synchronized, data-race free programs and never observe the reorderings. It is worth noting that weak consistency models are complex enough that researchers are still in the process of developing a rigorous semantics for them [67, 68]. And the proposed semantics are significantly more complicated than the standard semantics for multithreaded programs, which simply interleave the statements from parallel threads.

6.1   Short-Term Program Analysis Opportunities

In the short term, weak memory consistency models will be a fact of life for developers of multithreaded software. Most modern processors implement weak consistency models in hardware, and Java specifies a weak consistency model for multithreaded programs, in part because if threads can access shared data without synchronization, many standard compiler optimizations may change the order in which threads perform (and other threads potentially observe) accesses to shared data [78]. In this context, the alternative to a weak consistency model is to disable these optimizations unless the compiler performs the global analysis required to determine that parallel threads do not observe the reordered memory accesses [59, 64]. Requiring the extraction of this kind of global information as part of the standard compilation process is clearly problematic, primarily because it rules out optimized separate compilation.

Another approach is to develop analyses and transformations that restore the abstraction of a single consistent shared memory with no reordered writes. The basic idea is to analyze the program, discover situations in which the threads may observe reordered writes, then augment the program with additional instructions that prevent the hardware from reordering these writes [90, 63]. This research holds out the promise of providing the efficiency of a weak memory consistency model in the implementation combined with the abstraction of a single shared memory for the programmer. Because programs do not observe the effect of a weak consistency model unless they access shared data without explicit synchronization, we see these techniques as appropriate primarily for low-level programs that synthesize their own custom synchronization operations out of shared memory.

6.2   Impact on Existing Analysis Algorithms

Almost all existing analyses for multithreaded programs assume an interleaving model of concurrency. But weak consistency models generally increase the set of possible program behaviors as compared with the standard interleaving model, raising the possibility that existing analyses are unsound in the presence of weak consistency models. Furthermore, the complexity of the semantics for programs with weak consistency models increases the difficulty of developing provably sound analyses for these programs. We suspect that many existing analyses are sound for programs with weak consistency models [4, 93, 37, 57, 83], but this soundness is clearly inadvertent, in some cases a consequence of imprecision in the analysis, and not necessarily obvious to prove formally.

We expect the difficulty of dealing with weak memory consistency models to inspire multiphase approaches. The first phase will either verify the absence of data races or transform the program to ensure that it does not observe any of the possible reorderings. The subsequent phases will then assume the simpler interleaving model of concurrency. Another alternative would be to use an augmented type system that guarantees race-free programs (see Section 4). The analysis could use the type information to identify regions within which it could aggressively reorder accesses to optimize the program without changing the result that the program computes.

7   Conclusion

Multithreaded programs are significantly more complicated to analyze than sequential programs. Many analyses have focused on characterizing interactions between threads to detect safety problems such as data races and deadlock or to hide anomalies associated with weak memory consistency models. Future directions include generalizing abstractions and analyses to better handle constructs such as dynamically allocated memory, dynamic thread creation, procedures and methods, and threads as first-class objects. We also anticipate the further development of augmented type systems for race-free programs, which will reduce the potential interthread interactions that the analysis must consider and enable the development and use of more detailed, precise analyses.

References

1. S. Adve and K. Gharachorloo. Shared memory consistency models: a tutorial. *IEEE Computer*, 29(12):66–76, Dec. 1996.
2. A. Aiken and D. Gay. Barrier inference. In *Proceedings of the 25th Annual ACM Symposium on the Principles of Programming Languages*, Paris, France, Jan. 1998. ACM.
3. J. Aldrich, C. Chambers, E. Sirer, and S. Eggers. Static analyses for eliminating unnecessary synchronization from Java programs. In *Proceedings of the 6th International Static Analysis Symposium*, Sept. 1999.
4. L. O. Andersen. *Program Analysis and Specialization for the C Programming Language*. PhD thesis, DIKU, University of Copenhagen, May 1994.
5. D. Bacon, S. Graham, and O. Sharp. Compiler transformations for high-performance computing. *ACM Computing Surveys*, 26(4):345–420, Dec. 1994.
6. D. Bacon, R. Strom, and A. Tarafdar. Guava: A dialect of Java without data races. In *Proceedings of the 15th Annual Conference on Object-Oriented Programming Systems, Languages and Applications*, Portland, OR, Oct. 2000.
7. V. Balasundaram and K. Kennedy. A technique for summarizing data access and its use in parallelism enhancing transformations. In *Proceedings of the SIGPLAN '89 Conference on Program Language Design and Implementation*, Portland, OR, June 1989.
8. U. Banerjee. *Dependence Analysis for Supercomputing*. Kluwer Academic Publishers, Boston, MA, 1988.
9. U. Banerjee, R. Eigenmann, A. Nicolau, and D. Padua. Automatic program parallelization. *Proceedings of the IEEE*, 81(2):211–243, Feb. 1993.
10. A. Birrell. *Systems Programming with Modula-3*, chapter An Introduction to Programming with Threads. Prentice-Hall, Englewood Cliffs, N.J., 1991.
11. B. Blanchet. Escape analysis for object oriented languages. application to Java. In *Proceedings of the 14th Annual Conference on Object-Oriented Programming Systems, Languages and Applications*, Denver, CO, Nov. 1999.
12. J. Blieberger, B. Burgstaller, and B. Scholz. Symbolic dataflow analysis for detecting deadlocks in Ada tasking programs. In *Proceedings of the 5th International Conference on Reliable Software Technologies Ada-Europe 2000*, June 2000.
13. J. Bogda and U. Hoelzle. Removing unnecessary synchronization in Java. In *Proceedings of the 14th Annual Conference on Object-Oriented Programming Systems, Languages and Applications*, Denver, CO, Nov. 1999.
14. C. Boyapati and M. Rinard. A parameterized type system for race-free Java programs. In *Proceedings of the 16th Annual Conference on Object-Oriented Programming Systems, Languages and Applications*, Tampa Bay, FL, Oct. 2001.
15. P. Brinch-Hansen. The programming language Concurrent Pascal. *IEEE Transactions on Software Engineering*, SE-1(2):199–207, June 1975.
16. E. Bruneton and J. Pradat-Peyre. Automatic verification of concurrent Ada programs. In *Proceedings of the 4th International Conference on Reliable Software Technologies Ada-Europe 1999*, June 2000.
17. D. Callahan, K. Kennedy, and J. Subhlok. Analysis of event synchronization in a parallel programming tool. In *Proceedings of the 2nd ACM SIGPLAN Symposium on Principles and Practice of Parallel Programming*, Seattle, WA, Mar. 1990.
18. D. Callahan and J. Subhlok. Static analysis of low-level synchronization. In *Proceedings of the ACM SIGPLAN and SIGOPS Workshop on Parallel and Distributed Debugging*, Madison, WI, May 1988.

19. D. Chase, M. Wegman, and F. Zadek. Analysis of pointers and structures. In *Proceedings of the SIGPLAN '90 Conference on Program Language Design and Implementation*, pages 296–310, White Plains, NY, June 1990. ACM, New York.

20. G. Cheng, M. Feng, C. Leiserson, K. Randall, and A. Stark. Detecting data races in Cilk programs that use locks. In *Proceedings of the 10th Annual ACM Symposium on Parallel Algorithms and Architectures*, June 1998.

21. J. Choi, M. Gupta, M. Serrano, V. Sreedhar, and S. Midkiff. Escape analysis for Java. In *Proceedings of the 14th Annual Conference on Object-Oriented Programming Systems, Languages and Applications*, Denver, CO, Nov. 1999.

22. J. Chow and W. Harrison III. Compile time analysis of programs that share memory. In *Proceedings of the 19th Annual ACM Symposium on the Principles of Programming Languages*, Albuquerque, NM, Jan. 1992. ACM, New York.

23. J. Chow and W. Harrison III. State space reduction in abstract interpretation of parallel programs. In *Proceedings of the 1994 IEEE International Conference on Computer Language*, May 1994.

24. J. Corbett. Evaluating deadlock detection methods for concurrent software. *IEEE Transactions on Software Engineering*, 22(3), Mar. 1996.

25. J. Corbett. Using shape analysis to reduce finite-state models of concurrent Java programs. In *Proceedings of the International Symposium on Software Testing and Analysis*, Mar. 1998.

26. P. Cousot and R. Cousot. Abstract Interpretation: A Unified Lattice Model for Static Analysis of Programs by Construction or Approximation of Fixpoints. In *Conference Record of the 4th Annual ACM Symposium on the Principles of Programming Languages*, Los Angeles, CA, 1977.

27. P. Cousot and R. Cousot. *Automatic Program Construction Techniques*, chapter Invariance Proof Methods and Analysis Techniques for Parallel Programs. Macmillan Publishing Company, New York, NY, 1984.

28. D. Detlefs, K. R. Leino, G. Nelson, and J. Saxe. Extended static checking. Technical Report 159, Compaq Systems Research Center, 1998.

29. L. Dillon. Using symbolic execution for verification of Ada tasking programs. *ACM Transactions on Programming Languages and Systems*, 12(4), 1990.

30. P. Diniz and M. Rinard. Synchronization transformations for parallel computing. In *Proceedings of the 24th Annual ACM Symposium on the Principles of Programming Languages*, pages 187–200, Paris, France, Jan. 1997. ACM, New York.

31. P. Diniz and M. Rinard. Lock coarsening: Eliminating lock overhead in automatically parallelized object-based programs. *Journal of Parallel and Distributed Computing*, 49(2):2218–244, Mar. 1998.

32. A. Dinning and E. Schonberg. Detecting access anomalies in programs with critical sections. In *Proceedings of the ACM/ONR Workshop on Parallel and Distributed Debugging*, Santa Cruz, CA, May 1991.

33. E. Duesterwald and M. Soffa. Concurrency analysis in the presence of procedures using a data-flow analysis framework. In *Proceedings of the ACM Symposium on Analysis, Verification, and Testing*, Victoria, B.C., Oct. 1991.

34. S. Duri, U. Buy, R. Devarapalli, and S. Shatz. Application and experimental evaluation of state space reduction methods for deadlock analysis in Ada. *ACM Transactions on Software Engineering and Methodology*, 3(4), Oct. 1994.

35. M. Dwyer and L. Clarke. Data-flow analysis for verifying properties of concurrent programs. In *Proceedings of the 2nd ACM SIGSOFT Symposium on the Foundations of Software Engineering*, New Orleans, LA, Dec. 1994.

36. P. Emrath, S. Ghosh, and D. Padua. Event synchronization analysis for debugging parallel programs. In *Proceedings of Supercomputing '89*, Reno, NV, Nov. 1989. IEEE Computer Society Press, Los Alamitos, Calif.

37. M. Fahndrich, J. Foster, Z. Su, and A. Aiken. Partial online cycle elimination in inclusion constraint graphs. In *Proceedings of the SIGPLAN '98 Conference on Program Language Design and Implementation*, Montreal, Canada, June 1998.

38. P. Feautrier. Compiling for massively parallel architectures: A perspective. *Microprogramming and Microprocessors*, 1995.

39. A. Fisher and A. Ghuloum. Parallelizing complex scans and reductions. In *Proceedings of the SIGPLAN '94 Conference on Program Language Design and Implementation*, pages 135–144, Orlando, FL, June 1994. ACM, New York.

40. C. Flanagan and M. Abadi. Types for safe locking. In *Proceedings of the 8th European Symposium on Programming*, Amsterdam, The Netherlands, Mar. 2000.

41. C. Flanagan and S. Freund. Type-based race detection for Java. In *Proceedings of the SIGPLAN '00 Conference on Program Language Design and Implementation*, Vancouver, Canada, June 2000.

42. M. Frigo, C. Leiserson, and K. Randall. The implementation of the Cilk-5 multithreaded language. In *Proceedings of the SIGPLAN '98 Conference on Program Language Design and Implementation*, Montreal, Canada, June 1998.

43. R. Ghiya and L. Hendren. Is it a tree, a DAG or a cyclic graph? A shape analysis for heap-directed pointers in C. In *Proceedings of the 23rd Annual ACM Symposium on the Principles of Programming Languages*, pages 1–15, Jan. 1996.

44. A. Ghuloum and A. Fisher. Flattening and parallelizing irregular, recurrent loop nests. In *Proceedings of the 5th ACM SIGPLAN Symposium on Principles and Practice of Parallel Programming*, pages 58–67, Santa Barbara, CA, July 1995. ACM, New York.

45. P. Godefroid and P. Wolper. A partial approach to model checking. In *Proceedings of the Sixth Annual IEEE Symposium on Logic in Computer Science*, Amsterdam, The Netherlands, July 1991.

46. D. Grunwald and H. Srinivasan. Data flow equations for explicitly parallel programs. In *Proceedings of the 4th ACM SIGPLAN Symposium on Principles and Practice of Parallel Programming*, San Diego, CA, May 1993.

47. M. Gupta, S. Mukhopadhyay, and N. Sinha. Automatic parallelization of recursive procedures. In *Proceedings of the 1999 Conference on Parallel Algorithms and Compilation Techniques (PACT) '99*, Newport Beach, CA, Oct. 1999.

48. M. Hall, S. Amarasinghe, B. Murphy, S. Liao, and M. Lam. Detecting coarse-grain parallelism using an interprocedural parallelizing compiler. In *Proceedings of Supercomputing '95*, San Diego, CA, Dec. 1995. IEEE Computer Society Press, Los Alamitos, Calif.

49. C. Hauser, C. Jacobi, M. Theimer, B. Welch, and M. Weiser. Using threads in interactive systems: A case study. In *Proceedings of the Fourteenth Symposium on Operating Systems Principles*, Asheville, NC, Dec. 1993.

50. P. Havlak and K. Kennedy. An implementation of interprocedural bounded regular section analysis. *IEEE Transactions on Parallel and Distributed Systems*, 2(3):350–360, July 1991.

51. L. Hendren, J. Hummel, and A. Nicolau. Abstractions for recursive pointer data structures: Improving the analysis and transformation of imperative programs. In *Proceedings of the SIGPLAN '92 Conference on Program Language Design and Implementation*, San Francisco, CA, June 1992. ACM, New York.

52. M. Hill. Multiprocessors should support simple memory consistency models. *IEEE Computer*, 31(8), Aug. 1998.

53. F. Irigoin and R. Triolet. Supernode partitioning. In *Proceedings of the 15th Annual ACM Symposium on the Principles of Programming Languages*, San Diego, CA, Jan. 1988.

54. J. Kam and J. Ullman. Global data flow analysis and iterative algorithms. *Journal of the ACM*, 23(1):159–171, Jan. 1976.

55. G. Kildall. A unified approach to global program optimization. In *Conference Record of the Symposium on Principles of Programming Languages*. ACM, Jan. 1973.

56. J. Knoop and B. Steffen. Code motion for explicitly parallel programs. In *Proceedings of the 7th ACM SIGPLAN Symposium on Principles and Practice of Parallel Programming*, Atlanta, GA, May 1999.

57. J. Knoop, B. Steffen, and J. Vollmer. Parallelism for free: Efficient and optimal bitvector analyses for parallel programs. *ACM Transactions on Programming Languages and Systems*, 18(3):268–299, May 1996.

58. A. Krishnamurthy, D. Culler, A. Dusseau, S. Goldstein, S. Lumetta, T. von Eicken, and K. Yelick. Parallel programming in Split-C. In *Proceedings of Supercomputing '93*, Nov. 1993.

59. A. Krishnamurthy and K. Yelick. Analyses and optimizations for shared address space programs. *Journal of Parallel and Distributed Computing*, 38(2), Nov. 1996.

60. J. Larus and P. Hilfinger. Detecting conflicts between structure accesses. In *Proceedings of the SIGPLAN '88 Conference on Program Language Design and Implementation*, Atlanta, GA, June 1988. ACM, New York.

61. D. Lea. *Concurrent Programming in Java: Design Principles and Patterns*. Addison-Wesley, Reading, Mass., San Mateo, CA, 1996.

62. J. Lee, S. Midkiff, and D. Padua. A constant propagation algorithm for explicitly parallel programs. *International Journal of Parallel Programming*, 26(5), 1998.

63. J. Lee and D. Padua. Hiding relaxed memory consistency with compilers. In *Proceedings of the 2000 International Conference on Parallel Algorithms and Compilation Techniques*, Philadelphia, PA, Oct. 2000.

64. J. Lee, D. Padua, and S. Midkiff. Basic compiler algorithms for parallel programs. In *Proceedings of the 7th ACM SIGPLAN Symposium on Principles and Practice of Parallel Programming*, Atlanta, GA, May 1999.

65. B. Liblit and A. Aiken. Type systems for distributed data structures. In *Proceedings of the 27th Annual ACM Symposium on the Principles of Programming Languages*, Boston, MA, Jan. 2000.

66. D. Long and L. Clarke. Data flow analysis of concurrent systems that use the rendezvous model of synchronization. In *Proceedings of the ACM Symposium on Analysis, Verification, and Testing*, Victoria, B.C., Oct. 1991.

67. J. Maessen, Arvind, and X. Shen. Improving the Java memory model using CRF. In *Proceedings of the 15th Annual Conference on Object-Oriented Programming Systems, Languages and Applications*, Portland, OR, Oct. 2000.

68. J. Manson and W. Pugh. Core multithreaded semantics for Java. In *Proceedings of the Joint ACM Java Grande - ISCOPE 2001 Conference*, Stanford, CA, June 2001.

69. S. Masticola and B. Ryder. Static infinite wait anomaly detection in polynomial time. In *Proceedings of the 1990 International Conference on Parallel Processing*, St. Charles, IL, Aug. 1990.

70. S. Masticola and B. Ryder. Non-concurrency analysis. In *Proceedings of the 4th ACM SIGPLAN Symposium on Principles and Practice of Parallel Programming*, San Diego, CA, May 1993.

71. S. Midkiff and D. Padua. Compiler algorithms for synchronization. *IEEE Transactions on Computers*, 36(12):1485–1495, Dec. 1987.

72. S. Midkiff and D. Padua. Issues in the optimization of parallel programs. In *Proceedings of the 1990 International Conference on Parallel Processing*, pages II–105–113, 1990.

73. G. Naumovich, G. Avrunin, and L. Clarke. Data flow analysis for checking properties of concurrent Java programs. In *Proceedings of the 21st International conference on Software Engineering*, Los Angeles, CA, May 1999.

74. G. Naumovich, G. Avrunin, and L. Clarke. An efficient algorithm for computing MHP information for concurrent Java programs. In *Proceedings of the 7th ACM SIGSOFT Symposium on the Foundations of Software Engineering*, Toulouse, France, Sept. 1999.

75. G. Naumovich, L. Clarke, and J. Cobleigh. Using partial order techniques to improve performance of data flow analysis based verification. In *Proceedings of the ACM SIGPLAN-SIGSOFT Workshop on Program Analysis for Software Tools and Engineering*, Toulouse, France, Sept. 1999.

76. J. Ousterhout. Why threads are a bad idea (for most purposes). Invited Talk at the 1996 USENIX Technical Conference.

77. W. Pugh. A practical algorithm for exact array dependence analysis. *Commun. ACM*, 35(8):102–114, Aug. 1992.

78. W. Pugh. Fixing the Java memory model. In *Proceedings of the ACM 1999 Java Grande Conference*, San Francisco, CA, June 1999.

79. M. Rinard. Effective fine-grain synchronization for automatically parallelized programs using optimistic synchronization primitives. *ACM Transactions on Computer Systems*, 17(4):337–371, Nov. 1999.

80. M. Rinard and P. Diniz. Commutativity analysis: A new analysis technique for parallelizing compilers. *ACM Transactions on Programming Languages and Systems*, 19(6):941–992, Nov. 1997.

81. M. Rinard and M. Lam. The design, implementation, and evaluation of jade. *ACM Transactions on Programming Languages and Systems*, 20(3):483–545, May 1998.

82. E. Ruf. Effective synchronization removal for Java. In *Proceedings of the SIGPLAN '00 Conference on Program Language Design and Implementation*, Vancouver, Canada, June 2000.

83. R. Rugina and M. Rinard. Pointer analysis for multithreaded programs. In *Proceedings of the SIGPLAN '99 Conference on Program Language Design and Implementation*, Atlanta, GA, May 1999.

84. R. Rugina and M. Rinard. Symbolic bounds analysis of pointers, array indexes, and accessed memory regions. In *Proceedings of the SIGPLAN '00 Conference on Program Language Design and Implementation*, Vancouver, Canada, June 2000.

85. M. Sagiv, T. Reps, and R. Wilhelm. Solving shape-analysis problems in languages with destructive updating. *ACM Transactions on Programming Languages and Systems*, 20(1):1–50, Jan. 1998.

86. A. Salcianu and M. Rinard. Pointer and escape analysis for multithreaded Java programs. In *Proceedings of the 8th ACM SIGPLAN Symposium on Principles and Practice of Parallel Programming*, Snowbird, UT, June 2001.

87. V. Sarkar and B. Simons. Parallel program graphs and their classification. In *Proceedings of the Sixth Workshop on Languages and Compilers for Parallel Computing*, Portland, OR, Aug. 1993.

88. S. Savage, M. Burrows, G. Nelson, P. Solbovarro, and T. Anderson. Eraser: A dynamic race detector for multi-threaded programs. In *Proceedings of the*

Sixteenth Symposium on Operating Systems Principles, Saint-Malo, France, Oct. 1997.

89. D. Scales and M. S. Lam. The design and evaluation of a shared object system for distributed memory machines. In *Proceedings of the 1st USENIX Symposium on Operating Systems Design and Implementation.* ACM, New York, Nov. 1994.

90. D. Shasha and M. Snir. Efficient and correct execution of parallel programs that share memory. *ACM Transactions on Programming Languages and Systems*, 10(2), Apr. 1988.

91. H. Srinivasan, J. Hook, and M. Wolfe. Static single assignment for explicitly parallel programs. In *Proceedings of the 20th Annual ACM Symposium on the Principles of Programming Languages*, Jan. 1993.

92. G. Steele. Making asynchronous parallelism safe for the world. In *Proceedings of the 17th Annual ACM Symposium on the Principles of Programming Languages*, pages 218–231, San Francisco, CA, Jan. 1990. ACM, New York.

93. B. Steensgaard. Points-to analysis in almost linear time. In *Proceedings of the 23rd Annual ACM Symposium on the Principles of Programming Languages*, St. Petersburg Beach, FL, Jan. 1996.

94. N. Sterling. Warlock: A static data race analysis tool. In *Proceedings of the 1993 Winter Usenix Conference*, Jan. 1994.

95. R. N. Taylor. A general purpose algorithm for analyzing concurrent programs. *Commun. ACM*, 26(5):362–376, May 1983.

96. C. Tseng. Compiler optimizations for eliminating barrier synchronization. In *Proceedings of the 5th ACM SIGPLAN Symposium on Principles and Practice of Parallel Programming*, pages 144–155, Santa Barbara, CA, July 1995.

97. A. Valmari. A stubborn attack on state explosion. In *Proceedings of the 2nd International Workshop on Computer Aided Verification*, New Brunswick, NJ, June 1990.

98. J. Whaley and M. Rinard. Compositional pointer and escape analysis for Java programs. In *Proceedings of the 14th Annual Conference on Object-Oriented Programming Systems, Languages and Applications*, Denver, CO, Nov. 1999.

99. M. Young and R. Taylor. Combining static concurrency analysis with symbolic execution. *IEEE Transactions on Software Engineering*, 14(10), Oct. 1988.

100. H. Zhu and L. Hendren. Communication optimizations for parallel C programs. In *Proceedings of the SIGPLAN '98 Conference on Program Language Design and Implementation*, Montreal, Canada, June 1998.

Communication and Parallelism Introduction and Elimination in Imperative Concurrent Programs

Miquel Bertran, Francesc Babot, August Climent, and Miquel Nicolau

Informàtica La Salle, Universitat Ramon Llull, Barcelona
{miqbe,fbabot,augc,miqueln}@salleURL.edu

Abstract. Transformation rules of imperative concurrent programs, based on congruence and refinement relations between statements, are presented. They introduce and/or eliminate synchronous communication statements and parallelism in these programs. The development is made within a subset of SPL, a good representative of imperative notations for concurrent and reactive programs introduced by Manna and Pnueli. The paper shows that no finite set of transformation rules suffices to eliminate synchronous communication statements from programs involving the concatenation and parallelism operators only. An infinite set is given to suit this purpose, which can be applied recursively. As an important complement for the applications, a collection of *tactics*, for the acceleration of broader transformations, is described. Tactics apply a sequence of rules to a program with a specific transformation objective. The transformation rules and the tactics could be used in formal design to derive new programs from verified ones, preserving their properties, and avoiding the repetition of verifications for the transformed programs. As an example, the formal parallelization of a non-trivial distributed fast Fourier transform algorithm is outlined.

1 Introduction

A mathematical basis for the application of transformations to the design of parallel and distributed programs is introduced. The specific scenario of equivalence preserving formal transformations, introducing and/or eliminating synchronous communications and parallelism, is treated. We work in two broad transformations: *formal parallelization* and *formal communication simplification*. The former introduces internal synchronous communication and parallelism whereas the latter removes both. The basic constituent steps of formal parallelization and communication simplification are simple transformations, which have to correspond to congruences or other equivalence preserving relations between program statements. The soundness and meaning of them has to be mathematically established. Some sets of equivalence laws for concurrent programs are available in the literature, particularly in the area of process algebras. The books of Hoare and Milner [17, 27] contain some such sets. In the area of static analysis, transformations have been reported in [2] and methods to derive parallel codes have been treated in [11]. The works of Lamport and Hooman, reported in [21] and

P. Cousot (Ed.): SAS 2001, LNCS 2126, pp. 20–39, 2001.

[19] respectively, are related to the topic. However, these approaches are different to the one reported in the present work. The general problem of program analysis for communication elimination and introduction, at the syntactic level, of *imperative programs* is not treated in the above works and, up to our present knowledge, has not been dealt with in the literature either. Motivated by practical design, we wish to work at the *program level*, rather than at the process or specification levels. Therefore we are interested neither in process algebras nor in action based systems, but rather in *program state based* transformations. The transformations have to work for a concrete programming notation, which has to be chosen. It has to incorporate explicit parallelism and communication via channels. A good representative of this class is the *simple programming language* (SPL) used in the framework of Manna and Pnueli, presented in the books [23, 24]. SPL programs can be verified and/or model checked in the Stanford Temporal Prover (STeP) [5, 4]. SPL is similar to CSP [16] and OCCAM [17]. This in no way restricts the transformation approach to this specific framework. The transformations preserve properties and can be used in cooperation with other model checkers and program verifiers, such as for instance SPIN [18] and SMV [25], or in a broader design scenario where none of these tools is used but where the transformations would just allow the derivation of new programs from existing ones, by reusing and transforming them. As an illustration, consider the following SPL program, having top-level parallel or cooperating processes P_a, P and P_b. The inner process P is a concatenation whose first substatement is a parallel composition of two synchronous communication substatements with channels α and β. They match with synchronous communication substatements in processes P_a and P_b respectively.

$$\begin{bmatrix} \textbf{local} \quad a, b, x, y, z : \textbf{integer} \\ \textbf{local} \quad \alpha, \beta \qquad : \textbf{channel of integer} \\ \\ P_a :: [\textbf{produce } a; \ \alpha \Leftarrow a;] \\ \| \\ P :: \left[\ [\alpha \Rightarrow x \, \| \beta \Rightarrow y] \ ; \ \begin{bmatrix} z := x + y; \\ \textbf{consume } z; \end{bmatrix} \right] \\ \| \\ P_b :: [\textbf{produce } b; \ \beta \Leftarrow b;] \end{bmatrix}$$

The elimination of synchronous communications, and parallelism, would give the following equivalent and simpler program.

$$\begin{bmatrix} \textbf{local} \quad a, b, z : \textbf{integer} \\ [\textbf{produce } a; \ \textbf{produce } b; \ z := a + b; \ \textbf{consume } z;] \end{bmatrix}$$

This formal transformation needs laws such as $P;\ \textbf{skip} \approx \textbf{skip}\,;\ P \approx P$, associativity of parallelism, and a proper communication elimination law such as

$$[H^l \| H^r]; [u := e \| P^r]; [T^l \| T^r] \ \equiv \ [H^l; \alpha \Leftarrow e; T^l] \| [H^r; [\alpha \Rightarrow u \| P^r]; T^r]$$

These relations do not hold in SPL, but they are needed in order to carry out formal parallelization and communication simplification. A fundamental set of relations needed in both transformations is justified mathematically in this work. In addition, a collection of basic *tactics*, as used in STeP and other theorem provers, and which may have originated in LCF [15], is defined as a necessary complement of the rules. Tactics apply a sequence of transformation rules to a program with a specific transformation objective. They include the verification of applicability conditions, and accelerate the transformation process. They can be applied either interactively or from within a program, guaranteeing that the transformation always corresponds to the application of a sequence of rules. It is important to remark that notations such as CCS and OCCAM do not have such nice sets [17, 27]. The main reason for this is the existence of either non-determinism or the hidden action. This problem is analyzed in the present work for SPL, which does not have the needed set of rules either. As a result of the analysis a restriction is necessary to be imposed on SPL for endowing it with the desired rules. For convenience, we have also introduced a *nil* statement. The restriction endows the notation with an intuitive set of basic relations which, although they do not carry out directly communication elimination and/or introduction, they are needed for the application of the proper communication elimination and/or introduction transformations. Parallelism associativity, and *skip* and *nil* introduction/elimination relative to concatenation and parallelism are in the set. It is also shown that the set of communication elimination and introduction laws cannot be finite, and that in order to obtain a practical set of transformations, congruence relations are not sufficient in general. *Refinement relations* have to be taken into consideration. The notion of refinement that we work with is taken from [20]. In general, existing work in refinement [8, 7, 1, 13, 6, 22] has not been applied to programs with synchronous communications in the direction which we explore. This adds another motivation. Although a recursive algorithm exists for the application of the infinite set of reductions, the present work does not go into it. For illustration purposes a non-trivial distributed *fast fourier transform* (FFT) algorithm has been derived with the methods introduced in this work. The starting point is a sequential recursive algorithm.

2   Background Notions and Notation

2.1   Introduction

The meaning of statements will be defined in terms of state transition systems. Then, the equivalence of statements will be based on the equivalence of their associated transition systems. Some basic notions are needed for that, and are introduced in this section without much elaboration. The reader is referred to [23, 24] for further detail. A program denotes a *fair transition system* (FTS), which is the tuple $\langle V, \Sigma, \Theta, \mathcal{T}, \mathcal{J}, \mathcal{C} \rangle$. Its components are, respectively, the set of system variables, the set of states, the initial condition, the finite set of transitions, and the sets of *just* and *compassionate* transitions. The set $V = Y \cup \{\pi\}$, where π is the control variable, and $Y = \{y_1, \ldots, y_m\}$ is the set of *data variables*. A transition τ is a function $\tau : \Sigma \rightarrow 2^\Sigma$ mapping a state to a possibly empty set of successor states $\tau(s)$, it is characterized by a *transition relation* $\rho_\tau(V, V')$, which is a first order formula expressing the relation holding between a state s and its τ-successors s'. A transition is *just* (weakly fair) if when it is continuously enabled, then it is taken eventually. Consequently it will be taken an indefinite number of times as well. A transition is *compassionate* (strongly fair) if when enabled an indefinite number of times it is taken eventually. Consequently it will be taken an indefinite number of times as well. A *run* of a FTS is an infinite sequence of states $\sigma : s_0, s_1, s_2, \ldots$ satisfying *initiation* ($s_0 \models \Theta$) and *consecution* ($s_{j+1} \in \tau(s_j)$). A *computation* of a FTS is a *run* all of whose transitions satisfy their corresponding fairness requirements, expressed by the sets $\mathcal{J}$ and $\mathcal{C}$. In order to define a practical notion of equivalence between transition systems it is enough to consider observable parts. Then, a *reduced behavior* σ^r is obtained from a computation σ by retaining an *observable* part, relative to a set of observed variables $\mathcal{O}$, where $\pi \notin \mathcal{O}$, and eliminating from it stuttering steps (equivalent to the idling transition). $\mathcal{R}(\mathcal{S})$ is the set of all reduced behaviors of a transition system S. Two transition systems S_1 and S_2 are equivalent relative to a set $\mathcal{O}$ of observed variables, denoted by $S_1 \sim S_2$, if $\mathcal{R}(S_1) = \mathcal{R}(S_2)$. A system S_c *refines* system S_a, written $S_c \sqsubseteq S_a$, if every reduced behavior of S_c is also a reduced behavior of S_a.

2.2   The Notation

It is essential to define the precise notation to which the relations to be given apply. Since there are slight variations in the SPL notation throughout the two framework books, a schematic presentation of the subset of the SPL notation which we start with is included. Basically, the general selection statement has been restricted to only boolean and guarded communication selection forms. Also, in an initial attempt to obtain the above mentioned intuitive set of auxiliary relations, we have introduced a *nil* statement. The following table gives the definition of some basic statements of the notation:

Statement	Transition Relations	Fairness	Labels
$\ell : \mathbf{skip}; \hat{\ell} :$	$\rho_\ell :\ move(\ell, \hat{\ell}) \wedge pres(Y)$	$\mathcal{J}$	
$\ell : \mathbf{nil}; \hat{\ell} :$			$\ell \sim_L \hat{\ell}$
$\ell : \bar{u} := \bar{e}; \hat{\ell} :$	$\rho_\ell :\ move(\ell, \hat{\ell}) \wedge \bar{u}' = \bar{e}$ $\wedge pres(Y - \{\bar{u}\})$	$\mathcal{J}$	
$\ell : \alpha \Leftarrow e; \hat{\ell} :$ $m : \alpha \Rightarrow u; \hat{m} :$	$\rho_{<\ell,m>} :\ move(\{[\ell],[m]\}, \{[\hat{\ell}],[\hat{m}]\})$ $\wedge u' = e \wedge pres(Y - \{u\})$	$\mathcal{C}$	
$\ell : \mathbf{request}\ r; \hat{\ell} :$	$\rho_\ell :\ move(\ell, \hat{\ell}) \wedge r > 0 \wedge r' = r - 1$ $\wedge pres(Y - \{r\})$	$\mathcal{C}$	
$\ell : \mathbf{release}\ r; \hat{\ell} :$	$\rho_\ell :\ move(\ell, \hat{\ell}) \wedge r' = r + 1$ $\wedge pres(Y - \{r\})$	$\mathcal{J}$	
$\ell : \alpha \Leftarrow e; \hat{\ell} :$ α asynchronous	$\rho_\ell :\ move(\ell, \hat{\ell}) \wedge \alpha' = \alpha \cdot e$ $\wedge pres(Y - \{\alpha\})$	$\mathcal{J}$	
$\ell : \alpha \Rightarrow u; \hat{\ell} :$ α asynchronous	$\rho_\ell :\ move(\ell, \hat{\ell}) \wedge |\alpha| > 0 \wedge \alpha = u' \cdot \alpha'$ $\wedge pres(Y - \{\alpha\})$	$\mathcal{C}$	

Following again Manna and Pnueli, with each statement S we associate a finite set of transitions, and a finite set of control locations. The table gives the transition relation for each transition. An equivalence relation $\sim_L$, defined on statement labels, puts together labels which denote the same control location. A

location is an equivalence class of the label relation $\sim_L$. The location corresponding to label ℓ will be denoted by $[\ell]$. Usually, ℓ and $\hat{\ell}$ are the pre and post labels
of a statement S. The special variable $\pi \in V$ ranges over sets of locations. Its
value on a state denotes all the locations in the program that are currently active. The predicates $pres(U)$ and $move(L, \hat{L})$ express preservation of the values
of the variables in U, and movement of control from the set of control locations
L to $\hat{L}$. The skip, nil, and assignment statements correspond to the first three
lines of the table. Notice the no transition is associated with the nil statement,
which puts its pre and post labels in the same class of the label relation. With a
pair of synchronous communication statements, send and receive, over channel
α, a joint transition is associated. This transition is included in the compassion
set $\mathcal{C}$, as in reference [23]. Next, the table specifies two semaphore statements
and the two asynchronous communication statements.

A pair of synchronous communication statements is said to be *matching* if
their position in a program is such that the above joint transition $\rho_{<\ell,m>}$ could
be enabled. For instance a send and a receive statement over the same channel
may match but two send statements never do.

The semantics of some compound statements is given in the following table:

Statement	*Transition Relations*
$\ell : [\ell_1 : S_1; \hat{\ell}_1 \ldots ; \ell_m : S_m; \hat{\ell_m}]; \hat{\ell} :$	
$\ell : [[\ell_1 : S_1; \hat{\ell}_1] \| \ldots \| [\ell_m : S_m; \hat{\ell_m}]]; \hat{\ell} :$	$\rho_\ell^E : move(\{[\ell]\}, \{[\ell_1], \ldots, [\ell_m]\})$ $\wedge pres(Y)$
	$\rho_\ell^X : move(\{[\hat{\ell_1}], \ldots, [\hat{\ell_m}]\}, \{[\hat{\ell}]\})$ $\wedge pres(Y)$
$\ell : [c(\alpha_1), c_1; S_1 \text{ or } \ldots \text{ or } c(\alpha_m), c_m; S_m]; \hat{\ell} :$	$\rho_i : move(\ell, \ell_i) \wedge c_i \wedge \alpha_i' = \alpha_i \cdot e$ $\wedge pres(Y - \{\alpha_i\})$
	$\rho_i : move(\ell, \ell_i) \wedge c_i \wedge |\alpha_i| > 0$ $\wedge \alpha_i = u' \cdot \alpha_i' \wedge pres(Y - \{\alpha_i\})$
	$\rho_{<i,n>} : move(\{\ell, n\}, \{\ell_i, \hat{n}\})$ $\wedge c_i \wedge u' = e \wedge pres(Y - \{u\})$

The label relations associated with the concatenation statement are $\hat{\ell}_i \sim_L \ell_{i+1}$
for $i = 1..m - 1$, $\ell \sim_L \ell_1$, and $\hat{\ell} \sim_L \hat{\ell_m}$ The cooperation statement has
an entry and an exit transition, τ^E and τ^X associated with it. They are in the
justice set $\mathcal{J}$. No label relation is associated with this statement. Statements S_i
and S_j, $i \neq j$, of a cooperation statement are said to be *parallel*. Similarly for any
pair of their substatements, one in each. The three transitions which are shown
in the table for the communication selection statement are the possible *types*
of transitions depending on whether the communication statement $c(\alpha_i)$ is an
asynchronous send or receive, or a synchronous communication statement. The
fairness set of these transitions is the one indicated in the first table. The pre and
post labels ℓ_i and $\hat{\ell}_i$ of substatements S_i are not shown explicitly in the table. The
label relations associated with this statement are $\hat{\ell} \sim_L \hat{\ell}_1 \sim_L \ldots \sim_L \hat{\ell_m}$. The
boolean selection statement is the special case of the communication selection
statement, where the communication statements $c(\alpha_i)$ are nil, non-existent. The
general selection statement is not allowed.

The meaning of any program will be the FTS system which can be associated with the program using the statement semantics detailed above. Two programs are equivalent if their corresponding FTSs are equivalent. We proceed similarly with the notion of program refinement.

2.3   Relations between Statements

Transformation rules will correspond to congruence and refinement relations between statements. The meaning of these relations is defined next. Unless stated otherwise $\mathcal{O} = Y_1 \cap Y_2$. A *program context* $P[\ \_\ ]$ is a program P one of whose statements corresponds to a hole to be filled-in by an arbitrary statement S. With some abuse of notation $P[S]$ will denote a program context, where S denotes the arbitrary statement placed in the hole. In some design scenarios where synchronous communications are involved we need a more flexible notion. Before defining it we give some elementary concepts. Given a pair of matching synchronous communication statements, we say that one *matches* the other. When a joint synchronous communication transition is taken in a computation we say that a synchronous communication *event* has taken place. Two synchronous communication events are *ordered* if they take place in the same order in any computation. For instance, when the four synchronous communication statements giving rise to two communication events are parallel statements then the two communication events are not ordered.

Definition 1 (Flexible Program Context). *Let S be a statement having synchronous communication operations $com(\alpha_1), \ldots, com(\alpha_n)$ with channels $\alpha_1 \ldots, \alpha_n$ which are not local to S. These communication operations have to match synchronous communication statements parallel to S in any program context $F[S]$. We say that a program context $F[S]$ is a flexible program context with respect to the non-local communication statements of S when the statements parallel to S in $F[S]$ are disjoint with those in S and their matching communication statements are placed in the program in such a way that no order is imposed upon their corresponding communication events.*

Example: $F[S] = S \parallel \textbf{while } T \textbf{ do } c\bar{o}m(\alpha_1) \parallel \ldots \parallel \textbf{while } T \textbf{ do } c\bar{o}m(\alpha_n)$ where $c\bar{o}m(\alpha_i)$ is the synchronous communication statement which matches $com(\alpha_i)$, a substatement of S. The motivation for introducing this notion is the practical situation where we design a statement (program) by transformations and *after* we have obtained its desired form we proceed to the design of the parallel statements which will communicate with it without deadlock.

Two statements S_1 and S_2 are defined to be *congruent*, written as $S_1 \approx S_2$, if $P[S_1]$ and $P[S_2]$ are equivalent (that is, $P[S_1] \sim P[S_2]$) for all program contexts $P[S]$. Then both statements are interchangeable in any program. We say that statement S_c *refines* statement S_a, written as $S_c \sqsubseteq S_a$, if for all program contexts $P[S], P[S_c]$ refines $P[S_a]$ (that is, $P[S_c] \sqsubseteq P[S_a]$). We say that statement S_c is a *flexible refinement* of statement S_a, written as $S_c \sqsubseteq_F S_a$, if for all flexible program contexts $F[S]$, with respect to the external communication operations of S_a and S_c, $F[S_c] \sqsubseteq F[S_a]$.

3   Rules and Tactics for the Reduced Notation

3.1   Simple Cases

The first set of rules is based in the following congruences. Let $p_m(k)$, where $k = 1..m$, denote the k-th integer of a permutation of the list $\langle 1, 2, \ldots, m \rangle$. Then: $\mathbf{nil}; S \approx S$ $S; \mathbf{nil} \approx S$ $S_1 || \ldots || S_m \approx S_{p_m(1)} || \ldots || S_{p_m(m)}$ and $S_1; \ldots; S_k; \ldots; S_l; \ldots; S_m \approx S_1; \ldots; [S_k; \ldots; S_l]; \ldots; S_m$ hold. The justification of these congruences is simple, since from the semantic definition of the notation, given in section 2.2, it can be seen that both sides of their congruence symbols have the same associated FTS. The tactics based on the above laws are simple. Here are some of them:

Tactic 1 (Parallelism Permutation (ParPerm)). *Performs a permutation of the substatements of a parallelism (cooperation) statement.*
Inputs: *A program, P. The label k of the cooperation substatement of P where the permutation has to be applied. A list of naturals* ln *defining the desired permutation.*
Outputs: *A boolean,* done, *which takes the value true if the applicability conditions hold and the goal has been accomplished. The transformed program P′.*

Tactic 2 (Concatenation Association (ConcatAsso)). *Associates, as a single substatement, a sequence of contiguous substatements of a concatenation statement.*
Inputs: *A program, P. The label k of the concatenation substatement of P where the association has to be done. Two naturals* n1 *and* n2, $0 < n1 < n2$, *defining the first and the last substatement of the contiguous sequence.*
Outputs: *A boolean,* done, *which takes the value true if the applicability conditions hold and the goal has been accomplished. The transformed program P′.*

The inverse would be a concatenation flattening tactic *ConcatFlat*.

3.2   Rules of Skip

The following remarks make the mathematical justification of the rules for the introduction/elimination of the skip statement hard.

Remark 1 (Skip Concatenation Non-congruences). *Let S and $\tilde{S}$ be statements. Then* $S \not\approx S; \mathbf{skip}$ *and* $S; \tilde{S} \not\approx S; \mathbf{skip}; \tilde{S}$.   *Hence, in general* $S \not\approx \mathbf{skip}; S$

As an intuitive clue to justify this remark, deleting an skip statement may enable transitions associated with the statement which immediately follows it, particularly joint synchronous communication transitions formed with a statement parallel with it in some program context. This leads into an infinite number of enablings when the skip statement is within an infinite loop in the program context, and then some computation may be excluded from one side due to violation of the fairness requirements with respect to the enabled transition.

Remark 2 (Skip and Nil Cooperation Non-congruences). *Let S be a statement. Then* $S \not\approx S \parallel \mathbf{skip}$ *and* $S \not\approx S \parallel \mathbf{nil}$.

The proof of these remarks is given in appendix A. The following theorem is important since it identifies, within the reduced notation, the fairness assumptions about communication statements as being responsible for the irregular behavior of the *skip* statement, as in the above non-congruences. We remark, as the appendix shows, that without strong fairness the congruences would hold.

Theorem 1 (Concatenated Skip Deletion). *Let S be a statement distinct from the* nil *statement. Let S_{ncs} be a statement which is neither a communication selection, nor a synchronous communication, nor a* nil *statement. Then*

$$S; S_{ncs} \approx S; \mathbf{skip}; S_{ncs} .$$

The proof is given in appendix B.

Theorem 2 (Parallel Skip and Nil Deletion). *Let S be a statement distinct from the* nil *statement. Let S_{ncs} and S'_{ncs} be statements which are neither communication selection, nor synchronous communication, nor* nil *statements. Let $\tilde{S}$ be an arbitrary statement. Then*

$$S; S_{ncs}; \tilde{S}; S'_{ncs} \approx S; [\mathbf{skip}\|[S_{ncs}; \tilde{S}]]; S'_{ncs}$$
$$and \quad S; S_{ncs}; \tilde{S}; S'_{ncs} \approx S; [\mathbf{nil}\|[S_{ncs}; \tilde{S}]]; S'_{ncs} .$$

The proof is similar to the one of the previous lemma. Here the entry and exit transitions of the cooperation statement, which are of the skip type, play the same role as the transition associated with the *skip* statement in the previous theorem. We remark that the congruences of the two previous theorems also hold without the restriction when no transition associated with the communication statements is in the compassion set $\mathcal{C}$, as the proof in appendix B shows.

Lemma 1 (Associativity of Cooperation). *In general*

$$[S_1\|\dots\|S_k\|\dots\|S_l\|\dots\|S_m] \approx [S_1\|\dots\| [S_k\|\dots\|S_l] \|\dots\|S_m]$$

provided that the front statements of $S_k, \cdots, S_l$ are neither synchronous communication statements nor communication selection statements. Other congruences between cooperation statements with arbitrary associations of their substatements follow from the above congruence.

The proof of this congruence is similar to the one for the **skip** deletion lemma above. It is omitted due to space restrictions. We note that the entry and exit transitions associated with the main cooperation statement are present in both sides. The entry and exit transitions of the inner cooperation statement are present in one side only, therefore in moving from one side to the other these inner skip-type transitions are deleted. The outer exit transition prevents the situation which was possible in theorem 2 above. However, this is not the case for the inner entry transition.

4   Communication Elimination and Introduction

4.1   Restriction of SPL and New Tactics

The above results reduce the set of congruences in the notation introduced so far, since they prevent the deletion of *skip* and *nil* statements in general. One would always have to check whether or not a synchronous communication or a communications selection statement follows next to the *skip* statement. Furthermore, the congruences involving the cooperation statement which have **nil** as a substatement are needed in the process of synchronous communication elimination and introduction. They allow to transform programs to forms where the elimination-introduction laws can apply. With the objective of obtaining the needed set of congruences, which overcomes these drawbacks, we introduce the *delayed communications selection* statement as the following abbreviation:

$$[\, com(\alpha_1) \textbf{ provided } c_1; S_1 \textbf{ dor } \ldots \textbf{ dor } com(\alpha_m) \textbf{ provided } c_m; S_m \,]$$
$$=$$
$$\textbf{skip}; [\, com(\alpha_1) \textbf{ provided } c_1; S_1 \textbf{ or } \ldots \textbf{ or } com(\alpha_m) \textbf{ provided } c_m; S_m \,]$$

The restricted notation, to be used in the rest of this work, will not use communication selection statements but only delayed communication selection statements. Furthermore, an *skip* statement will also be inserted implicitly just before any isolated synchronous send or receive statement. These hidden *skip* statements will guarantee that the conditions of theorems 1, 2, and of lemma 1 will always hold. Therefore their congruences will also hold, and we will have associativity of cooperation and the intuitive congruences:

$$\textbf{skip}; S \approx S \,, \qquad S; \textbf{skip} \approx S \,, \qquad \textbf{skip} || S \approx S \,, \qquad \text{and} \qquad \textbf{nil } || S \approx S \,.$$

The introduction of hidden skip statements may be done easily by the compiler. Notice that what ultimately matters is the scheduling policy to be used with the programs. Therefore, an alternative way to justify the use of the above intuitive laws is to put all the transitions in the justice set $\mathcal{J}$, including the ones associated with the communication statements.

As a consequence of working in the restricted notation, lemma 1 holds and the tactics for the flattening and association in cooperation statements, *ParAsso* and *ParFlat* can be defined in the same way as tactics *ConcatAsso* and *ConcatFlat* respectively.

4.2   A Schema of Relations

This subsection considers the case of only two parallel processes, each one of them containing a synchronous communication statement matching each other. We start with a simple intuitive congruence relation.

Lemma 2 (Simple Communication Elimination and Introduction). *Let H^l and H^r be statements which do not have communication statements through synchronous channel α, and T^l and T^r be statements. Then,*
$$[H^l; \alpha \Leftarrow e; T^l] || [H^r; \alpha \Rightarrow u; T^r] \approx [H^l || H^r]; u := e; [T^l || T^r] \,.$$

This proof is omitted since the result is a special case of the schema of relations of theorem 4 below. The congruence $[\alpha \Leftarrow e || \alpha \Rightarrow u] \approx u := e$ is a special case obtained by making $H^l = H^r = T^l = T^r = \mathbf{nil}$.

Theorem 3 (Incompleteness of Any Finite Set of Laws). *No finite set of laws, congruences or refinement relations, suffices to syntactically eliminate a pair of synchronous communication statements from restricted SPL statements.*

Proof Outline. Consider the statement $[H^l; \alpha \Leftarrow e; T^l] || [H^r; [\alpha \Rightarrow u || P^r]; T^r]$ which is a simple extension of the left hand side of the congruence above, and where P^r is an arbitrary statement. The communication through synchronous channel α cannot be eliminated with the communications elimination lemma above. Restricting the statements to those constructible with concatenation and cooperation operators only, assume that we have found a relation $G \sqsubseteq [L || R]$ such that G has not the synchronous communication pair that communicates L and R, and that would eliminate the communication from the considered statement. Nevertheless, it would not be sufficient either since, consider the statement $L || [H ; [R||P] ; T]$ formed with the same L and R and where H does not contain synchronous communication statements through α. The assumed new law, which eliminated the communication from $L||R$ obtaining G, does not unify with the new statement due to the presence of P. Therefore, a new communication elimination law is needed. This reasoning can be iterated indefinitely.

Theorem 4 (Communication Elimination and Introduction). *In the following all parallel processes are assumed to be disjoint, in the sense that they only read their shared data variables and they do not communicate through asynchronous channels.*

- *Let T^l_k and T^r_k be statements. Let H^l_k and H^r_k be statements which do not have communication operations through synchronous channel α. In both definitions $k = 0, 1, \ldots$.*
- *Let $G^l_0 = [\alpha \Leftarrow e]$ and $G^r_0 = [\alpha \Rightarrow u]$, and for $k = 1, 2, \ldots$*

$$G^l_k = H^l_{k-1}; [G^l_{k-1} || P^l_{k-1}]; T^l_{k-1} \quad \text{and} \quad G^r_k = H^r_{k-1}; [G^r_{k-1} || P^r_{k-1}]; T^r_{k-1}$$

where statements P^l_k and P^r_k can be expressed as $P^l_k = P^{hl}_k; P^{ml}_k; P^{tl}_k$ and $P^r_k = P^{hr}_k; P^{mr}_k; P^{tr}_k$, and where any of the P processes may be $\mathbf{nil}$, in such a way that the following holds:

- *None of the P statements contain communication statements through channel α.*
- *P^{hl}_k communicates only with H^r_k and P^{hr}_k.*
- *P^{hr}_k communicates only with H^l_k and P^{hl}_k.*
- *P^{ml}_k communicates only with G_k, to be defined below, and P^{mr}_k.*
- *P^{mr}_k communicates only with G_k, to be defined below, and P^{ml}_k.*
- *P^{tl}_k communicates only with T^r_k and P^{tr}_k.*
- *P^{tr}_k communicates only with T^l_k and P^{tl}_k.*

– *Let* $G_0 = [u := e]$, *and*   *for* $k = 1, 2, \ldots$

$$G_k = [[H^l_{k-1}; P^{hl}_{k-1}]\|[H^r_{k-1}; P^{hr}_{k-1}]]; [G_{k-1}\|P^{ml}_{k-1}\|P^{mr}_{k-1}];$$

$$[[P^{tl}_{k-1}; T^l_{k-1}]\|[P^{tr}_{k-1}; T^r_{k-1}]]$$

Then $G_n \sqsubseteq_F [G^l_n\|G^r_n]$ *for* $n = 1, 2, \ldots$

The proof is not given due to paper length restrictions. We note that for quite a number of cases the refinement relation of the above lemmas can be a congruence relation. By making the required statements equal to the *nil* statement, the above lemma can be applied to a great variety of special cases where the cooperation statement at the right of the refinement symbol may be $G^l_n\|G^r_m$, where $n \neq m$. The following two tactics implement the recursive application of the above schema of laws.

Tactic 3 (Communication Elimination (ComElim)). *Given two matching synchronous communication statements within some cooperation statement of a program, transforms the program according to the lemma above, replacing the communication statements by their corresponding assignment.*
Inputs*: A program,* P. *The labels* k1 *and* k2 *of the matching pair of communication statements.*
Outputs*: A boolean,* done, *which takes the value true if the applicability conditions hold and the goal has been accomplished. The transformed program* P'.

Tactic 4 (Communication Introduction (ComIntro)). *Given an assignment statement within a program, transforms the program according to the lemma above, replacing the assignment statement by a pair of matching communication statements in parallel. If necessary, a new cooperation statement is introduced.*
Inputs*: A program,* P. *The label* k *of the assignment statement. The identifier* newc *of the channel. If the identifier is null, a suitable identifier is generated.*
Outputs*: A boolean,* done, *which takes the value true if the applicability conditions hold and the goal has been accomplished. The transformed program* P'.

5   Modular Procedures and Related Transformations

Both, modules and procedures, are needed in the applications. SPL modules are defined in reference [23], and they are extended for verification purposes in reference [14]. The notion of *modular procedure* combines the notions of module and of procedure. As used in the present work, it agrees with that of SPL module, but the possibility of referring to it at any point in a program is added. As modules, modular procedures can be composed in parallel. A reference statement, to a modular procedure, makes explicit all the names of the channels through which it interacts with processes parallel to the invocation statement. Also, it makes explicit the names of the variables shared with the rest of the program. The order of these names in the reference statement corresponds to their order within the modular procedure interface definition. From now on in the text, modular procedures will be referred to simply as *procedures*. In the following example two modes of interface statements will be used. Mode **out** specifies an output variable or channel to be written only in the current procedure, no statement parallel to the reference statement can write into the variable or send via the channel. Mode **external in** specifies the possibility that a statement parallel to the reference writes into the variable or sends via the channel. For the purposes of program transformation, we define the semantics of the reference statement to be consistent with the operation of replacement of this statement by the modular procedure body, possibly with a renaming of variables and channels, and with the reverse operation of encapsulation of a part of a program (a statement) within a procedure. Both operations are defined as transformation rules:

Rule 1 (Replace Procedure Reference (RepRef)). *Given a program* P *and the label* k *of a reference substatement within it, rule* RepRef *replaces the reference by the body of the procedure having the name specified in the reference statement. The names of variables and channels of the interface occurring in the body are changed by their corresponding names in the reference statement.*
Inputs: *A program,* P *which includes the declaration of the referred procedure. The label* k *of the reference statement.*
Outputs: *A boolean,* done, *which takes the value true if the applicability conditions hold and the goal has been accomplished. The transformed program* P'.

Rule 2 (Encapsulate within a Reference (EncRef)). *Given a program* P *and the label* k *of one of its statements, rule* EncRef *replaces the statement by a reference statement to an already defined procedure. The statement has to match with the procedure body, up to a relabeling of the names of variables and channels appearing in the procedure interface definition. This is checked as part of the applicability condition of the rule.*
Inputs: *A program,* P. *The label* k *of the statement. The name* name *of the procedure whose body has to replace the statement.*
Outputs: *A boolean,* done, *which takes the value true if the applicability conditions hold and the goal has been accomplished. The transformed program* P'.

6   Parallelization of an FFT

The architecture to be designed computes the discrete fourier transform (DFT) [31] of a vector f of order N. The DFT is defined as:

$$F_N[n] = \frac{1}{N} \sum_{m=0}^{N-1} f[m] w_N^{-mn} \quad , \quad n = 0, 1, ..., N-1 \tag{1}$$

where $w_N^n \stackrel{\text{def}}{=} e^{j\frac{2\pi n}{N}}$ and N is a power of 2, $N = 2^p$; $p = 0, 1, ...$ The computation is based on the Fast Fourier Transform (FFT) algorithm in its Decimation in Frequency (DF) variant [30, 33]. Its basic step is the computation of the two half order vectors f_0 and f_1 in terms of the original f by the equations:

$$f_0[m] = \frac{1}{2}(v_0[m] + v_1[m]) \tag{2}$$

$$f_1[m] = \frac{1}{2}(v_0[m] - v_1[m]) \times w_N^{-m} \tag{3}$$

for $m = 0, 1, ..., N/2 - 1$. Vectors v_0 and v_1 are of order $N/2$, and are defined as $v_0[m] = f[m]$, and $v_1[m] = f[m + N/2]$ for $m = 0, 1, \cdots, N/2 - 1$. They correspond to the lower and upper halves of vector f. The computation associated with the two formulas for a fixed m is known as *DF-butterfly*. Thus, the basic step computes $N/2$ butterflies. Then, the even and odd indexed components of F_N are obtained as the DFT of f_0 and f_1, respectively. The same procedure could be repeated to compute these DFTs of order $N/2$. The DF-FFT algorithm applies the basic step recursively until the order $N = 1$ is reached. Then, by equation (1) $F_1 = f$. It corresponds to the following procedure:

$$fout ::= FFT\ (fin, w, p)\ ::$$

$$\left[\begin{array}{lll} \textbf{out} & fout & : \textbf{vector}(p) \\ \textbf{external in}\ fin & : \textbf{vector}(p) \\ \textbf{external in}\ w & : \textbf{array}\ [k{:=}p..1]\ \textbf{of vector}(k-1) \\ \textbf{external in}\ p & : \textbf{integer} \\ \textbf{local} & f0, f1, fout0, fout1 : \textbf{vector}(p-1) \\ \left[\begin{array}{l} \textbf{when}\ p > 0\ \textbf{do} \\ \quad \left[\begin{array}{l} (f0, f1) := BStep\ (fin, w, p); \\ fout0 := FFT\ (f0, w, p-1); \\ fout1 := FFT\ (f1, w, p-1); \\ fout := (fout0, fout1) \end{array}\right] \\ \textbf{or} \\ \textbf{when}\ p = 0\ \textbf{do}\ [fout := fin] \end{array}\right] \end{array}\right]$$

From now on, the notation **vector**(p) will stand for **array** $[1..2^p]$ **of complex**. Procedure *BStep* corresponds to the basic step, and computes the two half-order vectors *f0* and *f1* in terms of the original vector *fin* by an iterative application of equations (2) and (3). The triangular matrix w contains the p vectors of the roots of the unity which are needed at each level of the computation tree. At the end of the computation the components of F_N are not ordered in *fout*. A communicating version of the *FFT* can be defined as:

$$\beta ::= ComFFT\ (\alpha, w, p)\ ::$$

$$\left[\begin{array}{lll} \textbf{out} & \beta & : \textbf{channel of vector}(p-1) \\ \textbf{external in}\ \alpha & : \textbf{channel of vector}(p) \\ \textbf{external in}\ w & : \textbf{array}\ [k := p..1]\ \textbf{of vector}(k-1) \\ \textbf{external in}\ p & : \textbf{integer} \\ \textbf{local} & in, out : \textbf{vector}(p) \\ \textbf{local} & f0, f1 : \textbf{vector}(p-1) \\ \left[\begin{array}{l} \alpha \Rightarrow in; \\ out ::= FFT\ (in, w, p); \\ (f0, f1) := out; \\ \beta \Leftarrow f0; \beta \Leftarrow f1; \end{array}\right] \end{array}\right]$$

It is valid for $p > 0$. It simply communicates its input and output vectors via synchronous channels. The output is formed by two half-order vectors in series via channel β. Similarly, for the basic step:

$$\beta ::= ComBStep\ (\alpha, w, p)\ ::\ \begin{bmatrix} \textbf{local}\ in\quad :\textbf{vector}(p) \\ \textbf{local}\ f0, f1 : \textbf{vector}(p-1) \\ \begin{bmatrix} \alpha \Rightarrow in; \\ (f0, f1) ::= BStep\ (in, w, p); \\ \beta \Leftarrow f0; \beta \Leftarrow f1 \end{bmatrix} \end{bmatrix}$$

The declaration of the interface variables has been omitted since it is the same as before. The same is done for the next procedure, which shares the same interface. A pipelined FFT architecture $SerialFFT$ is defined as:

$$\beta ::= SerialFFT\ (\alpha, w, p)\ ::$$

$$\begin{bmatrix} \textbf{local}\ f0, f1\quad :\textbf{vector}(p-1) \\ \textbf{local}\ k, l\qquad :\textbf{integer} \\ \textbf{local}\ \gamma\qquad\quad :\textbf{Array}\ [k := 0..p]\ \textbf{of channel of vector}(2^{p-k}) \\ \textbf{local}\ (\gamma(0), \alpha) :\textbf{equivalence} \\ [\ |||_{k:=0}^{p-1}\ \textbf{for}\ \ l := 1\ \textbf{to}\ \ 2^k\ \ \textbf{do}\ \gamma(k+1) ::= ComBStep\ (\gamma(k), w, p-k);] \\ || \\ \begin{bmatrix} \textbf{for}\ \ m := 1\ \textbf{to}\ \ 2^{p-1}\ \ \textbf{do}\ \gamma(p) \Rightarrow f0(m); \\ \textbf{for}\ \ m := 1\ \textbf{to}\ \ 2^{p-1}\ \ \textbf{do}\ \gamma(p) \Rightarrow f1(m); \\ \beta \Leftarrow f0; \beta \Leftarrow f1; \end{bmatrix} \end{bmatrix}$$

It is a pipeline architecture with p processes communicated via channels $\gamma(k)$, ended with a process which constructs vectors $f0$ and $f1$, and outputs them in sequence via channel β. Each one of the first p processes computes a number of basic steps in sequence, starting with one for the process corresponding to $k = 0$, and doubling the number of basic steps of their corresponding predecessors in the pipeline. With the above definitions, the following congruence holds:

Lemma 3 (Serial FFT Architecture). *For $p > 0$:*

$$[\beta ::= ComFFT\ (\alpha, w, p)] \approx [\beta ::= SerialFFT\ (\alpha, w, p)]$$

The set of observed variables is now $\mathcal{O} = \{var(\alpha), var(\beta)\}$, where $var(\alpha)$ means the variables associated with synchronous channel α via communication statements. The proof cannot be given due to paper length restrictions. It is carried out by induction on p. Both, the base case and the induction step are proved with transformations involving the tactics and rules which have been covered so far, plus some simple tactics for the rearrangement of sequences of parallel disjoint processes and iterations, and for the elimination of variables.

7   Conclusions and Future Work

The mathematical justification of a set of transformation rules for the elimination and introduction of synchronous communications and parallelism in imperative concurrent programs has been accomplished. A set of tactics has been defined for the application of the rules, they ease the generation of broader transformations guaranteeing that they are always consequence of a certain sequence of rule applications. As an illustration, a distributed FFT algorithm has been derived with the methods introduced in this work, starting from a sequential recursive version. It has been shown that an infinite set of relations is needed in general for the elimination of a matching pair of synchronous communication statements. All this has been worked out in the framework of Manna and Pnueli for reactive systems, and with the usual fairness assumptions. However, a restriction on the SPL notation has been needed, which is not important for the applications, and has endowed the notation with very intuitive congruences for the introduction and elimination of *skip* substatements in concatenation and cooperation statements. These are needed in conjunction with the proper elimination-introduction rules. The main treatment has been limited to programs formed with basic, concatenation, and cooperation statements. Although this is sufficient to show, as it has been done, that no finite set of relations is complete, the laws and tactics could be extended to general programs with selection statements. They could be incorporated into an interactive system complementing verification and model checking in an integrated formal design environment. This will form a good basis for an interactive transformation system. Nevertheless, more work is needed in the evaluation of heuristics to guide the rewriting. Once all this work is completed, repetition of verification and/or model checking for related programs may be avoided in many cases by carrying out communication and parallelism introduction-elimination transformations, forming part of a comprehensive formal design process.

Acknowledgements

We thank the criticisms of our work made by Dr. Toms Uribe during his visit to our department, and the encouragement received from the REACT group, lead by Prof. Zohar Manna, during our visit to Stanford University. The reviewers are also thanked for their comments which have improved the paper.

A   Proof of the Skip Non-congruences

Proof of Remark 1. In order to prove the first relation, define the program context $P[S]$ as the program shown below. Then $P[\alpha \Leftarrow T]$ always terminates under standard fairness. This is due to the synchronization between P_1 and P_3 imposed by the synchronous communication via channel α. Just after this transition is taken, the joint transition between the same two processes, but via β, is enabled. Since both communication statements occur within an indefinite loop in both processes, this enabling occurs an indefinite number of times.

local x, y, z, v : **boolean where** $x = T, y = T, z = T, v = T$
local $\alpha, \beta, \gamma, \delta$: **channel of boolean**

$$
P_1 :: \left[\begin{array}{l} k_0: \textbf{ while } x \textbf{ do} \\ \left[\begin{array}{lll} k_1: S; & k_2: & \left[\begin{array}{l} k_3: \ \beta \Rightarrow x; k_4: \ \alpha \Leftarrow F; k_5: \ \gamma \Leftarrow F \\ \textbf{or} \\ k_6: \ \gamma \Leftarrow T \end{array} \right] \\ k_7: \end{array} \right] \end{array} \right]
$$

$\parallel$

$$
P_2 :: \left[\begin{array}{l} \ell_0: \textbf{ while } y \textbf{ do} \\ \ [\ell_1: \ \gamma \Rightarrow y] \end{array} \right]
$$

$\parallel$

$$
P_3 :: \left[\begin{array}{l} m_0: \textbf{ while } z \textbf{ do} \\ \left[\begin{array}{lll} m_1: \ \alpha \Rightarrow z; & m_2: & \left[\begin{array}{l} m_3: \ \beta \Leftarrow F; m_4: \ \alpha \Rightarrow z; m_5: \ \delta \Leftarrow F \\ \textbf{or} \\ m_6: \ \delta \Leftarrow T \end{array} \right] \\ m_7: \end{array} \right] \end{array} \right]
$$

$\parallel$

$$
P_4 :: \left[\begin{array}{l} n_0: \textbf{ while } v \textbf{ do} \\ \ [n_1: \ \ \delta \Rightarrow v] \end{array} \right]
$$

But, since the joint transition associated with synchronous communication statements are in the compassion set (strongly fair), the synchronous communication via β has to be taken eventually. Once this occurs, the variables x, z, v, and y take the value false and the four processes terminate.

The communication via β may not occur in the program $P[\alpha \Leftarrow T; \textbf{skip}]$ since the presence of the new skip statement allows the existence of indefinite computations having no enabling of the communication via β.

This is so since now, due to the skip statement, the synchronization via channel α does not necessarily activate simultaneously the control locations corresponding to labels k_2 and m_2, consequently the joint transition of the synchronous communication via channel β may never be enabled. Therefore program $P[\alpha \Leftarrow T; \textbf{skip}]$ has a non-terminating computation. This proves the first non-congruence. The other two are consequences of the first. $\square$

The proof of the other remark is similar.

B   Proof of Theorem 1

A *reduced run* of a FTS is obtained from a run, as defined in section 2, in the same way that a reduced behavior was obtained from a computation in that section.

Definition 2 (Reduced Run). *Let* M *be a FTS, and* $\mathcal{O}$ *a set of observed variables, where* π *is not in* $\mathcal{O}$. *Then a reduced run* r^r *is obtained from a run* r *of* M *by retaining the observable part of all the states appearing in* r *and deleting any state which is equal to its predecessor but not equal to its successor.*

Therefore, stuttering steps are removed from the observable part of a run provided that they do not correspond to a terminal state. Notice also that a reduced run does not need to satisfy any fairness requirements. Then, reduced behaviors would be the subset of reduced runs which satisfy the fairness requirements. The concept of reduced run can be extended to programs, as the reduced run of the FTS associated with the program.

Lemma 4 (Skip Congruence in a Wide Sense). *Let $P[\_]$ be an arbitrary program context. Then, the sets of reduced runs of $P[S_1; S_2]$ and $P[S_1; \text{skip}; S_2]$ are identical. We express this fact by saying that the two concatenation statements are* congruent in the wide sense.

noindent**Proof.** Introduce m as the post-label of S_1 in $P[S_1; m : S_2]$ and of **skip** in $P[S_1; \ell : \text{skip}; m : S_2]$. Also, ℓ will be the post-label of S_1 in $P[S_1; \ell : \text{skip}; m : S_2]$

1. Consider a run r of $P[S_1; m : S_2]$. We obtain a run r' of $P[S_1; \ell : \text{skip}; m : S_2]$ by requiring that whenever control reaches m, which is now relabeled as ℓ, a skip transition τ_ℓ is taken immediately. Clearly, r' is a run of $P[S_1; \ell : \text{skip}; m : S_2]$ and the reduced runs of both r and r' are identical, since their only differences are at the transitions τ_ℓ which have been introduced in r', corresponding to the skip statement. These transitions have identical initial and final states. For each such pair of states in r', the run r has only one state. But the first of the two equal states of such pairs will be deleted when the corresponding reduced run is constructed, as it has been defined above. Then, the reduced runs of both r and r' will be equal.
2. The reverse direction is similar. $\square$

Let us describe the deletion of skip transitions τ_ℓ with some detail. The rest of this appendix will need and refer to it. A computation σ of $P[S_1; \ell : \text{skip}; m : S_2]$ will have state subsequences of the following form:

$$\ldots s_{i-f-1}, s_{i-f}, \ldots, s_i, s_{i+1}, \ldots, s_{i+n}, \ldots$$

where $s_{i-f}, \ldots, s_i$ are ℓ-states, in the sense that the control location corresponding to ℓ belongs to π in these states, s_{i-f-1} is not an ℓ-state. Also, states $s_{i+1}, \ldots, s_{i+n-1}$ are m-states, and the transition taken at s_i is the skip transition τ_ℓ, s_{i+n} is not an m-state. Hence, the last transition corresponding to S_1 is taken at state s_{i-f-1}, and a front transition of S_2 is taken at state s_{i+n-1}. It will be referred to later on as transition τ'. Let us construct now the state sequence σ' by deleting all τ_ℓ transitions from σ. This entails replacing ℓ by m in all the states of σ. This sequence of states will have subsequences of the form $\ldots s_{i-f-1}, s_{i-f}, \ldots, s_i \equiv s_{i+1}, \ldots, s_{i+n}, \ldots$ which will correspond to the above subsequences of σ. The states $s_{i-f}, \ldots, s_i \equiv s_{i+1}$ become now m-states by construction. States s_i and s_{i+1} collapse into the same state. The rest of the sequence remains the same, states $s_{i+2} \ldots, s_{i+n-1}$ continue being m-states.

For realistic schedulers we would like that the congruence of lemma 4 was true in a strict sense. In other words, that for an arbitrary program context $P[\_]$, the set of *reduced behaviors* for $P[S_1; m : S_2]$ and for $P[S_1; \ell : \text{skip}; m : S_2]$ were identical. This is not true due to remark 1 of section 3. However, the following lemma expresses the fact that it is true in one direction.

Lemma 5 (Sequential Skip Insertion). *Let $P[\_]$ be an arbitrary program context. Then, any reduced behavior of $P[S_1; S_2]$ is also a reduced behavior of $P[S_1; \textbf{skip}; S_2]$.*

The proof is not given due to paper length restrictions. It is based on the fact that the positions in which a transition τ is enabled or taken in both σ and σ' are the same when only skip transitions are inserted.

The reverse of lemma 5 is not true since, when deleting skip transitions from a computation, there is the possibility that some transition which was not enabled in the final state of the skip transition becomes enabled in the corresponding state obtained after the deletion. Hence, the satisfaction of fairness requirements may change for such transition. Next lemma characterizes the scenarios where the above may occur, and the transitions which are involved.

Lemma 6 (Unfairness Scenario). *The only way in which σ, a computation of $P[S_1; \ell : \textbf{skip}; m : S_2]$, can be fair to a transition τ but σ', the state sequence of $P[S; m : S_2]$ constructed by deleting τ_ℓ transitions as detailed above, be unfair to τ is if τ is enabled infinitely often in σ' but only finitely often in σ, and τ is taken only finitely many times in both.*

The proof is based on the fact that the deletion of the the skip transitions modifies states $s_{i-f}, ..., s_i$. This may enable transitions in these states which were not enabled in the corresponding states of σ.

Lemma 7 (Compassionate Transition). *If the state sequence σ' is unfair with respect to transition τ, which is enabled finitely often in $P[S_1; \ell : \textbf{skip}; m : S_2]$ but infinitely often in $P[S; m : S_2]$, then the control location corresponding to label m is visited an indefinite number of times, in both σ and σ'. Also, τ has to be a front transition of S_2 and compassionate (strongly fair).*

The proof is based mainly on the fact that the new enablings take place in at least one of the states of the sequence $s_{i-f}, ..., s_{i-1}$, which is preceded and followed by states where τ is not enabled, τ is enabled when control is at the location corresponding to m, and these sequences of states are finite.

Two transitions τ and τ' are *competing* if both are directly associated with the same selection statement. In addition, the two competing transitions may also correspond to a synchronous communication statement which does not form part of a selection statement, but which gives rise to two joint transitions with matching isolated communication statements which are parallel to it.

Lemma 8 (Disabling Transition). *A τ-disabling transition τ'' occurs in both σ and σ' in one of the states of their state subsequence $s_{i-f+1}, ..., s_{i-1}$. This transition should be competing with transition τ but should be parallel to the transitions associated with statement S_2.*

Proof. This has to be so since transition τ is enabled but not taken only in a subsequence of the state sequence $s_{i-f}, ..., s_{i-1}$. Therefore some transition τ'' is taken in one of these states, disabling transition τ. Transition τ'' has to be parallel to the transitions associated with S_2 since a front transition of this statement, τ', is taken in state s_{i+n-1} as it was pointed out before, and τ'' has to be taken in a prior state without moving control from the location corresponding to m. Transition τ'' disables transition τ, hence it should be competing with it. $\square$

Lemma 9 (Prohibited Statements). *Within the reduced notation, The only possibilities for statement S_2 which could give rise to the three transitions τ, τ' and τ'' identified above are a synchronous communication statement and a communication selection statement.*

We note that if this lemma is true then theorem 1 is also true. The proof is based on a review of the semantics of the notation as defined in section 2. $\square$

References

1. R.-J. Back, J. von Wright, *Refinement Calculus. A Systematic Introduction.* Springer-Verlag 1998.
2. S. Bensalem, M. Bozga, J.C. Fernandez, L. Ghirvu, Y. Lakhnech, *A Transformational Approach for Generating Non-Linear Invariants.* In J. Palsberg (Ed.), *Static Analysis*, Proc. 7th Intl. Symp. SAS 2000, Santa Barbara, CA, USA, June 29 - July 1, 2000. LNCS Vol. 1824, Springer, 2000, pp. 58-74.
3. M. Bertran, F. Alvarez-Cuevas, A. Duran, Communication Extended Abstract Types in the Refinement of Parallel Communicating Processes, in *Transformation-Based Reactive Systems Development*, LNCS v.1231, Springer, 1997.
4. N.S. Bjørner, A. Browne, M. Colón, B. Finkbeiner, Z. Manna, H.B. Sipma, and T.E. Uribe. Verifying Temporal Properties of Reactive Systems: A STeP Tutorial. *Formal Methods in System Design*, 16, 227-270, June 2000.
5. N.S. Bjørner, A. Browne, E. Chang, M. Colón, A. Kapur, Z. Manna, H.B. Sipma, and T.E. Uribe. STeP: The Stanford Temporal Prover, User's Manual. Technical Report STAN-CS-TR-95-1562, Computer Science Department, Stanford University, November 1995.
6. S.D. Brookes. 'Full abstraction for a shared variable parallel language', *Information and Computation*, 127(2):145-163, June 1996.
7. M. Broy, 'Functional Specification of Time-Sensitive Communicating Systems', *ACM Transactions on Software Engineering and Methodology*, 2(1),: 1-46, January 1993.
8. M. Broy, 'Refinement of Time', in M. Bertran and T. Rus (eds.), *Transformation-Based Reactive Systems Development*, Springer-Verlag, Lecture Notes in Computer Science 1231, 1997, pp. 44-63.
9. M. Broy, 'A Logical Basis for Component-Based Systems Engineering', *Tech. Report Inst. fr Informatik*, Tech. Univ. Munchen, Germany.
10. K.M. Chandy and J. Misra, *Parallel Program Design*, Addison Wesley, 1988.
11. Wei-Ngan Chin, Sian-Cheng Khoo, Z. Hu, M. Takeidu, *Deriving Parallel Codes via Invariants.* In J. Palsberg (Ed.), *Static Analysis*, Proc. 7th Intl. Symp. SAS 2000, Santa Barbara, CA, USA, June 29 - July 1, 2000. LNCS Vol. 1824, Springer, 2000, pp. 75-94.

12. E.M. Clarke, O. Grumberg, D.A. Peled, *Model Checking*, The MIT Press, 1999.
13. J. Dingel, 'A Trace-Based Refinement Calculus for Shared-Variable Parallel Programs', in A.Martin Haeberer (Ed.) *Algebraic Methodology and Software Technology*, AMAST'98, LNCS 1548, Springer-Verlag, pp. 231-247, 1998.
14. B. Finkbeiner, Z. Manna, H. Sipma, *Deductive Verification of Modular Systems*. In *Compositionality: The Significant Difference*, COMPOS'97, LNCS v. 1536, pp. 239-275, Springer 1998.
15. M. Gordon, A.J. Milner, Ch. P. Wadsworth, *Edinburgh LCF*, LNCS v.78, Springer-Verlag, 1979.
16. C.A.R. Hoare, 'Communicating Sequential Processes', *Communications of ACM*, Vol 21, pp 666-677, 1978.
17. C.A.R. Hoare, *Communicating Sequential Processes*, Prentice-Hall, Englewood Cliffs, N.J., 1985.
18. Gerald Holtzmann, *Design and Validation of Computer Protocols*, Prentice Hall, 1991.
19. J. Hooman, 'Extending Hoare Logic to Real-Time', *Formal Aspects of Computing*, 6A: 801-825, BCS, 1994.
20. Y. Kesten, Z. Manna, A. Pnueli, 'Temporal Verification of Simulation and Refinement', In REX Symposium *A Decade of Concurrency*, Lecture Notes in Computer Science 803, pp. 273-346, Springer-Verlag, 1994.
21. L. Lamport, 'The Temporal Logic of Actions', *ACM Trans. Progr. Lang. and Sys.*, 16(3):872-923.
22. B. Mahony, 'Using the Refinement Calculus for Dataflow Processes'. *Tech. Report 94-32*, Soft.Verification Research Centre, University of Queensland, October 94.
23. Z. Manna, A. Pnueli, *The Temporal Logic of Reactive and Concurrent Systems. Specification.* Springer-Verlag, 1991.
24. Z. Manna, A. Pnueli, *Temporal Verification of Reactive Systems. Safety.* Springer-Verlag, 1995.
25. K.L. McMillan, and D.L. Dill, *Symbolic Model Checking: An Approach to the State Explosion Problem*, Kluwer Academic, 1993.
26. R. Milner, *A Calculus of Communicating Systems*, Springer-Verlag, 1980.
27. R. Milner, *Communication and Concurrency*, Prentice-Hall 1989.
28. M.Muller-Olm, D.A. Schmit, B. Steffen, *Model Checking: A Tutorial Introduction*. In A.Cortesi, G.File (Eds.), *Static Analysis*, Proc. 6th Intl. Symp. SAS'99, Venice, Italy, September 22-24, 1999. LNCS, Vol 1694, Springer, 1999, pp. 330-354.
29. Wei-Ngan Chin, Sian-Cheng Khoo, Z. Hu, M. Takeidu, *Deriving Parallel Codes via Invariants*. In J. Palsberg (Ed.), *Static Analysis*, Proc. 7th Intl. Symp. SAS 2000, Santa Barbara, CA, USA, June 29 - July 1, 2000. LNCS Vol. 1824, Springer, 2000, pp. 75-94.
30. A.V. Oppenheim, R.W. Shafer, *Digital Signal Processing*, Prentice Hall, N.J., 1975.
31. A. Papoulis, *Signal Analysis*, McGraw-Hill, N.Y., 1977.
32. A. Podelski, *Model Checking as Constraint Solving*. In J. Palsberg (Ed.), *Static Analysis*, Proc. 7th Intl. Symp. SAS 2000, Santa Barbara, CA, USA, June 29 - July 1, 2000. LNCS Vol. 1824, Springer, 2000, pp. 22-37.
33. L.R. Rabiner, B. Gold, *Theory and Application of Digital Signal processing*, Prentice Hall, N.J., 1975.

Using Slicing to Identify Duplication in Source Code

Raghavan Komondoor[1] and Susan Horwitz[1,2]

[1] Computer Sciences Department
University of Wisconsin-Madison
Madison, WI 53706 USA
{raghavan,horwitz}@cs.wisc.edu
[2] IEI del CNR, Pisa Italy

Abstract. Programs often have a lot of duplicated code, which makes both understanding and maintenance more difficult. This problem can be alleviated by detecting duplicated code, extracting it into a separate new procedure, and replacing all the clones (the instances of the duplicated code) by calls to the new procedure. This paper describes the design and initial implementation of a tool that finds clones and displays them to the programmer. The novel aspect of our approach is the use of program dependence graphs (PDGs) and program slicing to find isomorphic PDG subgraphs that represent clones. The key benefits of this approach are that our tool can find non-contiguous clones (clones whose components do not occur as contiguous text in the program), clones in which matching statements have been reordered, and clones that are intertwined with each other. Furthermore, the clones that are found are likely to be meaningful computations, and thus good candidates for extraction.

1 Introduction

Programs undergoing ongoing development and maintenance often have a lot of duplicated code. The results of several studies [1, 12, 13] indicate that 7–23% of the source code for large programs is duplicated code. Duplication results in increased code size and complexity, making program maintenance more difficult. For example, when enhancements or bug fixes are done on one instance of the duplicated code, it may be necessary to search for the other instances in order to perform the corresponding modification. Lague et al [13] studied the development of a large software system over multiple releases and found that in fact, programmers often missed some copies of duplicated code when performing modifications.

A tool that finds clones (instances of duplicated code) can help alleviate these problems: the clones identified by the tool can be extracted into a new procedure, and the clones themselves replaced by calls to that procedure. In that case, there will be only one copy to maintain (the new procedure), and the fact that the procedure can be reused may cut down on future duplication. (Note that for a language like C with a preprocessor, macros can be used instead of procedures

P. Cousot (Ed.): SAS 2001, LNCS 2126, pp. 40–56, 2001.

if there is a concern that introducing procedures will result in unacceptable performance degradation.)

For an example illustrating clone detection and extraction, see Figure 1. The left column shows four fragments of code from the Unix utility *bison*. The four clones are indicated by the "++" signs. The function of the duplicated code is to grow the buffer pointed to by p if needed, append the current character c to the buffer and then read the next character. In the right column, the duplicated code has been extracted into a new procedure next_char, indicated by the "++" signs, and all four clones replaced by calls to this procedure. The four calls are indicated by "**" signs.

This paper describes the design and initial implementation of a tool for C programs that finds clones suitable for procedure extraction and displays them to the programmer. The novel aspect of the work is the use of *program dependence graphs* (PDGs) [9], and a variation on *program slicing* [19, 16] to find isomorphic subgraphs of the PDG that represent clones. The key benefits of a slicing-based approach, compared with previous approaches to clone detection that were based on comparing text, control-flow graphs, or abstract-syntax trees, is that our tool can find non-contiguous clones (i.e., clones whose statements do not occur as contiguous text in the program, such as in Fragments 1 and 2 in Figure 1), clones in which matching statements have been reordered, and clones that are intertwined with each other. Furthermore, the clones found using this approach are likely to be meaningful computations, and thus good candidates for extraction.

The remainder of this paper is organized as follows: Section 2 describes how our tool uses slicing to find clones, and the benefits of this approach. Section 3 describes an implementation of our tool, and some of the insights obtained from running the tool on real programs. Section 4 discusses related work, and Section 5 summarizes our results.

2 Slicing-Based Clone Detection

2.1 Algorithm Description

To find clones in a program, we represent each procedure using its program dependence graph (PDG) [9]. In the PDG, nodes represent program statements and predicates, and edges represent data and control dependences. The algorithm performs three steps (described in the following subsections):

Step 1: Find pairs of clones.
Step 2: Remove subsumed clones.
Step 3: Combine pairs of clones into larger groups.

Step 1: Find Pairs of Clones. We start by partitioning all PDG nodes into equivalence classes based on the syntactic structure of the statement/predicate that the node represents, ignoring variable names and literal values; two nodes

Fragment 1:

```
  while (isalpha(c) ||
      c == '_' || c == '-') {
++   if (p == token_buffer + maxtoken)
++      p = grow_token_buffer(p);
     if (c == '-') c = '_';
++   *p++ = c;
++   c = getc(finput);
  }
```

Fragment 2:

```
  while (isdigit(c)) {
++   if (p == token_buffer + maxtoken)
++      p = grow_token_buffer(p);
     numval = numval*20 + c - '0';
++   *p++ = c;
++   c = getc(finput);
  }
```

Fragment 3:

```
  while (c != '>') {
     if (c == EOF) fatal();
     if (c == '\n') {
       warn("unterminated type name");
       ungetc(c, finput);
       break;
     }
++   if (p == token_buffer + maxtoken)
++      p = grow_token_buffer(p);
++   *p++ = c;
++   c = getc(finput);
  }
```

Fragment 4:

```
  while (isalnum(c) ||
      c == '_' || c == '.') {
++   if (p == token_buffer + maxtoken)
++      p = grow_token_buffer(p);
++   *p++ = c;
++   c = getc(finput);
  }
```

Rewritten Fragment 1:

```
  while (isalpha(c) ||
      c == '_' || c == '-') {
     if (c == '-') c = '_';
**   next_char(&p, &c);
  }
```

Rewritten Fragment 2:

```
  while (isdigit(c)) {
     numval = numval*20 + c - '0';
**   next_char(&p, &c);
  }
```

Rewritten Fragment 3:

```
  while (c != '>') {
    if (c == EOF) fatal();
    if (c == '\n') {
    warn("unterminated type name");
    ungetc(c, finput);
    break;
    }
**next_char(&p, &c);
    }
```

Rewritten Fragment 4:

```
  while (isalnum(c) ||
      c == '_' || c == '.') {
**     next_char(&p, &c);
  }
```

Newly extracted procedure:

```
  void next_char(char **ptr_p,
                      char *ptr_c){
++ if (*ptr_p ==
        token_buffer + maxtoken)
++     *ptr_p =
        grow_token_buffer(*ptr_p);
++ *(*ptr_p)++ = *ptr_c;
++ *ptr_c = getc(finput);
  }
```

Fig. 1. Duplicated Code from *bison*.

in the same class are called matching nodes. Next, for each pair of matching nodes $(r1, r2)$, we find two isomorphic subgraphs of the PDGs that contain $r1$ and $r2$.

The heart of the algorithm that finds the isomorphic subgraphs is the use of backward slicing: starting from $r1$ and $r2$ we slice backwards in lock step, adding a predecessor (and the connecting edge) to one slice iff there is a corresponding, matching predecessor in the other PDG (which is added to the other slice). Forward slicing is also used: whenever a pair of matching loop or if-then-else predicates $(p1, p2)$ is added to the pair of slices, we slice forward one step from $p1$ and $p2$, adding their matching control-dependence successors (and the connecting edges) to the two slices. Note that while lock-step backward slicing is done from *every* pair of matching nodes in the two slices, forward slicing is done only from matching predicates. An example to illustrate the need for this kind of limited forward slicing is given in Section 2.2.

When the process described above finishes, it will have identified two isomorphic subgraphs (two matching "partial" slices) that represent a pair of clones. The process is illustrated using Figure 2, which shows the PDGs for the first two code fragments from Figure 1. (Function calls are actually represented in

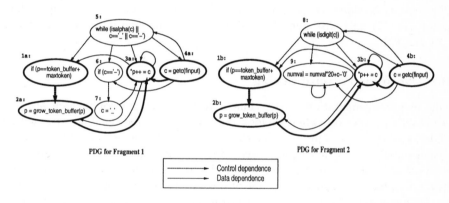

Fig. 2. Matching partial slices starting from `*p++ = c;`. The nodes and edges in the partial slices are shown in bold.

PDGs using multiple nodes: one for each actual parameter, one for the return value, and one for the call itself. For clarity, in this example we have treated function calls as atomic operations.) Nodes 3a and 3b match, so we can start with those two nodes. Slicing backward from nodes 3a and 3b along their incoming control-dependence edges we find nodes 5 and 8 (the two `while` nodes). However, these nodes do not match (they have different syntactic structure), so they are not added to the partial slices. Slicing backward from nodes 3a and 3b along their incoming data-dependence edges we find nodes 2a, 3a, 4a, and 7 in the first PDG, and nodes 2b, 3b, and 4b in the second PDG. Node 2a matches 2b, and node 4a matches 4b, so those nodes (and the edges just traversed to reach them) are added to the two partial slices. (Nodes $3a$ and $3b$ have already been added, so those nodes are not reconsidered.) Slicing backward from nodes $2a$ and $2b$, we find nodes $1a$ and $1b$, which match, so they (and the traversed edges) are added. Furthermore, nodes $1a$ and $1b$ represent if predicates; therefore we slice forward from those two nodes. We find nodes $2a$ and $2b$, which are already in the slices, so they are not reconsidered. Slicing backward from nodes $4a$ and $4b$, we find nodes 5 and 8, which do not match; the same two nodes are found when slicing backward from nodes $1a$ and $1b$.

The partial slices are now complete. The nodes and edges in the two partial slices are shown in Figure 2 using bold font. These two partial slices correspond to the clones of Fragments 1 and 2 shown in Figure 1 using "++" signs.

Step 2: Remove Subsumed Clones. A clone pair $(S1', S2')$ *subsumes* another clone pair $(S1, S2)$ iff $S1 \subseteq S1'$ and $S2 \subseteq S2'$. There is no reason for the tool to report subsumed clone pairs; therefore, this step removes subsumed clone pairs from the set of pairs identified in Step 1.

Step 3: Combine Pairs of Clones into Larger Groups. This step combines clone pairs into clone groups using a kind of transitive closure. For example, clone pairs $(S1, S2)$, $(S1, S3)$, and $(S2, S3)$ would be combined into the clone group $(S1, S2, S3)$.

2.2   Need for Forward Slicing

Our first implementation of the clone-detection tool did not include any forward slicing. However, when we looked at the clones that it found we saw that they sometimes were subsets of the clones that a programmer would have identified manually. In particular, we observed that conditionals and loops sometimes contain code that a programmer would identify as all being part of one logical operation, but that is not the result of a backward slice from any single node.

One example of this situation is error-handling code, such as the two fragments in Figure 3 from the Unix utility *tail*. The two fragments are identical except for the target of the final goto, and are reasonable candidates for extraction; they both check for the same error condition, and if it holds, they both perform the same sequence of actions: calling the error procedure, setting the global error variable, and freeing variable tmp. (The final goto should of course not be part of the extracted procedure; instead, that procedure would need to return a boolean value to specify whether or not the goto should be executed.) However, the two fragments cannot be identified as clones using only backward slicing, since the backward slice from any statement inside the if fails to include any of the other statements in the if. It is the forward-slicing step from the pair of matched if predicates that allows our tool to identify these two code fragments as clones.

Other examples where forward slicing is needed include loops that set the values of two related but distinct variables (e.g., the head and tail pointers of a

Fragment 1:   Fragment 2:

```
if (tmp->nbytes == -1)              if (tmp->nbytes == -1)
  {                                   {
    error (0, errno, "%s", filename);   error (0, errno, "%s", filename);
    errors = 1;                         errors = 1;
    free ((char *) tmp);                free ((char *) tmp);
    goto free_lbuffers;                 goto free_cbuffers;
  }                                   }
```

Fig. 3. Error-handling code from `tail` that motivates the use of forward slicing.

linked list). In such examples, although the entire loop corresponds to a single logical operation, backward slicing alone is not sufficient to identify the whole loop as a clone.

2.3   Preventing Clones that Cross Loops

Based on experience gained from applying the algorithm to real programs, we found that we needed a heuristic to prevent clones that "cross" loops; i.e., clones that include nodes both inside and outside a loop but not the loop itself. To illustrate this, consider the two code fragments (from *bison*) in Figure 4. The clones

Fragment 1:   Fragment 2:

```
     fp3 = lookaheadset + tokensetsize;    fp3 = base + tokensetsize;
     for (i = lookaheads(state);           ...
          i < k; i++) {                     if (rp) {
++       fp1 = LA +                             while ((j = *rp++) >= 0) {
++                i * tokensetsize;               ...
++       fp2 = lookaheadset;          ++          fp1 = base;
++       while (fp2 < fp3)            ++          fp2 = F +
++            *fp2++ |= *fp1++;       ++                   j * tokensetsize;
     }                               ++          while (fp1 < fp3)
                                     ++               *fp1++ |= *fp2++;
                                                  }
                                              }
```

Fig. 4. Two clones from *bison* that illustrates the heuristic that avoids "crossing" a loop. These clones also illustrate variable renaming and statement reordering.

identified by our tool are shown using "++" signs. Each of these clones modifies a portion of a bit array (`lookaheadset` / `base`) by performing a bit-wise *or* with the contents of another array (`LA` / `F`). The clones are identified by slicing back from the statement that does the bit-wise *or*. Note that the two initial assignments to `fp3` are matching statements that are data-dependence predecessors of matching nodes in the two clones (the nodes that represent the final `while` predicates). Therefore, the algorithm as described above in Section 2.1 would have included the two initial assignments in the clones. It would not, however, have included in the clones the `for` loop in the first fragment and the outer `while` loop in the second fragment because the predicates of those loops do not match.

The resulting clones would therefore contain the statements inside the loops and the assignments outside the loops, but not the loops themselves. This would make it difficult to extract the clones into a separate procedure. To prevent the algorithm from identifying "difficult" clones like these, we use a heuristic during the backward slicing step: when slicing back from two nodes that are inside loops, we add to the partial slices predecessor nodes that are outside the loops only if the loop predicates match (and so will also be added to the partial slices). That is why, as indicated in Figure 4, the initial assignments to `fp3` are not included in the clones identified by the tool.

2.4   Benefits of the Approach

As stated in the Introduction, the major benefits of a slicing-based approach to clone detection are the ability to find non-contiguous, reordered, and intertwined clones, and the likelihood that the clones that are found are good candidates for extraction. These benefits, discussed in more detail below, arise mainly because slicing is based on the PDG, which provides an abstraction that ignores arbitrary sequencing choices made by the programmer, and instead captures the important dependences among program components. In contrast, most previous approaches to clone detection used the program text, its control-flow graph, or its abstract-syntax tree, all of which are more closely tied to the (sometimes irrelevant) lexical structure.

Finding Non-contiguous, Reordered, and Intertwined Clones: One example of non-contiguous clones identified by our tool was given in Figure 1. By running a preliminary implementation of the proposed tool on some real programs, we have observed that non-contiguous clones that are good candidates for extraction (like the ones in Figure 1) occur frequently (see Section 3 for further discussion). Therefore, the fact that our approach can find such clones is a significant advantage over most previous approaches to clone detection.

Non-contiguous clones are a kind of *near* duplication. Another kind of near duplication occurs when the ordering of matching nodes is different in the different clones. The two clones shown in Figure 4 illustrate this. The clone in Fragment 2 differs from the one in Fragment 1 in two ways: the variables have been renamed (including renaming `fp1` to `fp2` and vice versa), and the order of the first and second statements (in the clones, not in the fragments) has been reversed. This renaming and reordering does not affect the data or control dependences; therefore, our approach finds the clones as shown in the figure, with the first and second statements in Fragment 1 that are marked with "++" signs matching the second and first statements in Fragment 2 that are marked with "++" signs.

The use of program slicing is also effective in finding intertwined clones. An example from the Unix utility *sort* is given in Figure 5. In this example, one clone is indicated by "++" signs while the other clone is indicated by "xx" signs. The clones take a character pointer (a/b) and advance the pointer past all blank characters, also setting a temporary variable (tmpa/tmpb) to point to the first non-blank character. The final component of each clone is an if predicate that uses the temporary. The predicates were the starting points of the slices used to find the two clones (the second one – the second-to-last line of code in the figure – occurs 43 lines further down in the code).

```
++ tmpa = UCHAR(*a),
xx tmpb = UCHAR(*b);
++ while (blanks[tmpa])
++    tmpa = UCHAR(*++a);
xx while (blanks[tmpb])
xx    tmpb = UCHAR(*++b);
++ if (tmpa == '-') {
      tmpa = UCHAR(*++a);
      ...
   }
xx else if (tmpb == '-') {
      if (...UCHAR(*++b)...) ...
```

Fig. 5. An Intertwined Clone Pair from *sort*.

Finding Good Candidates for Extraction: As discussed in the Introduction, the goal of our current research is to design a tool to help find clones to be extracted into new procedures. In this context, a good clone is one that is meaningful as a separate procedure (functionally) and that can be extracted out easily without changing program semantics. The proposed approach to finding clones is likely to satisfy both these criteria as discussed below.

Meaningful clones: In order for a code fragment to be meaningful as a separate procedure, it should perform a single conceptual operation (be highly cohesive [17]). That means it should compute a small number of outputs (outputs include values assigned to global variables and through pointer parameters, the value returned, and output streams written). Furthermore, all the code to be extracted should be relevant to the computation of the outputs (i.e., the backward slices from the statements that assign to the outputs should include the entire clone).

A partial slice obtained using backward slicing has a good chance of being cohesive because we start out from a single node and include only nodes that are relevant to that node's computation. However, in addition to being cohesive, a meaningful procedure should be "complete". In practice, we have found that there are examples (like the one in Figure 3) where backward slicing alone omits some relevant statements. Our use of forward slicing seems to address this omission reasonably well.

Extractable clones: A group of clones cannot be eliminated by procedure extraction if it is not possible to replace the clones by calls to the extracted procedure without changing program semantics. Such clone groups are said to be inextractable. Since semantic equivalence is, in general, undecidable, it is not always possible to determine whether a group of clones is extractable. In [11] we identified sufficient conditions under which a single, non-contiguous clone can be extracted by first moving its statements together (making it contiguous), then creating a new procedure using the contiguous statements, and finally replacing the clone with a call to the new procedure.

In the example in Figure 1, the duplicated code indicated by the "++" signs meets the extractability criteria of [11]. However, in the same example, if we wanted each clone to consist of just the two lines indicated by "++" signs below, we would face problems:

```
++    if (p == token_buffer + maxtoken)
          p = grow_token_buffer(p);
++    *p++ = c;
```

There is no obvious way of extracting out just these two lines because the statement `p = grow_token_buffer(p)` cannot be moved out of the way from in between the above two lines without affecting data and control dependences (and hence without affecting semantics).

Because backward slicing follows dependence edges in the PDG, it is more likely to avoid creating a "dependency gap" (e.g., including the statement `*p++ = c` and its dependence grandparent `if (p == token_buffer + maxtoken)`, but omitting its dependence parent `p = grow_token_buffer(p)`) than a text- or syntax-tree based algorithm that detects non-contiguous clones. The heuristic described in Section 2.3 is another aspect of our approach that helps avoid identifying inextractable clones.

3   Experimental Results

We have implemented a preliminary version of our proposed tool to find clones in C programs using the slicing-based approach described above. Our implementation uses CodeSurfer [10] to process the source code and build the PDGs. CodeSurfer also provides a GUI to display the clone groups identified by the tool using highlighting.

The implementation of Step 1 of the algorithm (finding clone pairs) is done in Scheme, because CodeSurfer provides a Scheme API to the PDGs. The other two steps of the algorithm (eliminating subsumed clone pairs, and combining clone pairs into clone groups) are done in C++.

We have run the tool on three Unix utilities, *bison*, *sort* and *tail*, and on four files from a graph-layout program used in-house by IBM. The results of these experiments are presented in the following subsections.

3.1   Unix Utilities

Figure 6 gives the sizes of the three Unix utilities (in lines of source code and in number of PDG nodes), and the running times for the three steps of the algorithm. Figure 7 presents the results of running the tool on those three programs; for each of eight clone size ranges, three sets of numbers are reported: the number of clone groups identified that contain clones of that size, and the max and mean numbers of clones in those groups (the median number of clones in the groups of each size range was always two). Our experience indicates that clones with fewer than five PDG nodes are too small to be good candidates for extraction, so they are ignored by our tool.

	Program Size		Running Times (elapsed time)		
	# of lines	# of PDG	find clone	eliminate subsumed	combine pairs
Program	of source	nodes	pairs (Scheme)	clone pairs (C++)	into groups(C++)
bison	11,540	28,548	1:33 hours	15 sec.	50 sec.
sort	2,445	5,820	10 min.	5 sec.	2 sec.
tail	1,569	2,580	40 sec.	1 sec.	2 sec.

Fig. 6. Unix Program Sizes and Running Times.

	Clone Size Ranges (# of PDG nodes)							
bison	5–9	10–19	20–29	30–39	40–49	50–59	60–69	70–227
# clone groups	513	164	34	16	9	9	6	49
max # clones in a group	61	26	11	2	2	2	2	4
mean # clones in a group	3.7	2.8	3.3	2	2	2	2	2.1
sort	5–9	10–19	20–29	30–39	40–48			
# clone groups	105	57	30	9	14			
max # clones in a group	17	8	6	3	2			
mean # clones in a group	3.0	2.8	2.4	2.1	2			
tail	5–9	10–19	20–29	30–39	40–49	50–59	60–69	70–85
# clone groups	21	4	0	0	4	1	0	2
max # clones in a group	12	8			3	2		2
mean # clones in a group	3.2	3.5			2.3	2		2

Fig. 7. Results of Running the Tool.

When run on the Unix utilities, the tool found a number of interesting clones, many of which are non-contiguous and some of which involve reordering and intertwining. These preliminary results seem to validate both the hypothesis that programs often include a significant amount of "near" duplication, and the potential of the proposed approach to find good quality clones.

Some examples of the interesting clones identified by the tool are listed below.

- The four-clone group shown in Figure 1, from *bison*.
- The two clones shown in Figure 4, from *bison*. These were part of a three-clone group. The third clone involved a different renaming of variables, and used the same statement ordering as the clone in Fragment 1.
- The pair of intertwined clones shown in Figure 5, from *sort*.
- A group of seven clones from *bison*, identical except for variable names. Two of the clones are shown in Figure 8. The clones were found by slicing back from the statement putc(',', ftable). This code prints the contents of an array (check / rrhs), ten entries to a line, separated by commas.

Fragment 1:
```
++  j = 10;
++  for (i=1; i < high; i++) {
++      putc(',', ftable);
++      if (j >= 10) {
++          putc('\n', ftable);
++          j = 1;
++      }
++      else
++          j++;
++      fprintf(ftable, "%6d", check[i]);
++  }
```

Fragment 2:
```
++  j = 10;
++  for (i=1; i < nrules; i++){
++      putc(',', ftable);
++      if (j >= 10) {
++          putc('\n', ftable);
++          j = 1;
++      }
++      else
++          j++;
++      fprintf(ftable, "%6d",
                        rrhs[i]);
++  }
```

Fig. 8. Seven Copies of this Clone Were Found in *bison*.

One limitation of the tool is that it often finds variants of the "ideal" clones (the clones that would be identified by a human) rather than finding exactly the ideal clones themselves. To illustrate this, consider the example in Figure 5. In that example, the ideal clones would not include the final if predicates; therefore, the clones found by the tool (which do include those predicates) are variants on the ideal ones. In the same example fragment, the tool also identifies a second pair of clones that is a slightly different variant of the ideal pair: this second pair includes everything in the ideal clones, does not include the if predicates, but does include the expressions UCHAR(*++a) and UCHAR(*++b) that occur in the last and fifth-to-last lines of code (the lines not marked with "++" or "xx" signs).

To further evaluate the tool we performed two studies, described below. The goals of the studies were to understand better:

a. whether the tool is likely to find (variants of) all of the ideal clones;
b. to what extent the tool finds multiple variants of the ideal clones rather than exactly the ideal ones;
c. how many "uninteresting" clones the tool finds (i.e., clones that are not variants of any ideal clone), and how large those clones are;
d. how often non-contiguous clones, intertwined clones, and clones that involve statement reordering and variable renaming occur in practice.

For the first study, we examined one file (*lex.c*) from *bison* by hand, and found four ideal clone groups. We then ran the tool on *lex.c*, and it identified forty-three clone groups. Nineteen of those groups were variants of the ideal clone groups (including several variants for each of the four ideal groups, so no ideal clones were missed by the tool), and the other twenty-four were uninteresting. More than half of the uninteresting clone groups (13 out of 24) had clones with fewer than 7 nodes (which was the size of the smallest ideal clone); the largest uninteresting clone had 9 nodes.

For the second study we examined all 25 clone groups identified by the tool for *bison* in the size range 30-49 (we chose an intermediate clone size in order to test the hypothesis that the uninteresting clones identified by the tool tend to be quite small). All but one of those 25 groups were variants of 9 ideal clone groups (i.e., only one of them was uninteresting).

In the two studies, we encountered a total of 11 ideal clone groups (two groups showed up in both studies) containing a total of 37 individual clones. Of those 37, 10 were non-contiguous. Two of the 11 ideal clone groups involved statement reordering, five involved variable renaming, and none involved intertwined clones.

3.2 IBM Code

The goals of the experiments using the IBM code were:

a. to see whether this code also contained non-contiguous, reordered, and intertwined clones;
b. to gather some quantitative data on the immediate effects of extracting clones.

Due to limitations of CodeSurfer, we were not able to process the entire IBM program. Therefore, we selected four (out of the 70+ files) and ran the tool on each of those files individually. The larger clones found by the tool were then examined manually (about 250 clone groups were examined), and the clones best-suited for extraction were identified. The "ideal" versions of those clones were (manually) extracted into macro definitions, which were placed in the same files, and each instance of a clone was replaced by a macro call. (Macros rather than procedures were used to avoid changing the running time of the program.) A total of 30 clone groups containing 77 "ideal" clones were extracted.

The results of the study are summarized in Figure 9, which gives, for each file:

- the size (in lines of source code and in number of PDG nodes);
- the running time for the tool (in all four cases, Step 1 of the algorithm – finding clone pairs – accounted for at least 90% of the running time);
- the number of clone groups that were extracted;
- the total number of extracted clones;
- the reduction in size of the file (in terms of lines of code);
- the average reduction in size for functions that included at least one extracted clone (in terms of lines of code).

	# of lines of source	# of PDG nodes	running time (elapsed)	# of clone groups extracted	total # of clones extracted	file size reduction	av. fn size reduction
file 1	1677	2235	1:02 min	3	6	1.9%	5.0%
file 2	2621	4006	7:49 min	12	24	4.7%	12.4%
file 3	3343	6761	5:15 min	3	7	2.1%	4.4%
file 4	3419	4845	13:00 min	12	40	4.9%	10.3%

Fig. 9. IBM File Sizes and Clone-Extraction Data.

Of the 30 clone groups that were extracted, 2 involved reordering of matching statements, 2 involved intertwined clones, and most of them involved renamed variables. Of the 77 extracted clones, 17 were non-contiguous.

3.3   Summary of Experimental Results

The results of our experiments indicate that our approach is capable of finding interesting clones that would be missed by other approaches. Many of these clones are non-contiguous and involve variable renaming; some also involve statement reordering and intertwining. The Unix-code studies also indicate that the tool is not likely to miss any clones that a human would consider ideal, and additionally is not likely to produce too many clones that a human would consider uninteresting (except very small ones). The IBM-code study provides some additional data about the amount of extractable duplicated code that may be found by our tool, and how extracting that code affects file and function sizes. Of course, the more important question is how duplicate code extraction affects the ease of future maintenance; unfortunately, such a study requires resources beyond those available to us (as noted in the Introduction, the work of [13] does provide a first step in that direction).

The two sets of studies also reveal that the current implementation often finds multiple variants of ideal clones rather than just the ideal ones. This may however not be a problem in practice; manually examining the 250 clone groups reported by the tool for the four IBM files and identifying the corresponding 30 ideal clone groups took only about 3 hours. Nevertheless, future work includes devising more heuristics (like the one described in Subsection 2.3) that will reduce the number of variants reported by the tool by finding clones that are closer to ideal.

As for the running time, although the tool is currently very slow, we believe that this is more a question of its implementation than of some fundamental problem with the approach. As indicated in the table in Figure 6, the bottleneck is finding clone pairs; one reason this step is so slow is that it is implemented in Scheme, and we use a Scheme interpreter, not a compiler. Another factor is that our primary concern has been to get an initial implementation running so that we can use the results to validate our approach (rather than trying to implement the algorithm as efficiently as possible). Future engineering efforts may reduce the time significantly. Furthermore, improvements that eliminate the generation of undesirable clones (e.g., variants of ideal clones) should speed up the tool. Finally, it may be possible (and profitable) to generate clone groups directly, rather than generating clone pairs and then combining them into groups (because for each clone group that contains n clones, we currently generate $(n^2 - n)/2$ clone pairs first).

4   Related Work

The long-term goal of our research project is a tool that not only finds clones, but also automatically extracts a user-selected group of clones into a procedure. A first step in that direction was an algorithm for semantics-preserving procedure extraction [11]. However, that algorithm only applies to a single clone; different techniques are needed to determine when and how a *group* of clones can be extracted into a procedure while preserving semantics. Also, while that work was related to the work presented here in terms of our over-all goal, it addressed a very different aspect, namely, how to do procedure extraction; there was no discussion of how to identify the code to be extracted, which is the subject of the current work.

Other related work falls into 3 main categories: work on clone detection, work on converting procedural code to object-oriented code, and work on subgraph isomorphism.

Clone Detection: Baker [1, 2] describes an approach that finds all pairs of matching "parameterized" code fragments. A code fragment matches another (with parameterization) if both fragments are contiguous sequences of source lines, and some global substitution of variable names and literal values applied to one of the fragments makes the two fragments identical line by line. Comments are ignored, as is whitespace within lines. Because this approach is text-based and line-based, it is sensitive to lexical aspects like the presence or absence of new lines, and the ordering of matching lines in a clone pair. Our approach does not have these shortcomings. Baker's approach does not find intertwined clones. It also does not (directly) find non-contiguous clones. A postpass can be used to group sets of matching fragments that occur close to each other in the source, but there is no guarantee that such sets belong together logically.

Kontogiannis et al [12] describe a dynamic-programming-based approach that computes and reports for every pair of `begin-end` blocks in the program the distance (i.e., degree of similarity) between the blocks. The hypothesis is that pairs with a small distance are likely to be clones caused by cut and paste activities. The distance between a pair of blocks is defined as the least costly sequence of insert, delete and edit steps required to make one block identical line-by-line to the other. This approach does not find clones in the sense of our approach, or Baker's approach. It only gives similarity measures, leaving it to the user to go through block pairs with high reported similarity and determine whether or not they are clones. Also, since it works only at the block level it can miss clone fragments that are smaller than a block, and it does not effectively deal with variable renamings or with non-contiguous or out-of-order matches.

Two other approaches that involve metrics are reported in [7, 14]. The approach of [7] computes certain features of code blocks and then uses neural networks to find similar blocks based on their features, while [14] uses function level metrics (e.g., number of lines of source, number of function calls contained, number of CFG edges, etc.) to find similar functions.

Baxter et al [4] find exact clones by finding identical abstract-syntax tree subtrees, and inexact clones by finding subtrees that are identical when variable names and literal values are ignored. Non-contiguous and out-of-order matches will not be found. This approach completely ignores variable names when asked to find inexact matches; this is a problem because ignoring variable names results in ignoring all data flows which itself could result in matches that are not meaningful computations worthy of extraction.

Debray et al [8] use the CFG to find clones in assembly-language programs for the purpose of code compression. They find matching clones only when they occur in different basic blocks, no intertwined clones, and only a limited kind of non-contiguous clones.

Converting Procedural Code to Object-Oriented Code: The primary goal of the work described by Bowdidge and Griswold in [6] is to help convert procedural code to object-oriented code by identifying methods. As part of this process, they do a limited form of clone detection. Given a variable of interest, the tool does forward slicing from all uses of the variable. The slices are subsequently decomposed into a set of (overlapping) paths, with each path stretching from the "root" node (i.e., the node that has the use of the variable) to the end point of the slice. Finally the paths obtained from all slices are overlayed visually on a single diagram (only the operators of the nodes are shown) with common prefixes drawn only once. Each common prefix is a set of isomorphic paths in the PDG and therefore represents a duplicated computation; the user selects the prefixes to be extracted. There are a few significant differences between their approach and ours. They report only isomorphic paths in the PDG, whereas we report isomorphic partial slices. Our observation is that most clones that are interesting and worthy of extraction are not simply paths in the PDG. Their diagram can be very large for large programs, making it tedious for the user to figure out what clones to extract. Finally, they do only forward slicing, which in our experience is not as likely to produce meaningful clones as a combination of backward and forward slicing; for example, of all the clones found by our tool that are illustrated in this paper, only the ones in Figures 3 and 5 correspond to forward slices.

Subgraph Isomorphism: A number of people have studied the problem of identifying maximal isomorphic subgraphs [3, 15, 5, 18]. Since this in general is a computationally hard problem, these approaches typically employ heuristics that seem to help especially when the graphs being analyzed are representations of molecules. In our approach we identify isomorphic partial slices, not general isomorphic subgraphs. We do this not only to reduce the computational complexity, but also because clones found this way seem more likely to be meaningful computations that are desirable as separate procedures.

5 Conclusions

We have described the design and implementation of a tool that finds duplicated code fragments in C programs and displays them to the programmer. The most innovative aspect of our work is the use of program-dependence graphs and program slicing, which allows our tool to find non-contiguous clones, intertwined clones, and clones that involve variable renaming and statement reordering.

Our implementation indicates that the approach is a good one; real code does include the kinds of clones that our tool is well-suited to handle (and that most previous approaches to clone detection would not be able to find), and the tool does find the clones that would be identified by a human. However, it currently finds many variants of the ideal clones. Future work includes developing heuristics to cut down on the number of variants identified, as well as to improve the running time of the implementation.

Acknowledgements

This work was supported in part by the National Science Foundation under grants CCR-9970707 and CCR-9987435, and by the IBM Center for Advanced Studies.

References

1. B. Baker. On finding duplication and near-duplication in large software systems. In *Proc. IEEE Working Conf. on Reverse Engineering*, pages 86–95, July 1995.
2. B. Baker. Parameterized duplication in strings: Algorithms and an application to software maintenance. *SIAM Jrnl. on Computing*, 26(5):1343–1362, Oct. 1997.
3. H. Barrow and R. Burstall. Subgraph isomorphism, matching relational structures and maximal cliques. *Information Processing Letters*, 4(4):83–84, Jan. 1976.
4. I. Baxter, A. Yahin, L. Moura, M. Sant'Anna, and L. Bier. Clone detection using abstract syntax trees. In *Int. Conf. on Software Maintenance*, pages 368–378, 1998.

5. D. Bayada, R. Simpson, A. Johnson, and C. Laurenco. An algorithm for the multiple common subgraph problem. *Jrnl. of Chemical Information and Computer Sciences*, 32(6):680–685, Nov.–Dec. 1992.
6. R. Bowdidge and W. Griswold. Supporting the restructuring of data abstractions through manipulation of a program visualization. *ACM Trans. on Software Engineering and Methodology*, 7(2):109–157, Apr. 1998.
7. N. Davey, P. Barson, S. Field, R. Frank, and D. Tansley. The development of a software clone detector. *Int. Jrnl. of Applied Software Technology*, 1(3-4):219–36, 1995.
8. S. Debray, W. Evans, R. Muth, and B. D. Sutter. Compiler techniques for code compaction. *ACM Trans. on Programming Languages and Systems*, 22(2):378–415, Mar. 2000.
9. J. Ferrante, K. Ottenstein, and J. Warren. The program dependence graph and its use in optimization. *ACM Trans. on Programming Languages and Systems*, 9(3):319–349, July 1987.
10. http://www.codesurfer.com.
11. R. Komondoor and S. Horwitz. Semantics-preserving procedure extraction. In *Proc. ACM Symp. on Principles of Programming Languages (POPL)*, pages 155–169, Jan. 2000.
12. K. Kontogiannis, R. Demori, E. Merlo, M. Galler, and M. Bernstein. Pattern matching for clone and concept detection. *Automated Software Engineering*, 3(1–2):77–108, 1996.
13. B. Lague, D. Proulx, J. Mayrand, E. Merlo, and J. Hudepohl. Assessing the benefits of incorporating function clone detection in a development process. In *Int. Conf. on Software Maintenance*, pages 314–321, 1997.
14. J. Mayrand, C. Leblanc, and E. Merlo. Experiment on the automatic detection of function clones in a software system using metrics. In *Proceedings of the Int. Conf. on Software Maintenance*, pages 244–254, 1996.
15. J. McGregor. Backtrack search algorithms and maximal common subgraph problem. *Software – Practice and Experience*, 12:23–34, 1982.
16. K. Ottenstein and L. Ottenstein. The program dependence graph in a software development environment. In *Proc. ACM SIGSOFT/SIGPLAN Software Engineering Symp. on Practical Software Development Environments*, pages 177–184, 1984.
17. W. Stevens, G. Myers, and L. Constantine. Structured design. *IBM Systems Jrnl.*, 13(2):115–139, 1974.
18. T. Wang and J. Zhou. Emcss: A new method for maximal common substructure search. *Jrnl. of Chemical Information and Computer Sciences*, 37(5):828–834, Sept.–Oct. 1997.
19. M. Weiser. Program slicing. *IEEE Trans. on Software Engineering*, SE-10(4):352–357, July 1984.

Soft Scheduling for Hardware

Richard Sharp[1,2] and Alan Mycroft[1]

[1] Computer Laboratory, Cambridge University
New Museums Site, Pembroke Street, Cambridge CB2 3QG, UK
[2] AT&T Laboratories Cambridge
24a Trumpington Street, Cambridge CB2 1QA, UK
am@cl.cam.ac.uk
rws26@cl.cam.ac.uk

Abstract. Hardware designs typically combine parallelism and resource-sharing; a circuit's correctness relies on shared resources being accessed mutually exclusively. Conventional high-level synthesis systems guarantee mutual exclusion by statically serialising access to shared resources during a compile-time process called *scheduling*. This approach suffers from two problems: (*i*) there is a large class of practical designs which cannot be scheduled statically; and (*ii*) a statically fixed schedule removes some opportunities for parallelism leading to less efficient circuits. This paper surveys the expressivity of current scheduling methods and presents a new approach which alleviates the above problems: first scheduling logic is automatically generated to resolve contention for shared resources dynamically; then static analysis techniques remove redundant scheduling logic.

We call our method Soft Scheduling to highlight the analogy with Soft Typing: the aim is to retain the flexibility of dynamic scheduling whilst using static analysis to remove as many dynamic checks as possible.

1 Introduction

At the structural level a hardware design can be seen as a set of interconnected resources. These resources run concurrently and are often shared.

The interaction between parallelism and resource-sharing leads to an obvious problem: how does one ensure that shared resources are accessed mutually exclusively? Existing silicon compilers solve the mutual exclusion problem by statically serialising operations during a compile-time *scheduling* phase (see Section 1.1). This paper describes an alternative approach:

We automatically generate circuitry to perform scheduling *dynamically* in a manner which avoids deadlock. Efficient circuits are obtained by employing *static* analysis to remove redundant scheduling logic.

Our method is to scheduling as Soft Typing [4] is to type checking (see Figure 1): the aim is to retain the flexibility of dynamic scheduling whilst using static analysis to remove as many dynamic checks as possible. To highlight this analogy we choose to call our method *Soft Scheduling*.

P. Cousot (Ed.): SAS 2001, LNCS 2126, pp. 57–72, 2001.

	Typing	Scheduling
Static	No dynamic checks required in object code. Not all valid programs pass type checker.	No scheduling logic required in final circuit. Not all valid programs can be scheduled statically.
Dynamic	Dynamic checking of argument types required each time a function is called. All valid programs can be run.	Scheduling logic required on each shared resource in the final circuit. All valid programs can be scheduled.
Soft	Fewer dynamic checks required (some removed statically). All valid programs can be run.	Less scheduling logic required (some removed statically). All valid programs can be scheduled.

Fig. 1. An Informal Comparison between Soft Scheduling and Soft Typing.

Although this paper considers the application of Soft Scheduling to hardware synthesis, the technique is also applicable to software compilation. Aldrich *et al.* [1] advocate a similar approach which uses static analysis to remove redundant synchronization from Java programs.

1.1   Conventional High-Level Synthesis

The hardware community refer to high-level, block-structured languages as *behavioural*. At a lower level, *structural* languages describe a circuit as a set of components, such as registers and multiplexers connected with wires and buses (e.g. RTL Verilog [9]). *High-level synthesis* (sometimes referred to as *behavioural synthesis*) is the process of compiling a behavioural specification into a structural hardware description language.

A number of behavioural synthesis systems have been developed for popular high-level languages (e.g. CtoV [20] and Handel [17]). Such systems typically translate high-level specifications into an explicitly parallel flow-graph representation where *allocation, binding* and *scheduling* [6] are performed:

- *Allocation* is typically driven by user-supplied directives and involves choosing which resources will appear in the final circuit (e.g. 3 adders, 2 multipliers and an ALU).
- *Binding* is the process of assigning operations in the high-level specification to low-level resources—e.g. the + in line 4 of the source program will be computed by adder_1 whereas the + in line 10 will be computed by the ALU.
- *Scheduling* involves assigning start times to operations in the flow-graph such that no two operations will attempt to access a shared resource simultaneously. Mutually-exclusive access to shared resources is ensured by statically serialising operations during scheduling.

The Contributions of this Paper

1. In contrast to conventional scheduling, we describe a method which generates logic to schedule shared resources dynamically. We show that (i) our approach is more expressive: all valid programs can be scheduled; and (ii) in some cases, our approach can generate more efficient designs by exploiting parallelism possibilities removed by static scheduling.
2. We describe a high-level static analysis that enables us to remove redundant scheduling logic and show that this can significantly improve the efficiency of generated circuits.

We have implemented Soft Scheduling as part of the FLaSH Synthesis System (see Section 1.2)—a novel hardware synthesis package being developed in conjunction with Cambridge University and AT&T Laboratories Cambridge. This paper presents Soft Scheduling in the framework of the FLaSH silicon compiler.

1.2   The FLaSH Synthesis System

In previous work we introduced a hardware description language, SAFL [15] (Statically Allocated Functional Language), and sketched its translation to hardware. An optimising silicon compiler (called FLaSH [18]—Functional Languages for Synthesising Hardware) has been implemented to translate SAFL into hierarchical RTL Verilog. The system has been tested on a number of designs, including a small commercial processor[1].

Although, for expository purposes, this paper describes our method in the framework of SAFL, Soft Scheduling techniques are applicable to any high-level Hardware Description Language which allows function definitions to be treated as shared resources (e.g. HardwareC [11], Balsa [7], Tangram [2]). Indeed we have extended SAFL with π-calculus [14] style channels and assignment without modifying the Soft Scheduling phase [19].

Outline of Paper. The remainder of this paper is structured as follows: Section 2 surveys existing scheduling techniques and explains the motivation for our research; the SAFL language and its translation to hardware are briefly outlined in Section 3; Section 4 presents the technical details of Soft Scheduling; some practical examples are described in Section 5.

2   Comparison with Other Work

Traditional high-level synthesis packages perform scheduling using a data-structure called a *sequencing graph*—a partial ordering which makes dependencies

---

[1] The instruction set of Cambridge Consultants XAP processor was implemented (see http://www.camcon.co.uk). We did not include the SIF instruction (a form of debugging breakpoint which transfers data to or from internal registers via a separately clocked serial interface).

between operations explicit. Recall that, in this context, scheduling is performed by assigning a start time to each operation in the graph such that operations which invoke a shared resource do not occur in parallel [6]. There are a number of problems with this approach:

1. The time taken to execute each operation in the sequencing graph must be bounded statically (and in general padded to this length). This restriction means that conventional scheduling techniques are not expressive enough to handle a large class of practical designs. For example, it is impossible to statically schedule an operation to perform a bus transaction of unknown length.
2. Since operations are scheduled statically one must be pessimistic about what *may* be invoked in parallel in order to achieve safety. This can inhibit parallelism in the final design by unnecessarily serialising operations.

Ku and De Micheli have proposed Relative Scheduling [10] which extends the method outlined above to handle operations with statically unbounded computation times. Their technique partitions a flow-graph into statically-schedulable segments separated by *anchor nodes*—nodes which have unbounded execution delays. Each segment is scheduled separately at compile-time. Finally, the compiler connects segments together by generating logic to signal the completion of anchor nodes dynamically.

In [12] Ku and De Micheli show how Relative Scheduling of shared resources is integrated into their Olympus Hardware Synthesis System [5]. Their method permits the scheduling of operations whose execution time is not statically bounded, hence alleviating Problem 1 (above). However, potential contention for shared resources is still resolved by serialising operations at compile time so Problem 2 remains. Furthermore, there is still a class of practical designs which cannot be scheduled by Olympus. Consider the following example.

Using || as a parallel composition operator and assuming suitable definitions of procedures Processor, DMA_Controller and Memory we would essentially like to describe the system of Figure 2 as:

```
Processor() || DMA_Controller() || Memory()
```

Since the operations corresponding to the invocation of the Processor and DMA_Controller both access a shared resource (Memory) the Olympus Synthesis System requires that the calls must be serialised. However, if neither the call to Processor() nor the call to DMA_Controller terminate[2], attempting to sequentialise the operations is futile; the correct operation of the system relies on their parallel interleaving. Soft Scheduling is expressive enough to cope with nonterminating operations: the FLaSH compiler automatically generates an arbiter to ensure mutually exclusive access to the Memory whilst allowing the Processor and DMA_Controller to operate in parallel (see Figure 2.ii). The following table summarises the expressivity of various scheduling methods.

---

[2] This is not merely a contrived example. In real designs both Processors and DMA Controllers are typically non-terminating processes which constantly update the machine state.

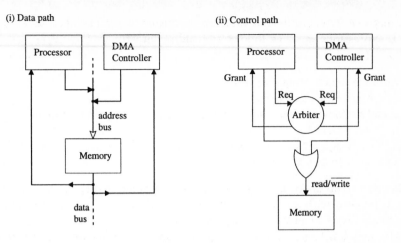

Fig. 2. A Hardware Design Containing a Memory Device Shared between a DMA Controller and a Processor.

	Bounded execution delays	Unbounded execution delays	Non-terminating operations
Static	✓	✗	✗
Relative	✓	✓	✗
Soft	✓	✓	✓

Although the technique of using arbiters to protect shared resources is widely employed, current hardware synthesis packages require arbitration to be coded at the *structural* level on an *ad hoc* basis. Since arbitration can impose an overhead both in terms of chip area and time, programmers often try to eliminate unnecessary locking operations manually. For large designs this is a tedious and error-prone task which often results in badly structured and less reusable code. In contrast the Soft Scheduling approach analyses a *behavioural* specification, automatically inserting arbiters on a where-needed basis. This facilitates readable and maintainable source code without sacrificing efficiency.

This paper does not discuss the SAFL language in depth. A detailed comparison of SAFL with other hardware description languages including Verilog, VHDL, MuFP, Lava, ELLA and Lustre can be found in [18].

3   An Overview of the SAFL Language

SAFL is a language of first order recurrence equations with an ML [13] style syntax. A user program consists of a sequence of function definitions:

$$\texttt{fun } f_1(\vec{x}) = e_1; \ \ldots; \ \texttt{fun } f_n(\vec{x}) = e_n$$

Programs have a distinguished function, main, (usually f_n) which represents an external world interface—at the hardware level it accepts values on an input

port and may later produce a value on an output port. The abstract syntax of
SAFL expressions, e, is as follows (we abbreviate tuples $(e_1, \ldots, e_k)$ as $\vec{e}$ and
similarly $(x_1, \ldots, x_k)$ as $\vec{x}$):

- variables: x; constants: c;
- user function calls: $f(\vec{e})$;
- primitive function calls: $a(\vec{e})$—where a ranges over primitive operators (e.g.
  +, -, <=, && etc.);
- conditionals: $e_1 \ ? \ e_2 \ : \ e_3$; and
- let bindings: let $\vec{x} = \vec{e}$ in e_0 end

In order to distinguish distinct call sites we assume that each abstract-syntax
node is labelled with a unique identifier, α, writing $f^\alpha(e_1, \ldots, e_k)$ to indicate a
call to function f at abstract-syntax node α.

Although functions can call other previously defined functions arbitrarily, the
only form of recursion allowed is tail-recursion. This allows us to statically allo-
cate the storage (e.g. registers and memories) required by a SAFL program [15].
Tail recursive calls are compiled into feedback loops at the circuit level.

SAFL is a call-by-value language. All function-call arguments and let-defini-
tions are evaluated in parallel. Operations can be sequenced using the let construct since the language semantics state that all let-declarations must terminate before the let-body is evaluated.

We compile SAFL to hardware in a *resource aware* manner. That is each
function definition is mapped into a single hardware-level *resource*; functions
which are called more than once become shared resources. For example, consider
the following SAFL code:

```
fun mult(x, y, acc) =
   if (x=0 or y=0) then acc
        else mult(x<<1, y>>1, if y.bit0 then acc+x else acc)

fun square(x) = mult(x, x, 0)
fun cube(x)   = mult(x, mult(x, x, 0), 0)
```

This SAFL specification describes a circuit containing a *single* shift-add multi-
plier shared between hardware-blocks to compute squares and cubes. Notice how
in contrast to traditional high-level synthesis (see Section 1.1) the resource aware
interpretation of SAFL specifications explicitly contains allocation and binding
information. (Although not of direct relevance to this paper, in [15] we show
how *fold/unfold* transformations [3] can be used to explore various allocation
and binding constraints.)

3.1   Translating SAFL to Hardware

As in Relative Scheduling [10] the FLaSH compiler generates logic to explicitly
signal the completion of operations. More precisely, each SAFL function definition, f, is compiled into a single resource, H_f, consisting of:

- logic to compute its body expression
- multiple control and data inputs: one control/data input-pair for each call site
- multiple control outputs (one to return control to each caller)
- a single data output (which is shared between all callers)

An example of function connectivity is given in Figure 3. In this example resource H_f is shared between H_g and H_h. Notice how H_f's data output is shared, but the control structure is duplicated on a per call basis.

To perform a call to resource H_f the caller places the argument values on its data input into H_f before triggering a call event on the corresponding control input. Some point later, when H_f has finished computing, the result of the call is placed on H_f's shared data-output and an event is generated on the corresponding control output. Full details of the translation to hardware can be found in [18].

4   Soft Scheduling: Technical Details

To protect shared resources the FLaSH compiler automatically generates scheduling logic to resolve conflicts dynamically (see Figure 3). The scheduling circuitry consists of two parts: (i) an arbiter to select which caller to service; and (ii) a locking mechanism to ensure the resource is accessed mutually exclusively. For the sake of brevity, this paper uses the term *arbiter* to refer to both the arbiter and locking structure.

Our approach is the hardware equivalent of using binary semaphores to protect critical regions in multi-threaded software. The analogy between arbiters and semaphores is explored further in [15] where a compilation function from SAFL to software is presented.

4.1   Removing Redundant Arbiters

Just because a resource is shared does not necessarily mean that arbitration is required. For example consider the following SAFL program:

```
fun f(x) = ...
fun g(x) = f(f(x))
```

In this case, the two calls to f cannot occur in parallel: the innermost call must complete before the outermost call can begin (recall that SAFL is a call-by-value language). We do not need to generate an arbiter to serialise the calls to H_f: from the structure of the program we can statically determine that the two calls will not try to access f simultaneously.

We use *Parallel Conflict Analysis* (see Section 4.2) in order to detect redundant arbiters. Removing unnecessary arbitration is important for two reasons:

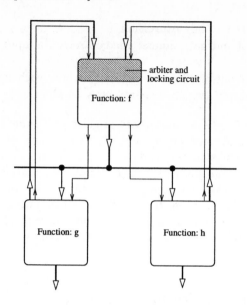

Fig. 3. A structural diagram of the hardware circuit corresponding to a shared function, f, called by functions g and h. Data buses are shown as thick lines, control wires as thin lines.

1. Arbitration takes time: in the current version of the FLaSH compiler arbitration adds one cycle latency to a call even if the requested resource is available at the time of call. Although we may accept this latency if it is small in comparison to the callee's average execution time, consider the case where the callee is a frequently used resource with a small execution delay. In this case an arbiter may significantly degrade the performance of the whole system (see Example 5.1).

2. Arbitration uses chip area: although the gate-count of an arbiter is typically small compared to the resource as a whole, the extra wiring complexity required to represent request and grant signals adds to the area of the final design.

Arbiters are inserted at the granularity of calls. This offers increased performance over inserting arbiters on a per-resource basis. For example, in a design containing a function, f, shared between five callers, we may infer that only two calls to f require an arbiter—the other three calls need not suffer the overhead of arbitration.

4.2   Parallel Conflict Analysis (PCA)

Parallel Conflict Analysis (PCA) is performed over the structure of a whole SAFL program in order to determine which function calls may occur in parallel. If a group of calls to the same function may occur in parallel then we say that the group is *conflicting*. We only need to synthesise logic to arbitrate between conflicting calls since, by definition, if a call f^α is not in a conflicting group then no other call to f can occur in parallel with f^α.

The result of PCA is a *conflict set*: a set of calls which require arbiters. For example, if the resulting conflict set is $\{f^1, f^2, f^5, g^{10}, g^{14}\}$ then we would synthesise two arbiters: one for the conflicting group $\{f^1, f^2, f^5\}$, the other for conflicting group $\{g^{10}, g^{14}\}$.

We now proceed to define PCA. Let e_f represent the body of function f. Let the predicate $RecursiveCall(f^\alpha)$ hold iff f^α is a recursive call (i.e. f^α occurs within the body of f). $\mathcal{C}[e]$ returns the set of non-recursive calls which may occur as a result of evaluating expression e:

$$\mathcal{C}[x] = \emptyset$$
$$\mathcal{C}[c] = \emptyset$$
$$\mathcal{C}[a(e_1, \ldots, e_k)] = \bigcup_{1 \leq i \leq k} \mathcal{C}[e_i]$$
$$\mathcal{C}[f^\alpha(e_1, \ldots, e_k)] = (\bigcup_{1 \leq i \leq k} \mathcal{C}[e_i]) \cup \begin{cases} \emptyset & \text{if } RecursiveCall(f^\alpha) \\ \{f^\alpha\} \cup \mathcal{C}[e_f] & \text{otherwise} \end{cases}$$
$$\mathcal{C}[\text{if } e_1 \text{ then } e_2 \text{ else } e_3] = \bigcup_{1 \leq i \leq 3} \mathcal{C}[e_i]$$
$$\mathcal{C}[\text{let } \vec{x} = \vec{e} \text{ in } e_0] = \bigcup_{0 \leq i \leq k} \mathcal{C}[e_i]$$

$PC(\mathcal{S}_1, \ldots, \mathcal{S}_n)$ takes sets of calls, $(\mathcal{S}_1, \ldots, \mathcal{S}_n)$, and returns the conflict set resulting from the assumption that calls in each $\mathcal{S}_i$ are evaluated in parallel with calls in each $\mathcal{S}_j$ $(j \neq i)$:

$$PC(\mathcal{S}_1, \ldots, \mathcal{S}_n) = \bigcup_{i \neq j} \{f^\alpha \in \mathcal{S}_i \mid \exists \beta.\ f^\beta \in \mathcal{S}_j\}$$

We are now able to define $\mathcal{A}[e]$ which returns the conflict set due to expression e:

$$\mathcal{A}[x] = \emptyset$$
$$\mathcal{A}[c] = \emptyset$$
$$\mathcal{A}[a(e_1, \ldots, e_k)] = PC(\mathcal{C}[e_1], \ldots, \mathcal{C}[e_k]) \cup \bigcup_{1 \leq i \leq k} \mathcal{A}[e_i]$$
$$\mathcal{A}[f(e_1, \ldots, e_k)] = PC(\mathcal{C}[e_1], \ldots, \mathcal{C}[e_k]) \cup \bigcup_{1 \leq i \leq k} \mathcal{A}[e_i]$$
$$\mathcal{A}[\text{if } e_1 \text{ then } e_2 \text{ else } e_3] = \bigcup_{1 \leq i \leq 3} \mathcal{A}[e_i]$$
$$\mathcal{A}[\text{let } \vec{x} = \vec{e} \text{ in } e_0] = PC(\mathcal{C}[e_1], \ldots, \mathcal{C}[e_k]) \cup \bigcup_{0 \leq i \leq k} \mathcal{A}[e_i]$$

Finally, for a program, p, consisting of a sequence of user-function definitions:

$$\text{fun } f_1(\ldots) = e_1; \quad \ldots; \quad \text{fun } f_n(\ldots) = e_n$$

$\mathcal{A}[\![p]\!]$ returns the conflict set resulting from program, p. The letter $\mathcal{A}$ is used since $\mathcal{A}[\![p]\!]$ represents the calls which require arbiters:

$$\mathcal{A}[\![p]\!] = \bigcup_{1 \leq k \leq n} \mathcal{A}[\![e_k]\!]$$

Notice that the equation for $\mathcal{C}[\![f^\alpha(e_1, \ldots, e_k)]\!]$ is a little unusual in that it is not defined compositionally. This reflects the fact that PCA depends on the global structure of a whole SAFL program as opposed to just the local structure of a function definition. $\mathcal{C}[\![\cdot]\!]$ is well-defined due to the predicate *RecursiveCall* and the source restrictions on SAFL which ensure that the call-graph is acyclic.

4.3   Integrating PCA into the FLaSH Synthesis System

After computing $\mathcal{A}[\![p]\!]$ at the abstract-syntax level the FLaSH Synthesis System translates p into an intermediate flow-graph representation which makes both control and data paths explicit [18]. At this level, the Call-nodes which require arbitration are tagged (i.e. we tag node, n, iff n represents Call f^α and $f^\alpha \in \mathcal{A}[\![p]\!]$).

When the circuit for H_f is generated only tagged calls to f are fed through an arbiter, other calls are merely multiplexed. If none of the calls to f are in $\mathcal{A}[\![p]\!]$ then H_f's arbiter is eliminated completely. As Section 5.1 shows, using Parallel Conflict Analysis to remove redundant arbitration can significantly improve the performance of a large class of designs.

4.4   Avoiding Deadlock

Deadlock occurs when there is a cycle of blocked processes each waiting for a lock held by the next process in the cycle. In the context of SAFL, where functions represent hardware-level resources, a deadlocked cycle of resources can only occur if we permit cycles in the call-graph (i.e. if we permit mutual recursion). Note that we do not have to worry about self-tail-recursion since it is simply treated as local loops and does not require locks.

Although the details are beyond the scope of this paper, in [15] we show how to deal with mutual recursion whilst avoiding deadlock. For the purposes of this paper it suffices to say that deadlock can be avoided simply by rejecting mutually recursive SAFL programs.

5   Examples and Results

We provide three practical examples of applying Soft Scheduling to SAFL hardware designs. Each example illustrates a different point: Example 5.1 demonstrates that using static analysis to remove redundant arbiters is critical to achieving efficient circuits; Example 5.2 highlights the extra expressivity of Soft

Scheduling over static scheduling techniques; Example 5.3 shows that dynamically controlling access to shared resources can lead to better performance than generating a single schedule statically.

5.1   Parallel FIR Filter

Finite Impulse Response (FIR) filters are commonly used in Digital Signal Processing where they are used to remove certain frequencies from a discrete-time sampled signal. Assuming the existence of functions read_next_value and write_value, an integer arithmetic FIR filter can be described in SAFL as follows:

```
fun mult1(x,y) = x*y
fun mult2(x,y) = x*y

fun FIR(x,y,z,w) =
    let val o1 = mult1(x,2)
        val o2 = mult2(y,3)
        val next = read_next_value()
    in
        let val o3 = mult1(x,7)
            val o4 = mult2(y,9)
        in write_value(o1 + o2 + o3 + o4);
            FIR(y,z,w,next)
        end
    end
```

Recall that the semantics of the let statement requires all val-declarations to be computed fully before the body is executed (see Section 3). Although this design contains two shared combinatorial multipliers, mult1 and mult2, the outermost let statement ensures that the calls to the shared multipliers do not occur in parallel. As a result Parallel Conflict Analysis infers that no arbitration is required.

The shared combinatorial multipliers, mult1 and mult2 take a single cycle to compute their result. Generating an arbiter for a shared resource adds an extra cycle latency to each call (irrespective of whether the resource is busy at the time of call). Thus, in this case, if we naively generated arbiters for all shared resources, the performance of the multipliers would be degraded by a factor of two.

This example illustrates the importance of using static analysis to remove redundant arbiters. For this design, using Parallel Conflict Analysis to remove unnecessary arbiters leads to a 50% speed increase over a policy which simply inserts arbiters on each shared resource.

5.2   Shared-Memory Multi-processor Architecture

Figure 4 contains SAFL code fragments describing a simple shared-memory multi-processor architecture. The system consists of two processors which have

```
type Instruction = {opcode:4,operand:12}
const WRITE=1, READ=0

extern Shared_memory(WriteSelect:1, Address:12, Data:16) : 16

extern instruction_mem1(Address:12) : 16
extern instruction_mem2(Address:12) : 16

(* Processor 1: Loads instructions from instruction_mem1 *)
fun proc1(PC:12, RX:16, RY:16, A:16) : unit =
  let val instr:Instruction = instruction_mem1(PC)
      val incremented_PC = PC + 2
   in
      case instr.opcode of
        1 => (* Load Accumulator From Register *)
             if instr.operand=1
               then proc1(incremented_PC,RX,RY,RX)
               else proc1(incremented_PC,RX,RY,RY)
      | 2 => (* Load Accumulator From Memory *)
             let val v = Shared_memory(READ, instr.operand, 0)
              in proc1(incremented_PC,RX,RY,v)
             end
      | 3 => (* Store Accumulator To Memory *)
             (Shared_memory(WRITE, instr.operand, A);
              proc1(incremented_PC,RX,RY,v))
        ... etc
  end

(* Processor 2: Loads instructions from instruction_mem2 *)
fun proc2(PC:12, RX:16, RY:16, A:16) : unit =
  let val instr:Instruction = instruction_mem2(PC)
      val incremented_PC = PC + 2
   in
      case instr.opcode of
        ....
      | 2 => (* Load Accumulator From Memory *)
             let val v = Shared_memory(READ, instr.operand, 0)
              in proc2(incremented_PC,RX,RY,v)
             end
      | 3 => (* Store Accumulator To Memory *)
             (Shared_memory(WRITE, instr.operand, A);
              proc2(incremented_PC,RX,RY,v))
        ... etc
  end

fun main() : unit = proc1(0,0,0,0) || proc2(0,0,0,0)
```

Fig. 4. Extracts from a SAFL Program Describing a Shared-Memory Multi-processor Architecture.

separate instruction memories but share a data memory. Such architectures are common in control-dominated embedded systems where multiple heterogenous processors perform separate tasks using a common memory to synchronise on shared data structures.

The example starts by defining the type of instructions (records containing 4-bit opcodes and 12-bit operands), declaring 2 constants and specifying the signatures of various (externally defined) memory functions. Bit-widths are specified explicitly using notation X:n to indicate that variable X represents an n-bit value. The bit-widths of function return values are also specified in this way (unit indicates a width of 0).

The function Shared_memory takes three arguments: WriteSelect indicates whether a read or a write is to be performed; Address specifies the memory location concerned; Data gives the value to be written (this argument is ignored if a read operation is performed). It always returns the value of memory location Address.

Functions proc1 and proc2 define two simple 16-bit processors. Argument PC represents the program counter, RX and RY represent processor registers and A is the accumulator. The processor state is updated on recursive calls—neither processor terminates.

The main function initialises the system by calling proc1 and proc2 in parallel with PC, RX, RY and A initialised to 0.

Since the SAFL code contains parallel non-terminating calls to proc1 and proc2 both of which share a single resource, neither static nor relative scheduling are applicable (see Section 2): this example cannot be synthesised using conventional silicon compilers.

Soft Scheduling is expressive enough to deal with non-terminating resources: a circuit is synthesised which contains an arbiter protecting the shared memory whilst allowing proc1 and proc2 to operate in parallel.

5.3   Parallel Tasks Sharing Graphical Display

Consider a hardware design which can perform a number of tasks in parallel with each task having the facility to update a graphical display. Many real-life systems have this structure. For example in preparation for printing an ink-jet printer performs a number of tasks in parallel: feed paper, reset position of print head, check ink levels etc. Each one of these tasks can fail in which case an error code is printed on the graphical display.

A controller for such a printer in SAFL may have the following structure:

```
extern display (data : 16) : unit

fun reset_head()  : unit = ...
                        if head_status <> 0 then
                            display(4) (* Error code 4 *)
                        else ...
```

```
fun feed_paper()   : unit = ... display(5) ...
fun check_ink()    : unit = ... display(6) ...

fun main()         : unit =
    (feed_paper() || reset_head() || check_ink());
    do_print();
    wait_for_next_job(); main()
```

Let us assume that each of the tasks terminates in a statically bounded time. Given this assumption, both static scheduling and Soft Scheduling can be used to ensure mutually exclusive access to display. It is interesting to compare and contrast the circuits resulting from the application of these different techniques.

Since the tasks may invoke a common resource, applying static scheduling techniques results in the tasks being serialised. In contrast, Soft Scheduling allows the tasks to operate in parallel and automatically generates an arbiter which dynamically schedules access to the shared display function.

Errors occur infrequently and hence contention for the display is rare. Under this condition, and assuming that the tasks take all roughly the same amount of time, Soft Scheduling yields a printer whose initialisation time is three times faster than an equivalent statically scheduled printer. More generally, for a system with n balanced tasks, Soft Scheduling generates designs which are n times faster.

6   Conclusions and Further Work

Soft Scheduling is a powerful technique which provides a number of advantages over current scheduling technology:

More expressive: in contrast to existing scheduling methods, Soft Scheduling can handle arbitrary networks of shared inter-dependent resources.

Increased efficiency: in some circumstances, controlling access to shared resources dynamically yields significantly better performance than statically choosing a single schedule (see Example 5.3).

Higher level of abstraction: current hardware synthesis paradigms require a designer to code arbiters explicitly at the structural level. Soft Scheduling abstracts mutual exclusion concerns completely, increasing the readability of source code without sacrificing efficiency.

One of the aims of the FLaSH Synthesis System is to facilitate the use of source-level program transformation in order to investigate a range of possible designs arising from a single specification. We have shown that *fold/unfold* transformations [3] can be applied to SAFL programs to explore various allocation/binding constraints [15]. In [16] we describe a SAFL transformation to partition a design into hardware and software parts. The simplicity of our transformation system is partly due to the resource abstraction provided by Soft Scheduling—transformations involving shared resources would be much more complex if locking and arbitration details had to be considered at the SAFL-level.

An arguable disadvantage of dynamic scheduling is that is makes the timing behaviour of the final circuit difficult to analyse. Since access to shared resources is resolved dynamically it becomes much harder to prove that real-time design constraints are met. In future work we intend to investigate (a) the incorporation of timing directives into the SAFL language; and (b) the static analysis of timing properties for dynamically scheduled hardware systems.

When the parallel interleaving of non-terminating resources is required dynamic scheduling is essential (see Example 5.2); in other cases dynamic scheduling can offer increased performance (see Example 5.3). However, for fine-grained sharing of smaller resources whose execution delays are known at compile-time (such as arithmetic units), static scheduling techniques are more appropriate. Soft Scheduling provides a powerful framework which strikes a compromise between the two approaches. The designer has the flexibility either:

– to describe a single static schedule (see Example 5.1) in which case dynamic arbitration is optimised away; or
– to leave scheduling details to the compiler (see Example 5.3) in which case dynamic arbitration is inserted where needed.

Acknowledgement

This research was supported by (UK) EPSRC grant GR/N64256: "A resource-aware functional language for hardware synthesis".

References

1. Aldrich, J., Chambers, C., Sirer, E., Eggers, S. Static Analyses for Eliminating Unnecessary Synchronization from Java Programs. Proceedings of the International Symposium on Static Analysis 1999. LNCS Vol. 1694, Springer Verlag.
2. Berkel, K. van. Handshake Circuits: an Asynchronous Architecture for VLSI Programming. International Series on Parallel Computation, Vol. 5. Published by Cambridge University Press, 1993.
3. Burstall, R.M. and Darlington, J. A Transformation System for Developing Recursive Programs, JACM 24(1).
4. Cartwright, R. and Fagan, M. Soft Typing. Proceedings of the ACM SIGPLAN 1991 Conference on Programming Language Design and Implementation
5. De Micheli, G., Ku, D., Mailhot, F., Truong, T. The Olympus Synthesis System for Digital Design. IEEE Design & Test Magazine, October 1990.
6. De Micheli, G. Synthesis and Optimization of Digital Circuits. Published by McGraw-Hill Inc., 1994.
7. Edwards, D., Bardsley, A. Balsa 3.0 User Manual. Available from http://www.cs.man.ac.uk/amulet/projects/balsa/
8. Hennessy, J., Patterson, D. Computer Architecture A Quantitative Approach. Published by Morgan Kaufmann Publishers, Inc. (1990) ; ISBN 1-55860-069-8

9. IEEE. Verilog HDL Language Reference Manual. IEEE Draft Standard 1364, October 1995.

10. Ku, D., De Micheli, G. Relative Scheduling Under Timing Constraints: Algorithms for High-Level Synthesis of Digital Circuits. IEEE Transactions on CAD/ICAS, June 1992.

11. Ku, D., De Micheli, G. HardwareC—a language for hardware design (version 2.0). Stanford University Technical Report No. CSL-TR-90-419.

12. Ku, D., De Micheli, G. Constrained Resource Sharing and Conflict Resolution in Hebe. Integration – The VLSI Journal, December 1991.

13. Milner, R., Tofte, M., Harper, R. and MacQueen, D. The Definition of Standard ML (Revised). MIT Press, 1997.

14. Milner, R. The Polyadic π-calculus: a tutorial. Technical Report ECS-LFCS-91-180, Laboratory for Foundations of Computer Science, University of Edinburgh, October 1991.

15. Mycroft, A. and Sharp, R. A Statically Allocated Parallel Functional Language. Proc. of the International Conference on Automata, Languages and Programming 2000. LNCS Vol. 1853, Springer-Verlag.

16. Mycroft, A. and Sharp, R. Hardware/Software Co-Design Using Functional Languages. Proc. of Tools and Algorithms for the Construction and Analysis of Systems 2001. LNCS Vol. 2031, Springer-Verlag.

17. Page, I. and Luk, W. Compiling Occam into Field-Programmable Gate Arrays. In Moore and Luk (eds.) FPGAs, pages 271-283. Abingdon EE&CS Books, 1991.

18. Sharp, R. and Mycroft, A. The FLaSH Compiler: Efficient Circuits from Functional Specifications. AT&T Technical Report tr.2000.3.
    Available from http://www.uk.research.att.com

19. Sharp, R. and Mycroft, A. A Higher Level Language For Hardware Synthesis. To appear: Proc. of Correct Hardware Design and Verification Methods (CHARME), 2001.

20. Tenison Tech EDA. CtoV Reference Manual.
    Available from http://www.tenisontech.com

Effective Strictness Analysis
with HORN Constraints

Kevin Glynn, Peter J. Stuckey, and Martin Sulzmann

Dept. of Computer Science and Software Engineering
The University of Melbourne, Victoria 3010, Australia
{keving,pjs,sulzmann}@cs.mu.oz.au

Abstract. We introduce a constraint-based framework for strictness analysis applicable to ML style languages supporting higher-order functions, let-style polymorphism and algebraic data types. The analysis produces strictness types for expressions in a program. A strictness type is defined using Boolean constraints. Perhaps surprisingly, the Boolean constraints that arise during analysis are in HORN, which makes the operations on them amenable to efficient implementation.
We have implemented the approach within a highly optimising Haskell compiler (GHC) and give a comparison with the current strictness analyser of GHC.

1 Introduction

In lazy functional programming languages expressions are evaluated only if they are needed. A function is strict in an argument if its value is undefined whenever the argument is undefined. Determining which arguments of a function are strict can be used by compilers to improve program performance by replacing call-by-need by call-by value. Hence there has been considerable interest in determining strictness of functions.

Mycroft [8] was the first person to consider strictness analysis of (first-order, flat-typed) functional programs. His approach to strictness analysis using abstract interpretation maps a function to a strictness function over Booleans. The undefined value is represented by *false* (which we shall write as $\perp$) while no information (all possible values including the undefined value) is represented by *true* (written $\top$). The translation to a Boolean function preserves just the function's behaviour on undefined values. The result of evaluating this function gives a safe approximation of the real function's behaviour.

For example, the strictness type of $+$, which is strict in both its arguments, is represented by the function

$$+ \, x \, y = x \wedge y$$

where $\wedge$ is Boolean conjunction.

The strictness of $+$ in its first argument is shown by the fact that $+ \perp \top = \perp$. This means that if the first argument is undefined the result of $+$ must be undefined.

The approach of Mycroft is pleasing, in that it simply maps each program construct to a Boolean version. So, for example, the functions

P. Cousot (Ed.): SAS 2001, LNCS 2126, pp. 73–92, 2001.

$$f :: \textbf{Int} \mapsto \textbf{Int} \mapsto \textbf{Int} \mapsto \textbf{Bool} \mapsto \textbf{Int}$$
$$f\ x\ y\ z\ b = \text{if } b \text{ then } x + y \text{ else } z$$
$$g :: \textbf{Int} \mapsto \textbf{Int} \mapsto \textbf{Bool} \mapsto \textbf{Int}$$
$$g\ x\ y\ b\ \ = f\ x\ y\ x\ b$$

are represented by the Boolean strictness functions

$$f : \textbf{Bool} \mapsto \textbf{Bool} \mapsto \textbf{Bool} \mapsto \textbf{Bool} \mapsto \textbf{Bool}$$
$$f\ x\ y\ z\ b = b \wedge ((+\ x\ y) \vee z) = b \wedge ((x \wedge y) \vee z)$$
$$g : \textbf{Bool} \mapsto \textbf{Bool} \mapsto \textbf{Bool} \mapsto \textbf{Bool}$$
$$g\ x\ y\ b\ \ = f\ x\ y\ x\ b = b \wedge ((x \wedge y) \vee x) = b \wedge x$$

where $\vee$ is Boolean disjunction. Note that we use the notation $\mapsto$ for function types to differentiate them from Boolean implication $\rightarrow$.

In general, a function f is detected to be strict in an argument if f called with that argument $\perp$ and all other arguments $\top$ returns $\perp$. For example, f is strict in b but not strict in x since $f\ \top\ \top\ \top\ \perp = \perp$ and $f\ \perp\ \top\ \top\ \top = \top$

The natural way to extend Mycroft's analysis to higher-order functions is to represent their strictness by higher-order Boolean functions, and this is indeed what Burn, Hankin and Abramsky [1] defined. Unfortunately, in practice manipulating higher-order Boolean function descriptions quickly becomes impractical.

Kuo and Mishra [7] instead suggested using constrained type expressions to express strictness. We take a similar approach in our framework, the strictness of a function is represented by a Boolean *relation*, rather than a function. The relation is represented by a two part description (C, τ), C is a Boolean Constraint and τ is the type annotated with the names of the Boolean variables. These variables. relate the Boolean constraints to the arguments and result of the function. We also write this in the style of a constrained type $\forall \bar{\delta}.C \Rightarrow \tau$ where $\bar{\delta}$ is a set of free variables, not bound in the function's environment, τ is the type component and C is the constraint component, restricting the set of possible instances of variables $\bar{\delta}$.

For example, we represent f above as

$$f : \forall\ b\ x\ y\ z\ r.\ (b \wedge ((x \wedge y) \vee z) \leftrightarrow r \Rightarrow x \mapsto y \mapsto z \mapsto b \mapsto r$$

Once we have made the step to relational descriptions, a key realization is that only one direction of the constraint information is required to determine the strictness information. Since $\top$ indicates no information the statement that $f\ \perp\ \top\ \top\ \top = \top$ conveys no information. It is the fact that $f\ \perp\ \top\ \top\ \top = \perp$ which demonstrates that f is strict in b. This information is still captured in the weaker relational description

$$f : \forall\ b\ x\ y\ z\ r.\ (b \wedge ((x \wedge y) \vee z) \rightarrow r \Rightarrow x \mapsto y \mapsto z \mapsto b \mapsto r$$

There are immediate advantages to keeping only the minimal amount of information:

- The resulting Boolean constraints are in HORN. For example, $(b \wedge ((x \wedge y) \vee z)) \to r$ is equivalent to $(b \to x \to y \to r) \wedge (b \to z \to r)$.[1] Algorithms for manipulating Horn formulae are more efficient than those for manipulating arbitrary Boolean formulae.
- The handling of if-then-else (and other "branching" constructs like case) is considerably simpler, the resulting strictness constraints can simply be conjoined. For example, consider the inference of a strictness type for f:

$$x + y : (x \to y \to r, \ r)$$
$$z : (z \to r, \ r)$$
$$\text{if b then x + y else z} : (b \to ((x \to y \to r) \wedge (z \to r)), \ r)$$
$$f : \forall b \ x \ y \ z \ r. \ (b \to x \to y \to r) \wedge (b \to z \to r) \Rightarrow$$
$$x \mapsto y \mapsto z \mapsto b \mapsto r$$

where for each subexpression we have written its strictness description on the right-hand side.

For functions with a first-order, flat type it is easy to show that our inference algorithms gives the same answers as that of Mycroft [8] and Burn *et al.* [1] (see Theorems 1, 3 and 4).

Type-based strictness analyses, such as the approach of Kuo and Mishra and ours, extend to higher-order functions in a natural way. Descriptions just relate the Boolean variables representing the various parts of the type. For example, the strictness types of twice f x = f (f x), id x = x and c3 x = 3 are

$$\text{twice} : \forall \delta_1 \delta_2 \delta_3 \delta_4. \ \delta_3 \to \delta_1 \wedge \delta_2 \to \delta_1 \wedge \delta_2 \to \delta_4 \Rightarrow (\delta_1 \mapsto \delta_2) \mapsto \delta_3 \mapsto \delta_4$$
$$\text{id} : \forall \delta_1 \delta_2. \ \delta_1 \to \delta_2 \Rightarrow \delta_1 \mapsto \delta_2$$
$$\text{c3} : \forall \delta_1 \delta_2. \ \delta_2 \Rightarrow \delta_1 \mapsto \delta_2$$

and the inference of strictness types for expressions twice id and twice c3 are straightforwardly obtained by matching arguments and conjoining the resulting constraints. That is

$$\text{twice id} : (\delta_1 \to \delta_2 \wedge \delta_3 \to \delta_1 \wedge \delta_2 \to \delta_1 \wedge \delta_2 \to \delta_4, \ \delta_3 \mapsto \delta_4) = (\delta_3 \to \delta_4, \ \delta_3 \mapsto \delta_4)$$
$$\text{twice c3} : (\delta_2 \wedge \delta_3 \to \delta_1 \wedge \delta_2 \to \delta_1 \wedge \delta_2 \to \delta_4, \ \delta_3 \mapsto \delta_4) = (\delta_4, \ \delta_3 \mapsto \delta_4)$$

Using Boolean constraints for strictness descriptions is advantageous since they are well understood, and operations like conjunction and existential quantification (both used in the above examples) are straightforward and have efficient implementations. Another advantage we claim for using well-understood constraint domains is that extensions of the system are easier to construct. Our approach to strictness analysis handles both let-style polymorphism and algebraic data types.

In this paper we present a strictness analyser for Haskell based on HORN constraints. It has been incorporated into the GHC Haskell compiler and handles the full Haskell 98 language. Although the implementation is still preliminary it is capable of analysing much more precise strictness information than the current GHC strictness analyser.

---

[1] We shall assume for the remainder of the paper that $\to$ is right associative and higher precedence than $\wedge$ and usually write Boolean constraints without brackets e.g. $b \to x \to y \to r \wedge b \to z \to r$.

The remainder of the paper is organized as follows. In the next section we define our strictness logic and its relation to the abstract interpretation framework of Burn *et al.* [1]. In particular, we prove equivalence on first-order, flat types to [1]. In Section 3 we give the inference algorithm for monomorphic programs. In Section 4 we extend the framework to handle let-style polymorphism and algebraic data types. In Section 5 we discuss our implementation in the GHC compiler and compare it with the current strictness analysis. Finally, in Section 6 we discuss related work and conclude.

2   Strictness Logic

For the moment, we assume that the underlying language is monomorphic:

Types $t ::= \mathbf{Int} \mid \mathbf{Bool} \mid t \mapsto t$
Expressions $e ::= x \mid \lambda x.e \mid e\,e \mid \mathsf{let}\ x = e\ \mathsf{in}\ e \mid \mathsf{fix}\ x\ \mathsf{in}\ e \mid \mathsf{if}\ e\ \mathsf{then}\ e\ \mathsf{else}\ e$

We will in later sections show how to incorporate ML-style polymorphism and algebraic data types.

We define a strictness logic in terms of a constraint-based type system. Strictness properties of expressions are specified by typing judgments which are of the form $C, \Gamma \vdash e : \eta$ where C is a strictness constraint, Γ is a strictness type environment assigning strictness types to the free variables of e and η is e's strictness type. We always assume that expression e is well-typed in the underlying type system.

Strictness Types

The structure of strictness types reflects the structure of the underlying type system.

Annotations $b ::= \delta \mid \perp \mid \top$
Strictness Types $\tau ::= b \mid \tau \mapsto \tau$
Type Schemes $\eta ::= \tau \mid \forall \bar{\delta}.C \Rightarrow \tau$

Our strictness analysis does not distinguish divergent functional expressions from functions that always diverge when applied to an argument. In rare cases this loses precision. If an analysis wishes to distinguish the two then a variable would also be attached to the $\mapsto$ type constructor. For example, this is required in our binding-time analysis [3].

We write $\bar{\delta} = fv(\eta)$ to refer to the free variables in a strictness type η. The constraint component C will be described shortly.

Strictness Constraints

Strictness constraints are in the class HORN of propositional formulas, additionally, we have conjunction and existential quantification. The language of constraints is as follows:

$$C ::= \perp \mid \top \mid \delta \mid \delta_1 \to \ldots \to \delta_n \mid C \wedge C \mid \exists \bar{\delta}.C$$

$$(\text{Var}) \ \frac{(x : \eta) \in \Gamma}{C, \Gamma \vdash x : \eta} \qquad (\text{Sub}) \ \frac{C, \Gamma \vdash e : \tau_2 \quad C \models [\![(\tau_2 \leq_s \tau_1)]\!]}{C, \Gamma \vdash e : \tau_1}$$

$$(\text{Abs}) \ \frac{C, \Gamma_x.x : \tau_1 \vdash e : \tau_2}{C, \Gamma_x \vdash \lambda x.e : \tau_1 \mapsto \tau_2} \qquad (\text{App}) \ \frac{C, \Gamma \vdash e_1 : (\tau_1 \mapsto \tau_2)}{C, \Gamma \vdash e_2 : \tau_1}{C, \Gamma \vdash e_1 e_2 : \tau_2}$$

$$(\text{Let}) \ \frac{C, \Gamma_x \vdash e_1 : \eta \quad C, \Gamma_x.x : \eta \vdash e_2 : \tau}{C, \Gamma_x \vdash \text{let } x = e_1 \text{ in } e_2 : \tau} \qquad (\exists \text{I}) \ \frac{C, \Gamma \vdash e : \tau \quad \bar{\delta} \notin fv(\Gamma, \tau)}{\exists \bar{\delta}.C, \Gamma \vdash e : \tau}$$

$$(\forall \text{I}) \ \frac{C \wedge D, \Gamma \vdash e : \tau \quad \bar{\delta} = fv(D, \tau) \backslash fv(\Gamma, C)}{C \wedge \exists \bar{\delta}.D, \Gamma \vdash e : \forall \bar{\delta}.D \Rightarrow \tau} \qquad (\forall \text{E}) \ \frac{C, \Gamma \vdash x : \forall \bar{\delta}.D \Rightarrow \tau \quad C \models [\bar{b}/\bar{\delta}]D}{C, \Gamma \vdash x : [\bar{b}/\bar{\delta}]\tau}$$

$$(\text{If}) \ \frac{C, \Gamma \vdash e : \delta \quad C, \Gamma \vdash e_1 : \tau_1 \quad C, \Gamma \vdash e_2 : \tau_2 \quad C \models \delta \to [\![(\tau_1 \leq_s \tau) \wedge (\tau_2 \leq_s \tau)]\!]}{C, \Gamma \vdash \text{if } e \text{ then } e_1 \text{ else } e_2 : \tau} \qquad (\text{Fix}) \ \frac{C, \Gamma_x.x : \eta \vdash e : \eta}{C, \Gamma_x \vdash \text{fix } x \text{ in } e : \eta}$$

Fig. 1. Strictness Typing Rules.

---

where $\bot$ denotes *false* and $\top$ denotes *true*. We write $C \models D$ to denote model-theoretic entailment among constraints C and D.

Structural strictness constraints $(\tau \leq_s \tau')$ are translated as follows:

$$[\![(\tau_1 \mapsto \tau_1' \leq_s \tau_2 \mapsto \tau_2')]\!] = [\![(\tau_1' \leq_s \tau_2')]\!] \wedge [\![(\tau_2 \leq_s \tau_1)]\!]$$
$$[\![(\delta_1 \leq_s \delta_2)]\!] = \delta_1 \to \delta_2$$

Note that types τ and τ' in structural constraints $(\tau \leq_s \tau')$ must always be of the same shape. This condition is enforced by requiring expressions to be well-typed in the underlying type system.

Typing Rules

Figure 1 defines the strictness logic. Most of its rules are straightforward. Γ_x denotes the environment obtained from Γ by excluding variable x. Rule (If) handles conditional expressions. Note that well-typing in the underlying system ensures that expression e is of type **Bool** and expressions e_1 and e_2 share the same underlying type. Therefore, their strictness types are of the same shape. The rule states that if the condition e is undefined, i.e. $C \models \delta \to \bot$, then the resulting type τ is unconstrained. If we have no information about the condition, i.e. $C \models \delta \to \top$, then we build the least upper bound of the strictness descriptions of e_1 and e_2. Note that the constraint $\delta \to [\![(\tau_1 \leq_s \tau) \wedge (\tau_2 \leq_s \tau)]\!]$ is in HORN. Rules ($\forall$I) and ($\forall$E) handle construction and elimination of polyvariant strictness types. Note that for now we only allow for polymorphism in the annotation variables (polyvariance). In Section 4, we show how to allow for polymorphism in the underlying language. Rule ($\exists$I) allows unnecessary strictness type variables in the constraint component of a typing judgment to be hidden.

Relationship to Abstract Interpretation

We relate our strictness logic to the strictness analysis by abstract interpretation of Burn *et al.* [1]. We show that for first-order programs our strictness logic is equivalent and for higher-order programs or logic is sound, which establishes the correctness of our analysis.

Strictness analysis by abstract interpretation interprets well-typed expressions in the complete partial order $\mathcal{V}$ where $\mathcal{V}$ is the least solution of the equation

$$\mathcal{V} = \mathbf{2} + \mathcal{V} \mapsto \mathcal{V}$$

where $\mathbf{2}$ is the two–point lattice $\{\bot, \top\}$ such that $\bot \leq \top$.

The abstraction of an expression e of type $\mathbf{Bool} \mapsto \mathbf{Int} \mapsto \mathbf{Int}$ would then be a function $[\![e]\!] :: \mathbf{2} \mapsto \mathbf{2} \mapsto \mathbf{2}$. The function $[\![\cdot]\!]$ on expressions is defined as follows (where ρ is a variable mapping from variables to values):

$$
\begin{aligned}
[\![x]\!]\rho &= \rho(x) \\
[\![\lambda u.e]\!]\rho &= \lambda v.[\![e]\!]\rho[u := v] \\
[\![e\,e']\!]\rho &= [\![e]\!]\rho([\![e']\!]\rho) \\
[\![\text{let } x = e \text{ in } e']\!]\rho &= [\![e']\!]\rho[x := [\![e]\!]\rho] \\
[\![\text{fix } x \text{ in } e]\!]\rho &= \text{fix}(\lambda v.[\![e]\!]\rho[x := v]) \\
[\![\text{if } e \text{ then } e_1 \text{ else } e_2]\!]\rho &= \begin{cases} \bot & \text{if } [\![e]\!]\rho = \bot \\ [\![e_1]\!]\rho \sqcup [\![e_2]\!]\rho & \text{otherwise} \end{cases}
\end{aligned}
$$

The meaning of strictness types is defined in terms of ideals in $\mathcal{V}$. Ideals are non-empty, downward-closed and limit-closed subsets of $\mathcal{V}$.

The function $[\![\cdot]\!]$ on closed strictness types is defined below. We say a type τ is a *monotype* if $fv(\tau) = \emptyset$. We let μ range over monotypes and ν over $\bot$ and $\top$.

$$
\begin{aligned}
[\![\bot]\!] &= \{\bot\} \\
[\![\top]\!] &= \{\bot, \top\} \\
[\![\mu \mapsto \mu']\!] &= \{f \in \mathcal{V} \mapsto \mathcal{V} \mid v \in [\![\mu]\!] \Rightarrow f\,v \in [\![\mu']\!]\} \\
[\![\forall \bar{\delta}.C \Rightarrow \tau]\!] &= \bigcap \{ [\![[\bar{\nu}/\bar{\delta}]\tau]\!] \mid \models [\bar{\nu}/\bar{\delta}]C \}
\end{aligned}
$$

Note that $[\![\eta]\!]$ is an ideal for a closed strictness type η. The strictness type system is sound, i.e. every satisfiable constraint has a monotype solution. The $(\leq_s)$ relation is coherent, i.e. if a type τ subsumes a type τ', written $\models (\tau \leq_s \tau')$, then the denotation of τ in the ideal model is a subset of the denotation of τ'.

Our first result concerns only first-order programs. We can show that our HORN-based strictness system is equivalent to Burn *et al.*'s abstract interpretation approach for first-order programs.

We observe that Burn *et al.*'s strictness descriptions for first-order functions, which are Boolean functions, can be viewed as constrained types in the Boolean domain. For example, the function + is described by the Boolean function $\delta_1 \mapsto \delta_2 \mapsto (\delta_1 \wedge \delta_2)$ which in turn can be viewed as $\forall \bar{\delta}.(\delta_1 \wedge \delta_2) \leftrightarrow \delta_3 \Rightarrow \delta_1 \mapsto \delta_2 \mapsto \delta_3$. We can be more specific. Every first-order function f can be described by $\forall \bar{\delta}.P \leftrightarrow \delta_n \Rightarrow \delta_1 \mapsto \dots \delta_n$ where P is a positive boolean formulae where the class of positive boolean formulas (POS) is defined as:

$$P ::= \bot \mid \top \mid \delta \mid P \wedge P \mid P \vee P \mid \exists \bar{\delta}.P$$

We further observe that we can weaken the strictness description of first-order functions without losing any information.

Lemma 1 (Equivalence between HORN and POS Types). *Let P be a boolean expression in POS. Let $\eta = \forall \bar{\delta}.P \leftrightarrow \delta_n \Rightarrow \delta_1 \mapsto \dots \mapsto \delta_n$ be a polymorphic strictness type such that $fv(\eta) = \emptyset$. Then, $P \to \delta_n$ is in HORN and*

$$[\![\forall \bar{\delta}.P \leftrightarrow \delta_n \Rightarrow \delta_1 \mapsto \dots \mapsto \delta_n]\!] = [\![\forall \bar{\delta}.P \to \delta_n \Rightarrow \delta_1 \mapsto \dots \mapsto \delta_n]\!]$$

This allows us to establish the result that HORN-based inference is sound and complete wrt. Burn *et al.*'s abstract interpretation approach for first-order programs.

A variable environment ρ *models* a closed typing environment Γ, written $\rho \models \Gamma$, if for all $x : \eta \in \Gamma$, $\rho(x) \in [\![\eta]\!]$. We write $\Gamma \models e : I$ iff for all ρ where $\rho \models \Gamma$ we have that $[\![e]\!]\rho \in I$ where I is an ideal.

Theorem 1 (Soundness and Completeness of First-Order Programs). *Let e be a first-order program, η a strictness type, Γ a strictness environment such that $fv(\Gamma, \eta) = \emptyset$. Then, $true, \Gamma \vdash e : \eta$ iff $\Gamma \models e : I$ where $I = [\![\eta]\!]$.*

For higher-order programs we can say that we are sound with respect to Burn *et al.*.

Theorem 2 (Soundness of Higher-Order Programs). *Let $C, \Gamma \vdash e : \eta$ be a valid typing judgment. Let ϕ be a substitution such that $\phi\Gamma$ and $\phi\eta$ are closed and $\models \phi C$. Let ρ be a variable environment such that $\rho \models \phi\Gamma$. Then $[\![e]\!]\rho \in [\![\phi\eta]\!]$.*

3   Inference

We assume that we are given a well-typed program, each subexpression annotated with its underlying type. We write $(e :: t)$ to denote that expression e has the underlying type t.

Strictness inference computes the missing strictness information for a type-annotated expression $(e :: t)$. We first compute the shape of e's strictness type from the underlying type t. We introduce judgments of the form $t \vdash \tau$ which state that τ is a strictness type with the same shape as t. The rules are as follows:

$$\text{(Bool)} \ \frac{\delta \text{ is fresh}}{\textbf{Bool} \vdash \delta} \qquad \text{(Int)} \ \frac{\delta \text{ is fresh}}{\textbf{Int} \vdash \delta} \qquad \text{(Arrow)} \ \frac{t_1 \vdash \tau_1 \quad t_2 \vdash \tau_2}{t_1 \mapsto t_2 \vdash \tau_1 \mapsto \tau_2}$$

$$\text{(Var)} \quad \frac{(x : \forall \bar{\delta}.C \Rightarrow \tau) \in \Gamma \quad \bar{\delta}' \text{ new}}{\Gamma, x :: t \vdash_{inf} ([[\bar{\delta}'/\bar{\delta}]C], [\bar{\delta}'/\bar{\delta}]\tau)}$$

$$\text{(Var-}\lambda\text{)} \quad \frac{(x : \tau) \in \Gamma \quad t \vdash \tau'}{C = [[(\tau \leq_s \tau')]]} \quad \frac{}{\Gamma, x :: t \vdash_{inf} (C, \tau')}$$

$$\text{(Abs)} \quad \frac{t_1 \vdash \tau_1}{\Gamma_x.x : \tau_1, e :: t_2 \vdash_{inf} (C, \tau_2)}{\Gamma_x, \lambda x.e :: t_1 \mapsto t_2 \vdash_{inf} (C, \tau_1 \mapsto \tau_2)}$$

$$\text{(App)} \quad \frac{\begin{array}{c} \Gamma, e_1 :: t_1 \vdash_{inf} (C_1, \tau_1) \\ \Gamma, e_2 :: t_2 \vdash_{inf} (C_2, \tau_2) \\ t_3 \vdash \tau_3 \\ C = C_1 \land C_2 \land [[(\tau_1 \leq_s \tau_2 \mapsto \tau_3)]] \end{array}}{\Gamma, ((e_1 :: t_1)(e_2 :: t_2)) :: t_3 \vdash_{inf} (C, \tau_3)}$$

$$\text{(Let)} \quad \frac{\begin{array}{c} \Gamma_x, e_1 :: t_1 \vdash_{inf} (C_1, \tau_1) \\ gen(C_1, \Gamma_x, \tau_1) = (C_0, \eta_0) \\ \Gamma_x.x : \eta_0, e_2 :: t_2 \vdash_{inf} (C_2, \tau_2) \\ C = C_0 \land C_2 \end{array}}{\Gamma_x, (\text{let } x = (e_1 :: t_1) \text{ in } e_2) :: t_2 \vdash_{inf} (C, \tau_2)}$$

$$\text{(}\exists\text{Intro)} \quad \frac{\Gamma, e :: t \vdash_{inf} (C, \tau)}{\bar{\delta} = fv(C) \backslash fv(\Gamma, \tau)}{\Gamma, e :: t \vdash_{inf} (\exists \bar{\delta}.C, \tau)}$$

$$\text{(If)} \quad \frac{\begin{array}{c} \Gamma, e :: \textbf{Bool} \vdash_{inf} (C_0, \delta) \quad t \vdash \tau \\ \Gamma, e_1 :: t \vdash_{inf} (C_1, \tau_1) \quad \Gamma, e_2 :: t \vdash_{inf} (C_2, \tau_2) \\ C = C_0 \land C_1 \land C_2 \land (\delta \rightarrow [[(\tau_1 \leq_s \tau) \land (\tau_2 \leq_s \tau)]]) \end{array}}{\Gamma, (\text{if } e \text{ then } e_1 \text{ else } e_2 :: t) \vdash_{inf} (C, \tau)}$$

$$\text{(Fix)} \quad \frac{\begin{array}{c} t \vdash \tau \quad \bar{\delta} = fv(\tau) \\ \eta_0 = \forall \bar{\delta}.true \Rightarrow \tau \\ \mathcal{F}(\Gamma_x.x : \eta_0, e :: t) = (C, \tau) \end{array}}{\Gamma_x, (\text{fix } x :: t \text{ in } e) :: t \vdash_{inf} (C, \tau)}$$

Fig. 2. Strictness Inference.

In Figure 2 we define the inference algorithm which is formulated as a deduction system over clauses of the form

$$\Gamma, e :: t \vdash_{inf} (C, \tau)$$

with a strictness environment Γ and a type-annotated expression $e :: t$ as input, and a strictness constraint C and a strictness type τ as output. We note that an algorithm in the style of $\mathcal{W}$ can be straightforwardly derived from this specification.

All rules are syntax-directed except rule ($\exists$Intro). This rule is justified by the corresponding rule in the logical system and can be applied at any stage of the inference process. Rule (Var-λ) handles lambda-bound variables and rule (Var) handles the instantiation of let-bound variables. Rule (Let) introduces annotation polymorphism. We define a generalisation function giving the generalised type scheme and the generalised constraint. Let C be a constraint, Γ a type environment, and τ a type. Then

$$gen(C, \Gamma, \tau) = (\exists \bar{\delta}.C, \forall \bar{\delta}.C \Rightarrow \tau)$$

where $\bar{\delta} = fv(C, \tau) \backslash fv(\Gamma)$. Note that we push the whole constraint C into the type scheme (we could be more efficient by pushing in only the *affected* constraints).

In rule (If), the constraint $\delta \rightarrow [\![(\tau_1 \leq_s \tau) \wedge (\tau_2 \leq_s \tau)]\!]$, where $[\![(\tau_1 \leq_s \tau) \wedge (\tau_2 \leq_s \tau)]\!] = (\delta_1 \rightarrow \delta_1') \wedge \ldots \wedge (\delta_n \rightarrow \delta_n')$, translates to $\delta \rightarrow ((\delta_1 \rightarrow \delta_1') \wedge \ldots \wedge (\delta_n \rightarrow \delta_n'))$ which is equivalent to $\delta \rightarrow \delta_1 \rightarrow \delta_1' \wedge \ldots \wedge \delta \rightarrow \delta_n \rightarrow \delta_n'$. Hence, all constraints we generate are in HORN.

With (Fix), we follow Dussart, Henglein and Mossin [2], performing a Kleene-Mycroft iteration until a fixpoint is found. We define $(\forall \bar{\delta}_1.C_1 \Rightarrow \tau_1) \leq (\forall \bar{\delta}_2.C_2 \Rightarrow \tau_2)$ iff $C_2 \models \exists \bar{\delta}_1.(C_1 \wedge [\![(\tau_1 \leq_s \tau_2)]\!])$. W.l.o.g. we assume there are no name clashes between $\bar{\delta}_1$ and $\bar{\delta}_2$. Define

$$\mathcal{F}(\Gamma_x.x : \eta_i, e :: t) = \begin{cases} \mathcal{F}(\Gamma_x.x : \eta_{i+1}, e :: t) & \text{if } \eta_i < \eta_{i+1} \\ (C, \tau) & \text{if } \eta_i = \eta_{i+1} \end{cases}$$

where $\Gamma_x.x : \eta_i, e :: t \vdash_{inf} (C, \tau)$ and $(\cdot, \eta_{i+1}) = gen(C, \Gamma_x.x : \eta_i, \tau)$. Clearly, the sequence $\eta_o \leq \ldots \leq \eta_i \leq \ldots$ is finite.

Example 1. Let $t = \textbf{Int} \mapsto \textbf{Int} \mapsto \textbf{Int} \mapsto \textbf{Int}$. Consider the inference for km :: t.

km x y z = if z == 1 then x - y else km y x (z - 1)

Let $\Gamma = \{x : \delta_x, y : \delta_y, z : \delta_z, km : \forall \delta_1 \delta_2 \delta_3 \delta_4.\ true \Rightarrow \delta_1 \mapsto \delta_2 \mapsto \delta_3 \mapsto \delta_4\}$ plus strictness types for 1, == and −.

$$\Gamma, 1 :: \textbf{Int} \vdash_{inf} (\delta_5, \delta_5)$$

(App) $\Gamma, z == 1 :: \textbf{Bool} \vdash_{inf} (\delta_5 \rightarrow \delta_z \rightarrow \delta_6 \wedge \delta_5, \delta_6)$

($\exists$Intro) $\Gamma, z == 1 :: \textbf{Bool} \vdash_{inf} (\delta_z \rightarrow \delta_6, \delta_6)$

(App)($\exists$Intro)$\Gamma, z - 1 :: \textbf{Int} \vdash_{inf} (\delta_z \rightarrow \delta_7, \delta_7)$

(App)($\exists$Intro)$\Gamma, x - y :: \textbf{Int} \vdash_{inf} (\delta_x \rightarrow \delta_y \rightarrow \delta_8, \delta_8)$

(Var) $\Gamma, km :: t \vdash_{inf} (true, \delta_1 \mapsto \delta_2 \mapsto \delta_3 \mapsto \delta_4)$

(App)$\Gamma, km\ y\ x\ (z\text{-}1) :: \textbf{Int} \vdash_{inf} (\delta_y \rightarrow \delta_1 \wedge \delta_x \rightarrow \delta_2 \wedge \delta_7 \rightarrow \delta_3 \wedge \delta_4 \rightarrow \delta_9 \wedge$
$$\delta_z \rightarrow \delta_7, \delta_9)$$

(If) $\Gamma, \text{if} \ldots :: \textbf{Int} \vdash_{inf} (\delta_y \rightarrow \delta_1 \wedge \delta_x \rightarrow \delta_2 \wedge \delta_7 \rightarrow \delta_3 \wedge \delta_4 \rightarrow \delta_9 \wedge$
$$\delta_z \rightarrow \delta_7 \wedge \delta_z \rightarrow \delta_6 \wedge \delta_x \rightarrow \delta_y \rightarrow \delta_8 \wedge$$
$$\delta_6 \rightarrow \delta_8 \rightarrow \delta_r \wedge \delta_6 \rightarrow \delta_9 \rightarrow \delta_r, \delta_r)$$

($\exists$Intro) $\Gamma, \text{if} \ldots :: \textbf{Int} \vdash_{inf} (\delta_y \rightarrow \delta_1 \wedge \delta_x \rightarrow \delta_2 \wedge \delta_z \rightarrow \delta_3 \wedge$
$$\delta_4 \rightarrow \delta_z \rightarrow \delta_r \wedge \delta_x \rightarrow \delta_y \rightarrow \delta_z \rightarrow \delta_r, \delta_r)$$

(Abs)$\times$3 $\Gamma, km :: t \vdash_{inf} (\delta_y \rightarrow \delta_1 \wedge \delta_x \rightarrow \delta_2 \wedge \delta_z \rightarrow \delta_3 \wedge \delta_4 \rightarrow \delta_z \rightarrow \delta_r \wedge$
$$\delta_x \rightarrow \delta_y \rightarrow \delta_z \rightarrow \delta_r, \delta_x \mapsto \delta_y \mapsto \delta_z \mapsto \delta_r)$$

($\exists$Intro) $\Gamma, km :: t \vdash_{inf} (\delta_x \rightarrow \delta_y \rightarrow \delta_z \rightarrow \delta_r, \delta_x \mapsto \delta_y \mapsto \delta_z \mapsto \delta_r)$

In the last step we obtain the first approximation of km in the fixpoint iteration. We can evaluate the next iteration by adding the constraint $\delta_1 \rightarrow \delta_2 \rightarrow \delta_3 \rightarrow \delta_4$

to the constraints from the (Var) step onward. This time in the last step the elimination of variables $\{\delta_1, \delta_2, \delta_3, \delta_4\}$ results in the same description. Hence the fixpoint is reached and we have

$$\mathsf{km} : \forall \delta_x \delta_y \delta_z \delta_r. \; \delta_x \to \delta_y \to \delta_z \to \delta_r \Rightarrow \delta_x \mapsto \delta_y \mapsto \delta_z \mapsto \delta_r$$

That is km is strict in all arguments.

We can prove soundness and completeness results for well-typed programs. Soundness states that every deduction derived by the inference system can also be derived in the logical system:

Theorem 3 (Soundness of Inference). *Let* $\Gamma, e :: t \vdash_{inf} (C, \tau)$. *Then* $C, \Gamma \vdash e : \tau$.

Completeness states that every deduction derivable in the logical system is subsumed by a deduction in the inference system:

Theorem 4 (Completeness of Inference). *Let* $C, \Gamma \vdash e : \forall \bar{\delta}_1.C_1 \Rightarrow \tau_1$ *and* $(e :: t)$ *be the type-annotated version of expression* e *such that* τ_1 *is of shape* t. *Then* $\Gamma, e :: t \vdash_{inf} (C_2, \tau_2)$ *for some* $C_2, \tau_2, \bar{\delta}_2$ *such that* $\bar{\delta}_2 = fv(C_2, \tau_2) \backslash fv(\Gamma)$ *and* $C \wedge C_1 \models \exists \bar{\delta}_2.(C_2 \wedge \llbracket (\tau_2 \leq_s \tau_1) \rrbracket)$.

3.1 Constraint-Based Fixpoints

If we are willing to give up some accuracy in the presence of polymorphic recursion in strictness types then we can replace the (Fix) rule by a simpler rule which just ensures that the constraints generated will be above the least fixpoint. This is similar to the (FIX) rule of Kuo and Mishra [7] (they only gave a constraint based fixpoint rule, no iterative fixpoint rule).

The following rule forces all recursive invocations to have the same strictness type which must be a super-type of the strictness type of the recursively defined expression.

$$(\text{FixC}) \quad \frac{t \vdash \tau' \quad \Gamma_x.x : \tau', e :: t \vdash_{inf} (C_1, \tau) \quad t \vdash \tau''}{C = C_1 \wedge \llbracket (\tau \leq_s \tau') \rrbracket \wedge \llbracket (\tau \leq_s \tau'') \rrbracket}{\Gamma_x, (\text{fix } x :: t \text{ in } e) :: t \vdash_{inf} (C, \tau'')}$$

The "shortcut" of stipulating $(\tau \leq_s \tau')$ may have the unfortunate side-effect of introducing constraints amongst the arguments to a function. An example of this phenomenon appears in Example 2 below. A simple way of eliminating such constraints is to couch the result in terms of a fresh binding-time type τ'', with the constraint $(\tau \leq_s \tau'')$.

This approach may lose accuracy, since it forces the strictness of the arguments in the recursive call to be the same as the strictness for the overall function. It finds a correct but imprecise strictness type for the function.

Example 2. We illustrate the constraint-based fixpoint rule on km starting from the second last inference step of Example 1. Let $\tau' = \delta_1 \mapsto \delta_2 \mapsto \delta_3 \mapsto \delta_4$ and

$\tau'' = \delta_x'' \mapsto \delta_y'' \mapsto \delta_z'' \mapsto \delta_r''$. The (FixC) rule proceeds by adding the constraints $[\![(\delta_x \mapsto \delta_y \mapsto \delta_z \mapsto \delta_r \leq_s \delta_1 \mapsto \delta_2 \mapsto \delta_3 \mapsto \delta_4)]\!]$ and $[\![(\delta_x \mapsto \delta_y \mapsto \delta_z \mapsto \delta_r \leq_s \delta_x'' \mapsto \delta_y'' \mapsto \delta_z'' \mapsto \delta_r'')]\!]$ to those inferred in the second last inference step of Example 1 as follows:

$$\Gamma, \mathsf{km} :: t \vdash_{inf} (\delta_y \rightarrow \delta_1 \wedge \delta_x \rightarrow \delta_2 \wedge \delta_z \rightarrow \delta_3 \wedge \delta_4 \rightarrow \delta_z \rightarrow \delta_r \wedge$$
$$\delta_x \rightarrow \delta_y \rightarrow \delta_z \rightarrow \delta_r, \delta_x \mapsto \delta_y \mapsto \delta_z \mapsto \delta_r)$$

(FixC) $\Gamma_{km}, \mathsf{fix\ km\ in\ \ldots} :: t \vdash_{inf} (\delta_y \rightarrow \delta_1 \wedge \delta_x \rightarrow \delta_2 \wedge \delta_z \rightarrow \delta_3 \wedge \delta_4 \rightarrow \delta_z \rightarrow \delta_r \wedge$
$$\delta_x \rightarrow \delta_y \rightarrow \delta_z \rightarrow \delta_r \wedge \delta_1 \rightarrow \delta_x \wedge \delta_2 \rightarrow \delta_y \wedge$$
$$\delta_3 \rightarrow \delta_z \wedge \delta_4 \rightarrow \delta_r \wedge \delta_x'' \rightarrow \delta_x \wedge \delta_y'' \rightarrow \delta_y \wedge$$
$$\delta_z'' \rightarrow \delta_z \wedge \delta_r \rightarrow \delta_r'', \delta_x'' \mapsto \delta_y'' \mapsto \delta_z'' \mapsto \delta_r'')$$

($\exists$Int) $\Gamma_{km}, \mathsf{fix\ km\ in\ \ldots} :: t \vdash_{inf} (\delta_x'' \rightarrow \delta_y'' \rightarrow \delta_z'' \rightarrow \delta_r'', \delta_x'' \mapsto \delta_y'' \mapsto \delta_z'' \mapsto \delta_r'')$

Note the spurious consequence $\delta_x \leftrightarrow \delta_y$ that arises on the variables of τ in addition to the correct answer $\delta_x \rightarrow \delta_y \rightarrow \delta_z \rightarrow \delta_r$. This is eliminated when we couch the results in terms of fresh type τ''.

For this example the constraint-based fixpoint leads to no loss of accuracy since the strictness of the two arguments x and y which were forced to be equal were already equal. Notice that this is an example where the approach of Kuo and Mishra [7] loses accuracy.

The rule is not complete wrt. the logic in Section 2. The result using (FixC) for the function h x y b = if b then x else h x (h y x b) b is

$$h : \forall\ x\ y\ b.\ b \rightarrow x \rightarrow r \wedge b \rightarrow y \rightarrow r \Rightarrow x \mapsto y \mapsto b \mapsto r$$

rather than $h : \forall\ x\ y\ b.\ b \rightarrow x \rightarrow r \Rightarrow x \mapsto y \mapsto b \mapsto r$. However, the (FixC) rule is sound.

Theorem 5 (Soundness of FixC). *Let* $\Gamma, e :: t \vdash_{inf} (C, \tau)$ *using (FixC). Then* $C, \Gamma \vdash e : \tau$.

4   Polymorphism and Algebraic Data Types

Any realistic program analysis needs to be able to handle additional language features such as polymorphism and algebraic data types. We first extend our strictness analysis to ML-style polymorphism. Thereafter, we describe our handling of algebraic data types.

4.1   Polymorphism

In previous work [3], we have already described how to extend Dussart *et al*'s binding-time analysis [2] to programs which are polymorphic in their underlying types. Fortunately, most of the methods and concepts introduced for the binding-time analysis of polymorphic programs carry over to the strictness analysis described in this paper.

We assume that the underlying type language is now polymorphic, as follows:

$$\textbf{Types} \qquad t ::= \alpha \mid \textbf{Int} \mid \textbf{Bool} \mid t \mapsto t$$
$$\textbf{Type Schemes } \sigma ::= t \mid \forall \bar{\alpha}.t$$

Example 3. Consider the following polymorphic program:

sel :: $\forall \bar{\alpha}.\textbf{Bool} \mapsto (\alpha_1 \mapsto \alpha_2) \mapsto (\alpha_1 \mapsto \alpha_2) \mapsto \alpha_1 \mapsto \alpha_2$
sel b f g x = if b then f x else g x

which either applies function f or function g to value x, depending on the boolean expression b.

The strictness description of sel is as follows:

$$\forall \delta, \bar{\beta}. \begin{array}{l} \beta_{13} \to \beta_{11} \wedge \delta \to \beta_{21} \to \beta_{23} \wedge \\ \beta_{13} \to \beta_{12} \wedge \delta \to \beta_{22} \to \beta_{23} \end{array} \Rightarrow \delta \mapsto (\beta_{11} \mapsto \beta_{21}) \mapsto (\beta_{12} \mapsto \beta_{22}) \mapsto \beta_{13} \mapsto \beta_{23}$$

We use the convention that variables β refer to strictness variables which correspond to a polymorphic variable in the underlying system. For example, strictness variables β_{11}, β_{12} and β_{13} correspond to variable α_1. Note that although we still use HORN constraints, constraints of the form $\beta_{13} \to \beta_{11}$ now express structural relationships between instances of β_{13} and β_{11}. In a system without Boolean constraints, we would write $(\beta_{13} \leq_s \beta_{11})$ instead. The advantage of using Booleans is that we do not need to introduce any new primitive constraints. For example, the constraint $\delta \to \beta_{21} \to \beta_{23}$ states that if $\delta = \top$ then $(\beta_{21} \leq_s \beta_{23})$ must hold, otherwise the relationship between instances of β_{21} and β_{23} is unaffected.

Assume that we apply function sel in the following context:

$$\text{sel'} = \text{sel } \sharp \text{ } (\textbf{Int} \mapsto \textbf{Int}) \text{ } (\textbf{Int} \mapsto \textbf{Int})$$

sel' b f g e :: $\textbf{Int} \mapsto \textbf{Int}$		: (C, τ)
b	:: $\textbf{Bool}$	: (C_b, δ_b)
f	:: $(\textbf{Int} \mapsto \textbf{Int}) \mapsto (\textbf{Int} \mapsto \textbf{Int})$	: $(C_f, (\delta_{f1} \mapsto \delta_{f2}) \mapsto (\delta_{f3} \mapsto \delta_{f4}))$
g	:: $(\textbf{Int} \mapsto \textbf{Int}) \mapsto (\textbf{Int} \mapsto \textbf{Int})$	: $(C_g, (\delta_{g1} \mapsto \delta_{g2}) \mapsto (\delta_{g3} \mapsto \delta_{g4}))$
e	:: $\textbf{Int} \mapsto \textbf{Int}$	: $(C_e, \delta_{e1} \mapsto \delta_{e2})$

where $\sharp$ denotes polymorphic type application, instantiating polymorphic variables α_1 and α_2 with $\textbf{Int} \mapsto \textbf{Int}$. Note that we have type-annotated all expressions and written all strictness descriptions on the right-hand side.

We obtain the strictness description (C, τ) of expression sel' b f g e as follows. We perform the following substitutions on the type component of sel

$$\begin{array}{ll} \beta_{11} = \delta_{f1} \mapsto \delta_{f2} & \beta_{21} = \delta_{f3} \mapsto \delta_{f4} \\ \beta_{12} = \delta_{g1} \mapsto \delta_{g2} & \beta_{22} = \delta_{g3} \mapsto \delta_{g4} \\ \beta_{13} = \delta_{e1} \mapsto \delta_{e2} & \beta_{23} = \delta_1 \mapsto \delta_2 \end{array}$$

which gives $\tau = \beta_{23} = \delta_1 \mapsto \delta_2$. On the constraint side, it must hold that all relations which hold for polymorphic strictness variables carry over to their instances. For example, the constraint $\beta_{13} \to \beta_{11}$ generates the constraint $[\![(\delta_{e1} \mapsto$

$\delta_{e2} \leq_s \delta_{f1} \mapsto \delta_{f2})]$ and $\delta \to \beta_{21} \to \beta_{23}$ generates the constraint $\delta \to [(\delta_{f3} \mapsto \delta_{f4} \leq_s \delta_1 \mapsto \delta_2)]$. We find

$$
C = \begin{array}{l}
\delta_{f1} \to \delta_{e1} \wedge \delta_{e2} \to \delta_{f2} \wedge \delta_{g1} \to \delta_{e1} \wedge \delta_{e2} \to \delta_{g2} \wedge \\
\delta \to \delta_1 \to \delta_{f3} \wedge \delta \to \delta_{f4} \to \delta_2 \wedge \\
\delta \to \delta_1 \to \delta_{g3} \wedge \delta \to \delta_{g4} \to \delta_2 \wedge \\
C_b \wedge C_f \wedge C_g \wedge \delta_b \to \delta
\end{array}
$$

In general, the method for building an instance of a strictness type scheme is as follows. We first relate polymorphic strictness variables to corresponding polymorphic variables in the underlying system. To this purpose, we introduce judgments $\Delta \vdash \tau : t$ where Δ is a shape environment associating strictness variables β to type variables α. Judgments $\Delta \vdash \tau : t$ are derived as follows:

$(\mathbf{Bool}_\delta)\ \Delta \vdash \delta : \mathbf{Bool}$ $(\mathbf{Bool}_\top)\ \Delta \vdash \top : \mathbf{Bool}$ $(\mathbf{Bool}_\bot)\ \Delta \vdash \bot : \mathbf{Bool}$

$$
(\beta)\ \frac{(\beta : \alpha) \in \Delta}{\Delta \vdash \beta : \alpha} \qquad (\mathrm{Arrow})\ \frac{\Delta \vdash \tau_1 : t_1 \quad \Delta \vdash \tau_2 : t_2}{\Delta \vdash \tau_1 \mapsto \tau_2 : t_1 \mapsto t_2}
$$

For brevity, we omit rules $(\mathbf{Int}_\delta)$, $(\mathbf{Int}_\top)$ and $(\mathbf{Int}_\bot)$.

We note that shape inference is decidable. Given a strictness type τ with underlying type t, we denote by $\tau, t \vdash \Delta$ the algorithm to infer the most general shape environment Δ. Given a shape environment Δ and underlying type t, we denote by $\Delta, t \vdash \tau$ the algorithm to infer the most general strictness type τ. We refer to [3] for more details.

Example 4. Coming back to the example above, relating the strictness description of sel with its underlying type, we find that $\Delta = \{\beta_{11} : \alpha_1, \beta_{12} : \alpha_1, \beta_{13} : \alpha_1, \beta_{21} : \alpha_2, \beta_{22} : \alpha_2, \beta_{23} : \alpha_2\}$.

Consider a polymorphic expression with strictness type $\forall \bar{\beta}, \bar{\delta}.C \Rightarrow \tau$ and underlying type $\forall \bar{\alpha}.t$. Apply this expression to a sequence of (underlying) instantiation types $\bar{t}$. First, compute the shape environment Δ from $\tau, t \vdash \Delta$. Then, for each pair (β_{ij}, α_i) where $\Delta \vdash \beta_{ij} : \alpha_i$ we generate a fresh τ_{ij} such that $\Delta, t_i \vdash \tau_{ij}$. This gives us a sequence of (strictness) instantiation types $\bar{\tau}$. Finally, we must build the instantiated constraint $[\bar{\tau}/\bar{\beta}]C$.

For each strictness constraint involving polymorphic variables, we need to generate the appropriate instantiated constraints. We observe that there are two possible kinds of polymorphic constraints:

$$
\begin{array}{l}
(1)\ \delta_1 \to \ldots \to \delta_n \to \beta \to \beta' \\
(2)\ \delta_1 \to \ldots \to \delta_n \to \beta
\end{array}
$$

where n possibly equals zero. We have already seen constraints of the first kind. Constraints of the second kind state that if we have no information about $\delta_1, \ldots, \delta_n$ (that is $\delta_1, \ldots \delta_n = \top$), then we do not have any information about β either. Such constraints prove to be useful if our analysis is not able to state any results.

Example 5. Consider an imported function $\mathrm{im} :: \forall \alpha.\alpha \mapsto \alpha \mapsto \alpha$ with no analysis information available. The best we can do is to assign im the following strictness type

$$\mathrm{im} : \forall \beta_1 \beta_2 \beta_3. \ \beta_3 \Rightarrow \beta_1 \mapsto \beta_2 \mapsto \beta_3$$

which states that we do not have any information about im's strictness behaviour.

We proceed by querying which relations hold and add in the appropriate constraints. The structure of the constraints allows us to avoid testing for certain combinations. For example, given a constraint $\delta \to \beta \to \beta'$ we know that variables δ and β must appear in a negative position and variable β' in a positive position of the type component.

We define *polarities* recursively: β appears in *positive* position in τ (written $\tau[\beta^+]$) iff $\tau = \beta$, or else $\tau = \tau_1 \mapsto \tau_2$ and either $\tau_1[\beta^-]$ or $\tau_2[\beta^+]$. Similarly, β appears in *negative* position in τ (written $\tau[\beta^-]$) iff $\tau = \tau_1 \mapsto \tau_2$ and $\tau_1[\beta^+]$ or $\tau_2[\beta^-]$.

We define the query relation for the first kind of constraints as follows

$$\mathcal{T}_{\alpha_i}(\Delta, \tau, \bar{\tau}_i) = \left\{ \delta_1 \to \cdots \to \delta_n \to [\![(\tau_{ij} \leq_s \tau_{ik})]\!] \,\middle|\, \begin{array}{l} \Delta \vdash \beta_{ij} : \alpha_i, \tau[\beta_{ij}^-], \\ \Delta \vdash \beta_{ik} : \alpha_i, \tau[\beta_{ik}^+], \\ \tau[\delta_1^-], \ldots, \tau[\delta_n^-] \\ C \models \delta_1 \to \cdots \to \delta_n \to \beta_{ij} \to \beta_{ik} \end{array} \right\}$$

In a similar style, we handle constraints of the second kind. We define

$$|\beta| = \beta \qquad |\delta| = \delta \qquad |\tau \mapsto \tau'| = |\tau'|$$

Then, the query relation for the second kind of constraints is as follows

$$\mathcal{T}'_{\alpha_i}(\Delta, \tau, \bar{\tau}_i) = \left\{ \delta_1 \to \cdots \to \delta_n \to |\tau_{ij}| \,\middle|\, \begin{array}{l} \Delta \vdash \beta_{ij} : \alpha_i, \tau[\beta_{ij}^+], \\ \tau[\delta_1^-], \ldots, \tau[\delta_n^-] \\ C \models \delta_1 \to \cdots \to \delta_n \to \beta_{ij} \end{array} \right\}$$

Note that it is sufficient to just constrain the final result of a function.

For example, assume that we have $\delta \to \beta$ and β is instantiated by $(\delta_1 \mapsto \delta_2) \mapsto (\delta_3 \mapsto \delta_4)$. Then, it is sufficient to add in $\delta \to \delta_4$ only.

Both query relations can be implemented efficiently which ensures the effectiveness of analysing polymorphically typed programs.

$$\mathcal{T}(\Delta, \tau, \bar{\tau}) = \bigwedge\nolimits_{\alpha_i \in range(\Delta)} (\mathcal{T}_{\alpha_i}(\Delta, \tau, \bar{\tau}_i) \wedge \mathcal{T}'_{\alpha_i}(\Delta, \tau, \bar{\tau}_i))$$

The resultant inference rule for polymorphic application is as follows

$$\text{(Var--Inst)} \ \frac{\begin{array}{c} x : \forall \bar{\beta}, \bar{\delta}.C \Rightarrow \tau \in \Gamma \quad t' = [\bar{t}/\bar{\alpha}]t \quad \tau, t \vdash \Delta \\ \text{for each } \Delta \vdash \beta_{ij} : \alpha_i \text{ generate} \Delta, t_i \vdash \tau_{ij} \\ C' = [\![[\bar{\delta}'/\bar{\delta}]C]\!] \wedge \mathcal{T}(\Delta, \tau, \bar{\tau}) \quad \tau' = [\bar{\tau}/\bar{\beta}, \bar{\delta}'/\bar{\delta}]\tau \quad \bar{\delta}' \text{ new} \end{array}}{\Gamma, ((x :: \forall \bar{\alpha}.t) \ \sharp \ \bar{t}) :: t' \vdash_{inf} (C', \tau')}$$

where $(x :: \forall \bar{\alpha}.t) \ \sharp \ \bar{t}$ denotes instantiation of polymorphic variables $\bar{\alpha}$ by types $\bar{t}$.

We have omitted the details of building strictness types which are polymorphic in annotation and underlying types. It is straightforward to adjust the corresponding rules (Let), ($\forall$I) and ($\exists$I). We refer to previous work [3] for a detailed development.

4.2   Algebraic Data Types

We first show how to handle non-recursive data types [2]

$$data\, \mathsf{Maybe}\, \alpha = \mathsf{Just}\, \alpha \mid \mathsf{Error}\, \mathbf{Int}$$

which translates to the following strictness data type

$$\mathsf{Maybe}^{\delta_1}\, \beta\, \delta_2 = \mathsf{Just}\, \beta \mid \mathsf{Error}\, \delta_2$$

The top-most annotation δ_1 tells us whether the data type is totally undefined (when $\delta_1 = \bot$), or (when $\delta_2 = \top$) the constructor may be known, but some of the arguments of the constructor are possibly undefined. The strictness variable β represents the strictness behaviour of α and δ_2 represents the strictness behaviour of Error's integer argument.

Value constructors are translated as follows:

$$\mathsf{Just}\ :\forall \beta, \delta_1, \delta_2.\ \delta_1 \Rightarrow \beta \mapsto \mathsf{Maybe}^{\delta_1}\, \beta\, \delta_2$$
$$\mathsf{Error} :\forall \beta, \delta_1, \delta_2.\ \delta_1 \Rightarrow \delta_2 \mapsto \mathsf{Maybe}^{\delta_1}\, \beta\, \delta_2$$

Note that for Just we do not constrain δ_2 and for Error we do not constrain β.

In general, a non-recursive data type

$$data\, T\, \bar{\alpha} = k_1 \bar{t}_1 \mid \ldots \mid k_n \bar{t}_n$$

translates to

$$T^{\delta}\, \bar{\beta}\, \bar{\delta} = k_1 \bar{\tau}_{k_1} \mid \ldots \mid k_n \bar{\tau}_{k_n}$$

where each α_i is represented by β_i and $\bar{\tau}_{k_i}$ results from $\Delta, \bar{t}_i \vdash \bar{\tau}_{k_i}$ where $\Delta = \{\beta_i : \alpha_i\}$ and $\bar{\delta}$ are the freshly introduced annotation variables in $\bar{\tau}_{k_1}, \ldots, \bar{\tau}_{k_n}$.

Each value constructor $k_i : \forall \bar{\alpha}.t_{i1} \mapsto \ldots \mapsto t_{im} \mapsto T\, \bar{\alpha}$ translates to

$$\forall \bar{\beta}, \bar{\delta}.\ \delta \Rightarrow \tau_{i1} \mapsto \ldots \mapsto \tau_{im} \mapsto T^{\delta}\, \bar{\beta}\, \bar{\delta}$$

We find the following inference rule for case expressions:

$$\Gamma, e :: T\, \bar{t}' \vdash_{inf} (C_0, T^{\delta}\, \bar{\tau}'\, \bar{\delta}')$$
$$\bar{\tau}', \bar{t}' \vdash \Delta \quad \Delta, \bar{t}' \vdash \bar{\tau}'' \quad \Delta, t \vdash \tau \quad \bar{\delta}''\ \text{fresh}$$

(Case) $\quad \Gamma.\bar{x}_i : [\bar{\tau}''/\bar{\beta}, \bar{\delta}''/\bar{\delta}]\bar{\tau}_{k_i}, e_i : t \vdash_{inf} (C_i, \tau_i''') \quad \text{for } i = 1..n$

$$\frac{C = C_0 \wedge \bigwedge_{i=1}^{n} C_i \wedge [\![(\bar{\tau}' \leq_s \bar{\tau}'')]\!] \wedge [\![(\bar{\delta}' \leq_s \bar{\delta}'')]\!] \wedge \delta \to (\bigwedge_{i=1}^{n} [\![(\tau_i''' \leq_s \tau)]\!])}{\Gamma, (\mathsf{case}\, e :: T\, \bar{t}'\, \mathsf{of}\, k_1 \bar{x}_1 \Rightarrow e_1 \mid \ldots \mid k_n \bar{x}_n \Rightarrow e_n) :: t \vdash_{inf} (C, \tau)}$$

---

[2] We note that non-recursive data types could be encoded as functions, this would give the same strictness information.

For recursive algebraic data types, we only consider the strictness properties of the top-most constructor. In effect, all information we have about recursive components is discarded. For example, the list description $[\beta]^\delta$ is interpreted as: δ describes the strictness behaviour of the topmost list constructor (so if it is $\perp$ then the whole list is $\perp$) while β describes the strictness of the element in the first cons cell. So, if a list-consuming function is strict in δ then it is safe to evaluate the list as far as its first constructor (i.e. to *weak head normal form*) before the function is applied. If the function is also strict in β then the element in the head of the list can also be evaluated before the function is applied.

There have been many proposals for finding more accurate information for recursive data types, usually in the context of lists. For example, *head-strictness* [13], *spine-strictness* (the shape of the expression is required) and *full-strictness* (all components of the expression are required) [12, 5]. We are currently investigating extensions to our analysis method to support these properties.

5   Implementation and Empirical Results

We have built a prototype implementation of the strictness analysis presented here for the Haskell compiler, GHC. The analysis engine is written in Haskell, while the Boolean constraints are handled by a specialized HORN constraint solver written in C, which represents Horn clauses as graphs with directed hyper-edges. It supports the operations of: conjunction, existential quantification, copying and renaming. For polymorphic application we provide specialized support for efficiently determining (a minimal set of) conjunctions $(\delta_1 \wedge \cdots \wedge \delta_n)$ such that $(\delta_1 \wedge \cdots \wedge \delta_n) \rightarrow (\beta_1 \rightarrow \beta_2)$ based on finding paths from β_1 to β_2.

GHC's current strictness analysis [10] is based on the abstract interpretation approach of Burn *et al.* [1], made practical by a widening operation which eliminates all but weak-head normal form information about higher-order types and algebraic data types with more than a single constructor. The strictness analysis produces a strictness description for functional variables which is used by a later pass to optimise these functions safely. The description assigns each argument one of S (for strict in weak head normal form, L (for lazy) and $U(d_1, \ldots, d_n)$ for a strict argument of a *product* type (one with only a single constructor), where d_i is the strictness description for argument i of the constructor. For example, the strictness descriptions for + is SS (for unboxed integers), snd is $U(LS)$ (strict in the pair and its second part) and f (from the introduction) is $LLLS$ (strict only in b). These strictness descriptions are written to an interface file for use in analysing modules which import analysed functions.

This approach appears very weak, it loses all information about application of functional arguments. This would seem very unfortunate because even simple Haskell programs often have implicit higher-order arguments because of type classes and their translation to dictionary passing. The simple function double x = x + x with type double :: Num a $\Rightarrow$ a $\mapsto$ a becomes, after processing, something like (for simplicity the Num dictionary is drastically simplified)

```
doubleCore :: (a ↦ a ↦ a, a ↦ a ↦ a) ↦ a ↦ a
doubleCore (plus,minus) x = plus x x
```

and the GHC strictness description discovered is $U(SL)L$ (strict in the plus part of the dictionary, but not in x). This apparent weakness is often avoided by aggressive inlining. Hence although we might expect doubleInt = (Int) double to be given an L strictness description (no information), this only happens if inlining of double is switched off. Inlining of double plus dictionary specialization results in GHC's current analyser finding the desired S strictness description.

Currently, we do not write or read our strictness descriptions to/from the interface file, instead we use GHC's strictness info to build a (weak) Boolean strictness description for imported functions.

We can show that we are at least as accurate as GHC's current strictness analyser by mapping our Boolean strictness types to the simple sequences above and comparing the number of S and U annotations that occur. Note that this mapping throws away a considerable amount of the strictness information we have in our descriptions. We find all the strictness results that GHC finds. In addition, we often improve GHC's information.

Table 1. Comparison with GHC Built-In Strictness Analysis.

Program	Functions	Lines	GHC Comp (secs)	Fix %+Time	Strict	FixC %+Time	Strict
bspt	271	2141	29.21	3473%	71	1193%	4-47
cacheprof	331	2151	37.64	662%	4	111%	4
compress2	19	198	4.49	88%	—	94%	0-4
ebnf2ps	485	2927	34.78	1394%	42	77%	41-34
fem	103	1286	27.19	38%	2	37%	6-7
fluid	278	2401	34.74	124%	22	52%	18-50
gamteb	48	701	15.83	30%	4	24%	4-8
gg	292	812	19.81	89%	9	40%	12-20
grep	148	356	5.11	150%	2	83%	8-10
hidden	233	521	17.44	49%	63	36%	64-15
hpg	319	2067	15.32	2419%	133	416%	14-96
infer	398	584	13.33	237%	12	84%	14-80
lift	1943	2043	7.75	5%	1	0%	3-35
maillist	10	175	1.59	51%	4	32%	9-9
mkhprog	75	803	4.56	76%	15	44%	0-19
pic	96	527	13.26	30%	25	23%	5-11
prolog	164	539	7.01	227%	22	60%	14-31
reptile	205	1522	20.35	55%	14	37%	4-14
rsa	14	74	2.03	11%	1	11%	1
symalg	38	1146	16.79	212%	2	8%	5-8
imaginary	97	318	11.03	163%	15	47%	17-20
spectral	3385	21709	240.66	703%	384	44%	145-397

Our experimental results are shown in Table 1, giving benchmark name (from the nofib suite) size (in no. of functions and lines), and original GHC compilation time. The data for each fixpoint rule is: the increase in compilation time when our strictness analysis phase is added, and the increase in number of U and

S annotations found. Using (Fix) we are uniformly more accurate than GHC, but this is not the case for (FixC). An entry x-y indicates x U+S annotations found by (FixC) where GHC found L, and y U+S annotations found by GHC where (FixC) found L. Two smaller `nofib` benchmark suites `imaginary` and `spectral` are shown in one summary line for space reasons.

The purpose of the comparison is mainly to show that the analysis is feasible, on a large and varied suite of programs. Our approach would already improve GHC's current approach. We emphasize that the descriptions we are calculating carry much more strictness information.

Overall, we were surprised by the accuracy of the current analysis for GHC given its simplicity. Clearly, the GHC implementors have ensured that the strictness analysis phase is well-integrated into the compiler as a whole and provides exactly the information they require. Of course, in the comparison we are favouring GHC by only comparing on the information it collects. By writing and reading our strictness information to/from the interface file we should be able to improve our accuracy significantly. Better handling of recursive data types should also lead to much more accuracy. The (FixC) approach currently loses too much strictness information. Investigations so far suggest that (FixC) loses considerable information when the recursive call has an always constructed algebraic data type. Unfortunately, since basic types, such as **Ints**, are boxed this is very common. We are investigating how to avoid this information loss.

The analysis times are large, but not infeasible. At present, the large analysis times seem to be caused by very large algebraic data types in combination with deeply nested bindings caused by GHC's aggressive inlining. Our current implementation is only a prototype and there are a number of obvious places for improvement: early elimination of variables during analysis; building a more efficient constraint solver; and, gracefully losing information when the analysis begins to take too much time. Another possibility worth investigating is a hybrid (Fix)/(FixC) approach which uses `FixC` after a certain number of fixpoint iterations. Arguably, the (Fix) implementation could be used now in a highly optimizing compilation mode where we are willing to pay (considerable) time for the best possible performance.

6   Conclusion and Related Work

There is a huge amount of theoretical work of strictness analysis, but very little of it has translated into practice. Our aim with this work was to see how far we could go in producing an accurate strictness analyser for a real programming language while remaining practical.

The starting point for the work presented here is our binding-time analysis using Boolean constraints [3]. The constraints that arise in strictness analysis are more complex (Horn formulae rather than simple implications) but the approaches are quite similar. Indeed, the two implementations share a considerable amount of code. We claim the analysis we have built is (almost) practical, and accurate compared to other implemented analysers.

Other implemented strictness analyses include Jensen *et al.* [4] which implements Burn *et al.*'s abstract interpretation approach using chaotic fixpoint iterations (which give a demand-driven evaluation of function descriptions that makes the higher-order function descriptions far more tractable). Unfortunately, the chaotic fixpoint approach does not handle separate modular compilation, and the only experimental data they give is for very small programs. Seward [11] developed an abstract interpretation based strictness analysis in GHC which was capable of analysing large programs. The approach is essentially first-order, and loses precision for polymorphic functions. Results are given for small programs, and it is not clear how effective it is in practice.

The Clean functional language has a well regarded strictness analyser which finds strictness information by a process of abstract reduction [9]. It is not easy to compare our results with this system. The system is more complex than the system presented here and consequently difficult to show correct, and implement.

The theoretical approaches that are most similar to ours are that of Kuo and Mishra [7], who gave the first constraint-based strictness analysis, and first used constraint-based fixpoints. They also gave an informal discussion of handling let-style polymorphism. Their approach is weak because it does not express conjunctive strictness information directly, but needs to do case by case analysis.

Wright [14] employs an annotated type-system to express strictness properties. In contrast to our system, he annotates function instead of base-types and he requires the full Boolean domain.

The closest work to ours is probably Jensen's framework for strictness [6]. He uses an inference system similar to ours to determine strictness types. Conditional properties are expressed using a ? operator, where $\phi?\psi$ is interpreted as $\perp$ if $\psi = \perp$ and ϕ otherwise. For example, the strictness of f from the introduction is (in a format as close to ours as possible)

$$\text{f} : \forall \delta_1 \delta_2 \delta_3 \delta_4. \ (\delta_1 \mapsto \delta_2 \mapsto \delta_3 \mapsto \delta_4 \mapsto (\delta_2 \wedge \delta_3)?\delta_4) \wedge (\delta_1 \mapsto \delta_2 \mapsto \delta_3 \mapsto \delta_4 \mapsto \delta_1?\delta_4)$$

Clearly, the conditional expressions $\phi?\delta$ play the same role as δ in our (If) rule $\delta \rightarrow [\![(\tau_1 \leq_s \tau) \wedge (\tau_2 \leq_s \tau)]\!]$. However, the constraints in Jensen's approach are complicated and he needs to define meaning of new operators and rules for constraint simplification. For example, he reduces the constraint $\delta_1?\delta_2 \leq \delta_3 \wedge C$ to the (disjunctive) set of constraints $\{\delta_1 \leq \delta_3 \wedge C, \ \delta_2 = \perp \wedge C\}$ where each new constraint represents one possible way of proving the original constraint. This can be avoided by simply using well-understood Boolean constraints.

Jensen's work is based on ranked intersection types, which may appear to be much more expressive than the strictness types we consider. However, we conjecture that his approach captures no more useful strictness information. At least for the examples in Jensen's paper the two approaches give equivalent strictness information. There is no implementation of Jensen's approach that we are aware of, and the approach does not tackle let-style polymorphism and algebraic data structures.

We have presented an accurate and feasible strictness analysis based on HORN constraints, which we believe will eventually form the basis of a robust and practical strictness analysis in everyday use in a real compiler. In future work, we will investigate the exact connection of our work with that of Jensen, Wright and others.

Acknowledgements

We thank Harald Søndergaard and the anonymous referees for their valuable comments.

References

1. G. L. Burn, C. L. Hankin, and S. Abramsky. The theory and practice of strictness for higher order functions. *Science of Computer Programming*, 7:249–278, 1986.
2. D. Dussart, F. Henglein, and C. Mossin. Polymorphic recursion and subtype qualifications: Polymorphic binding-time analysis in polynomial time. In A. Mycroft, editor, *Proc. Second Int. Symp. Static Analysis*, volume 983 of *LNCS*, pages 118–135. Springer-Verlag, 1995.
3. K. Glynn, P. J. Stuckey, M. Sulzmann, and H. Søndergaard. Boolean constraints for binding-time analysis. To appear in *Second Symposium on Programs as Data Objects (PADO-II)*, volume 2053 of *LNCS*. Springer-Verlag, 2001.
4. K. Jensen, P. Hjæresen, and M. Rosendahl. Efficient strictness analysis for haskell. In *Proceedings of the First International Static Analysis Symposium*, volume 864 of *LNCS*, pages 346–362. Springer-Verlag, 1994.
5. T. Jensen. Disjunctive program analysis for algebraic data types. *ACM Trans. on Programming Languages and Systems*, 19(5):751–803, 1997.
6. T. Jensen. Inference of polymorphic and conditional strictness properties. In *Proc. Twenty-Fifth ACM SIGPLAN-SIGACT Symp. on Principles of Programming Languages*. ACM Press, 1998.
7. T. Kuo and P. Mishra. Strictness analysis: A new perspective based on type inference. In *Functional Programming Languages and Computer Architecture*, pages 260–272, September 1989.
8. A. Mycroft. *Abstract Interpretation and Optimising Transformations for Applicative Programs*. PhD thesis, University of Edinburgh, 1981.
9. E. Nocker. Strictness analysis using abstract reduction. In *Proceedings Conference on Functional Programming Languages and Computer Architectures (FPCA '93)*. ACM Press, 1993.
10. S. Peyton Jones and W. Partain. Measuring the effectiveness of a simple strictness analyser. In Hammond and O'Donnell, editors, *Functional Programming, Glasgow 1993*, Springer Workshops in Computer Science, pages 201–220, 1993.
11. J. Seward. Beyond prototype implementations: Polymorphic projection analysis for glasgow haskell. In *Proceedings of the Second International Static Analysis Symposium*, volume 983 of *LNCS*, pages 382–399. Springer-Verlag, 1995.
12. P. Wadler. Strictness analysis on non-flat domains. In S. Abramsky and C.L. Hankin, editors, *Abstract Interpretation of Declarative Languages*, pages 266–275. Ellis Horwood, 1987.
13. P. Wadler and J. Hughes. Projections for strictness analysis. In *Proceedings of the 3rd International Conference on Functional Programming Languages and Computer Architecture*, volume 274 of *LNCS*, pages 385–407. Springer, 1987.
14. D.A. Wright. A new technique for strictness analysis. In *Proceedings of TAPSOFT*, volume 494 of *LNCS*, pages 235–258. Springer, 1991.

Applying Static Analysis Techniques for Inferring Termination Conditions of Logic Programs

Fred Mesnard[1] and Ulrich Neumerkel[2]

[1] Iremia - Université de La Réunion, France
fred@univ-reunion.fr
[2] Institut für Computersprachen - Technische Universität Wien, Austria
ulrich@complang.tuwien.ac.at

Abstract. We present the implementation of cTI, a system for universal left-termination *inference* of logic programs.

Termination inference generalizes termination analysis/checking. Traditionally, a termination analyzer tries to prove that a given class of queries terminates. This class must be provided to the system, requiring user annotations. With termination inference such annotations are no longer necessary. Instead, all provably terminating classes to all related predicates are inferred at once.

The architecture of cTI is described[1] and some optimizations are discussed. Running times for classical examples from the termination literature in LP and for some middle-sized logic programs are given.

1   Introduction

Termination is a crucial aspect of program verification. It is of particular importance for logic programs [31, 3], since there are *a priori* no syntactic restrictions to queries. In fact, most predicates do not terminate for the most general queries. Termination has been the subject of many works in the last fifteen years in the logic programming community [45, 4, 38]. Contrary to other languages there are two notions of termination for logic programs [45]: existential and universal termination. To illustrate them assume we use a standard Prolog engine. Existential termination means that either the computation finitely fails or produces *one* solution in finite time. When asked for further solutions, it may loop. On the other hand, universal termination means that the computation yields all solutions and fails in finite time (if we repeatedly ask for further solutions). Although existential termination plays an important rôle for normal logic programs, it has severe drawbacks: it is not instantiation-closed (*i.e.*, a goal may existentially terminate, but some of its instances may not terminate), hence it is not and-compositional (*i.e.*, two goals may existentially terminate, but not their conjunction), finally it

---

[1] A preliminary version of this paper was presented at the Workshop on Parallelism and Implementation Technology for Constraint Logic Programming Languages (ed. Ines de Castro Dutra), CL'2000, London.

P. Cousot (Ed.): SAS 2001, LNCS 2126, pp. 93–110, 2001.
© Springer-Verlag Berlin Heidelberg 2001

depends on the textual order of clauses. Universal termination has none of these brittle properties.

Existential termination has been the subject of only a few efforts [45, 28, 27, 32] whereas most research focused on universal termination. There are two main directions (see [22] for a survey): characterizing termination [4, 1, 38] and finding weaker but decidable sufficient conditions that lead to actual algorithms, e.g. [44, 37, 46] and [17] using complexity upper bounds. While our research belongs to both streams, we focus in this paper on the implementation of our approach. A companion paper positions our approach in the theoretical setting of acceptability for constraint logic programming [35].

Our main contribution compared to automated termination analysis [29, 18, 43, 11] is that we *infer* sufficient universal termination conditions from the text of any Prolog program. Inference implies that we adopt a bottom-up approach to termination. *There is no need to define a class of queries of interest.* We point out that giving a class of queries is imposed by all other works we are aware of. If required, these classes can be easily simulated within our framework.

Our system, cTI (*constraint-based Termination Inference*), is available at URL http:www.complang.tuwien.ac.at/cti and has been realized in SICStus Prolog. The only correctness requirement we currently impose on ISO-Prolog [20] programs is that they must not create infinite rational terms. Hence we consider execution with occur check or NTSO (*not subject to occur check*) programs [21] that are safely executed with any standard complying system. cTI is also used within the LP environment GUPU [36].

In Section 2 we present cTI informally with an example analysis. The central fixpoint algorithms for computing models are covered in Section 3. Our scheme to determine level-mappings is given in Section 4. Finally, Section 5 presents an empirical evaluation.

2   An Overview of cTI

Our aim is to compute classes of queries for which universal left termination is guaranteed.

Definition 1. *Let P be a Prolog program and q a predicate symbol of P. A termination condition for q is a set TC_q of goals of the form $\leftarrow q(\tilde{t})$ such that, for any goal $G \in TC_q$, each derivation of P and G using the left-to-right selection rule is finite.*

Our analyzer uses three main constraint structures (see [25, 26] for a presentation of the CLP paradigm): Herbrand terms (CLP($\mathcal{H}$)) for the initial program P, non-negative integers (CLP($\mathbb{N}$)) and booleans (CLP($\mathcal{B}$)) for approximating P. The correspondence between these structures relies on *approximations* [33], which are a simple form of abstract interpretation [13, 14], also called *abstract compilation*. We illustrate our method to infer termination conditions by using the predicates app/3, app3/4, and nrev/2.

app([], X, X).   nrev([], []).   app3(X, Y, Z, U) ←
app([E|X], Y, [E|Z]) ←   nrev([E|X], Y) ←   app(X, Y, V),
    app(X, Y, Z).   nrev(X, Z),   app(V, Z, U).
                   app(Z, [E], Y).

1. The initial Prolog program P is mapped to $P^{\mathbb{N}}$, a program in CLP($\mathbb{N}$) using an approximation based on a symbolic norm. In our example, we use the term-size norm[2]:

$$\|t\|_{\text{term-size}} = \begin{cases} 1 + \sum_{i=1}^{n} \|t_i\|_{\text{term-size}} & \text{if } t = f(t_1, \ldots, t_n), n > 0 \\ 0 & \text{if } t \text{ is a constant} \\ t & \text{if } t \text{ is a variable} \end{cases}$$

E.g.$\|f(0,0)\|_{\text{term-size}} = 1$. All non-monotonic elements of the program are approximated by monotone constructs. E.g., Prolog's unsound negation \+G is approximated by ((G,false);true). The approximation maintains that if a goal in $P^{\mathbb{N}}$ is terminating, then also the corresponding original goals in P terminate.

app$_{\mathbb{N}}$(0, X, X).   nrev$_{\mathbb{N}}$(0, 0).   app3$_{\mathbb{N}}$/4
app$_{\mathbb{N}}$(1+E+X,Y,1+E+Z) ←   nrev$_{\mathbb{N}}$(1+E+X,Y) ←   same as
    app$_{\mathbb{N}}$(X, Y, Z).   nrev$_{\mathbb{N}}$(X, Z),   app3/4
                  app$_{\mathbb{N}}$(Z, 1+E, Y).

2. In $\mathbb{N}$ we compute a model of all predicates. The model describes with a finite conjunction of linear equalities and inequalities the inter-argument relations *post* that hold for every solution. The actual computation is performed with CLP($\mathbb{Q}$), using a generic fixpoint calculator with standard widening detailed in Section 3. In our example the least model is found. In general, however, only a less precise model is determined. With the help of such a numeric model, for each recursive predicate p (the only source of potential non-termination), we compute a valid level mapping called μ_p, see Section 4. For instance, the intuitive meaning of $\mu_{\text{app}}^{\mathbb{N}}$ is: for any ground recursive clause defining *app*$_{\mathbb{N}}$, the first and the third argument decrease. Section 4 explains more precisely how the model in $\mathbb{N}$ is taken into account (roughly speaking, it helps for dealing with variables that are local to a clause and that reappear in recursive calls). As *app3*$_{\mathbb{N}}$ is not recursive, we set its level mapping to 0.

(least) models   level mappings

$$post_{\text{app}}^{\mathbb{N}}(x,y,z) \equiv x+y=z \qquad\qquad \mu_{\text{app}}^{\mathbb{N}}(x,y,z) \equiv min(x,z)$$

$$post_{\text{nrev}}^{\mathbb{N}}(x,y) \equiv x=y \qquad\qquad\quad \mu_{\text{nrev}}^{\mathbb{N}}(x,y) \equiv x$$

$$post_{\text{app3}}^{\mathbb{N}}(x,y,z,u) \equiv x+y+z=u \qquad \mu_{\text{app3}}^{\mathbb{N}}(x,y,z,u) \equiv 0$$

---

[2] cTI applies the term-size norm by default. All ISO-predefined predicates are pre-analyzed for this norm. But a similar analysis of any *pure* Prolog programs can be done using *any* linear norm, and remains correct. Note that the resulting boolean termination conditions should then be lifted to termination conditions with respect to the chosen linear norm.

3. $P^{\mathbb{N}}$ is mapped to $P^{\mathcal{B}}$, a program in CLP($\mathcal{B}$). Here 1 means that an argument is bounded wrt the considered norm, while 0 means that this information is unknown. Note that the obtained program no longer maintains the same termination property. Its sole purpose is to determine the actual dependencies of boundedness within the program. The simplified structure allows us to always compute the least model. For each predicate, its previously computed linear level mapping is represented by a single boolean term.

$app_{\mathcal{B}}(1, X, X).$
$app_{\mathcal{B}}(1 \wedge E \wedge X, Y, 1 \wedge E \wedge Z) \leftarrow$
$\qquad app_{\mathcal{B}}(X, Y, Z).$

$nrev_{\mathcal{B}}(1, 1).$
$nrev_{\mathcal{B}}(1 \wedge E \wedge X, Y) \leftarrow$
$\qquad nrev_{\mathcal{B}}(X, Z),$
$\qquad app_{\mathcal{B}}(Z, 1 \wedge E, Y).$

$app3_{\mathcal{B}}(X,Y,Z,U) \leftarrow$
$\qquad app_{\mathcal{B}}(X,Y,V),$
$\qquad app_{\mathcal{B}}(V,Z,U).$

least models $\qquad\qquad\qquad$ level mappings

$$post^{\mathcal{B}}_{app}(x,y,z) \quad \equiv (x \wedge y) \leftrightarrow z \qquad \mu^{\mathcal{B}}_{app}(x,y,z) \quad \equiv x \vee z$$
$$post^{\mathcal{B}}_{nrev}(x,y) \quad \equiv x \leftrightarrow y \qquad\qquad \mu^{\mathcal{B}}_{nrev}(x,y) \quad \equiv x$$
$$post^{\mathcal{B}}_{app3}(x,y,z,u) \equiv (x \wedge y \wedge z) \leftrightarrow u \qquad \mu^{\mathcal{B}}_{app3}(x,y,z,u) \equiv 1$$

4. Using the informations obtained in $P^{\mathcal{B}}$, boolean termination conditions are determined with the following boolean μ-calculus formulæ taking level mappings and boundedness propagation (at each program point) into account. The greatest fixpoint νT is determined with a μ-solver [12].

$$pre_{app} = \nu T.\lambda(x,y,z).$$
$$\begin{cases} \mu^{\mathcal{B}}_{app}(x,y,z) \\ \wedge \forall e,x',z'.[(x \leftrightarrow (1 \wedge e \wedge x')) \wedge (z \leftrightarrow (1 \wedge e \wedge z'))] \rightarrow T(x',y,z') \end{cases}$$

$$pre_{nrev} = \nu T.\lambda(x,y).$$
$$\begin{cases} \mu^{\mathcal{B}}_{nrev}(x,y) \\ \wedge \forall e,x',z.[(x \leftrightarrow (1 \wedge e \wedge x'))] \rightarrow T(x',z) \\ \wedge \forall e,x',z.[(x \leftrightarrow (1 \wedge e \wedge x')) \wedge post^{\mathcal{B}}_{nrev}(x',z)] \rightarrow pre_{app}(z, 1 \wedge e, y) \end{cases}$$

$$pre_{app3} = \nu T.\lambda(x,y,z,u).$$
$$\begin{cases} \mu^{\mathcal{B}}_{app3}(x,y,z,u) \\ \wedge \forall v.1 \rightarrow pre_{app}(x,y,v) \\ \wedge \forall v.post^{\mathcal{B}}_{app}(x,y,v) \rightarrow pre_{app}(v,z,u) \end{cases}$$

Let us try to intuitively explain such a boolean μ-calculus formula. First, we want at least one level mapping to be bounded. Second, if there is a call to a clause and if its first (from left to right) i body atoms succeed, then, after including their success, the call to the $i + 1$-th body atom must terminate. Third, we are interested in the largest solution. Solving the equations of our example gives:

$$pre_{app}(x,y,z) \quad \equiv x \vee z$$
$$pre_{nrev}(x,y) \quad \equiv x$$
$$pre_{app3}(x,y,z,u) \equiv (x \wedge y) \vee (x \wedge u)$$

5. These boolean termination conditions lift to termination conditions (see Definition 1) with the following interpretation, where the c's are CLP($\mathcal{H}$) constraints:

- any goal $\leftarrow c$, app(X,Y,Z) left-terminates if X or Z are ground in c.
- any goal $\leftarrow c$, nrev(X,Y) left-terminates if X is ground in c.
- any goal $\leftarrow c$, app3(X,Y,Z,U) left-terminates if either X and Y are ground in c or X and U are ground in c.

The correctness of the analysis, first described in [33], is based on the following result (see [35] for details and proofs). Let $\bar{p}$ denote the equivalence class of p with respect to mutual recursion seen as an equality relation, $\tilde{x}$ denote a tuple of distinct variables, and $\forall F$ denote the universal closure of the formula F.

Theorem 1. *(Correctness)*

- *Let P be a logic program and Q a query. Let $P^{\mathbb{N}}$ and $Q^{\mathbb{N}}$ be their images by the term-size norm. If any left derivation of $P^{\mathbb{N}}$ and $Q^{\mathbb{N}}$ is finite, then any left derivation of P and Q is finite.*
- *We consider now left termination of $P^{\mathbb{N}}$ in CLP($\mathbb{N}$). Let Π_P be the set of predicate symbols defined in $P^{\mathbb{N}}$. Assume that:*
  - $\forall p \in \Pi_P$, $post_p^{\mathcal{B}}$ *has been computed (see point 3 above and Section 3);*
  - $\forall p \in \Pi_P$, $\mu_p^{\mathcal{B}}$ *is a boolean representation of some valid level mappings for p (see point 3 above and Section 4);*
  - *p is defined by m_p rules r_k $(1 \leq k \leq m_p)$:*
    $$p(\tilde{x}) \leftarrow c_{k,0}, p_{k,1}(\tilde{x}_{k,1}), c_{k,1}, \ldots, c_{k,n_k-1}, p_{k,n_k}(\tilde{x}_{k,n_k}), c_{k,n_k}$$
  - *for each $q \not\subseteq \bar{p}$ that appears in the rules defining $\bar{p}$, a termination condition pre_q has been computed.*

  If the set of boolean terms $\{pre_p\}_{p \in \bar{p}}$ verifies:

$$\forall p \in \bar{p} \begin{cases} \forall [pre_p(\tilde{x}) \to \mu_p^{\mathcal{B}}(\tilde{x})] \\ \forall k,j, 1 \leq k \leq m_p, 1 \leq j \leq n_k : \\ \quad \forall \{[pre_p(\tilde{x}) \wedge c_{k,0}^{\mathcal{B}} \wedge \bigwedge_{i=1}^{j-1}(post_{p_{k,i}}^{\mathcal{B}}(\tilde{x}_{k,i}) \wedge c_{k,i}^{\mathcal{B}})] \to pre_{p_{k,j}}(\tilde{x}_{k,j})\} \end{cases}$$

  then $\{pre_p\}_{p \in \bar{p}}$ is a boolean termination condition for $\bar{p}$.

We note that the boolean system defined in Theorem 1 can be used not only to *check* if a set of boolean terms is a set of boolean termination conditions but also to *infer* such set, with the help of a μ-calculus solver (see point 4 above). Finally, it remains to lift the computed boolean termination conditions to termination conditions (see point 5 above).

3   Fixpoint Computations

As motivated in Section 2, we have to compute some models of two versions of the initial program: $P^{\mathbb{N}}$, the CLP($\mathbb{N}$) version, and $P^{\mathcal{B}}$, the CLP($\mathcal{B}$) version. To this aim, we have developed an abstract immediate consequence operator U_P being similar to the well-known T_P. (An similar approach tailored to CLP($\mathbb{R}$) has been described in [23].) In this section we rely on numerous results in abstract interpretation [13, 16, 14, 15].

3.1 The Algorithm

The key of our abstract computation is the notion of *rational interpretation* for a predicate symbol p:

Definition 2. *Let P be a program with predicate symbol p. We call a rational interpretation of p an equivalence of the form: $p(\tilde{x}) \leftrightarrow c(\tilde{x})$ where $c(\tilde{x})$ is a (finite) constraint such that $vars(c(\tilde{x})) \subseteq \tilde{x}$. We extend this notion to P: a rational interpretation of P is a set I containing exactly one rational interpretation for each predicate symbol p of P.*

We denote by $\mathcal{I}$ the set of all rational interpretations. To compute a rational interpretation being a model of P we define below an operator U_P. We assume, without loss of generality for those computations, that the rules are of the form $p(\tilde{x}) \leftarrow c, p_1(\tilde{x_1}), \dots, p_n(\tilde{x_n})$ where c is the *only* constraint of the rule. Let $\bigvee$ be an associative-commutative operator which generalizes disjunction in the following sense: for any constraints $c_1(\tilde{x})$ and $c_2(\tilde{x})$, $\bigvee(c_1, c_2)$ is a constraint over $\tilde{x}$ such that $\forall[c_1 \vee c_2 \rightarrow \bigvee(c_1, c_2)]$.

Definition 3. *U_P is a function on $\mathcal{I}$ defined for any rational interpretation I of a program P by:*

$$U_P(I) = \{p(\tilde{x}) \leftrightarrow \bigvee\nolimits_{cl(p)} \left(\exists_{-\tilde{x}}(c \wedge \bigwedge\nolimits_{1 \leq i \leq n} c_i) \right) \mid$$
$$cl(p) = (p(\tilde{x}) \leftarrow c, p_1(\tilde{x_1}), \dots, p_n(\tilde{x_n})) \in P$$
$$\forall i \in [1, n]\ p_i(\tilde{x_i}) \leftrightarrow c_i \in I\}$$

We define the successive powers of U_P as usual. It turns out that U_P is monotone and continuous. Now let us establish a link between the meaning of a program P and the U_P operator. First, we give a ground semantics of a rational interpretation:

Definition 4. *Let I be a rational interpretation, we define the semantics of I by: $[I] = \{p(\tilde{d}) \mid p(\tilde{x}) \leftrightarrow c(\tilde{x}) \in I, \tilde{d} \in \tilde{D}_\chi, \models_\chi c(\tilde{d})\}$ where D_χ is the domain of computation.*

For any interpretation I, we have: $T_P([I]) \subseteq [U_P(I)]$. Now, as a fixpoint I of U_P verifies $T_P([I]) \subseteq [U_P(I)] = [I]$, we get: any fixpoint of U_P is a model of P.

For CLP($\mathcal{B}$), we set $\bigvee(c_1, c_2) = c_1 \vee c_2$. Hence we have $T_P([I]) = [U_P(I)]$ which justifies the use of U_P for computing the least boolean model ($= \mathrm{lfp}(U_P)$) of P. Figure 1 presents an algorithm for the U_P operator.

3.2 Widenings

For CLP($\mathbb{Q}$), we set $\bigvee(c_1, c_2) = convex{-}hull(c_1, c_2)$. Computing $\mathrm{lfp}(U_P)$ diverges in the general case. Therefore a *widening* operator (∇) [13] is required to enforce convergence at the expense of precision. cTI uses widening only for computations in CLP($\mathbb{Q}$) since the least boolean model is finitely reached. However, we coded a *generic* fixpoint calculator for both CLP($\mathbb{Q}$) and CLP($\mathcal{B}$) [9, 24, 34]. A simple widening can be found in [16]. We use an equivalent definition [39]:

---

function $U_P(I) : J$

Require: I, a rational interpretation of P

Ensure: $J = U_P(I)$, a rational interpretation of P

1:   $J \leftarrow \emptyset$
2:   **for all** clause $p(\tilde{x}) \leftarrow c, p_1(\tilde{x}_1), \ldots, p_n(\tilde{x}_n) \in P$ **do**
3:     **for** $i = 1$ **to** n **do**
4:       **let** $p_i(\tilde{x}_i) \leftrightarrow c_i \in I$
5:     **end for**
6:     **let** $p(\tilde{x}) \leftrightarrow c' \in J$
7:     $c \leftarrow \bigvee(c', \exists_{-\tilde{x}}(c \wedge c_1 \wedge \ldots \wedge c_n))$
8:     $J \leftarrow update(J, p(\tilde{x}) \leftrightarrow c))$
9:   **end for**
10: **return** J

Fig. 1. U_P, a T_P-Like Operator.

Definition 5. *Let S_1 and S_2 be two sets of linear inequalities defining two polyhedra in $\mathbb{Q}^n$. Then: $S_1 \triangledown S_2 = \{\beta \in S_1 \mid S_2 \Rightarrow \beta\}$*

Fig. 2 presents an algorithm for successive iterations of U_P until it reaches a fixpoint. In cTI's current implementation *prec* is set to 3 for CLP($\mathbb{Q}$).

It remains to be shown that $I_n = \texttt{ite\_U}_P(prec)$ is a model of P. First, note that, by induction on k, $I_k \subseteq I_{k+1}$. So we have in fact an equality when we reach line 11 for the last time: $I_n = I_{n-1}$. Then the last assignment for I_n is either line 7 if $n \leq prec$. In this case, we have $I_n = U_P(I_n)$ hence $T_P([I_n]) \subseteq [I_n]$. Or the last assignment for I_n is line 9: $I_n \leftarrow I_n \triangledown U_P(I_n) \supseteq U_P(I_n)$ by definition of any widening operator $\triangledown$. But we know that $T_P([I]) \subseteq [U_P(I)]$ for all I. Again, $T_P([I_n]) \subseteq [I_n]$.

3.3 Optimizations

Since the fixpoint computation engine is used twice, generic optimizations applicable to both have a substantial effect. The current optimization takes all unit clauses defining the predicate symbols of the analyzed scc into account in a single pass and then processes only the non-unit clauses of the scc. Table 1 compares the runtime of the non-optimized version of U_P and the optimized version. Note that we also replace the union operator $\bigvee$ of line 7 of the algorithm presented in Fig. 1 by a convex hull (in both versions for CLP($\mathbb{Q}$), opt and nopt), which can be easily coded via projection in CLP($\mathbb{Q}$) using a technique first described in [5], and later in [6].

4 Computing Level-Mappings

One key concept in many approaches for termination lies in the use of *level mappings*, *i.e.*, mappings from ground atoms to natural numbers. Moreover, we are

---

function ite_$U_P(prec) : I_n$

Require: *prec*, a non-negative integer
Ensure: I_n, a rational interpretation such that lfp(U_P) $\subseteq I_n$

```
 1: n ← 0
 2: I_n ← ∅
 3: repeat
 4:    I ← U_P(I_n)
 5:    n ← n + 1
 6:    if n ≤ prec then
 7:        I_n ← I
 8:    else
 9:        I_n ← I_{n-1} ∇ I
10:    end if
11: until I_n ⊆ I_{n-1}
12: return I_n ;
```

Fig. 2. An algorithm to finitely reach a super set of lfp(U_P).

interested here in *valid* level mappings, which decrease at each recursive call. cTI uses an improvement of an already known technique for their automatic generation. K. Sohn and A. Van Gelder described in 1991 [41] an algorithm (SVG) based on linear programming which ensures the existence of valid linear level mappings. This method, despite its power, does not seem to have attracted the attention of researchers interested in automating termination analysis. Hence, we recall it after some preliminaries. Then, the remaining subsections propose an extensions to SVG.

4.1 Preliminaries

We consider pure CLP($\mathbb{N}$) programs, with three predefined symbols for constraints: $=$, $\geq$, and $\leq$ and their standard meaning. Those programs are abstractions of (constraint) logic programs using (fixed or inferred) norms. We assume that clauses are written in flat form: $p_0(\tilde{x}_0) \leftarrow c_0, p_1(\tilde{x}_1), c_1, \ldots, c_{l-1}, p_l(\tilde{x}_l), c_l$, with $i \neq j \rightarrow \tilde{x}_i \cap \tilde{x}_j = \emptyset$ (where $\emptyset$ denotes the empty set). In this presentation we will only consider the case of directly recursive predicates. cTI itself is also able to treat the general case. We write p/n as a shorthand for *a predicate symbol p with arity(p) = n*. Note that we frequently switch to CLP($\mathbb{Q}^+$) as some computational problems in this structure are much cheaper (e.g. satisfiability). There is clearly a loss in the precision of the analysis: results are correct but not complete. From now on, we write CLP for CLP($\mathbb{N}$) or CLP($\mathbb{Q}^+$). Section 3 showed how we can compute a model M_P for a CLP program P, where each predicate $p(\tilde{x})$ is defined as a (finite) conjunction $c_p(\tilde{x})$ of CLP constraints. We use this model to simplify the program P.

Table 1. Impact of the Optimization on the Analysis Times.

times in [s]	$Post_N$			$Post_B$		
Programs	opt	nopt	gain	opt	nopt	gain
ANN	1.07	1.33	20%	0.46	0.65	29%
BID	0.17	0.27	37%	0.09	0.14	35%
BOYER	2.55	3.48	27%	0.25	0.48	48%
BROWSE	0.37	0.35	-5%	0.12	0.15	20%
CREDIT	0.12	0.19	37%	0.07	0.13	46%
MINISSAEXP	2.98	2.74	-9%	0.73	1.17	38%
PEEPHOLE	1.24	1.35	8%	0.47	0.63	25%
PLAN	0.13	0.20	35%	0.09	0.13	31%
QPLAN	1.52	1.88	19%	0.62	0.86	28%
RDTOK	1.22	0.70	-74%	0.26	0.29	10%
READ	1.05	1.26	17%	0.34	0.50	32%
WARPLAN	0.82	0.96	15%	0.27	0.37	27%
average			11%			31%
min.			-74%			10%
max.			37%			48%

Definition 6. *Let M_P be a model of the CLP program P. The definition of a predicate p is simplified with respect to M_P when, for the clauses defining p/n, we add to the right of each predicate $q(\tilde{x})$ (including p) its model $c_q(\tilde{x})$ relative to M_P. Moreover, those predicates $q/m \neq p/n$ which appear in the bodies are replaced by true (e.g. the dummy constraint $0 = 0$). Hence we end with a finite set of CLP clauses of the form: $p(\tilde{x}_0) \leftarrow c_0, p(\tilde{x}_1), c_1, \ldots, c_{l-1}, p(\tilde{x}_l), c_l$. The simplified program is denoted P_M^{simpl}.*

We are interested in the automatic discovery of valid linear level mappings in such a program. We therefore give definitions for the required notions.

Definition 7. *Let p/n be a recursive predicate symbol of a CLP program P. A linear level mapping μ for $p(x_1, \ldots, x_n)$ is a linear relation $\sum_{i=1}^{n} \mu_i x_i$, where the coefficients μ_i are non-negative integers.*

Such linear level mappings should satisfy a property ensuring their usefulness for left-termination:

Definition 8. *A linear level mapping μ for p is valid with respect to $P_{M_P}^{simpl}$ if for each recursive clause $p(\tilde{x}_0) \leftarrow c_0, p(\tilde{x}_1), c_1, \ldots, c_{l-1}, p(\tilde{x}_l), c_l$ defining p in P_M^{simpl}, for $k = 0$ to $l - 1$, we have $\bigwedge_{i=0}^{k} c_i \rightarrow \mu^T \tilde{x}_0 \geq 1 + \mu^T \tilde{x}_{k+1}$, where μ^T denotes the transpose of the vector μ.*

4.2   The Algorithm SVG

Let us first quickly review the algorithm of Sohn and Van Gelder. It aims at checking the existence of one valid linear level mapping. SVG starts with a pure

CLP program P and a constrained goal. A top-down boundedness analysis (see [33,34]) reveals the calling modes of each predicate. Arguments are detected as either bounded (denoted b) or unbounded (u). A CLP model M is computed and P is simplified to P_M^{simpl}. Then SVG examines each recursive procedure p/n in turn (the precise order does not matter). Let us symbolically define the level mapping for $p(x_1, \ldots, x_n)$ as $\mu^T \tilde{x} = \sum_{1 \leq i \leq n} \mu_i^{u \ or \ b} x_i$ where $\mu_i^u = 0$ if x_i is labelled as unbounded with respect to the calling mode of p/n and $\mu_i^b \geq 0$ if x_i is labelled as bounded. Each clause r_i is processed. For one such clause, say $p(\tilde{x}_0) \leftarrow c_0, p(\tilde{x}_1), c_1, \ldots, c_{l-1}, p(\tilde{x}_l), c_l$, l simplified rules (for $k = 0$ to $k = l - 1$) are constructed: $p(\tilde{x}_0) \leftarrow \left[\bigwedge_{0 \leq j \leq k} c_j \right] p(\tilde{x}_{k+1})$. One can assume that the constraint $C_{i,k} = \bigwedge_{0 \leq j < k} c_j$ is satisfiable, already projected onto $\tilde{x}_0 \cup \tilde{x}_{k+1}$, only contains inequalities of the form $\leq$, and implies $\tilde{x}_0 \geq 0$ and $\tilde{x}_{k+1} \geq 0$. Such a simplified rule gives rise to the following (pseudo-)linear programming problem

$$minimize \ \theta = \mu^T (\tilde{x}_0 - \tilde{x}_k) \ subject \ to \ C_{i,k} \tag{1}$$

A valid linear level mapping μ exists (at least for this recursive call of this clause) if $\theta^* \geq 1$ where θ^* denotes the minimum of the objective function. Unfortunately, because of the symbolic constants μ, (1) is *not* a linear programming problem. The *clever* idea of Sohn and Van Gelder is to consider its dual form:

$$maximize \ \eta = \tilde{y}\beta \ subject \ to \ \tilde{y} \geq 0 \wedge \tilde{y}A \geq (\mu, -\mu) \tag{2}$$

where β and A are automatically derived while switching to the dual form of (1). By duality theory (see [40] for instance), we have $\theta^* = \eta^*$. Now, the authors observe that μ appears linearly in the dual problem (it is not true for (1)) because no μ_i appears in A. Hence (2) can be rewritten, by adding $\eta \geq 1$ and $\tilde{\mu}^b \geq 0 \wedge \tilde{\mu}^u = 0$, as S_{ij}, a set of linear inequations. If the conjunction $S_p = \bigwedge_{i,j} S_{ij}$ for each recursive call and for each clause defining p/n is satisfiable, then there exists a valid linear level mapping for p/n.

4.3   An Extension of SVG

Instead of checking satisfiability of S_p, we can project it onto μ (we do not need the top-down boundeness analysis explained in subsection 4.2, all arguments are assumed bounded). Hence we get in one constraint *all* the valid linear level mappings. It remains to compute the maximal elements of $\Pi_\mu(S_p)$, given the partial order: $\mu^1 \succeq \mu^2$ if $\forall i \in [1, n]$ $\mu_i^1 \neq 0 \rightarrow \mu_i^2 \neq 0$.

Example 1. For app/3, let $\mu(x, y, z) = ax + by + cz$. We have $\Pi_\mu(S_p) = \{a + c \geq 1\}$. There are two maximal elements: $\mu^1(x, y, z) = x$ and $\mu^2(x, y, z) = z$.

In some sense, given a model for a program, this extension is complete in CLP($\mathbb{Q}^+$) (mainly because there are complete algorithms for linear programming and projection). But a more precise model can lead to more maximal elements. Hence the precision of the inferred CLP model is important. From an implementation point of view, this algorithm heavily relies on the costly projection operator. In our experience a good strategy is to project constraints as soon as possible.

5   Running cTI

5.1   Standard Programs from the Termination Literature in LP

Tables 2 and 3 presents timings and results of cTI using some standard LP termination benchmarks, where the following abbreviations mean:

- *program*: the name of the analyzed program. We add a star to some names to pin-point that we manually tune cTI, by selecting the list-size norm (instead of the term-size norm) with *prec* = 4 (instead of *prec* = 3) (see Section 3.2);
- *top-level predicate*: the predicate of interest;
- *Others: checked*: the class of queries checked by the analyzers of [19, 29, 43];
- *result*: the best result (y > n) among [19, 29, 43];
- *cTI: inferred*: the termination condition inferred by cTI (1 means that any call to the predicate terminates, 0 means that cTI can not find a terminating mode for that predicate);
- *cTI time*: the running time for cTI to infer termination conditions.

The Mergesort Mystery Reconsidered. For MERGESORT (and similarly for MERGE-SORT_AP), we encountered a well known problem that has been solved using additional program transformations in [30]. The actual problem is *split*/3 that splits a list (first argument) in two sublists (second and third argument) whose lengths are *almost* equal.

```
split([],[],[]).
split([E|X],[E|Y],Z) :- split(X,Z,Y).
```

Using the term-size norm, cTI obtains the following models depending on the precision of the numeric abstract interpreter However, these models are not strong enough for inferring termination. We note that the result obtained for *prec* = 3 is already the best interpretation possible with term-size. The fluctuation of the size of the list elements blurs any finer measuring. Evidently, there is no chance for improvement as long as we stay with the term-size norm and the (unmodified) original program.

$$prec \leq 2 : post^{\text{IN}}_{\text{split}}(x, y, z) \equiv true$$
$$prec \geq 3 : post^{\text{IN}}_{\text{split}}(x, y, z) \equiv x = y + z$$

However, by switching to the list-size norm defined below we obtain a sufficiently precise model for proving termination. Note that the missing information is the fact that the length of the two split lists differ at most by one. Therefore, both elements decrease if there are at least two elements in *x*.

$$\|t\|_{\text{list-size}} = \begin{cases} 1 + \|u\|_{\text{list-size}} & \text{if } t = [s|u] \\ t & \text{if } t \text{ is a variable} \\ 0 & \text{otherwise} \end{cases}$$

Table 2. Programs from [22, 2], cTI 0.40, Athlon 750 MHz, 256Mb, SICStus 3.8.4.

program	Others			cTI	
	top-level predicate	checked	result	inferred	time[s]
PERMUTE	permute(x,y)	x	yes	x	0.15
DUPLICATE	duplicate(x,y)	x	yes	$x \vee y$	0.05
SUM	sum(x,y,z)	$x \wedge y$	yes	$x \vee y \vee z$	0.18
MERGE	merge(x,y,z)	$x \wedge y$	yes	$(x \wedge y) \vee z$	0.26
DIS-CON	dis(x)	x	yes	x	0.24
REVERSE	reverse(x,y,z)	$x \wedge z$	yes	x	0.08
APPEND	append(x,y,z)	$x \wedge y$	yes	$x \vee z$	0.09
LIST	list(x)	x	yes	x	0.01
FOLD	fold(x,y,z)	$x \wedge y$	yes	y	0.10
LTE	goal	1	yes	1	0.13
MAP	map(x,y)	x	yes	$x \vee y$	0.09
MEMBER	member(x,y)	y	yes	y	0.03
MERGESORT	mergesort(x,y)	x	no	0	0.43
MERGESORT*	mergesort(x,y)	x	no	x	0.57
MERGESORT_AP	mergesort_ap(x,y,z)	x	yes	z	0.79
MERGESORT_AP*	mergesort_ap(x,y,z)	x	yes	$x \vee z$	0.92
NAIVE_REV	naive_rev(x,y)	x	yes	x	0.12
ORDERED	ordered(x)	x	yes	x	0.04
OVERLAP	overlap(x,y)	$x \wedge y$	yes	$x \wedge y$	0.05
PERMUTATION	permutation(x,y)	x	yes	x	0.15
QUICKSORT	quicksort(x,y)	x	yes	x	0.39
SELECT	select(x,y,z)	y	yes	$y \vee z$	0.08
SUBSET	subset(x,y)	$x \wedge y$	yes	$x \wedge y$	0.09
SUBSET	subset(x,y)	y	no	$x \wedge y$	0.09
SUM	sum(x,y,z)	z	yes	$y \vee z$	0.12

$$prec \leq 2 : post_{\text{split}}^{\text{IN}}(x, y, z) \equiv true$$

$$prec = 3 : post_{\text{split}}^{\text{IN}}(x, y, z) \equiv x = y + z$$

$$prec \geq 4 : post_{\text{split}}^{\text{IN}}(x, y, z) \equiv x = y + z \wedge 0 \leq y - z \leq 1$$

5.2 Middle-Sized Programs

Table 5 presents timings of cTI using some standard benchmarks[3] from the LP program analysis community. We have chosen twelve middle-sized well-known logic programs. Almost all the programs are taken from [8] except CREDIT, PLAN and MINISSAEXP. Table 4 describes them, where the following abbreviations mean:

---

[3] collected by Naomi Lindenstrauss, www.cs.huji.ac.il/~naomil and also available at www.complang.tuwien.ac.at/cti/bench.

Table 3. Plümer's Programs [37], cTI 0.40, Athlon 750 MHz, 256Mb, SICStus 3.8.4.

	Plümer			cTI	
program	top-level predicate	checked	result	inferred	time[s]
PL1.1	append(x,y,z)	$x \wedge y$	yes	$x \vee z$	0.08
PL1.1	append(x,y,z)	z	yes	$x \vee z$	0.08
PL1.2	perm(x,y)	x	yes	x	0.16
PL2.3.1	p(x,y)	x	no	0	0.01
PL3.5.6	p(x)	1	no	x	0.05
PL3.5.6A	p(x)	1	yes	x	0.06
PL4.0.1	append3(x,y,z,v)	$x \wedge y \wedge z$	yes	$x \wedge y \vee x \wedge v$	0.10
PL4.4.3	merge(x,y,z)	$x \wedge y$	yes	$x \wedge y \vee z$	0.26
PL4.4.6A	perm(x,y)	x	yes	x	0.12
PL4.5.2	s(x,y)	x	no	0	0.17
PL4.5.3A	p(x)	x	no	0	0.01
PL6.1.1	qsort(x,y)	x	yes	x	0.39
PL7.2.9	mult(x,y,z)	$x \wedge y$	yes	$x \wedge y$	0.21
PL7.6.2A	reach(x,y,z)	$x \wedge y \wedge z$	no	0	0.14
PL7.6.2B	reach(x,y,z,t)	$x \wedge y \wedge z \wedge t$	no	0	0.22
PL7.6.2C	reach(x,y,z,t)	$x \wedge y \wedge z \wedge t$	yes	$z \wedge t$	0.29
PL8.2.1	mergesort(x,y)	x	no	0	0.43
PL8.2.1*	mergesort(x,y)	x	no	x	0.58
PL8.2.1A	mergesort(x,y)	x	yes	x	0.47
MERGESORT_T	mergesort(x,y)	x	yes	x	0.94
PL8.3.1	minsort(x,y)	x	no	$x \wedge y$	0.26
PL8.3.1A	minsort(x,y)	x	yes	x	0.24
PL8.4.1	even(x)	x	yes	x	0.13
PL8.4.2	e(x,y)	x	yes	x	0.52

- *lines* is the number of lines of the Prolog program in pure form (e.g. no disjunction), with one predicate symbol per line and no blank line;
- *facts* and *rules* denote, respectively, the numbers of facts (unit clauses) and rules (non-unit clauses) in the program;
- *sccs* gives the number of strongly connected components (sccs, *i.e.* cycles of mutually recursive predicate symbols) in the call graph;
- *length* denotes the number of predicate symbols in the longest cycle in the call graph;
- *vars* denotes the sum of the arities of the predicate symbols of the longest cycle in the call graph.

The first five columns of Table 5 indicate the time for computing:

- a model $Post_{\mathbb{N}}$ (section 3);
- the constraint defining the level mapping μ (section 4);
- the concrete level mapping;
- the least model $Post_B$;
- the boolean termination conditions.

Table 4. Informations about Analyzed Programs.

Program	lines	facts	rules	sccs	length	vars
ANN	571	101	99	44	2	7
BID	108	24	26	20	1	4
BOYER	275	63	78	25	2	5
BROWSE	107	4	29	15	1	6
CREDIT	108	33	24	24	1	4
MINISSAEXP	870	42	237	101	5	17
PEEPHOLE	322	72	80	11	2	5
PLAN	64	12	17	16	1	4
QPLAN	403	63	87	38	3	11
RDTOK	285	7	57	12	4	12
READ	299	15	75	17	7	33
WARPLAN	304	43	68	33	3	14

The timings are minimum execution times over ten iterations. Next we give:

- the total runtime (including all syntactic transformations);
- the speed of the analysis (the average number of analyzed lines of code in one second);
- the quality of the analysis, computed as the ratio of the number of relations which have a non-empty termination condition over the total number of relations.

Let us comment on the results of Table 5.

The speed of the analysis is surprisingly slower for PEEPHOLE than for the other programs. A more careful look on its code shows that its call graph contains 5 cycles of length 2, which slow down the computation of the constraints defining the level mapping.

We note that cTI was able to prove that BID, CREDIT, and PLAN are *left-terminating* (see [3], every ground atom left-terminates). For any such program P, T_P has only one fixpoint ([3], Theorem 8.13), which helps proving partial correctness. Moreover, the ground semantics of such a program is decidable (Prolog is the decision procedure!), which helps testing and validating the program.

On the other hand, when the quality of the analysis is less than 100%, it means that there exists at least one scc where the inferred termination condition is 0. Such sccs are clearly identified, which may help the programmer. Here are some reasons why cTI may fail: potential non-termination, unknown predicate in the code (assumed to be non-terminating by cTI), poor numeric model, non-existence of a linear level mapping for a predicate, inadequate norm, etc. Also, the analysis of the sccs which depend on a failed one is likely to fail.

Table 5. Middle-Sized Programs, cTI 0.40, Athlon 750 MHz, 256Mb, SICStus 3.8.4.

times in [s] program	$Post_N$	C_μ	μ	$Post_B$	TC	total time	lines/sec	quality %
ANN	1.07	2.62	0.17	0.46	0.13	5.01	114	48
BID	0.17	0.33	0.03	0.09	0.04	0.79	136	100
BOYER	2.55	0.36	0.03	0.25	0.05	3.53	78	85
BROWSE	0.37	1.01	0.08	0.12	0.03	1.81	59	60
CREDIT	0.12	0.18	0.04	0.07	0.03	0.61	177	100
MINISSAEXP	3.51	6.02	0.73	1.10	0.35	12.33	70	68
PEEPHOLE	1.24	9.78	0.14	0.47	0.12	12.08	27	93
PLAN	0.13	0.32	0.03	0.09	0.03	0.71	90	100
QPLAN	1.52	4.32	0.23	0.62	0.16	7.3	55	68
RDTOK	1.22	0.95	0.07	0.26	0.05	2.92	98	44
READ	1.05	5.25	0.03	0.34	0.16	6.87	44	52
WARPLAN	0.82	1.67	0.03	0.27	0.03	3.18	96	36
mean	23%	54%	2%	7%	2%	100%	87	71%

6   Conclusion

We have presented the main algorithms of cTI, our bottom-up left-termination inference tool for logic programs and given some running times for standard LP termination programs and middle-sized logic programs. The analysis requires three fixpoint computations and the inference of well-founded orders. We have described some optimizations and measured their impacts.

We have compared the quality of the results obtained by cTI with three other top-down termination checkers (we point out that the system Ciao-Prolog [7] adopts another approach for termination, based on complexity analysis [17]). Our termination inference tool is able in all the examples[4] presented above to infer as least as large a class of terminating queries (although we manually tuned cTI three times). On the other hand, the running times of cTI are also larger, but termination inference is a much more general problem than termination checking. In the worst case, an exponential number of termination checks are needed to simulate termination inference.

Right now, cTI cannot directly infer termination for some programs, e.g. CHAT, as suggested by P. Tarau. A more detailed look to this program written by F.C.N. Pereira and D.H.D. Warren shows that it contains one scc of 30 mutually recursive predicate symbols with 8 arguments per predicate symbol on the average. We cannot compute a numeric model for CHAT using the constraint solver CLP($\mathbb{Q}$) of SICStus Prolog in reasonable time. So we add for each computation which may be too costly (see also [10]) a timeout and if necessary we are able to return a value which does not destroy the correctness of the analysis (this is another widening!). The point is that the theoretical framework [35] only

---

[4] TermiLog is sometimes able to prove termination whereas cTI is not, and *vice versa*.

requires to have a CLP(ℕ) model and an upper approximation of the CLP($\mathcal{B}$) least model. The drawback of this approach is that, in such a case, the quality of the inference is deteriorated. As a side effect, *the running time of cTI is now linear with respect to the number of sccs in the call graph*. We point out that CHAT is one of the very few examples we know which requires such a mechanism (F. Henderson notified us of a similar scc in the code of the Mercury compiler [42]). Finally, Table 5 points out that most ($> 75\%$) of the analysis time lies in numeric computations. As a last resort we might consider to use specialized C libraries for polyhedra manipulations and a simplex solver optimized to projection.

We are also developing another line of research where we try to prove the *optimality* of the termination conditions computed by cTI. Instead of looking for general classes of logic programs for which the analysis is complete, we try, for each particular (pure) logic program, to prove that the termination condition derived by cTI is as general as it can be (with respect to the language describing the termination conditions and independently from the analysis). We have already implemented a prototype of the analyzer (called nTI for *non-Termination Inference*, available at the same URL than cTI) and its formalization is in progress.

Acknowledgements: We thank the readers of this paper for their useful comments.

References

1. K. R. Apt and D. Pedreschi. Reasoning about termination of pure Prolog programs. *Information and computation*, 1(106):109–157, 1993.
2. K. R. Apt and D. Pedreschi. Modular termination proofs for logic and pure Prolog programs. In G. Levi, editor, *Advances in Logic Programming Theory*, pages 183–229. Oxford University Press, 1994.
3. K.R. Apt. *From Logic Programming to Prolog*. Prentice Hall, 1997.
4. K.R. Apt and D. Pedreschi. Studies in pure Prolog: Termination. In J.W. LLOYD, editor, *Proc. of the Symp. in Computational Logic*, pages 150–176. Springer, 1990.
5. B. De Backer and H. Beringer. A clp language handling disjunctions of linear constraints. In *Proc. of ICLP'93*, pages 550–563. MIT Press, 1993.
6. F. Benoy and A. King. Inferring argument size relationships with CLP(R). In J. P. Gallagher, editor, *Logic Program Synthesis and Transformation*, volume 1207 of *LNCS*. Springer-Verlag, 1997.
7. F. Bueno, D. Cabeza, M. Carro, M. Hermenegildo, P. López-Garcia, and G. Puebla. The Ciao Prolog System. Reference Manual. The Ciao System Documentation Series–TR CLIP3/97.1, School of Computer Science, Technical University of Madrid (UPM), August 1997. System and on-line version of the manual available at http://clip.dia.fi.upm.es/Software/Ciao/.
8. F. Bueno, M. Garcia de la Banda, and M. Hermenegildo. Effectiveness of global analysis in strict independence-based automatic program parallelization. In *Proc. of the 1994 Intl. Symp. on Logic Programming*, pages 320–336. MIT Press, 1994.
9. M. Carlsson. Boolean constraints in SICStus Prolog. Technical Report T91:09, Swedish Institute of Computer Science, 1994.
10. M. Codish. Worst-case groundness analysis using positive boolean functions. *Journal of Logic Programming*, 41(1):125–128, 1999.

11. M. Codish and C. Taboch. A semantics basis for termination analysis of logic programs. *Journal of Logic Programming*, 41(1):103–123, 1999.

12. S. Colin, F. Mesnard, and A. Rauzy. Constraint logic programming and mu-calculus. *ERCIM/COMPULOG Workshop on Constraints*, 1997.

13. P. Cousot and R. Cousot. Abstract interpretation: a unifed lattice model for static analysis of programs by construction or approximation of fixpoints. In *Proc. of the 4th Symp. on Principles of Programming Languages*, pages 238–252. ACM, 1977.

14. P. Cousot and R. Cousot. Abstract interpretation and application to logic programs. *Journal of Logic Programming*, 13(2,3):103–179, 1992.

15. P. Cousot and R. Cousot. Comparing the Galois connection and widening/narrowing approaches to abstract interpretation. In *Proc. of PLILP'92*, volume 631 of *LNCS*. Springer-Verlag, 1992.

16. P. Cousot and N. Halbwachs. Automatic discovery of linear restraints among variables of a program. In *Proc. of the 5th Symp. on Principles of Programming Languages*, pages 84–96. ACM, 1978.

17. S. K. Debray, P. Lopez-Garcia, M. Hermenegildo, and N.-W. Lin. Estimating the computational cost of logic programs. In B. Le Charlier, editor, *LNCS*, volume 864, pages 255–265. Springer-Verlag, 1994. Proc. of SAS'94.

18. S. Decorte. *Enhancing the power of termination analysis of logic programs through types and constraints*. PhD thesis, Katholieke Universiteit Leuven, 1997.

19. S. Decorte, D. De Schreye, and H. Vandecasteele. Constraint-based termination analysis of logic programs. *ACM Transactions on Programming Languages and Systems*, 21(6):1136–1195, 1999.

20. P. Deransart, A. Ed-Dbali, and L. Cervoni. *Prolog: The standard, reference manuel*. Springer-Verlag, 1996.

21. P. Deransart, G. Ferrand, and M. Téguia. NSTO programs (not subject to occur-check). *Proc. of the Int. Logic Programming Symp.*, pages 533–547, 1991.

22. D. DeSchreye and S. Decorte. Termination of logic programs : the never-ending story. *Journal of Logic Programming*, 19-20:199–260, 1994.

23. M. Handjieva. Stan: a static analyzer for CLP(R) based on abstract interpretation. In R. Cousot and D. Schmidt, editors, *Proc. of SAS'96*, volume 1145 of *LNCS*. Springer-Verlag, 1996.

24. C. Holzbaur. OFAI clp(q,r) manual, edition 1.3.3. Technical Report TR-95-09, Austrian Research Institute, 1995.

25. J. Jaffar and J-L. Lassez. Constraint logic programming. In *Proc. of the 14th Symp. on Principles of Programming Languages*, pages 111–119. ACM, 1987.

26. J. Jaffar and M. J. Maher. Constraint logic programming: a survey. *Journal of Logic Programming*, 19:503–581, 1994.

27. K.-K. Lau, M. Ornaghi, A. Pettorossi, and M. Proietti. Correctness of logic program transformation based on existential termination. In J. W. Lloyd, editor, *Proc. of the 1995 Intl. Logic Programming Symp*, pages 480–494. MIT Press, 1995.

28. G. Levi and F. Scozzari. Contributions to a theory of existential termination for definite logic programs. In M. Alpuente and M. I. Sessa, editors, *Proc. of the GULP-PRODE'95 Joint Conf. on Declarative Programming*, pages 631–641, 1995.

29. N. Lindenstrauss and Y. Sagiv. Automatic termination analysis of logic programs. In L. Naish, editor, *Proc. of the 14th Intl. Conf. on Logic Programming*, pages 63–77. MIT Press, 1997.

30. N. Lindenstrauss, Y. Sagiv, and A. Serebrenik. Unfolding the mystery of mergesort. In N. Fuchs, editor, *Proc. of LOPSTR'97*, volume 1463 of *LNCS*. Springer-Verlag, 1998.

31. J. W. Lloyd. *Foundations of Logic Programming*. Springer-Verlag, 1987.
32. M. Marchiori. Proving existential termination of normal logic programs. In *Proc. of AMAST*, volume 1101 of *LNCS*, pages 375–390, 1996.
33. F. Mesnard. Inferring left-terminating classes of queries for constraint logic programs by means of approximations. In M. J. Maher, editor, *Proc. of the 1996 Joint Intl. Conf. and Symp. on Logic Programming*, pages 7–21. MIT Press, 1996.
34. F. Mesnard. Entailment and projection for CLP($\mathcal{B}$) and CLP($\mathbb{Q}$) in SICStus Prolog. *1st Intl. Workshop on Constraint Reasoning for Constraint Programming*, 1997.
35. F. Mesnard and S. Ruggieri. On proving left termination of constraint logic programs. Technical report, Université de La Réunion, 2001. Submitted for publication.
36. U. Neumerkel. GUPU: A Prolog course environment and its programming methodology. In M. Maher, editor, *Proc. of JICSLP'96*, page 549. MIT Press, 1996. http://www.complang.tuwien.ac.at/ulrich/gupu/.
37. L. Plümer. Termination proofs for logic programs. *LNAI*, 446, 1990.
38. S. Ruggieri. *Verification and Validation of Logic Programs*. PhD thesis, Università di Pisa, 1999.
39. H. Sağlam. *A Toolkit for Static Analysis of Constraint Logic Programs*. PhD thesis, University of Bristol, 1997.
40. A. Schrijver. *Theory of linear and integer programming*. Wiley, 1986.
41. K. Sohn and A. Van Gelder. Termination detection in logic programs using argument sizes. In *Proc. of the 1991 Intl. Symp. on Principles of Database Systems*, pages 216–226. ACM, 1991.
42. Z. Somogyi, F. Henderson, and T. Conway. The execution algorithm of Mercury, an efficient purely declarative Logic Programming language. *The Journal of Logic Programming*, 29(1–3):17–64, 1996.
43. C. Speirs, Z. Somogyi, and H. Søndergaard. Termination analysis for Mercury. In P. van Hentenrick, editor, *Proc. of the 1997 Intl. Symp. on Static Analysis*, volume 1302 of *LNCS*. Springer-Verlag, 1997.
44. J. D. Ullman and A. Van Gelder. Efficient tests for top-down termination of logical rules. *Communications of the ACM*, pages 345–373, 1988.
45. T. Vasak and J. Potter. Characterization of terminating logic programs. In *Proc. of the 1986 Intl. Symp. on Logic Programming*, pages 140–147. IEEE, 1986.
46. K. Verschaetse. *Static termination analysis for definite Horn clause programs*. PhD thesis, Dept. Computer Science, K.U. Leuven, 1992.

An Abstract Analysis of the Probabilistic Termination of Programs

David Monniaux

LIENS, 45 rue d'Ulm
75230 Paris cedex 5, France
http://www.di.ens.fr/~monniaux

Abstract. It is often useful to introduce probabilistic behavior in programs, either because of the use of internal random generators (probabilistic algorithms), either because of some external devices (networks, physical sensors) with known statistics of behavior. Previous works on probabilistic abstract interpretation have addressed safety properties, but somehow neglected probabilistic termination. In this paper, we propose a method to automatically prove the probabilistic termination of programs using exponential bounds on the tail of the distribution. We apply this method to an example and give some directions as to how to implement it. We also show that this method can also be applied to make unsound statistical methods on average running times sound.

1 Introduction

In this paper, we propose an analysis scheme for probabilistic programs, with the goal of proving probabilistic termination and other probabilistic properties.

1.1 Goals

It is in general difficult to automatically prove liveness properties of programs; nevertheless, the availability of probabilistic informations makes that task easier. In this paper, we shall address the cases of termination where the probability of taking a loop k times decreases at least exponentially with k. Such cases happen, for instance, in waiting loops on hardware peripherals where the probability that the busy peripheral will become ready over a period of time is a constant. However, we address cases where the constant in the exponential is unknown. Our analysis tries to derive automatically suitable constants for the exponential bound.

An obvious application of this analysis is to prove that the probability of non-termination is zero. Other applications include improvements on statistical methods to derive average execution times.

Our analysis is explained on block-structured programs. A reason for this is that the control-flow structure of a block-structured program is generally apparent from its syntactic structure, whereas converting the program to a probabilistic transition system would hide that structure. It is nevertheless possible to

P. Cousot (Ed.): SAS 2001, LNCS 2126, pp. 111–126, 2001.

apply the method to a probabilistic transition system, considering it as a single while loop, although the results may not be very satisfactory.

As usual with abstract interpretation, our analysis is sound, that is, any result it gives is proven to be correct (provided that the implementation of the analysis is correct, of course). On the other hand, because of the essential undecidability of non-trivial program properties, our analyzer is forced to give non-optimal results. Careful experimentation and heuristics may then improve the analysis.

1.2 Related Works

Several analyses have been proposed to prove the termination of non-probabilistic programs. Generally speaking, proving the termination of a program is done by showing that some value taken in a well-founded ordered set decreases strictly as the program proceeds [7]. The problem is to detect the appropriate value and the appropriate order. We follow this general principle by showing that the probability that the loop count or execution time reaches k is bounded by a strictly decreasing function of k whose limit is 0; the choice of an exponential is natural since the distribution we wish to approximate is exactly exponential in some simple cases (where the control graph of the program is a Markov chain, as in §6.1).

We use the framework of abstract interpretation of probabilistic programs defined in our earlier work [8]. However, that work did not address the problem of probabilistic termination except perhaps in its most trivial cases (where there exists a constant number of iterations after which the program always terminate, regardless of the inputs). Here, we address a specific case (loops whose iteration count or total execution time follow a distribution bounded from above by a decreasing exponential) that was not addressed by our previous methods, yet is of common practical interest. Nevertheless, the analysis described in this paper can be "mixed" with the analysis described in [8]; both are likely to be implemented in the same system.

1.3 Overview of the Paper

In section 2, we explain the probabilistic concrete semantics that we analyze. In section 3, we explain how to apply abstract interpretation to such a semantics. In section 4, we give a first abstract domain able to express properties such as the exponential decrease of the tail of the distribution of an integer variable. In section 5, we explain how to build a more complex, but much more precise domain using elements of the former domain as building blocks. In section 6, we show on a simple example what kind of results the analysis achieves, and we explain how such an analysis can improve the mathematical soundness of experimental average time estimations.

2   Concrete Semantics

We take the same concrete semantics as in earlier papers [5, 6, 8]. For the sake of clarity and self-containedness, we shall summarize them here.

We shall express probabilities using *measures* [11, §1.18]. We shall begin by a few classical mathematical definitions.

2.1   Measures

The basic objects we shall operate on are measures.

- $\mathcal{P}(X)$ is the power-set of X.
- A *σ-algebra* is a subset of $\mathcal{P}(X)$ that contains $\emptyset$ and is stable by countable union and complementation (and thus contains X and is stable by countable intersection).
- A set X with a σ-algebra σ_X defined on it is called a *measurable space* and the elements of the σ-algebra are the *measurable subsets*. We shall often mention measurable spaces by their name, omitting the σ-algebra, if no confusion is possible.
- If X and Y are measurable spaces, $f : X \to Y$ is a *measurable function* if for all W measurable in Y, $f^{-1}(W)$ is measurable in X.
- A *positive measure* is a function μ defined on a σ-algebra σ_X whose range is in $[0, \infty]$ and which is countably additive. μ is countably additive if, taking $(A_n)_{n \in \mathbb{N}}$ a disjoint collection of elements of σ_X, then $\mu(\cup_{n=0}^{\infty} A_n) = \sum_{n=0}^{\infty} \mu(A_n)$. To avoid trivialities, we assume $\mu(A) < \infty$ for at least one A. The *total weight* of a measure μ is $\mu(X)$. μ is said to be *concentrated* on $A \subseteq X$ if for all B, $\mu(B) = \mu(B \cap A)$. We shall note $\mathcal{M}_+(X)$ the positive measures on X.
- A *probability measure* is a positive measure of total weight 1. A *σ-finite* measure is a measure μ so that there exists a countable partition $X = \sqcup_{k=1}^{\infty} X_k$ so that $\mu(X_k) < \infty$ for all k. This is a technical condition that will be met every time in our cases.
- Given two σ-finite measures measures μ and μ' on X and X' respectively, we note $\mu \otimes \mu'$ the product measure [11, definition 7.7], defined on the product σ-algebra $\sigma_X \times \sigma_{X'}$. The characterizing property of this product measure is that $\mu \otimes \mu'(A \times A') = \mu(A).\mu'(A')$ for all measurable sets A and A'.

Our semantics shall be expressed as continuous linear operators between measure spaces.

2.2   Semantics of Arithmetic Operators

Let us consider an elementary program statement c so that $[\![c]\!] : X \to Y$, X and Y being measurable spaces. We shall also suppose that $[\![c]\!]$ is measurable, which is a purely technical requirement.

To $[\![c]\!]$ we associate the following linear operator $[\![c]\!]_p$:

$$[\![c]\!]_p : \left| \begin{array}{l} \mathcal{M}_+(X) \to \mathcal{M}_+(Y) \\ \mu \quad\quad \mapsto \lambda W.\mu([\![c]\!]^{-1}(W)) \end{array} \right. .$$

2.3   Random Inputs or Generators

An obvious interest of probabilistic semantics is to give an accurate semantics to assignment such as x:=random();, where random() is a function that, each time it is invoked, returns a real value uniformly distributed between 0 and 1, independently of previous calls.[1] We therefore have to give a semantics to constructs such as x:=random();, where random returns a value in a measured space R whose probability is given by the measure μ_R and is independent of all other calls and previous states.

We decompose this operation into two steps:

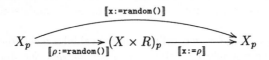

The second step is a simple assignment operator, addressed by the generic semantics for arithmetic operators. The first step is a product of measures:

$$[\![\rho\text{:=random()}]\!] : \left| \begin{array}{l} X_p \to (X \times R)_p \\ \mu \mapsto \mu \otimes \mu_R \end{array} \right. . \tag{1}$$

In the rest of the paper, when dealing with random generators, we shall focus on this product operation.

2.4   Tests and Loops

We restrict ourselves to test and loop conditions b so that $[\![b]\!]$ is measurable. $[\![b]\!]$ is the set of environments matched by condition b. It is obtained inductively from the set of environment matched by the atomic tests (e.g. comparisons):

- $[\![b_1 \text{ or } b_2]\!] = [\![b_1]\!] \cup [\![b_2]\!]$
- $[\![b_1 \text{ and } b_2]\!] = [\![b_1]\!] \cap [\![b_2]\!]$
- $[\![\text{not } b]\!] = [\![b]\!]^C$

The semantics of tests is:

$$[\![\text{if } c \text{ then } e_1 \text{ else } e_2]\!]_p(\mu) = [\![e_1]\!]_p \circ \phi_{[\![c]\!]}(\mu) + [\![e_2]\!]_p \circ \phi_{[\![c]\!]^C}(\mu) \tag{2}$$

---

[1] Of course, functions such as the POSIX C function drand48() would not fulfill such requirements, since they are pseudo-random generators whose output depends on an internal state that changes each time the function is invoked, thus the probability laws of successive invocations are not independent. However, ideal random generators are quite an accurate approximation for most analyses.

where $\phi_W(\mu) = \lambda X.\mu(X \cap W)$. The semantics for the while loop is:

$$[\![\text{while } c \text{ do } e]\!]_p(\mu) = \sum_{n=0}^{\infty} \phi_{[\![c]\!]^C} \circ ([\![e]\!]_p \circ \phi_{[\![c]\!]})^n(\mu)$$

$$= \phi_{[\![c]\!]^C} \left(\sum_{n=0}^{\infty} ([\![e]\!]_p \circ \phi_{[\![c]\!]})^n(\mu) \right)$$

$$= \phi_{[\![c]\!]^C} \left(\lim_{n \to \infty} (\lambda \mu'.\mu + [\![e]\!]_p \circ \phi_{[\![c]\!]}(\mu'))^n(\lambda X.0) \right) \quad (3)$$

Limits and infinite sums are taken according to the set-wise topology [3, §III.10]. We refer the reader to the extended version of [8] for the technical explanations on continuity and convergence.

3 Abstract Semantics

We first give the vocabulary and notations we use for abstractions in general (the reader is invited to consult [2] for further details). We then explain the particular treatment of probabilistic semantics.

3.1 Summary of Abstraction

Let us consider a preordered set $X^\sharp$ and a monotone function $\gamma_X : X^\sharp \to \mathcal{P}(X)$. $x^\sharp \in X^\sharp$ is said to be an *abstraction* of $x^b \subset X$ if $x^b \subseteq \gamma_X(x^\sharp)$. γ_X is called the *concretization function*. The triple $\langle \mathcal{P}(X), X^\sharp, \gamma_X \rangle$ is called an *abstraction*. $\mathcal{P}(X)$ is the *concrete domain* and $X^\sharp$ the *abstract domain*. Such definitions can be extended to any preordered set X^b besides $\mathcal{P}(X)$.

Let us now consider two abstractions $\langle \mathcal{P}(X), X^\sharp, \gamma_X \rangle$ and $\langle \mathcal{P}(Y), Y^\sharp, \gamma_Y \rangle$ and a function $f : X \to Y$. $f^\sharp$ is said to be *an abstraction of f* if

$$\forall x^\sharp \in X^\sharp \; \forall x \in X \; x \in \gamma_X(x^\sharp) \Rightarrow f(x) \in \gamma_Y(f^\sharp(x^\sharp)) \quad (4)$$

More generally, if $\langle X^b, X^\sharp, \gamma_X \rangle$ and $\langle Y^b, Y^\sharp, \gamma_Y \rangle$ are abstractions and $f^b : X^b \to Y^b$ is a monotone function, then $f^\sharp$ is said to be *an abstraction of f^b* if

$$\forall x^b \in X^b \; \forall x^\sharp \in X^\sharp \; x^b \sqsubseteq \gamma_X(x^\sharp) \Rightarrow f^b(x^b) \sqsubseteq \gamma_X(f^\sharp(x^\sharp)) \quad (5)$$

Algorithmically, elements in $X^\sharp$ will have a machine representation. To any program construct c we shall attach an effectively computable function $[\![c]\!]^\sharp$ so that $[\![c]\!]^\sharp$ is an abstraction of $[\![c]\!]$. Given a machine description of a superset of the inputs of the programs, the abstract version yields a superset of the outputs of the program. If a state is not in this superset, this means that, for sure, the program cannot reach this state.

Let us take an example, the *domain of intervals*: if $X^\sharp = Y^\sharp = T^3$ where $T = \{(a,b) \in \mathbb{Z} \cup \{-\infty, +\infty\} \mid a \leq b\} \cup \{\bot\}$, $\gamma(a,b) = \{c \in \mathbb{Z} \mid a \leq c \leq b\}$ and γ induces a preorder $\sqsubseteq_T$ over T and, point-wise, over $X^\sharp$, then we can take $[\![\text{x:=y+z}]\!]^\sharp((a_x, b_x), (a_y, b_y), (a_z, b_z)) = ((a_y + a_z, b_y + b_z), (a_y, b_y), (a_z, b_z))$.

3.2 Turning Fixpoints of Affine Operators into Fixpoints of Monotone Set Operators

Equation 3 shows that the semantics of loops are given as infinite sums or, equivalently, as fixpoints of some affine operators. In non-probabilistic semantics, the semantics of loops is usually the fixpoint of some monotone operator on the concrete lattice, which get immediately abstracted as fixpoints on the abstract lattice. The approximation is not so evident in the case of this sum; we shall nevertheless see how to deal with it using fixpoints on the abstract lattice.

Defining μ_n recursively, as follows: $\mu_0 = \lambda X.0$ and $\mu_{n+1} = \psi\mu_n$, with $\psi(\nu) = \mu + [\![e]\!]_p \circ \phi_{[\![c]\!]}(\nu)$, we can rewrite equation 3 as $[\![\texttt{while } c \texttt{ do } e]\!]_p (\mu) = \phi_{[\![c]\!]^c}(\lim_{n\to\infty} \mu_n)$. We wish to approximate this limit in the measure space by an abstract element.

We get this approximation by finding a subset L of $\mathcal{P}(\mathcal{M}_+(X))$ that:

- contains any element of the sequence (μ_n),
- is stable by ψ,
- is topologically closed.

Then $\lim_{n\to\infty} \mu_n \in L$.

Let us take $N \in \mathbb{N}$. Let us note $+^\sharp$ an abstraction of the sum operation on measures, $0^\sharp$ an abstraction of the null measure and $\psi^\sharp(\nu^\sharp) = W^\sharp + [\![e]\!]_p^\sharp \circ \phi_{[\![c]\!]}^\sharp(\nu^\sharp)$.

Let us take $\mu \in W^\sharp$. By abstraction, $\mu_N \in \gamma(\psi^{\sharp N}(0^\sharp))$.

Let us suppose that we have an "approximate least fixpoint" operation $\mathrm{lfp}^\sharp$: $(X^\sharp \xrightarrow{\text{monotonic}} X^\sharp) \to X^\sharp$. By "approximate least fixpoint" we mean that if $\phi^\sharp$ is an abstraction of ϕ, then $\mathrm{lfp}^\sharp \phi^\sharp$ is an abstraction of $\mathrm{lfp}\, \phi$. The next sub-section will explain how to implement such an operation using widening operators.

Let us consider $L = \gamma\left(\mathrm{lfp}^\sharp X^\sharp \mapsto \psi^{\sharp N}(0^\sharp) \sqcup (W^\sharp +^\sharp [\![e]\!]^\sharp (\phi_{[\![c]\!]}^\sharp(X)))\right)$. L contains μ_N and is stable by ψ.

We can therefore take:

$$[\![\texttt{while } c \texttt{ do } e]\!]^\sharp (W^\sharp) = \phi_{[\![c]\!]^c}^\sharp \left(\mathrm{lfp}^\sharp X^\sharp \mapsto \psi^{\sharp N}(0^\sharp) \sqcup (W^\sharp +^\sharp [\![e]\!]^\sharp (\phi_{[\![c]\!]}^\sharp(X)))\right),$$
(6)

3.3 Approximation of Least Fixpoints

As noted before, we need an "approximate least fixpoint" operation $\mathrm{lfp}^\sharp$: $(X^\sharp \xrightarrow{\text{monotonic}} X^\sharp) \to X^\sharp$. We shall see here that such an operation can be implemented using widening operators ([2]; see §4.4, 5.4 for the widening operators that we propose for our particular application).

A *widening operator* $\nabla : X^\sharp \times X^\sharp \to X^\sharp$ is such that

- for all $x^\sharp$, $y^\sharp$, $x^\sharp \sqcup y^\sharp \sqsubseteq x^\sharp \nabla y^\sharp$;
- for any ascending sequence $(y_n^\sharp)$ and any $x_0^\sharp$, the sequence $(x_n^\sharp)$ defined by $x_{n+1}^\sharp = x_n^\sharp \nabla y_n^\sharp$ is ultimately stationary.

Informally, a widening operator is a kind of "convergence accelerator" for ascending sequences of elements of the lattice; it allows obtaining in finite time an over-approximation of the limit of the sequence (which can be reached in infinite time).

Let us suppose we have a monotonic $\phi : X \to X$ and an abstraction of it $\phi^\sharp : X^\sharp \to X^\sharp$. Let us define $x_0^\sharp = \bot$ and $x_n^\sharp = x_n^\sharp \nabla \phi^\sharp(x_n^\sharp)$. Since ∇ is a widening operator, $x_n^\sharp$ is ultimately stationary. Let us call $L^\sharp$ its limit. We have $L^\sharp = L^\sharp \nabla \phi^\sharp(L^\sharp)$. Since ∇ is a widening operator, $\phi^\sharp(L^\sharp) \sqsubseteq L^\sharp \nabla \phi^\sharp(L^\sharp) = L^\sharp$. Let us apply γ (monotonic) to both sides of the inequality: $\gamma \circ \phi^\sharp(L^\sharp) \sqsubseteq \gamma(L^\sharp)$. Since $\phi^\sharp$ is an abstraction of ϕ, $\phi \circ \gamma(L^\sharp) \sqsubseteq \gamma \circ \phi^\sharp(L^\sharp)$. It follows that $\phi(\gamma(L^\sharp)) \sqsubseteq \gamma(L^\sharp)$. By Tarski's theorem [2, §4.1], lfp $\phi = \bigsqcap_{\phi(x) \sqsubseteq x} x$ and thus lfp $\phi \sqsubseteq \gamma(L^\sharp)$. $\gamma L^\sharp$ is thus an upper approximation of the least fixpoint of ϕ, obtained by a finite computation using the widening operator.

4   Basic Abstract Domain and Abstract Operations

We wish to represent sets of (sub)probability measures symbolically. In this section, we give a basic abstract domain expressing exponentially decreasing tails of probabilistic distributions on integers. This abstract domain is not very satisfactory by itself (it is very crude when it comes to loops), but is a basis for the definition of a more complex domain (section 5).

4.1   Abstract Domain

Let V be the set of variables. Each element of the abstract domain E is a tuple of coefficients. Those coefficients will represent three kinds of known facts on the measures:

- an upper bound W on their total weight;
- upper bounds on the intervals of probable variation for the integer variables: for any variable v, the probability that v is outside $[a_v, b_v]$ is 0; of course, a_b and/or b_v can be infinite ($a_v \le b_v$);
- for each integer variable v, some data C_v on its exponential decreasing: either none or a pair $(\alpha_v, \beta_v) \in \mathbb{R}_+ \times [0, 1[$ meaning that the probability that variable v is k is bounded by $\alpha_v \beta_v^k$.

$\gamma_E(W, (a_v, b_v)_{v \in V}, (C_v)_{v \in V})$ is the set of all measures matching the above conditions. We shall note $\mu(condition)$ for the application of the measure μ to the set of environments matching condition $condition$. The three conditions above then get written as:

$$\mu \in \gamma_E(W, (a_v, b_v)_{v \in V}, (C_v)_{v \in V}) \iff$$
$$\begin{cases} \mu(\text{true}) \le W \\ \forall v \in V\ \mu(v \notin [a_v, b_v]) = 0 \\ \forall v \in V\ C_v = (\alpha_v, \beta_v) \Rightarrow \forall k \in \mathbb{Z}\ \mu(v = k) \le \alpha_v \beta_v^k \end{cases} \quad (7)$$

4.2 Arithmetic Operations

We do not provide an abstract operator for each of the basic operations that a program may encounter; for instance, we say nothing of multiplication. In cases that are not described, we just apply interval propagation [1] and set $C_v =$ none for every modified variable v. In some case, we shall provide only for some cases, while some others can be handled by using the symmetry of the operation and reverting to a described case.

We focus on the operations that will be most useful for our analysis goals (number of iterations taken in a loop, number of used CPU cycles). For instance, we consider the case of the arithmetic plus since it will be used to count loop iterations or program cycles, whereas multiplication is of little use for such tasks.

Arithmetic Plus. We define here the abstract operation $(W, (a_v, b_v)_{v \in V},$ $(C_v)_{v \in V}) \mapsto (W', (a'_v, b'_v)_{v \in V}, (C'_v)_{v \in V}) = z := \text{x+y}_p^\sharp.(W, (a_v, b_v)_{v \in V}, (C_v)_{v \in V})$.
The distribution after applying an arithmetic plus obeys the following convolution equation:

$$([\![\text{x+y}]\!]_p . \mu)(z = t) = \sum_{k \in \mathbb{Z}} \mu(\text{x} = k \wedge \text{y} = t - k). \tag{8}$$

Let us suppose that $\mu \in \gamma_E(W, (a_v, b_v)_{v \in V}, (C_v)_{v \in V})$; we want to produce $(W', (a'_v, b'_v)_{v \in V}, (C'_v)_{v \in V})$ so that $([\![\text{x+y}]\!]_p . \mu \in \gamma_E(W', (a'_v, b'_v)_{v \in V}, (C'_v)_{v \in V})$.

Obviously we can take $W' = W$, $a'_z = a_x + a_y$, $b'_z = b_x + b_y$, and $b'_v = b_v$ and $C'_v = C_v$ for all $v \neq z$.

We therefore have four cases:

- $C_x =$ none and $C_y =$ none, then $C'_z =$ none;
- $C_x =$ none and $C_y = (\alpha_y, \beta_y)$. We then have $\mu(x = k \wedge y = t - k) \leq \alpha_y \beta_y^{t-k}$ if $k \in [a_x, b_x]$ $\mu(x = k \wedge y = t - k) = 0$ otherwise. Inequality 8 then yields $\mathbb{P}(x + y = t) \leq \alpha_y \sum_{k=a_x}^{b_x} \beta_y^{t-k}$.
   Let $\alpha'_z = \alpha_y \beta_y^{-b_x} \frac{\beta_y^{b_x - a_x + 1} - 1}{\beta_y - 1}$ and $\beta'_z = \beta_y$. In particular, if $b_x = a_x$ (variable x is actually a constant), then $\alpha'_z = \alpha_y \beta_y^{-b_x}$.
   Then $([\![\text{x+y}]\!]_p . \mu)(z = t) \leq \alpha'_z \beta'_z{}^t$. If $\alpha'_z = \infty$, we take $C'_z =$ none else we take $C'_z = (\alpha'_z, \beta'_z)$.
- $C_x = (\alpha_x, \beta_x)$ and $C_y =$ none; this is *mutatis mutandis* the previous case.
- $C_x = (\alpha_x, \beta_x)$ and $C_y = (\alpha_y, \beta_y)$; we then apply the previous cases and take the greatest lower bound of both.

4.3 Random Generation

We define here the abstract operation $(W, (a_v, b_v)_{v \in V}, (C_v)_{v \in V}) \mapsto (W', (a'_v, b'_v)_{v \in V}, (C'_v)_{v \in V}) = \rho := \text{random}_p^\sharp.(W, (a_v, b_v)_{v \in V}, (C_v)_{v \in V})$.

Let us recall that $\rho := \text{random}_p.\mu = \mu \otimes \mu_R$ where μ_R is the distribution of the generator. Let us note W_R the total weight of μ_R (it can be less than 1, see §5.3). We take $W' = W_R.W$, and for any variable v except ρ, $a'_v = a_v$ and $b'_v = b_v$; if $C_v = (\alpha_v, \beta_v)$ then $C'_v = (W_R.\alpha_v, \beta_v)$, else $C'_v =$ none. If the generator has an integer output and is bounded in $[a_R, b_R]$, then $a'_\rho = a_R$ and $b'_\rho = b_R$. $C'_\rho =$ none.

4.4   Flow Control

As with preceding operations, we only define the cases that will be actually used for our analysis goals. Other cases are handled by simple interval propagation and setting C_v to none for every modified variable v.

Least Upper Bound. We define here the abstract operation $((W, (a_v, b_v)_{v \in V}, (C_v)_{v \in V}), (W', (a'_v, b'_v)_{v \in V}, (C'_v)_{v \in V})) \mapsto (W'', (a''_v, b''_v)_{v \in V}, (C''_v)_{v \in V})$ noted as $(W, (a_v, b_v)_{v \in V}, (C_v)_{v \in V}) \sqcup^{\sharp} (W', (a'_v, b'_v)_{v \in V}, (C'_v)_{v \in V})$.

Given $(W, (a_v, b_v)_{v \in V}, (C_v)_{v \in V})$ and $(W', (a'_v, b'_v)_{v \in V}, (C'_v)_{v \in V})$, we want $(W'', (a''_v, b''_v)_{v \in V}, (C''_v)_{v \in V})$ so that $\gamma_E(W, (a_v, b_v)_{v \in V}, (C_v)_{v \in V}) \cup \gamma_E(W', (a'_v, b'_v)_{v \in V}, (C'_v)_{v \in V}) \subseteq \gamma_E(W'', (a''_v, b''_v)_{v \in V}, (C''_v)_{v \in V})$ with little loss of precision. Let us take $W'' = \max(W, W')$ and for all v:

- $a''_v = \min(a_v, a'_v)$ and $b''_v = \max(b_v, b'_v)$
- if $C_v = (\alpha_v, \beta_v)$ and $C'_v = (\alpha'_v, \beta'_v)$ then we take $\beta''_v = \max(\beta_v, \beta'_v)$ and $\alpha''_v = \max(\alpha_v \beta_v^{a''_v}, \alpha'_v \beta'_v{}^{a''_v}).\beta''_v{}^{-a''_v}$.
- if $C_v = $ none or $C'_v = $ none then $C''_v = $ none.

Widening. As noted before (§3.3), we need some widening operators to approximate least fixpoints.

We shall define here the abstract operation $((W, (a_v, b_v)_{v \in V}, (C_v)_{v \in V}), (W', (a'_v, b'_v)_{v \in V}, (C'_v)_{v \in V})) \mapsto (W'', (a''_v, b''_v)_{v \in V}, (C''_v)_{v \in V})$ noted as $(W, (a_v, b_v)_{v \in V}, (C_v)_{v \in V}) \nabla_E (W', (a'_v, b'_v)_{v \in V}, (C'_v)_{v \in V})$.

$(W, (a_v, b_v)_{v \in V}, (C_v)_{v \in V}) \nabla_E (W', (a'_v, b'_v)_{v \in V}, (C'_v)_{v \in V})$ should be higher than $(W, (a_v, b_v)_{v \in V}, (C_v)_{v \in V}) \sqcup_E (W', (a'_v, b'_v)_{v \in V}, (C'_v)_{v \in V})$. We also require the sequence defined inductively by $\mu'_{n+1} = \mu'_n \nabla \mu_n^{\sharp}$ to be stationary, for any sequence $(\mu_n^{\sharp})_{n \in \mathbb{N}}$. The main interest of such an operator is the computation of least fixpoints (see §3.3).

We shall use a widening operator $\nabla_{\mathbb{R}}$ on the reals:

- $x \nabla_{\mathbb{R}} y = \infty$ if $x < y$;
- $x \nabla_{\mathbb{R}} y = y$ otherwise.

Intuitively, using this operator means that if a sequence of real coefficients keeps of ascending, we get an upper approximation of it using $+\infty$.

Let us take $W'' = \max(W, W')$ and for all v:

- if $a_v > a'_v$, $a''_v = -\infty$ else $a''_v = a_v$;
- if $b_v < b'_v$, $b''_v = +\infty$ else $b''_v = a_v$;
- two cases:
  - If $a''_v = +\infty$ or $C_v = $ none or $C'_v = $ none then $C''_v = $ none.
  - Otherwise, if $C_v = (\alpha_v, \beta_v)$ and $C'_v = (\alpha'_v, \beta'_v)$ then we take $\beta''_v = \exp(-(-\ln \beta_v) \nabla_{\mathbb{R}} (-\ln \beta'_v))$ and $\alpha''_v = (\alpha_v \beta_v^{a''_v} \nabla_{\mathbb{R}} \alpha'_v \beta'_v{}^{a''_v})).\beta''_v{}^{-a''_v}$. If $\alpha''_v < \infty$ then $C''_v = (\alpha''_v, \beta''_v)$, otherwise $C''_v = $ none.

Addition. We shall define here the abstract operation $((W, (a_v, b_v)_{v \in V}, (C_v)_{v \in V})$, $(W', (a'_v, b'_v)_{v \in V}, (C'_v)_{v \in V})) \mapsto (W'', (a''_v, b''_v)_{v \in V}, (C''_v)_{v \in V})$ noted as $(W, (a_v, b_v)_{v \in V}, (C_v)_{v \in V}) +^{\sharp} (W', (a'_v, b'_v)_{v \in V}, (C'_v)_{v \in V})$.

Two cases are of particular interest:

- For all $t \in \mathbb{Z}$, $\mu(v = t) \leq \alpha_v \beta_v^t$, $t \notin [a_v, b_v] \Rightarrow \mu(v = t)$, $t \notin [a'_v, b'_v] \Rightarrow \mu'(v = t)$ and $\mu'(\text{true}) \leq W'$.

  Two cases:
  - $b'_v < a'_v$; then let us take $\alpha''_v = \max(\alpha_v, W'.\beta_v^{-b'_v})$ and $\beta''_v = \beta_v$, then $\mu + \mu(t = v) \leq \alpha''_v \beta_v''^t$ (see Fig. 1 for an example);
  - otherwise, let us take $\alpha''_v = \alpha_v, W' + \beta_v^{b'_v}$ and $\beta''_v = \beta_v$, then $\mu + \mu(t = v) \leq \alpha''_v \beta_v''^t$.

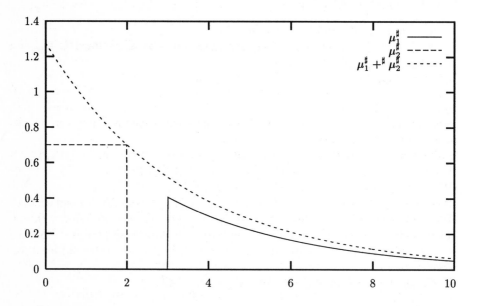

Fig. 1. Abstract addition of measures. $C_x = (1, 0.3)$, $a_x = 3$, $b_x = +\infty$, $W' = 0.7$, $C'_x = \text{none}$, $a'_x = 0$, $b'_x = 2$. For the sake of readability, the discrete distributions are extended to continuous ones. The near-vertical slopes are artefacts of the plotting software replacing vertical slopes.

- For all $t \in \mathbb{Z}$, $t \notin [a_v, b_v] \Rightarrow \mu(v = t)$, $t \notin [a'_v, b'_v] \Rightarrow \mu'(v = t)$, where $a'_v > b_v$. Let us take $\beta''_v = (W/W')^{\frac{1}{b'_v - b_v}}$ and $\alpha''_v = W.\beta_v''^{b_v}$, then $\mu + \mu(t = v) \leq \alpha''_v \beta_v''^t$ (see Fig. 2 for an example).

4.5   Machine Reals in Our Abstract Domain

Our abstract domain makes ample use of real numbers: each coefficient α_v or β_v is *a priori* a real number. A possible implementation of these coefficients is

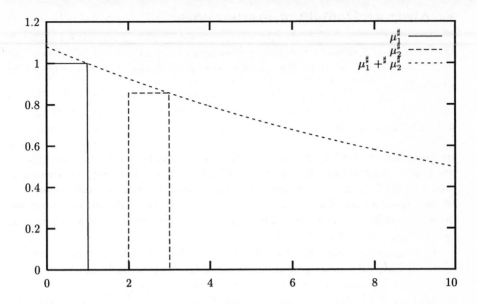

Fig. 2. Abstract addition of measures. $C_x =$ none, $a_x = 0$, $b_x = 1$, $W = 1$, $a'_x = 2$, $b'_x = 3$, $W' = 0.856$.

machine reals (IEEE 754 or similar); another is rational numbers as quotients of arbitrary-precision integers. We discuss here the possible consequences of the use of machine reals for the implementation of those coefficients.

The use of machine reals leads to two implementation problems. The first problem is that it is difficult to ascertain the loss of precision induced by machine reals throughout computations: how can the user be convinced that the output of the analyzer is sound? This can be worked around by using directed rounding modes.

A more annoying problem, relevant in implementation, is the fact that accrued imprecisions may lead to "drift", especially when using directed rounding modes. By "drift", we mean that a sequence of real numbers that, mathematically speaking, should appear to be stationary may be strictly ascending in the floating-point approximation. In that case, our widening operator on the reals $\nabla_{\mathbb{R}}$ (§4.4) may jump prematurely to $+\infty$.

It may be desirable to consider that small changes in some real coefficients do not indicate that the coefficient is actually changing but rather indicate some loss of precision. We expect the current work on abstract domains for real numbers [10] to provide better solutions to that problem.

5 Abstract Domain of Finite Sums

The preceding domain is not yet very suitable to handle random generation. In this section, we lift it to the domain of its finite sums. This is similar to [8, section 4].

5.1 Definition

We shall define another domain S and another concretization function γ_S. S consists of finite tuples of elements of E or, more interestingly, of a reduced product [2, §4.2.3.3] P of E and another domain D. For our subsequent examples, we shall use for P the product of E and the lattice of real intervals (for real variables). γ_P is the concretization function for this reduced product: $\gamma_P(e^{\sharp}, d^{\sharp}) = \gamma_E(e^{\sharp}) \cap \gamma_D(d^{\sharp})$.

As a running example we shall use for D the lifted domain of real intervals: to each real variable v we attach an interval $[a_v, b_v]$, with possibly infinite bounds. The probability that variable v is outside $[a_v, b_v]$ is zero.

Items of S are therefore finite tuples of elements of P. The concretization function γ_S is defined as follows: $\mu \in \gamma_S(p_1^{\sharp}, ..., p_n^{\sharp})$ if and only if there exist $\mu_1 \in \gamma_P(p_1), ..., \mu_n \in \gamma_P(p_n)$ so that $\mu = \sum_{k=1}^n \mu_k$.

5.2 Arithmetic Operations

Deterministic Operations. Basic operations are handled by linearity: since for any program construct P its semantics $[\![P]\!]_p$ is a linear operator, it follows that if $\mu \in \gamma_S(p_1^{\sharp}, ..., p_n^{\sharp})$ then $[\![P]\!]_p . \mu \in \gamma_S([\![P]\!]_p^{\sharp} . p_1^{\sharp}, \ldots, [\![P]\!]_p^{\sharp} . p_n^{\sharp})$.

The abstract operator is therefore constructed:

$$[\![P]\!]_p^{\sharp} (p_1^{\sharp}, ..., p_n^{\sharp}) = ([\![P]\!]_p^{\sharp} . p_1^{\sharp}, \ldots, [\![P]\!]_p^{\sharp} . p_n^{\sharp}).$$

5.3 Random Operations

Let us consider a random generator G operating according to the distribution μ_R. The semantics of the random operation is $[\![\texttt{random}]\!]_p . \mu = \mu \otimes \mu_R$ (Equ. 1). We shall suppose that our underlying domain P has an abstract operation $\otimes^{\sharp}$.

Let us suppose that $\mu_R = \sum_{i=1}^N \mu_i$. Then $\mu \otimes \mu_R = \sum_{i=1}^N \mu \otimes \mu_i$ thus if $\mu \in \gamma_S([\![P]\!]_p^{\sharp} . p_1^{\sharp}, \ldots, [\![P]\!]_p^{\sharp} . p_n^{\sharp})$ then $\mu \otimes \mu_R \in \gamma_S([\![P]\!]_p^{\sharp} . p_1^{\sharp} \otimes^{\sharp} \mu_1^{\sharp}, \ldots, [\![P]\!]_p^{\sharp} . p_1^{\sharp} \otimes^{\sharp} \mu_N^{\sharp}, \ldots, [\![P]\!]_p^{\sharp} . p_n^{\sharp} \otimes^{\sharp} \mu_1^{\sharp}, \ldots, [\![P]\!]_p^{\sharp} . p_n^{\sharp} \otimes^{\sharp} \mu_N^{\sharp})$.

As an example, let us consider the case of an uniform random generator in $[0, 1]$. Let us "cut" it into N equal sub-segments: let us note μ_R the uniform measure on $[0, 1]$. $\mu_R = \sum_{i=1}^N \mu_i$ with $\mu_i(X) = \mu_R(X \cap [(i-1)/N; i/N])$. For the abstraction of $\mu \mapsto \mu \otimes \mu_i$ over our example for the domain P: $(e, (d_1, \ldots, d_n)) \mapsto (e, (d_1, \ldots, d_n, [(i-1)/N; i/N]))$.

5.4   Flow Control

$$[\![\text{while } c \text{ do } e]\!]^{\sharp}(W^{\sharp}) = \phi^{\sharp}_{[\![c]\!]^{c}}(\text{lfp}^{\sharp} X^{\sharp} \mapsto W^{\sharp} \sqcup [\![e]\!]^{\sharp}(\phi^{\sharp}_{[\![c]\!]}(X^{\sharp}))).$$

Addition. Addition is very simple:

$$(p_1, \ldots, p_n) +^{\sharp} (p'_1, \ldots, p'_{n'}) = (p_1, \ldots, p_n, p'_1, \ldots, p'_{n'}) \tag{9}$$

Loops. For accuracy reasons, we wish $[\![\text{while } b \text{ do } e]\!]^{\sharp}.(p^{\sharp}_1, \ldots, p^{\sharp}_n)$ to operate separately on each component $p^{\sharp}_1, \ldots, p^{\sharp}_n$. We thus define an auxiliary function $H^{\sharp}$ so that $[\![\text{while } b \text{ do } e]\!]^{\sharp}.(p^{\sharp}_1, \ldots, p^{\sharp}_n) = (H^{\sharp}.p^{\sharp}_1, \ldots, H^{\sharp}.p^{\sharp}_n)$. $H^{\sharp}$ is defined following equation 6:

$$H^{\sharp}(W^{\sharp}) = \phi^{\sharp}_{[\![c]\!]^{c}}(\text{lfp}^{\sharp} X^{\sharp} \mapsto \text{merge}(W^{\sharp} \sqcup W^{\sharp} +^{\sharp} [\![e]\!]^{\sharp}(\phi^{\sharp}_{[\![c]\!]}(X)))).$$

where $\text{merge}(p_1, \ldots, p_n) = (p_1 +^{\sharp} \cdots +^{\sharp} p_n)$.

We construct the "approximate least fixpoint operation" $\text{lfp}^{\sharp}(f^{\sharp})$ as follows: we consider the sequence $u^{\sharp}_0 = (0)$, $u^{\sharp}_{n+1} = u^{\sharp}_n \nabla_P f^{\sharp}(u^{\sharp}_n)$. All elements of the sequences are 1-tuples of elements of P. If ∇_P is a widening operator for the domain P, then this sequence is stationary, and its limit is an approximation of the least fixpoint of $f^{\sharp}$.

Such a ∇_P operator can be defined as follows: $(e, d) \nabla_P(e', d') = (e \nabla_E e', d \nabla_D d')$ where ∇_E is the widening operator defined at §4.4.

6   Examples and Applications

6.1   Proof of Probabilistic Termination

Let us consider the following program:

```
double x, y;
int k = 0;
do
{
  x = uniform()+uniform();
  y = uniform();
  k++;
}
while(x < 1.4 || y < 0.2)
```

uniform() is assumed to be a random generator uniformly distributed in $[0, 1]$. In this simple case, the probability that the loop is taken is independent of the input data and of the number of iterations done so far. Furthermore, we can compute it mathematically (0.856), with our knowledge of the distribution of the random variables and the computation of an integral.

Let us examine here what happens if we apply the above method, dividing the random generator into $N = 20$ sub-segments of equal length (§5.3). At the end of the first iteration, after the merge, the analyzer establishes that the probability of reaching 1 iteration is less than 0.8805.[2] Applying the last case of §4.4, we obtain $a_k = 1$, $b_k = 2$, $\beta_k = 0.8805$, $\alpha_k \approx 1.1357$. After another iteration, we obtain $a_k = 1$, $b_k = 3$, $\beta_k = 0.8805$, $\alpha_k \approx 1.1357$. The analyzer widens to $a_k = 1$, $b_k = \infty$, $\beta_k = 0.8805$, $\alpha_k \approx 1.1357$, which is stable.

We have therefore established that the probability that $k = x$ at the beginning of the body of the loop is less than 0.8805^{k-1}. That is of course not as good as the exact computation, but still offers a reasonable bound.

6.2   Statistical Inference of Average Running Times

It is often needed to derive statistical facts such as average running times for real-time systems. Results achieved by the preceding method can be too rough to give precise estimates; nevertheless, they can help in making mathematically accurate some experimental statistical results.

Intuitively, to get the average running time of a system, we should take a large number n of random samples $(x_k)_{1 \leq k \leq n}$ for the input (distributed according to the supposed or inferred distribution on the inputs of the system). Let us call $R(x)$ the running time on input x; we then hope to have an approximation of the means $\bar{R}$ by taking $\frac{1}{n} \sum_{k=1}^{n} R(x_k)$.

Unfortunately, this method is not mathematically sound, essentially because R is not bounded, or rather because we have no information as to the very large values of R (the "tail" of the distribution). For instance, let us suppose that R is 0 for 99.99% of the input values and V for 0.01% of the input values. With 90% probability, the experimental average obtained by the Monte-Carlo method using 1000 samples will be 0, whereas the correct value is $V/10000$. As V can be arbitrarily large, this means we cannot gain any confidence interval on the result.

On the other hand, if, using the analysis described in this paper, we can show that the tail of the distribution decreases exponentially, we can get a confidence bound. Let us note $\mathbb{P}(A)$ the probability of an event A. Let us suppose that our analysis has established that the probability of running a loop at least k times is less than $\alpha.\beta^k$. Let $N \geq 1$. Let us run the program n times, stopping each time when either the loop terminates or it has been executed N times. Let us consider the random variable R where $R(x)$, the number of iterations the program takes when run on input x. We wish to determine $\bar{R} = \sum_{k=0}^{\infty} k.\mathbb{P}(R = k)$. To achieve this, we split the sum in two parts: $\bar{R} = \bar{R}_{\leq N} + \bar{R}_{>N}$ where $\bar{R}_{\leq N} = \sum_{k=0}^{N} k.\mathbb{P}(R = k)$ and $\bar{R}_{>N} = \sum_{k=N+1}^{\infty} k.\mathbb{P}(R = k)$.

---

[2] This result has been computed automatically by the Absinthe abstract interpreter http://cgi.dmi.ens.fr/cgi-bin/monniaux/absinthe.

We wish to obtain an upper bound on $\bar{R}_{>N}$.

$$\sum_{k=a}^{b} k.\beta^k = \frac{1}{(\beta - 1)^2} \cdot \left[\beta^{b+1}\left((b+1)(\beta - 1) - \beta\right) - \beta^a\left(a(\beta - 1) - \beta\right)\right] \quad (10)$$

and thus

$$\sum_{k=a}^{\infty} k\beta^k = \frac{\beta^a}{(\beta - 1)^2} \cdot (\beta - a(\beta - 1)) \quad (11)$$

Therefore $\bar{R}_{>N} \leq \alpha.\frac{\beta^{N+1}}{(\beta-1)^2}\cdot(\beta - (N+1)(\beta - 1))$.

On the other hand, $\bar{R}_{<N}$ can be estimated experimentally [9]. Let us consider the random variable R^*: $R^*(x) = 0$ if $R(x) > N$ and $R^*(x) = R(x)/N$ if $R(x) < N$; this is a random variable whose range is a subset of $[0, 1]$. It is therefore possible to apply to R^* the various techniques known for estimating the expectation of such random variables (such as Chernoff-Hoeffding bounds [4] or simple Gaussian confidence intervals, using the Central Limit Theorem). We then obtain $\bar{R}_{<N} = N.\bar{R}^*$.

We therefore obtain a confidence upper bound on $\bar{R}$ by adding together the confidence intervals obtained on $\bar{R}_{\leq N}$ and $\bar{R}_{>N}$.

7   Conclusions and Future Work

We have proposed a method to analyze automatically the termination of certain kinds of computer programs. This analysis outputs probabilistic invariants of loops, especially on the distribution of the number of loop iterations done or the number of program cycles used. The invariants obtained can be used in several ways, including:

- proofs of probabilistic termination,
- proofs of soundness of experimental statistical methods.

The analysis is proved to be sound, as it is set in a framework of abstract interpretation suitable for probabilistic programs. It has been partially implemented in an automatic analyzer for a subset of the C programming language. We plan to implement it fully in an analyzer for industrial embedded systems, where it could serve as a quick method to validate active waiting loops and similar constructs.

This analysis deals with a particular kind of probabilistic distributions, for example typical of the running time of a program waiting for data with probabilistic timings on a network. Other kinds of distributions, such as the normal (Gaussian) one, are of particular interest when analyzing embedded systems — for instance, to model error propagation. We plan to give analyses suitable for such distributions.

References

1. P. Cousot and R. Cousot. Abstract intrepretation: a unified lattice model for static analysis of programs by construction or approximation of fixpoints. In *Conference Record of the 4th ACM Symposium on Principles of Programming Languages*, pages 238–252, Los Angeles, CA, January 1977.
2. Patrick Cousot and Radhia Cousot. Abstract interpretation and application to logic programs. *J. Logic Prog.*, 2-3(13):103–179, 1992.
3. J.L. Doob. *Measure Theory*, volume 143 of *Graduate Texts in Mathematics*. Springer-Verlag, 1994.
4. Wassily Hoeffding. Probability inequalities for sums of bounded random variables. *J. Amer. Statist. Assoc.*, 58(301):13–30, 1963.
5. D. Kozen. Semantics of probabilistic programs. In *20th Annual Symposium on Foundations of Computer Science*, pages 101–114, Long Beach, Ca., USA, October 1979. IEEE Computer Society Press.
6. D. Kozen. Semantics of probabilistic programs. *Journal of Computer and System Sciences*, 22(3):328–350, 1981.
7. Chin Soon Lee, Neil D. Jones, and Amir M. Ben-Amram. The size-change principle for program termination. In *ACM Symposium on Principles of Programming Languages*, volume 28, pages 81–92. ACM press, January 2001.
8. David Monniaux. Abstract interpretation of probabilistic semantics. In *Seventh International Static Analysis Symposium (SAS'00)*, number 1824 in Lecture Notes in Computer Science. Springer-Verlag, 2000. Extended version on the author's web site.
9. David Monniaux. An abstract Monte-Carlo method for the analysis of probabilistic programs (extended abstract). In *28th Symposium on Principles of Programming Languages (POPL '01)*, pages 93–101. Association for Computer Machinery, 2001.
10. Éric Goubault. Static analyses of floating-point operations. In *Static Analysis (SAS'01)*, Lecture Notes in Computer Science, pages 234–259, Springer-Verlag, July 2001.
11. Walter Rudin. *Real and Complex Analysis*. McGraw-Hill, 1966.

Watchpoint Semantics: A Tool for Compositional and Focussed Static Analyses

Fausto Spoto

Dipartimento Scientifico e Tecnologico
Strada Le Grazie, 15, Ca' Vignal, 37134 Verona, Italy
spoto@sci.univr.it

Abstract. We abstract a denotational trace semantics for an imperative language into a compositional and focussed *watchpoint semantics*. Every abstraction of its computational domain induces an abstract, still compositional and focussed watchpoint semantics. We describe its implementation and instantiation with a domain of signs. It shows that its space and time costs are proportional to the number of watchpoints and that abstract compilation reduces those costs significantly.

1 Introduction

A *compositional* analysis of a complex statement is defined in terms of that of its components. Then the analysis of a procedure depends only on that of the procedures it calls and the analysis of a huge program can be easily kept up-to-date. This is important if a local change is applied to the program, during debugging or as a consequence of program transformation. A *focussed* or *demand-driven* analysis is *directed* to a given set of program points, called *watchpoints*, and has a cost (in space and time) proportional to their number. This is important if only those points are relevant. For instance, zero information is typically useful only before a division. Class information for object-oriented programs is typically useful only before a method call. During debugging the programmer wants to analyse a program in very few points, with a cost proportional to their number.

Our first contribution here is the definition of a compositional and focussed *watchpoint semantics*, as an abstract interpretation (AI) [6] specified by the watchpoints of interest of a more concrete trace semantics. An optimality result (Equation (4)) states that no precision is lost by this abstraction w.r.t. the information at the watchpoints. The *computational domain* is identified as a data structure with some operations. The second contribution states that every AI of the computational domain induces an abstraction of the watchpoint semantics. This reduces the problem of static analysis to that of the development of abstract domains. The third contribution is the description of our implementation of the watchpoint semantics instantiated for sign analysis. It shows that the space and time costs of the analysis are proportional to the number of watchpoints. The final contribution is to show that abstract compilation [11] leads to a significant improvement in the time and space costs of the analysis.

P. Cousot (Ed.): SAS 2001, LNCS 2126, pp. 127–145, 2001.

1.1   Related Works

Traditionally, compositionality is synonym with denotational semantics. But the usual denotational semantics [16] provides an input/output characterisation of procedures which is too *abstract* to observe their internal behaviour. This has been recognised in [5], where Cousot models information at internal program points through a more concrete, denotational *trace semantics*. Here, a procedure is denoted by a map from an initial *state* to a *trace* of states representing its execution from the initial state. Our trace semantics is a instance of the *maximal trace semantics* of [5]. Even [4] observes that traces contain more information than a traditional input/output denotation w.r.t. software pipelining, loop-invariant removal and data alias detection. That framework is however based on an operational definition. In [15] an operational trace semantics is defined and abstracted through AI into an *abstract trace semantics*. The abstraction of a trace is a (regular) tree, because of the non-deterministic nature of the abstract semantics. Information at program points (what they call the *collecting semantics*) is extracted from those trees *after* the fixpoint of the semantics is reached. Thus, their analysis is *not* focussed, since the whole trace semantics (the abstract trees) must be computed and then projected on program points. This is justified by the fact that they are interested in properties of traces, like those considered in the context of model-checking. However, for properties of states, like in sign, interval, class and security context analysis of variables (and, more generally, in all those analyses called *first-order* in [12], page 210), trees are not needed and can be safely abstracted into sets of states.

Abstract denotational semantics need a representation of the abstract input/output behaviour of a procedure. Since abstract inputs can partially overlap, the *meaning* or, in abstract interpretation words, the concretisation of an abstract denotation is not so easily devisable. In Section 6 we show a solution when the abstract domain elements can be written in terms of *union-irreducible* elements. For the general case, we rely on the *functional partitioning* technique defined in [1].

Focussed or demand-driven frameworks for analysis have been developed in the past. In [2] backward propagation of assertions was applied to the debugging of a high-order imperative language. In [8, 9, 13] backward dataflow analysis from a given query is defined and shown more efficient than an *exhaustive*, unfocussed analysis. The analyses in [8, 9] are provably as precise as the corresponding unfocussed versions for *distributive finite dataflow problems*, while our optimality result (Equation (4)) holds for every abstract domain. Queries can be checked to hold in a given program point, but cannot be computed by the analysis. It is not shown how those analyses scale w.r.t. the number of queries. No notion of computational domain is defined, which makes harder the definition of new abstract analyses. Abstract compilation cannot be applied because those analyses are not compositional. In [1] it is studied a very general and abstract way of looking at the problem of localised analyses in a given set of program points. However, its actual application to a real programming language is not tackled there.

Abstract compilation (AC) was born and applied only in the context of the analysis of logic programs [3, 11]. It is an optimised computation of the fixpoint of an abstract semantics where at the i-th iteration part of the analysis is *compiled* when it becomes clear that it will not change at the $(i + 1)$-th iteration.

Our work has been heavily influenced by the systematic construction of semantics for logic programming from the observable property of interest [10]. There, semantics for resultants, call patterns and computed answers of logic programs are derived through AI of the very concrete semantics of SLD-derivations. In particular, the call pattern semantics collects the information in some program points only.

1.2   Plan of the Paper

Section 2 introduces some preliminary notations. Section 3 defines the simple imperative language used in the paper. Section 4 defines the concrete trace semantics which is then abstracted into our watchpoint semantics of Section 5 and its collecting version. Section 6 shows how every abstract interpretation of the concrete computational domain induces an abstract watchpoint semantics. Section 7 describes our implementation of the watchpoint semantics instantiated for sign analysis. Section 8 concludes. Proofs are omitted.

2   Preliminaries

A *sequence* of elements from a set S is denoted by $\mathsf{seq}(S)$. The cardinality of a set S is denoted by $\#S$. A definition like $S = \langle a, b \rangle$, with a and b meta-variables, silently defines the selectors $s.a$ and $s.b$ for $s \in S$. For instance, Definition 8 defines $t.w$ and $t.s$ for $t \in \mathcal{T}_\tau^w$. An element $x \in X$ will often stand for the singleton $\{x\} \subseteq X$.

The domain (codomain) of a function f is $\mathsf{dom}(f)$ ($\mathsf{cd}(f)$). A total (partial) function is denoted by $\mapsto$ ($\to$). We denote by $[v_1 \mapsto t_1, \ldots, v_n \mapsto t_n]$ a function f whose domain is $\{v_1, \ldots, v_n\}$ and such that $f(v_i) = t_i$ for $i = 1, \ldots, n$. Its update is $f[d_1/w_1, \ldots, d_m/w_m]$, where the domain can be potentially enlarged. By $f|_s$ ($f|_{-s}$) we denote the restriction of f to $s \subseteq \mathsf{dom}(f)$ (to $\mathsf{dom}(f) \setminus s$).

A pair $(C, \le)$ is a *poset* if $\le$ is reflexive, transitive and antisymmetric on C. A poset is a *complete lattice* when *least upper bounds* (lub) and *greatest lower bounds* (glb) always exist, a *complete partial order* (CPO) when lubs exist for the non-empty chains (totally ordered subsets). A CPO is *pointed* when it has a bottom element. A map is *additive* when it preserves all lubs. If $f(x) = x$ then x is a *fixpoint* of f. If a least fixpoint exists, it is denoted by $\mathsf{lfp}(f)$.

Let $(C, \le)$ and $(A, \preceq)$ be two posets (the concrete and the abstract domain). A *Galois connection* [6, 7] is a pair of monotonic maps $\alpha : C \mapsto A$ and $\gamma : A \mapsto C$ such that $\gamma\alpha$ is extensive and $\alpha\gamma$ is reductive. It is a *Galois insertion* when $\alpha\gamma$ is the identity map, i.e., when the abstract domain does not contain *useless* elements. This is equivalent to α being onto, or γ one-to-one. The *abstraction* α

and the *concretisation* γ determine each other. If C and A are complete lattices and α is additive, it is the abstraction map of a Galois connection.

An abstract operator $\hat{f} : A^n \to A$ is *correct* w.r.t. $f : C^n \to C$ if $\alpha f \gamma \preceq \hat{f}$. For each operator f, there exists an *optimal* (most precise) correct abstract operator $\hat{f}$ defined as $\hat{f} = \alpha f \gamma$. If $\hat{f}\alpha = \alpha f$, we say that $\hat{f}$ is α-*optimal* w.r.t. f, i.e., $\hat{f}$ computes the same abstract information as f.

In AI, the *semantics* of a program is the fixpoint of some $f : C \mapsto C$, where C is the computational domain [5]. Its *collecting version* [6] works over *properties* of C, i.e., over $\wp(C)$ and is the fixpoint of the powerset extension of f. If f is defined through suboperations, their powerset extensions *and* $\cup$ (which merges the semantics of the branches of a conditional) induce the extension of f.

3   A Simple Language

Our language is left expandable at the price of some redundancy in the definitions. Integers are its only basic type, with two operations ($=$ and $+$). Booleans are implemented as integers (*false* is represented by a negative integer and *true* by any other integer). We do not have procedures but only functions. Those limitations are just meant to simplify the presentation. Our framework can be extended to cope with those missing items.

Definition 1. *Let* Id *be a set of* identifiers *and* $\mathcal{F} \subseteq Id$ *a finite set of* function symbols. *Expressions* $\mathcal{E}$ *and* commands $\mathcal{C}$ *are defined by the grammar*

$$e ::= i \mid v \mid f(v_1, \ldots, v_n) \mid e = e \mid e + e$$
$$c ::= (v := e) \mid c;c \mid \texttt{let } v{:}t \texttt{ in } c \mid \texttt{if } e \texttt{ then } c \texttt{ else } c \mid \texttt{while } e \texttt{ do } c$$

with $Type = \{int\}$, $Int = \mathbb{Z}$, $t \in Type$, $i \in Int$, $f \in \mathcal{F}$ *and* $v, v_1, \ldots, v_n \in Id$.

A typing gives types to a finite set of variables. The map *Pars* binds every function to the typing (its signature) and the list of its parameters. This list provides the order of the variables in the definition of the function. The function *Code* binds a function symbol to its (syntactically correct and type-checked) code. Local variables are always introduced by a `let` construct.

Definition 2. *We define* $Typing = \{\tau : Id \to Type \mid \mathrm{dom}(\tau) \text{ is finite}\}$, $Code = (\mathcal{F} \mapsto \mathcal{C})$ *and* $Pars = (\mathcal{F} \mapsto \mathrm{seq}(Id) \times Typing)$. *If* $p \in Pars$ *and* $f \in \mathcal{F}$, *then* $p(f) = \langle s, \tau \rangle$, *where* $f \in s$ *and* $\mathrm{dom}(\tau) = s$. *The variable* f *holds the return value of the function, like in Pascal.*

A program is specified by $\mathcal{F}$ and two elements in *Code* and *Pars*. In the following, we assume that we have a program $P = \langle \mathcal{F}, c, p \rangle$.

Expressions have a type in a typing. In our case, $\mathrm{type}_\tau(e) = int$ for $e \in \mathcal{E}$.

Example 1. Figure 10(a) gives a representation of the program for computing the n-th Fibonacci number (lines introduced by % are comments and will be discussed later). Note that the name `fib` of the (only) function in the program is used to hold its result value. Moreover, it is described by the *Pars* map p of the program.

$$\text{nop}_\tau : \Sigma_\tau \mapsto \Sigma_\tau$$

$$\text{get\_int}_\tau^i : \Sigma_\tau \mapsto \Sigma_{\tau[int/res]} \qquad \text{with } res \notin \text{dom}(\tau),\ i \in Int$$

$$\text{get\_var}_\tau^v : \Sigma_\tau \mapsto \Sigma_{\tau[\tau(v)/res]} \qquad \text{with } v \in \text{dom}(\tau),\ res \notin \text{dom}(\tau)$$

$$\text{put\_var}_\tau^v : \Sigma_\tau \mapsto \Sigma_{\tau|_{-res}} \qquad \text{with } res \in \text{dom}(\tau),\ v \in \text{dom}(\tau),\ v \neq res,\ \tau(v) = \tau(res)$$

$$=_\tau, +_\tau\, :\, \Sigma_\tau \mapsto (\Sigma_\tau \mapsto \Sigma_\tau) \qquad \text{with } res \in \text{dom}(\tau),\ \tau(res) = int$$

$$\text{scope}_\tau^{f,v_1,\ldots,v_{\#p(f).s-1}} : \Sigma_\tau \mapsto \Sigma_{p(f).\tau|_{-f}}$$

$$\text{with } p(f).s \setminus f = \langle \iota_1,\ldots,\iota_n \rangle \text{ and } \{v_1,\ldots,v_{\#p(f).s-1}\} \subseteq \text{dom}(\tau)$$

$$\text{unscope}_\tau^f : \Sigma_\tau \mapsto (\Sigma_{p(f).\tau|_f} \rightarrow \Sigma_{\tau[p(f).\tau(f)/res]}) \qquad \text{with } res \notin \text{dom}(\tau)$$

$$\text{restrict}_\tau^{vs} : \Sigma_\tau \mapsto \Sigma_{\tau|_{-vs}} \qquad \text{with } vs \subseteq \text{dom}(\tau)$$

$$\text{expand}_\tau^{v:t} : \Sigma_\tau \mapsto \Sigma_{\tau[t/v]} \qquad \text{with } v \notin \text{dom}(\tau),\ t \in Type$$

$$\text{is\_true}_\tau, \text{is\_false} \subseteq \wp(\Sigma_\tau) \qquad \text{with } \tau(res) = int\ .$$

$$\text{nop}_\tau(\sigma) = \sigma \qquad\qquad \text{get\_int}_\tau^i(\sigma) = \sigma[i/res]$$

$$\text{get\_var}_\tau^v(\sigma) = \sigma[\sigma(v)/res] \qquad \text{put\_var}_\tau^v(\sigma) = \sigma[\sigma(res)/v]|_{-res}$$

$$+_\tau(\sigma_1)(\sigma_2) = \sigma_2[\sigma_1(res) + \sigma_2(res)/res] \qquad =_\tau(\sigma_1)(\sigma_2) = \begin{cases} \sigma_2[1/res] & \text{if } \sigma_1(res) = \sigma_2(res) \\ \sigma_2[-1/res] & \text{if } \sigma_1(res) \neq \sigma_2(res) \end{cases}$$

$$\text{scope}_\tau^{f,v_1,\ldots,v_n}(\sigma) = [\iota_1 \mapsto \sigma(v_1),\ldots,\iota_n \mapsto \sigma(v_n)] \qquad \text{where } \langle \iota_1,\ldots,\iota_n \rangle = p(f).s \setminus f$$

$$\text{unscope}_\tau^f(\sigma_1)(\sigma_2) = \sigma_1[\sigma_2(f)/res] \qquad \text{restrict}_\tau^{vs}(\sigma) = \sigma|_{-vs} \qquad \text{expand}_\tau^{v:t}(\sigma) = \sigma[\text{init}(t)/v]$$

$$\text{is\_true}_\tau(\sigma) \text{ if and only if } \sigma(res) \geq 0 \qquad \text{is\_false}_\tau(\sigma) \text{ if and only if } \sigma(res) < 0$$

$$\text{init}(int) = 0\ .$$

Fig. 1. The signature and implementation of the operations over the states.

4   Trace Semantics

The computational domain of states described here is used below to define a trace semantics for our language. Each of its abstractions will induce an abstraction of that semantics (Section 6), as usual in AI (see for instance [14]). More complex notions of states could be used here, maybe dealing with locations and memory.

Definition 3. *Let* $Value = Int$ *and* $\Sigma = \cup_{\tau \in Typing}\Sigma_\tau$ *where, for* $\tau \in Typing$, *states* $\sigma \in \Sigma_\tau$ *map variables to values consistent with their declared type, i.e.,*

$$\Sigma_\tau = \left\{ \sigma \;\middle|\; \begin{array}{l} \sigma \in \text{dom}(\tau) \mapsto Value \text{ and} \\ \text{for every } v \in \text{dom}(\tau) \text{ if } \tau(v) = int \text{ then } \sigma(v) \in Int \end{array} \right\}.$$

States are endowed with the operations shown in Figure 1.

In the operations of Figure 1, the variable *res* holds intermediate results. The nop operation does nothing. The get_int (get_var^v) operation loads an integer (the value of v) in *res*. The put_var^v operation copies the value of *res* in v. There is no result, then *res* is removed. For every binary operation like = and +, there is an operation on states. The operations scope and unscope are used before and after a call to a function f, respectively. The former creates a new state in which

f can execute. Its typing $p(f).\tau|_{-f}$ describes the input parameters (the variable f is not among them). The latter copies in the variable res of the state before the call, i.e., its first argument, the result of f, i.e., the variable f of its second argument. The operation expand (restrict) adds (removes) variables from a state. The is_true (is_false) predicate checks whether res contains $true$ ($false$).

Since res plays a major role, we introduce the following abbreviations.

Definition 4. *For $\tau \in Typing$, $\sigma \in \Sigma_\tau$ and $e \in \mathcal{E}$, let $\tau^e = \tau[\text{type}_\tau(e)/res]$ and $\llcorner\sigma\lrcorner_\tau = \text{restrict}_\tau^{res}(\sigma)$ (τ will be always omitted).*

We define now an instance of the *maximal trace semantics* of [5].

Definition 5. *A trace $t \in \mathcal{T}$ is a non-empty sequence in Σ. A convergent trace $\sigma_1 \to \cdots \to \sigma_n$ represents a terminated computation, a finite divergent trace $\sigma_1 \to \cdots \to \tilde{\sigma}_n$ a yet non-terminated computation and an infinite divergent trace $\sigma_1 \to \cdots \to \sigma_n \to \cdots$ a divergent computation. Arrows are given labels $l \in Label$, like in $\to^l$, meaning that the interpreter was then in a watchpoint labelled with l (see Section 5). We assume $\to$ is given a hidden mark $\_ \notin Label$.*

The first state of $t \in \mathcal{T}$ is $\text{fst}(t)$. The predicate $\text{div}(t)$ means that t is divergent. If $\neg\,\text{div}(t)$, the last state of t is $\text{lst}(t)$. For $l \in Label$ and $\sigma \in \Sigma$, we let $\sigma \in_l t$ mean that σ occurs in t before an arrow $\to^l$.

The $\sqsubseteq$ ordering on traces (extension of finite divergent traces) is the minimal relation such that $t_1 \sqsubseteq t_2$ if $t_1 = t_2$ or (t_1 is finite divergent and $t_2 = \underline{t_1} \to^l t'$ for some $t' \in \mathcal{T}$ and $l \in Label \cup \{\_\}$), where $\underline{t_1}$ is t_1 deprived of the tilde sign.

Expressions and commands are *denoted* by a map from an initial state to a trace t. In the first case, if $\neg\,\text{div}(t)$ then $\text{lst}(t)(res)$ is the value of the expression.

Proposition 1. *Given $\tau, \tau' \in Typing$, we expand the $\sqsubseteq$ ordering on traces to*

$$C_{\tau,\tau'} = \{c \in \Sigma_\tau \mapsto \mathcal{T}_{\tau'} \mid \text{for every } \sigma \in \Sigma_\tau \text{ we have } \text{fst}(c(\sigma)) = \sigma\} . \quad (1)$$

The pair $\langle C_{\tau,\tau'}, \sqsubseteq \rangle$ is a pointed CPO whose bottom is $\perp_{C_{\tau,\tau'}} = \lambda\sigma \in \Sigma_\tau.\tilde{\sigma}$.

Interpretations denote every $f \in \mathcal{F}$ with an element of $C_{p(f).\tau|_{-f},p(f).\tau|_f}$. Indeed, its input variables are $p(f).s \setminus f$ and its output variable is named f.

Example 2. The program of Figure 10(a) is denoted by an interpretation which denotes fib with an element of $C_{[n\mapsto int],[fib\mapsto int]}$.

Definition 6. *The interpretations $\mathcal{I}$ are maps $I : \mathcal{F} \mapsto (\Sigma \to \mathcal{T})$ such that $I(f) \in C_{p(f).\tau|_{-f},p(f).\tau|_f}$ for $f \in \mathcal{F}$. The $\sqsubseteq$ ordering is point-wise extended to $\mathcal{I}$.*

Proposition 2. *The semantic operations on denotations of Figure 2 (the subscripts will be usually omitted) are monotonic w.r.t. $\sqsubseteq$.*

The operation $[op]$ applies an operation op from Figure 1. The operation $?$ joins the denotation E of an expression with that of one of two commands, depending on is_true and is_false on the final states of E. Since commands do not receive a partial result in res, we restrict those states through $\llcorner\lrcorner$. The operations $\otimes$

$$[op] : C_{\tau,\tau'}, \text{ with } \tau, \tau' \in Typing, \; op : \Sigma_\tau \to \Sigma_{\tau'}$$

$$?_\tau : C_{\tau,\tau[int/res]} \times C_{\tau,\tau}^2 \mapsto C_{\tau,\tau}, \text{ with } \tau \in Typing, \; res \notin dom(\tau)$$

$$\otimes_{\tau,\tau',\tau''} : (C_{\tau,\tau'} \times C_{\tau',\tau''}) \mapsto C_{\tau,\tau''}, \text{ with } \tau, \tau', \tau'' \in Typing$$

$$\otimes_{bop,\tau} : C_{\tau,\tau[t_1/res]} \times C_{\tau,\tau[t_2/res]} \mapsto C_{\tau,\tau'}$$

$$\text{with } \tau, \tau' \in Typing, \; res \notin dom(\tau), \; t_1, t_2 \in Type,$$

$$\text{and } bop_{\tau[t_1/res]} : \Sigma_{\tau[t_1/res]} \mapsto (\Sigma_{\tau[t_2/res]} \to \Sigma_{\tau'})$$

$$\bowtie_\tau (f(v_1, \ldots, v_{\#p(f)-1})) : \mathcal{I} \mapsto C_{\tau,\tau}, \text{ with } \tau \in Typing, \; \{v_1, \ldots, v_{\#p(f)-1}\} \subseteq dom(\tau)$$

$$[op]_{\tau,\tau'}(\sigma) = \begin{cases} \sigma \to op(\sigma) & \text{if } op(\sigma) \text{ is defined} \\ \sigma \to \tilde{\sigma} & \text{otherwise} \end{cases}$$

$$?_\tau(E, S_1, S_2)(\sigma) = \begin{cases} E(\sigma) & \text{if div}(E(\sigma)) \\ E(\sigma) \to S_1(\llcorner lst(E(\sigma)) \lrcorner) \\ \quad \text{if } \neg \text{div}(E(\sigma)) \text{ and is\_true}_{\tau[int/res]}(lst(E(\sigma))) \\ E(\sigma) \to S_2(\llcorner lst(E(\sigma)) \lrcorner) \\ \quad \text{if } \neg \text{div}(E(\sigma)) \text{ and is\_false}_{\tau[int/res]}(lst(E(\sigma))) \end{cases}$$

$$(S_1 \otimes_{\tau,\tau',\tau''} S_2)(\sigma) = \begin{cases} S_1(\sigma) & \text{if div}(S_1(\sigma)) \\ S_1(\sigma) \to S_2(lst(S_1(\sigma))) & \text{otherwise.} \end{cases}$$

$$(S_1 \otimes_{bop,\tau} S_2)(\sigma) = \begin{cases} S_1(\sigma) & \text{if div}(S_1(\sigma)) \\ S_1(\sigma) \to S_2(\llcorner l_1 \lrcorner) & \text{if } \neg \text{div}(S_1(\sigma)) \text{ and div}(S_2(\llcorner l_1 \lrcorner)) \\ S_1(\sigma) \to S_2(\llcorner l_1 \lrcorner) \to \tilde{l_2} \\ \quad \text{if } \neg \text{div}(S_1(\sigma)), \neg \text{div}(S_2(\llcorner l_1 \lrcorner)) \\ \quad \text{and } bop_{\tau[t_1/res]}(l_1)(l_2) \text{ is undefined} \\ S_1(\sigma) \to S_2(\llcorner l_1 \lrcorner) \to bop_{\tau[t_1/res]}(l_1)(l_2) & \text{otherwise.} \end{cases}$$

$$\text{where } l_1 = lst(S_1(\sigma)) \text{ and } l_2 = lst(S_2(\llcorner l_1 \lrcorner))$$

$$\bowtie_\tau (f(v_1, \ldots, v_n))(I)(\sigma) = \begin{cases} \sigma \to i & \text{if div}(i) \\ \sigma \to i \to \text{unscope}_\tau^f(\sigma)(lst(i)) & \text{otherwise} \end{cases}$$

$$\text{where } i = I(f)(\text{scope}_\tau^{f,v_1,\ldots,v_n}(\sigma)).$$

Fig. 2. The signature and the implementation of the semantic operations.

and $\otimes_{bop}$ join two denotations S_1 and S_2. Divergent traces in S_1 are not joined, since they represent an incomplete computation. Moreover, $\otimes_{bop}$ applies a binary operation bop to the final states of S_1 and S_2 ($\llcorner \lrcorner$ removes res from the final states of S_1). The operation $\bowtie$ calls a function by using an interpretation.

Example 3. Assume that τ is such that Σ_τ contains exactly three distinct states σ_1, σ_2 and σ_3. Consider $S_1, S_2 \in C_{\tau,\tau}$ such that

$$S_1(\sigma_1) = \sigma_1 \to \sigma_2 \to^{l_1} \sigma_3 \qquad\qquad S_2(\sigma_1) = \sigma_1 \to \tilde{\sigma}_2$$
$$S_1(\sigma_2) = \sigma_2 \to^{l_2} \tilde{\sigma}_1 \qquad\qquad S_2(\sigma_2) = \sigma_2 \to^{l_3} \sigma_3 \to^{l_2} \tilde{\sigma}_1$$
$$S_1(\sigma_3) = \sigma_3 \to^{l_2} \sigma_1 \to^{l_3} \sigma_3 \qquad\qquad S_2(\sigma_3) = \sigma_3 \to^{l_1} \tilde{\sigma}_1 \,.$$

Let $S = S_1 \otimes S_2$. We have

$$S(\sigma_1) = \sigma_1 \to \sigma_2 \to^{l_1} \sigma_3 \to \sigma_3 \to^{l_1} \tilde{\sigma}_1 \qquad\qquad S(\sigma_2) = \sigma_2 \to^{l_2} \tilde{\sigma}_1$$
$$S(\sigma_3) = \sigma_3 \to^{l_2} \sigma_1 \to^{l_3} \sigma_3 \to \sigma_3 \to^{l_1} \tilde{\sigma}_1 \,.$$

$$\mathcal{E}_\tau[\![i]\!]I = [\text{get\_int}_\tau^i]$$
$$\mathcal{E}_\tau[\![v]\!]I = [\text{get\_var}_\tau^v]$$
$$\mathcal{E}_\tau[\![e_1 = e_2]\!]I = \mathcal{E}_\tau[\![e_1]\!]I \otimes_= \mathcal{E}_\tau[\![e_2]\!]I$$
$$\mathcal{E}_\tau[\![e_1 + e_2]\!]I = \mathcal{E}_\tau[\![e_1]\!]I \otimes_+ \mathcal{E}_\tau[\![e_2]\!]I$$
$$\mathcal{E}_\tau[\![f(v_1,\ldots,v_n)]\!]I = \bowtie_\tau (f(v_1,\ldots,v_n))(I) \;.$$

$$\mathcal{C}_\tau[\![v := e]\!]I = \mathcal{E}_\tau[\![e]\!]I \otimes [\text{put\_var}_{\tau^e}^v] \qquad \mathcal{C}_\tau[\![c_1;c_2]\!]I = \mathcal{C}_\tau[\![c_1]\!]I \otimes \mathcal{C}_\tau[\![c_2]\!]I$$
$$\mathcal{C}_\tau[\![\texttt{let } v:t \texttt{ in } c]\!]I = [\text{expand}_\tau^{v:t}] \otimes \mathcal{C}_{\tau[t/v]}[\![c]\!]I \otimes [\text{restrict}_{\tau[t/v]}^v]$$
$$\mathcal{C}_\tau[\![\texttt{if } e \texttt{ then } c_1 \texttt{ else } c_2]\!]I = ?(\mathcal{E}_\tau[\![e]\!]I, \mathcal{C}_\tau[\![c_1]\!]I, \mathcal{C}_\tau[\![c_2]\!]I)$$
$$\mathcal{C}_\tau[\![\texttt{while } e \texttt{ do } c]\!]I = \text{lfp}_{C_{\tau,\tau}} \lambda fix.?(\mathcal{E}_\tau[\![e]\!]I, \mathcal{C}_\tau[\![c]\!]I \otimes fix, [\text{nop}_\tau]) \;.$$

Fig. 3. The rules of our denotational trace semantics.

By using the above operations, we build a denotational semantics for our language. The map $\mathcal{E}_\tau[\![e]\!] : I \mapsto C_{\tau,\tau^e}$ is shown in Figure 3 (for τ^e, see Definition 4). The basic cases of the denotation of an expression are immediate. For cases like $e_1 \ bop \ e_2$, the denotations of the two expressions are joined through $\otimes_{bop}$. For function call, we use $\bowtie$. The map $\mathcal{C}_\tau[\![]\!] : C \times \mathcal{I} \mapsto C_{\tau,\tau}$ is shown in Figure 3. The denotation of an assignment applies put_var to the final environments of the denotation of the right hand side. The introduction of a local variable v evaluates the code in a state expanded with v. Conditionals are modelled through the ? operation. A while command is denoted by a least fixpoint over a conditional [16]. It is well-defined since both $\mathcal{C}[\![]\!]$ and $\mathcal{E}[\![]\!]$ are monotonic (Proposition 2), and because of Proposition 1. It is the least upper bound of an ascending transfinite chain which starts from $\perp_{C_{\tau,\tau}}$.

The semantics of a program is a least fixpoint defined through $\mathcal{C}[\![]\!]$ [16]. Namely, for every $f \in \mathcal{F}$ we initialise (expand) the variable f, we compute the denotation of its code and we remove all the variables except f.

Definition 7. *By Props. 1 and 2, the semantics of $P = \langle \mathcal{F}, c, p \rangle$ is defined as $\mathcal{S}_P = \bigsqcup_o I_P^o$ where, letting $\tau = p(f).\tau$, $f \in \mathcal{F}$, i finite ordinal and l limit ordinal,*

$$I_P^0(f) = \perp_{C_{\tau|_{-f},\tau|_f}}, \quad I_P^{i+1}(f) = [\text{expand}_{\tau|_{-f}}^{f:\tau(f)}] \otimes \mathcal{C}_\tau[\![c(f)]\!]I_P^i \otimes [\text{restrict}_\tau^{\text{dom}(\tau)\backslash f}], \quad I_P^l(f) = \bigsqcup_{m < l} I_P^m(f) \;.$$

5   Watchpoint Semantics

We specify a program point of interest (a *watchpoint*) through the command watchpoint(l), with $l \in Label$. We expand the rules in Figure 3 with

$$\mathcal{C}_\tau[\![\texttt{watchpoint}(l)]\!]I = [watch]_{\tau,l} \;.$$

For $\tau \in Typing$ and $l \in Label$, $[watch]_{\tau,l} \in C_{\tau,\tau}$ creates a $\rightarrow^l$ transition, i.e.,

$$[watch]_{\tau,l}(\sigma) = \sigma \rightarrow^l \sigma \;. \tag{2}$$

Note that the typing τ_l in a watchpoint l is statically known.

Assume we are not interested in the states before an unnamed transition, but only in those before $\to^l$ with $l \in Label$, which can be selected through a map

$$w : \mathcal{T} \mapsto (Label \mapsto \wp(\Sigma))$$

(for its explicit definition, see Definition 9) pointwise extended to denotations (Eq. (1)) and interpretations (Def. 6). Instead of computing $w(\mathcal{S}_P)$ (Def. 7), we want to *push* w *inside* the semantics, i.e., compute the abstract *watchpoint semantics induced* by the abstraction w.

5.1   Why a New Semantics

Given $t \in \mathcal{T}$, by definition $w(t)$ is more *abstract* than t, and requires less space (memory) to be stored. Let $\varsigma(x)$ be the space needed to store x. Since we are particularly interested in the case when the program to be analysed is huge and the number of watchpoints is relatively small, we can assume that

$$\varsigma(w(t)) \ll \varsigma(t) \tag{3}$$

for $t \in \mathcal{T}$. Assume we want to compute $w(t)$ where t is a trace for the command $c_1; c_2$, i.e., the concatenation of a trace t_1 generated by c_1 and a trace t_2 generated by c_2 from $\mathsf{lst}(t_1)$. We can compute t_1, abstract it in $w(t_1)$, compute t_2, abstract it in $w(t_2)$ and *merge* $w(t_1)$ and $w(t_2)$ into $w(t)$. For this we need *at most* $m_1 = \max\{\varsigma(t_1) + \varsigma(w(t_1)), \varsigma(w(t_1)) + \varsigma(w(t_2)) + \varsigma(t_2)\}$ space (we never hold both t_1 and t_2 in memory at the same time). Instead, if we compute t and *then* $w(t)$, we need *at least* $m_2 = \varsigma(t) + \varsigma(w(t)) = \varsigma(t_1) + \varsigma(t_2) + \varsigma(w(t_1)) + \varsigma(w(t_2))$ space. Since $m_1 \leq m_2$, *pushing* w *inside* the semantics induces a lighter calculation.

This claim does not work for the time of the analysis, since a state depends on its predecessors in a trace. Hence all states must be considered during the computation of the semantics, not just those before a $\to^l$ transition. But the watchpoint semantics reduces the cost in time of the analysis for other reasons.

1. A more abstract fixpoint computation might require fewer iterations, and hence less space and time. Section 7 shows that this is very often the case.
2. Consider while e do c, where c contains some watchpoints, c is denoted by d and e by d'. If we *unfold* d after d' until the fixpoint (Fig. 3), we then need to *scan* a trace looking for the $\to^l$ transitions. If, instead, we had a denotation $w(d)$ such that $w(d)(\sigma) = w(d(\sigma))$, we could just merge, during the fixpoint calculation, the states for the same watchpoints, without scanning any trace.
3. Dealing with smaller data structures (as shown before) leads in general to faster analyses. From Equation (3), this could mean sometimes that virtual memory is not needed by the analyser, i.e., swapping is avoided.
4. Analyses based on a trace semantics use *widening* to avoid dealing with infinite traces. For instance, [4] and [15] use regular trees, which add complexity to the analyser. A watchpoint semantics does not need such a widening.

Consider how the analysis scales with the number of watchpoints. Of course, fewer watchpoints means lighter data structures, i.e., less space requirements.

W.r.t. time, fewer watchpoints means faster analysis for points 1 and 3 above. Finally since, for every watchpoint l, we need to compute the union (join) of the states before a $\rightarrow^l$ transition, it even means fewer joins, i.e., a faster analysis.

These considerations have been experimentally verified in Section 7.

5.2 The Semantics

We define here in detail the watchpoint semantics. To observe the states in the watchpoints, we can abstract the traces in sets of states, one for each watchpoint. But this abstraction induces too coarse optimal abstract operations, since the $\otimes$ operation (Figure 2) joins the traces through their last state. Thus, for better precision, we abstract the traces in *watchpoint traces*, i.e., a set of states for every watchpoint, collected into an element of $\mathcal{W}^w$, and a set for the final states.

Definition 8. *Let*

$$\mathcal{W}^w = \{w \in Label \mapsto \wp(\Sigma) \mid given \ l \in Label \ we \ have \ w(l) \in \wp(\Sigma_{\tau_l})\} \ .$$

A $w \in \mathcal{W}^w$ is finite if $w(l)$ is finite for every $l \in Label$. The set $\mathcal{W}^w$ is a complete lattice ordered w.r.t. the pointwise extension of $\subseteq$. Lub and glb are (pointwise) $\cup$ and $\cap$, its bottom is $\bot = \lambda l \in Label.\emptyset$.

The set of watchpoint traces *is $\mathcal{T}^w = \cup_{\tau \in Typing} \mathcal{T}^w_\tau$ where, for $\tau \in Typing$,*

$$\mathcal{T}^w_\tau = \{\langle w, s \rangle \mid w \in \mathcal{W}^w, \ s \in \Sigma_\tau \cup \{\sim\} \ and \ if \ s \neq \sim \ then \ w \ is \ finite\} \ .$$

They are ordered as $\langle w, s \rangle \sqsubseteq^w \langle w, s \rangle$ and $\langle w, \sim \rangle \sqsubseteq^w \langle w', s \rangle$ if and only if $w \subseteq w'$.

Elements of $\mathcal{W}^w$ are extentionally represented as $[l_1 \mapsto \Sigma_1, \ldots, l_n \mapsto \Sigma_n]$, meaning that the label l_i is mapped to the set of states Σ_i for $i = 1, \ldots, n$. If a label is not contained in that enumeration, it is assumed that it is mapped to $\emptyset$.

Example 4. We have

$$\langle [l_1 \mapsto \{\sigma_3\}, l_3 \mapsto \{\sigma_2\}], \sim \rangle \sqsubseteq^w \langle [l_1 \mapsto \{\sigma_1, \sigma_3\}, l_2 \mapsto \{\sigma_2\},]l_3 \mapsto \{\sigma_2, \sigma_3\}], \sigma_1 \rangle \ .$$

A watchpoint trace $\langle w, s \rangle$ with $s \neq \sim$ represents all convergent traces which end with s and contain exactly the watchpoints in w. If $s = \sim$, instead, it represents all divergent traces which contain exactly the watchpoints in w.

Definition 9. *Given $t \in \mathcal{T}$, we define $w(t) \in \mathcal{W}^w$ and $\alpha^w : \mathcal{T} \mapsto \mathcal{T}^w$ as*

$$w(t)(l) = \{\sigma \mid \sigma \in_l t\} \qquad for \ every \ l \in Label.$$

$$\alpha^w(t) = \begin{cases} \langle w(t), \sim \rangle & if \ \mathsf{div}(t) \\ \langle w(t), \mathsf{lst}(t) \rangle & otherwise. \end{cases}$$

Example 5. Let $Label = \{l_1, l_2\}$. Then

$$\alpha^w(\sigma_1 \rightarrow \sigma_2 \rightarrow^{l_1} \sigma_3 \rightarrow \sigma_4 \rightarrow^{l_2} \sigma_5 \rightarrow^{l_1} \sigma_6) = \langle [l_1 \mapsto \{\sigma_2, \sigma_5\}, l_2 \mapsto \{\sigma_4\}], \sigma_6 \rangle$$

$$\alpha^w(\sigma_1 \rightarrow \sigma_2 \rightarrow^{l_1} \sigma_3 \rightarrow \sigma_4 \rightarrow^{l_2} \sigma_5 \rightarrow^{l_1} \tilde{\sigma}_6) = \langle [l_1 \mapsto \{\sigma_2, \sigma_5\}, l_2 \mapsto \{\sigma_4\}], \sim \rangle \ .$$

$$[op]^w(\sigma) = \begin{cases} \langle \bot, op(\sigma) \rangle & \text{if } op(\sigma) \text{ is defined} \\ \langle \bot, \sim \rangle & \text{otherwise,} \end{cases} \qquad [watch]_l^w(\sigma) = \langle \bot[\{\sigma\}/l], \sigma \rangle$$

$$?^w(E, S_1, S_2)(\sigma) = \begin{cases} E(\sigma) & \text{if } E(\sigma).s = \sim \\ \langle E(\sigma).w \cup S_1(\llcorner E(\sigma).s \lrcorner).w, S_1(\llcorner E(\sigma).s \lrcorner).s \rangle \\ \quad \text{if } E(\sigma).s \neq \sim \text{ and is\_true}_{\tau[int/res]}(E(\sigma).s) \\ \langle E(\sigma).w \cup S_2(\llcorner E(\sigma).s \lrcorner).w, S_2(\llcorner E(\sigma).s \lrcorner).s \rangle \\ \quad \text{if } E(\sigma).s \neq \sim \text{ and is\_false}_{\tau[int/res]}(E(\sigma).s) \end{cases}$$

$$(S_1 \otimes^w S_2)(\sigma) = \begin{cases} S_1(\sigma) & \text{if } S_1(\sigma).s = \sim \\ \langle S_1(\sigma).w \cup S_2(S_1(\sigma).s).w, S_2(S_1(\sigma).s).s \rangle & \text{otherwise.} \end{cases}$$

$$(S_1 \otimes^w_{bop} S_2)(\sigma) = \begin{cases} S_1(\sigma) & \text{if } S_1(\sigma).s = \sim \\ \langle S_1(\sigma).w \cup S_2(\llcorner S_1(\sigma).s \lrcorner).w, \sim \rangle \\ \quad \text{if } S_1(\sigma).s \neq \sim \text{ and } (S_2(\llcorner S_1(\sigma).s \lrcorner).s).s = \sim \text{ or } b \text{ is undefined}) \\ \langle S_1(\sigma).w \cup S_2(\llcorner S_1(\sigma).s \lrcorner).w, b \rangle & \text{otherwise,} \end{cases}$$

$$\text{with } b = bop_{\tau[t_1/res]}(S_1(\sigma).s)(S_2(\llcorner S_1(\sigma).s \lrcorner).s)$$

$$\bowtie^w (f(v_1, \ldots, v_n))(I)(\sigma) = \begin{cases} \langle i.w, \sim \rangle & \text{if } i.s = \sim \\ \langle i.w, \text{unscope}^f(\sigma)(i.s) \rangle & \text{otherwise,} \end{cases} \quad i = I(f)(\text{scope}^{f,v_1,\ldots,v_n}(\sigma)) \ .$$

Fig. 4. The operations on watchpoint traces.

We define now the abstract counterpart of the set $C_{\tau,\tau'}$ of Equation (1).

Proposition 3. *Let $\tau, \tau' \in Typing$ and $W_{\tau,\tau'} = \Sigma_\tau \mapsto \mathcal{T}^w_{\tau'}$. The $\sqsubseteq^w$ order (α^w) is pointwise extended to $W_{\tau,\tau'}$ $(C_{\tau,\tau'})$. The pair $\langle W_{\tau,\tau'}, \sqsubseteq^w \rangle$ is a pointed CPO with bottom $\lambda\sigma \in \Sigma_\tau.\langle \bot, \sim \rangle$, and α^w is well-defined, onto, strict and additive.*

Proposition 4. *The operations in Fig. 4, whose signatures are the α^wabstraction of those in Fig. 2, are monotonic and α^w-optimal w.r.t. those in Fig. 2.*

Example 6. Consider the concrete denotations of Example 3. Let $S_1^w = \alpha^w(S_1)$, $S_2^w = \alpha^w(S_2)$ and $S^w = \alpha^w(S)$. We have

$$S_1^w(\sigma_1) = \langle [l_1 \mapsto \{\sigma_2\}], \sigma_3 \rangle \qquad\qquad S_2^w(\sigma_1) = \langle \bot, \sim \rangle$$
$$S_1^w(\sigma_2) = \langle [l_2 \mapsto \{\sigma_2\}], \sim \rangle \qquad\qquad S_2^w(\sigma_2) = \langle [l_2 \mapsto \{\sigma_3\}, l_3 \mapsto \{\sigma_2\}], \sim \rangle$$
$$S_1^w(\sigma_3) = \langle [l_2 \mapsto \{\sigma_3\}, l_3 \mapsto \{\sigma_1\}], \sigma_3 \rangle \quad S_2^w(\sigma_3) = \langle [l_1 \mapsto \{\sigma_3\}], \sim \rangle \ .$$

Moreover, we have that S^w is

$$S^w(\sigma_1) = \langle [l_1 \mapsto \{\sigma_2, \sigma_3\}], \sim \rangle \qquad\qquad\qquad S^w(\sigma_2) = \langle [l_2 \mapsto \{\sigma_2\}], \sim \rangle$$
$$S^w(\sigma_3) = \langle [l_1 \mapsto \{\sigma_3\}, l_2 \mapsto \{\sigma_3\}, l_3 \mapsto \{\sigma_1\}], \sim \rangle \ ,$$

which is *exatcly* $S_1^w \otimes^w S_2^w$.

Like in Section 4, we define a *watchpoint semantics* $\mathcal{S}_P^w$. By Propositions 3 and 4, it computes the same information about watchpoints as our trace semantics, i.e.,

$$\alpha^w(\mathcal{S}_P) = \mathcal{S}_P^w \ . \tag{4}$$

$$[op]^{co}(\eta) = \langle \bot, op(\eta) \rangle \qquad [watch]_l^{co}(\eta) = \langle \bot[\eta/l], \eta \rangle$$

$$?^{co}(E, S_1, S_2)(\eta) = \langle E(\eta).w \cup S_1(\llcorner \eta_t \lrcorner).w \cup S_2(\llcorner \eta_f \lrcorner).w, S_1(\llcorner \eta_t \lrcorner).\eta \cup S_2(\llcorner \eta_f \lrcorner).\eta \rangle$$

where $\eta_t = \text{is\_true}_{\tau[int/res]}(E(\eta).\eta)$ and $\eta_f = \text{is\_false}_{\tau[int/res]}(E(\eta).\eta)$

$$(S_1 \otimes^{co} S_2)(\eta) = \langle S_1(\eta).w \cup S_2(S_1(\eta).\eta).w, S_2(S_1(\eta).\eta).\eta \rangle$$

$$(S_1 \otimes_{bop}^{co} S_2)(\eta) = \langle S_1(\eta).w \cup S_2(\llcorner S_1(\eta).\eta \lrcorner).w, bop_{\tau[t_1/res]}(S_1(\eta).\eta)(S_2(\llcorner S_1(\eta).\eta \lrcorner).\eta) \rangle$$

$$\bowtie^{co}(f(v_1, \ldots, v_n))(I)(\eta) = \langle i.w, \text{unscope}^f(\eta)(i.\eta) \rangle, \quad \text{where } i = I(f)(\text{scope}^{f, v_1, \ldots, v_n}(\eta)).$$

Fig. 5. The operations on collecting watchpoint traces.

The *collecting* or *static* semantics [6] $\mathcal{S}_P^{\wp(w)}$ is the powerset lifting of $\mathcal{S}_P^w$. It works over $\wp(W_{\tau,\tau'})$, i.e., it models properties of watchpoint denotations. Since we are interested in properties of states, we define below a semantics $\mathcal{S}_P^{co}$ which works over watchpoint traces of sets of states. It is an AI of $\mathcal{S}_P^{\wp(w)}$ and will be called *collecting* though, strictly speaking, the real collecting semantics is $\mathcal{S}_P^{\wp(w)}$.

Definition 10. *The set of* collecting watchpoint traces $\mathcal{T}^{co} = \cup_{\tau \in Typing} \mathcal{T}_\tau^{co}$ *where, letting* $\tau \in Typing$ *and* $\mathcal{W}^{co} = \mathcal{W}^w$ *(Definition 8)* $\mathcal{T}_\tau^{co} = \{\langle w, \eta \rangle \mid w \in \mathcal{W}^{co} \text{ and } \eta \in \wp(\Sigma_\tau)\}$, *is ordered as* $\langle w_1, \eta_1 \rangle \sqsubseteq^{co} \langle w_2, \eta_2 \rangle$ *iff* $w_1 \subseteq w_2$ *and* $\eta_1 \subseteq \eta_2$.

Denotations are identified by their values on singleton sets. Denotations with more than one argument will be useful at the end of this section. This is formalised below.

Proposition 5. *Let* $n \geq 1$ *and* $\tau_1, \ldots, \tau_n, \tau' \in Typing$. *Let* $CO_{\tau_1, \ldots, \tau_n, \tau'}$ *be*

$$\left\{ \begin{array}{l|l} co \in \wp(\Sigma_{\tau_1}) \mapsto \cdots & co(\eta_1) \cdots (\eta_n) = \langle \cup_{\sigma_1 \in \eta_1, \ldots, \sigma_n \in \eta_n} co(\{\sigma_1\}) \cdots (\{\sigma_n\}).w, \\ \cdots \mapsto \wp(\Sigma_{\tau_n}) \mapsto \mathcal{T}_{\tau'}^{co} & \cup_{\sigma_1 \in \eta_1, \ldots, \sigma_n \in \eta_n} co(\{\sigma_1\}) \cdots (\{\sigma_n\}).\eta \end{array} \right\}. \quad (5)$$

The $\sqsubseteq^{co}$ *order of Definition 10 is pointwise extended to denotations* CO. *The pair* $\langle CO_{\tau_1, \ldots, \tau_n, \tau'}, \sqsubseteq^{co} \rangle$ *is a complete lattice with bottom* $\lambda \eta_1 \cdots \lambda \eta_n.\langle \bot, \emptyset \rangle$.

A collecting watchpoint trace represents a set of watchpoint traces. This abstraction induces optimal abstract counterparts of the operations in Figure 4.

Proposition 6. *Let* $\alpha^{co} : \wp(\mathcal{T}^w) \mapsto \mathcal{T}^{co}$ *be* $\alpha^{co}(S) = \langle \cup_{t \in S} t.w, \{t.s \mid t \in S \text{ and } t.s \neq \sim\} \rangle$. *Its extension* $\alpha^{co} : \wp(W_{\tau,\tau'}) \mapsto CO_{\tau,\tau'}$, *for* $\tau, \tau' \in Typing$, *given by* $(\alpha^{co}(W))(\eta) = \alpha^{co}(\{w(\sigma) \mid w \in W \text{ and } \sigma \in \eta\})$ *for* $\eta \in \wp(\Sigma_\tau)$, *is well-defined, onto, strict and additive (hence, the abstraction of a Galois insertion).*

Proposition 7. *The operations in Figure 5 are monotonic and* α^{co}*-optimal w.r.t. the pointwise extension of those in Figure 4.*

We define a *collecting watchpoint semantics* $\mathcal{S}_P^{co}$. We have $\mathcal{S}_P^{co} = \alpha^{co}(\mathcal{S}_P^{\wp(w)})$.

The operations in Figure 5 use objects in $\wp(\Sigma)$ (like $S_1(\eta).\eta$ in $\otimes^{co}$), $\mathcal{W}^{co}$ (like $S_1(\eta).w$ in $\otimes^{co}$) and CO (like S_1 in $\otimes^{co}$). To simplify the abstraction of Section 6, we *compile* them in terms of smaller operations over CO only, given in Figure 6. The compilation is shown in Figure 7.

Proposition 8. *The operations in Figure 5 and those in Figure 7 are the same.*

$$[op] : CO_{\tau_1,\cdots,\tau_n,\tau'}, \text{ if } op : \Sigma_{\tau_1} \mapsto \cdots \Sigma_{\tau_n} \mapsto \Sigma_{\tau'} \qquad\qquad [watch]_l : CO_{\tau,\tau}$$
$$.w : CO_{\tau,\tau'} \mapsto CO_{\tau,\tau'}$$
$$\circ : CO_{\tau_1,\ldots,\tau_n,\tau'} \times CO_{\tau,\tau_1} \cdots \times CO_{\tau,\tau_n} \mapsto CO_{\tau,\tau'} \qquad\qquad \cup : CO_{\tau,\tau'}^2 \mapsto CO_{\tau,\tau'}$$

$$[op] = \lambda\eta_1 \ldots \lambda\eta_n.\langle \bot, op(\eta_1, \cdots, \eta_n)\rangle \qquad\qquad [watch]_l = \lambda\eta.\langle \bot[\eta/l], \eta\rangle$$
$$T.w = \lambda\eta.\langle T(\eta).w, \emptyset\rangle \qquad\qquad T \circ (T_1,\ldots,T_n) = \lambda\eta.T(T_1(\eta).\eta)\cdots(T_n(\eta).\eta)$$
$$T_1 \cup T_2 = \lambda\eta.\left\langle \begin{matrix} T_1(\eta).w \cup T_2(\eta).w, \\ T_1(\eta).\eta \cup T_2(\eta).\eta \end{matrix} \right\rangle .$$

Fig. 6. A minimal set of operations over CO.

$$\llcorner T \lrcorner = [\text{restrict}^{res}] \circ T , \qquad [op]^{co} = [op] , \qquad [watch]_l^{co} = [watch]_l$$
$$?^{co}(E, S_1, S_2) = E.w \cup (S_1 \circ \llcorner T_t \lrcorner) \cup (S_2 \circ \llcorner T_f \lrcorner)$$
$$\text{where } T_t = [\text{is\_true}_{\tau[int/res]}] \circ E \text{ and } T_f = [\text{is\_false}_{\tau[int/res]}] \circ E$$
$$S_1 \otimes^{co} S_2 = S_1.w \cup (S_2 \circ S_1)$$
$$S_1 \otimes_{bop}^{co} S_2 = S_1.w \cup (S_2 \circ \llcorner S_1 \lrcorner).w \cup [bop_{\tau[t_1/res]}] \circ (S_1, S_2 \circ \llcorner S_1 \lrcorner)$$
$$\bowtie^{co} (f(v_1,\ldots,v_n))(I) = T_i.w \cup [\text{unscope}^f] \circ ([nop], T_i) \qquad \text{where } T_i = I(f) \circ [\text{scope}^{f,v_1,\cdots,v_n}].$$

Fig. 7. The operations in Figure 5 in terms of those in Figure 6.

6   From Abstract Domains to Abstract Semantics

We show here how every abstraction of the domain of states (Definition 3) induces an abstraction of the denotations CO (Equation (5)) and of their operations (Figure 6) and hence of the collecting watchpoint semantics of last section. This reduces the definition of a static analysis to the definition of abstract states.

Every abstract denotational semantics works over abstract denotations which are maps from abstract inputs to abstract outputs. In our watchpoint semantics, the abstract outputs are actually abstract traces. The problem here is how to define the concretisation of such abstract denotations. If a concrete state belongs to two abstract inputs, how should it behave in the concretisation? We do not consider this problem in details here, since it has already been studied in a more general setting. Consider for instance the *functional partitioning* technique in [1]. Instead, we assume here that in the lattice of abstract states there exists a set of *union-irreducible* states in terms of which all other abstract states can be expressed. This condition holds for the case of sign analysis shown in Section 7.

For $\tau \in Typing$, let $\langle D_\tau, \sqsubseteq\rangle$ be a complete lattice and α^{D_τ} and γ^{D_τ} the abstraction and concretisation maps of a Galois insertion from $\langle \wp(\Sigma_\tau), \subseteq\rangle$ to $\langle D_\tau, \sqsubseteq\rangle$ (typings will be often omitted).

Definition 11. *Let $\mathcal{W}^a = \{w \in Label \mapsto D \mid \text{for } l \in Label \text{ we have } w(l) \in D_{\tau_l}\}$. The set of abstract watchpoint traces is $\mathcal{T}^a = \cup_{\tau \in Typing}\mathcal{T}_\tau^a$ where*

$$\mathcal{T}_\tau^a = \{\langle w, d\rangle \mid w \in \mathcal{W}^a \text{ and } d \in D_\tau\} \qquad \text{for every } \tau \in Typing,$$

$$[op]^a = \lambda d_1 \ldots \lambda d_n.\langle \bot, \alpha^D(op(\gamma^D(d_1), \ldots, \gamma^D(d_n)))\rangle \qquad [watch]_l^a = \lambda d.\langle \bot[d/l], d\rangle$$

$$T.w^a = \lambda d.\langle T(d).w, \emptyset\rangle$$

$$T \circ^a (T_1, \ldots, T_n) = \lambda d. \sqcup_{d' \in S}^a T(T_1(d')) \cdots (T_n(d')) , \qquad \text{with } S \in \rho(d)$$

$$T_1 \cup^a T_2 = \lambda d. \left\langle \begin{array}{c} T_1(d).w \cup^D T_2(d).w, \\ T_1(d).d \cup^D T_2(d).d \end{array} \right\rangle \qquad \cup^D \text{ is the best approximation of } \cup \text{ over } D.$$

Fig. 8. The generic abstract counterparts of the operations of Figure 6.

ordered as $\langle w_1, d_1 \rangle \sqsubseteq^a \langle w_2, d_2 \rangle$ if and only if $w_1 \sqsubseteq^a w_2$ (pointwise) and $d_1 \sqsubseteq^a d_2$. The map α^D is expanded to $\mathcal{T}_\tau^{co}$ as $\alpha^D(\langle w, \eta\rangle) = \langle \lambda l.\alpha^{D_{\tau_l}}(w(l)), \alpha^{D_\tau}(\eta)\rangle$.

Definition 12. Let $\tau \in Typing$. The union-reductions of $d \in D_\tau$ are

$$\rho(d) = \{S \in \wp(D_\tau) \mid \gamma^D(d) = \cup_{d' \in S}\gamma^D(d') \text{ and } \#\rho(d') = 1 \text{ for every } d' \in S\} .$$

If $\#\rho(d) = 1$ (i.e., $\rho(d) = \{\{d\}\}$) we say that d is union-irreducible. If every $d \in D_\tau$ is such that $\rho(d) \neq \emptyset$, we say that D_τ is union-reducible.

Proposition 9. Assume that D_τ is union-reducible for every $\tau \in Typing$. Given $n \geq 1$ and $\tau_1, \ldots, \tau_n, \tau' \in Typing$, let $A_{\tau_1,\ldots,\tau_n,\tau'}$ be

$$\left\{ a \in D_{\tau_1} \mapsto \cdots D_{\tau_n} \mapsto D_{\tau'} \,\middle|\, \begin{array}{l} a \text{ is monotonic and given } 1 \leq i \leq n \text{ and } S \in \rho(d_i) \\ a(d_1)\cdots(d_i)\cdots(d_n) = \sqcup_{d' \in S}^{D_{\tau'}} a(d_1)\cdots(d')\cdots(d_n) \end{array} \right\}, \quad (6)$$

i.e., denotations in $A_{\tau_1,\ldots,\tau_n,\tau'}$ are identified by the union-irreducible elements. Let $\alpha^a : CO_{\tau_1,\ldots,\tau_n,\tau'} \mapsto A_{\tau_1,\ldots,\tau_n,\tau'}$ be $\alpha^a(co) = \alpha^D co \gamma^D$. The set $A_{\tau_1,\ldots,\tau_n,\tau'}$ is a complete lattice with bottom $\lambda d_1 \ldots \lambda d_n.\langle \bot, \bot_{D_{\tau'}}\rangle$ and α^a is well-defined, onto, strict and additive (hence, the abstraction map of a Galois insertion).

Proposition 10. Assume that D_τ is union-reducible for every $\tau \in Typing$. The operations in Figure 8 are the best approximations over A of those in Figure 6 (note that $\circ^a$ is not the composition of functions).

In conclusion, given a union-reducible abstraction D_τ of $\wp(\Sigma_\tau)$ for every $\tau \in Typing$, and the best approximations over D of the powerset extension of the operations of Figure 1 (used in $[op]^a$) and of $\cup$, we obtain an abstract watchpoint semantics, correct w.r.t. the collecting watchpoint semantics of Subsection 5.2. As said before, similar results can be obtained in the more general case of non-union-reducible lattices by using the functional partitioning technique of [1].

7   Implementation

We describe here our implementation in Prolog of the watchpoint semantics of Sections 5 and 6 instantiated with sign analysis. It can be downloaded from http://www.sci.univr.it/~spoto/watch.tar.gz. We have chosen Prolog for fast prototyping, and sign analysis because it is a well-known, simple analysis.

$$\mathrm{nop}_\tau^s(\varsigma) = \varsigma \qquad\qquad (\mathrm{get\_int}_\tau^i)^s(\varsigma) = \begin{cases} \varsigma[+/res] & \text{if } i \geq 0 \\ \varsigma[-/res] & \text{if } i < 0 \end{cases}$$

$$(\mathrm{get\_var}_\tau^v)^s(\varsigma) = \varsigma[\varsigma(v)/res] \qquad (\mathrm{put\_var}_\tau^v)^s(\varsigma) = \varsigma[\varsigma(res)/v]|_{-res}$$

$$=_\tau^s(\varsigma_1)(\varsigma_2) = \begin{cases} \varsigma_2[-/res] & \text{if } \varsigma_1(res) = - \\ & \text{and } \varsigma_2(res) = + \\ & \text{or vice versa} \\ \varsigma_2[u/res] & \text{otherwise} \end{cases} \qquad +_\tau^s(\varsigma_1)(\varsigma_2) = \begin{cases} \varsigma_2[+/res] & \text{if } \varsigma_1(res) = \varsigma_2(res) = + \\ \varsigma_2[-/res] & \text{if } \varsigma_1(res) = \varsigma_2(res) = - \\ \varsigma_2[u/res] & \text{otherwise} \end{cases}$$

$$(\mathrm{scope}_\tau^{f,v_1,\ldots,v_n})^s(\varsigma) = [\iota_1 \mapsto \varsigma(v_1), \ldots, \iota_n \mapsto \varsigma(v_n)] \quad \text{where } \langle \iota_1, \ldots, \iota_n \rangle = p(f).s \setminus f$$

$$(\mathrm{unscope}_\tau^f)^s(\varsigma_1)(\varsigma_2) = \varsigma_1[\varsigma_2(f)/res] \qquad (\mathrm{restrict}_\tau^{vs})^s(\varsigma) = \varsigma|_{-vs} \qquad (\mathrm{expand}_\tau^{v:t})^s(\varsigma) = \varsigma[+/v]$$

$$\mathrm{is\_true}_\tau^s(\varsigma) = \begin{cases} \mathrm{empty} & \text{if } \varsigma(res) = - \\ \varsigma[+/res] & \text{otherwise} \end{cases} \qquad \mathrm{is\_false}_\tau^s(\varsigma) = \begin{cases} \mathrm{empty} & \text{if } \varsigma(res) = + \\ \varsigma[-/res] & \text{otherwise} \end{cases}$$

$$\cup_\tau^s(\mathrm{empty})(x) = \cup_\tau^s(x)(\mathrm{empty}) = x \qquad \cup_\tau^s(\varsigma_1)(\varsigma_2) = \lambda v \in \mathrm{dom}(\tau). \begin{cases} \varsigma_1(v) & \text{if } \varsigma_1(v) = \varsigma_2(v) \\ u & \text{otherwise.} \end{cases}$$

Fig. 9. The abstract operations over the domain of signs.

The module `analyser.pl` implements the fixpoint calculation (Figure 3 and Definition 7) by using the semantic operations (Figures 7 and 8) implemented in the module `semantic.pl`. The module `typing.pl` manipulates typings. The module `domain.pl` implements the abstract counterparts of the operations of Figure 1. Only this module depends from the domain of analysis.

Our domain for sign analysis is similar to that in [6].

Definition 13. *For every* $\tau \in \mathit{Typing}$, *let* $S_\tau = \{\mathrm{empty}\} \cup \{\varsigma : \mathrm{dom}(\tau) \mapsto \{+, -, u\}\}$. *The abstraction map* $\alpha : \wp(\Sigma_\tau) \mapsto S_\tau$ *is such that, for* $X \neq \emptyset$ *and* $v \in \mathrm{dom}(\tau)$,

$$\alpha(\emptyset) = \mathrm{empty} \qquad \alpha(X)(v) = \begin{cases} + & \text{if } \sigma(v) \geq 0 \text{ for every } \sigma \in X \\ - & \text{if } \sigma(v) < 0 \text{ for every } \sigma \in X \\ u & \text{otherwise.} \end{cases}$$

Let $\leq$ *be reflexive and let* $+ \leq u$ *and* $- \leq u$. *The set* S_τ *is ordered as* $\mathrm{empty} \sqsubseteq^s s$ *for every* $s \in S_\tau$ *and* $\varsigma_1 \sqsubseteq^s \varsigma_2$ *if and only if* $\varsigma_1(v) \leq \varsigma_2(v)$ *for every* $v \in \mathrm{dom}(\tau)$. *The optimal counterparts over* S *of the powerset extension of the operations in Fig. 1 are (all but* $\cup^s$*) strict on* empty. *Otherwise, they are given in Figure 9.*

Given $\tau \in \mathit{Typing}$, the union-irreducible elements of S_τ are empty and those $\varsigma \in S_\tau$ such that $\varsigma(v) \neq u$ for every $v \in \mathrm{dom}(\tau)$. If $\varsigma(v) = u$ for some $v \in \mathrm{dom}(\tau)$, instead, the concretisation of ς can be shown to be the union of the concretisations of $\varsigma[+/v]$ and $\varsigma[-/v]$. Therefore, we have

$$\rho(\mathrm{empty}) = \{\mathrm{empty}\} \qquad \rho(\varsigma) = \left\{ \varsigma' \;\middle|\; \begin{array}{l} \text{for all } v \in \mathrm{dom}(\tau) \text{ we have } \varsigma'(v) \neq u \\ \text{and if } \varsigma(v) \neq u \text{ then } \varsigma(v) = \varsigma'(v) \end{array} \right\}.$$

By the results of Section 6, the abstract denotations are maps whose domain is made of empty and of all ς which never bind a variable to u. The values for the other elements of S_τ are induced.

$\mathcal{F} = \{\texttt{fib}\}$

$p(\texttt{fib}) = \langle\langle\texttt{fib}, \texttt{n}\rangle, [\texttt{fib} \mapsto int, \texttt{n} \mapsto int]\rangle$

$c(\texttt{fib}) =$ if $(\texttt{n} =< 1)$ then
    %watchpoint(p1);
    fib := 1
  else
    %watchpoint(p2);
    let n1 : int in let n2 : int in
    %watchpoint(p3);
    n1 := n − 1;
    %watchpoint(p4);
    n2 := n − 2;
    %watchpoint(p5);
    fib := fib(n1) + fib(n2);
  %watchpoint(p6)

(a)

```
| ? − interpret.
Analysing [fib] : iteration 1
Analysing [fib] : iteration 2
fixpoint reached

Procedure : fib

Input : empty Output : empty
Watchpoints : p3 : empty

Input : [+] Output : [+]
Watchpoints : p3 : [+, +, +, +]

Input : [−] Output : [+]
Watchpoints : p3 : empty
```

(b)

Fig. 10. The Fibonacci procedure and one of its possible analyses.

Elements of S_τ are implemented as the term empty or lists of +, − and u, ordered alphabetically w.r.t. the names in $\text{dom}(\tau)$. For instance, if $\tau = [a \mapsto int, c \mapsto int, b \mapsto int]$ then $\varsigma = [a \mapsto +, c \mapsto −, b \mapsto u]$ is implemented as [+,u,-]. We are aware of cleverer implementations, but in this paper we focus on the semantics.

The input of the analyser is a Prolog term which represents the abstract syntax of a program. Figure 10(a) shows a program for the n-th Fibonacci number, with six possible watchpoints. The file fib.pl contains its abstract syntax. We download it with [fib]. and we analyse it with interpret. Figure 10(b) shows the result when only watchpoint p_3 is not commented. The input of fib is the value of n, its output is the value of the variable fib at its end. As you can see, if we start with an empty set of states we never reach watchpoint p_3. If we start with a state where n is positive, the output is positive and we reach watchpoint p_3 with a state where fib, n, n1 and n2 are positive. Indeed the initial value of a variable is 0 and in the else branch we have $n > 1$. Finally, if we start with a state where n is negative, the output is positive and watchpoint p_3 is never reached. Indeed, if $n < 0$ the then branch is executed. If we start with an unknown value for n we would obtain the least upper bound of the last two cases.

7.1   The Costs in Space and in Time of the Analysis

To estimate the space used by our analyser independently from its implementation, we count the number of Prolog atoms contained in the denotations it computes (*weight*). Fig. 11 gives the weight for the analysis of fib (Fig. 10(a)) and pi (a Monte Carlo algorithm computing π), as a function of the number of active watchpoints. For now, consider only the lines marked with *Abstract Interpretation*. Horizontally, an integer like 3 means that only watchpoints p_1, p_2 and p_3 were active. As you can see, the weight grows with the number of active watchpoints. When passing from 0 watchpoints to 1 watchpoint in Fig. 11(a)

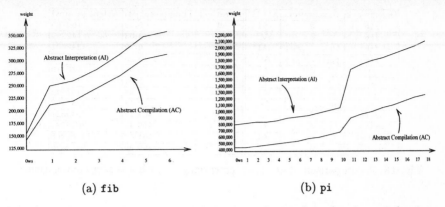

Fig. 11. The cost in space of the analysis w.r.t. the number of active watchpoints.

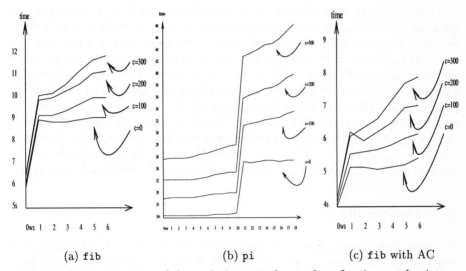

Fig. 12. The cost in time of the analysis w.r.t. the number of active watchpoints.

and from 10 watchpoints to 11 in Fig. 11(b) one more iteration is needed to reach the fixpoint. Thus less watchpoints *does* mean less iterations (Subs. 5.1).

We expect the time of the analysis to grow with the number of watchpoints, proportionally with the cost of the abstract join (Subs. 5.1). Fig. 12 confirms this. The constant c is a fictitious cost added to the computation of the join. Note that domains more realistic than signs usually feature complex joins. Note again the jump when one more iteration is needed for the fixpoint calculation. The benchmark `nested` shows the same behaviour of Fig. 12. But if a benchmark does not contain recursive predicates nor conditionals nor iterative constructs, then the time for its analysis is independent from the number of watchpoints, like for `arith`, whose abstract execution tree is actually a finite trace.

Note that [4], [5] and [15] do not provide a link to an implementation.

Benchmark	Watchpoints	AI/AC	Iterations	Time (seconds)	Weight (atoms)
fib	$\emptyset$	AI	2	5.92	160795
fib	$\emptyset$	AC	2	4.03	142299
fib	$\{p_1,\ldots,p_6\}$	AI	3	9.19	349631
fib	$\{p_1,\ldots,p_6\}$	AC	3	5.28	305363
pi	$\emptyset$	AI	2	16.61	833419
pi	$\emptyset$	AC	2	8.91	463294
pi	$\{p_1,\ldots,p_{18}\}$	AI	3	25.93	2107643
pi	$\{p_1,\ldots,p_{18}\}$	AC	3	10.58	1287127
arith	$\emptyset$	AI	1	303.12	7049327
arith	$\emptyset$	AC	1	308.42	7049327
nested	$\emptyset$	AI	3	661.43	14253268
nested	$\emptyset$	AC	3	369.99	8419626

Fig. 13. A comparison of abstract interpretation with abstract compilation.

7.2 Abstract Compilation

In Figure 10(a) we note that the denotation of the `then` branch is independent from the partial denotation computed for `fib`. Thus, it does not need to be computed at every iteration, like, instead, that of the `else` branch, which contains two calls to `fib`. However, its first part, till the watchpoint p_5, does not contain recursive calls, and can be safely analysed only once. Those optimisations are examples of abstract compilation (AC). Our analyser uses AC by invoking the goal `compile`. The result is like that in Figure 10(b), with smaller space and time costs, as Figures 11 and 12(c) show for weight (space) and time, respectively. Moreover, Figure 12(c) shows that the time still depends from the number of watchpoints and the cost of the join. Finally, Figure 13 shows that AC leads very often to major improvements, but is of no help with the *flat* benchmark `arith`.

8 Conclusions

We have shown that, if we are interested in the analysis of a program in a small set of *watchpoints*, it is worth abstracting a trace semantics in a lighter, compositional and still as precise *watchpoint semantics*. We have shown through an implementation that it is *focussed*, i.e., its complexity grows with the number of watchpoints, and that abstract compilation improves significantly the fixpoint calculation.

The analysis process is defined as a fixpoint computation. For better efficiency, if a set of call patterns is known for some functions, this computation can be done *on demand*, simulating a top-down analysis. This means that the abstract denotations are enriched at fixpoint computation time whenever the behaviour of a function for a new input is needed.

Our results apply to the modular analysis of large programs and to the analysis inside smart cards, where memory requirements must be kept small.

References

1. F. Bourdoncle. Abstract Interpretation by Dynamic Partitioning. *Journal of Functional Programming*, 2(4):407–423, 1992.
2. F. Bourdoncle. Abstract Debugging of High-Order Imperative Languages. In *Proceedings of the 1993 SIGPLAN Conference on Programming Language Design and Implementation*, pages 46–55, Albuquerque, New Mexico, June 1993. ACM Press.
3. M. Codish and B. Demoen. Deriving Polymorphic Type Dependencies for Logic Programs Using Multiple Incarnations of Prop. In *Proc. of the first International Symposium on Static Analysis*, volume 864 of *Lecture Notes in Computer Science*, pages 281–296. Springer-Verlag, 1994.
4. C. Colby and P. Lee. Trace-based Program Analysis. In *Proc. of POPL'96*, pages 195–207, St. Petersburg, FLA, USA, January 1996. ACM Press.
5. P. Cousot. Constructive Design of a Hierarchy of Semantics of a Transition System by Abstract Interpretation. In S. Brookes and M. Mislove, editors, *Proc. of the 13th Conf. on Mathematical Foundations of Programming Semantics (MFPS XIII)*, volume 6 of *Electronic Notes on Theoretical Computer Science*, Pittsburgh, PA, USA, March 1997. Elsevier Science Publishers. Available at `http://www.elsevier.nl/locate/entcs/volume6.html`.
6. P. Cousot and R. Cousot. Abstract Interpretation: A Unified Lattice Model for Static Analysis of Programs by Construction or Approximation of Fixpoints. In *Proc. of POPL'77*, pages 238–252, 1977.
7. P. Cousot and R. Cousot. Systematic Design of Program Analysis Frameworks. In *6th ACM Symp. on Principles of Programming Languages*, pages 269–282, 1979.
8. E. Duesterwald, R. Gupta, and M. Soffa. Demand-Driven Computation of Interprocedural Data Flow. In *Proceedings of POPL'95*, pages 37–48, San Francisco, CA, January 1995.
9. E. Duesterwald, R. Gupta, and M. Soffa. A Practical Framework for Demand-Driven Interprocedural Data Flow Analysis. *TOPLAS*, 19(6):992–1030, 1997.
10. M. Gabbrielli, G. Levi, and M. C. Meo. Resultants Semantics for PROLOG. *Journal of Logic and Computation*, 6(4):491–521, 1995.
11. M. Hermenegildo, W. Warren, and S.K. Debray. Global Flow Analysis as a Practical Compilation Tool. *Journal of Logic Programming*, 13(2 & 3):349–366, 1992.
12. F. Nielson, H. R. Nielson, and C. Hankin. *Principles of Program Analysis*. Springer-Verlag, 1999.
13. T. Reps, S. Horwitz, and M. Sagiv. Precise Interprocedural Dataflow Analysis via Graph Reachability. In *Proceedings of POPL'95*, pages 49–61, San Francisco, CA, January 1995.
14. M. Sagiv, T. Reps, and R. Wilhelm. Solving Shape-Analysis Problems in Languages with Destructive Updates. In *Proc. of POPL'96*, pages 16–31, St. Petersburg, FLA, USA, January 1996. ACM Press.
15. D. A. Schmidt. Trace-based Abstract Interpretation of Operational Semantics. *Journal of LISP and Symbolic Computation*, 10(3):237–271, 1998.
16. G. Winskel. *The Formal Semantics of Programming Languages*. The MIT Press, 1993.

Parameterizing a Groundness Analysis of Logic Programs

Lunjin Lu

Department of Computer Science and Engineering
Oakland University, Rochester, MI 48309, USA
l2lu@oakland.edu
Phone: +248-370-2225, FAX: +248-370-4625

Abstract. We present a parametric groundness analysis whose input and output are parameterized by a set of groundness parameters. The result of the analysis can be instantiated for different uses of the program. It can also be used to derive sufficient conditions for safely removing groundness checks for built-in calls in the program. The parametric groundness analysis is obtained by generalizing a non-parametric groundness analysis that uses the abstract domain Con. It is shown to be as precise as the non-parametric groundness analysis for any possible values for the groundness parameters. Experimental results of a prototype implementation of the parametric groundness analysis are given.
Keywords: Abstract Interpretation, Groundness Analysis, Logic programs.

1 Introduction

In logic programming [30, 1], a real world problem is modeled as a set of axioms and a general execution mechanism is used to solve the problem. While this allows a problem to be solved in a natural and declarative manner, the general execution mechanism incurs a performance penalty for most programs. This motivated much research into semantic based analysis of logic programs [20]. Groundness analysis is one of the most important analyses for logic programs. It provides answers to questions such as whether, at a program point, a variable is definitely bound to a ground term - a term that contains no variables. This is useful not only to an optimizing compiler but also to other program manipulation tools. There have been many methods proposed for groundness analysis [36, 43, 22, 6, 14, 46, 17, 34, 17, 2, 3, 29, 25, 9, 8, 44].

This paper presents a new groundness analysis whose input and output are parameterized by a number of groundness parameters, hence called parametric groundness analysis. These parameters represent groundness information that is not available before analysis but can be provided after analysis. Providing such information *instantiates* the result of analysis. Instantiability implies reusability. A program module such as a library program can be analyzed once and the result be instantiated for different uses of the program module. This improves the efficiency of analysis. Instantiability also makes the new groundness analysis

P. Cousot (Ed.): SAS 2001, LNCS 2126, pp. 146–164, 2001.

amenable to program modifications since modules that are not changed need not be re-analyzed. Groundness parameters in the input and the output of the new groundness analysis makes it easier to derive a sufficient condition under which groundness checks for built-in calls in the program can be safely removed.

The parametric groundness analysis is obtained by generalizing a groundness analysis based on the abstract domain Con [43]. Con is the least precise abstract domain for groundness analysis. The parametric groundness analysis is thus less precise than a groundness analysis that uses a more precise abstract domain namely Pos [34], Def [22] or EPos [24]. However, a Con-based groundness analysis is much more efficient than groundness analyzers based on more precise abstract domains. By generalizing a Con-based groundness analysis, we obtain a parametric groundness analysis that is more efficient and scalable.

The parametric groundness analysis is performed by abstract interpretation [18, 19]. Abstract interpretation is a methodology for static program analysis whereby a program analysis is viewed as the execution of the program over a nonstandard data domain. A number of frameworks have been brought about for abstract interpretation of logic programs [37, 5, 6, 27, 28, 35, 39, 33]. An abstract interpretation framework is an analysis engine that takes care of algorithmic issues that are common to a class of analyses, allowing the designer of an analysis to focus on issues that are specific to the analysis. This greatly simplifies the design and the presentation of a new analysis. The parametric groundness analysis will be presented in the abstract interpretation framework in [31]. The adaptation to other frameworks [37, 5, 6, 27, 28, 35, 39, 33] can be easily made.

The remainder of the paper is organized as follows. Section 2 gives motivation for the parametric groundness analysis through an example. Section 3 gives basic notations and briefly describes the abstract interpretation framework in [31]. Section 4 reformulates a non-parametric groundness analysis that is generalized in section 5 to obtain the new groundness analysis. Section 6 provides performance results of a prototype implementation. In section 7, we compare our work with related work. Section 8 concludes the paper. Proofs are omitted due to space limit.

2 Motivation

In groundness analysis, we are interested in knowing which variables will be definitely instantiated to ground terms and which variables are not when the execution of the program reaches a program point. We use g and u to represent these two groundness modes of a variable. Let $MO \overset{def}{=} \{g, u\}$ and $\trianglelefteq$ be defined as $g \trianglelefteq g$, $g \trianglelefteq u$ and $u \trianglelefteq u$. $\langle MO, \trianglelefteq \rangle$ is a complete lattice with infimum g and supremum u. Let ∇ and $\triangle$ be the least upper bound and the greatest lower bound operators on $\langle MO, \trianglelefteq \rangle$ respectively.

Example 1. Consider the program and the initial goal in Figure 1. Let $\textcircled{a} : Q \implies \textcircled{b} : R$ denote that if Q holds at the program point $\textcircled{a}$ then R holds whenever the execution reaches the program point $\textcircled{b}$. Let $X \mapsto m$ denote that the groundness

$\leftarrow$ ⓐ $treesort(Li, Lo)$. ⓑ

$treesort(Li, Lo) \leftarrow list\_to\_tree(Li, T), tree\_to\_list(T, Lo)$.

$insert(I, void, tr(I, void, void))$.
$insert(I, tr(E, L, R), tr(E, Ln, R)) \leftarrow$ ⓒ $I < E, insert(I, L, Ln)$.
$insert(I, tr(E, L, R), tr(E, L, Rn)) \leftarrow$ ⓓ $I >= E, insert(I, R, Rn)$.

$insert\_list([H|L], T, Tn) \leftarrow insert(H, T, Tm), insert\_list(L, Tm, Tn)$.
$insert\_list([], T, T)$.

$list\_to\_tree(L, T) \leftarrow insert\_list(L, void, T)$.

$tree\_to\_list(T, L) \leftarrow tree\_to\_list\_aux(T, [], L)$.

$tree\_to\_list\_aux(void, L, L)$.
$tree\_to\_list\_aux(tr(I, L, R), O, N) \leftarrow$
$\qquad\qquad tree\_to\_list\_aux(R, O, L1), tree\_to\_list\_aux(L, [I|L1], N)$.

Fig. 1. The treesort program from [21]. Circled letters are not part of the program but locate program points.

mode of X is m. A groundness analysis infers the following statements.

$$ⓐ : (Li \mapsto \mathsf{g}) \wedge (Lo \mapsto \mathsf{g}) \Longrightarrow ⓒ : (I \mapsto \mathsf{g}) \wedge (E \mapsto \mathsf{g})$$
$$ⓐ : (Li \mapsto \mathsf{g}) \wedge (Lo \mapsto \mathsf{u}) \Longrightarrow ⓒ : (I \mapsto \mathsf{g}) \wedge (E \mapsto \mathsf{g})$$
$$ⓐ : (Li \mapsto \mathsf{u}) \wedge (Lo \mapsto \mathsf{g}) \Longrightarrow ⓒ : (I \mapsto \mathsf{u}) \wedge (E \mapsto \mathsf{u})$$
$$ⓐ : (Li \mapsto \mathsf{u}) \wedge (Lo \mapsto \mathsf{u}) \Longrightarrow ⓒ : (I \mapsto \mathsf{u}) \wedge (E \mapsto \mathsf{u})$$

These statements must be inferred independently from each other. The groundness of I and E at the point ⓒ depends on the groundness of Li and Lo at the point ⓐ in such a way that I and E are ground at point ⓒ iff Li is ground at point ⓐ. Thus, it will be desirable to have a groundness analysis which infers the following statement

$$ⓐ : (Li \mapsto \alpha) \wedge (Lo \mapsto \beta) \Longrightarrow ⓒ : (I \mapsto \alpha) \wedge (E \mapsto \alpha) \qquad (1)$$

where α and β are groundness parameters ranging over MO. ∎

Such an analysis is parametric in the sense that its input ⓐ $: (Li \mapsto \alpha) \wedge (Lo \mapsto \beta)$ and its output ⓒ $: (I \mapsto \alpha) \wedge (E \mapsto \alpha)$ are parameterized.

Statement (1) can be instantiated as follows. When the parameters α and β are assigned groundness modes from MO, the groundness of Li and Lo at the point ⓐ and the groundness of I and E at the point ⓒ are obtained by instantiation. The first statement inferred by the non-parametric groundness analysis is obtained from (1) by assigning g to both α and β. Instantiations can be made for four different assignments of groundness modes to α and β.

Statement (1) can also be used to infer a sufficient condition on α and β under which the run-time check on the groundness of I and E in the built-in call $I < E$ at the point ⓒ can be safely removed. Specifically, if α is assigned g then the run-time check can be safely removed. With a non-parametric groundness analysis, one needs to analyze the program for four times to infer the sufficient condition.

3   Preliminaries

Lattice Theory. A poset is a tuple $\langle A, \sqsubseteq \rangle$ where A is a set and $\sqsubseteq$ is a reflexive, anti-symmetric and transitive relation on A. Let $B \subseteq A$ and $u \in A$. u is an upper bound of B if $b \sqsubseteq u$ for each $b \in B$. u is a least upper bound of B if $u \sqsubseteq u'$ for any upper bound u' of B. The least upper bound of B, if exists, is unique and denoted $\sqcup B$. Lower bounds and the greatest lower bound are defined dually. $\sqcap B$ denotes the greatest lower bound of B.

A complete lattice is a poset $\langle A, \sqsubseteq \rangle$ such that $\sqcup B$ and $\sqcap B$ exist for any $B \subseteq A$. A complete lattice is denoted $\langle A, \sqsubseteq, \bot, \top, \sqcap, \sqcup \rangle$ where $\bot \overset{def}{=} \sqcup \emptyset$ and $\top \overset{def}{=} \sqcap \emptyset$. Let $\langle A, \sqsubseteq, \bot, \top, \sqcap, \sqcup \rangle$ be a complete lattice and $B \subseteq A$. B is a Moore family if $\top \in B$ and $(x_1 \sqcap x_2) \in B$ for any $x_1 \in B$ and $x_2 \in B$.

Let $\langle A, \sqsubseteq_A \rangle$ and $\langle B, \sqsubseteq_B \rangle$ be two posets. A function $f : A \mapsto B$ is monotonic if $f(a_1) \sqsubseteq_B f(a_2)$ for any $a_1 \in A$ and $a_2 \in A$ such that $a_1 \sqsubseteq_A a_2$. Let $X \subseteq A$. We define $f(X) \overset{def}{=} \{f(x) \mid x \in X\}$. We sometimes use Church's lambda notation for functions, so that a function f will be denoted $\lambda x.f(x)$.

Logic Programming. Let Σ be a set of *function symbols*, Π a set of *predicate symbols*, $\mathcal{V}$ a denumerable set of variables and $\mathcal{U} \subseteq \mathcal{V}$. The set $\mathcal{T}_{\Sigma,\mathcal{U}}$ of *terms* over Σ and $\mathcal{U}$ is the smallest set containing x in $\mathcal{U}$ and $f(t_1, \cdots, t_n)$ with $f/n \in \Sigma$, $n \geq 0$ and $t_i \in \mathcal{T}_{\Sigma,\mathcal{U}}$ for $1 \leq i \leq n$. The set $\mathcal{A}_{\Pi,\Sigma,\mathcal{U}}$ of *atoms* over Π and $\mathcal{T}_{\Sigma,\mathcal{U}}$ consists of $p(t_1, \cdots, t_n)$ with $p/n \in \Pi$, $n \geq 0$ and $t_i \in \mathcal{T}_{\Sigma,\mathcal{U}}$ for $1 \leq i \leq n$. Let $vars(O)$ denote the set of variables in O. A substitution is a mapping $\theta : \mathcal{V} \mapsto \mathcal{T}_{\Sigma,\mathcal{V}}$ such that $\{x \in \mathcal{V} \mid x \neq \theta(x)\}$, denoted $dom(\theta)$, is finite. The range of θ is $range(\theta) \overset{def}{=} \cup_{X \in dom(\theta)} vars(\theta(X))$. $\theta \lceil \mathcal{U}$ is a substitution such that $(\theta \lceil \mathcal{U})(x) = \theta(x)$ for $x \in \mathcal{U}$ and $(\theta \lceil \mathcal{U})(x) = x$ for $x \notin \mathcal{U}$. A substitution $\theta : \mathcal{V} \mapsto \mathcal{T}_{\Sigma,\mathcal{V}}$ is uniquely extended to a homomorphism $\theta : \mathcal{T}_{\Sigma,\mathcal{V}} \mapsto \mathcal{T}_{\Sigma,\mathcal{V}}$. A renaming substitution is a bijective mapping from $\mathcal{V}$ to $\mathcal{V}$. Let Sub be the set of idempotent substitutions.

An *equation* is a formula $l = r$ where either $l, r \in \mathcal{T}_{\Sigma,\mathcal{V}}$ or $l, r \in \mathcal{A}_{\Pi,\Sigma,\mathcal{V}}$. The set of all equations is denoted Eqn. For a set of equations $E \in \wp(\mathsf{Eqn})$, a unifier of E is a substitution such that $\theta(l) = \theta(r)$ for each $(l = r) \in E$. E is called unifiable if E has a unifier. A unifier θ of E is a most general unifier if for any other unifier σ of E there is a substitution η such that $\sigma = \eta \circ \theta$ where $\circ$ denotes function composition. All most general unifiers of E are equivalent modulo renaming. Let $mgu : \wp(\text{Eqn}) \mapsto Sub \cup \{fail\}$ return either a most general unifier for E if E is unifiable or $fail$ otherwise. $mgu(\{l = r\})$ is also written as $mgu(l, r)$. Let $\theta \circ fail \overset{def}{=} fail$ and $fail \circ \theta \overset{def}{=} fail$ for any $\theta \in Sub \cup \{fail\}$.

Let VI be the set of variables of interest. VI is usually the set of the variables occurring in the program. We will use a fixed renaming substitution Ψ such that $\Psi(VI) \cap VI = \emptyset$. Ψ is called a tagging substitution in [38].

Abstract Interpretation. Two semantics of the program are involved in abstract interpretation. One is called concrete and the other abstract. In a compositional definition of semantics, the concrete semantics is defined in terms of a group of semantic functions $f_i : D_i \mapsto E_i$ and the abstract semantics is defined in terms of another group of semantic function $f_i^{\sharp} : D_i^{\sharp} \mapsto E_i^{\sharp}$ such that each abstract semantic function $f_i^{\sharp}$ simulates its corresponding concrete semantic function f_i. To prove the correctness of the abstract semantics (the program analysis) with respect to the concrete semantics is reduced to proving the correctness of each abstract semantic function $f_i^{\sharp}$ with respect to its corresponding concrete semantic function f_i. The latter can be done using the Moore family approach [19] when concrete domains D_i and E_i are complete lattices. Let $\gamma_{D_i^{\sharp}} : D_i^{\sharp} \mapsto D_i$ and $\gamma_{E_i^{\sharp}} : E_i^{\sharp} \mapsto E_i$ be monotonic functions such that $\gamma_{D_i^{\sharp}}(D_i^{\sharp})$ and $\gamma_{E_i^{\sharp}}(E_i^{\sharp})$ are Moore families. Then $f_i^{\sharp} : D_i^{\sharp} \mapsto E_i^{\sharp}$ is correct with respect to $f_i : D_i \mapsto E_i$ iff $f_i(\gamma_{D_i^{\sharp}}(x^{\sharp})) \sqsubseteq_{E_i} \gamma_{E_i^{\sharp}}(f_i^{\sharp}(x^{\sharp}))$ for each $x^{\sharp} \in D_i^{\sharp}$.

Abstract Interpretation Framework. The abstract interpretation framework in [31] which we use to present the parametric groundness analysis is based on a concrete semantics of logic programs that is defined in terms of two operators on $(\wp(Sub), \subseteq)$. One is the set union $\cup$ and the other is $UNIFY$ defined as follows. Let $a_1, a_2 \in A_{\Pi, \Sigma, VI}$ and $\Theta_1, \Theta_2 \in \wp(Sub)$.

$$UNIFY(a_1, \Theta_1, a_2, \Theta_2) = \{unify(a_1, \theta_1, a_2, \theta_2) \neq fail \mid \theta_1 \in \Theta_1 \wedge \theta_2 \in \Theta_2\}$$

where $unify(a_1, \theta_1, a_2, \theta_2) \overset{def}{=} mgu(\rho(\theta_1(a_1)), \theta_2(a_2)) \circ \theta_2$ and ρ is a renaming substitution satisfying $(vars(\theta_1) \cup vars(a_1)) \cap (vars(\theta_2) \cup vars(a_2)) = \emptyset$.

Specializing the framework for a program analysis consists in designing an abstract domain $\langle ASub, \sqsubseteq \rangle$, a monotonic function $\gamma_{ASub} : ASub \mapsto \wp(Sub)$ such that $\gamma_{ASub}(ASub)$ is a Moore family and an abstract operator $AUNIFY$ on $\langle ASub, \sqsubseteq \rangle$ such that, for any $a_1, a_2 \in A_{\Pi, \Sigma, VI}$ and any $\pi_1, \pi_2 \in ASub$,

$$UNIFY(a_1, \gamma_{ASub}(\pi_1), a_2, \gamma_{ASub}(\pi_2)) \subseteq \gamma_{ASub}(AUNIFY(a_1, \pi_1, a_2, \pi_2))$$

since monotonicity of γ_{ASub} implies that $\gamma_{ASub}(\pi_1) \cup \gamma_{ASub}(\pi_2) \subseteq \gamma_{ASub}(\pi_1 \sqcup \pi_2)$ where $\sqcup$ is the least upper bound operator on $\langle ASub, \sqsubseteq \rangle$. Elements of $ASub$ are called abstract substitutions since they describe sets of substitutions. The abstract operator $AUNIFY$ is called abstract unification operator as its main functionality is to simulate unification.

4   Non-parametric Groundness Analysis

This section reformulates the groundness analysis presented in [43] that uses the abstract domain for groundness proposed in [36]. The reformulated groundness analysis will be used in section 5 to obtain the parametric groundness analysis.

4.1   Abstract Domain

A set of substitutions is described by associating each variable in VI with a groundness mode from MO. The abstract domain is thus $\langle \mathsf{Con}, \sqsubseteq_{\mathsf{Con}} \rangle$ where $\mathsf{Con} \overset{def}{=} VI \mapsto \mathsf{MO}$ and $\sqsubseteq_{\mathsf{Con}}$ is the pointwise extension of $\unlhd$.[1] $(\mathsf{Con}, \sqsubseteq_{\mathsf{Con}})$ is a complete lattice. The set of substitutions described by an abstract substitution in Con is given by a function $\gamma_{\mathsf{Con}} : \mathsf{Con} \mapsto \wp(\mathsf{Sub})$ defined as follows.

$$\gamma_{\mathsf{Con}}(\theta^{\sharp}) \overset{def}{=} \{\theta \mid \forall X \in VI.((\theta^{\sharp}(X) = \mathsf{g}) \to (vars(\theta(X)) = \emptyset)\}$$

γ_{Con} is a monotonic function from $\langle \mathsf{Con}, \sqsubseteq_{\mathsf{Con}} \rangle$ to $\langle \wp(\mathsf{Sub}), \subseteq \rangle$. A substitution θ is said to satisfy an abstract substitution $\theta^{\sharp}$ if $\theta \in \gamma_{\mathsf{Con}}(\theta^{\sharp})$.

The abstract unification operator for the non-parametric groundness analysis also deals with groundness of renamed variables. Let $VI^{\dagger} \overset{def}{=} VI \cup \Psi(VI)$. We define $\mathsf{Con}^{\dagger} \overset{def}{=} VI^{\dagger} \mapsto \mathsf{MO}$ and $\gamma_{\mathsf{Con}}^{\dagger}(\theta^{\sharp}) \overset{def}{=} \{\theta \mid \forall X \in VI^{\dagger}.((\theta^{\sharp}(X) = \mathsf{g}) \to (vars(\theta(X)) = \emptyset)\}$.

Lemma 1. $\gamma_{\mathsf{Con}}(\mathsf{Con})$ and $\gamma_{\mathsf{Con}}^{\dagger}(\mathsf{Con}^{\dagger})$ are Moore families.   ∎

4.2   Abstract Unification

Algorithm 1 defines the abstract unification operator $AUNIFY_{\mathsf{Con}}$ for the non-parametric groundness analysis. Given $\theta^{\sharp}, \sigma^{\sharp} \in \mathsf{Con}$ and $a_1, a_2 \in A_{\Pi, \Sigma, VI}$, the renaming substitution Ψ is first applied to a_1 and $\theta^{\sharp}$ to obtain $\Psi(a_1)$ and $\Psi(\theta^{\sharp})$, and $\Psi(\theta^{\sharp})$ and $\sigma^{\sharp}$ are combined to obtain $\zeta^{\sharp} = \Psi(\theta^{\sharp}) \cup \sigma^{\sharp}$. Note that $\zeta^{\sharp} \in \mathsf{Con}^{\dagger}$ and a substitution satisfying $\zeta^{\sharp}$ satisfies both $\Psi(\theta^{\sharp})$ and $\sigma^{\sharp}$. $E_0 = mgu(\Psi(a_1), a_2)$ is then computed. If $E_0 = \textit{fail}$ then the algorithm returns $\{X \mapsto \mathsf{g} \mid X \in VI\}$ - the infimum of $\langle \mathsf{Con}, \sqsubseteq_{\mathsf{Con}} \rangle$. Otherwise, the algorithm continues. $\eta^{\sharp} = DOWN_{\mathsf{Con}}(E_0, \zeta^{\sharp})$ is then computed. If a variable X occurs in t, (Y/t) in E_0 and Y is ground in $\zeta^{\sharp}$ then X is ground in $\eta^{\sharp}$. Then $\beta^{\sharp} = UP_{\mathsf{Con}}(\eta^{\sharp}, E_0)$ is computed. If Y/t in E_0 and all variables in t are ground in $\eta^{\sharp}$ then Y is ground in $\beta^{\sharp}$. The algorithm finally restricts $\beta^{\sharp}$ to VI and returns the result.

Algorithm 1. Let $\theta^{\sharp}, \sigma^{\sharp} \in \mathsf{Con}$, $a_1, a_2 \in A_{\Pi, \Sigma, VI}$.

$$AUNIFY_{\mathsf{Con}}(a_1, \theta^{\sharp}, a_2, \sigma^{\sharp}) \overset{def}{=}$$
$$\begin{cases} let & E_0 = mgu(\Psi(a_1), a_2) \ in \\ if & E_0 \neq fail \\ then & UP_{\mathsf{Con}}(E_0, DOWN_{\mathsf{Con}}(E_0, \Psi(\theta^{\sharp}) \cup \sigma^{\sharp})) \!\restriction\! VI \\ else & \{X \mapsto \mathsf{g} \mid X \in VI\} \end{cases}$$

---

[1] An element f in Con is represented as $\{x \in VI \mid f(x) = \mathsf{g}\}$ in the literature.

$$DOWN_{\mathsf{Con}}(E,\zeta^{\sharp}) \stackrel{def}{=} \lambda X. \begin{cases} \zeta^{\sharp}(X), & if\ X \notin range(E) \\ \zeta^{\sharp}(X) \triangle (\triangle_{(Y/t)\in E \wedge X \in vars(t)}\zeta^{\sharp}(Y)), & otherwise. \end{cases}$$

$$UP_{\mathsf{Con}}(E,\eta^{\sharp}) \stackrel{def}{=} \lambda X. \begin{cases} \eta^{\sharp}(X), & if\ X \notin dom(E) \\ \eta^{\sharp}(X) \triangle (\nabla_{Y \in vars(E(X))}\zeta^{\sharp}(Y)), & otherwise. \end{cases}$$

The following theorem states the correctness of the non-parametric groundness analysis.

Theorem 1. *For any* $\theta^{\sharp}, \sigma^{\sharp} \in$ Con *and any* $a_1, a_2 \in \mathcal{A}_{\Pi,\Sigma,VI}$,

$$UNIFY(a_1, \gamma_{\mathsf{Con}}(\theta^{\sharp}), a_2, \gamma_{\mathsf{Con}}(\sigma^{\sharp})) \subseteq \gamma_{\mathsf{Con}}(AUNIFY_{\mathsf{Con}}(a_1, \theta^{\sharp}, a_2, \sigma^{\sharp}))$$

∎

5   Parametric Groundness Analysis

The input and the output of the parametric groundness analysis by necessity contains a set Para of groundness parameters. They are instantiated after analysis by an assignment of groundness modes to groundness parameters - a function from Para to MO. Therefore, the parametric groundness analysis needs to propagate groundness information encoded by groundness parameters in such a way that instantiating its output by a groundness assignment κ obtains the same groundness information as first instantiating its input by κ and then performing the non-parametric groundness analysis.

5.1   Abstract Domain

We first consider how to describe groundness of a variable in the presence of groundness parameters. In the non-parametric groundness analysis, groundness of a variable is described by a groundness mode from MO. Propagation of groundness reduces to computing the least upper bounds and greatest lower bounds of groundness modes from MO. In the parametric groundness analysis, groundness descriptions of a variable contain parameters and hence the least upper bound and greatest lower bound of groundness descriptions cannot evaluated to an element of MO or an element of Para during analysis. We resolve this problem by delaying the least upper bound and the greatest lower bound computations. This requires that groundness of a variable be described by an expression formed of elements of MO, elements of Para, the least upper bound operator ∇ and the greatest lower bound operator $\triangle$. It can be shown that

Observation 1. *Any expression formed as above is equivalent to an expression of the form* $\nabla_{i\in I}(\triangle_{j\in J_i}\alpha_i^j)$ *where* $\alpha_i^j \in$ Para. ∎

Expression $\nabla_{i\in I}(\triangle_{j\in J_i}\alpha_i^j)$ is represented as a set S of subsets of groundness parameters. Let $S = \{S_1, S_2, \cdots, S_n\}$, $S_i = \{\alpha_i^1, \alpha_i^2, \cdots, \alpha_i^{k_i}\}$. S stands for

$\nabla_{1 \leq i \leq n}(\triangle_{1 \leq j \leq k_i} \alpha_i^j)$ which is a function from (Para $\mapsto$ MO) to MO defined as $\mathcal{S}(\kappa) \stackrel{def}{=} \nabla_{1 \leq i \leq n}(\triangle_{1 \leq j \leq k_i} \kappa(\alpha_i^j))$. For any $\kappa \in$ (Para $\mapsto$ MO), $\emptyset(\kappa) = g$ since $\nabla \emptyset = g$ and $\{\emptyset\}(\kappa) = u$ as $\nabla(\triangle \emptyset) = u$. Thus, $\emptyset$ and $\{\emptyset\}$ represent modes g and u respectively. There may be two parametric groundness descriptions $\mathcal{S}_1$ and $\mathcal{S}_2$ such that $\mathcal{S}_1(\kappa) = \mathcal{S}_2(\kappa)$ for any $\kappa \in$ (Para $\mapsto$ MO). We follow the normal practice in program analysis of identifying those descriptions that have the same denotation. Define relations $\ll$ and $\cong$ on $\wp(\wp(\text{Para}))$ as $\mathcal{S}_1 \ll \mathcal{S}_2 \stackrel{def}{=} \forall \mathcal{S}_1 \in \mathcal{S}_1.\exists \mathcal{S}_2 \in \mathcal{S}_2.(\mathcal{S}_2 \subseteq \mathcal{S}_1)$ and $\mathcal{S}_1 \cong \mathcal{S}_2 \stackrel{def}{=} (\mathcal{S}_1 \ll \mathcal{S}_2) \wedge (\mathcal{S}_2 \ll \mathcal{S}_1)$. Then $\cong$ is an equivalence relation on $\wp(\wp(\text{Para}))$. The domain of parametric groundness descriptions is $\langle \text{PMO}, \preceq \rangle$ where

$$\text{PMO} \stackrel{def}{=} \wp(\wp(\text{Para}))_{/\cong}$$

$$\preceq \stackrel{def}{=} \ll_{/\cong}$$

$\langle \text{PMO}, \preceq \rangle$ is a complete lattice with its infimum being $[\emptyset]_\cong$ and its supremum being $[\{\emptyset\}]_\cong$. The least upper bound of $[\mathcal{S}_1]_\cong$ and $[\mathcal{S}_2]_\cong$ is $[\mathcal{S}_1]_\cong \oplus [\mathcal{S}_2]_\cong = [\mathcal{S}_1 \cup \mathcal{S}_2]_\cong$ and the greatest lower bound of $[\mathcal{S}_1]_\cong$ and $[\mathcal{S}_2]_\cong$ is $[\mathcal{S}_1]_\cong \otimes [\mathcal{S}_2]_\cong = [\{S_1 \cup S_2 \mid S_1 \in \mathcal{S}_1 \wedge S_2 \in \mathcal{S}_2\}]_\cong$. A parametric groundness description $[\mathcal{S}]_\cong \in$ PMO is a function from (Para $\mapsto$ MO) to MO defined as $[\mathcal{S}]_\cong(\kappa) \stackrel{def}{=} \mathcal{S}(\kappa)$. In other words, a parametric groundness description is instantiated to a non-parametric groundness description - a groundness mode in MO by a groundness assignment.

Let $|X|$ be the number of elements in set X and $size([\mathcal{S}]_\cong) \stackrel{def}{=} \Sigma_{S \in \mathcal{S}}|S|$. It can be shown that

Lemma 2. *The height of* PMO *is* $\mathcal{O}(2^{|\text{Para}|})$ *and* $size([\mathcal{S}]_\cong)$ *is* $\mathcal{O}(|\text{Para}|2^{|\text{Para}|})$ *for any* $[\mathcal{S}]_\cong \in$ PMO. ∎

A parametric abstract substitution is a function that maps a variable in VI to a groundness description in PMO. The domain of parametric abstract substitutions is $\langle \text{PCon}, \sqsubseteq_{\text{PCon}} \rangle$ where $\text{PCon} \stackrel{def}{=} VI \mapsto \text{PMO}$ and $\sqsubseteq_{\text{PCon}}$ is the pointwise extension of $\preceq$. $\langle \text{PCon}, \sqsubseteq_{\text{PCon}} \rangle$ is a complete lattice with its infimum being $\{x \mapsto [\emptyset]_\cong \mid x \in VI\}$. A parametric abstract substitution $\theta^\sharp \in$ PCon can be thought of as a function from (Para $\mapsto$ MO) to Con defined as $\theta^\sharp(\kappa) \stackrel{def}{=} \lambda X \in VI.((\theta^\sharp(X))(\kappa))$, that is, a parametric abstract substitution is instantiated to a non-parametric abstract substitution by a groundness assignment. The meaning of a parametric abstract substitution is given by γ_{PCon} : PCon $\mapsto$ ((Para $\mapsto$ MO) $\mapsto \wp(\text{Sub})$) defined as follows.

$$\gamma_{\text{PCon}}(\theta^\sharp) \stackrel{def}{=} \lambda \kappa.\{\theta \mid \forall x \in VI.((\theta^\sharp(x)(\kappa) = g) \to (vars(\theta(x)) = \emptyset))\}$$

Example 2. Let $\text{Para} = \{\alpha, \beta, \gamma\}$ and $VI = \{x, y, z\}$. $\theta^\sharp = \{x \mapsto [\{\{\alpha, \gamma\}\}]_\cong, y \mapsto [\{\{\beta, \gamma\}\}]_\cong, z \mapsto [\{\{\alpha, \gamma\}, \{\beta, \gamma\}\}]_\cong\}$ is a parametric abstract substitution and

$\gamma_{\mathsf{PCon}}(\theta^{\sharp})$ is the following function from groundness assignments to sets of substitutions.

$$\left\{ \begin{array}{l} \{\alpha \mapsto \mathsf{g}, \beta \mapsto \mathsf{g}, \gamma \mapsto \mathsf{g}\} \mapsto \{\theta \in \mathsf{Sub} \mid vars(\theta(x)) = vars(\theta(y)) = vars(\theta(z)) = \emptyset\} \\ \qquad\qquad \vdots \\ \{\alpha \mapsto \mathsf{u}, \beta \mapsto \mathsf{u}, \gamma \mapsto \mathsf{u}\} \mapsto \mathsf{Sub} \end{array} \right\}$$

∎

Let $\mathsf{PCon}^{\dagger} \stackrel{def}{=} VI^{\dagger} \mapsto \mathsf{PMO}$ and $\gamma_{\mathsf{PCon}}^{\dagger}(\theta^{\sharp}) \stackrel{def}{=} \lambda\kappa.\{\theta \mid \forall x \in VI^{\dagger}.((\theta^{\sharp}(x)(\kappa) = \mathsf{g}) \to (vars(\theta(x)) = \emptyset))\}$.

Lemma 3. $\gamma_{\mathsf{PCon}}(\mathsf{PCon})$ *and* $\gamma_{\mathsf{PCon}}^{\dagger}(\mathsf{PCon}^{\dagger})$ *are Moore families.* ∎

5.2 Abstract Unification

Algorithm 2 defines an abstract unification operator for the parametric groundness analysis. It is obtained from that for the non-parametric groundness analysis by replacing non-parametric groundness descriptions with parametric groundness descriptions, ∇ and $\triangle$ by $\oplus$ and $\otimes$ respectively, and renaming $AUNIFY_{\mathsf{Con}}$, $DOWN_{\mathsf{Con}}$ and UP_{Con} into $AUNIFY_{\mathsf{PCon}}$, $DOWN_{\mathsf{PCon}}$ and UP_{PCon} respectively.

Algorithm 2. *Let* $\theta^{\sharp}, \sigma^{\sharp} \in \mathsf{PCon}$, $a_1, a_2 \in \mathcal{A}_{\Pi,\Sigma,VI}$.

$$AUNIFY_{\mathsf{PCon}}(a_1, \theta^{\sharp}, a_2, \sigma^{\sharp}) \stackrel{def}{=}$$
$$\left\{ \begin{array}{l} let \quad E_0 = mgu(\Psi(a_1), a_2) \ in \\ if \quad\ E_0 \neq fail \\ then \ UP_{\mathsf{PCon}}(E_0, DOWN_{\mathsf{PCon}}(E_0, \Psi(\theta^{\sharp}) \cup \sigma^{\sharp}))\!\upharpoonright VI \\ else \ \{X \mapsto [\emptyset]_{\simeq} \mid X \in VI\} \end{array} \right.$$

$$DOWN_{\mathsf{PCon}}(E, \zeta^{\sharp}) \stackrel{def}{=} \lambda X. \left\{ \begin{array}{ll} \zeta^{\sharp}(X), & if\ X \notin range(E) \\ \zeta^{\sharp}(X) \ \otimes\ (\bigotimes_{(Y/t)\in E \wedge X \in vars(t)} \zeta^{\sharp}(Y)), & otherwise. \end{array} \right.$$

$$UP_{\mathsf{PCon}}(E, \eta^{\sharp}) \stackrel{def}{=} \lambda X. \left\{ \begin{array}{ll} \eta^{\sharp}(X), & if\ X \notin dom(E) \\ \eta^{\sharp}(X) \ \otimes\ (\bigoplus_{Y \in vars(E(X))} \zeta^{\sharp}(Y)), & otherwise. \end{array} \right.$$

Lemma 4. *The time complexity of* $AUNIFY_{\mathsf{PCon}}$ *is* $\mathcal{O}(|VI|^2|\mathsf{Para}|^2 2^{|\mathsf{Para}|})$ *and that of* $\sqcup_{\mathsf{PCon}}$ *is* $\mathcal{O}(|VI||\mathsf{Para}|^2 2^{|\mathsf{Para}|})$ *where* $\sqcup_{\mathsf{PCon}}$ *is the least upper bound operator on* PCon. ∎

Example 3. This example illustrates how $AUNIFY_{\mathsf{PCon}}$ works. Let

$$\begin{aligned} VI &= \{X, Y, Z\} \\ A &= g(X, f(Y, f(Z, Z)), Y) \\ B &= g(f(X, Y), Z, X) \\ \theta^{\sharp} &= \{X \mapsto \{\{\alpha_1, \alpha_2\}\}, Y \mapsto \{\{\alpha_1, \alpha_3\}\}, Z \mapsto \{\{\alpha_2, \alpha_3\}\}\} \\ \sigma^{\sharp} &= \{X \mapsto \{\{\alpha_1\}, \{\alpha_2\}\}, Y \mapsto \{\{\alpha_2, \alpha_3\}\}, Z \mapsto \{\emptyset\}\} \end{aligned}$$

Suppose $\Psi = \{X \mapsto X_0, Y \mapsto Y_0, Z \mapsto Z_0\}$. We have

$$\Psi(A) = g(X_0, f(Y_0, f(Z_0, Z_0)), Y_0)$$
$$\Psi(\theta^\sharp) = \{X_0 \mapsto \{\{\alpha_1, \alpha_2\}\}, Y_0 \mapsto \{\{\alpha_1, \alpha_3\}\}, Z_0 \mapsto \{\{\alpha_2, \alpha_3\}\}\}$$
$$\zeta^\sharp \ = \Psi(\theta^\sharp) \cup \sigma^\sharp$$
$$= \left\{ \begin{array}{l} X_0 \mapsto \{\{\alpha_1, \alpha_2\}\}, Y_0 \mapsto \{\{\alpha_1, \alpha_3\}\}, Z_0 \mapsto \{\{\alpha_2, \alpha_3\}\}, \\ X \mapsto \{\{\alpha_1\}, \{\alpha_2\}\}, Y \mapsto \{\{\alpha_2, \alpha_3\}\}, Z \mapsto \{\emptyset\} \end{array} \right\}$$

and

$$E_0 = eq \circ mgu(\Psi(A), B) = \{X_0 = f(Y_0, Y), Z = f(Y_0, f(Z_0, Z_0)), X = Y_0\}$$

and

$$\eta^\sharp = DOWN_{\mathsf{PCon}}(E_0, \zeta^\sharp)$$
$$= \left\{ \begin{array}{l} X_0 \mapsto \{\{\alpha_1, \alpha_2\}\}, Y_0 \mapsto \{\{\alpha_1, \alpha_2, \alpha_3\}\}, Z_0 \mapsto \{\{\alpha_2, \alpha_3\}\}, \\ X \mapsto \{\{\alpha_1\}, \{\alpha_2\}\}, Y \mapsto \{\{\alpha_1, \alpha_2, \alpha_3\}\}, Z \mapsto \{\emptyset\} \end{array} \right\}$$
$$\beta^\sharp = UP_{\mathsf{PCon}}(E_0, \eta^\sharp)$$
$$= \left\{ \begin{array}{l} X_0 \mapsto \{\{\alpha_1, \alpha_2, \alpha_3\}\}, Y_0 \mapsto \{\{\alpha_1, \alpha_2, \alpha_3\}\}, Z_0 \mapsto \{\{\alpha_2, \alpha_3\}\}, \\ X \mapsto \{\{\alpha_1, \alpha_2, \alpha_3\}\}, Y \mapsto \{\{\alpha_1, \alpha_2, \alpha_3\}\}, Z \mapsto \{\{\alpha_2, \alpha_3\} \end{array} \right\}$$

Finally,

$$AUNIFY_{\mathsf{PCon}}(A, \theta^\sharp, B, \sigma^\sharp)$$
$$= \beta^\sharp \!\upharpoonright VI$$
$$= \{X \mapsto \{\{\alpha_1, \alpha_2, \alpha_3\}\}, Y \mapsto \{\{\alpha_1, \alpha_2, \alpha_3\}\}, Z \mapsto \{\{\alpha_2, \alpha_3\}\}\}$$

∎

   The following theorem states that instantiating the output of the parametric groundness analysis by a groundness assignment obtains the same groundness information as first instantiating its input by the same groundness assignment and then performing the non-parametric groundness analysis.

Theorem 2. Let $[S_1]_\simeq, [S_2]_\simeq \in PMO$, $\theta^\sharp, \sigma^\sharp \in PCon$, $\eta^\sharp, \zeta^\sharp \in PCon^\dagger$, $a_1, a_2 \in A_{\Pi, \Sigma, VI}$ and $E \in \wp(Eqn)$. For any $\kappa \in (Para \mapsto MO)$,

(a) $([S_1]_\simeq \otimes [S_2]_\simeq)(\kappa) = (S_1(\kappa) \triangle S_2(\kappa))$ and $([S_1]_\simeq \oplus [S_2]_\simeq)(\kappa) = (S_1(\kappa) \nabla S_2(\kappa))$;
(b) $(DOWN_{\mathsf{PCon}}(E, \zeta^\sharp))(\kappa) = DOWN_{\mathsf{Con}}(E, \zeta^\sharp(\kappa))$;
(c) $(UP_{\mathsf{PCon}}(E, \eta^\sharp))(\kappa) = UP_{\mathsf{Con}}(E, \eta^\sharp(\kappa))$; and
(d) $(AUNIFY_{\mathsf{PCon}}(a_1, \theta^\sharp, a_2, \sigma^\sharp))(\kappa) = AUNIFY_{\mathsf{Con}}(a_1, \theta^\sharp(\kappa), a_2, \sigma^\sharp(\kappa))$.

∎

   The following theorem establishes the correctness of the parametric groundness analysis.

Theorem 3. For any $a_1, a_2 \in A_{\Pi, \Sigma, VI}$, $\kappa \in (Para \mapsto MO)$, and $\theta^\sharp, \sigma^\sharp \in PCon$,

$$UNIFY(a_1, \gamma_{\mathsf{PCon}}(\theta^\sharp)(\kappa), a_2, \gamma_{\mathsf{PCon}}(\sigma^\sharp)(\kappa)) \subseteq \gamma_{\mathsf{PCon}}(AUNIFY_{\mathsf{PCon}}(a_1, \theta^\sharp, a_2, \sigma^\sharp))(\kappa)$$

∎

6   Implementation

We have implemented the parametric groundness analysis and the abstract interpretation framework in SWI-Prolog. The abstract interpretation framework is implemented using O'Keefe's least fixed-point algorithm [40]. Both the abstract interpretation framework and the parametric groundness analysis are implemented as meta-interpreters using ground representations for program variables and groundness parameters.

6.1   An Example

Example 4. The following is the permutation sort program from [45] (Chapter 3) and the result of the parametric groundness analysis. The sets are represented by lists. $V \mapsto T$ is written as V/T in the results, α as alpha and β as beta. Program points marked (a) and (b) will be referred to later.

```
:-  %[Li/[[alpha]],Lo/[[beta]]]                                        (a)
   sort(Li,Lo).
     %[Li/[[alpha]],Lo/[[alpha,beta]]]

select(X,[X|Xs],Xs).
     %[X/[[alpha,beta]],Xs/[[alpha]]]
select(X,[Y|Ys],[Y|Zs]) :-
     %[X/[[beta]],Y/[[alpha]],Ys/[[alpha]],Zs/[[]]]
   select(X,Ys,Zs).
     %[X/[[alpha,beta]],Y/[[alpha]],Ys/[[alpha]],Zs/[[alpha]]]

ordered([]).
     %[]
ordered([X]).
     %[X/[[alpha,beta]]]
ordered([X,Y|Ys]) :-
     %[X/[[alpha,beta]],Y/[[alpha,beta]],Ys/[[alpha,beta]]]            (b)
   X=<Y,
     %[X/[],Y/[],Ys/[[alpha,beta]]]
   ordered([Y|Ys]).
     %[X/[],Y/[],Ys/[]]

permutation(Xs,[Z|Zs]) :-
     %[Xs/[[alpha]],Z/[[beta]],Zs/[[beta]],Ys/[[]]]
   select(Z,Xs,Ys),
     %[Xs/[[alpha]],Z/[[alpha,beta]],Zs/[[beta]],Ys/[[alpha]]]
   permutation(Ys,Zs).
     %[Xs/[[alpha]],Z/[[alpha,beta]],Zs/[[alpha,beta]],Ys/[[alpha]]]
permutation([],[])
     %[].

sort(Xs,Ys) :-
     %[Xs/[[alpha]],Ys/[[beta]]]
```

```
permutation(Xs,Ys),
   %[Xs/[[alpha]],Ys/[[alpha,beta]]]
ordered(Ys).
   %[Xs/[[alpha]],Ys/[[alpha,beta]]]
```

The top-level goal is $sort(Li, Lo)$ and the input abstract substitution at program point (a) is $\{Li \mapsto \{\{\alpha\}\}, Lo \mapsto \{\{\beta\}\}\}$. It says that groundness mode of Li is α and that of Lo is β. The parametric groundness analysis infers an abstract substitution for every other program points. The abstract substitution at program point (b) associates the parametric groundness description $\alpha \triangle \beta$ with variables X, Y and Ys. The result can be instantiated by any of four groundness assignments in $\{\alpha, \beta\} \mapsto$ MO. Let $\kappa = \{\alpha \mapsto g, \beta \mapsto u\}$. Then κ instantiates the input abstract substitution to $\{Li \mapsto g, Lo \mapsto u\}$ and the abstract substitution at program point (b) to $\{X \mapsto g, Y \mapsto g, Ys \mapsto g\}$. This indicates that if the goal $sort(Li, Lo)$ is called with Li being ground then X, Y and Ys are ground when $(X <= Y)$ is invoked.

Since the abstract substitution at program point (b) maps both X and Y to $\alpha \triangle \beta$, it is obvious that if either α or β is assigned g then X and Y are ground before the execution of $X =< Y$ and the run-time groundness check at program point (b) can be eliminated. ∎

6.2 Performance

The SWI-Prolog implementation of the parametric groundness analysis has been tested with a set of benchmark programs. The experiments were done on an 1.0GHz Dell Desktop running Windows 2000 Professional and SWI-Prolog 3.4.0.

Table 1 shows time performance of the implementation. All but the last row corresponds to a specific input. The input consists of a program, a goal and an input abstract substitution that specifies the groundness of the variables in the goal. The program and the goal are listed in the first and the third columns. The input abstract substitution associates each variable in the goal with a different groundness parameter. For instance, the abstract substitution for the first row is $\{X \mapsto \{\{\alpha\}\}, Y \mapsto \{\{\beta\}\}\}$. The second column lists the size of the program measured in the number of program points in the program. Each fact p is treated as a clause $p \leftarrow true$ which has two program points. The fourth column is the time in seconds spent on the input. The last row gives the total size of the programs and the total time.

Table 1 indicates that the prototype parametric groundness analyzer spends an average of 1.72 seconds to process one thousand program points. This is an acceptable speed for most logic programs. We believe that there is still room for improving the time performance through a better implementation because both meta-programming and ground representation of variables significantly slow the prototype.

The same table compares the performance of the parametric groundness analysis with that of the non-parametric groundness analysis presented in [43] which uses a subset of VI as an abstract substitution. The subset contains those variables that are definitely ground under all substitutions described by the abstract

Table 1. Performance of Parametric Groundness Analysis.

Program	Points	Goal	Poly (sec)	Mono (sec)	Ratio	Assign- ments
Buggy Quick Sort	38	qs(A, B)	0.038	0.016	2.375	4
Exponentiation	27	exp(A, B, C)	0.01	0.009	1.111	8
Factorial	25	factorial(A, B)	0.008	0.005	1.6	4
Graph Connectivity	50	connected(A, B)	0.012	0.009	1.333	4
Heapify Binary Trees	27	heapify(A, B)	0.043	0.015	2.867	4
Improved Quick Sort	22	iqsort(A, B)	0.025	0.009	2.778	4
Interchange Sort	24	sort(A, B)	0.015	0.005	3	4
List Insertion	23	insert(A, B, C)	0.01	0.008	1.25	8
Permutation Sort	26	sort(A, B)	0.018	0.008	2.25	4
QuickSort with D-List	22	quicksort(A, B)	0.027	0.012	2.25	4
Tree Sort	34	treesort(A, B)	0.038	0.014	2.714	4
ann	653	go(A)	0.911	0.541	1.684	2
asm	904	asm_PIL(A, B)	1.188	0.855	1.389	4
boyer	351	tautology(A)	0.269	0.16	1.681	2
browse	132	q	0.073	0.06	1.217	1
chat	1368	chat_parser	4.326	2.554	1.694	1
cs_r	348	pgenconfig(A)	0.649	0.42	1.545	2
disj_r	180	top(A)	0.103	0.088	1.17	2
dnf	95	go	0.285	0.239	1.192	1
ga	503	test_ga	0.541	0.531	1.019	1
gabriel	131	main(A, B)	0.122	0.072	1.694	4
kalah	298	play(A, B)	0.215	0.144	1.493	4
life	115	lift(A, B, C, D)	0.04	0.04	1	16
mastermind	238	play	0.13	0.1	1.3	1
meta	110	interpret(A)	0.139	0.073	1.904	2
nand	624	main(A)	1.117	0.921	1.213	2
naughts_and_crosses	137	play(A)	0.067	0.042	1.595	2
nbody	454	go(A, B)	0.404	0.235	1.719	4
neural	382	test(A, B)	0.257	0.119	2.16	4
peep	541	comppeepopt(A, B, C)	1.07	0.538	1.989	8
press	455	test_press(A, B)	1.624	0.626	2.594	4
queens	33	queens(A, B)	0.01	0.007	1.429	4
read	500	read(A, B)	1.863	1.219	1.528	4
reducer	408	try(A, B)	0.719	0.426	1.688	4
ronp	110	puzzle(A)	0.097	0.05	1.94	2
sdda	355	do_sdda(test, A, B, C)	0.462	0.23	2.009	8
semi	216	go(A, B)	0.773	0.382	2.024	4
serialize	50	go(A)	0.083	0.033	2.515	2
simple_analyzer	560	main(A)	0.716	0.39	1.836	2
tictactoe	286	play(A)	0.34	0.263	1.293	2
tree order	39	v2t(A, B, C)	0.038	0.021	1.81	8
tsp	153	tsp(A, B, C, D, E)	0.164	0.087	1.885	32
zebra	64	zebra(A, B, C, D, E, F, G)	0.048	0.025	1.92	128
	11111		19.087		1.78	7.4

substitution. This allows operators on abstract substitutions to be optimized. The non-parametric groundness analysis is implemented in the same way as the parametric groundness analysis.

The number of different groundness assignments for the parametric groundness analysis is two to the power of the number of groundness parameters. Each assignment corresponds to a non-parametric groundness analysis that is performed and measured. The fifth column lists the average time in seconds spent on these non-parametric groundness analyses. The sixth column lists the ratio of the fourth column and the fifth column. The seventh column lists the number of groundness assignments.

The table shows that the time the parametric groundness analysis takes is from 1.0 to 3.0 times that the non-parametric groundness analysis takes. On average, the parametric groundness analysis is 78% slower. This is due to the fact that the parametric groundness descriptions are more complex than the non-parametric groundness descriptions. The abstract unification operator and the least upper bound operator for the parametric groundness are more costly than those for the non-parametric groundness analysis.

The result of the parametric groundness analysis is much more general than that of the non-parametric groundness analysis. It can be instantiated as many times as there are different groundness assignments. The average number of groundness assignments is 7.4 which is 4.2 times the average performance ratio 1.78. In order to derive a sufficient condition for safely removing groundness checks for builtin calls, the non-parametric groundness analysis must be run as many times as the number of groundness assignments. In this case, the parametric groundness analysis is 4.2 times better.

7 Related Work

The parametric groundness analysis has been obtained from a non-parametric groundness analysis that uses a simple groundness domain. As groundness is useful both in compile-time program optimizations and in improving the precision of other program analyses, more powerful groundness domains have been studied. These domains consists of propositional formulae over program variables that act as propositional variables. Dart uses the domain Def of definite propositional formulae to capture groundness dependency between variables [22]. For instance, the definite propositional formula $x \leftarrow (y \wedge z)$ represents the groundness dependency that x is bound to a ground term if y and z are bound to ground terms. Def consists of propositional formulae whose models are closed under set intersection [17]. Marriott and Søndergaard use the domain Pos (also called Prop) of positive propositional formulae [34]. A propositional formula f is positive if f is true when all propositional variables in f are true. Pos is strictly more powerful than Def. It has been further studied in [17, 2, 3] and has several implementations [29, 25, 8, 4].

Giacobazzi and Scozzari reconstruct Def and Pos from Con via Heyting completion [23, 42] where Con is a subdomain of Pos and consists of propositional formulae that are conjunctions of propositional variables. The Sharing domain proposed by Jacobs and Langen for sharing analysis [26, 27] also contains groundness information. Cortesi et. al prove that groundness information contained in Sharing is exactly that captured by Def [16, 15]. Codish and Søndergaard recently discover that Sharing is isomorphic to Pos in structure [10].

Pos-based analyzers using binary decision diagrams have been shown [25] to be precise and efficient for benchmark programs. However, Pos-based analyzers do not come with any efficiency guarantee as they require in the worst case exponential number of iterations or exponentially large data structures [11]. More abstract domains [22, 12, 24] have been proposed, offering different trade-offs between the precision and the efficiency of analysis.

Pos-based goal-independent groundness analyzers enjoys a favorable property of being condensing [27, 34]. An analysis F that infers output information $F(P, \phi)$ from a program P and input information ϕ is condensing if $F(P, \phi \wedge \psi) = F(P, \phi) \wedge \psi$ for any P, ϕ and ψ. Thus, a condensing analysis can be performed with partial input information ϕ and its output be conjoined with additional input information ψ to obtain the output that would result from analyzing the program with complete input information $\phi \wedge \psi$. Thus, a Pos-based goal-independent groundness analysis is also parametric since its result can be instantiated by logic conjunction. [34] and [8] present two approaches to perform condensing goal-independent groundness analysis using program transformation and bottom-up evaluation. An atomic call in the transformed program in [34] contains both variables of interest at a program point in the original program and variables in the query. Thus, the abstract domain for goal-independent groundness analysis in [34] is $Pos_{(Para \cup VI)}$ since variables in the query play the role of groundness parameters. Similar argument can be made of [8].

Groundness analyzers in [25, 17] use Pos with top-down abstract interpretation frameworks to perform goal-dependent groundness analysis [25, 17]. These analyzers project a Pos formula onto variables occurring in the clause to which the program point belongs. This makes them fail to capture groundness dependency between variables at a program point and variables in a query. Let Pos_X denote the set of positive Boolean functions over X - the set of propositional variables. The following fix should make a top-down Pos-based groundness analysis condensing and hence parametric. The abstract domain Pos_{VI} is extended to $Pos_{(Para \cup VI)}$ and the projection operation $\lambda f. \exists_{VI}. f$ is replaced with $\lambda f. \exists_{(Para \cup VI)}. f$.

Though Pos-based groundness analysis is parametric and more precise than the parametric groundness analysis, the parametric groundness analysis is more efficient. The cost of an analysis is determined by the number of iterations performed and cost of operations performed in each iteration. The height of $Pos_{(Para \cup VI)}$ (abstract domain in a Pos-based goal-dependent groundness analysis) is $\mathcal{O}(2^{|VI|}2^{|Para|})$ [3]. The height of PCon (abstract domain in the parametric groundness analysis) is $\mathcal{O}(|VI|2^{|Para|})$. Therefore, the number of iterations performed in the parametric groundness analysis is much less than those performed in a Pos-based groundness analysis. Abstract operations $AUNIFY_{PCon}$ and $\sqcup_{PCon}$

are also much less expensive than $\vee$, $\wedge$ and existential quantification on positive Boolean functions over (Para $\cup$ VI) in a Pos-based groundness analysis. Therefore, the parametric groundness analysis is more efficient than a Pos-based groundness analysis. Furthermore, the parametric groundness analysis has the same asymptotic time and space complexity as a Con-based groundness analysis when it is used with Para $= \emptyset$. Thus, it only pays more cost than a Con-based analysis when it infers more general results.

$$append([\,], L, L).$$
$$append([H|L_1], L_2, [H|L_3]) \leftarrow append(L_1, L_2, L_3).\textcircled{b}$$

$$\leftarrow \textcircled{a}\ append(Xs, Ys, Zs).\textcircled{c}$$

Fig. 2. The append Program.

It is interesting to note that the parametric groundness analysis also captures some groundness dependency among variables.

Example 5. For the program and the goal in Figure 2, the parametric groundness analysis infers

$$\textcircled{a} : \{Xs \mapsto \{\{\alpha\}\}, Ys \mapsto \{\{\beta\}\}, Zs \mapsto \{\{\gamma\}\}\}$$
$$\implies \textcircled{c} : \{Xs \mapsto \{\{\alpha, \gamma\}\}, Ys \mapsto \{\{\beta, \gamma\}\}, Zs \mapsto \{\{\alpha, \gamma\}, \{\beta, \gamma\}\}\}$$

This implies that whenever Xs and Ys are bound to ground terms at point $\textcircled{c}$, Zs is bound to a ground term at the same point. In order to bind Xs to a ground term, g must be assigned to either α or γ. In order to bind Ys to a ground term, g must be assigned to either β or γ. Any groundness assignment satisfying the above two conditions will evaluate $\{\{\alpha, \gamma\}, \{\beta, \gamma\}\}$ to g. So, we have $Xs \wedge Ys \rightarrow Zs$ in Pos. Similarly, we can infer $Xs \wedge Ys \leftarrow Zs$. ∎

In general, if the abstract substitution at a program point assign $\mathcal{R}_j$ to Y_j for $1 \leq j \leq l$ and $\mathcal{S}_i$ to X_i for $1 \leq i \leq k$ and $\oplus_{1 \leq j \leq l} \mathcal{R}_j \preceq \oplus_{1 \leq i \leq k} \mathcal{S}_k$ then the Pos like proposition $\wedge_{1 \leq i \leq k} X_i \rightarrow \wedge_{1 \leq j \leq l} Y_j$ holds at the program point. Thus the parametric groundness analysis also captures groundness dependency between program variables. However, the degree to which the parametric groundness analysis captures this kind of groundness dependency is limited. In particular, when Para $= \emptyset$, the parametric groundness analysis degenerates to the non-parametric groundness analysis which does not capture this kind of groundness dependency.

There have also been effort in analyzing logic programs to discover type dependency between program variables [7, 32, 13]. Though groundness modes in MO can be thought of as types, it is not beneficial to apply a type dependency analysis to infer groundness dependency. Abstract domains for type dependency analyses in [7, 32, 13] are more complex and hence abstract operations are more costly than those required in a groundness dependency analysis. Furthermore, their abstract domains have infinite increasing chains and they must employ a widening operator. [32] obtains a parametric type analysis from a nonparametric type analysis. Since types have much rich structures than groundness modes, equational constraints over parametric types need be incorporated into its abstract domain in order to propagate precisely type dependency. This makes abstract operations costly. As there are infinite number of assignments of types to type parameters, loss of precision is incurred when abstract operations in the parametric type analysis mimicks those in the non-parametric type analysis. The parametric groundness analysis presented in this paper has a much simpler abstract domain and abstract operations that mimicks precisely those in the non-parametric groundness analysis.

8   Conclusion

We have presented a new groundness analysis, called parametric groundness analysis, that infers groundness of variables parameterized by groundness parameters that can be instantiated after analysis. The parametric groundness analysis is obtained by generalizing a non-parametric groundness analysis. Experimental results with a prototype implementation of the analysis are promising. The parametric groundness analysis is as precise as the non-parametric groundness analysis.

The parametric groundness analysis is theoretically faster but less precise than a Pos based groundness analysis. As future work, we would like to compare experimentally the time and the precision of the parametric groundness analysis with those of Pos based groundness analyses.

References

1. K.R. Apt. Logic programming. In J.V. Leeuwen, editor, *Handbook of Theoretical Computer Science: (Volume B) Formal Models and Semantics*, pages 493–574. Elsevier Science Publishers B.V., 1990.
2. T. Armstrong, K. Marriott, P. Schachte, and H. Søndergaard. Boolean functions for dependency analysis: Algebraic properties and efficient representation. *Lecture Notes in Computer Science*, 864:266–280, 1994.
3. T. Armstrong, K. Marriott, P. Schachte, and H. Søndergaard. Two classes of Boolean functions for dependency analysis. *Science of Computer Programming*, 31(1):3–45, 1998.
4. R. Bagnara and P. Schachte. Factorizing equivalent variable pairs in ROBDD-based implementations of *Pos*. Lecture Notes in Computer Science, 1548:471–485, 1999.
5. M. Bruynooghe. A practical framework for the abstract interpretation of logic progams. *Journal of Logic Programming*, 10(2):91–124, 1991.
6. M. Codish, D. Dams, and Yardeni E. Derivation and safety of an abstract unification algorithm for groundness and aliasing analysis. In K. Furukawa, editor, *Proceedings of the Eighth International Conference on Logic Programming*, pages 79–93. The MIT Press, 1991.

7. M. Codish and B. Demoen. Deriving polymorphic type dependencies for logic programs using multiple incarnations of Prop. *Lecture Notes in Computer Science*, 864:281–297, 1994.

8. M. Codish and B. Demoen. Analysing logic programs using "Prop"-ositional logic programs and a magic wand. *Journal of Logic Programming*, 25(3):249–274, 1995.

9. M. Codish, A. Mulkers, M. Bruynooghe, M. García de la Banda, and M. Hermenegildo. Improving abstract interpretations by combining domains. In PEPM93 [41], pages 194–205.

10. M. Codish and H. Søndergaard. The boolean logic of set sharing analysis. *Lecture Notes in Computer Science*, 1490:89–101, 1998.

11. Michael Codish. Worst-case groundness analysis using positive boolean functions. *The Journal of Logic Programming*, 41(1):125–128, 1999.

12. Michael Codish, Andy Heaton, Andy King, Muhamed Abo-Zaed, and Pat Hill. Widening Positive Boolean functions for Goal-dependent Groundness Analysis. Technical Report 12-98, Computing Laboratory, May 1998.

13. Michael Codish and Vitaly Lagoon. Type dependencies for logic programs using aci-unification. *Journal of Theoretical Computer Science*, 238:131–159, 2000.

14. A. Cortesi and G. Filé. Abstract interpretation of logic programs: an abstract domain for groundness, sharing, freeness and compoundness analysis. In *Proceedings of the Symposium on Partial Evaluation and Semantics-based Program Manipulation*, pages 52–61, New Haven, Connecticut, USA, 1991.

15. A. Cortesi, G. Filé, R. Giacobazzi, C. Palamidessi, and F. Ranzato. Complementation in abstract interpretation. *ACM Transactions on Programming Languages and Systems*, 19(1):7–47, 1997.

16. A. Cortesi, G. Filé, and W. Winsborough. Comparison of abstract interpretations. In *Proceedings of the 19th Int. Colloquium on Automata, Languages and Programming ICALP'92*, pages 523–534. Springer Verlag, 1992.

17. A. Cortesi, G. Filé, and W. Winsborough. Optimal groundness analysis using propositional logic. *Journal of Logic Programming*, 27(2):137–168, 1996.

18. P. Cousot and R. Cousot. Abstract interpretation: a unified framework for static analysis of programs by construction or approximation of fixpoints. In *Proceedings of the fourth annual ACM symposium on Principles of programming languages*, pages 238–252. The ACM Press, 1977.

19. P. Cousot and R. Cousot. Systematic design of program analysis frameworks. In *Proceedings of the sixth annual ACM symposium on Principles of programming languages*, pages 269–282. The ACM Press, 1979.

20. P. Cousot and R. Cousot. Abstract interpretation and application to logic programs. *Journal of Logic Programming*, 13(1, 2, 3 and 4):103–179, 1992.

21. M. A. Covington, D. Nute, and A. Vellino. *PROLOG PROGRAMMING IN DEPTH*. Scott, Foresman & Co., 1988.

22. P.W. Dart. On derived dependencies and connected databases. *Journal of Logic Programming*, 11(2):163–188, 1991.

23. R. Giacobazzi and F. Scozzari. Intuitionistic Implication in Abstract Interpretation. In *Proceedings of Programming Languages: Implementations, Logics and Programs*, pages 175–189. Springer-Verlag, 1997. LNCS 1292.

24. Andy Heaton, Muhamed Abo-Zaed, Michael Codish, and Andy King. Simple, efficient and scalable groundness analysis of logic programs. *The Journal of Logic Programming*, 45(1-3):143–156, 2000.

25. P. Van Hentenryck, A. Cortesi, and B. Le Charlier. Evaluation of the Domain PROP. *Journal of Logic Programming*, 23(3):237–278, 1995.

26. D. Jacobs and A. Langen. Accurate and Efficient Approximation of Variable Aliasing in Logic Programs. In Ewing L. Lusk and Ross A. Overbeek, editors, *Proceedings of the North American Conference on Logic Programming*, pages 154–165, Cleveland, Ohio, USA, 1989.

27. D. Jacobs and A. Langen. Static analysis of logic programs for independent and parallelism. *Journal of Logic Programming*, 13(1–4):291–314, 1992.

28. T. Kanamori. Abstract interpretation based on Alexander Templates. *Journal of Logic Programming*, 15(1 & 2):31–54, 1993.

29. B. Le Charlier and P. Van Hentenryck. Groundness analysis of Prolog: implementation and evaluation of the domain Prop. In PEPM93 [41], pages 99–110.

30. J.W. Lloyd. *Foundations of Logic Programming*. Springer-Verlag, 1987.

31. L. Lu. Abstract interpretation, bug detection and bug diagnosis in normal logic programs. PhD thesis, University of Birmingham, 1994.

32. L. Lu. A polymorphic type analysis in logic programs by abstract interpretation. *Journal of Logic Programming*, 36(1):1–54, 1998.

33. K. Marriott and H. Søndergaard. Bottom-up dataflow analysis of normal logic programs. *Journal of Logic Programming*, 13(1–4):181–204, 1992.

34. K. Marriott and H. Søndergaard. Precise and efficient groundness analysis for logic programs. *ACM Letters on Programming Languages and Systems*, 2(1–4):181–196, 1993.

35. K. Marriott, H. Søndergaard, and N.D. Jones. Denotational abstract interpretation of logic programs. *ACM Transactions on Programming Languages and Systems*, 16(3):607–648, 1994.

36. C. Mellish. Some global optimisations for a Prolog compiler. *Journal of Logic Programming*, 2(1):43–66, 1985.

37. C. Mellish. Abstract interpretation of Prolog programs. In S. Abramsky and C. Hankin, editors, *Abstract interpretation of declarative languages*, pages 181–198. Ellis Horwood Limited, 1987.

38. K. Muthukumar and M. Hermenegildo. Compile-time derivation of variable dependency using abstract interpretation. *Journal of Logic Programming*, 13(1, 2, 3 and 4):315–347, 1992.

39. U. Nilsson. Towards a framework for the abstract interpretation of logic programs. In *Proceedings of the International Workshop on Programming Language Implementation and Logic Programming*, pages 68–82. Springer-Verlag, 1988.

40. R. A. O'Keefe. Finite fixed-point problems. In J.-L. Lassez, editor, *Proceedings of the fourth International Conference on Logic programming*, volume 2, pages 729–743. The MIT Press, 1987.

41. *ACM SIGPLAN Symposium on Partial Evaluation and Semantics-Based Program Manipulation*. The ACM Press, 1993.

42. F. Scozzari. Logical optimality of groundness analysis. *Lecture Notes in Computer Science*, 1302:83–97, 1997.

43. H. Søndergaard. An application of abstract interpretation of logic programs: occur check problem. *Lecture Notes in Computer Science*, 213:324–338, 1986.

44. H. Søndergaard. Immediate fixpoints and their use in groundness analysis. *Lecture Notes in Computer Science*, 1180:359–370, 1996.

45. L. Sterling and E. Shapiro. *The Art of Prolog*. The MIT Press, 1986.

46. R. Sundararajan and J.S. Conery. An abstract interpretation scheme for groundness, freeness, and sharing analysis of logic programs. In R. Shyamasundar, editor, *Proceedings of 12th Conference on Foundations of Software Technology and Theoretical Computer Science*, pages 203–216. Springer-Verlag, 1992.

Finite-Tree Analysis
for Constraint Logic-Based Languages*

Roberto Bagnara[1], Roberta Gori[2], Patricia M. Hill[3], and Enea Zaffanella[1]

[1] Department of Mathematics, University of Parma, Italy
{bagnara,zaffanella}@cs.unipr.it
[2] Department of Computer Science, University of Pisa, Italy
gori@di.unipi.it
[3] School of Computing, University of Leeds, U. K.
hill@comp.leeds.ac.uk

Abstract. Logic languages based on the theory of rational, possibly infinite, trees have much appeal in that rational trees allow for faster unification (due to the omission of the occurs-check) and increased expressivity. Note that cyclic terms can provide a very efficient representation of grammars and other useful objects. Unfortunately, the use of infinite rational trees has problems. For instance, many of the built-in and library predicates are ill-defined for such trees and need to be supplemented by run-time checks whose cost may be significant. Moreover, some widely-used program analysis and manipulation techniques are only correct for those parts of programs working over finite trees. It is thus important to obtain, automatically, a knowledge of those program variables (the *finite variables*) that, at the program points of interest, will always be bound to finite terms. For these reasons, we propose here a new data-flow analysis that captures such information. We present a parametric domain where a simple component for recording finite variables is coupled with a generic domain (the parameter of the construction) providing sharing information. The sharing domain is abstractly specified so as to guarantee the correctness of the combined domain and the generality of the approach.

1 Introduction

The intended computation domain of most logic-based languages[1] includes the algebra (or structure) of *finite trees*. Other (constraint) logic-based languages, such as Prolog II and its successors [10, 12], SICStus Prolog [36], and Oz [34], refer to a computation domain of *rational trees*. A rational tree is a possibly infinite tree with a finite number of distinct subtrees and, as is the case for finite trees,

---

* This work has been partly supported by MURST project "Certificazione automatica di programmi mediante interpretazione astratta." Some of this work was done during visits of the fourth author to Leeds, funded by EPSRC under grant M05645.

[1] That is, ordinary logic languages, (concurrent) constraint logic languages, functional logic languages and variations of the above.

P. Cousot (Ed.): SAS 2001, LNCS 2126, pp. 165–184, 2001.

where each node has a finite number of immediate descendants. These properties will ensure that rational trees, even though infinite in the sense that they admit paths of infinite length, can be finitely represented. One possible representation makes use of connected, rooted, directed and possibly cyclic graphs where nodes are labeled with variable and function symbols as is the case of finite trees.

Applications of rational trees in logic programming include graphics [18], parser generation and grammar manipulation [10, 21], and computing with finite-state automata [10]. Other applications are described in [20] and [23]. Going from Prolog to CLP, [31] combines constraints on rational trees and record structures, while the logic-based language *Oz* allows constraints over rational and feature trees [34]. The expressive power of rational trees is put to use, for instance, in several areas of natural language processing. Rational trees are used in implementations of the HPSG formalism (Head-driven Phrase Structure Grammar) [32], in the ALE system (Attribute Logic Engine) [8], and in the ProFIT system (Prolog with Features, Inheritance and Templates) [19].

While rational trees allow for increased expressivity, they also come equipped with a surprising number of problems. As we will see, some of these problems are so serious that rational trees must be used in a very controlled way, disallowing them in any context where they are "dangerous". This, in turn, causes a secondary problem: in order to disallow rational trees in selected contexts one must first detect them, an operation that may be expensive.

The first thing to be aware of is that almost any semantics-based program manipulation technique developed in the field of logic programming —whether it be an analysis, a transformation, or an optimization— assumes a computation domain of *finite trees*. Some of these techniques might work with the rational trees but their correctness has only been proved in the case of finite trees. Others are clearly inapplicable. Let us consider a very simple Prolog program:

```
list([]).
list([_|T]) :- list(T).
```

Most automatic and semi-automatic tools for proving program termination and for complexity analysis agree on the fact that list/1 will terminate when invoked with a ground argument. Consider now the query

```
?- X = [a|X], list(X).
```

and note that, after the execution of the first rational unification, the variable X will be bound to a rational term containing no variables, i.e., the predicate list/1 will be invoked with X ground. However, if such a query is given to, say, SICStus Prolog, then the only way to get the prompt back is by pressing ^C. The problem stems from the fact that the analysis techniques employed by these tools are only sound for finite trees: as soon as they are applied to a system where the creation of cyclic terms is possible, their results are inapplicable. The situation can be improved by combining these termination and/or complexity analyses by a finiteness analysis providing the precondition for the applicability of the other techniques.

The implementation of built-in predicates is another problematic issue. Indeed, it is widely acknowledged that, for the implementation of a system that provides real support for the rational trees, the biggest effort concerns proper handling of built-ins. Of course, the meaning of 'proper' depends on the actual built-in. Built-ins such as copy_term/2 and ==/2 maintain a clear semantics when passing from finite to rational trees. For others, like sort/2, the extension can be questionable:[2] both raising an exception and answering Y = [a] can be argued to be "the right reaction" to the query

```
?- X = [a|X], sort(X, Y).
```

Other built-ins do not tolerate infinite trees in some argument positions. A good implementation should check for finiteness of the corresponding arguments and make sure "the right thing" —failing or raising an appropriate exception— always happens. However, such behavior appears to be uncommon. A small experiment we conducted on six Prolog implementations with queries like

```
?- X = 1+X, Y is X.
?- X = [97|X], name(Y, X).
?- X = [X|X], Y =.. [f|X].
```

resulted in infinite loops, memory exhaustion and/or system thrashing, segmentation faults or other fatal errors. One of the implementations tested, SICStus Prolog, is a professional one and implements run-time checks to avoid most cases where built-ins can have catastrophic effects.[3] The remaining systems are a bit more than research prototypes, but will clearly have to do the same if they evolve to the stage of production tools. Again, a data-flow analysis aimed at the detection of those variables that are definitely bound to finite terms would allow to avoid a (possibly significant) fraction of the useless run-time checks. Note that what has been said for built-in predicates applies to libraries as well. Even though it may be argued that it is enough for programmers to know that they should not use a particular library predicate with infinite terms, it is clear that the use of a "safe" library, including automatic checks which ensure that such predicates are never called with an illegal argument, will result in more robust systems. With the appropriate data-flow analyses, safe libraries do not have to be inefficient libraries.

Another serious problem is the following: the ISO Prolog standard term ordering cannot be extended to rational trees [M. Carlsson, Personal communication, October 2000]. Consider the rational trees defined by A = f(B, a) and B = f(A, b). Clearly, A == B does not hold. Since the standard term ordering is total, we must have either A @< B or B @< A. Assume A @< B. Then f(A, b) @< f(B, a), since the ordering of terms having the same principal functor is inherited by the ordering of subterms considered in a left-to-right fashion. Thus B @< A must hold, which is a contradiction. A dual contradiction

---

[2] Even though sort/2 is not required to be a built-in by the standard, it is offered as such by several implementations.

[3] SICStus 3.8.5 still loops on ?- X = [97|X], name(Y, X).

is obtained by assuming B @< A. As a consequence, applying one of the Prolog term-ordering predicates to one or two infinite terms may cause inconsistent results, giving rise to bugs that are exceptionally difficult to diagnose. For this reason, any system that extends ISO Prolog with rational trees ought to detect such situations and make sure they are not ignored (e.g., by throwing an exception or aborting execution with a meaningful message). However, predicates such as the term-ordering ones are likely to be called a significant number of times, since they are often used to maintain structures implementing ordered collections of terms. This is another instance of the efficiency issue mentioned above.

In this paper, we present a parametric abstract domain for finite-tree analysis, denoted by $H \times P$. This domain combines a simple component H (the *finiteness* component), recording the set of definitely finite variables, with a generic domain P (the parameter of the construction), providing sharing information. The term "sharing information" is to be understood in its broader meaning, which includes variable aliasing, groundness, linearity, freeness and any other kind of information that can improve the precision on these components, such as explicit structural information. Several domain combinations and abstract operators, characterized by different precision/complexity trade-offs, have been proposed to capture these properties (see [5] for an account of some of them). By giving a generic specification for this parameter component, in the style of the *open product* construct proposed in [14], it is possible to define and establish the correctness of the abstract operators on the finite-tree domain independently from any particular domain for sharing analysis.

The paper is structured as follows. The required notations and preliminary concepts are given in Section 2. The finite-tree domain is then introduced in Section 3: Section 3.1 provides the specification of the parameter domain P; Section 3.2 defines the abstraction function for the finiteness component H; Section 3.3 defines the abstract unification operator for $H \times P$. A description of some ongoing work on the subject is given in Section 4 where a possible instance of the parameter P is also specified. We conclude in Section 5.

A longer version of this paper with proofs of the results presented here is available as a technical report [1].

2   Preliminaries

2.1   Infinite Terms and Substitutions

For a set S, $\wp(S)$ is the powerset of S, whereas $\wp_f(S)$ is the set of all the *finite* subsets of S. Let *Sig* denote a possibly infinite set of function symbols, ranked over the set of natural numbers. It is assumed that *Sig* contains at least one function symbol having rank 0 and one having rank greater than 0. Let *Vars* denote a denumerable set of variables, disjoint from *Sig*. Then *Terms* denotes the free algebra of all (possibly infinite) terms in the signature *Sig* having variables in *Vars*. Thus a term can be seen as an ordered labeled tree, possibly having some infinite paths and possibly containing variables: every inner node is labeled with a function symbol in *Sig* with a rank matching the number of the node's immediate descendants, whereas every leaf is labeled by either a variable in *Vars* or a function symbol in *Sig* having rank 0 (a constant).

If $t \in \textit{Terms}$ then $\mathrm{vars}(t)$ and $\mathrm{mvars}(t)$ denote the set and the multiset of variables occurring in t, respectively. We will also write $\mathrm{vars}(o)$ to denote the set of variables occurring in an arbitrary syntactic object o. If a occurs more than once in a multiset M we write $a \in M$.

Suppose $s, t \in \textit{Terms}$: s and t are *independent* if $\mathrm{vars}(s) \cap \mathrm{vars}(t) = \varnothing$; if $y \in \mathrm{vars}(t)$ and $\neg(y \in \mathrm{mvars}(t))$ we say that variable y *occurs linearly in* t, more briefly written using the predication $\mathrm{occ\_lin}(y, t)$; t is said to be *ground* if $\mathrm{vars}(t) = \varnothing$; t is *free* if $t \in \textit{Vars}$; t is *linear* if, for all $y \in \mathrm{vars}(t)$, we have $\mathrm{occ\_lin}(y, t)$; finally, t is a *finite term* (or *Herbrand term*) if it contains a finite number of occurrences of function symbols. The sets of all ground, linear and finite terms are denoted by *GTerms*, *LTerms* and *HTerms*, respectively. As we have specified that *Sig* contains function symbols of rank 0 and rank greater than 0, $\textit{GTerms} \cap \textit{HTerms} \neq \varnothing$ and $\textit{GTerms} \setminus \textit{HTerms} \neq \varnothing$.

A *substitution* is a total function $\sigma \colon \textit{Vars} \to \textit{HTerms}$ that is the identity almost everywhere; in other words, the *domain* of σ,

$$\mathrm{dom}(\sigma) \stackrel{\mathrm{def}}{=} \{\, x \in \textit{Vars} \mid \sigma(x) \neq x \,\},$$

is finite. Given a substitution $\sigma \colon \textit{Vars} \to \textit{HTerms}$, we overload the symbol 'σ' so as to denote also the function $\sigma \colon \textit{HTerms} \to \textit{HTerms}$ defined as follows, for each term $t \in \textit{HTerms}$:

$$\sigma(t) \stackrel{\mathrm{def}}{=} \begin{cases} t, & \text{if } t \text{ is a constant symbol;} \\ \sigma(t), & \text{if } t \in \textit{Vars}; \\ f\big(\sigma(t_1), \dots, \sigma(t_n)\big), & \text{if } t = f(t_1, \dots, t_n). \end{cases}$$

If $x \in \textit{Vars}$ and $t \in \textit{HTerms} \setminus \{x\}$, then $x \mapsto t$ is called a *binding*. The set of all bindings is denoted by *Bind*. Substitutions are denoted by the set of their bindings, thus a substitution σ is identified with the (finite) set

$$\{\, x \mapsto \sigma(x) \mid x \in \mathrm{dom}(\sigma) \,\}.$$

We denote by $\mathrm{vars}(\sigma)$ the set of variables occurring in the bindings of σ.

A substitution is said to be *circular* if, for $n > 1$, it has the form

$$\{x_1 \mapsto x_2, \dots, x_{n-1} \mapsto x_n, x_n \mapsto x_1\},$$

where $x_1, \dots, x_n$ are distinct variables. A substitution is in *rational solved form* if it has no circular subset. The set of all substitutions in rational solved form is denoted by *RSubst*.

If $t \in \textit{HTerms}$, we write $t\sigma$ to denote $\sigma(t)$ and $t[x/s]$ to denote $t\{x \mapsto s\}$.

The composition of substitutions is defined in the usual way. Thus $\tau \circ \sigma$ is the substitution such that, for all terms $t \in \textit{HTerms}$,

$$(\tau \circ \sigma)(t) = \tau\big(\sigma(t)\big)$$

and has the formulation

$$\tau \circ \sigma = \left\{\, x \mapsto x\sigma\tau \mid x \in \operatorname{dom}(\sigma), x \neq x\sigma\tau \,\right\} \cup \left\{\, x \mapsto x\tau \mid x \in \operatorname{dom}(\tau) \setminus \operatorname{dom}(\sigma) \,\right\}.$$

As usual, σ^0 denotes the identity function (i.e., the empty substitution) and, when $i > 0$, σ^i denotes the substitution $(\sigma \circ \sigma^{i-1})$.

For each $\sigma \in RSubst$, $s \in HTerms$, the sequence of finite terms

$$\sigma^0(s), \sigma^1(s), \sigma^2(s), \ldots$$

converges to a (possibly infinite) term, denoted $\sigma^\infty(s)$ [25, 29]. Therefore, the function rt: $HTerms \times RSubst \to Terms$ such that

$$\mathrm{rt}(s, \sigma) \overset{\mathrm{def}}{=} \sigma^\infty(s)$$

is well defined. Note that, in general, this function is not a substitution: while having a finite domain, its "bindings" $x \mapsto t$ can map a domain variable x into a term $t \in Terms \setminus HTerms$.

2.2   Equations

An *equation* is of the form $s = t$ where $s, t \in HTerms$. *Eqs* denotes the set of all equations. A substitution σ may be regarded as a finite set of equations, that is, as the set $\left\{\, x = t \mid x \mapsto t \in \sigma \,\right\}$. We say that a set of equations e is in *rational solved form* if $\left\{\, s \mapsto t \mid (s = t) \in e \,\right\} \in RSubst$. In the rest of the paper, we will often write a substitution $\sigma \in RSubst$ to denote a set of equations in rational solved form (and vice versa).

Languages such as Prolog II, SICStus and Oz are based on $\mathcal{RT}$, the theory of rational trees [10, 11]. This is a syntactic equality theory (i.e., a theory where the function symbols are uninterpreted), augmented with a *uniqueness axiom* for each substitution in rational solved form. Informally speaking these axioms state that, after assigning a ground rational tree to each non-domain variable, the substitution uniquely defines a ground rational tree for each of its domain variables. Thus, any set of equations in rational solved form is, by definition, satisfiable in $\mathcal{RT}$. Note that being in rational solved form is a very weak property. Indeed, unification algorithms returning a set of equations in rational solved form are allowed to be much more "lazy" than one would usually expect. We refer the interested reader to [27, 28, 30] for details on the subject.

Given a set of equations $e \in \wp_f(Eqs)$ that is satisfiable in $\mathcal{RT}$, a substitution $\sigma \in RSubst$ is called a *solution for e in $\mathcal{RT}$* if $\mathcal{RT} \vdash \forall(\sigma \to e)$, i.e., if every model of the theory $\mathcal{RT}$ is also a model of the first order formula $\forall(\sigma \to e)$. If in addition $\mathrm{vars}(\sigma) \subseteq \mathrm{vars}(e)$, then σ is said to be a *relevant* solution for e. Finally, σ is a *most general solution for e in $\mathcal{RT}$* if $\mathcal{RT} \vdash \forall(\sigma \leftrightarrow e)$. In this paper, the set of all the relevant most general solution for e in $\mathcal{RT}$ will be denoted by mgs(e).

2.3   The Concrete Domain

Throughout the paper, we assume a knowledge of the basic concepts of abstract interpretation theory [15, 16].

For the purpose of this paper, we assume a concrete domain constituted by pairs of the form (Σ, V), where V is a finite set of *variables of interest* and Σ is a (possibly infinite) set of substitutions in rational solved form.

Definition 1. (The Concrete Domain.) *Let* $\mathcal{D}^{\flat} \stackrel{\text{def}}{=} \wp(RSubst) \times \wp_{\mathrm{f}}(Vars)$. *If* $(\Sigma, V) \in \mathcal{D}^{\flat}$, *then* (Σ, V) *represents the (possibly infinite) set of first-order formulas* $\left\{\, \exists \Delta \,.\, \sigma \mid \sigma \in \Sigma, \Delta = \mathrm{vars}(\sigma) \setminus V \,\right\}$ *where* σ *is interpreted as the logical conjunction of the equations corresponding to its bindings.*

Concrete domains for constraint languages would be similar. If the analyzed language allows the use of constraints on various domains to restrict the values of the variable leaves of rational trees, the corresponding concrete domain would have one or more extra components to account for the constraints (see [2] for an example).

The concrete element $\left(\{\{x \mapsto f(y)\}\}, \{x, y\}\right)$ expresses a dependency between x and y. In contrast, $\left(\{\{x \mapsto f(y)\}\}, \{x\}\right)$ only constrains x. The same concept can be expressed by saying that in the first case the variable name 'y' matters, but it does not in the second case. Thus, the set of variables of interest is crucial for defining the meaning of the concrete and abstract descriptions. Despite this, always specifying the set of variables of interest would significantly clutter the presentation. Moreover, most of the needed functions on concrete and abstract descriptions preserve the set of variables of interest. For these reasons, we assume the existence of a set $VI \in \wp_{\mathrm{f}}(Vars)$ that contains, at each stage of the analysis, the current variables of interest.[4] As a consequence, when the context makes it clear that $\Sigma \in \wp(RSubst)$, we will write $\Sigma \in \mathcal{D}^{\flat}$ as a shorthand for $(\Sigma, VI) \in \mathcal{D}^{\flat}$.

3   An Abstract Domain for Finiteness Analysis

Finite-tree analysis applies to logic-based languages computing over a domain of rational trees where cyclic structures are allowed. In contrast, analyses aimed at occurs-check reduction [17, 35] apply to programs that are meant to compute on a domain of finite trees only, but have to be executed over systems that are either designed for rational trees or intended just for the finite trees but omit the occurs-check for efficiency reasons. Despite their different objectives, finite-tree and occurs-check analyses have much in common: in both cases, it is important to detect all program points where cyclic structures can be generated.

---

[4] This parallels what happens in the efficient implementation of data-flow analyzers. In fact, almost all the abstract domains currently in use do not need to represent explicitly the set of variables of interest. In contrast, this set is maintained externally and in a unique copy, typically by the fixpoint computation engine.

Note however that, when performing occurs-check reduction, one can take advantage of the following invariant: all data structures generated so far are finite. This property is maintained by transforming the program so as to force finiteness whenever it is possible that a cyclic structure could have been built.[5] In contrast, a finite-tree analysis has to deal with the more general case when some of the data structures computed so far may be cyclic. It is therefore natural to consider an abstract domain made up of two components. The first one simply represents the set of variables that are guaranteed not to be bound to infinite terms. We will denote this *finiteness component* by H (from *Herbrand*).

Definition 2. (The Finiteness Component.) *The* finiteness component *is the set* $H \overset{\text{def}}{=} \wp(VI)$ *partially ordered by reverse subset inclusion.*

The second component of the finite-tree domain should maintain any kind of information that may be useful for computing finiteness information.

It is well-known that sharing information as a whole, therefore including possible variable aliasing, definite linearity, and definite freeness, has a crucial role in occurs-check reduction so that, as observed before, it can be exploited for finite-tree analysis too. Thus, a first choice for the second component of the finite-tree domain would be to consider one of the standard combinations of sharing, freeness and linearity as defined, e.g., in [5, 6, 22]. However, this would tie our specification to a particular sharing analysis domain, whereas the overall approach seems to be inherently more general. For this reason, we will define a finite-tree analysis based on the abstract domain schema $H \times P$, where the generic *sharing component* P is a parameter of the abstract domain construction. This approach can be formalized as an application of the *open product* operator [14].

3.1   The Parameter Component P

Elements of P can encode any kind of information. We only require that substitutions that are equivalent in the theory $\mathcal{RT}$ are identified in P.

Definition 3. (The Parameter Component.) *The parameter component P is an abstract domain related to the concrete domain $\mathcal{D}^\flat$ by means of the concretization function* $\gamma_P \colon P \to \wp(RSubst)$ *such that, for all $p \in P$,*

$$\Big(\sigma \in \gamma_P(p) \wedge \big(\mathcal{RT} \vdash \forall(\sigma \leftrightarrow \tau) \big) \Big) \implies \tau \in \gamma_P(p).$$

The interface between H and P is provided by a set of predicates and functions that satisfy suitable correctness criteria. Note that, for space limitations, we will only specify those abstract operations that are useful to define abstract unification on the combined domain $H \times P$. The other operations needed for a full description of the analysis, such as renamings, upper bound operators and projections, are very simple and, as usual, do not pose any problems.

---

[5] Such a requirement is typically obtained by replacing the unification with a call to `unify_with_occurs_check/2`. As an alternative, in some systems based on rational trees it is possible to insert, after each problematic unification, a finiteness test for the generated term.

Definition 4. (Abstract Operators on P.) *Let $s, t \in HTerms$ be finite terms. For each $p \in P$, we define the following predicates:*
s and t are independent *in p if and only if* $\text{ind}_p : HTerms^2 \to Bool$ *holds for (s, t), where*

$$\text{ind}_p(s, t) \implies \forall \sigma \in \gamma_P(p) : \text{vars}(\text{rt}(s, \sigma)) \cap \text{vars}(\text{rt}(t, \sigma)) = \varnothing;$$

s and t share linearly *in p if and only if* $\text{share\_lin}_p : HTerms^2 \to Bool$ *holds for (s, t), where*

$$\text{share\_lin}_p(s, t) \implies \forall \sigma \in \gamma_P(p) :$$
$$\forall y \in \text{vars}(\text{rt}(s, \sigma)) \cap \text{vars}(\text{rt}(t, \sigma)) :$$
$$\text{occ\_lin}(y, \text{rt}(s, \sigma)) \wedge \text{occ\_lin}(y, \text{rt}(t, \sigma));$$

t is ground *in p if and only if* $\text{ground}_p : HTerms \to Bool$ *holds for t, where*

$$\text{ground}_p(t) \implies \forall \sigma \in \gamma_P(p) : \text{rt}(t, \sigma) \in GTerms;$$

t is ground-or-free *in p if and only if* $\text{gfree}_p : HTerms \to Bool$ *holds for t, where*

$$\text{gfree}_p(t) \implies \forall \sigma \in \gamma_P(p) : \text{rt}(t, \sigma) \in GTerms \vee \text{rt}(t, \sigma) \in Vars;$$

s and t are or-linear *in p if and only if* $\text{or\_lin}_p : HTerms^2 \to Bool$ *holds for (s, t), where*

$$\text{or\_lin}_p(s, t) \implies \forall \sigma \in \gamma_P(p) : \text{rt}(s, \sigma) \in LTerms \vee \text{rt}(t, \sigma) \in LTerms;$$

s is linear *in p if and only if* $\text{lin}_p : HTerms \to Bool$ *holds for s, where*

$$\text{lin}_p(s) \overset{\text{def}}{\iff} \text{or\_lin}_p(s, s).$$

For each $p \in P$, the following functions compute subsets of the set of variables of interest:
the function $\text{share\_same\_var}_p : HTerms \times HTerms \to \wp(VI)$ *returns a set of variables that may share with the given terms via the same variable. For each $s, t \in HTerms$,*

$$\text{share\_same\_var}_p(s, t) \supseteq \left\{ y \in VI \,\middle|\, \begin{array}{l} \exists \sigma \in \gamma_P(p) \,. \\ \quad \exists z \in \text{vars}(\text{rt}(y, \sigma)) \,. \\ \qquad z \in \text{vars}(\text{rt}(s, \sigma)) \cap \text{vars}(\text{rt}(t, \sigma)) \end{array} \right\};$$

the function $\text{share\_with}_p : HTerms \to \wp(VI)$ *yields a set of variables that may share with the given term. For each $t \in HTerms$,*

$$\text{share\_with}_p(t) \overset{\text{def}}{=} \left\{ y \in VI \mid y \in \text{share\_same\_var}_p(y, t) \right\}.$$

The function $\text{amgu}_P \colon P \times Bind \to P$ *correctly captures the effects of a binding on an element of* P. *For each* $(x \mapsto t) \in Bind$ *and* $p \in P$, *let*

$$p' \stackrel{\text{def}}{=} \text{amgu}_P(p, x \mapsto t).$$

For all $\sigma \in \gamma_P(p)$, *if* $\tau \in \text{mgs}(\sigma \cup \{x = t\})$, *then* $\tau \in \gamma_P(p')$.

As it will be shown in Section 4.1, some of these generic operators can be directly mapped into the corresponding abstract operators defined for well-known sharing analysis domains. However, the specification given in Definition 4, besides being more general than a particular implementation, also allows for a modular approach when proving correctness results.

3.2   The Abstraction Function for H

When the concrete domain is based on the theory of finite trees, idempotent substitutions provide a finitely computable *strong normal form* for domain elements, meaning that different substitutions describe different sets of finite trees.[6] In contrast, when working on a concrete domain based on the theory of rational trees, substitutions in rational solved form, while being finitely computable, no longer satisfy this property: there can be an infinite set of substitutions in rational solved form all describing the same set of rational trees (i.e., the same element in the "intended" semantics). For instance, the substitutions

$$\sigma_n = \{x \mapsto \overbrace{f(\cdots f(x)\cdots)}^{n}\}$$

for $n = 1, 2, \ldots$, all map the variable x into the same rational tree (which is usually denoted by f^ω).

Ideally, a strong normal form for the set of rational trees described by a substitution $\sigma \in RSubst$ can be obtained by computing the limit σ^∞. The problem is that we may end up with $\sigma^\infty \notin RSubst$, as σ^∞ can map domain variables to infinite rational terms.

This poses a non-trivial problem when trying to define a "good" abstraction function, since it would be really desirable for this function to map any two equivalent concrete elements to the same abstract element. As shown in [24], the classical abstraction function for set-sharing analysis [13, 26], which was defined for idempotent substitutions only, does not enjoy this property when applied, as it is, to arbitrary substitutions in rational solved form. A possibility is to look for a more general abstraction function that allows to obtain the desired property. For example, in [24] the sharing-group operator sg of [26] is replaced by an occurrence operator, occ, defined by means of a fixpoint computation. We now provide a similar fixpoint construction defining the finiteness operator.

---

[6] As usual, this is modulo the possible renaming of variables.

Definition 5. (Finiteness Functions.) *For each* $n \in \mathbb{N}$, *the* finiteness func-tion $\text{hvars}_n \colon RSubst \to \wp(Vars)$ *is defined, for each* $\sigma \in RSubst$, *by*

$$\text{hvars}_0(\sigma) \stackrel{\text{def}}{=} Vars \setminus \text{dom}(\sigma)$$

and, for $n > 0$, *by*

$$\text{hvars}_n(\sigma) \stackrel{\text{def}}{=} \text{hvars}_{n-1}(\sigma) \cup \big\{\, y \in \text{dom}(\sigma) \,\big|\, \text{vars}(y\sigma) \subseteq \text{hvars}_{n-1}(\sigma) \,\big\}.$$

For each $\sigma \in RSubst$ and each $i \geq 0$, we have $\text{hvars}_i(\sigma) \subseteq \text{hvars}_{i+1}(\sigma)$ and also that $Vars \setminus \text{hvars}_i(\sigma) \subseteq \text{dom}(\sigma)$ is a finite set. By these two properties, the following fixpoint computation is well defined and finitely computable.

Definition 6. (Finiteness Operator.) *For each* $\sigma \in RSubst$, *the* finiteness operator $\text{hvars} \colon RSubst \to \wp(Vars)$ *is given by* $\text{hvars}(\sigma) \stackrel{\text{def}}{=} \text{hvars}_\ell(\sigma)$ *where* $\ell \stackrel{\text{def}}{=} \ell(\sigma) \in \mathbb{N}$ *is such that* $\text{hvars}_\ell(\sigma) = \text{hvars}_n(\sigma)$ *for all* $n \geq \ell$.

The following proposition shows that the hvars operator precisely captures the intended property.

Proposition 1. *If* $\sigma \in RSubst$ *and* $x \in Vars$ *then*

$$x \in \text{hvars}(\sigma) \iff \text{rt}(x, \sigma) \in HTerms.$$

Example 1. Consider $\sigma \in RSubst$, where

$$\sigma = \big\{ x_1 \mapsto f(x_2), x_2 \mapsto g(x_5), x_3 \mapsto f(x_4), x_4 \mapsto g(x_3) \big\}.$$

Then,

$$\begin{aligned}
\text{hvars}_0(\sigma) &= Vars \setminus \{x_1, x_2, x_3, x_4\}, \\
\text{hvars}_1(\sigma) &= Vars \setminus \{x_1, x_3, x_4\}, \\
\text{hvars}_2(\sigma) &= Vars \setminus \{x_3, x_4\} \\
&= \text{hvars}(\sigma).
\end{aligned}$$

Thus, $x_1 \in \text{hvars}(\sigma)$, although $\text{vars}(x_1\sigma) \subseteq \text{dom}(\sigma)$.

The abstraction function for H can then be defined in the obvious way.

Definition 7. (The Abstraction Function for H.) *The abstraction function* $\alpha_H \colon RSubst \to H$ *is defined, for each* $\sigma \in RSubst$, *by*

$$\alpha_H(\sigma) \stackrel{\text{def}}{=} VI \cap \text{hvars}(\sigma).$$

The concrete domain $\mathcal{D}^\flat$ *is related to* H *by means of the abstraction function* $\alpha_H \colon \mathcal{D}^\flat \to H$ *such that, for each* $\Sigma \in \wp(RSubst)$,

$$\alpha_H(\Sigma) \stackrel{\text{def}}{=} \bigcap \big\{\, \alpha_H(\sigma) \,\big|\, \sigma \in \Sigma \,\big\}.$$

Since the abstraction function α_H is additive, the concretization function is given by its adjoint [15]:

$$\gamma_H(h) \stackrel{\text{def}}{=} \left\{ \sigma \in RSubst \mid \alpha_H(\sigma) \supseteq h \right\}.$$

With these definitions, we have the desired result: equivalent substitutions in rational solved form have the same finiteness abstraction.

Theorem 1. *If $\sigma, \tau \in RSubst$ and $\mathcal{RT} \vdash \forall(\sigma \leftrightarrow \tau)$, then $\alpha_H(\sigma) = \alpha_H(\tau)$.*

3.3   Abstract Unification on $H \times P$

The abstract unification for the combined domain $H \times P$ is defined by using the abstract predicates and functions as specified for P as well as a new finiteness predicate for the domain H.

Definition 8. (Abstract Unification on $H \times P$.) *A term $t \in HTerms$ is a finite tree in h if and only if the predicate $\text{hterm}_h \colon HTerms \to Bool$ holds for t, where $\text{hterm}_h(t) \stackrel{\text{def}}{=} \text{vars}(t) \subseteq h$.*

The function $\text{amgu}_H \colon (H \times P) \times Bind \to H$ captures the effects of a binding on an H element. Let $\langle h, p \rangle \in H \times P$ and $(x \mapsto t) \in Bind$. Then

$$\text{amgu}_H\big(\langle h, p \rangle, x \mapsto t\big) \stackrel{\text{def}}{=} h',$$

where

$$
h' \stackrel{\text{def}}{=}
\begin{cases}
h \cup \text{vars}(t), & \text{if } \text{hterm}_h(x) \wedge \text{ground}_p(x); \\
h \cup \{x\}, & \text{if } \text{hterm}_h(t) \wedge \text{ground}_p(t); \\
h, & \text{if } \text{hterm}_h(x) \wedge \text{hterm}_h(t) \\
& \quad \wedge \text{ind}_p(x, t) \wedge \text{or\_lin}_p(x, t); \\
h, & \text{if } \text{hterm}_h(x) \wedge \text{hterm}_h(t) \\
& \quad \wedge \text{gfree}_p(x) \wedge \text{gfree}_p(t); \\
h \setminus \text{share\_same\_var}_p(x, t), & \text{if } \text{hterm}_h(x) \wedge \text{hterm}_h(t) \\
& \quad \wedge \text{share\_lin}_p(x, t) \\
& \quad \wedge \text{or\_lin}_p(x, t); \\
h \setminus \text{share\_with}_p(x), & \text{if } \text{hterm}_h(x) \wedge \text{lin}_p(x); \\
h \setminus \text{share\_with}_p(t), & \text{if } \text{hterm}_h(t) \wedge \text{lin}_p(t); \\
h \setminus \big(\text{share\_with}_p(x) \cup \text{share\_with}_p(t)\big), & \text{otherwise.}
\end{cases}
$$

The abstract unification function $\text{amgu} \colon (H \times P) \times Bind \to H \times P$, for any $\langle h, p \rangle \in H \times P$ and $(x \mapsto t) \in Bind$, is given by

$$\text{amgu}\big(\langle h, p \rangle, x \mapsto t\big) \stackrel{\text{def}}{=} \Big\langle \text{amgu}_H\big(\langle h, p \rangle, x \mapsto t\big), \text{amgu}_P(p, x \mapsto t) \Big\rangle.$$

In the computation of h' (the new finiteness component resulting from the abstract evaluation of a binding) there are eight cases based on properties holding for the concrete terms described by x and t.

1. In the first case, the concrete term described by x is both finite and ground. Thus, after a successful execution of the binding, any concrete term described by t will be finite. Note that t could have contained variables which may be possibly bound to cyclic terms just before the execution of the binding.
2. The second case is symmetric to the first one. Note that these are the only cases when a "positive" propagation of finiteness information is correct. In contrast, in all the remaining cases, the goal is to limit as much as possible the propagation of "negative" information, i.e., the possible cyclicity of terms.
3. The third case exploits the classical results proved in research work on occurs-check reduction [17, 35]. Accordingly, it is required that both x and t describe finite terms that do not share. The use of the implicitly disjunctive predicate or_lin$_p$ allows for the application of this case even when neither x nor t are known to be definitely linear. For instance, as observed in [17], this may happen when the component P embeds the domain Pos for groundness analysis.[7]
4. The fourth case exploits the observation that cyclic terms cannot be created when unifying two finite terms that are either ground or free. Ground-or-freeness [5] is a safe, more precise and inexpensive replacement for the classical freeness property when combining sharing analysis domains.
5. The fifth case applies when unifying a linear and finite term with another finite term possibly sharing with it, provided they can only share linearly (namely, all the shared variables occur linearly in the considered terms). In such a context, only the shared variables can introduce cycles.
6. In the sixth case, we drop the assumption about the finiteness of the term described by t. As a consequence, all variables sharing with x become possibly cyclic. However, provided x describes a finite and linear term, all finite variables independent from x preserve their finiteness.
7. The seventh case is symmetric to the sixth one.
8. The last case states that term finiteness is preserved for all variables that are independent from both x and t. Note that this case is only used when none of the other cases apply.

The following result, together with the assumption on amgu$_P$ as specified in Definition 4, ensures that abstract unification on the combined domain $H \times P$ is correct.

Theorem 2. *Let* $\langle h, p \rangle \in H \times P$ *and* $(x \mapsto t) \in Bind$, *where* $\{x\} \cup vars(t) \subseteq VI$. *Let also* $\sigma \in \gamma_H(h) \cap \gamma_P(p)$ *and* $h' = amgu_H(\langle h, p \rangle, x \mapsto t)$. *Then*

$$\tau \in mgs(\sigma \cup \{x = t\}) \implies \tau \in \gamma_H(h').$$

---

[7] Let t be y. Let also P be Pos. Then, given the Pos formula $\phi \stackrel{\text{def}}{=} (x \vee y)$, both ind$_\phi(x, y)$ and or_lin$_\phi(x, y)$ satsify the conditions in Definition 4. Note that from ϕ we cannot infer that x is definitely linear and neither that y is definitely linear.

4   Ongoing and Further Work

4.1   An Instance of the Parameter Domain *P*

As discussed in Section 3, several abstract domains for sharing analysis can be
used to implement the parameter component *P*. One could consider the well-
known set-sharing domain of Jacobs and Langen [26]. In such a case, all the
non-trivial correctness results have already been established in [24]: in particular, the abstraction function provided in [24] satisfies the requirement of Definition 3 and the abstract unification operator has been proven correct with respect
to rational-tree unification. Note however that, since no freeness and linearity
information is recorded in the plain set-sharing domain, some of the predicates
of Definition 4 need to be grossly approximated.

Therefore, a better choice would be to consider the abstract domain *SFL* [5]
(see also [6]) that represents possible sharing. This domain incorporates the
set-sharing domain of Jacobs and Langen with definite freeness and linearity information; the information being encoded by two sets of variables, one satisfying
the property of freeness and the other, the property of linearity.

Definition 9. (The Set-Sharing Domain *SH*.) *The set SH is defined by*
$SH \stackrel{\text{def}}{=} \wp(SG)$, *where* $SG \stackrel{\text{def}}{=} \wp(VI) \setminus \{\varnothing\}$ *is the set of* sharing groups. *SH is
ordered by subset inclusion.*

Definition 10. (The Domain *SFL*.) *Let* $F \stackrel{\text{def}}{=} \wp(VI)$ *and* $L \stackrel{\text{def}}{=} \wp(VI)$ *be
partially ordered by reverse subset inclusion. The domain SFL is defined by the
Cartesian product* $SFL \stackrel{\text{def}}{=} SH \times F \times L$ *ordered by '$\leq_S$', the component-wise
extension of the orderings defined on the sub-domains.*

Note that a complete definition, besides explicitly dealing with the set of relevant variables *VI*, would require the addition of a bottom element $\bot$ representing
the semantics of those program fragments that have no successful computations.

In the next definition we introduce a few well-known operations on the set-
sharing domain *SH*. These will be used to define the operations on the domain
SFL.

Definition 11. (Abstract Operators on *SH*.) *For each sh $\in$ SH and each
$V \subseteq VI$, the extraction of the relevant component of sh with respect to V is
given by the function* rel: $\wp(VI) \times SH \to SH$ *defined as*

$$\mathrm{rel}(V, sh) \stackrel{\text{def}}{=} \{\, S \in sh \mid S \cap V \neq \varnothing \,\}.$$

For each sh $\in$ SH and each $V \subseteq VI$, the function $\overline{\mathrm{rel}}$: $\wp(VI) \times SH \to SH$
gives the irrelevant component of sh with respect to V. It is defined as

$$\overline{\mathrm{rel}}(V, sh) \stackrel{\text{def}}{=} sh \setminus \mathrm{rel}(V, sh).$$

The function $(\cdot)^\star \colon SH \to SH$, *called* star-union, *is given, for each* $sh \in SH$, *by*

$$sh^\star \stackrel{\text{def}}{=} \left\{ S \in SG \ \middle| \ \exists n \ge 1 \ . \ \exists T_1, \ldots, T_n \in sh \ . \ S = \bigcup_{i=1}^n T_i \right\}.$$

For each $sh_1, sh_2 \in SH$, *the function* bin$\colon SH \times SH \to SH$, *called* binary union, *is given by*

$$\text{bin}(sh_1, sh_2) \stackrel{\text{def}}{=} \{ \, S_1 \cup S_2 \mid S_1 \in sh_1, S_2 \in sh_2 \, \}.$$

It is now possible to define the implementation, on the domain *SFL*, of all the predicates and functions specified in Definition 4.

Definition 12. (Abstract Operators on *SFL*.) *For each* $d = \langle sh, f, l \rangle \in SFL$, *for each* $s, t \in HTerms$, *where* $\text{vars}(s) \cup \text{vars}(t) \subseteq VI$, *let* $R_s = \text{rel}(\text{vars}(s), sh)$ *and* $R_t = \text{rel}(\text{vars}(t), sh)$. *Then*

$$\text{ind}_d(s, t) \stackrel{\text{def}}{=} \big(R_s \cap R_t = \varnothing \big);$$

$$\text{ground}_d(t) \stackrel{\text{def}}{=} \big(\text{vars}(t) \subseteq VI \setminus \text{vars}(sh) \big);$$

$$\text{occ\_lin}_d(y, t) \stackrel{\text{def}}{=} \text{ground}_d(y) \vee \Big(\text{occ\_lin}(y, t) \wedge (y \in l)$$
$$\wedge \, \forall z \in \text{vars}(t) : \big(y \ne z \implies \text{ind}_d(y, z) \big) \Big);$$

$$\text{share\_lin}_d(s, t) \stackrel{\text{def}}{=} \forall y \in \text{vars}(R_s \cap R_t) :$$
$$y \in \text{vars}(s) \implies \text{occ\_lin}_d(y, s)$$
$$\wedge \, y \in \text{vars}(t) \implies \text{occ\_lin}_d(y, t);$$

$$\text{free}_d(t) \stackrel{\text{def}}{=} \exists y \in VI \ . \ (y = t) \wedge (y \in f);$$

$$\text{gfree}_d(t) \stackrel{\text{def}}{=} \text{ground}_d(t) \vee \text{free}_d(t);$$

$$\text{lin}_d(t) \stackrel{\text{def}}{=} \forall y \in \text{vars}(t) : \text{occ\_lin}_d(y, t);$$

$$\text{or\_lin}_d(s, t) \stackrel{\text{def}}{=} \text{lin}_d(s) \vee \text{lin}_d(t);$$

$$\text{share\_same\_var}_d(s, t) \stackrel{\text{def}}{=} \text{vars}(R_s \cap R_t);$$

$$\text{share\_with}_d(t) \stackrel{\text{def}}{=} \text{vars}(R_t).$$

The function amgu$_S \colon SFL \times Bind \to SFL$ *captures the effects of a binding on an element of SFL. Let* $d = \langle sh, f, l \rangle \in SFL$ *and* $(x \mapsto t) \in Bind$, *where* $V_{xt} = \{x\} \cup \text{vars}(t) \subseteq VI$. *Let* $R_x = \text{rel}(\{x\}, sh)$ *and* $R_t = \text{rel}(\text{vars}(t), sh)$. *Let also*

$$sh' \stackrel{\text{def}}{=} \overline{\text{rel}}(V_{xt}, sh) \cup \text{bin}\big(S_x, S_t \big),$$

$$S_x \stackrel{\text{def}}{=} \begin{cases} R_x, & \text{if } \text{free}_d(x) \vee \text{free}_d(t) \vee \big(\text{lin}_d(t) \wedge \text{ind}_d(x, t) \big); \\ R_x^\star, & \text{otherwise}; \end{cases}$$

$$S_t \stackrel{\text{def}}{=} \begin{cases} R_t, & \text{if } \text{free}_d(x) \vee \text{free}_d(t) \vee \big(\text{lin}_d(x) \wedge \text{ind}_d(x,t)\big); \\ R_t^\star, & \text{otherwise;} \end{cases}$$

$$f' \stackrel{\text{def}}{=} \begin{cases} f, & \text{if } \text{free}_d(x) \wedge \text{free}_d(t); \\ f \setminus \text{vars}(R_x), & \text{if } \text{free}_d(x); \\ f \setminus \text{vars}(R_t), & \text{if } \text{free}_d(t); \\ f \setminus \text{vars}(R_x \cup R_t), & \text{otherwise;} \end{cases}$$

$$l' \stackrel{\text{def}}{=} \big(VI \setminus \text{vars}(sh')\big) \cup f' \cup l'';$$

$$l'' \stackrel{\text{def}}{=} \begin{cases} l \setminus \big(\text{vars}(R_x) \cap \text{vars}(R_t)\big), & \text{if } \text{lin}_d(x) \wedge \text{lin}_d(t); \\ l \setminus \text{vars}(R_x), & \text{if } \text{lin}_d(x); \\ l \setminus \text{vars}(R_t), & \text{if } \text{lin}_d(t); \\ l \setminus \text{vars}(R_x \cup R_t), & \text{otherwise.} \end{cases}$$

Then $\text{amgu}_S(d, x \mapsto t) \stackrel{\text{def}}{=} \langle sh', f', l' \rangle.$

It is worth noting that, when observing the term finiteness property, set-sharing is strictly more precise than pair-sharing, since a set-sharing domain is strictly more precise when computing the functions share_same_var_p and share_lin_p.[8] This observation holds regardless of the pair-sharing variant considered, including ASub [9, 35], *PSD* [3] and Sh^{PSh} [33].

It remains for us to establish that the relations and functions given in Definition 12 satisfy all the requirements of Definitions 3 and 4. This will require a proof of the correctness, with respect to rational unification, of the abstract operators defined on the domain *SFL*, thereby generalizing and extending the results proved in [24] for the set-sharing domain of Jacobs and Langen.

Note that the domain *SFL* is not the target of the generic specification given in Definition 4; more powerful sharing domains can also satisfy this schema, including all the enhanced combinations considered in [5]. For instance, as the predicate gfree_d defined on *SFL* does not fully exploit the disjunctive nature of its generic specification gfree_p, the precision of the analysis may be improved by adding a domain component explicitly tracking ground-or-freeness, as proposed in [5]. The same argument applies to the predicate or_lin_d, with respect to or_lin_p, when considering the combination with the groundness domain *Pos*.

In order to provide an experimental evaluation of the proposed finiteness analysis, we are implementing $H \times P$ where the P component is the *SFL* domain extended with some of the enhancements described in [5]. One of these

---

[8] For the expert: consider the abstract evaluation of the binding $x \mapsto y$ and the description $\langle h, d \rangle \in H \times SFL$, where $h = \{x, y, z\}$ and $d = \langle sh, f, l \rangle$ is such that $sh = \{\{x, y\}, \{x, z\}, \{y, z\}\}$, $f = \varnothing$ and $l = \{x, y, z\}$. Then $z \notin \text{share\_same\_var}_d(x, y)$ so that we have $h' = \{z\}$. In contrast, when using a pair-sharing domain such as *PSD*, the element d is equivalent to $d' = \langle sh', f, l \rangle$, where $sh' = sh \cup \{\{x, y, z\}\}$. Hence we have $z \in \text{share\_same\_var}_{d'}(x, y)$ and $h' = \varnothing$. Thus, in sh the information provided by the lack of the sharing group $\{x, y, z\}$ is redundant when observing pair-sharing and groundness, but it is not redundant when observing term finiteness.

enhancements uses information about the actual structure of terms. It has been shown in [2] that this structural information, provided by integrating the generic Pattern($\cdot$) construction with *SFL*, can have a key role in improving the precision of sharing analysis and, in particular, allowing better identification where cyclic structures may appear. Thus, it is expected that structural information captured using Pattern($H \times P$) can improve the precision of finite-tree analysis; both with respect to the parametric component P and the finiteness component H itself.

4.2   Term-Finiteness Dependencies

The parametric domain $H \times P$ captures the negative aspect of term-finiteness, that is, the circumstances under which finiteness can be lost. When a binding has the potential for creating one or more rational terms, the operator amgu$_H$ removes from h all the variables that may be bound to non-finite terms. However, term-finiteness has also a positive aspect: there are cases where a variable is guaranteed to be bound to a finite term and this knowledge can be propagated to other variables. Guarantees of finiteness are provided by several built-ins like `unify_with_occurs_check/2`, `var/1`, `name/2`, all the arithmetic predicates, and so forth. SICStus Prolog also provides an explicit `acyclic_term/1` predicate.

The term-finiteness information provided by the h component of $H \times P$ does not capture the information concerning how finiteness of one variable affects the finiteness of other variables. This kind of information, usually termed *relational information*, is very important as it allows the propagation of positive finiteness information. An important source of relational information comes from *dependencies*. Consider the terms $t_1 \stackrel{\text{def}}{=} f(x)$, $t_2 \stackrel{\text{def}}{=} g(y)$, and $t_3 \stackrel{\text{def}}{=} h(x,y)$: it is clear that, for each assignment of rational terms to x and y, t_3 is finite if and only if t_1 and t_2 are so. We can capture this by the Boolean formula $t_3 \leftrightarrow (t_1 \wedge t_2)$. The reasoning is based on the following facts:

1. t_1, t_2, and t_3 are finite terms, so that the finiteness of their instances depends only on the finiteness of the terms that take the place of x and y.
2. t_3 *covers* both t_1 and t_2, that is, vars(t_3) $\supseteq$ vars(t_1) $\cup$ vars(t_2); this means that, if an assignment to the variables of t_3 produces a finite instance of t_3, that very same assignment will necessarily result in finite instances of t_1 and t_2. Conversely, an assignment producing non-finite instances of t_1 or t_2 will forcibly result in a non-finite instance of t_3.
3. Similarly, t_1 and t_2, taken together, cover t_3.

The important point to notice is that the indicated dependency will continue to hold for any further simultaneous instantiation of t_1, t_2, and t_3. In other words, such dependencies are preserved by forward computations (since they proceed by consistently instantiating program variables).

Consider the abstract binding $x \mapsto t$ where t is a finite term such that vars(t) = $\{y_1, \ldots, y_n\}$. After this binding has been successfully performed, the destinies of x and t concerning term-finiteness are tied together forever. This tie can be described by the dependency formula

$$x \leftrightarrow (y_1 \wedge \cdots \wedge y_n), \tag{1}$$

meaning that x will be bound to a finite term if and only if, for each $i = 1$, $\ldots, n$, y_i is bound to a finite term. While the dependency expressed by (1) is a correct description of any computation state following the application of the binding $x \mapsto t$, it is not as precise as it could be. Suppose that x and y_k are indeed the same variable. Then (1) is logically equivalent to

$$x \to (y_1 \wedge \cdots \wedge y_{k-1} \wedge y_{k+1} \wedge \cdots \wedge y_n). \tag{2}$$

Correct: whenever x is bound to a finite term, all the other variables will be bound to finite terms. The point is that x has just been bound to a non-finite term, irrevocably: no forward computation can change this. Thus, the implication (2) holds vacuously. The precise and correct description for the state of affairs caused by the cyclic binding is, instead, the negated atom $\neg x$, whose intuitive reading is "x is not (and never will be) finite."

Following the intuition outlined above, in [4] we have studied a domain, whose carrier is the set of all Boolean functions, for representing and propagating finiteness dependencies. We believe that coupling this new domain with $H \times P$ can greatly improve the precision of the analysis.

5 Conclusion

Several modern logic-based languages offer a computation domain based on rational trees. On the one hand, the use of such trees is encouraged by the possibility of using efficient and correct unification algorithms and by an increase in expressivity. On the other hand, these gains are countered by the extra problems rational trees bring with themselves and that can be summarized as follows: several built-ins, library predicates, program analysis and manipulation techniques are only well-defined for program fragments working with finite trees.

In this paper we propose an abstract-interpretation based solution to the problem of detecting program variables that can only be bound to finite terms. The rationale behind this is that applications exploiting rational trees tend to do so in a very controlled way. If the analysis we propose proves to be precise enough, then we will have a practical way of taking advantage of rational trees while minimizing the impact of their disadvantages.

References

1. R. Bagnara, R. Gori, P. M. Hill, and E. Zaffanella. Finite-tree analysis for constraint logic-based languages. Quaderno 251, Dipartimento di Matematica, Università di Parma, 2001. Available at http://www.cs.unipr.it/~bagnara/.
2. R. Bagnara, P. M. Hill, and E. Zaffanella. Efficient structural information analysis for real CLP languages. In M. Parigot and A. Voronkov, editors, *Proceedings of the 7th International Conference on Logic for Programming and Automated Reasoning (LPAR 2000)*, volume 1955 of *Lecture Notes in Computer Science*, pages 189–206, Reunion Island, France, 2000. Springer-Verlag, Berlin.

3. R. Bagnara, P. M. Hill, and E. Zaffanella. Set-sharing is redundant for pair-sharing. *Theoretical Computer Science*, 2001. To appear.

4. R. Bagnara, E. Zaffanella, R. Gori, and P. M. Hill. Boolean functions for finite-tree dependencies. Quaderno 252, Dipartimento di Matematica, Università di Parma, 2001. Available at http://www.cs.unipr.it/~bagnara/.

5. R. Bagnara, E. Zaffanella, and P. M. Hill. Enhanced sharing analysis techniques: A comprehensive evaluation. In M. Gabbrielli and F. Pfenning, editors, *Proceedings of the 2nd International ACM SIGPLAN Conference on Principles and Practice of Declarative Programming*, pages 103–114, Montreal, Canada, 2000. Association for Computing Machinery.

6. M. Bruynooghe, M. Codish, and A. Mulkers. A composite domain for freeness, sharing, and compoundness analysis of logic programs. Technical Report CW 196, Department of Computer Science, K.U. Leuven, Belgium, July 1994.

7. J. A. Campbell, editor. *Implementations of Prolog*. Ellis Horwood/Halsted Press/Wiley, 1984.

8. B. Carpenter. *The Logic of Typed Feature Structures with Applications to Unification-based Grammars, Logic Programming and Constraint Resolution*, volume 32 of *Cambridge Tracts in Theoretical Computer Science*. Cambridge University Press, New York, 1992.

9. M. Codish, D. Dams, and E. Yardeni. Derivation and safety of an abstract unification algorithm for groundness and aliasing analysis. In K. Furukawa, editor, *Logic Programming: Proceedings of the Eighth International Conference on Logic Programming*, MIT Press Series in Logic Programming, pages 79–93, Paris, France, 1991. The MIT Press.

10. A. Colmerauer. Prolog and infinite trees. In K. L. Clark and S. Å. Tärnlund, editors, *Logic Programming, APIC Studies in Data Processing*, volume 16, pages 231–251. Academic Press, New York, 1982.

11. A. Colmerauer. Equations and inequations on finite and infinite trees. In *Proceedings of the International Conference on Fifth Generation Computer Systems (FGCS'84)*, pages 85–99, Tokyo, Japan, 1984. ICOT.

12. A. Colmerauer. An introduction to Prolog-III. *Communications of the ACM*, 33(7):69–90, 1990.

13. A. Cortesi and G. Filé. Sharing is optimal. *Journal of Logic Programming*, 38(3):371–386, 1999.

14. A. Cortesi, B. Le Charlier, and P. Van Hentenryck. Combinations of abstract domains for logic programming: Open product and generic pattern construction. *Science of Computer Programming*, 38(1–3), 2000.

15. P. Cousot and R. Cousot. Abstract interpretation: A unified lattice model for static analysis of programs by construction or approximation of fixpoints. In *Proceedings of the Fourth Annual ACM Symposium on Principles of Programming Languages*, pages 238–252, 1977.

16. P. Cousot and R. Cousot. Abstract interpretation frameworks. *Journal of Logic and Computation*, 2(4):511–547, 1992.

17. L. Crnogorac, A. D. Kelly, and H. Søndergaard. A comparison of three occur-check analysers. In R. Cousot and D. A. Schmidt, editors, *Static Analysis: Proceedings of the 3rd International Symposium*, volume 1145 of *Lecture Notes in Computer Science*, pages 159–173, Aachen, Germany, 1996. Springer-Verlag, Berlin.

18. P. R. Eggert and K. P. Chow. Logic programming, graphics and infinite terms. Technical Report UCSB DoCS TR 83-02, Department of Computer Science, University of California at Santa Barbara, 1983.

19. G. Erbach. ProFIT: Prolog with Features, Inheritance and Templates. In *Proceedings of the 7th Conference of the European Chapter of the Association for Computational Linguistics*, pages 180–187, Dublin, Ireland, 1995.

20. M. Filgueiras. A Prolog interpreter working with infinite terms. In Campbell [7], pages 250–258.

21. F. Giannesini and J. Cohen. Parser generation and grammar manipulation using Prolog's infinite trees. *Journal of Logic Programming*, 3:253–265, 1984.

22. W. Hans and S. Winkler. Aliasing and groundness analysis of logic programs through abstract interpretation and its safety. Technical Report 92-27, Technical University of Aachen (RWTH Aachen), 1992.

23. S. Haridi and D. Sahlin. Efficient implementation of unification of cyclic structures. In Campbell [7], pages 234–249.

24. P. M. Hill, R. Bagnara, and E. Zaffanella. Soundness, idempotence and commutativity of set-sharing. *Theory and Practice of Logic Programming*, 2001. To appear. Available at http://arXiv.org/abs/cs.PL/0102030.

25. B. Intrigila and M. Venturini Zilli. A remark on infinite matching vs infinite unification. *Journal of Symbolic Computation*, 21(3):2289–2292, 1996.

26. D. Jacobs and A. Langen. Accurate and efficient approximation of variable aliasing in logic programs. In E. L. Lusk and R. A. Overbeek, editors, *Logic Programming: Proceedings of the North American Conference*, MIT Press Series in Logic Programming, pages 154–165, Cleveland, Ohio, USA, 1989. The MIT Press.

27. J. Jaffar, J-L. Lassez, and M. J. Maher. Prolog-II as an instance of the logic programming scheme. In M. Wirsing, editor, *Formal Descriptions of Programming Concepts III*, pages 275–299. North-Holland, 1987.

28. T. Keisu. *Tree Constraints*. PhD thesis, The Royal Institute of Technology, Stockholm, Sweden, May 1994.

29. A. King. Pair-sharing over rational trees. *Journal of Logic Programming*, 46(1–2):139–155, 2000.

30. M. J. Maher. Complete axiomatizations of the algebras of finite, rational and infinite trees. In *Proceedings, Third Annual Symposium on Logic in Computer Science*, pages 348–357, Edinburgh, Scotland, 1988. IEEE Computer Society.

31. K. Mukai. *Constraint Logic Programming and the Unification of Information*. PhD thesis, Department of Computer Science, Faculty of Engineering, Tokio Institute of Technology, 1991.

32. C. Pollard and I. A. Sag. *Head-Driven Phrase Structure Grammar*. University of Chicago Press, Chicago, 1994.

33. F. Scozzari. Abstract domains for sharing analysis by optimal semantics. In J. Palsberg, editor, *Static Analysis: 7th International Symposium, SAS 2000*, volume 1824 of *Lecture Notes in Computer Science*, pages 397–412, Santa Barbara, CA, USA, 2000. Springer-Verlag, Berlin.

34. Gert Smolka and Ralf Treinen. Records for logic programming. *Journal of Logic Programming*, 18(3):229–258, 1994.

35. H. Søndergaard. An application of abstract interpretation of logic programs: Occur check reduction. In B. Robinet and R. Wilhelm, editors, *Proceedings of the 1986 European Symposium on Programming*, volume 213 of *Lecture Notes in Computer Science*, pages 327–338. Springer-Verlag, Berlin, 1986.

36. Swedish Institute of Computer Science, Programming Systems Group. *SICStus Prolog User's Manual*, release 3 #0 edition, 1995.

Applications of Extended Static Checking

K. Rustan M. Leino

Compaq Systems Research Center
130 Lytton Ave., Palo Alto, CA 94301, USA
rustan.leino@compaq.com

Abstract. Extended static checking is a powerful program analysis technique. It translates into a logical formula the hypothesis that a given program has some particular desirable properties. The logical formula, called a verification condition, is then checked with an automatic theorem prover. The extended static checking technique has been built into a couple of program checkers. This paper discusses other possible applications of the technique to the problem of producing quality software more quickly.

1 Extended Static Checking

The use of software plays a large role in our lives, directly and indirectly. We wish it were cheaper to create software, easier to produce software that is correct, and quicker to get to market with new or updated software. A research goal is therefore to improve program quality and programmer productivity.

Many attempts have been made to increase productivity in software development. Perhaps the most successful attempts have been ones that have influenced the design of programming languages. A language can force programs to follow certain programming disciplines. For example, the discipline of storing in each variable values of only one type has been enormously successful. It has led to the development of type systems, type declarations, and type checkers. In fact, type checking has become such a standard occurrence in popular languages that we tend to think of type errors as simple typographic errors rather than thinking about the great damage that such errors might have caused at run time. A type checker is usually applied at the time a program is compiled, which means the errors it catches are found early in the development cycle, which drastically decreases the cost of the errors.

Another example of a programming discipline that has influenced the vast majority of programs being written today is the abstinence from use of arbitrary control-flow jumps. Useful jump disciplines have been incorporated into for example if statements, loops, exceptions, and dynamically dispatched method calls, whereas arbitrary goto statements have ceased to be supported. Because modern high-level languages do not provide constructs for doing arbitrary jumps, the programming errors that stem from arbitrary jumps can be avoided altogether. In this way, good programming disciplines have influenced the design of

P. Cousot (Ed.): SAS 2001, LNCS 2126, pp. 185–193, 2001.

programming languages, which in turn have a strong influence on the kinds of programs programmers write and the kinds of errors they are likely to introduce.

Another attack on programming errors involves forms of program analysis beyond traditional type checking. The program analysis technique that I focus on in this paper is *extended static checking* (ESC). Drawing from program verification technology, ESC translates a given program (or part of a program) into a logical formula called a *verification condition*. The idea is that the verification condition holds if and only if the program satisfies certain desirable properties. The verification condition is then passed to a theorem prover that searches for counterexamples to the verification condition. Each counterexample corresponds to an error condition in the program.

Two program checkers that use this ESC technique are the extended static checkers for Modula-3 (ESC/Modula-3) [8] and for Java (ESC/Java) [10, 15].

Although extended static checking shares its building blocks with program verification, there's a fundamental difference between the two techniques: the goal of program verification is to prove the full functional correctness of the given program, whereas the goal of ESC is merely to find certain common errors, like null dereferences and array index bounds errors. This difference has far-reaching consequences.

One consequence is that the task of the theorem prover can be expected to be simpler than in program verification. Indeed, in ESC/Modula-3 and ESC/Java, this simplicity has allowed the underlying theorem prover to be entirely automatic. This means that users of ESC-based tools do not need the expertise to drive an interactive mechanical theorem prover; in fact, users don't even need to know about the underlying theorem prover.

Another important consequence of the difference between the goals of ESC and program verification is that the user-supplied specifications can be expected to be simpler. Indeed, in ESC/Java, for example, these light-weight specifications, called *annotations*, revolve around programming concepts and ordinary Java boolean expressions; in contrast, proof strategies and user-defined theories, which are unfamiliar to most programmers, are neither supported nor needed.

A third important consequence of ESC's non-goal of proving the full correctness of the program is that the ESC technique can allow a verification condition generator to be designed to make use of assumptions that are not checked. For example, it may be convenient to assume that no arithmetic overflows occur in the program, or that the object being initialized by a constructor is not dangerously "leaked" to an accessible location before all subclass constructors have completed their initializing actions. If assumptions are not checked, the resulting checking is *unsound*—if the assumptions are violated by the program, then ESC may have missed some of the errors that it was looking for (*cf.* [13]). On the upside, the unsoundness can be chosen by the tool designer to further simplify the task of the theorem prover and to further simplify the annotation language. It is prudent to assume only those conditions that are less likely to be violated in practice.

The level of automation in ESC is reminiscent of type checking. In fact, the name extended static checking comes from the idea that the technique is applied in ways similar to how static type checking is applied, but yielding an extended set of checks. There are more similarities: both static type checking and extended static checking can perform *modular checking*, that is, the checking can proceed module by module, without needing global program information. Modular checking is possible because type checking and ESC rely on annotations that specify module boundaries. For example, a type checker can deal with a call to a procedure P by knowing only the type signature of P (note in particular that the implementation of P is not needed to reason about the call), and the type signature is supplied by the programmer as a type declaration.

ESC annotations are a great feature. Let me list some of their benefits.

One benefit is that annotations allow programmers to write down their design decisions, for example declaring the intention that a certain pointer variable is always non-null or that a certain parameter is expected to be a valid index into a particular array. Not only does writing down the annotations document the design decisions, but it allows ESC to enforce them.

Another benefit is that the modular checking enabled by the annotations can make tools based on ESC scalable. The smaller bodies of code that are analyzed as units permit ESC-based checkers to perform a more detailed analysis. In contrast, whole-program analyses are forced to abstract from the actual code or approximate the behavior of the code in order to scale to large programs. For example, the tool PREfix approximates program behavior by considering only a fixed number of execution paths through each function [4], SLAM abstracts the program behavior by reducing the program's state space to a finite set of predicates [1], and abstract interpretation is a technique for automatically finding an abstraction of the program [5]. While abstraction can be good and is in many situations sufficient to do useful checking, modular checking affords a tool the luxury of using more details.

While annotations have great benefits, the experience with ESC/Java has shown that not everyone embraces the use of annotations. Far from it. The dominant cost in using ESC is the task of supplying annotations. The jury is still out on whether the benefits of ESC at the current required level of annotation outweigh its cost. But regardless of whether the ESC tools built so far are cost effective, one can apply the ESC technique differently from how it is applied in the checkers ESC/Modula-3 and ESC/Java. Different applications of ESC can adjust the required level of annotation differently and can maybe even change how annotations are perceived. In the rest of this paper, I discuss four such possible applications.

2   New Applications of the ESC Technique

2.1   Changing the Unit of Modularity

The checkers ESC/Modula-3 and ESC/Java perform modular checking at the level of separate routines. That is, these checkers analyze the implementation of one routine using only the specifications, not the implementations, of routines that are called. This approach follows the ideas behind procedural abstraction in that the specifications explicitly establish a contract between callers and the implementation of each routine. Because programmers tend to divide their code into reasonably-sized routines to limit the complexity of each routine, the approach of using routines as the unit of modularity naturally imposes comfortable limits on the amount of code that is analyzed at a time.

However, sometimes this level of granularity may not be ideally suited. For example, in object-oriented languages like Java, the program checker can often use the code of a private method in lieu of (or in addition to) a specification of the method. This suggests that one could use the class, rather than the routine, as the unit of modularity. By enlarging the unit of modularity in this way, this approach would reduce the annotation burden. In Java, one can even consider going a step further, making the package (which is a set of classes and interfaces) be the unit of modularity.

While enlarging the unit of modularity has the benefit that less annotation is needed, the cost is that verification conditions grow bigger, and the number of execution paths to consider through the code can grow dramatically.

So, new applications of ESC can reduce the annotation burden by adopting a different unit of modularity. This is similar to the approach taken by the type system in ML, where type inference reduces the need for manual type annotations on every function [17].

2.2   Using ESC as a Subroutine

Another promising application of the ESC technique is as a precise subroutine for analyzing a small piece of code in the context of a more encompassing checker. Let me mention two current efforts in this application area.

Houdini is a program checker that first infers annotations for a given (unannotated) program and then invokes ESC/Java on the annotated program to find possible errors [11]. The inferred annotations reduce the number of spurious warnings produced by the call to ESC/Java. Houdini also makes use of ESC/Java in its inference algorithm: it iteratively calls ESC/Java as a subroutine in order to discover annotations that are consistent with the program.

Another ongoing research effort is to use the tool Daikon's run-time profiling and statistical invariant inference [9] to create annotations that are then checked by ESC/Java [19]. By using ESC as a subroutine, the inferred likely invariants can be checked for all program inputs, not just the inputs used during the run-time profiling.

2.3   Annotation Checkers

Another application of the ESC technique can be found by applying a tool like ESC/Java in a particular, limited way. By default, ESC/Java warns about the possible misapplication of language primitives (like null dereferences and array bounds errors) whenever it cannot establish that such errors won't occur. For an unannotated program, this leads to a large number of warnings, which is not useful to programmers.

An alternative is to permanently turn these warnings off (which ESC/Java's command-line switches permit), letting the tool check only that the program is consistent with the given annotations. The resulting tool, an *annotation checker*, will then produce no warnings on an unannotated program. However, as soon as an annotation is added, the checker goes to work. This mode of checking, although it won't find checked run-time errors, lets programming teams ease their way into using the ESC checker. Even though annotations are required in order for the tool to do any actual checking, the annotation burden that otherwise arises from checking the use of language primitives is avoided. Stated differently, users get only what they pay for.

It is worth pointing out a particular specification paradigm that seems ideally suited for an annotation checker. The paradigm specifies a protocol that clients of a given class must satisfy. For example, consider a class representing character input streams and containing the operations *open*, *getChar*, *unGetChar*, and *close*. Suppose the intended use of these operations is as follows: *open* must be applied before any other operations are applied, no operations are allowed after applying *close*, and *unGetChar* is allowed only if the previous operation applied to the stream was *getChar*. To specify this protocol, we can introduce two boolean object fields *isOpen* and *isUnGettable* (ESC/Java allows the declaration of *ghost fields* for when the fields don't need to be seen by the compiler) and specify the four methods as follows:

/*@ **modifies** *isOpen, isUnGettable*; **ensures** *isOpen* */
void *open*(*String filename*);

/*@ **requires** *isOpen*; **modifies** *isUnGettable*; **ensures** *isUnGettable* */
int *getChar*( );

/*@ **requires** *isOpen* & *isUnGettable*; **modifies** *isUnGettable*; */
void *unGetChar*( );

/*@ **requires** *isOpen*; **modifies** *isOpen, isUnGettable*; */
void *close*( );

where **requires** specifies a method's precondition, **modifies** specifies which variables the method may modify, and **ensures** specifies the method's postcondition.

In summary, simple protocols like the one above can easily be specified in annotations. An annotation checker then checks that any specified protocol is observed by clients. While one can write protocol specifications like this one using special languages for abstract state machines (see *e.g.* AsmL [2] and Vault [6]), the ESC technique can perform a detailed semantical analysis and allows such protocol specifications to co-exist with other kinds of specifications.

2.4   Programming Language Design

As history shows, programming language design, for those languages that attract users, is one of the most effective ways to influence software development practices. The application of the ESC technique in programming language design seems intriguing, notably in cases where the analysis to be performed is mostly local to a routine or when the annotation overhead is small. I will outline three specific example applications, and will then discuss some obstacles that must be overcome to make these applications a reality.

A primary goal of programming language design is to find grammatical restrictions, static checks, and an execution semantics that together guarantee certain invariants at run time. For example, static and dynamic type checks can guarantee the invariant that variables hold values of their declared types. One can take the type systems of today's popular languages a step further by distinguishing between non-null types and may-be-null types. For example, let the type $T-$ represent the set of objects of a class T (or of a subclass of T), and let the type $T+$ indicate the union of that set and the special object **null**. A dynamic type cast of an expression e from $T+$ to $T-$ gives rise to a run-time check that e does not evaluate to the value **null**. The languages Java, Modula-3, and C++ provide only type $T+$, whereas the language CLU (see *e.g.* [16]) provides the type $T-$ and allows type $T+$ to be defined using a tagged union. Perhaps a reason for why this null-value discrimination in types has not yet found its way into more languages is that it is awkward (in the language definition and in programs) to have to have a special construct for breaking up the tagged union into two cases. More natural may be simply to use an ordinary if statement and compare the value of a $T+$ expression with **null** before using the expression as a $T-$ expression. The ESC technique may see a useful application here, because it could do a precise analysis of each routine implementation, producing an error for any possible dereference of **null** or possible assignment of **null** to a $T-$ variable. That is, the language would sport both types $T-$ and $T+$, but would require programmers to insert a dynamic type cast from $T+$ to $T-$ only when ESC would otherwise have produced an error.

Let's consider a second example. Uninitialized local variables is a problem in some languages, like C, and lint-like checkers are wise to warn about situations when this is a possible error. To prevent such errors, Java builds in a "definite assignment" rule that guarantees that every local variable is initialized (to a value of the variable's type) before it is used. The rule usually does well, but not for a code segment like

```
int x;
if (B) { ...assign to x... }
...
if (C) { ...use x... }
```

where condition C evaluates to true only if the first if statement's then clause is executed. The coarseness of Java's definite assignment rule will cause the compiler to report an error for this code segment (likewise, any coarse lint-like checker will produce a spurious warning). In these cases, one might have wished for a dynamic check instead, but programmers are forced to add a "dummy" assignment to x before the first if statement. If the programmer's assumption about condition C is mistaken, then the dummy assignment will have introduced an error that is harder to catch. Here, the more detailed analysis of the ESC technique can come to the rescue (see *e.g.* ESC/Java's **uninitialized** annotation [15]).

As a third example, we may consider including language support for specifying and checking protocols like those referred to in the previous subsection.

To realize any of these improvements in language design through applications of the ESC technique, one must overcome some obstacles. I'll describe the three primary obstacles.

A first obstacle is that ESC checking can be unsound. For a language to guarantee certain program invariants, the ESC technique had better be applied only in sound ways. One may be able to achieve soundness, but the challenge is to do so while retaining the power of the ESC technique and keeping annotation to a bare minimum.

Another obstacle is the possible need to know which variables a routine can modify. For instance, to enforce a protocol like the one in the example in Section 2.3, one needs to know whether or not a call can modify *isOpen*. Specifying the possible modifications of a routine is difficult, because it adds complexity to the annotation language [12, 14, 18]. In fact, to ensure soundness, one may need to introduce a discipline for alias confinement [7], which may in turn require knowing which variables a routine can read [3].

A third obstacle is that to include ESC checks among the static checks prescribed by a programming language, the language definition must include enough of a description of the verification condition generator and theorem prover that all compilers will agree on which programs are to be accepted. For example, if the language definition were to leave the strength of the theorem prover unspecified, then a program accepted by a compiler with a powerful theorem prover might not be accepted by a compiler with a more impoverished theorem prover. There is hope, however: a language may define the generation of verification conditions into some decidable mathematical domain. For example, if the verification conditions are formulas in first-order logic with uninterpreted function symbols and equality, then a compiler can use any sound and complete decision procedure for congruence closure—the language definition would cleanly say what needs to be checked, not how it is to be checked. Restricting verification conditions to decidable domains limits the power of the ESC technique (*cf.* [13]), but in the case of language design, such limitations may be appropriate.

3   Conclusion

Extended static checking is a powerful program analysis technique. To date, the primary application of the technique has been to standalone program checkers that search for misapplications of language primitives, perform modular checking routine by routine, and require annotations. This paper has sketched some new application areas of the ESC technique. One of these areas for which the potential gain is particularly high is programming language design, but several research challenges remain to make this application a reality. By exploring various applications of the ESC technique, possibly in combination with other techniques, we can hope to reduce the cost in producing quality software.

Acknowledgments

I am grateful to Cormac Flanagan, Raymie Stata, and Marcos Aguilera for contributing ideas and feedback in various discussions on the subject of this paper, and to Tony Hoare for articulating in an inspiring way some important correlations between programming language design and program correctness.

References

1. Thomas Ball and Sriram K. Rajamani. Automatically validating temporal safety properties of interfaces. In *Proceedings SPIN 2001*, 2001. To appear.
2. Mike Barnett, Egon Börger, Yuri Gurevich, Wolfram Schulte, and Margus Veanes. Using abstract state machines at Microsoft: A case study. In *Abstract State Machines, Theory and Applications, International Workshop, ASM 2000*, volume 1912 of *Lecture Notes in Computer Science*, pages 367–379. Springer, 2000.
3. John Boyland. Alias burying: Unique variables without destructive reads. *Software—Practice & Experience*, To appear.
4. William R. Bush, Jonathan D. Pincus, and David J. Sielaff. A static analyzer for finding dynamic programming errors. *Software—Practice & Experience*, 30:775–802, 2000.
5. Patrick Cousot and Radhia Cousot. Abstract interpretation: a unified lattice model for static analysis of programs by construction or approximation of fixpoints. In *Conference Record of the Fourth Annual ACM Symposium on Principles of Programming Languages*, pages 238–252. ACM, January 1977.
6. Rob DeLine and Manuel Fähndrich. Vault project home page. On the web at http://research.microsoft.com/vault/, 2001.
7. David L. Detlefs, K. Rustan M. Leino, and Greg Nelson. Wrestling with rep exposure. Research Report 156, Digital Equipment Corporation Systems Research Center, July 1998.
8. David L. Detlefs, K. Rustan M. Leino, Greg Nelson, and James B. Saxe. Extended static checking. Research Report 159, Compaq Systems Research Center, December 1998.
9. Michael D. Ernst, Adam Czeisler, William G. Griswold, and David Notkin. Quickly detecting relevant program invariants. In *Proceedings of the 22nd International Conference on Software Engineering (ICSE 2000), Limerick, Ireland*, June 2000.
10. Extended Static Checking for Java home page. On the web at http://research.compaq.com/SRC/esc/, November 2000.
11. Cormac Flanagan and K. Rustan M. Leino. Houdini, an annotation assistant for ESC/Java. In José Nuno Oliveira and Pamela Zave, editors, *FME 2001: Formal Methods for Increasing Software Productivity*, volume 2021 of *Lecture Notes in Computer Science*, pages 500–517. Springer, March 2001.

12. K. Rustan M. Leino. Data groups: Specifying the modification of extended state. In *Proceedings of the 1998 ACM SIGPLAN Conference on Object-Oriented Programming, Systems, Languages, and Applications (OOPSLA '98)*, volume 33, number 10 in *SIGPLAN Notices*, pages 144–153. ACM, October 1998.

13. K. Rustan M. Leino. Extended static checking: A ten-year perspective. In Reinhard Wilhelm, editor, *Informatics—10 Years Back, 10 Years Ahead*, volume 2000 of *Lecture Notes in Computer Science*, pages 157–175. Springer, January 2001.

14. K. Rustan M. Leino and Greg Nelson. Data abstraction and information hiding. Research Report 160, Compaq Systems Research Center, November 2000.

15. K. Rustan M. Leino, Greg Nelson, and James B. Saxe. ESC/Java user's manual. Technical Note 2000-002, Compaq Systems Research Center, November 2000.

16. Barbara Liskov and John Guttag. *Abstraction and Specification in Program Development*. MIT Electrical Engineering and Computer Science Series. MIT Press, 1986.

17. Robin Milner, Mads Tofte, and Robert Harper. *The Definition of Standard ML*. MIT Press, 1990.

18. Peter Müller. *Modular Specification and Verification of Object-Oriented Programs*. PhD thesis, FernUniversität Hagen, 2001. Available from http://www.informatik.fernuni-hagen.de/pi5/publications.html.

19. Jeremy W. Nimmer and Michael D. Ernst. Static verification of dynamically detected program invariants: Integrating Daikon and ESC/Java. In preparation, MIT, 2001.

Cleanness Checking of String Manipulations in C Programs via Integer Analysis

Nurit Dor[1]*, Michael Rodeh[2], and Mooly Sagiv[1]

[1] School of Computer Science, Tel-Aviv University, Israel
{nurr,msagiv}@post.tau.ac.il
[2] IBM Research Laboratory in Haifa

Abstract. All practical C programs use structures, arrays, and/or strings. At runtime, such objects are mapped into consecutive memory locations, hereafter referred to as *buffers*. Many software defects are caused by buffer overflow — unintentional access to memory outside the intended object. String manipulation is a major source of such defects. According to the FUZZ study, they are the cause of most UNIX failures. We present a new algorithm for statically detecting buffer overflow defects caused by string manipulations in C programs. In many programs, our algorithm is capable of precisely handling destructive memory updates, even in the presence of overlapping pointer variables which reference the same buffer at different offsets. Thus, our algorithm can uncover defects which go undetected by previous works. We reduce the problem of checking string manipulation to that of analyzing integer variables.

A prototype of the algorithm has been implemented and applied to statically uncover defects in real C applications, i.e., errors which occur on some inputs to the program. The applications were selected without a priori knowledge of the number of string manipulation errors. A significant number of string manipulation errors were found in every application, further indicating the extensiveness of such errors. We are encouraged by the fact that our algorithm reports very few *false alarms*, i.e., warnings on errors that never occur at runtime.

1 Introduction

Strings are frequently used in C programs, despite being one of the most unsafe type. Many software defects result from misusing strings, pointers to strings and standard C string functions (e.g., gets(), strcpy()). We refer to such bugs as *string-manipulation cleanness violations*, since they should not exist in any "reasonable" program, independent of the program specification. In general, we say that an expression is *unclean* if there exists an input to the program on which the result of the expression is undefined according to ANSI C semantics [10]. An expression is *clean* when no such input exists. A program is *clean* when

---

* This research was supported by a grant from the Ministry of Science, Israel and by the RTD project IST-1999-20527 "DAEDALUS" of the European FP5 programme.

P. Cousot (Ed.): SAS 2001, LNCS 2126, pp. 194–212, 2001.

it contains only clean expressions. Thus, the behavior of a clean C program is always predictable and does not depend on the environment.

String-manipulation cleanness violations lead to many nasty bugs. For example, we have found that 60% of the UNIX failures reported in the 1995 FUZZ study [13] are due to string-manipulation cleanness violations. In Nov. 1988, the Internet worm incident used a buffer overflow in fingerd to attack 60,000 computers [16]. Furthermore, CERT advisories indicate that buffer overflows account for up to 50% of today's software vulnerabilities [18].

1.1 Main Results

In this paper, we describe an algorithm that discovers potentially unclean string-manipulation expressions. Figure 1 shows three interesting erroneous C functions analyzed by our algorithm. Unclean expressions are underlined. Figure 1(a) shows an example of overlapping. After statement l_2, p overlaps s by 5, i.e., p points to the sixth character in the string pointed to by s. This implies that after statement l_3, which destructively updates p, s points to a 12-character string and that the expression at l_4 is unclean — it copies 13 bytes (including null) into a 10-byte array. Our static analysis algorithm detects this.

```
void simple () {
    char s[20],t[10],*p;

    l1:strcpy(s,"Hello");
    l2:p = s+5;
    l3:strcpy(p, " world!");
    l4:strcpy(t,s);
}

            (a)


/* web2c [strpascal.c] */
void null_terminate (char *s) {
    l1: while (*s != ' ')
    l2:        s++;

    l3: *s = 0;
}
            (b)
```

```
/* web2c [fixwrites.c] */
#define BUFSIZ 1024
char buf[BUFSIZ];

char* insert_long (char *cp) {
    char temp[BUFSIZ];
    int i;

    l1: for (i=0; &buf[i] < cp; ++i)
    l2:     temp[i] = buf[i];

    l3:strcpy (&temp[i],"(long)");
    l4:strcpy (&temp[i + 6], cp);
    l5:strcpy (buf, temp);
    l6:return cp + 6;
}
            (c)
```

Fig. 1. Unclean string manipulation functions. Unclean expressions are underlined. The function simple is from [18] and the other two functions are from web2c 6.1.

A typical error of accessing a string without bound-checking is shown in Figure 1(b). If the string pointed to by s does not contain a blank, s will be incremented beyond the allocated bounds. Our algorithm analyzes pointer arithmetic and reports a potentially unclean expression at l_2.

It is quite challenging to find unclean expressions in the function `insert_long` shown in Figure 1(c) without reporting false alarms. As shown in Section 3, our algorithm achieves that. This function inserts the string `"(long)"` at offset `cp` by copying the data up to `cp` into a temporary array, appending the string `"(long)"` and appending the remainder of the string. When invoked, `cp` overlaps `buf`. A buffer overflow occurs at l_3 and/or l_4 if not enough space is left in `temp`. Therefore, these expressions are flagged as potentially unclean. In addition, our algorithm verifies that all the other expressions `buf[i]`, `temp[i]`, and `strcpy(buf, temp)` are clean. Knowing that `buf` and `cp` overlap and analyzing the condition at statement l_1 is necessary in order to validate that the access to `buf[i]` is within bounds, and so is `temp[i]` (since `i` is less than `BUFSIZ`).

Technically, we propose to *reduce* the problem of checking string-manipulation cleanness violations to that of analyzing integer variables — a problem with many known solutions. Although the problem of string-manipulation cleanness checking is to verify that accesses are within bounds, it is more complicated than array bounds checking. The domain of string programs requires that the analysis is capable of tracking the following features of the C programming language: (i) handling standard C functions such as `strcpy()` and `strlen()` which perform unbounded number of loop iterations in a rather precise way; (ii) statically estimating the length of strings (in addition to the size of allocated arrays). This length is dynamically changed based on the index of the first null character; and (iii) simultaneously analyzing pointer and integer values is required in order to precisely handle pointer arithmetic and destructive updates. Our analysis is the first with these capabilities. The overlapping information enables our method to handle destructive updates in a rather precise way. When updating a pointer value such as *p=0, the overlapping information between p and another pointer, say q, is used to compute the effect of the update on the length of q. In particular, this paper reports three main results:

1. A source-to-source transformation that produces an instrumented C program which `asserts` when a string-manipulation cleanness violation occurs. The transformation is described in Section 2.
2. In Section 3, we show that the integer analysis algorithm of Cousot and Halbwachs [5] can be used to analyze the instrumented program to find all potentially unclean string expressions in a rather precise way. Methods with lower complexity such as range analysis [3] can also be used.
3. We have implemented both the source-to-source transformation and the static analysis algorithms and applied them to real C programs (Section 4). The experimental results are quite encouraging. We analyze real programs and locate nontrivial software defects with only a few false alarms.

In the following subsections we elaborate on these results.

A Source-to-Source C Transformation. We describe a source-to-source program transformation that produces an instrumented C program which dynamically checks that expressions are clean using `assert` statements. For example, the instrumented version of Figure 1(a) shown in Figure 2 will abort at $cond_4$ indicating that the expression strcpy(t, s) at l_4 of the original program is unclean. The details of the transformation technique are explained in Section 2.

```
void simple () {
    char s[20];  int s_len=0, s_alloc=20;
    char *p;     int p_len=0, p_alloc=0;
    char t[10];  int t_len=0, t_alloc=10;
                 int p_overlap_s = 0;

                 cond₁:assert(s_alloc > 5);
    l₁:strcpy(s,"Hello");
                 post₁₁:s_len = 5;

                 cond₂:assert(s_alloc >= 5);
    l₂:p = s+5;
                 post₂₁:p_overlaps_s = 5;
                 post₂₂:p_len = s_len - 5;
                 post₂₃:p_alloc = s_alloc - 5;

                 cond₃:assert(p_alloc > 7);
    l₃:strcpy(p, " world!");
                 post₃₁:p_len = 7;
                 post₃₂:s_len = p_len + p_overlaps_s;

                 cond₄:assert(t_alloc > s_len);
    l₄:strcpy(t,s);
                 post₄₁:t_len = s_len;
}
```

Fig. 2. The instrumented function simple from Figure 1(a). Added instrumentation code is indented and appears in boldface.

If the original program is clean, then the instrumented program yields the same results. However, if the original program contains an unclean string expression, then the instrumented program will abort on an assert statement, while the result of the original program is undefined.

The idea of instrumenting programs to dynamically check cleanness is not new. For example, SafeC [1] and [12] also instruments the C source with assertions. Purify [14] instruments the executable files. These tools instrument every physical buffer by extending it with additional information and checking this additional information at runtime. Our approach is to instrument the program, adding computations on new integer variables, but analyze them at compile time.

Applying Integer Analysis. The static problem is to analyze the instrumented program and to mark potentially unclean expressions by detecting that an `assert` statement may not hold. We aim at a *conservative* solution, i.e., one that never misses an unclean string manipulation. Since our goal is to prove that conservative static cleanness checking of realistic C programs is feasible, while generating only a small number of false alarms, we use a rather expensive but precise integer analysis that detects linear restraints among the integer variables that our transformation introduces [5]. The integer analysis is conservative thus resulting in an algorithm that detects all unclean string manipulations.

A Prototype Implementation. We analyzed functions with massive string manipulations from three different applications: (i) `fixoutput` — a checker for the output of a lexical analyzer; (ii) `agrep` — a `grep` application; and (iii) `web2c` — a converter from TeX, Metafont, and other related WEB programs to C. A total of 19 errors were detected with only four false alarms. (See Table 3 and Section 4.3 for more information on the analysis results).

1.2   Related Work

Many academic and commercial projects aim at producing tools that detect string-manipulation cleanness violations at runtime, e.g., [14, 1, 12]. Due to the overhead of runtime checking, these tools are usually not used in production. Moreover, their effectiveness strongly depends on the input tested, and these checks do not assure against future bugs on different inputs. There are tools that directly identify cleanness violations leading to security vulnerabilities such as StackGuard [6].

An unpublished success story in program analysis is the usage of the AST ToolKit to identify 23 string violation bugs in Office 10 by scanning syntax trees [19]. An extension to LCLint, a widely used static checking tool, which checks for buffer overflow vulnerabilities is presented in [11]. Following the approach of LCLint, their aim is a scalable tool by using lightweight techniques. Procedures are annotated with constraints on the allocated space and on the string length. The loop body is analyzed once and then some heuristics are used to estimate the number of loop iterations and their effect on the constraints.

In [18] Wagner et al. present an algorithm that statically identifies string-manipulation cleanness violations and apply it to uncover nontrivial defects in real software. This algorithm is based on flow insensitive analysis, and thus can handle large programs. However, it achieves that at the price of generating many false alarms , and, even worse, many errors are missed. For example, as observed in [18], the bug in Figure 1(a) (which our algorithm correctly identifies) is skipped by their method because it does not handle pointer arithmetic. Indeed, in analyzing the reasons behind their false alarms, they have identified four needed techniques: flow-sensitivity, context-sensitivity, pointer analysis and linear invariants. Our method includes pointer analysis and linear invariants. It is flow-sensitive and annotations are used to analyze function calls.

To summarize, the above static tools do not guarantee conservative result and produce false alarms. In contrast, since our method is conservative we *assure* against certain defects and the user is relieved from the need to test against them. Our method is heavier than these tools but can identify cleanness errors resulting from destructive updates. Also, dynamic cleanness tools can benefit from our analysis which identifies cases were runtime checks are redundant. The reader is referred to [18] for additional references.

Limitations. Our instrumentation does not handle multi-dimensional arrays, structures and multilevel pointers. These features can be handled by combining our method with instrumentation inside buffers, e.g., as done by SafeC. Our static analysis algorithm can handle these constructs conservatively, e.g., using the methods described in [20].

Code size increase due to the transformation is bounded by $O(m*n^2)$, where m is the number of statements and n is the number of variables. However, applying a very simple flow-insensitive analysis prior to the transformation phase (see Section 2.2) allows maintaining much lower code increase in practice for all our benchmark programs.

Our cleanness algorithm does not currently check the cleanness of subtraction expressions (i.e., $p = q + exp$ when $exp < 0$). This is an easy extension which we choose to omit in this paper.

The main limitation of our prototype implementation is the handling of function calls. Obviously, cleanness checking should yield only a few false alarms, if at all. Therefore, since we currently rely on an expensive static technique, we avoid interprocedural analysis and allow preconditions and postconditions of each function to be specified (see Section 4.1). Our initial experience indicates that even a straightforward implementation of the algorithm handles mid-size programs and that it is easy to provide annotations for these programs. We have no experience with large programs.

2   The Transformation

The instrumented program contains the original program with additional variables and statements. Figure 2 shows the instrumented function of Figure 1(a). The instrumented code is indented and appears in boldface. For reasons of clarity, we omitted some of the instrumented code and discuss it later in Section 2.3.

A *string variable* is either a pointer to char, such as p in the example, or an array of characters such as s and t. For every string variable, v, two integer variables are added, v_len and v_alloc. The first holds the length of the string v (excluding the null-terminator) and the second holds the allocated size of the buffer pointed to by v. These integers are initialized depending on the declaration and the initialization of the variable v.

We say that a pointer variable p *overlaps* a pointer variable q by i if p points to the same physical buffer as q but at an offset of i bytes. That is, $p = q + i$. Note that if p overlaps q by i then q overlaps p by $-i$. For every pair of string variables, v_1 and v_2, an integer variable $v_1\_overlaps\_v_2$ is added to hold the overlapping index between them. To reduce the number of overlapping variables a pre-transformation analysis is applied to detect variables that cannot overlap, see Section 2.2.

In addition to the integer variables, Boolean variables are added to indicate the status of the variable: (i) is_v_alloc indicates whether variable v is allocated; (ii) is_v_null indicates whether the data pointed to by v is a null-terminated string; and (iii) is_v_1_overlaps_v_2 indicates whether variables v_1 and v_2 overlap.

For every statement, st, there is a cleanness condition that is checked via an assert statement prior to statement st. The cleanness condition is generated in a syntax-directed fashion and is labeled as $cond_{st}$. For example, the cleanness condition of statement strcpy(dst,src) is that the length of src is less than the allocated size of dst. This guarantees that there is sufficient space to copy the string src and the null-terminator byte.

Every statement st is followed by statements that update the instrumented variables. These are labeled as $post_{st}$. In the example this is rather straight-forward. After statement l_1, the length of s is updated. After statement l_2, p_overlaps_s, the length and the allocated size of p are set. After statement l_3 the length of p is updated. In addition, since p overlaps s, the length of s is also updated.

2.1 Simplifier

The first phase of the transformation is a C-to-C simplifier which transforms every expression that may be unclean into a statement by assigning its value into a new variable. For example, the expressions &temp[i] and &temp[i+6] in statements l_3 and l_4 in Figure 1(c) are assigned to two new variables. This serves to mark that the first expression overlaps temp and the second expression overlaps both temp and the first expression. With the overlapping information we can precisely handle the destructive updates at statements l_3 and l_4 and compute their effect on the length of temp.

2.2 Preliminary Analysis

The number of overlap variables added by the transformation can be quadratic in the number of string variables. However, in a typical program the number of variables that do overlap is small. Only assignments and function calls may generate overlapping variables. A preliminary intraprocedural flow-insensitive analysis is performed to detect which variables may overlap. This is done by using a union-find algorithm which assumes that if a may overlap b and b may overlap c then a may overlap c. This algorithm is overly conservative. For example, it assumes that the result value of a function call may overlap any of the input parameters and that every pair of global string variables may overlap. Even so, the experimental results described in Section 4 show that the number of overlapping variables is dramatically reduced.

2.3   Transformation of Statements

Table 1(a)-(c) shows the transformation of basic statements. The original statement appears is boldfaced, its cleanness condition, if any, is written above the statement and the update statements of the instrumented variables are written below the statement.

The assignment of a constant string to variable `dst` is fairly simple. There is no cleanness condition to check. The instrumented variables are updated according to the length of the constant which is known at the transformation time. All `dst`-overlapping variables are set to false. This is safe even in the presence of two pointers to the same constant string (the same label in the data section) since no updates can take place in the data section.

Assignment of pointer arithmetic is one of the most complicated statement types to instrument. Following [10, pp.205], we verify that the result of a pointer arithmetic is within bounds or at the first location beyond the rightmost character. The allocation size of `dst` is computed using the allocation size of `src`. Since `src_len` holds the position of the first null byte in the string starting at `src`, only if `dst` is set in between `src` and the null-terminator then the length of `dst` is computed using the length of `src`. In other cases the length of `dst` is computed using the macro `RECOMPUTE` shown in Table 2. This macro computes the length by calling `strlen()` and sets the Boolean variable `is_null` to true if the null-terminator is within bounds. We try to minimize the use of this macro since it cannot be analyzed statically in a precise manner.

Assignments create overlapping. We set the overlapping variable between the `dst` and `src` of the statement and also between `dst` and any other `dst`-overlapping variable according to its `src`-overlapping.

Destructive updates such as `src[i] = c` can come in two flavors: the assignment of ascii 0 (a null-terminator) and the assignment of any other character. For assignments of a null-terminator, we check whether the length of `src` has been changed. This happens when the current length (if it exists) is greater than `i`. Every destructive update to `str` may affect the length of variable `a` that overlaps `str`. The macro `DESTRUCTIVE_UPDATE` (shown in Table 2) detects if `a` has been affected and if so updates the length of `a`. In some cases the macro `RECOMPUTE` must be used to compute the new length of `a`. The case of a non-null character assignment is simpler since only the case where the null-terminator is removed affects the instrumented variables.

Table 1(d)-(g) lists the transformation code of a few common standard C functions which are rather straightforward: `malloc()` sets the allocation to the new allocation size and eliminates any existing overlapping; `strcpy(dst,src)` sets the length of `dst`; `strlen(src)` checks that `src` is null-terminating and assigns `src_len` to the lefthand side; `strcat(dst,src)` checks that both parameters are null-terminating and computes the new length of `dst`. In every destructive update overlapping variables are updated. Some cleanness conditions verify only the `is_null` variable since we already maintain the invariant `is_null` → `is_alloc`. Due to space limitation we do not show the transformation code of the more complicated C library functions.

Table 1. The transformation code of basic statements: (a) assignment of a string constant, (b) pointer arithmetic and, (c) an update to an index in the array; and of a few C library functions: (d) `malloc()`, (e) `strcpy()`, (f) `strlen()`, and (g) `strcat()`. The original statement appears in boldface.

<table>
<tr>
<td>

dst = *string-const*;
is_dst_alloc = true;
dst_alloc = length of *string-const*+1;
is_dst_null = true;
dst_len = length of *string-const*;
FOREACH variable a
   is_dst_overlaps_a = false;

(a)

---

assert(is_src_alloc && i < src_alloc);
src[i] = *exp*;
if(*exp* == 0) {
  if(!is_src_null || src_len > i) {
    is_src_null = true;
    src_len = i; }
  FOREACH variable a
    DESTRUCTIVE_UPDATE(a,src); }
else {
  if(is_src_null && i == src_len)
    RECOMPUTE(src);
  FOREACH variable a
    DESTRUCTIVE_UPDATE(a,src); }

(c)

</td>
<td>

assert (is_src_alloc && $exp \leq$ src_alloc);
dst = **src** + *exp*;
is_dst_alloc = true;
dst_alloc = src_alloc - *exp*;
if(is_src_null && src_len $\geq exp \geq 0$) {
  is_dst_null = true;
  dst_len = src_len - *exp*; }
else
  RECOMPUTE(dst);
is_dst_overlaps_src = true;
dst_overlaps_src = *exp*;
FOREACH variable a
  is_dst_overlaps_a = is_src_overlaps_a;
  dst_overlaps_a = *exp* + src_overlaps_a;

(b)

</td>
</tr>
<tr>
<td>

dst = **malloc(**exp**)**;
if (dst) {
  dst_alloc = *exp*;
  is_dst_alloc = true; }
else
  is_dst_alloc = false;
is_dst_null = false;
FOREACH variable a
  is_dst_overlaps_a = false;

(d)

</td>
<td>

assert (is_dst_alloc && is_src_null &&
      src_len < dst_alloc);
strcpy(dst,src);
is_dst_null = true;
dst_len = src_len;
FOREACH variable a
    DESTRUCTIVE_UPDATE(a,dst);

(e)

</td>
</tr>
<tr>
<td>

assert(is_src_null);
i = **strlen(src)**;
i = src_len;

(f)

</td>
<td>

assert(is_src_null && is_dst_null &&
    dst_alloc > dst_len+src_len);
strcat(dst,src);
dst_len = dst_len + src_len;
FOREACH variable a
    DESTRUCTIVE_UPDATE(a,dst);

(g)

</td>
</tr>
</table>

Table 2. The macros' code used in the transformation.

```
#define RECOMPUTE(str)
    str_len = strlen(str);
    is_str_null = (str_len < str_alloc ? true : false);
```

```
#define DESTRUCTIVE_UPDATE(a,dst)
    if(is_a_overlaps_dst)
        if(is_dst_null &&
           (a_overlaps_dst ≤ len_dst) && /*a is between dst and the first null*/
           ( !is_a_null || a_overlaps_dst ≥ - a_len)
                                { /*a is before dst or has a new nul */
                    is_a_null = true;
                    a_len = dst_len - a_overlaps_dst; }
        else RECOMPUTE(a);
```

Function Calls. Function calls are treated by passing additional parameters in a dynamic array pointed to by a global variable. The array contains the length and allocated size of every string parameter and the overlapping information of every pair of string parameters. Similarly, upon return, the information is passed back along with additional information on the return value and its overlapping with the string parameters. Cases where either the callee or the caller is not instrumented are handled similarly to the approach described in [12].

Derived Expressions. To enhance the precision of the static analysis the following expressions are replaced by equivalent expressions that use the instrumented variables:

$$*str == 0 \qquad \equiv (\text{is\_str\_null} \&\& \text{str\_len} == 0)$$
$$*str == c \ (c \not\equiv 0) \equiv ((!\text{is\_str\_null} \ || \ \text{str\_len} > 0) \&\& *str == c)$$
$$p \ - \ q \qquad \equiv \text{p\_overlaps\_q}$$
$$p \ > \ q \qquad \equiv \text{p\_overlaps\_q} > 0$$

The first two are conditions on the length of the string. Pointer comparisons and subtractions are replaced by expressions over the appropriate **overlap** variable.

Proving that our transformation preserves the semantics of clean C programs involves establishing certain invariants on the value of the auxiliary instrumentation variables. For example, in the transformation shown in Table 1(f) the value of src_len is the same as the result of the call to strlen().

3   Static Analysis

Our static algorithm detects all the potentially unclean string manipulations. It analyzes the instrumented program and identifies **assert** statements that may be violated. The algorithm is *conservative*, i.e., if there exists an input on which an assertion in the instrumented program is violated, the algorithm will identify this assertion. However, it may yield false alarms by identifying potentially-violated expressions even for assertions in the instrumented program that are never violated.

Our algorithm is iterative. It simultaneously processes Boolean and integer variables by analyzing the program control flow graph and computing conservative information at every node. It then[1] checks if any of the assertions are potentially violated and produces appropriate messages.

To analyze Boolean variables a three-valued domain is used [4]. The value $\top$ results from joining `true` and `false`. The analysis handles Boolean assignments and conditions.

$$buf\_alloc = BUFSIZ$$
$$temp\_alloc = BUFSIZ$$
$$cp\_overlaps\_buf = BUFSIZ - cp\_alloc$$
$$cp\_alloc \geq cp\_len + 1$$
$$cp\_alloc \leq BUFSIZ - 2$$
$$cp\_len \geq 0$$
$$i = 1$$

(a)

$$buf\_alloc = BUFSIZ$$
$$temp\_alloc = BUFSIZ$$
$$cp\_overlaps\_buf = BUFSIZE - cp\_alloc$$
$$cp\_alloc \geq cp\_len + 1$$
$$cp\_alloc \leq BUFSIZ - 1 - i$$
$$cp\_len \geq 0$$
$$i \geq 1$$
$$i \leq 2$$

(b)

$$buf\_alloc = BUFSIZ$$
$$temp\_alloc = BUFSIZ$$
$$cp\_overlaps\_buf = BUFSIZE - cp\_alloc$$
$$cp\_alloc \geq cp\_len + 1$$
$$cp\_len \geq 0$$
$$i \leq BUFSIZ - 1 - cp\_alloc$$
$$i \geq 1$$

(c)

Fig. 3. Application of widening when analyzing the loop in `insert_long`. (c) displays the result of the widening operation applied to (a) and (b), the static information arising at the first and second iterations, respectively.

---

[1] The implementation carries out the check simultaneously.

3.1   Integer Analysis

We use a linear relation analysis algorithm which discovers linear inequalities among numerical variables [5, 8]. This method identifies linear inequalities of the form: $\Sigma_{i=1}^{n} c_i x_i + b \geq 0$, where x_i is a variable and c_i and b are constants.

In the analysis of the function insert_long (see Figure 1(c)), the algorithm detects the inequalities shown in Figure 3(c) upon entry into the loop body (after at least one execution of the loop body[2]). For simplicity, we only show the relevant (in)equalities. The first five (in)equalities are derived from the declarations of the string variables and from the function's precondition. The last two inequalities constrain the loop induction variable i. Note that i is always less than BUFSIZ which is important to avoid reporting false alarms while accessing temp[i] and buf[i].

Figure 4 demonstrates how our static algorithm identifies the unclean expression strcpy(&temp[i], "(long)") in function insert_long. For reasons of clarity, we omitted constraints that are irrelevant to the assert verified. From this information, one can understand that when the allocation size of the parameter cp is less than or equal to 6, a buffer overflow occurs at l_3. For each potential cleanness violation, the algorithm locates the constraints on the variables (of the instrumented program) where the violation occurs. Of course, in a practical tool these errors need to be reported in terms of the original program.

---

l_{3_1}: tmp1 = temp + i ;
$cond_3$: assert(tmp1_alloc > 6)
                    error: the assertion may be violated when:
                            i = BUFSIZ - cp_alloc
                            tmp1_alloc = cp_alloc
                            cp_alloc $\leq$ 6
l_3: strcpy (tmp1 ,"(long)") ;

Fig. 4. A report of a potentially unclean expression strcpy(&temp[i], "(long)") in insert_long (see Figure 1(c)) by the static analysis algorithm. (Expression l_{3_1} is added by the simplifier.)

Technically, linear inequalities are represented by a closed convex polyhedron (a polyhedron, for short) which has two representations: (i) a *system of linear inequalities* $P = \{X | AX \geq B\}$, where A is an $m \times n$-matrix, B is an m-vector, and n is the number of numerical variables; (ii) a *system of generators* which can be viewed as a geometric representation. See [5, 8] for more information.

---

[2] Our simplification step transforms all loops into do-while loops with surrounding conditional statements.

Upon termination of the iterative algorithm, the polyhedron at every control flow node conservatively represents the inequalities that are guaranteed to hold whenever the control reaches the respective point. The polyhedron at function entry is $\top$ indicating that no inequalities are known to hold. We then proceed as follows:

Assignments. Every assignment generates a new polyhedron from the polyhedron before the statement. Linear assignments of the form $x = \Sigma_{i=1}^{n} c_i x_i + b$ are handled by substituting $\Sigma_{i=1}^{n} c_i x_i + b$ for x in the polyhedron before the assignment and then normalizing. Other assignments are handled conservatively by removing inequalities of affected variables from the polyhedra.

$$buf\_alloc = BUFSIZ$$
$$temp\_alloc = BUFSIZ$$
$$cp\_overlaps\_buf = 0$$
$$cp\_alloc = BUFSIZ$$
$$cp\_len \leq BUFSIZ - 1$$
$$cp\_len \geq 0$$
$$i = 0$$

(a)

$$buf\_alloc = BUFSIZ$$
$$temp\_alloc = BUFSIZ$$
$$cp\_alloc = BUFSIZ - i$$
$$cp\_overlaps\_buf = i$$
$$cp\_alloc \geq cp\_len + 1$$
$$cp\_alloc \leq BUFSIZ - 1$$
$$cp\_len \geq 0$$

(b)

$$buf\_alloc = BUFSIZ$$
$$temp\_alloc = BUFSIZ$$
$$cp\_overlaps\_buf = i$$
$$cp\_alloc = BUFSIZ - i$$
$$cp\_len \geq 0$$
$$i \geq 0$$

(c)

Fig. 5. The result of join operation at l_3 in the analysis of insert_long. (c) shows the result of joining (a) which corresponds to the case the loop was not executed and (b) which assumes that the loop was executed.

Program Conditions. It is very important to analyze conditions in order to avoid many false alarms. A non-linear condition is handled conservatively by assuming that both branches may occur. A linear condition cond is handled by: (i) creating a polyhedron that represents cond and intersecting it with the polyhedron before the conditional statement to conservatively determine the polyhedron at the true-branch, and (ii) creating a polyhedron that represents !cond and intersecting it with the polyhedron before the conditional statement to conservatively determine the polyhedron at the false-branch. The polyhedron for cond and !cond are conservatively determined. Since we only have to deal with integers, negations can be handled more precisely than general numerical variables. For example, we have the following equivalence: $!(\Sigma_{i=1}^{n}c_ix_i + b \geq 0) \equiv (\Sigma_{i=1}^{n}(-c_i)x_i + (-b - 1)) \geq 0$.

Control Flow Merges and Loops. When two control flow edges are merged, a new polyhedron "including" both polyhedra is computed. Figure 5 shows the result of the join operation at l_3 in the analysis of insert_long. Figure 5(a) shows the polyhedron corresponding to the case where the loop is not executed. In this case, i is 0 and cp_overlaps_buf is 0, indicating that cp and buf both point to the same location. Figure 5(b) shows the polyhedron corresponding to the end of the execution of the loop. Thus, cp and &buf[i] point to the same location, which implies that i is equal to cp_overlaps_buf. The result of the join operation is shown in Figure 5(c). The resultant polyhedron includes the case where i is greater than zero and is equal to cp_overlaps_buf.

Loops present a more involved situation. In order to guarantee that the algorithm terminates, a widening operation is used on loop back edges. The resultant polyhedron is defined by those constraints which are satisfied by both polyhedra. Figure 3 demonstrates a widening operation at the loop in insert_long. Figure 3(a) shows the polyhedron describing the first execution of the loop, where i equals 1. Figure 3(b) shows the polyhedron describing the second execution of the loop, where i is between 1 and 2. The result of the widening is shown in Figure 3(c) in which the boundaries of i are relaxed, i is at least 1 and less than BUFSIZ − cp_alloc.

Widening operations may cause a loss of precision which in turn, may lead to false alarms. As a partial remedy a narrowing operation is performed by analyzing the loop body again without a widening operation.

4 Experimental Results

To investigate the usability of our approach in terms of false alarms and cost, we implemented our algorithm for a large subset of C.

4.1 User Annotations

As our prototype implementation analyzes one function at a time we allow function prototypes to be annotated with preconditions and postconditions in the style of Icontract [15] and ESC Java [2]. Preconditions and postconditions are written as C expressions without function calls but with the following extra built-in expressions on strings:

len(*str*) —   The length of string variable *str*
is_null(*str*) —   Is *str* null-terminated?
alloc(*str*) —   The allocation size of string variable *str*
is_alloc(*str*) —   Is *str* allocated?
is_overlap(*a*,*str*) — Are *a* and *str* overlapping?
overlaps(*a*,*str*) — The overlapping index of *a* from *str*

In addition, for ease of annotating, there are some shorthand annotation expressions. For example:

string(s) $\equiv$ (is_alloc(s) && is_null(s) && len(s) $\geq$ 0 &&
                    len(s) < alloc(s))
overlap_leq(a,b,i) $\equiv$ (is_overlap(a,b) && overlaps(a,b) $\leq$ i &&
                    alloc(b) == alloc(a) + overlap(a,b))
overlap_geq(a,b,i) $\equiv$ (is_overlap(a,b) && overlaps(a,b) $\geq$ i &&
                    alloc(b) == alloc(a) + overlap(a,b))

Postcondition expressions use a special syntax pre@e to denote the value of the expression e at the function entry. Thus, a postcondition x = pre@x +1 indicates that the value of the variable x after the call is equal to the value of x before the call plus one. Finally, postcondition expressions can use a designated variable return denoting the return value of the function.

PRE(string(cp) && alloc(cp) <= BUFSIZ &&
        overlap_leq(cp,buf,BUFSIZ-1) && overlap_geq(cp,buf,0))
char* insert_long (char *cp)
POST(len(cp) == pre@len(cp) + 6 && return == pre@cp + 6)

Fig. 6. The annotation of insert_long.

Annotations can be written in a separate header file with the function prototype. The analysis conservatively checks the precondition expression when an invocation of a function is processed. Then, it assumes that the postcondition expression holds after the call. The precondition expression is assumed to hold when the body of the function is analyzed, and a warning is issued when the postcondition is not guaranteed to hold at the exit of the function.

The annotated prototype for the function insert_long (shown in Figure 1(c)) is given in Figure 6. This annotation is one of the most difficult annotations written in our study. Usually, annotations indicate string data types for parameters and return values. In this example, the precondition indicates that cp is a string and its allocation is not greater than BUFSIZ. The last two overlapping expressions in the precondition indicate that cp may only point to locations within buf. The postcondition of this function is obvious.

4.2   Prototype Implementation

Our algorithm was implemented for a subset of C. The first phase is the simplifier implemented under SUIF [17]. It generates a new C file. As described in Section 2.1, every expression that may be unclean is transformed into a statement. Also, for ease of implementation the following simplifications are applied: (i) complex expressions are replaced by a set of sequential expressions; (ii) function calls in expressions are transformed into statements; (iii) arguments in function calls are transformed into simple expressions (variables or constants); (iv) all types of loop statements are replaced by do-while statements. The simplified C file is annotated and is the input to the transformation phase implemented under EDG's C-backend [7].

The pre-transformation step (described in Section 2.2) marks which string variables may overlap and generates a control flow graph. The main idea is to generate a "slice" of the program which only includes those parts of the program which are relevant to the analysis and control flow statements. It includes *string-related* integer variables. An integer variable i is *string-related* if it is used: (i) as an index to a string variable, e.g., str[i], (ii) in a pointer arithmetic expression, e.g., str+i, (iii) in a function call returning a string variable, e.g., malloc(i), or (iv) as a parameter to a function that also has a string parameter, e.g., strncpy(dst,src,i).

The static analysis phase is implemented in C using the polyhedra library [9]. The final output of the static analysis is a list of potentially unclean expressions. The analysis provides a description of potentially-violated assert statements in the format shown in Figure 4. The instrumented program provides a conceptual tool in order to validate whether an error message is a false alarm — assertions which are flagged by the static analysis algorithm but cannot be violated by any program input.

When our static analysis algorithm identifies an assertion violation, it flags an error (in the form shown in Figure 4). After reporting the error it (optimistically) assumes that the assertion condition holds on subsequent execution paths to avoid repetitive error messages. This is in line with the instrumented program that aborts at the first violated assertion. For example, our algorithm does not flag the expression cp+6 at l_6 in Figure 1(c) as unclean. This expression is unclean when the allocation size of the buffer pointed to by cp is less than 6. In this case, strcpy(&temp[i],"(long)") at l_3 is also unclean and must be executed prior to l_6. However, both expressions in l_3 and l_4 are detected as unclean since they can be violated on different inputs.

4.3   Results

Table 3 presents the analysis results. Columns 3–5 provide source information: (i) number of lines of simplified code, (ii) number of nodes in the analyzed CFG, and (iii) number of string variables in the function including global variables. The ratio between LOC and CFG indicates the fragment of the program analyzed. In some cases, such as backup and insert_long, all statements are string manipulations. In others, such as main, a small fraction is analyzed.

Table 3. The Experimental Results. The column named "Annotations" indicates the level of difficulty of annotating the function: S - simple, M - moderate and D - difficult.

App.	Function	Source code info				Static Analysis				Messages	
		LOC	CFG	Strings	Annotations	Overlap	Vars	CPU sec	Space MB	False Alarms	Errors
fixoutput	flush	19	11	6	S	15	30	0.4	1.2	0	0
	getchar	33	31	8	D	15	36	3.0	5.1	0	3
	backup	22	28	6	D	6	22	0.6	0.7	0	0
	getstr	50	42	7	D	6	28	8.0	9.2	0	0
	main	403	157	10	S	10	44	309.9	99.5	0	0
agrep	extend_re	30	14	11	S	28	54	3.2	9.6	0	0
	init	45	19	3	S	1	9	0.3	0.3	0	0
	coutline	22	12	10	M	28	61	1.4	4.4	0	0
	m_short	187	109	14	M	78	125	279.8	242.7	0	5
web2c	fprint_pascal_string	29	10	3	S	1	9	0.1	0.1	0	2
	null_terminate	11	7	2	S	0	5	0.1	0.1	0	2
	space_terminate	12	9	2	S	0	5	0.1	0.1	0	0
	extendfilename	17	13	4	S	1	11	0.3	0.6	0	2
	remove_newline	18	11	12	S	29	56	0.8	3.4	0	0
	insert_long	21	25	14	D	78	110	19.6	38.8	0	2
	join	44	27	13	M	29	60	8.9	16.0	3	1
	skip_balanced	72	24	9	S	28	53	2.8	5. 2	1	0
	bare	85	57	9	M	28	53	13.8	17.1	0	2

Column 6 indicates the level of difficulty of annotating the functions. For most functions it was rather straightforward (marked as "Simple"). In some functions, additional preconditions are needed to avoid false alarms, such as on the allocation size of the parameter (marked as "Moderate"). Certain functions, such as insert_long shown in Figure 1(c), required introducing preconditions on the overlapping between parameters and/or global variables (marked as "Difficult").

Columns 7–10 show some statistics on the analysis: (i) the number of overlapping variables[3]; (ii) the total number of integer variables in the analysis: it includes two variables per string, the string-related integer variables, and the overlap variables; (iii) the elapsed CPU time of the analysis in seconds on a Pentium 366 with 128MB running Windows 2000; and (iv) the maximum size of allocated memory during the analysis in MBytes.

From a user point of view, the most important information appears in columns 11–12 that show the number of false alarms vs. the number of errors found. We

---

[3] The maximum number of overlap variables is $n * (n - 1)/2$, where n is the number of string variables. Only flush requires that many variables.

verified errors by running the program with an appropriate input. A total of 19 errors were detected. Ten errors are due to unsafe pointer arithmetic resulting in a pointer beyond the bounds of the buffer. These errors are due to assumptions that a certain character appears in the string, such as in the function null_terminate shown in Figure 1(b) which assumes that there is a blank in the string. Five errors are due to unsafe calls to standard C functions, such as the calls to strcpy() in insert_long. The remaining four errors are updates of a single character out of the buffer bounds, such as the expression *s = 0 in null_terminate.

In the function join the analysis produced three false alarms due to a complex condition in a for loop. In this case the widening operation causes loss of important constraints. The false alarm in skip_balanced occurs because it safely assumes that it is invoked with a balanced number of parentheses in the input parameter. This is verified in a prior call to a different function. This example demonstrates that in some cases it is hard to separate cleanness from correctness — in order to show that this function is clean we need to verify correctness, i.e., that the implementation correctly checks that the input string contains a balanced number of parentheses. Fortunately, in most of the analyzed examples, this is not the case, i.e., cleanness does not depend on correctness.

5   Conclusions

We have shown that real software defects can be identified by conservative static analysis tools in a realistic subset of C. The analysis produces very few false alarms. It assures against certain defects and the user is relieved from the need to test against them. The analysis combines pointer and integer analysis resulting in a rather precise information.

In the future we intend to analyze the instrumented program with different integer analysis techniques including interval analysis and other linear relation analyses. We also plan to generalize our method for a larger subset of C. Another fruitful area of research is automatically generating procedure annotations.

Acknowledgments

We would like to thank Bertrand Jeannet and Nicolas Halbwachs for providing us the polyhedra library and for their support. Thanks to Alex Warshavsky for his assistance in the prototype implementation and for many technical insights. Thanks to Rastislav Bodik, David Evans, John Field, G. Ramalingam, and Reinhard Willhelm for their helpful comments.

References

1. T. Austin, S. Breach, and G. Sohi. Efficient detection of all pointer and array access errors. In *SIGPLAN Conf. on Prog. Lang. Design and Impl.*, 1994.
2. Compaq Systems Research Center. Compaq extended static checker for Java. Available at http://research.compaq.com/SRC/esc/, 2000.
3. P. Cousot and R. Cousot. Static determination of dynamic properties of programs. In *Proc. 2nd. Int. Symp on Programming*, Paris, Apr. 1976.
4. P. Cousot and R. Cousot. Abstract interpretation: A unified lattice model for static analysis of programs by construction of approximation of fixed points. In *Symp. on Princ. of Prog. Lang.*, pages 238–252, New York, NY, 1977. ACM Press.
5. P. Cousot and N. Halbwachs. Automatic discovery of linear constraints among variables of a program. In *ACM Symp. on Princ. of Prog. Lang.*, 1978.
6. C. Cowan, P. Wagle, C. Pu, S. Beattie, and J. Walpole. Buffer overflows: attacks and defenses for the vulnerability of the decade. In *In Proc. of the DARPA Information Survivability Conference and Expo*, 1999.
7. Edison Design Group. C++ front end. Available at http://www.edg.com/.
8. N. Halbwachs, Y. Proy, and P. Roumanoff. Verification of real-time systems using linear relation analysis. *Formal Methods in System Design*, 11(2):157–185, 1997.
9. B. Jeannet. New polka library. Available at http://www-verimag.imag.fr/~bjeannet/newpolka-english.html.
10. B. W. Kernighan and D. M. Ritchie. *The C programming language*. Prentice-Hall, Englewood Cliffs, NJ 07632, USA, 1988.
11. D. Larochelle and D. Evans. Statically detecting likely buffer overflow vulnerabilities. In *To appear in 10th USENIX Security Symposium*, 2001.
12. A. Loginov, S. Yong, S. Horwitz, and T. Reps. Debugging via run-time type checking. In *Proc. of Fundamental Approaches to Softw. Eng. (FASE)*, 2001.
13. B. Miller, D. Koski, C. Lee, V. Maganty, R. Murthy, A. Natarajan, and J. Steidl. Fuzz revisited: A re-examination of the reliability of Unix utilities and services, 1995. Available at http://www.cs.wisc.edu/~bart/fuzz/fuzz.html.
14. Rational Inc. Purify software. Available at http://www.purify.com, 1995.
15. Reliable Systems. Icontract – design by contract. Available at http://www.reliable-systems.com/, 1999.
16. E. Spafford. The internet worm: Crisis and aftermath. In *Communications of the ACM, June 1989. 165*, pages 678–687, June 1989.
17. SUIF. Suif compiler system. Available at http://suif.stanford.edu/.
18. D. Wagner, J. Foster, E. Brewer, and A. Aiken. A first step towards automated detection of buffer overrun vulnerabilities. In *Symposium on Network and Distributed Systems Security (NDSS '00) San Diego, CA*, Feb. 2000.
19. D. Weise. Personal communication. Nov. 2000.
20. S. Yong, S. Horwitz, and T. Reps. Pointer analysis for programs with structures and casting. In *SIGPLAN Conf. on Prog. Lang. Design and Impl.*, 1999.

Solving Regular Tree Grammar Based Constraints[*]

Yanhong A. Liu[1], Ning Li[2], and Scott D. Stoller[1]

[1] Computer Science Dept., State University of New York, Stony Brook, NY 11794
[2] Computer Science Dept., University of Wisconsin, Madison, WI 53706
{liu,stoller}@cs.sunysb.edu, ning@cs.wisc.edu

Abstract. This paper describes the precise specification, design, analysis, implementation, and measurements of an efficient algorithm for solving regular tree grammar based constraints. The particular constraints are for dead-code elimination on recursive data, but the method used for the algorithm design and complexity analysis is general and applies to other program analysis problems as well. The method is centered around Paige's finite differencing, i.e., computing expensive set expressions incrementally, and allows the algorithm to be derived and analyzed formally and implemented easily. We propose higher-level transformations that make the derived algorithm concise and allow its complexity to be analyzed accurately. Although a rough analysis shows that the worst-case time complexity is cubic in program size, an accurate analysis shows that it is linear in the number of live program points and in other parameters, including mainly the arity of data constructors and the number of selector applications into whose arguments the value constructed at a program point might flow. These parameters explain the performance of the analysis in practice. Our implementation also runs two to ten times as fast as a previous implementation of an informally designed algorithm.

1 Introduction

Regular tree grammar based methods are important for program analysis, especially for analyzing programs that use recursive data structures [22, 29, 17, 37, 25]. Basically, a set of grammar-based constraints is constructed from the program and a user query and is then simplified according to a set of simplification rules to produce the solution. Usually, the constraints are constructed in linear time in the size of the program, and the efficiency of the analysis is determined by the constraint-simplification algorithms.

This paper describes the precise specification, design, analysis, implementation, and measurements of an efficient algorithm for solving regular tree grammar based constraints. The particular constraints are for dead-code elimination on recursive data, but the method used for the algorithm design and complexity analysis is general and applies to other program analyses as well.

The method is centered around Paige's finite differencing [31, 34, 32], i.e., computing expensive set expressions incrementally. It starts with a fixed-point

---

[*] This work is supported in part by ONR under grants N00014-99-1-0132, N00014-99-1-0358, and N00014-01-1-0109, by NSF under grants CCR-9711253 and CCR-9876058, and by a Motorola University Partnership in Research Grant.

P. Cousot (Ed.): SAS 2001, LNCS 2126, pp. 213–233, 2001.

specification of the problem, then applies (1) dominated convergence at the higher level [8] to transform fixed-point expressions into loops, (2) finite differencing [34, 32] to transform expensive set expressions in loops into incremental operations, and (3) real-time simulation at the lower level [33, 7] to transform sets and set operations to use efficient data structures. This method allows the algorithm to be derived and analyzed formally and implemented easily.

We first give a precise fixed-point specification of the problem. We then transform it into a loop and apply finite differencing completely systematically, making all the steps explicit. At the higher level, we study new transformations that make the derived algorithm concise and allow its complexity to be analyzed accurately. The complexity analysis captures the exact contribution of each parameter. In particular, although a rough analysis shows that the worst-case time complexity is cubic in program size, an accurate analysis shows that it is linear in the number of live program points and in other parameters, including mainly the arity of data constructors and the number of selector applications into whose arguments the value constructed at a program point might flow. These parameters explain the performance of the analysis in practice. At the lower level, we show that real-time simulation using based representation [33] applies only partially to our application, and we discuss data structure choices and the trade-offs. In particular, our accurate complexity analysis at the higher-level suggests that combination with unbased representation works well in our application, and our experiments support this. Our implementation runs two to ten times as fast as a previous implementation of an informally designed algorithm [25].

The main contributions of this work include

(1) the application of a powerful, systematic transformational design methodology that leads from a precise high-level fixed-point specification of a nontrivial problem to a highly efficient algorithmic solution,
(2) the identification of parameters in problem instances and the precise expression of the algorithm complexity in terms of these parameters, and
(3) the implementation and experiments that help confirm the accuracy of the complexity analysis and compare the efficiency of the algorithm with that of an informally designed algorithm.

It is not the goal of this paper to show a drastically new algorithm or algorithm design method. Instead, since program analysis is a central recurring task in all kinds of program manipulation, and static analysis is naturally described as computing fixed points, the goal is to show the systematic nature of the design method in the hope that it can be more widely used for developing analysis algorithms, to allow easier correctness proof, algorithm understanding, performance analysis and comparison, and implementation. At the same time, through such usage, one may further improve the design method, for example, as we study the transformations and accurate complexity analyses enabled by Theorem 1.

2   Problem Specification

The Specification from the Application. We first look at the grammar constraints and the simplification algorithm for the dead-code elimination application in [25].[1] There, regular tree grammars, called liveness patterns, represent projection functions that project out components of values and parts of programs that are of interest.

The grammar constraints constructed from a given program or given in a user query consist of productions of the following standard forms:

$$N \to d \qquad \text{dead form,} \qquad \text{where } d \text{ is a special constant}$$
$$N \to l \qquad \text{live form,} \qquad \text{where } l \text{ is a special constant}$$
$$N \to c(N_1, ..., N_k) \text{ constructor form, where } c \text{ is from a set of constructors and}$$
$$\text{may have arity 0}$$

and the following extended forms:

$$N' \to N \qquad \text{copy form}$$
$$N' \to c_i^{-1}(N) \qquad \text{selector form}$$
$$N' \to [N]R' \qquad \text{conditional form,}$$

where R' is of forms l, $c(N_1, ..., N_k)$, and N''. Symbols d, l, and c's are terminals, and symbols N, $N_1, ..., N_k$, N', N'' are nonterminals. The extended forms are simplified away using the algorithm below, where R is of forms l and $c(N_1, ..., N_k)$, which are called good forms.

> **input**: productions P of standard forms and extended forms;
> **repeat**
>   if P contains $N' \to N$ and $N \to R$, add $N' \to R$ to P;
>   if P contains $N' \to c_i^{-1}(N)$ and $N \to l$, add $N' \to l$ to P;
>   if P contains $N' \to c_i^{-1}(N)$ and $N \to c(N_1, ..., N_k)$, add $N' \to N_i$ to P;   (1)
>   if P contains $N' \to [N]R'$ and $N \to R$, add $N' \to R'$ to P;
> **until** no more productions can be added;
> **output**: the resulting productions in P that are of good forms.

Throughout the paper, we use R' to denote right-side forms l, $c(N_1, ..., N_k)$, and N''. We use R to denote right-side good forms l and $c(N_1, ..., N_k)$; when R is a variable whose value could be an N form, it is accompanied by a test to ensure that its value is a good form.

In the application, extended forms are constructed from programs: for each program construct below on the left, the corresponding productions on the right are constructed, where a nonterminal associated with (at the left upper corner of) a program point denotes the liveness pattern for the values at that point.

---

[1] The presentation here includes minor notational changes and simplifications. In particular, in [25], the condition in the first production for a binding expression is unnecessary.

function definition:

$f({}^{N_1}v_1, ..., {}^{N_n}v_n) \triangleq e$ $\qquad$ $N_i \rightarrow N_i'$ for $i = 1..n$ and for each occurrence of ${}^{N_i'}v_i$ in e

data construction:

${}^{N}c({}^{N_1}e_1, ..., {}^{N_n}e_n)$ $\qquad$ $N_i \rightarrow c_i^{-1}(N)$ for $i = 1..n$

selector application:

${}^{N}c_i^{-1}({}^{N_1}e)$ $\qquad$ $N_1 \rightarrow [N]c(\overbrace{d, ..., d}^{i-1}, N, \overbrace{d, ..., d}^{n-i})$ for c of arity n

tester application:

${}^{N}c?({}^{N_1}e)$ $\qquad$ $N_1 \rightarrow [N]c(\overbrace{d, ..., d}^{n})$ for each possible c of arity n

primitive operation:

${}^{N}p({}^{N_1}e_1, ..., {}^{N_n}e_n)$ $\qquad$ $N_i \rightarrow [N]l$ for $i = 1..n$

conditional:

^{N}if ${}^{N_1}e_1$ then ${}^{N_2}e_2$ else ${}^{N_3}e_3$ $\quad$ $N_1 \rightarrow [N]l,\ N_2 \rightarrow N,\ N_3 \rightarrow N$

binding:

^{N}let $u = {}^{N_1}e_1$ in ${}^{N_2}e_2$ $\qquad$ $N_1 \rightarrow N_1'$ for each free occurrence of ${}^{N_1'}u$ in $e_2,\ N_2 \rightarrow N$

function application:

${}^{N}f({}^{N_1}e_1, ..., {}^{N_n}e_n)$ $\qquad$ $N_i \rightarrow [N]N_i'$ for $i = 1..n,\ N' \rightarrow N$

where $f({}^{N_1'}v_1, ..., {}^{N_n'}v_n) = {}^{N'}e$

Standard forms are given in user queries to indicate program points of interest and liveness patterns of interest at those points. For example, a user query $N \rightarrow l$ indicates that the entire value at point N is of interest. Simplification aims to add standard forms that capture the effects of extended forms. After simplification, program points whose associated nonterminals do not have a right-side good form are identified as dead. Appendix A gives a small example program together with the constructed grammar, a user query, and the simplification result.

All the production forms here are the same as or similar to those studied by many people. For example, standard forms are as in [14, 22, 9], copy forms are common in grammars, selector forms are first seen in [22], and conditional forms have counterparts in [3, 17]. Overall, the constraints here extend those by Jones and Muchnick [22].

Notation. We use a set-based language. It is based on SETL [41, 42] extended with a fixed-point operation by Cai and Paige [8]; we allow sets of heterogeneous elements and extend the language with pattern matching. Primitive data types are sets, tuples, and maps, i.e., binary relations represented as sets of 2-tuples. Their syntax and operations on them are summarized below:

$\{X_1, ..., X_n\}$	a set with elements $X_1,...,X_n$
$[X_1, ..., X_n]$	a tuple with elements $X_1,...,X_n$ in order
$\{[X_1, Y_1], ..., [X_n, Y_n]\}$	a map that maps X_1 to Y_1, ..., X_n to Y_n
$\{\}$	empty set
$S \cup T,\ S - T$	union and difference, respectively, of sets S and T
S with X, S less X	$S \cup \{X\}$ and $S - \{X\}$, respectively
$S \subseteq T$	whether S is a subset of T
X in S, X notin S	whether or not, respectively, X is an element of S
$\#S$	number of elements in set S
$T(I)$	I'th component of tuple T
dom M	domain of map M, i.e., $\{X : [X, Y] \text{ in } M\}$
$M\{X\}$	image set of X under map M, i.e., $\{Y : [Z, Y] \text{ in } M \mid Z = X\}$
inv M	inverse of map M, i.e., $\{[Y, X] : [X, Y] \text{ in } M\}$

We use the notation below for pattern matching against constants and tuples. The second returns false if X is not a tuple of length n; otherwise, it binds Y_i to the ith component of X if Y_i is an unbound variable, and otherwise, recursively tests whether the ith component of X matches Y_i, until either a test fails or all unbound variables in the pattern become bound.

X **of** c, where c is a constant   whether X is constant c
X **of** $[Y_1, ..., Y_n]$ whether X matches pattern $[Y_1, ..., Y_n]$

We use the notation below for set comprehension. Y_i's enumerate elements of all S_i's; for each combination of $Y_1, ..., Y_n$, if the Boolean value of expression Z is true, then the value of expression X forms an element of the resulting set. Each Y_i can be a tuple, in which case an enumerated element of S_i is first matched against it.

$\{X : Y_1 \textbf{ in } S_1, ..., Y_n \textbf{ in } S_n \mid Z\}$ set former
$\{X : Y_1 \textbf{ in } S_1, ..., Y_n \textbf{ in } S_n\}$ abbreviation of $\{X : Y_1 \textbf{ in } S_1, ..., Y_n \textbf{ in } S_n \mid true\}$
$\{Y \textbf{ in } S \mid Z\}$ abbreviation of $\{Y : Y \textbf{ in } S \mid Z\}$

LFP $_{\subseteq, X}(F(Y), Y)$ denotes the minimum element Y, with respect to partial ordering $\subseteq$, that satisfies the condition $X \subseteq Y$ and $F(Y) = Y$. We abbreviate $X := X \textbf{ op } Y$ as $X \textbf{ op } := Y$. Also, we abbreviate $X_1 := Y; ...; X_n := Y$ as $X_1, ..., X_n := Y$.

A Set-Based Fixed-Point Specification. We represent the right-side R' forms as follows:

$$l \qquad\qquad \text{as } l, \text{ where } l \text{ is a special constant}$$
$$c(N_1, ..., N_k) \text{ as } [c, [N_1, ..., N_k]] \qquad\qquad (2)$$
$$N \qquad\qquad \text{as } N$$

and represent the productions as follows:

$$N' \to R' \qquad \text{as } [N', \text{representation of } R']$$
$$N' \to c_i^{-1}(N) \text{ as } [N', c, i, N] \qquad\qquad (3)$$
$$N' \to [N]R' \text{ as } [N', N, \text{representation of } R']$$

This representation allows us to distinguish all the production forms by simple pattern matching against constants and tuples of different lengths. We also need to tell whether an R' form is an R form or an N form, so for convenience, we define:

$$R' \text{ isR} = R' \textbf{ of } l \textbf{ or } R' \textbf{ of } [C, T]$$
$$R' \text{ isN} = \textbf{not } (R' \textbf{ of } l \textbf{ or } R' \textbf{ of } [C, T]) \qquad\qquad (4)$$

The simplification algorithm in (1) can be specified as follows. The input is a set P of productions in the new representation. The **repeat**-loop computes the minimum set Q that satisfies $P \subseteq Q$ and $F(Q) \subseteq Q$, where $F(Q)$ captures, line-by-line, the four rules in the loop body:

$$
\begin{aligned}
F(Q) = \;& \{[N', R] : [N', N] \textbf{ in } Q, [N, R] \textbf{ in } Q \mid R \text{ isR}\} \cup \\
& \{[N', l] : [N', C, I, N] \textbf{ in } Q, [N, l] \textbf{ in } Q\} \cup \\
& \{[N', T(I)] : [N', C, I, N] \textbf{ in } Q, [N, [C, T]] \textbf{ in } Q\} \cup \\
& \{[N', R'] : [N', N, R'] \textbf{ in } Q, [N, R] \textbf{ in } Q \mid R \text{ isR}\}
\end{aligned} \qquad (5)
$$

Since $F(Q) \subseteq Q$ iff $F(Q) \cup Q = Q$, the loop computes

$$\mathbf{LFP}_{\subseteq,P}(F(Q) \cup Q, Q) \qquad (6)$$

The output is the set O of resulting productions whose right side is a good form:

$$O = \{[N, R] \text{ in } \mathbf{LFP}_{\subseteq,P}(F(Q) \cup Q, Q) \mid R \text{ is} R\} \qquad (7)$$

Note that $G = \lambda Q.F(Q) \cup Q$ is monotone, i.e., if $Q_1 \subseteq Q_2$ then $G(Q_1) \subseteq G(Q_2)$, and is inflationary at P, i.e., $P \subseteq G(P)$.

The representation of constraints using SETL tuples is immaterial to the problem. However, efficient algorithms for simplifying the constraints require the use of auxiliary maps, as discussed in Section 4; both for discovering such auxiliary expressions and for systematically manipulating them, uniform notation helps.

3   Approach

The method has three steps: (1) dominated convergence, (2) finite differencing, and (3) real-time simulation.

Dominated convergence [8] transforms a set-based fixed-point specification into a **while**-loop. The idea is to perform a small update operation in each iteration. The fixed-point expression $\mathbf{LFP}_{\subseteq,P}(F(Q) \cup Q, Q)$ in (7) is transformed into the following **while**-loop, making use of $\lambda Q.F(Q) \cup Q$ being monotone and inflationary at P:

$$
\begin{aligned}
&Q := P; \\
&\textbf{while exists } p \text{ in } F(Q) - Q \qquad\qquad (8) \\
&\quad Q \textbf{ with} := p;
\end{aligned}
$$

This code is followed by

$$O = \{[N, R] \text{ in } Q \mid R \text{ is} R\}; \qquad (9)$$

Finite differencing [34, 32] transforms expensive set operations in a loop into incremental operations. The idea is to replace expensive expressions $exp_1, ..., exp_n$ in a loop $LOOP$ with fresh variables $E_1, ..., E_n$, respectively, and maintain the invariants $E_1 = exp_1, ..., E_n = exp_n$ by inserting appropriate initializations or updates to $E_1, ..., E_n$ at each assignment in $LOOP$. We denote the transformed loop as

$$\Delta E_1, ..., E_n \langle LOOP \rangle$$

For our program (8) and (9) from Step 1, expensive expressions, i.e., non-constant-time expressions here, are the one that computes O and others that are needed for computing $F(Q) - Q$. We use fresh variables to hold their values. These variables are initialized together with the assignment $Q := P$ and are updated incrementally as Q is augmented by p in each iteration. Liu [23] gives references to much work that exploited related ideas.

Real-time simulation [33, 7] selects appropriate data structures for representing sets so that operations on them can be implemented efficiently. The idea is to design sophisticated linked structures based on how sets and set elements are accessed, so that each operation can be performed in constant time with at most a constant (a small fraction) factor of overall space overhead.

4   Finite Differencing

Identifying Expensive Subexpressions. The output O in (9) and expensive subexpressions used to compute O need to be computed incrementally in the loop. The latter expressions are $E1$ to $E4$, one for each of the sets in $F(Q)$ in (5), and W, the workset:

$$E1 = \{[N', R] : [N', N] \text{ in } Q, [N, R] \text{ in } Q \mid R \text{ is} R\}$$
$$E2 = \{[N', l] : [N', C, I, N] \text{ in } Q, [N, l] \text{ in } Q\}$$
$$E3 = \{[N', T(I)] : [N', C, I, N] \text{ in } Q, [N, [C, T]] \text{ in } Q\} \tag{10}$$
$$E4 = \{[N', R'] : [N', N, R'] \text{ in } Q, [N, R] \text{ in } Q \mid R \text{ is} R\}$$
$$W = F(Q) - Q = E1 \cup E2 \cup E3 \cup E4 - Q$$

Thus, the overall computation becomes

$$\Delta O, E1, E2, E3, E4, W \; \langle \; Q := P;$$
$$\textbf{while exists } p \textbf{ in } W \tag{11}$$
$$Q \textbf{ with } := p; \; \rangle$$

Discovering Auxiliary Expressions. To compute $E1$ to $E4$ incrementally with respect to Q **with** $:= p$, the following auxiliary expressions $E11$ to $E41$ are maintained. Expression $E11$ maps N to N' if there is a production of form $N' \rightarrow N$. Expression $E21$ maps N to N' and expression $E31$ maps $[c, N]$ to $[N', i]$ if there is a production of the form $N' \rightarrow c_i^{-1}(N)$. Expression $E41$ maps N to $[N', R']$ if there is a production of form $N' \rightarrow [N]R'$.

$$E11 = \{[N, N'] : [N', N] \text{ in } Q \mid N \text{ is} N\}$$
$$E21 = \{[N, N'] : [N', C, I, N] \text{ in } Q\}$$
$$E31 = \{[[C, N], [N', I]] : [N', C, I, N] \text{ in } Q\} \tag{12}$$
$$E41 = \{[N, [N', R']] : [N', N, R'] \text{ in } Q\}$$

These expressions are introduced for differentiating $E1$ to $E4$, respectively. For example, $E11$ is introduced for differentiating $E1$ in (10) after adding an element $[N, R]$ in Q—we need to add $[N', R]$ to $E1$ for all $[N', N]$ in Q, i.e., for all N' in $E11\{N\}$. These expressions can be obtained systematically based on the set formers in (10): after adding an element corresponding to one enumerator, create based on the other enumerator a map from variables that are already bound to variables yet unbound. For example, consider $E3$ and adding an element $[N, [C, T]]$ in Q. Then, for $[N', C, I, N]$ in Q, variables C and N are bound, and N' and I are not. So, we create a map from $[C, N]$ to $[N', I]$ for each $[N', C, I, N]$ in Q, which is $E31$. Now, the overall computation becomes

$$\Delta O, E1, E2, E3, E4, W, E11, E21, E31, E41 \; \langle \; Q := P;$$
$$\textbf{while exists } p \textbf{ in } W \tag{13}$$
$$Q \textbf{ with } := p; \; \rangle$$

These auxiliary maps provide, at a high level, the indexing needed to support efficient incremental updates.

Transforming Loop Body. We apply finite differencing to the loop body. This means that we differentiate O, $E1$ to $E4$, W, and $E11$ to $E41$ with respect to Q with $:= p$ in (13):

$$\Delta O, E1, E2, E3, E4, W, E11, E21, E31, E41 \; \langle \; Q \text{ with} := p; \; \rangle \qquad (14)$$

Based on the elements added to W, which is through $E1$ to $E4$, p can be of forms $[N, l]$, $[N, [C, T]]$, and $[N', N]$ where N *is*N. For each form of p, we determine how the sets O, $E1$ to $E4$, and $E11$ to $E41$ are updated. Also, for each of the forms, we do two things to update W. First, with anything added into $E1$ to $E4$, if it is not in Q, then it is added to W. Second, remove p from W. We obtain the following complete code for the loop body:

```
Q with := p;
W less := p;
case p of
    [N, R], where R isR :                                        //if p is N→ R
        O with := [N, R];
        E1 ∪ := {[N', R] : N' in E11{N}};                        //add N'→ R for all N'→ N
        W  ∪ := {[N', R] : N' in E11{N} | [N', R] notin Q};
        E4 ∪ := {[N', R'] in E41{N}};                            //add N'→ R' for all N'→ [N]R'
        W  ∪ := {[N', R'] in E41{N} | [N', R'] notin Q};
    [N, l] :                                                     //if p is N→ l
        E2 ∪ := {[N', l] : N' in E21{N}};                        //add N'→ l for all N'→ C_I^{-1}(N)
        W  ∪ := {[N', l] : N' in E21{N} | [N', l] notin Q};
    [N, [C, T]] :                                                //if p is N→ C(T(1), ..., T(k))
        E3 ∪ := {[N', T(I)] : [N', I] in E31{[C, N]}};           //add N'→ T(I) for all N'→ C_I^{-1}(N)
        W  ∪ := {[N', T(I)] : [N', I] in E31{[C, N]} | [N', T(I)] notin Q};
    [N', N], where N isN :                                       //if p is N'→ N
        E1 ∪ := {[N', R] : R in O{N}};                           //add N'→ R for all N→ R
        W  ∪ := {[N', R] : R in O{N} | [N', R] notin Q};
        E11 with := [N, N'];
```
(15)

These updates are keys for achieving high efficiency: after adding a new production, we consider only productions that are directly affected.

Initialization. Sets O, $E1$ to $E4$, W, and $E11$ to $E41$ need to be initialized together with $Q := P$ in (13). To do this, we add each p from P into Q one by one, and update each of these sets incrementally as in the loop body. We have the same four cases of p as in the loop body (15) and the cases for two additional forms of p, namely $[N', C, I, N]$ and $[N', N, R]$. We obtain the following complete code for initialization:

```
O, E1, E2, E3, E4, W, E11, E21, E31, E41, Q := {};
for p in P
    Q with := p;
    W less := p;
    case p of
        same four cases of p as in the loop body
        [N', C, I, N] :                                          //if p is N'→ C_I^{-1}(N)
            E2 ∪ := {[N', l] : l in Q{N}};                       //add N'→ l for all N→ l
            W  ∪ := {[N', l] : l in Q{N} | [N', l] notin Q};
            E21 with := [N, N'];
            E3 ∪ := {[N', T(I)] : [C, T] in Q{N}};               //add N'→ T(I) for all N→ C(T(1), ..., T(k))
            W  ∪ := {[N', T(I)] : [C, T] in Q{N} | [N', T(I)] notin Q};
            E31 with := [[C, N], [N', I]];
        [N', N, R'] :                                            //if p is N'→ [N]R'
            E4 ∪ := {[N', R'] : R in Q{N} | R isR};              //add N'→ R' for all N→ R
            W  ∪ := {[N', R'] : R in Q{N} | R isR, [N', R'] notin Q};
            E41 with := [N, [N', R']];
```
(16)

Dead-Code Elimination. Since only O is the desired output, it is easy to see that $E1$ to $E4$ are not needed, i.e., they are dead. Furthermore, Q can be eliminated using the equivalences:

$$[N, R] \text{ in } Q, \text{ where } R \text{ } isR \iff [N, R] \text{ in } O$$
$$[N', N] \text{ in } Q, \text{ where } N \text{ } isN \iff [N, N'] \text{ in } E11$$

We obtain the following complete algorithm:

```
O, W, E11, E21, E31, E41 := {};
for p in P
  W less := p;
  case p of
    same four cases of p as in the loop body
    [N', C, I, N] :
      W ∪ := {[N', l] : l in O{N} | [N', l] notin O};
      E21 with := [N, N'];
      W ∪ := {[N', T(I)] : [C, T] in O{N} | [T(I), N'] notin E11};
      E31 with := [[C, N], [N', I]];
    [N', N, R'] :
      W ∪ := {[N', R'] : R in O{N} | if R' isR then [N', R'] notin O else [R', N'] notin E11};
      E41 with := [N, [N', R']];
  while exists p in W                                                              (17)
    W less := p;
    case p of
      [N, R], where R isR :
        O with := [N, R];
        W ∪ := {[N', R] : N' in E11{N} | [N', R] notin O};
        W ∪ := {[N', R'] in E41{N} | if R' isR then [N', R'] notin O else [R', N'] notin E11};
      [N, l] :
        W ∪ := {[N', l] : N' in E21{N} | [N', l] notin O};
      [N, [C, T]] :
        W ∪ := {[N', T(I)] : [N', I] in E31{[C, N]} | [T(I), N'] notin E11};
      [N', N], where N isN :
        W ∪ := {[N', R] : R in O{N} | [N', R] notin O};
        E11 with := [N, N'];
```

where $W \cup := \{X : Y \text{ in } S \mid Z\}$ is implemented as

$$
\begin{aligned}
&\textbf{for } Y \textbf{ in } S \\
&\quad \textbf{if } Z \textbf{ then} \\
&\qquad W \textbf{ with} := X;
\end{aligned}
\qquad (18)
$$

Complexity Analysis. For now, we assume that set initialization $S := \{\}$, retrieval of an arbitrary element in a set by **for** or **while** or an indexed element by $T(I)$, element addition and deletion S **with/less** X, and associative access X **notin** S and $M\{X\}$ each takes $\mathcal{O}(1)$ time; Section 6 describes how to achieve this. Other operations clearly take $\mathcal{O}(1)$ time.

Besides input size $\#P$ and output size $\#O$, i.e., the number of productions in input and output, respectively, we use the following parameters. The meanings of these parameters are based on how the constraints were constructed. Note that sets $E11$ to $E41$ only grow during the computation, so we consider their values at the end.

- Let a be the maximum of $\#E21\{N\}$, $\#E31\{[C, N]\}$, and $\#E41\{N\}$ for any N and C.
  Meaning: In the application, a is the maximum of the arities of constructors, primitive functions, and user-defined functions and the number of possible outermost constructors in the argument of a tester (such as *null*). In

fact, $\#E21\{N\}$ and $\#E31\{[C, N]\}$ are bounded by the maximum arity of constructors only.

– Let h be the maximum number of nonterminals to the left of a nonterminal:

$$h = \max\nolimits_{N \text{ in dom } E11} \#E11\{N\} \tag{19}$$

Meaning: In the application, for productions built from programs, $\#E11\{N\} \leq 2$ for any N (2 for a conditional expression, 1 for a binding expression and a function call, 0 for others). However, $E11$ and h may grow during simplification.

– Let g be the maximum number of good forms a nonterminal goes to:

$$g = \max\nolimits_{N \text{ in dom } O} \#O\{N\} \tag{20}$$

Meaning: In the application, a good form is either l or the right side of a constructor form constructed at the argument of a selector or a tester, and testers together generate no more than a constructor forms. Thus, g corresponds to the maximum of a and the maximum number of selector applications into whose arguments the value constructed at a program point might flow.

– Let r be the size of the domain of O:

$$r = \#\mathbf{dom}\ O \tag{21}$$

Meaning: In the application, r is the number of live program points. Note that $\#O \leq r * g$.

– Let n be the number of nonterminals in P.

Meaning: In the application, n is the number of program points plus the number of nonterminals introduced in a user query. A user query usually has a small number of productions, and at most $a+1$ productions are constructed at each program point, so usually $\#P \leq n * a$.

Parameter n is not used in the precise complexity analysis, but it best captures program size. Also, n bounds h, and $\#P$ bounds g; the latter is because all good forms are in the given productions, so there are at most $\#P$ of them.

The complexity is the sum of (i) a constant for each element considered for addition to W, as in all the assignments to W, (ii) a constant for each element in W, as in the iterations, and (iii) a constant for each element in P, as in the initialization. Clearly, (ii) is bounded by (i), and (iii) is $\mathcal{O}(\#P)$. The total for (i) is the sum of (c1) to (c8) below, where (c1) to (c5) are for cases 1 to 4 in both the iteration and initialization, and (c6) to (c8) are for cases 5 and 6 in the initialization, explained below.

cases 1-3:	$\Sigma_{[N,R] \text{ in } O} \#E11\{N\}$	(c1)
	$\Sigma_{[N,l] \text{ in } O} \#E21\{N\}$	(c2)
	$\Sigma_{[N,[C,T]] \text{ in } O} \#E31\{[C, N]\}$	(c3)
	$\Sigma_{[N,R] \text{ in } O} \#E41\{N\}$	(c4)
case 4:	$\Sigma_{[N,N'] \text{ in } E11} \#O\{N\}$	(c5)
case 5:	$\Sigma_{[N',C,I,N] \text{ in } P} \#\{l \text{ in } O\{N\}\}$	(c6)
	$\Sigma_{[N',C,I,N] \text{ in } P} \#\{[C,T] \text{ in } O\{N\}\}$	(c7)
case 6:	$\Sigma_{[N',N,R'] \text{ in } P} \#\{R \text{ in } O\{N\}\}$	(c8)

For each p of form $[N, R]$, all N' in $E11\{N\}$ and all $[N', R']$ in $E41\{N\}$ are considered; since each p of form $[N, R]$ is added to set O, the total complexity for case 1 is (c1) plus (c4). The other cases are similar.

Using the parameters introduced above, we have

$$(c1) \le h * \#O \quad (c2) \le a * r \quad (c3) \le a * \#O \quad (c4) \le a * \#O \tag{22}$$

Note that

$$(c1) = (c5) = \Sigma_{N \text{ in dom } O} \#E11\{N\} * \#O\{N\} \tag{23}$$

A second way of estimating (c1) and (c5) is

$$
\begin{aligned}
(c1) = (c5) &\le \#\{[N, N'] \text{ in } E11 \mid N \text{ in dom } O\} * g && \text{by (23)} \\
&= \#\{[N', N] \text{ in } Q \mid N \text{ in dom } O\} * g && \text{by definition of } E11 \\
&\le (\#\{[N', N] \text{ in } P \mid N \text{ in dom } O\}+ && \text{those of form } [N', N] \text{ in } P \\
&\quad \#\{[N', N] \text{ in } E3 \mid N \text{ in dom } O\}+ && \text{those of form } [N', N] \text{ in } E3 \\
&\quad \#\{[N', N] \text{ in } E4 \mid N \text{ in dom } O\}) * g && \text{those of form } [N', N] \text{ in } E4 \text{ where } N \text{ is} N \\
& && \text{these three contribute all of form } [N', N] \text{ in } Q \\
&\le (r + (c3) + (c4)) * g \\
&\le (r + a * \#O + a * \#O) * g
\end{aligned}
\tag{24}
$$

Therefore, (c1) and (c5) are $\mathcal{O}(\#O * g * a)$. Thus, the sum of (c1) through (c5) is $\mathcal{O}(\#O*(h+a))$, using the first way of estimating (c1) and (c5), and $\mathcal{O}(\#O*g*a)$, using the second way. Also,

$$(c6), (c7), (c8) \le g * \#P \tag{25}$$

Thus, the total complexity of (i) to (iii) is $\mathcal{O}(\#O*\min(h+a, g*a)+\#P*g+\#P)$, which is

$$\mathcal{O}(\#O * \min(h + a, g * a) + \#P * g) \tag{26}$$

since $\#O \ne 0$ and thus $g \ne 0$ in the application.

In the application, productions in P with right sides in good forms are from the user query; if we assume there is a constant number of them, then (c6) to (c8) are $\mathcal{O}(\#P)$, and the total complexity is $\mathcal{O}(\#O * \min(h + a, g * a) + \#P)$.

5   Higher-Level Design and Analysis

Avoiding Duplication of Code for Initialization. Algorithm (17) duplicates the code in the loop body in the initialization. Cai and Paige [8] proposed a high-level transformation that can drastically simplify the initialization and do all the work in the loop body. By Theorem 5 in [8], the fixed-point expression (6) is equivalent to

$$\mathbf{LFP}_{\subseteq, \{\}}(P \cup F(Q) \cup Q, Q) \tag{27}$$

which can be transformed into

$$
\begin{aligned}
&Q := \{\}; \\
&\textbf{while exists } p \text{ in } P \cup F(Q) - Q \\
&\quad Q \textbf{ with} := p;
\end{aligned}
\tag{28}
$$

This merges the initialization for $Q := P$ into the iteration and thus avoids code duplication. However, this merging reduces the accuracy of the complexity analysis. The complexity analysis is similar to that in Section 4. The total complexity is again $\mathcal{O}(\#O * \min(h + a, g * a) + \#P * g)$. We can not obtain

$\mathcal{O}(\#O * \min(h + a, g * a) + \#P)$ here, even if we have the additional assumption about the user query, because (c6) to (c8) are now from the main loop, where g is not bounded by a constant.

We propose a general method that not only eliminates code duplication completely but also yields overall even smaller code and more accurate complexity. The method is to merge into the main loop only the cases in the initialization that must be handled in the main loop, not the cases that are needed only in initialization. Our method is supported by the following theorem.

Theorem 1. *For all $P_0 \subseteq P$, $\mathbf{LFP}_{\subseteq,P_0}((P - P_0) \cup F(Q) \cup Q, Q)$ exists if and only if $\mathbf{LFP}_{\subseteq,P}(F(Q) \cup Q, Q)$ exists, and if they exist, they are equal.*

Proof. $\mathbf{LFP}_{\subseteq,P_0}((P - P_0) \cup F(Q) \cup Q, Q) = \mathbf{LFP}_{\subseteq,\{\}}(P_0 \cup (P - P_0) \cup F(Q) \cup Q, Q)$
$= \mathbf{LFP}_{\subseteq,\{\}}(P \cup F(Q) \cup Q, Q) = \mathbf{LFP}_{\subseteq,P}(F(Q) \cup Q, Q)$. $\square$

We apply Theorem 1 with $P_0 = \{p \textbf{ in } P \mid p \textbf{ of } [N', C, I, N] \textbf{ or } p \textbf{ of } [N', N, R']\}$. The fixed-point expression (6) is equivalent to $\mathbf{LFP}_{\subseteq,P_0}(P - P_0 \cup F(Q) \cup Q, Q)$. Transforming this into a **while**-loop and applying finite differencing yields the following complete algorithm, which has the same iteration as in algorithm (17) and initializes O and $E11$ to $\{\}$, $E21$ through $E41$ for p in P_0 as in (17), and W to $P - P_0$:

$$
\begin{aligned}
&O, W, E11, E21, E31, E41 := \{\}; \\
&\textbf{for } p \textbf{ in } P \\
&\quad \textbf{case } p \textbf{ of} \\
&\quad\quad [N', C, I, N] : \\
&\quad\quad\quad E21 \textbf{ with} := [N, N']; \\
&\quad\quad\quad E31 \textbf{ with} := [[C, N], [N', I]]; \\
&\quad\quad [N', N, R'] : \\
&\quad\quad\quad E41 \textbf{ with} := [N, [N', R']]; \\
&\quad\quad \textbf{other} : \\
&\quad\quad\quad W \textbf{ with} := p; \\
&\quad\text{same iteration as in algorithm (17)}
\end{aligned}
\tag{29}
$$

The complexity analysis is the same as in Section 4, except that the corresponding (c6) to (c8) in (i) equal zero here, and (ii) here is bounded by the sum of (ii) and (iii) there. Thus, the total complexity is

$$\mathcal{O}(\#O * \min(h + a, g * a) + \#P) \tag{30}$$

which is better than the complexity (26) obtained for (17).

Handling Multiple Queries. In the application, there can be many queries about a program. We can transform the above algorithm, so that initialization is done once in linear time in the size of the program, and simplification after each query takes time roughly linear in the number of live program points. In particular, initialization can be done concurrently with the construction of the productions.

Let P_0 be the set of productions constructed from the given program; it contains only productions of copy, selector, and conditional forms. Let P_1 be the set of productions from a user query; they are all in good forms. Thus, based on Theorem 1, initialization using P_0 followed by simplification using P_1 can be specified as

$$\mathbf{LFP}_{\subseteq,P_0}(P_1 \cup F(Q) \cup Q, Q) \tag{31}$$

which is transformed into

$$Q := P_0;$$
$$\textbf{while exists } p \textbf{ in } P_1 \cup F(Q) - Q \qquad\qquad (32)$$
$$Q \textbf{ with} := p;$$

Applying finite differencing in a similar way as above yields an algorithm that takes

$$\mathcal{O}(\#O * \min(h + a, g * a)) \qquad\qquad (33)$$

time for simplification after a query.

An Optimization to Conditional Forms. For production p of form $[N, R]$ where R is$R$, we can add the following updates at the end of handling that form, so as to avoid unnecessarily enabling any conditional form more than once:

$$Q \quad - := \{[N', N, R'] \textbf{ in } Q\}$$
$$E41 - := \{[N, [N', R']] \textbf{ in } E41\}$$

Then the assignment to Q will be deleted by dead-code elimination, and the assignment to $E41$ is simply $E41\{N\} := \{\}$. This optimization can be applied to all algorithms derived above.

For complexity analysis, we only need to change formula (c4) to

$$\Sigma_{N \textbf{ in dom } O} \#E41\{N\} \qquad\qquad (\text{c4'})$$

Therefore, (c4') $\leq a*r$. This does not change the overall asymptotic complexities.

For handling multiple queries, since this optimization updates $E41$ in the iteration, we need to preserve $E41$ after the initialization. To do this, we simply use a new set $E41'$ to function as $E41$ in the iteration: insert $E41' := E41$ immediately before the iteration, which can be a pointer assignment, and in the iteration, replace all uses of $E41$ by $E41'$. This does not change the complexity.

6   Lower-Level Implementation and Experiments

We consider implementation of the two best algorithms, (29) for one query and the algorithm obtained from (32) for multiple queries. The same data structures for representing sets are suitable for both. All sets involved are clearly finite based on the analysis in Sections 4 and 5.

Low-Level Set Operations. All the sets constructed in our algorithms are in fact maps, i.e., sets of pairs. To make this explicit, we do the following three groups of replacements in order:

1) **while exists** Z **in** M	with	**while exists** X **in dom** M
...Z...		**while exists** Y **in** $M\{X\}$
		...[X, Y]...
2) M **with** $:= [X, Y]$	with	$M\{X\}$ **with** $:= Y$
M **less** $:= [X, Y]$	with	$M\{X\}$ **less** $:= Y$
$[X, Y]$ **notin** M	with	Y **notin** $M\{X\}$
3) S **with** $:= X$	with	**if** X **notin** S
		S **with** $:= X$

The first two groups clearly treat the domain of a map M as a set and the image of M at each element X as a set. The third guarantees that an addition is only for an element not located in the set; in general, similar replacements are done for deletions as well, but the only deletion in our algorithms is for an arbitrary element retrieved from the same set and thus already located in it. We do not need to transform **for**-loops in our algorithms, since they enumerate sets of tuples that are only read; we introduce pattern matching to make components of these tuples explicit, so other replacements apply in the loop body.

After the replacements, all the set operations are restricted to those described in Section 4, with the above guarantees about elements added or deleted. To support the complexity analysis in Sections 4 and 5, each of these operations needs to be done in $\mathcal{O}(1)$ time.

Data Structure Selection. Consider using a singly linked list for each of the domain and image sets of O, W, and $E11$ to $E41$. Let each element in a domain linked list contain a pointer to its image linked list, i.e., represent a map as a linked list of linked lists. It is easy to see that all operations except indexed retrieval and associative access can be done in worst-case $\mathcal{O}(1)$ time. The indexed retrievals are for tuples never updated and can be implemented using arrays. However, an associative access would take linear time if a linked list is naively traversed. A classical approach is to use hash tables instead of linked lists. This gives average, rather than worst-case, $\mathcal{O}(1)$ time for each operation, and has an overhead of computing hashing related functions for each operation.

Paige et al. [33, 7] describe a technique for designing linked structures that support associative access in worst-case $\mathcal{O}(1)$ time with little space overhead. Consider

> **for** X **in** W or **while exists** X **in** W
> ...X **in** S... or ...X **notin** S... or ...$M\{X\}$... where the domain of M is S

We want to locate value X in S after it has been located in W. The idea is to use a finite universal set B, called a base, to store values for both W and S, so that retrieval from W also locates the value in S. B is represented as a set (this set is only conceptual) of records, with a K field storing the key (i.e., value). Set S is represented using a S field of B: records of B whose keys belong to S are connected by a linked list where the links are stored in the S field; records of B whose keys are not in S store a special value for undefined in the S field. Set W is represented as a separate linked list of pointers to records of B whose keys belong to W. Thus, an element of S is represented as *a field in* the record, and S is said to be *strongly based* on B; and element of W is represented as *a pointer to* the record, and W is said to be *weakly based* on B. This representation allows an arbitrary number of weakly based sets but only a constant number of strongly based sets. Essentially, base B provides a kind of indexing.

Our **while**-loop retrieves elements from the domain of W and locates these elements in the domains of O and $E11$ to $E41$. For example, at $O\{N\}$ in case 4 in the main loop, nonterminal N needs to be located in the domain of O. We use a base B for the set of nonterminals. The domain of W is weakly based on B, and the domains of O and $E11$ to $E41$ are strongly based on B. The only exception is that the domain of $E31$ needs a two-element key of the form $[C, N]$, but in the application, each N has only one corresponding C, so we simply use N as the key and record the corresponding C in a separate field to be checked against.

Our algorithms test whether a value is not in the images of O, W, and $E11$ to $E41$ at any element in their domains, so there are $\mathcal{O}(n)$ sets that need to be strongly based, and thus the based-representation method does not apply here. We describe three representations for these images and discuss the trade-offs.

Data Structure Choices and Trade-Offs. The images of O, W, and $E11$ to $E41$ can be implemented using arrays, linked lists, hash tables, or a combination of linked lists and hash tables.

First, for the $\mathcal{O}(n)$ images of each of O, W, $E11$ to $E41$, we may make them strongly based using an array of fields. This includes making a base $B2$ for the set of good forms. Each membership test takes worst-case $\mathcal{O}(1)$ time. However, this requires a total of quadratic space. Quadratic initialization time can be avoided using the technique in [1, Exercise 2.12].

Second, we may use a singly linked list for each of the images of O, W, and $E11$ to $E41$. Such a list is called unbased representation [33] if it is a list of elements rather than a list of pointers to the elements in some base. Due to other associative accesses in the main loop body, any mention of a nonterminal (in images of W, $E11$, and $E21$, in domains of the images of $E31$, and in domains and images of the images of $E41$) should be implemented as a pointer to an element in base B. We also make a base $B2$ for the set of good forms (where nonterminals in the arguments of constructor forms are also implemented as pointers to elements in B), and represent any mention of a good form (in images of O and W and in images of the images of $E41$) as a pointer to an element in $B2$; use of $B2$ avoids an extra factor of a in the time complexity for comparing constructor forms if specialized constructor forms are not used. Linked-list representation incurs no asymptotic space overhead, but each membership test takes worst-case $\mathcal{O}(l)$ time where l is the length of such a linked list. Based on parameters introduced in Section 4, we know that $l = a$ for the images of $E21$, $E31$, and $E41$, $l = h$ for the images of $E11$, and $l = g$ for the images of O. Also, each element in W either has a right side in a good form or is a copy form, and thus $l = g + f$ for the images of W, where f is the dual of h, i.e., it is the maximum number of nonterminals to the right of a nonterminal:

$$f = \max_{N \text{ in dom (inv } E11)} \#(\textbf{inv } E11)\{N\} \tag{34}$$

In the application, f is bounded by the maximum of $g+1$, the number of live call sites of any function, and the number of live occurrences of any formal parameter or bound variable. For (29) and the algorithm obtained from (32), the time for initialization is increased by a factor of a, and the time for the main loop is increased by a factor of $h + g + f$. This representation works well if h, g, and f are small. It works well for all our examples except a contrived worst-case example.

Third, we may maintain a hash table for each of the image sets. This achieves the time complexities analyzed in Sections 4 and 5, but they become average-case, rather than worst-case, complexities.

Finally, we can use linked lists when the images are small, and use hash tables when the images are larger. This achieves the same complexities analyzed in Sections 4 and 5, also for average case.

Experiments. We implemented the simplification algorithm obtained from (32) with the optimization to conditional forms and used it to replace a previous algorithm in a prototype system for dead-code analysis and elimination [25]. The prototype system is implemented using the Synthesizer Generator [36], and the simplification algorithms are written in a dialect of Scheme. We have used the system to analyze dozens of examples. Table 1 reports measurements of the most relevant parameters—as defined in the complexity analysis in Section 4, plus c4' in Section 5 and f in Section 6—and simplification times from analyzing 14 programs with 25 different queries using the new simplification algorithm.

Programs `bigfun`, `minmax`, and `biggerfun` are examples from [25]. `worst`, `worst10`, and `worst20` are examples contrived to demonstrate the worst-case cubic-time complexity. `incsort` and `incout` are incremental programs for selection sort and outer product, respectively, derived using incrementalization [27], where dead code after incrementalization is to be eliminated. `cachebin` and `cachelcs` are dynamic-programming programs for binomial coefficients and longest common subsequences, respectively, derived using cache-and-prune [26, 24], where cached intermediate results that are not used are to be pruned. `calend`, `symbdiff`, `takr`, and `boyer` are taken from the Internet Scheme Repository [21]. `calend` is a collection of calendrical functions [10]. `takr` is a 100-function version of TAK that tries to defeat cache memory effects. `symbdiff` does symbolic differentiation. `boyer` is a logic programming benchmark.

The queries are in the form $N \rightarrow l$, where N corresponds to the return value of a function in the second column of Table 1. In general, especially for libraries, such as the `calend` example, there may be multiple functions of interest; we included an example where we picked 22 functions at once.

First of all, the analysis is effective, reflected in the resulting number of live program points r compared to the total number of program points n. For some examples, the program after dead-code elimination is even asymptotically faster [25]. We also observe: 1) $\#P$ ranges from $1.02n$ to $1.56n$, 2) a is consistently very small, 3) h varies widely, 4) g and f are typically quite small, 5) $\#O$ is roughly linear in r and in g. Whether the observations about g and f hold for large programs need more experiments, but regardless, the measurements help confirm that the second way of estimating (c1) and (c5), not using h, better explains the running time in practice.

The simplification time after initialization, in milliseconds, with and without garbage-collection time, is measured on a SUN station SPARC 20 with 60 MHz CPU and 256 MB main memory. The times in Table 1 are for when linked lists are used for images of O, W, and $E11$ to $E41$. We also measured the times for hash tables and for linked lists combined with hash tables; both of these are slower. Optimization to conditional forms gives up to 15% speedup.

We can see that the simplification time is very much linear in c=(c1)+(c2)+(c3)+(c4), that is, it is roughly linear in $\#O$ with a small factor from g, and thus, it is linear in r and quadratic in g. Being close to linear in r rather than n is important, especially for analyzing libraries. Again, experiments measuring *g* for large programs are needed, but our measurements confirm the accurate complexities analyzed in terms of the identified parameters.

Table 1. Measurements for Example Programs.

program name	user query	#P	#O	n	r	a	h	g	f	c1,c5	c2	c3	c4	c4'	c	simp. time w/gc	no gc
bigfun	lenf	48	47	36	23	2	2	3	3	40	0	4	24	14	68	.002	.001
minmax	getlen	112	89	81	31	3	2	5	11	76	0	8	48	23	132	.006	.005
minmax	getmin	112	149	81	49	3	2	8	11	129	2	38	72	33	241	.010	.007
biggerfun	evef	115	114	84	64	2	2	5	10	86	2	14	64	45	166	.008	.007
biggerfun	oddf	115	115	84	56	2	2	6	6	94	2	16	60	36	172	.008	.007
worst	f	28	69	24	24	2	4	4	4	64	0	0	21	12	85	.005	.004
worst10	f	70	419	59	59	2	11	11	11	407	0	0	133	33	540	.028	.018
worst20	f	130	1429	109	109	2	21	21	21	1407	0	0	463	63	1870	.097	.068
incsort	sort	144	132	108	49	3	2	11	5	139	2	20	98	29	259	.010	.007
incsort	sort'	144	33	108	24	3	2	5	5	24	6	0	15	11	45	.002	.001
incout	out	152	53	117	30	5	2	4	3	43	4	0	24	18	71	.003	.002
incout	out'	152	77	117	55	5	2	5	4	56	8	0	48	36	112	.005	.004
cachebin	bin	91	113	74	67	3	4	5	5	105	0	51	65	41	221	.009	.006
cachelcs	lcs	140	205	117	89	4	6	7	5	214	0	152	104	88	470	.018	.014
calend	gregorian-	1840	228	1551	192	5	12	4	25	178	0	66	115	111	359	.018	.015
calend	islamic-	1840	418	1551	346	5	12	4	25	339	4	144	199	189	686	.034	.024
calend	eastern-	1840	460	1551	375	5	24	4	25	380	4	186	207	197	777	.038	.030
calend	yahrzeit	1840	484	1551	428	5	11	4	25	373	0	108	293	290	774	.038	.030
calend	22 functions	1861	1604	1551	1352	5	37	4	25	1329	41	614	791	777	2775	.13	.10
symbdiff	deriv	1974	7636	1264	1221	3	65	13	65	11045	28	206	6639	855	17918	.59	.48
symbdiff	derivations-x	1974	7784	1264	1261	3	65	13	65	11214	30	206	6686	878	18136	.60	.48
takr	tak99	4005	2800	2804	2800	3	4	1	5	3000	0	0	2200	2200	5200	.23	.21
takr	run-takr	4005	2804	2804	2804	3	5	1	5	3004	0	0	2203	2203	5207	.23	.21
boyer	setup	4496	4513	4347	3755	3	106	8	6	1152	3496	1316	92	31	6056	.29	.23
boyer	setup,run-boyer	4497	39501	4347	4302	3	924	25	13	83925	3684	38370	1377	254	127356	4.9	3.2

gregorian-: gregorian->absolute   islamic-: islamic-date   eastern-: eastern-orthodox-christmas

7   Related Work and Conclusion

Regular tree grammar based constraints have been used for analyzing recursive data in other applications and go back at least to Reynolds [38] and Schwartz [40]. Related work includes flow analysis for memory optimization by Jones and Muchnick [22], binding-time analysis for partial evaluation by Mogensen [29], set-based analysis of ML by Heintze [17], type inference by Aiken et al. [2,3], backward slicing by Reps and Turnidge [37], and set-based analysis for debugging Scheme by Flanagan and Felleisen [13]. Some of these are general type inference and are only shown to be decidable [3] or take exponential time in the worst case [2]. For others, either a cubic time complexity is given based on a simple worst-case analysis of a relatively straightforward algorithm [17,13], or algorithm complexity is not discussed explicitly [22,29,37].

Constraints have also been used for other analyses, in particular, analyses handling mainly higher-order functions or pointers. This includes higher-order binding-time analysis by Henglein [20], Bondorf and Jørgensen [6], and Birkedal and Welinder [4,5], points-to analysis by Steensgaard [44], and control flow analysis for special cases by Heintze and McAllester [19]. The last restricts type sizes and has a linear time complexity, and the others use union-find algorithms [20] and have an almost linear time complexity. These analyses either do not consider recursive data structures [20,44], or use bounded domains [6,4,5,19] and are thus less precise than grammar constraints constructed based on uses of recursive data in their contexts.

People study methods to speed up the cubic-time analysis algorithms. For example, Heintze [16] describes implementation techniques such as dependency directed updating and special representations, which has the same idea as incremental update by finite differencing and efficient access by real-time simulation. Flanagan and Felleisen [13] study techniques for component-wise simplification. Fähndrich et al. [11] study a technique for eliminating cycles in the inclusion constraint graphs. Su et al. [45] study techniques for reducing redundancies caused by transitivity in the constraint graphs. These improvements are all found to be very effective. Moreover, sometimes a careful implementation of a worst-case cubic-time [18, 25] (or quadratic-time [43]) analysis algorithm seems to give nearly linear behavior [18, 43, 25]. Our work in this paper is a start in the formal study of the reasons.

Our analysis adds edges through selecting components of constructions and enabling conditions, and our application also has the cycle and redundancy problems caused by dynamic transitivity, as studied in [11, 45]. However, our algorithm still proceeds in a linear fashion. That is, if we have constraints $N_1 \to N_2, ..., N_{k-1} \to N_k$, we do not add any edges $N_i \to N_j$ for any i, j such that $1 \leq i \leq j \leq k$; only when a new $N_k \to R$ is added, we add an $N_{k-1} \to R$ if it is not already added and subsequently an $N_{k-2} \to R$ and so on. This formalizes Heintze's algorithm [16]. For comparison, a future work would be to formalize the algorithms in [11, 45]. It will also be interesting to formalize and compare with [47]. As our problem is related to computing Datalog queries, it will be worthwhile to see to what degree McAllester's complexity results for Datalog queries [28] could be applied; note, however, that those results are obtained based on extensive hashing and thus are for average cases, not worst cases. Compared with the magic-sets transformation [46], finite differencing or incrementalization [23] based methods derive more specialized algorithms and data structures, yielding more efficient programs, often asymptotically better.

To summarize, for the problem of dead-code elimination on recursive data, this paper shows that formal specification, design, and analysis lead to an efficient algorithm with exact complexity factors. Clearly, there is a large body of work on all kinds of program analysis algorithms [30], from type inference algorithms, e.g., [35], to efficient fixed-point computation, e.g., [12]. Precise and unified specification, design, and complexity analysis of all kinds of program analysis algorithms deserve much further study. We believe that such study can benefit greatly from the approach of Paige et al. [34, 32, 8, 33, 7], as illustrated in this work, and from the more formal characterization by Goyal [15].

References

1. A. V. Aho, J. E. Hopcroft, and J. D. Ullman. *The Design and Analysis of Computer Algorithms*. Addison-Wesley, Reading, Mass., 1974.
2. A. Aiken and B. R. Murphy. Static type inference in a dynamically typed language. In *Conference Record of the 18th Annual ACM Symposium on Principles of Programming Languages*. ACM, New York, Jan. 1991.
3. A. Aiken, E. Wimmers, and T. Lakshman. Soft typing with conditional types. In *Conference Record of the 21st Annual ACM Symposium on Principles of Programming Languages*. ACM, New York, Jan. 1994.
4. L. Birkedal and M. Welinder. Binding-time analysis for standard ML. In *Proceedings of the ACM SIGPLAN Workshop on Partial Evaluation and Semantics-Based*

Program Manipulation, Technical Report 94/9, pages 61–71. Department of Computer Science, The University of Melbourne, June 1994.

5. L. Birkedal and M. Welinder. Binding-time analysis for Standard ML. *Lisp and Symbolic Computation*, 8(3):191–208, Sept. 1995.

6. A. Bondorf and J. Jørgensen. Efficient analyses for realistic off-line partial evaluation. *Journal of Functional Programming*, 3(3):315–346, July 1993.

7. J. Cai, P. Facon, F. Henglein, R. Paige, and E. Schonberg. Type analysis and data structure selection. In B. Möller, editor, *Constructing Programs from Specifications*, pages 126–164. North-Holland, Amsterdam, 1991.

8. J. Cai and R. Paige. Program derivation by fixed point computation. *Sci. Comput. Program.*, 11:197–261, Sept. 1988/89.

9. P. Cousot and R. Cousot. Formal language, grammar and set-constraint-based program analysis by abstract interpretation. In *Proceedings of the 7th International Conference on Functional Programming Languages and Computer Architecture*, pages 170–181. ACM, New York, June 1995.

10. N. Dershowitz and E. M. Reingold. Calendrical calculations. *Software—Practice and Experience*, 20(9):899–928, Sept. 1990.

11. M. Fähndrich, J. S. Foster, Z. Su, and A. Aiken. Partial online cycle elimination in inclusion constraint graphs. In *Proceedings of the ACM SIGPLAN '98 Conference on Programming Language Design and Implementation*, pages 85–96. ACM, New York, June 1998.

12. C. Fecht and H. Seidl. Propagating differences: An efficient new fixpoint algorithm for distributive constraint systems. In C. Hankin, editor, *Proceedings of the 7th European Symposium on Programming*, volume 1381 of *Lecture Notes in Computer Science*, pages 90–104. Springer-Verlag, Berlin, 1998.

13. C. Flanagan and M. Felleisen. Componential set-based analysis. *ACM Trans. Program. Lang. Syst.*, 21(2):370–416, Mar. 1999.

14. F. Gecseg and M. Steinb. *Tree Automata*. Akademiai Kiado, Budapest, 1984.

15. D. Goyal. *A Language Theoretic Approach to Algorithms*. PhD thesis, Department of Computer Science, New York University, Jan. 2000.

16. N. Heintze. Practical aspects of set based analysis. In K. Apt, editor, *Proceedings of the Joint International Conference and Symposium on Logic Programming*, pages 765–779. The MIT Press, Cambridge, Mass., Nov. 1992.

17. N. Heintze. Set-based analysis of ML programs. In *Proceedings of the 1994 ACM Conference on LISP and Functional Programming*, pages 306–317. ACM, New York, June 1994.

18. N. Heintze and J. Jaffar. Set constraints and set-based analysis. In *Proceedings of the 2nd International Workshop on Principles and Practice of Constraint Programming*, volume 874 of *Lecture Notes in Computer Science*, pages 281–298. Springer-Verlag, Berlin, 1994.

19. N. Heintze and D. McAllester. Linear-time subtransitive control flow analysis. In *Proceedings of the ACM SIGPLAN '97 Conference on Programming Language Design and Implementation*. ACM, New York, June 1997.

20. F. Henglein. Efficient type inference for higher-order binding-time analysis. In *Proceedings of the 5th International Conference on Functional Programming Languages and Computer Architecture*, volume 523 of *Lecture Notes in Computer Science*, pages 448–472. Springer-Verlag, Berlin, Aug. 1991.

21. The Internet Scheme Repository.
http://www.cs.indiana.edu/scheme-repository/.

22. N. D. Jones and S. S. Muchnick. Flow analysis and optimization of LISP-like structures. In S. S. Muchnick and N. D. Jones, editors, *Program Flow Analysis*, pages 102–131. Prentice-Hall, Englewood Cliffs, N.J., 1981.

23. Y. A. Liu. Efficiency by incrementalization: An introduction. *Higher-Order and Symbolic Computation*, 13(4):289–313, Dec. 2000.
24. Y. A. Liu and S. D. Stoller. Dynamic programming via static incrementalization. In *Proceedings of the 8th European Symposium on Programming*, volume 1576 of *Lecture Notes in Computer Science*, pages 288–305. Springer-Verlag, Berlin, Mar. 1999.
25. Y. A. Liu and S. D. Stoller. Eliminating dead code on recursive data. In SAS 1999 [39], pages 211–231.
26. Y. A. Liu, S. D. Stoller, and T. Teitelbaum. Static caching for incremental computation. *ACM Trans. Program. Lang. Syst.*, 20(3):546–585, May 1998.
27. Y. A. Liu and T. Teitelbaum. Systematic derivation of incremental programs. *Sci. Comput. Program.*, 24(1):1–39, Feb. 1995.
28. D. McAllester. On the complexity analysis of static analyses. In SAS 1999 [39], pages 312–329.
29. T. Mogensen. Separating binding times in language specifications. In *Proceedings of the 4th International Conference on Functional Programming Languages and Computer Architecture*, pages 12–25. ACM, New York, Sept. 1989.
30. F. Nielson, H. R. Nielson, and C. Hankin, editors. *Principles of Program Analysis*. Springer-Verlag, 1999.
31. R. Paige. *Formal Differentiation: A Program Synthesis Technique*, volume 6 of *Computer Science and Artificial Intelligence*. UMI Research Press, Ann Arbor, Michigan, 1981. Revision of Ph.D. dissertation, New York University, 1979.
32. R. Paige. Programming with invariants. *IEEE Software*, 3(1):56–69, Jan. 1986.
33. R. Paige. Real-time simulation of a set machine on a RAM. In *Computing and Information, Vol. II*, pages 69–73. Canadian Scholars Press, 1989. Proceedings of ICCI '89: The International Conference on Computing and Information, Toronto, Canada, May 23-27, 1989.
34. R. Paige and S. Koenig. Finite differencing of computable expressions. *ACM Trans. Program. Lang. Syst.*, 4(3):402–454, July 1982.
35. J. Rehof. *The Complexity of Simple Subtyping Systems*. PhD thesis, DIKU, University of Copenhagen, Copenhagen, Denmark, Apr. 1998.
36. T. Reps and T. Teitelbaum. *The Synthesizer Generator: A System for Constructing Language-Based Editors*. Springer-Verlag, New York, 1988.
37. T. Reps and T. Turnidge. Program specialization via program slicing. In O. Danvy, R. Glück, and P. Thiemann, editors, *Proceedings of the Dagstuhl Seminar on Partial Evaluation*, volume 1110 of *Lecture Notes in Computer Science*, pages 409–429. Springer-Verlag, Berlin, 1996.
38. J. C. Reynolds. Automatic computation of data set definitions. In A. J. H. Morrell, editor, *Information Processing 68: Proceedings of IFIP Congress 1968*, volume 1, pages 456–461. North-Holland, Amsterdam, 1969.
39. *Proceedings of the 6th International Static Analysis Symposium*, volume 1694 of *Lecture Notes in Computer Science*. Springer-Verlag, Berlin, Sept. 1999.
40. J. T. Schwartz. Optimization of very high level languages – I: Value transmission and its corollaries. *Journal of Computer Languages*, 1(2):161–194, 1975.
41. J. T. Schwartz, R. B. K. Dewar, E. Dubinsky, and E. Schonberg. *Programming with Sets: An Introduction to SETL*. Springer-Verlag, Berlin, New York, 1986.
42. W. K. Snyder. The SETL2 Programming Language. Technical report 490, Courant Institute of Mathematical Sciences, New York University, Sept. 1990.
43. B. Steensgaard. Points-to analysis by type inference of programs with structures and unions. In T. Gyimothy, editor, *Proceedings of the 6th International Conference on Compiler Construction*, volume 1060 of *Lecture Notes in Computer Science*, pages 136–150. Springer-Verlag, Berlin, 1996.

44. B. Steensgaard. Points-to analysis in almost linear time. In *Conference Record of the 23rd Annual ACM Symposium on Principles of Programming Languages*, pages 32–41. ACM, New York, Jan. 1996.
45. Z. Su, M. Fähndrich, and A. Aiken. Projection merging: Reducing redundancies in inclusion constraint graphs. In *Conference Record of the 27th Annual ACM Symposium on Principles of Programming Languages*, pages 81–95. ACM, New York, Jan. 2000.
46. J. D. Ullman. *Principles of Database and Knowledge-Base Systems*, volume II. Computer Science Press, New York, 1988.
47. D. M. Yellin. Speeding up dynamic transitive closure for bounded degree graphs. *Acta Informatica*, 30(4):369–384, July 1993.

A   An Example Program

Program. A program is a set of recursive function definitions, together with a set of constructor definitions, each with the corresponding tester and selectors.

$$f(x) \quad \overset{\triangle}{=} \quad \text{if } null(x) \text{ then } nil \text{ else } cons(g(car(x)), f(cdr(x)));$$
$$g(x) \quad \overset{\triangle}{=} \quad x * x * x * x * x;$$
$$len(x) \quad \overset{\triangle}{=} \quad \text{if } null(x) \text{ then } 0 \text{ else } 1 + len(cdr(x));$$
$$lenf(x) \quad \overset{\triangle}{=} \quad len(f(x));$$

$$cons \quad : \quad cons?(car, cdr);$$
$$nil \quad : \quad null();$$

Labeled Program. The program is labeled, with a distinct nonterminal associated with each program point, as follows:

$$f(^{N_{36}}x) \quad \overset{\triangle}{=} N_{35} \text{:if } ^{N_{34}} null(^{N_{33}}x) \text{ then } ^{N_{32}} nil \text{ else } ^{N_{31}} cons(^{N_{30}} g(^{N_{29}} car(^{N_{28}}x)), ^{N_{27}} f(^{N_{26}} cdr(^{N_{25}}x)));$$
$$g(^{N_{24}}x) \quad \overset{\triangle}{=} N_{23} {:} N_{22} {:} N_{21} {:} N_{20} {:} N_{19} {:} x * ^{N_{18}} {:} x * ^{N_{17}} {:} x * ^{N_{16}} {:} x * ^{N_{15}} {:} x;$$
$$len(^{N_{14}}x) \overset{\triangle}{=} N_{13} \text{:if } ^{N_{12}} null(^{N_{11}}x) \text{ then } ^{N_{10}} 0 \text{ else } ^{N_9} {:} N_8 {:} 1 + ^{N_7} {:} len(^{N_6} cdr(^{N_5}x));$$
$$lenf(^{N_4}x) \overset{\triangle}{=} N_3 {:} len(^{N_2} f(^{N_1}x));$$

Constructed Grammar. The grammar constructed from the given program is

$$N_{36} \to N_{33}, N_{36} \to N_{28}, N_{36} \to N_{25}, N_{33} \to [N_{34}] cons(N_0, N_0), N_{33} \to [N_{34}] nil(), N_{34} \to [N_{35}] L, N_{32} \to N_{35},$$

$$N_{28} \to [N_{29}] cons(N_{29}, N_0), N_{29} \to [N_{30}] N_{24}, N_{23} \to N_{30}, N_{30} \to car(N_{31}),$$
$$N_{25} \to [N_{26}] cons(N_0, N_{26}), N_{26} \to [N_{27}] N_{36}, N_{35} \to N_{27}, N_{27} \to cdr(N_{31}), N_{31} \to N_{35},$$

$$N_{24} \to N_{19}, N_{24} \to N_{18}, N_{24} \to N_{17}, N_{24} \to N_{16}, N_{24} \to N_{15}, N_{19} \to [N_{20}] L, N_{18} \to [N_{20}] L, N_{20} \to [N_{21}] L,$$
$$N_{17} \to [N_{21}] L, N_{21} \to [N_{22}] L, N_{16} \to [N_{22}] L, N_{22} \to [N_{23}] L, N_{15} \to [N_{23}] L,$$

$$N_{14} \to N_{11}, N_{14} \to N_5, N_{11} \to [N_{12}] cons(N_0, N_0), N_{11} \to [N_{12}] nil(), N_{12} \to [N_{13}] L, N_{10} \to N_{13},$$
$$N_8 \to [N_9] L, N_5 \to [N_6] cons(N_0, N_6), N_6 \to [N_7] N_{14}, N_{13} \to N_7, N_7 \to [N_9] L, N_9 \to N_{13},$$
$$N_4 \to N_1, N_1 \to [N_2] N_{36}, N_{35} \to N_2, N_2 \to [N_3] N_{14}, N_{13} \to N_3, N_0 \to D$$

User Query. A user query is

$$N_3 \to L$$

Simplification Result. The output of simplification, sorted by nonterminal number, is

$$N_{36} \to nil(), N_{36} \to cons(N_0, N_0), N_{36} \to cons(N_0, N_{26}), \quad N_{11} \to nil(), N_{11} \to cons(N_0, N_0),$$
$$N_{35} \to nil(), N_{35} \to cons(N_0, N_0), N_{35} \to cons(N_0, N_6), \quad N_{10} \to L,$$
$$N_{34} \to L, \qquad\qquad\qquad\qquad\qquad\qquad\qquad\qquad N_9 \to L,$$
$$N_{33} \to nil(), N_{33} \to cons(N_0, N_0), \qquad\qquad\qquad\quad N_8 \to L,$$
$$N_{32} \to nil(), N_{32} \to cons(N_0, N_0), N_{32} \to cons(N_0, N_6), \quad N_7 \to L,$$
$$N_{31} \to nil(), N_{31} \to cons(N_0, N_0), N_{31} \to cons(N_0, N_6), \quad N_6 \to nil(), N_6 \to cons(N_0, N_0), N_6 \to cons(N_0, N_6),$$
$$N_{27} \to nil(), N_{27} \to cons(N_0, N_0), N_{27} \to cons(N_0, N_6), \quad N_5 \to cons(N_0, N_6),$$
$$N_{26} \to nil(), N_{26} \to cons(N_0, N_0), N_{26} \to cons(N_0, N_{26}), \quad N_4 \to nil(), N_4 \to cons(N_0, N_0), N_4 \to cons(N_0, N_{26}),$$
$$N_{25} \to cons(N_0, N_{26}), \qquad\qquad\qquad\qquad\qquad\qquad N_3 \to L,$$
$$N_{14} \to nil(), N_{14} \to cons(N_0, N_0), N_{14} \to cons(N_0, N_6), \quad N_2 \to nil(), N_2 \to cons(N_0, N_0), N_2 \to cons(N_0, N_6),$$
$$N_{13} \to L, \qquad\qquad\qquad\qquad\qquad\qquad\qquad\qquad N_1 \to nil(), N_1 \to cons(N_0, N_0), N_1 \to cons(N_0, N_{26}),$$
$$N_{12} \to L, \qquad\qquad\qquad\qquad\qquad\qquad\qquad\qquad N_0 \to D$$

Nonterminals N_{15} to N_{24} and N_{28} to N_{30} do not have a right-side good form. The corresponding program points are dead.

Static Analyses of the Precision of Floating-Point Operations

Eric Goubault*

LIST (CEA - Recherche Technologique)
DTSI-SLA, CEA F91191 Gif-sur-Yvette Cedex

Abstract. Computers manipulate approximations of real numbers, called floating-point numbers. The calculations they make are accurate enough for most applications. Unfortunately, in some (catastrophic) situations, the floating-point operations lose so much precision that they quickly become irrelevant. In this article, we review some of the problems one can encounter, focussing on the IEEE754-1985 norm. We give a (sketch of a) semantics of its basic operations then abstract them (in the sense of abstract interpretation) to extract information about the possible loss of precision. The expected application is abstract debugging of software ranging from simple on-board systems (which use more and more on-the-shelf micro-processors with floating-point units) to scientific codes. The abstract analysis is demonstrated on simple examples and compared with related work.

1 Introduction

Everybody knows that computers calculate numerical results which are mostly wrong, yet they are intensively used for simulating highly complex physical processes and for predicting their behavior. Transcendental numbers (like π and e) cannot be represented exactly in a computer, since machines only use finite implementations of numbers (floating-point numbers instead of mathematical real numbers); they are truncated to a given number of decimals. Less known is that the usual algebraic laws (associativity for instance) that we use when thinking about numbers are no longer true in general when it comes to manipulating floating-point numbers.

It is actually surprising that very few studies on static analysis of floating-point operations or on their semantic foundations have been carried out. Our point of view in this article is that there are "numerical bugs" that a programmer can encounter, and that some are amenable to automatic detection using static analysis of the source code, using abstract interpretation. This new sort of bug includes what is normally called bug, i.e. run-time errors (here for instance, uncaught numerical exceptions), but also more subtle ones about the relevance of the numerical calculations that are made. We advocate that it is as much

---

* This work was supported by the RTD project IST-1999-20527 "DAEDALUS". This paper follows a seminar given at Ecole Normale Supérieure in June 1998.

P. Cousot (Ed.): SAS 2001, LNCS 2126, pp. 234–259, 2001.

of a bug to terminate on a "segmentation fault" as to terminate with a completely meaningless numerical result (which might be used to control a physical apparatus with catastrophic consequences).

This problem is not very well-known to programmers of non-scientific codes. Let us just give one example showing this is also of importance for the non-scientific computing world. On the 25th of February 1991, during the Gulf war, a Patriot anti-missile missed a Scud in Dharan which in turn crashed onto an American barracks, killing 28 soldiers. The official enquiry report (GAO/IMTEC-92-26) attributed this to a fairly simple "numerical bug". An internal clock that delivers a tick every tenth of a second controlled the missile. Internal time was converted in seconds by multiplying the number of ticks by $\frac{1}{10}$ in a 24 bits register. But $\frac{1}{10} = 0.00011001100110011001100 \cdots$ in binary format, i.e. is not represented in an exact manner in memory. This produced a truncating error of about 0.000000095 (decimal), which made the internal computed time drift with respect to ground systems. The battery was in operation for about 100 hours which made the drift of about 0.34 seconds. A Scud flies at about 1676m/s, so the clock error corresponded to a localization error of about 500 meters. The proximity sensors supposed to trigger the explosion of the anti-missile could not find the Scud and therefore the Scud fell and hit the ground, exploding onto the barracks.

Actually, more and more critical or on-board systems are using on-the-shelf floating-point units which used not to be approved beforehand. Therefore we believe that static analysis of floating-point operations is going to be very important in the near future, for safety-critical software as well as for numerical applications in the large.

These kinds of problems are better-known in scientific computing, at least when modeling the physical phenomena to be simulated. What we mean is that in many cases, the discretizations of the (continuous) problems that are modeled are sufficiently stable so that little truncation errors do not overly affect the result of their simulation. Unfortunately, it is difficult to find the exact semantics of floating-point operations, and even using some well-behaved numerical schemes, some unpredictable numerical errors can show up. Also some problems are inherently ill-conditioned, meaning that their sensitivity to numerical errors are very high. In this latter case it is in general very difficult to assess the relevance of the numerical simulation even by hand.

Organization of the Paper. In Sect. 2, we will explain what model of floating-point arithmetic we want to analyze (IEEE754-1985). We carry on in Sect. 2.1 by explaining what kind of properties we want to synthesize by the analysis. Then in Sect. 2.2 we give the syntax and informal meaning of a simple imperative toy language manipulating floating-point numbers; we give a first sketch of a formal semantics in Sect. 2.3 (that we refine in Sect. 3.2).

In Sect. 3 we present a few abstract domains that are candidate for the abstract interpretation of the concrete semantics. We give an example of abstract analysis in Sect. 4. We give some directions for improvement in Sect. 5.1 and compare with existing related work in Sect. 6. We conclude by giving some future directions of work in Sect. 7.

2   The IEEE 754 Norm

The IEEE754-1985 norm specifies how real numbers are represented in *memory*[1] using floating-point numbers, see [Gol91,Kah96]. The norm itself relies on a simple observation:

Lemma 1.

$$\mathcal{F} : (s, \quad f, \quad k) \to s(1+f)2^k$$
$$\{-1,1\} \times [0,1[\times \mathbb{N} \to \mathbb{R}^*$$

is a bijection with inverse:

$$\mathbb{R}^* \to \{-1,1\} \times [0,1[\times \mathbb{N}$$
$$\mathcal{G} : x \quad \to (s(x), \quad f(x), \quad k(x))$$

with $s(x)$ being the sign of x, $k(x) = \lfloor log_2(|x|) \rfloor$ where $\lfloor u \rfloor$ denotes the integral part[2] of u and log_2 is the logarithm in base 2, and $f(x) = \frac{|x|}{2^{k(x)}} - 1$.

Taking a representation with a fixed number of bits K for exponents (function $k(x)$) and a fixed number of bits N for the mantissa (function $f(x)$ or $m(x) = 1 + f(x)$), the norm defines several kinds of floating-point numbers,

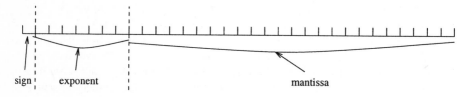

Fig. 1. Representation of a floating-point number in memory.

- The standard numbers, $r = s*n*2^{k+1-N}$, with $s \in \{-1,1\}, 1-2^K < k < 2^K$, $0 \le n < 2^N$ normalized so that, $r = s*2^k(1+f)$ with $f < 1$,
- Denormalized numbers (to manage "underflow" in a gradual manner), $r = s*n*2^{k+1-N} = s*2^k(0+f)$ with $k = 2 - 2^K$ and $0 < n < 2^{N-1}$ i.e. $0 < f < 1$,
- $+\infty$ and $-\infty$ (notice that their inverses, $+0$ et -0 are also there),

---

[1] But not in the registers of micro-processors.
[2] i.e. the greatest integer less or equal than x. We will also use $\lceil u \rceil$ which is the least integer greater or equal than x.

– NaN "Not a Number" signed or not (which are the results of dubious operations such as $0 * \infty$).

Normalized numbers come in several versions, according to different choices of K and N, so allowing more or less precision at will. Simple precision (REAL*4, float) has $K = 7$ and $N = 24$, double precision (REAL*8, double) has $K = 10$, $N = 53$, and double extended (REAL*10 etc., long double) has $K \geq 14, N \geq 64$.

Just to give an order of magnitude of the numbers we are talking about, let us show a few examples. For a simple float, the maximum normalized number is $3.40282347 * 10^{38}$, the minimum positive normalized number is $1.17549435 * 10^{-38}$, the maximum denormalized number is $1.17549421 * 10^{-38}$ minimum positive denormalized number is $1.40129846 * 10^{-45}$. Around 1, the maximal error ("unit in the last place", or ulp, or $ulp(1)$) is 2^{-23} for a simple float, i.e. about $1.19200928955 * 10^{-7}$.

The norm also specifies some properties of some of the computations we can make on floating-point numbers. For instance, the norm specifies that $+, -, *, /,$ $\sqrt{\ }$ are computed with an inaccuracy that cannot go beyond the ulp around the exact result (if there is no "overflow").

The norm allows the user to use different round-off methods. One can use round-off towards zero, round-off towards the nearest, round-off towards plus infinity, and round-off towards minus infinity. A more subtle rule is that when we have the choice between two roundings (in the round-off towards the nearest mode), we choose the even mantissa. In fact, the norm even specifies[3] that $x.y$ (where . is one of the floating-point operations $+$, $-$, $*$, $/$, $\sqrt{\ }$ on floating-point numbers x and y) is the rounding (in the corresponding rounding mode) of $x \circ y$ (where $\circ$ is the corresponding operation in $\mathbb{R}$).

The conversions are to be given an explicit semantics as well. More annoying is that we should take care of the order of evaluation (in conflict with compiler optimizations!), since the round-offs destroy associativity in general.

Caveats. As we said in the beginning of this section, the norm specifies what happens in memory but not in processor registers. There are conversions between memory and registers that we have to know about. In general, (except M680x0 and Ix86/Ix87 where all operations are computed in double extended before round-off), registers are like main memory. There can be some differences with RISC processors as well, like the IBM Power PC or Apple Power Macintosh, because of the use of compound instructions (multiply-add etc.) which do not use the same round-off methods. Most of the machines follow the norm anyway but not all the compilers in particular concerning the way they handle (or do not handle!) arithmetic exceptions (underflow etc.). CRAY used to have a different arithmetic, which is a problem for actual applicability of our methods for scientific computing. Hopefully, it seems that it is now converging towards the norm. We have seen cases in which porting a scientific code to a computer with a different arithmetic produces dramatic changes.

---

[3] This is done using extra "guard digits" for computation by the processor of the operations.

Another problem is to know how to deal with the other mathematical operations (like the ones in `<math.h>` in C). In general we have to know the algorithm or its specifications (sometimes given by library providers). The problem of having "good" libraries of transcendantal functions is well-known in the literature, as the "Table makers' dilemna" [LMT98]. In this article we will stick to the core of the norm, and consider only "simple" operations.

2.1   Examples and Properties of Interest

Our aim is to be able to analyze at compile-time the way floating-point operations are used or mis-used.

What we intend to automatically find is at least the exceptions that might be raised (and not caught), like "Overflow", "Underflow" and "NaN". This could be handled with other well-known analyses (interval analysis as used in Syntox [Bou92], polyhedra [CH78] etc.) so we will not describe this part so much. What we really would like to find is some not too pessimistic information about the precision of the values of the variables. This leads to estimates of branching reliability in tests and in expecting to partially solve some difficult termination problems (see Example 1).

Example 1. Consider the expression $x = \frac{c_1 b_2 - c_2 b_1}{a_1 b_2 - a_2 b_1}$ which leads on an UltraSparc in simple precision, for $c_1 = 0$, $c_2 = 1$, $b_1 = -46099201$, $b_2 = -35738642$, $a_1 = 37639840$ and $a_2 = 29180479$, to $x = 1046769994$ (the true result is $x = -46099201$). This is an example of a problem known as "cancellation". The control flow might be wrong after this instruction, if it were followed by the (somewhat unlikely!) instructions:

```
if (x==-46099201) { ... }
else { ... }
```

or non-termination could happen since this could be the termination test of a loop.

Here are some simple (and classic) examples of stable and unstable numerical computations:

Example 2. Consider the following two implementations of the computation of the nth power of the gold number ($g = \frac{\sqrt{5}-1}{2}$). The first one on the left (program (A)) relies on the simple property that if u_n is the nth power of the gold number, $u_{n+2} = u_n - u_{n+1}$. The second one, on the right hand side (program (B)), is the brute force approach.

```
main()
{float x,y,z;
  int i;
  x=1;
  y=(sqrt(5)-1)/2;
  for (i=1;i<=20;i++) {
    z=x;
    x=y;
    y=z-y;
    printf("phi^%d=%f\n",i,x);}}
```

```
main()
{float t;
  int i;
  t=1;
  for (i=1;i<=20;i++) {
    t=t*(sqrt(5)-1)/2;
    printf("phi^%d=%f\n",i,t);}}
```

Program (A) gives the following results:

```
phi^1=0.618034
phi^2=0.381966
phi^3=0.236068
phi^4=0.145898
phi^5=0.090170
phi^6=0.055728
phi^7=0.034442
phi^8=0.021286
phi^9=0.013156
phi^10=0.008130
```

```
phi^11=0.005026
phi^12=0.003103
phi^13=0.001923
phi^14=0.001180
phi^15=0.000743
phi^16=0.000437
phi^17=0.000306
phi^18=0.000131
phi^19=0.000176
phi^20=-0.000045
```

Which of course does not make much sense! The fact is that the numerical scheme used on program (A) is not well-conditioned, meaning that it is very sensitive to the initial inaccuracy. In fact the initial inaccuracy on the computation of $(\sqrt(5)-1)/2$ which is of the order of $ulp(1)$ at most, is increased at each iteration and becomes more important than the real result.

Program (B) leads to the following results,

```
phi^1=0.618034
phi^2=0.381966
phi^3=0.236068
phi^4=0.145898
phi^5=0.090170
phi^6=0.055728
phi^7=0.034442
phi^8=0.021286
phi^9=0.013156
phi^10=0.008131
```

```
phi^11=0.005025
phi^12=0.003106
phi^13=0.001919
phi^14=0.001186
phi^15=0.000733
phi^16=0.000453
phi^17=0.000280
phi^18=0.000173
phi^19=0.000107
phi^20=0.000066
```

Which is in fact completely acceptable. Take now program (C) below which looks like program (A) (at least it does not look simpler):

```
x=1;
y=-1.0/3.0;
for (i=1;i<=20;i++) {
  z=x;
  x=y;
```

```
y=(x+z)/6; }
```

The results that are computed are accurate (they are roundings of $\left(-\frac{1}{3}\right)^n$):

```
phi^1=-0.333333                    phi^11=-0.000006
phi^2=0.111111                     phi^12=0.000002
phi^3=-0.037037                    phi^13=-0.000001
phi^4=0.012346                     phi^14=0.000000
phi^5=-0.004115                    phi^15=-0.000000
phi^6=0.001372                     phi^16=0.000000
phi^7=-0.000457                    phi^17=-0.000000
phi^8=0.000152                     phi^18=0.000000
phi^9=-0.000051                    phi^19=-0.000000
phi^10=0.000017                    phi^20=0.000000
```

This "numerical scheme" is well-conditioned, i.e. stable.

2.2   A Language

In the language we consider in this paper, we confine ourselves to simple floating-point operations (which are fully specified in the IEEE754-1985 norm), with one type of floating-point number only (no double precision nor cast here),

$$
\begin{array}{lll}
\text{Expr} = & \text{cste} & \text{constant real expression} \\
& X & \text{variable } X \in \text{Var} \\
& \text{Expr} + \text{Expr} & \text{sum} \\
& \text{Expr} * \text{Expr} & \text{product} \\
& \text{Expr} - \text{Expr} & \text{difference} \\
& \text{Expr}/\text{Expr} & \text{division} \\
& \sqrt{\text{Expr}} & \text{square root} \\
& (\text{Expr}) & \text{bracketing}
\end{array}
$$

The idea is that the evaluation of arithmetic expressions is determined by the syntax (left to right, innermost to outermost evaluation here). We confine ourselves in this paper to very simple test expressions, as follows,

$$
\begin{array}{lll}
\text{test} = & X == 0 & \text{zero} \\
& X > 0 & \text{strict positivity} \\
& X \geq 0 & \text{positivity}
\end{array}
$$

Instructions are,

$$
\begin{array}{ll}
\text{Instr} = X = \text{Expr} & \text{assignment for } X \in \text{Var} \\
\quad \text{if test then block else block} & \text{conditional statement} \\
\quad \text{while test block} & \text{while loop}
\end{array}
$$

We have used in the examples "equivalent" C forms of a program in that syntax. Blocks of instructions are concatenations of instructions,

$$
\begin{array}{ll}
\text{block} = \emptyset & \text{empty block} \\
\quad \text{Instr; block} & \text{block concatenation}
\end{array}
$$

Finally a program P is just a block.

2.3   A (Almost) Standard Concrete Semantics

We plunge floating-point numbers (parameterized here by N and K, the length of the binary words representing respectively the mantissa and the exponent) into Val which is the union of the (mathematical) real numbers $\mathbb{R}$ extended with values $\{\infty, -\infty, NaN, \omega, \upsilon, \delta, \sigma\}$ which stand respectively for $+\infty$ and $-\infty$ (mathematical infinities, coming from a compactification of the set of reals for instance), NaN, a special element denoting the value "not a number", and ω denoting overflow, υ, underflow, δ, division by zero error and σ is the error resulting from taking the square root of a strictly negative number. The semantics is given as a transition system, where states are elements of $Ctrl \times Env$ where $Env = Var \rightarrow Val$ and $Ctrl$ is the text of the program yet to be executed. The semantics also depends on the round-off mode $\mathcal{M} : Val \rightarrow Val$ (a partial function[4]) and on the use (or not) of some standard handlers in case of overflow, taken care of by a (partial) function $\mathcal{E} : Val \rightarrow Val$. By convention, all our (partial) functions (if not otherwise stated) will not be defined on "errors" ω, υ, δ and σ, nor on NaN and will be the identity on ∞ and $-\infty$. For the sake of simplicity, we will consider only normalized floating-point numbers and will not use signed NaN nor signed zero. We re-define now the following mathematical functions acting on Val,

- We "overload" the exponent function we had at Lemma 1; $k : Val \rightarrow Val$ is the exponent (partial) function with, $k(\infty) = k(-\infty) = \infty$, $k(x) = max(\lfloor log_2(\mid x \mid)\rfloor, 2 - 2^K)$ if $x \in \mathbb{R}$, $x \neq 0$, $k(0) = 0$, $k(x) = \perp$ (i.e. not defined) in all other cases. This enables us to have the right f (as in lemma 1) function and thus the right underflow mechanism.

- $\mathcal{M}(x) = s\left(\frac{\lfloor 2^N f(x)\rfloor}{2^N} + 1\right) 2^{k(x)}$ (this is the rounding towards zero mode, which we write when there is a risk of ambiguity $\mathcal{M}_0$), other modes include:
  $\mathcal{M}(x) = s\left(\frac{s\lceil 2^N sf(x)\rceil}{2^N} + 1\right) 2^{k(x)}$ (rounding towards plus infinity or $\mathcal{M}_+$),
  and $\mathcal{M}(x) = s\left(\frac{s\lfloor 2^N sf(x)\rfloor}{2^N} + 1\right) 2^{k(x)}$ (rounding towards minus infinity or $\mathcal{M}_-$),

- $\mathcal{E}(x) = \omega$ if $\mid x \mid > 2^{2^K+1} - 2^{2^K - N}$, $\mathcal{E}(x) = \upsilon$ if $\mid x \mid < 2^{2-2^K}$ (so that we are not dealing here with "gradual underflow" or denormalized numbers), otherwise $\mathcal{E}(x) = x$ (this is the "no handler" option).

We look at the semantics of an expression Expr. Given $\rho \in Env$,

$$
\begin{aligned}
[\![\text{cste}]\!]^f \rho & = \mathcal{E} \circ \mathcal{M}(\text{cste}) \\
[\![X]\!]^f \rho & = \rho(X) \\
[\![\text{Expr}_1 + \text{Expr}_2]\!]^f \rho & = [\![\text{Expr}_1]\!]^f \rho +^f [\![\text{Expr}_2]\!]^f \rho \\
[\![\text{Expr}_1 * \text{Expr}_2]\!]^f \rho & = [\![\text{Expr}_1]\!]^f \rho *^f [\![\text{Expr}_2]\!]^f \rho \\
[\![\text{Expr}_1 / \text{Expr}_2]\!]^f \rho & = [\![\text{Expr}_1]\!]^f \rho /^f [\![\text{Expr}_2]\!]^f \rho \\
[\![\text{Expr}_1 - \text{Expr}_2]\!]^f \rho & = [\![\text{Expr}_1]\!]^f \rho -^f [\![\text{Expr}_2]\!]^f \rho \\
[\![\sqrt{\text{Expr}}]\!]^f \rho & = \sqrt{[\![\text{Expr}]\!]^f}^f
\end{aligned}
$$

---

[4] We write in an equivalent manner $\mathcal{M}(x) = \perp$ and $\mathcal{M}(x)$ undefined.

where the functions $+^f$, $*^f$, $/^f$, $-^f$ and $\sqrt{}^f$ are defined as follows,

- $a +^f b = \mathcal{E} \circ \mathcal{M}(a + b)$
- $a *^f b = \mathcal{E} \circ \mathcal{M}(ab)$
- $a -^f b = \mathcal{E} \circ \mathcal{M}(a - b)$ if a and b are not both the same infinity. In the latter case, $a -^f b = NaN$.
- $a/^f b = \mathcal{E} \circ \mathcal{M}(\frac{a}{b})$ if $b \neq 0$. If $b = 0$ then $a/^f b = \delta$.
- $\sqrt{a}^f = \mathcal{E} \circ \mathcal{M}(\sqrt{a})$ if $a \geq 0$ otherwise $\sqrt{a}^f = \sigma$.

Assignments have the following semantics: $[\![X = \texttt{Expr}]\!]^f \rho = \rho[X \leftarrow [\![\texttt{Expr}]\!]^f \rho]$ where $\rho[u \leftarrow v]$ denotes the new environment in which $\rho(u)$ is now equal to v, whereas all other variables are mapped to the values they had by ρ. Tests are also quite straightforward ($[\![\texttt{test}]\!]_f$ is a boolean value indicating whether the test is true or not). Transitions from state $(\texttt{Instr}; Prog, \rho)$ to $(Prog, \rho')$ are now rather easy to write down, given the evaluation of expressions above. We spare the reader the details, given that this is rather standard (in SOS style [Plo81] for instance). In order to be able to write the abstract semantics in an easier manner in the sequel, we suppose that all expressions are decomposed into sequences of single operations (like $+$, $-$ etc. respecting the evaluation strategy). For instance, the assignment x=y*z+2 will be supposed to be decomposed using an auxiliary variable t as t=y*z; x=t+2. This refines the transition system described above by splitting the transition representing the evaluation of a (complex) expression into a sequence of transitions, one for each simple floating-point operation.

Notations. In the sequel, operations $+^f$, $-^f$ etc. (respectively $+$, $-$ etc.) will have to be understood as the floating-point (respectively "real") operations. We will also introduce new operations $+^b$, $-^b$ etc. and $\oplus$, $\ominus$ etc. (next section) and $+^a$, $-^a$ etc., that are "abstractions" of these operations.

3   Abstract Domains

A correct (in the sense of abstract interpretation) domain for abstracting the semantics above is given by intervals of floating-point numbers (in the style of F. Bourdoncle's Syntox integer interval analyzer [Bou90]). Basically the "best" correct abstract operations (forward semantics) are:

- the abstraction of the $+$ operation is $[a, b] \oplus [c, d] = [\mathcal{M}'_-(a +^f c), \mathcal{M}'_+(b +^f d)]$
- for subtraction: $[a, b] \ominus [c, d] = [\mathcal{M}'_-(a -^f d), \mathcal{M}'_+(b -^f c)]$
- for multiplication: $[a, b] \otimes [c, d] = [\mathcal{M}'_-(min(a *^f c, a *^f d, b *^f c, b *^f d)),$
  $\mathcal{M}'_+(max(a *^f c, a *^f d, b *^f c, b *^f d))]$
- for the inverse (here $d \geq c > 0$): $inv^o([c, d]) = [\mathcal{M}'_-(1/^f d), \mathcal{M}'_+(1/^f c)]$
- for the square root: $\sqrt{[c, d]}^o = [\mathcal{M}'_-(\sqrt{c}^f), \mathcal{M}'_+(\sqrt{d}^f)]$ (when $c, d \geq 0$)
- For tests, one should be cautious with the rule for strict positivity: $[\![X > 0]\!]\rho = (\rho(X) \geq 2^{2-2^K})$.

where $\mathcal{M}'$ is the rounding function on the analyzer's internal representation of floating-point numbers, $+^f$, $-^f$ etc. are the floating-point operations on the target architecture where the program which is statically analyzed should be run, and K is the corresponding number of bits used for representing exponents. In general, we can (should?) hope for the analyzer to have a better precision than the target architecture[5], and in that case we can simplify the rules above (forgetting about the $\mathcal{M}'$ in the right-hand side of the definitions). This semantics has been implemented as part of the abstract domains used in the static analyzer TWO (ESPRIT project 28940), but is obviously very unsuitable for having a precise information on floating-point operations. Actually, we used an even less precise semantics in that we supposed we did not know the rounding mode in the analyzed program, so we had to assume the worst case which is, for instance in the case of the abstraction of addition: $[a,b] \oplus [c,d] = [\mathcal{M}_-(a+b), \mathcal{M}_+(c+d)]$ where $\mathcal{M}$ is the rounding function corresponding to the target architecture (or a suitable approximation of).

The experiments (described in [GGP$^+$01]) show that this kind of analysis behaves poorly on floating-point code. The figure of about ten percent of the lines (which use floating-point operations) of a code being signaled as potential run-time errors (over-pessimistic warnings about the possibility of getting to an erroneous state, like overflow, division by zero etc.) is not uncommon. Using this semantics though, we are able to find real "subtle" bugs such as for the program: if (x>0) y=1/x*x, where there might be a division by zero error[6] (for instance when $x = 2^{2-2^K}$). Also this abstract semantics is sufficient to get good estimates of the 20th iteration of program (B) of example 2. It is of order $[\rho_0 - 2^{-23}, \rho_0 + 2^{-23}]^{20}$ i.e. about $[6.61067063328 * 10^{-5}, 6.61072163724 * 10^{-5}]$. Also the numerical bug of the Patriot as explained in the introduction would certainly have been found by such interval analyzers, with correct floating-point semantics.

But interval semantics is always very conservative and pessimistic: it might even incorporate the error of computation of the analyzer itself ($\mathcal{M}'$)! Secondly, it aggregates in the abstract value both the magnitude of the expected result and the inaccuracy error. Also it does not take care of dependencies between the values and especially between the errors. For instance, $x - x$ will always lead in such abstractions to a strictly positive error except if x is a singleton interval (i.e. a constant). What we really need is a relational abstraction at least on inaccuracy values.

3.1   Domain of Affine Forms

The idea here is to trace instructions (or locations in the program) that create round-off errors. We associate with each location and variable the way this control point makes the variable lose precision. This is loosely based on ideas

---

[5] One could actually use multi-precision numbers instead of IEEE 754 double or extended double types for representing intervals in the static analyzer.

[6] This is an example taken from a seminar by Alain Deutsch in 1998.

from affine arithmetic [VACS94] (used in simulation of programs, not in static analysis).

The abstract values (notwithstanding error values) are, $x = a_0 + a_1\epsilon_1 + \cdots + a_n\epsilon_n$, the ϵ_i are variables, intended to represent random values with range $]-ulp(1), ulp(1)[$[7], associated with each location (describing the loss of precision at that point), the a_i being in an abstract domain $\mathcal{A}$ (for example real or floating-point intervals) abstracting $\wp(\mathbb{R} \cup \{\infty, -\infty\})$, through (for instance) a Galois Connection [CC92a] $\wp(\mathbb{R} \cup \{\infty, -\infty\}) \xleftarrow[\gamma]{\alpha} \mathcal{A}$. Basically a_0 should be an abstraction of the intended result if the program was manipulating real numbers, and the a_i ($i \geq 1$) represent abstractions of each small error due to the "ith operation" in the program.

Let us make this more precise by setting first $\mathcal{L}$, the set of all locations in the programs to be analyzed (i.e. all elements in $Ctrl$ in the concrete semantics given in Sect. 2.3) $\mathcal{L} = \{\epsilon_i \mid i \in L\}$ (L is the set of indices used to describe elements of $\mathcal{L}$) that we will identify in the sequel with a subset of $\mathbb{N}$. The affine forms domain, parameterized by $\mathcal{A}$ and $\mathcal{L}$ is the domain $\mathcal{D}$ defined as follows, $\mathcal{D} = \{a_0 + \sum_{i \in L} a_i\epsilon_i \mid a_0, a_i \in \mathcal{A}, i \in L\}$ and the order is defined component-wise, $a_0 + \sum_{i \in L} a_i\epsilon_i \leq a'_0 + \sum_{i \in L} a'_i\epsilon_i$ if $a_0 \leq_{\mathcal{A}} a'_0$ and $a_i \leq_{\mathcal{A}} a'_i$ for all $i \in L$.

Therefore, if $\mathcal{A}$ is a lattice, then $\mathcal{D}$ is a lattice with component-wise operations. Similarly, widenings and narrowings [CC92b] defined in $\mathcal{A}$ can be extended in a component-wise manner to generate widenings and narrowings on $\mathcal{D}$. In general the classical widenings on intervals are not very subtle. We define the following family of widenings as: $[a, b] \nabla_k [c, d] = [e, f]$ with $\begin{cases} e = c - 2^k(a - c) & \text{if } c < a \\ e = a & \text{otherwise} \end{cases}$ and $\begin{cases} f = d + 2^k(d - b) & \text{if } d > b \\ f = a & \text{otherwise} \end{cases}$. This is only a widening if we suppose that the boundaries of our intervals use a finite precision arithmetic (bounded multi-precision for instance).

We can now define a concretization function $\Gamma : \mathcal{D} \to \wp(\mathbb{R} \cup \{\infty, -\infty\})$ by $\Gamma(a_0 + \sum_{i \in L} a_i\epsilon_i) = \gamma(a_0) + \sum_{i \in L} \gamma(a_i)*] - ulp(1), ulp(1)[$.

The problem is that there is no way we can hope for a very strong correctness condition (we will give it in detail in Sect. 3.3) for an analysis based on $\mathcal{D}$ with respect to the concrete semantics given in Sect. 2.3, because we have not specified in the concrete semantics what the "real" result should be. Therefore there is no best choice to what a_0 should be (hence the same problem holds for the a_i, $i \in L$)[8]. We should in fact have designed a non-standard concrete semantics that remembers the inaccuracy of the computations, which we shall see now.

---

[7] Notice that if we assume the default rounding mode, we could actually use a smaller interval i.e. $[-ulp(1)/2, ulp(1)/2]$.

[8] Mathematically, suppose we have a corresponding abstraction $A : \wp(Val) \to \mathcal{D}$ making (A, Γ) into a Galois connection. Suppose for instance that $\mathcal{A}$ is the interval domain, and consider $\Gamma(u_1 = [0, 0] + [1, 1]\epsilon_1) =]-ulp(1), ulp(1)[$ and $\Gamma(u_2 = [0, 0] + [1, 1]\epsilon_2) =]-ulp(1), ulp(1)[$ as well. But $\Gamma(u_1 \cap u_2) = \Gamma([0, 0]) = [0, 0]$ is not equal to $\Gamma(u_1) \cap \Gamma(u_2) =]-ulp(1), ulp(1)[$, so there cannot be a left-adjoint to Γ.

3.2   A Non-standard Semantics

We slightly change the semantics of Sect. 2.3 so that environments are now of the form $\rho : \text{Var} \to (Val \times Val)$ (we will write $\rho = (\underline{\rho}, \overline{\rho})$). So $\rho(X) = (\underline{X}, \overline{X})$ where X is any variable, and the intended meaning is that $\underline{X}$ is the semantics we had in Sect. 2.3 and $\overline{X}$ is the intended "real" computation (i.e. using real numbers and not floating point numbers). For the sake of simplicity, we only carry on the concrete and abstract semantics without dealing with NaN nor run-time errors, hence dropping the $\mathcal{E}$ part of the semantics. For expressions for instance, we find the new concrete operators:

- $a +^b b = (\mathcal{M}(a + b), a + b)$
- $a *^b b = (\mathcal{M}(ab), ab)$
- $a -^b b = (\mathcal{M}(a - b), a - b)$
- $a/^b b = (\mathcal{M}(\frac{a}{b}), \frac{a}{b})$ if $b \neq 0$.

The rest of the semantics is pretty much the same, "executing in parallel" the program with floating-point operations, and the program with operations in $\mathbb{R}$, but without observing precisely the steps in the "real" computation. For instance, we have a transition from $(x = \text{Expr}; Prgm, (\underline{\rho}, \overline{\rho}))$ to $(Prgm, ([x = \text{Expr}]^f \underline{\rho}, [x = \text{Expr}]\overline{\rho}))$ where $[.]^f$ is the "floating-point" semantics given in Sect. 2.3, and $[.]$ is a similar semantics, but with operations and numbers in $\mathbb{R}$ (the "ideal semantics"). The more difficult part of the semantics is tests (also while loops of course since they include tests). The problem is that a test in the floating-point semantics might well not give the same result as the test in the real number semantics (as in example 1), leading to a different flow of execution in the two semantics. We choose in that case to stop computing the real number semantics: for instance there is a transition from $(if \ (x < 0) \ x = x + 1 \ else \ x = x - 1, (x \leftarrow -10^{-37}, x \leftarrow 0))$ to $(x = x + 1, (x \leftarrow -10^{-37}, \perp))$ and then to $(\emptyset, (x \leftarrow 1, \perp))^9$. This actually corresponds to a synchronized product [Arn92] (with synchronization between two transitions being only allowed when the two have the same labels) of the transition system corresponding to the floating-point semantics with another, corresponding to an "observer", which is the real number semantics.

From this semantics, we can construct an even more detailed semantics which will be our final non-standard semantics, and which goes (briefly) as follows. We define inductively the notion of "inaccuracy" coming from a location (i.e. a transition) that we identify with a "formal" variable ϵ_i. Consider a trace s of execution from an initial environment $(\underline{\rho}, \overline{\rho})$. Suppose this trace goes through locations ϵ_1 to ϵ_{j-1} and that variables x and y are computed on this trace; we suppose we can write formally (this is the induction step of the definition) $x = x_0 + \sum_{i=1}^{j-1} x_i \epsilon_i$ and $y = y_0 + \sum_{i=1}^{j-1} y_i \epsilon_i$ where ϵ_i is a formal variable of magnitude $\epsilon = ulp(1)$. x_0 (respectively y_0) is the value computed with the semantics of real numbers on s from $\overline{\rho}$. x_i is the magnitude (divided by ϵ) of the error of the computed result in the semantics of floating-point numbers starting at $\underline{\rho}$, due

---

[9] We say in that case that this test is "unstable".

to the rounding operation at instruction ϵ_i. Then suppose we extend the trace s with operation $z = x.y$. This derived semantics computes $z = z_0 + \sum_{i=1}^{j} z_i \epsilon_i$ with z_i being a function of the x_k and y_l ($1 \leq k \leq j-1$ and $1 \leq l \leq j-1$). This semantics is fully described in the forthcoming article [Mar01]. Now we are going to abstract the coefficients z_i.

3.3 Abstract Semantics

We particularize $\mathcal{D}$ with $\mathcal{A}$ being the interval lattice (but this is easy to generalize on any non-relational abstract domain) and $\mathcal{L}$ being the set of locations (identified again with a subset of $\mathbb{N}$). We will only deal here with a forward abstract semantics that we call $[\![.]\!]^a$. Of course, having a backward abstract semantics would enable us to gain more precision during analysis, using iterates of forward and backward iterates [CC92a], but this is outside the scope of the paper.

The semantics of expressions is defined using operations $+^a$, $-^a$, $*^a$, inv^a, $\sqrt{}^a$ as follows: let $x = [a_0, b_0] + \sum_{i=1}^{n} [a_i, b_i] \epsilon_i$, $y = [c_0, d_0] + \sum_{i=1}^{n} [c_i, d_i] \epsilon_i$ be two affine forms. We are trying to find a good abstraction for an operation . on x and y at location j, giving[10] the result $z = z_0 + \sum_{i=1}^{n} z_i \epsilon_i$. The abstract semantic functions are (using $\oplus$, $\otimes$ etc. of Sect. 3, where we assume $\mathcal{M}' = \mathcal{M}$):

$$x +^a y \stackrel{def}{=} ([a_0, b_0] \oplus [c_0, d_0]) + \sum_{i=1}^{j-1} ([a_i, b_i] \oplus [c_i, d_i]) \, \epsilon_i + (\alpha \circ \Gamma(x) \oplus \alpha \circ \Gamma(y)) \epsilon_j$$

This merely translates the fact that the "real value" of the sum should be in the sum of the (floating-point) intervals containing the real values of x and y. The errors from ϵ_i must be over-approximated by the sum of the errors for computing x and y at ϵ_i. The last term (factor of ϵ_j) is due to the rounding of the "real" sum operation at ϵ_j. Because of the IEEE-754 standard, its magnitude is at most $ulp(z)$ where z is the floating-point sum of x and y. It is easy to see that it is less or equal than $(\alpha \circ \Gamma(x) \oplus \alpha \circ \Gamma(y)) \epsilon_j$. The other rules are:

$$x -^a y \stackrel{def}{=} ([a_0, b_0] \ominus [c_0, d_0]) + \sum_{i=1}^{j-1} ([a_i, b_i] \ominus [c_i, d_i]) \, \epsilon_i + (\alpha \circ \Gamma(x) \ominus \alpha \circ \Gamma(y)) \epsilon_j$$

$$x \times^a y \stackrel{def}{=} [a_0, b_0] \otimes [c_0, d_0] + \sum_{i=1}^{j-1} (([a_i, b_i] \otimes \alpha \circ \Gamma(y)) \oplus (\alpha \circ \Gamma(x) \otimes [c_i, d_i])) \, \epsilon_i$$
$$+ (\alpha \circ \Gamma(x) \otimes \alpha \circ \Gamma(y)) \epsilon_j$$

$$inv(x)^a \stackrel{def}{=} inv^o([a_0, b_0]) - inv^o(\alpha \circ \Gamma(x) \otimes \alpha \circ \Gamma(x)) \otimes \sum_{i=1}^{j-1} [a_i, b_i] \epsilon_i$$
$$+ inv^o(\alpha \circ \Gamma(x)) \epsilon_j$$

---

[10] Note that we have used a suitable relabelling of control points, identifying them with an interval of integers.

$$\sqrt{x}^a \stackrel{def}{=} \sqrt{[a_0, b_0]}^o + inv^o([2,2] \otimes \sqrt{\alpha \circ \Gamma(x)}^o) \otimes \sum_{i=1}^{j-1} [a_i, b_i] \epsilon_i + \sqrt{\alpha \circ \Gamma(x)}^o \epsilon_j$$

The correctness of this semantics with respect to the semantics of Sect. 2.3 is expressed as follows; let x and y be two affine forms, and let $.^f$ (respectively h^f) be any of the operations $+^f$, $-^f$, $*^f$, (respectively inv^f, $\sqrt{}^f$) then $\Gamma(x).^f\Gamma(y) \subseteq \Gamma(x.^a y)$ (respectively $\Gamma(h^f(x)) \subseteq h^a(\Gamma(x)))$.

Addition and subtraction rules are easy, even if they are too approximate in fact because we always say that the operation might create an inaccuracy of up to one ulp around the result (which is at most, by the IEEE 754 norm of $ulp(| x.y |) \leq | x.y | ulp(1))$.

Let us show for instance the correctness of $\times^a$. Take $U = U_0 + \sum_{i=1}^{j-1} U_i \epsilon_i$ and $V = V_0 + \sum_{i=1}^{j-1} V_i \epsilon_i$ two affine forms, with $U_i = [a_i, b_i]$ and $V_i = [c_i, d_i]$. Let $u \in \Gamma(U)$ and $v \in \Gamma(V)$. We write $u = u_0 + \sum_{i=1}^{j-1} u_i \epsilon$ (where $\epsilon = ulp(1)$) and $v = v_0 + \sum_{i=1}^{j-1} v_i \epsilon$ where $u_i \in \gamma(U_i)$ and $v_i \in \gamma(V_i)$. We consider $u \times^f v = \mathcal{M}(uv)$. We have $uv = u_0 v_0 + \sum_{i=1}^{j-1} uv_i \epsilon + \sum_{i=1}^{j-1} vu_i \epsilon$, so,

$$\mathcal{M}(u \times v) \leq uv + | uv | \epsilon$$
$$\leq u_0 v_0 + \sum_{i=1}^{j-1}(uv_i + vu_i)\epsilon + | uv | \epsilon$$
$$\leq max([a_0, b_0] \otimes [c_0, d_0]) +$$
$$\sum_{i=1}^{j-1}(max(\Gamma(U) \otimes [c_i, d_i] + [a_i, b_i] \otimes \Gamma(V)))\epsilon$$
$$+ max(| \Gamma(U)\Gamma(V) |)\epsilon$$

Which shows one part of the inclusion. The rest is left to the reader.

For the formula for inv, the abstraction is correct since $x \to \frac{1}{x}$ is concave on its domain of definition, so it can be safely approximated on an interval $[a, b]$ by (for $x \in [a, b]$, $x + \delta \in [a, b]$):

$$\frac{1}{x} - \frac{1}{a^2}\delta \leq \frac{1}{x + \delta} \leq \begin{cases} \frac{1}{a} - \frac{1}{qb}\delta & \text{if } ab > 0 \\ \frac{1}{b} - \frac{1}{ab}\delta & \text{if } ab < 0 \end{cases}$$

Same proof with square root, but this time the function is convex so we approximate it on $[a, b]$ by:

$$\sqrt{a} + \frac{1}{\sqrt{a} + \sqrt{b}}\delta \leq \sqrt{x + \delta} \leq \sqrt{x} + \frac{1}{2\sqrt{x}}\delta$$

Of course, there are other ways to give lower and upper bounds to these computations. The choice we have taken is that the individual coefficients of the ϵ_i should reflect the magnitude of the error coming from the computation at ϵ_i in the total error on a trace of computation. Of course this depends on the "formal derivatives" that appear in these formulae.

The correctness of this semantics with respect to the semantics of Sect. 3.2 is as follows (more details in the forthcoming article [Mar01]). On the set of paths that $Prgm$ can execute from a set of initial environments, x (respectively y) has real value in $[a_0, b_0]$ (respectively $[c_0, d_0]$) and errors coming from location

ϵ_i $(i \in \{1, \cdots, j-1\})$ are in $[a_i, b_i]$ (respectively $[c_i, d_i]$), then on the set of paths that $Prgm; z = x.y$ can execute from the same environment, z has real value in z_0, and the error coming from location ϵ_i is in z_i plus the error in the computation of the operation . itself (represented by ϵ_j). The effect of adding the operation $z = x.y$ on the magnitude of the error coming from location ϵ_i $(i < j)$ is reflected by the derivative of the operation in question.

We have not spoken of the abstract semantics of constants and tests. Constants are easy to abstract, the IEEE754-1985 rules dealing with constants are very precise and we can determine for sure whether we lose precision or not. Tests are more complex. We use local decreasing iterations as in [Gra92]. For instance suppose we want to interpret $x == y$. The corresponding abstract operator $==^a$ will be the greatest fixed point of the functional F on affine forms, which to every pair of affine forms $(x = x_0 + \sum_i x_i\epsilon_i, y = y_0 + \sum_i y_i\epsilon_i)$ associates $(x' = x'_0 + \sum_i x'_i\epsilon_i, y' = y'_0 + \sum_i y'_i\epsilon_i)$ with (each component of the functional is in $\mathcal{A}$, i.e. here the lattice of intervals)

$$\begin{cases} x'_0 = x_0 \cap (\Gamma(y -^a \sum_i x_i\epsilon_i)) \\ x'_i = x_i \\ y'_0 = y_0 \cap (\Gamma(x -^a \sum_i y_i\epsilon_i)) \\ y'_i = y_i \end{cases}$$

This is not the best abstraction (on the coefficients of ϵ_i) but it is enough to show that some tests might be unstable (when the order of magnitude of the x_i or y_i is not negligible with respect to x_0 and y_0 respectively).

4   An Example

Let us decorate now the different floating-point operations for program (A):

```
x=1;
y=(sqrt(5)!1! -1 !2!)/2 !3!; !4!

for(i=1;i<20;i++){
  z=x;
  x=y;
  y=z-y; !5!
}
```

The semantics using affine forms[11] goes as follows; first for the locations before the loop:

$$!1! : \sqrt{5} = [2.236068, 2.236069] + [2.236068, 2.236069]\epsilon_1$$
$$!2! : \sqrt{5} - 1 = [1.236068, 1.236069] + [2.236068, 2.236069]\epsilon_1 +$$
$$[1.2360676, 1.2360684]\epsilon_2$$

---

[11] This comes from a library programmed in C by Nicolas Regal in 1999 [Reg99].

$$!3! : \frac{1}{2} = [0.5, 0.5] + [0.5, 0.5]\epsilon_3$$

$$!4! : \frac{\sqrt{5} - 1}{2} = [0.618033936, 0.618034058] + [1.118033936, 1.118034058]\epsilon_1$$
$$+ [0.6180338176, 0.6180342272]\epsilon_2 + [0.6180340736, 0.6180342784]\epsilon_3$$
$$+ [0.6180340736, 0.6180342784]\epsilon_4$$
$$= y$$

(Notice that $\frac{1}{2}$ is blindly over-approximated. This could be done exactly in a more refined semantics). We can then look at the abstract values on the first unfolding of the loop. For instance, in the first loop we find the abstract value for y to be:

$$[0.381966004, 0.381966126] + [-1.118033935, -1.118033813]\epsilon_1 +$$

$$[-0.6180341760, -0.6180337664]\epsilon_2 + [-0.6180342272, -0.6180340224]\epsilon_3 +$$

$$[-0.6180342272, -0.6180340224]\epsilon_4 + [0.3819656448, 0.3819658240]\epsilon_5$$

(concretization is [0.38196568,0.38196583]). Then,

$$[0.236067780, 0.236068024] + [2.236067872, 2.236068116]\epsilon_1 +$$

$$[1.2360676352, 1.2360684544]\epsilon_2 + [1.2360681472, 1.2360685568]\epsilon_3 +$$

$$[1.2360681472, 1.2360685568]\epsilon_4 + [-0.1458974464, -0.1458969344]\epsilon_5$$

(concretization is [0.23606846,0.23606873]) Then,

$$[0.145897995, 0.145898346] + [-3.354102050, -3.354101562]\epsilon_1 +$$

$$[-1.854102528, -1.8541012992]\epsilon_2 + [-1.854102528, -1.8541021184]\epsilon_3 +$$

$$[-1.854102528, -1.8541021184]\epsilon_4 + [0.2917938944, 0.2917948160]\epsilon_5$$

(concretization is [0.14589696,0.14589734]) Then,

$$[0.090169434, 0.090170029] + [5.590169434, 5.590170411]\epsilon_1 +$$

$$[3.090168832, 3.0901712896]\epsilon_2 + [3.0901702656, 3.0901714944]\epsilon_3 +$$

$$[3.0901702656, 3.0901714944]\epsilon_4 + [-0.2016236672, -0.2016221184]\epsilon_5$$

(concretization is [0.09017118,0.09017179]) Then again (the fifth time we go around the loop):

$$[0.055727959, 0.055728913] + [-8.944272460, -8.944270507]\epsilon_1 +$$

$$[-4.9442738176, -4.9442693120]\epsilon_2 + [-4.9442742272, -4.9442717696]\epsilon_3 +$$

$$[-4.9442742272, -4.9442717696]\epsilon_4 + [0.2573515008, 0.2573540352]\epsilon_5$$

(concretization is [0.05572883,0.05573179]). We see that the coefficients of the ϵ_i up to $i = 4$ get bigger and bigger as the expected value gets smaller and smaller. The subtraction in control point 5 does not lose much precision as such. This means the loop magnifies the initial error of computation of y at each turn. This is an example of bad-conditioning. For the well-conditioned example computing $(-1/3)^n$, the computation with affine forms would show there is no problem.

Of course, in general we cannot unfold loops like that in a static analyzer. After some number of unfoldings, we use our widening operator, which would predict a huge potential loss of precision. We need better widening operators in general.

5   Improvements

5.1   Affine Interval Transformations

The idea is to consider that the semantics creates dependencies between the a_i coefficients (due to an inaccuracy at location i) that we can approximate by linear dependencies. This choice is motivated by the fact that a great deal of numerical codes compute affine operations (also quadratic sometimes in finite elements methods). It is also motivated by the fact that we know in general how to linearize errors, and we know how to manipulate affine constraints (which are used for instance in [Kar76] in static analysis).

We call T an affine transformation on the space generated by $\{\epsilon_1, \cdots, \epsilon_n\}$ if there exists a $n \times n$ matrix A, and an n-dimensional vector B such that for all vectors X, $T(X) = AX + B$. We can represent such a transformation by the pair (A, B). We abstract a set of affine transformations by abstracting its sets of coefficients in A and B by an element of $\mathcal{A}$. In fact the semantics of Sect. 3.2 gives a set of such transformations each over-approximating the effect of each trace.

For instance, setting $\mathcal{A}$ to be the interval domain,

$$\alpha\left(\left\{\left(\begin{pmatrix} 1 & 2 \\ 0 & 1 \end{pmatrix}, \begin{pmatrix} 3 \\ 4 \end{pmatrix}\right), \left(\begin{pmatrix} 1 & 3 \\ 0 & 2 \end{pmatrix}, \begin{pmatrix} 3 \\ 5 \end{pmatrix}\right)\right\}\right) = \left(\begin{pmatrix} [1,1] & [2,3] \\ [0,0] & [1,2] \end{pmatrix}, \begin{pmatrix} [3,3] \\ [4,5] \end{pmatrix}\right)$$

The abstract domain of affine error dependence $\mathcal{T}$ is therefore isomorphic to $\mathcal{A}^{(nm)^2+nm}$ (n is the number of control points, m is the number of variables) with component-wise ordering. This means that as for affine intervals, if $\mathcal{A}$ is a lattice, then $\mathcal{T}$ is a lattice with intersection and union computed pointwise etc.

The concretization function G goes from $\mathcal{T}$ to the set of all (concrete) affine transformations. $G(A') = (a'_{i,j})_{1 \leq i,j \leq nm}, B' = (b'_j)_{1 \leq j \leq nm}$ is the set of affine transformations $(A = (a_{i,j})_{1 \leq i,j \leq nm}, B = (b_j)_{1 \leq j \leq nm})$ with $a_{i,j} \in \gamma_A(a'_{i,j})$ (for all $1 \leq i, j \leq nm$) and $b_j \in \gamma_A(b'_j)$ (for all $1 \leq j \leq nm$).

What is important to see now is that these abstract affine transformations act on elements of $\mathcal{D}$, because we can use the semantics of the operations $+, *$ in $\mathcal{A}$ to compute a safe approximation of $\{AX + B/(A, B) \subseteq G(A', B'), X \in G(X')\}$.

For instance, the instruction $x + y = z$ at instruction j will be written in matrix form as (we only represent a sub-block of the complete matrix here):

$$
\begin{array}{c}
 \\
\epsilon_0(x) \\
... \\
... \\
\epsilon_n(x) \\
\epsilon_0(y) \\
... \\
... \\
\epsilon_n(y) \\
\epsilon_0(z) \\
... \\
... \\
\epsilon_n(z) \\
\epsilon_j(z)
\end{array}
\begin{array}{c}
\begin{array}{ccccccccc}
\epsilon_0(x) & & ... & ... & \epsilon_n(x) & \epsilon_0(y) & ... & ... & \epsilon_n(y) & & \epsilon_j
\end{array} \\
\left(
\begin{array}{ccccccccc}
1 & & & & & & & & \\
 & 1 & & & & & & & \\
 & & 1 & & & & & & \\
 & & & 1 & & & & & \\
 & & & & 1 & & & & \\
 & & & & & 1 & & & \\
 & & & & & & 1 & & \\
 & & & & & & & 1 & \\
1 & & & & 1 & & & & \\
 & 1 & & & & 1 & & & \\
 & & 1 & & & & 1 & & \\
 & & & 1 & & & & 1 & \\
 & & & & & & & & \gamma \circ \Gamma(x) \oplus \gamma \circ \Gamma(y)
\end{array}
\right)
\end{array}
$$

We do not write the other rules since they are the transcription of what we have seen for affine interval forms, on affine interval matrices.

5.2   Principle of the Improvement

Let $\mathcal{X}$ be the product of the domain $Var \to \mathcal{D}$ (each variable is associated with an affine interval) with $\mathcal{T}$. An abstract value in $\mathcal{X}$ is a pair $(f = \lambda x.a_0(x) + \sum_{i \in L} a_i(x)\epsilon_i, (A, B))$ which describes an abstract state at some location ϵ_j for which the value of variable x is in $\gamma(a_0(x))$ plus inaccuracy errors of order $\gamma(a_i(x))$ coming from control point i, together with the abstract affine transformation approximating the way these inaccuracy errors have been transformed by the instructions just before location ϵ_j. This extra information added to f would not be necessary if the control flow of the program we are analyzing was acyclic. It is only when we need infinite least fixed point iterations that we can benefit from the approximation of the transformation of errors that take place at certain control points (given by (A, B)) to widen the iterations. So in practice, the abstract affine transformations will be managed at some suitable widening points as defined for instance in [Bou90,Bou93] (heads of loops, return sites in case of inter-procedural analysis of mutually recursive functions).

We use this extra-information for getting better widening operators. In fact we approximate the abstract affine transformation by a transformation that multiplies by an upper approximation of the spectral radius of the transformation (A, B). We can then look at the asymptotic value: $lim_{n \to \infty} A^n X_0 + \frac{A^{n+1} - Id}{A - Id} B$.

Unfortunately, most of the 'interesting properties" that we might want to compute on $G(A', B')$ are NP-complete. Among these interesting properties are, the property of having all the transformations invertible, or the determination of the spectrum of all the transformations ("spectral portrait"). So we need to approximate further, so that we can compute in an efficient manner a good upper approximation of the spectral radius of (A, B).

"Any" norm on matrices can be used to determine an approximation of the spectral radius. If $A = (a_{i,j})_{1 \leq i,j \leq n}$, $\|A\|_1 = \sum_{i,j} |a_{i,j}|$, $\|A\|_2 = \sqrt{\sum_{i,j} |a_{i,j}|^2}$, $\cdots$, $\|A\|_\infty = \max\{|a_{i,j}|\}$ can all be used because, the maximal norm of its eigenvalues is $\lambda_{max} \leq \|A\|$ ($n\|A\|$ in the last case). This is not a very precise though.

There are in fact better algorithms to calculate this spectral radius. A very famous method (iterative power) is as follows. Let $A = (a_{i,j})_{1 \leq i,j \leq n}$ be a matrix, u any non-null vector, and $(q_k)_{k \geq 0}$ the sequence, $q_0 = \frac{u}{\|u\|_2}$, $\cdots$ $q_k = \frac{Aq_{k-1}}{\|Aq_{k-1}\|_2}$, $\cdots$ q_k converges (when $k \to +\infty$) towards the greatest norm of the eigenvalues of A. Unfortunately this is not of much use in an abstract calculus since we do not know if any of the iterates are upper-approximations of the spectral radius. We have only a weaker result, about the convergence of the (q_k) sequence.

There is a nicer approximation which only uses "lattice-theoretic" notions. It is called the "Gerschgorin discs":

Lemma 2. *Let $A = (a_{i,j})_{1 \leq i,j \leq n}$ be a matrix. The spectrum of A is contained in $D_1 \cap D_2$ (in the complex plane) with,*

- $D_1 = \cup_{1 \leq i \leq n} D_{1,i}$,
- $D_2 = \cup_{1 \leq j \leq n} D_{2,j}$,
- $D_{1,i}$ *is the circle with center $a_{i,i}$, radius $r_{1,i} = \sum_{1 \leq j \leq n, j \neq i} |a_{i,j}|$,*
- $D_{2,j}$ *is the circle with center $a_{j,j}$, radius $r_{2,j} = \sum_{1 \leq i \leq n, i \neq j} |a_{i,j}|$.*

A good approximation of the biggest absolute value of the eigenvalues of *real* A is thus,

$$G(A) = \max\{|a_{i,i}| + \max\{r_{1,i}, r_{2,i}\}/1 \leq i \leq n\}$$

Consider again the example 2 and in particular program (A). The analysis using affine transformations basically discovers something that numericians are used to. At each loop the errors on x, y et z are given by the affine transformation (we give here only a sub-block of the complete matrix),

$$\begin{pmatrix} \delta'_x \\ \delta'_y \\ \delta'_z \end{pmatrix} = \begin{pmatrix} 0 & 1 & 0 \\ 1 & -1 & 0 \\ 1 & 0 & 0 \end{pmatrix} \begin{pmatrix} \delta_x \\ \delta_y \\ \delta_z \end{pmatrix} + \begin{pmatrix} 0 \\ \alpha \\ 0 \end{pmatrix}$$

with at the first iteration of the loop $\delta_y = \epsilon = 2^{-23}$, and α is the error due to the rounding of operation $-$ in the loop.

$$A = \begin{pmatrix} 0 & 1 & 0 \\ 1 & -1 & 0 \\ 1 & 0 & 0 \end{pmatrix}$$

We find $G(A) = 2$ (instead of $1.6180 \cdots$). Then we have to notice that $\alpha \leq 2^{-24}$. In fact the affine transformation has two non-null eigenvalues $\rho_1 =$

$\frac{-1+\sqrt{5}}{2}$ and $\rho_0 = \frac{-1-\sqrt{5}}{2} < -1$. Therefore the error at the 20th iteration of order $\frac{\epsilon}{\rho_1-\rho_0}\rho_1^{20} + \frac{|\rho_1^{21}|-1}{\rho_1-1}\alpha$ (about $4 * 10^{-4} + 2.4 * 10^{-3}$) bigger than ρ_0^{20} (about $6.6 * 10^{-5}$).

Of course to do this we need a reduced product with at least an interval analysis on the integer variables (to determine the right number of loops). This will not be described here.

Note that program (C) has $G(A) = 1$ (instead of $1/2$ which is the exact greatest eigenvalue), hence the inaccuracy does not increase at each iteration of the loop.

6   Related Work

To our knowledge, there are two main types of tools that are used to help the programmer compute with floating-point operations (see [BMMM95,CCF96,DM97] for general references).

The first type of tool uses alternative arithmetic implementations to better match the "ideal" semantics of reals. For instance, interval arithmetic [GL70], [Moo79] implements a real number as an interval of floating-point numbers containing it. Multi-precision arithmetic [KJ93,Sco89] uses variable length floating-point numbers to approximate at best real number computations. Rational arithmetic [Bak75,Cle74,HCL+68,Kla93,KM83,KM88,Sch83] implements exact arithmetic for rational numbers, which can be used to approximate real numbers, for instance using continued fractions [KM85,RT73,Sei83,Vui90]. These methods do not solve the problem in all cases; interval arithmetic might lead to very imprecise (but true) results[12], multi-precision arithmetic and rational arithmetic may be very costly to perform on real scientific codes[13].

A new and promising line of research uses domain theory and fractal encoding of exact real numbers [ES98,EP97,Eda97,PEE97,PE98]. We do not know yet how we can use these ideas for static analysis purposes.

Another approach is at the heart of the CADNA software [Che95]. It is known as the perturbation method (CESTAC) or stochastic arithmetic [CV88,CV92], [Vig96]. The idea is that round-off errors can be modeled as quasi-Gaussian distributions of some sort, and that a simple statistic test (Student test) can estimate its parameters, thus enabling to give better approximations of real number computations. This method and tool is probably one of the most favored among the code programmers, since it is quite precise. But it has lead to some criticisms, see [Kah91] for example. We review some of its central ideas more

---

[12] See Sect. 3 for examples of that phenomenon.

[13] And they do not solve the problem in general, see [CC94] where the following classical dynamical system example by J. M. Muller $U_{n+1} = 111 - \frac{1130}{U_n} + \frac{3000}{U_n U_{n-1}}$ with $U_0 = 2$ and $U_1 = -4$ leads, with floating-point numbers of finite precision up to a hundred decimal digits, to 100 whereas the exact value for the limit is 6. Limits of some other dynamical systems [Bea91] can only be computed by exact real numbers, i.e. infinite precision arithmetic!

in detail in Sect. 6.2. A similar approach (still stochastic but in a "backwards" manner) has been implemented and tested under the name "Precise" [CCT00]. We thought of using similar probabilistic ideas as a basis of a static analysis but at the moment there seems to be no way to ensure (even probabilistically) the correctness of the approach. Very important work is being carried out on the foundations of probabilistic abstract interpretation [Mon00,Mon01] which we might use for this purpose later on.

In some applications (image synthesis etc.), some algorithmic geometry has been specifically designed, like for CGAL, [BCD+99] in order to use in a very controlled manner the IEEE 754 floating-point numbers for some computations. We do not know yet how to use this for our purposes.

On the more mathematical side, let us mention the work done in automatic differentiation (which could lead to interesting connections with our work) [Gri00] and some specific studies of the precision of some numerical schemes, for which we direct the reader to the general reference [Hig96] and also to the article [LN97].

We know of only one example of a static analyzer (such as we are discussing in this article), that not only tries to give more precise results on one execution, or give some hint about the precision on one execution, but rather assesses a property valid for all (or a large class of) executions. This analyzer [ACFG92] actually uses abstract interpretation. We will explain the abstraction chosen more in detail in next section.

6.1   Another Abstract Interpretation

The abstract interpreter [ACFG92] is based on the following underlying concrete model. Floating-point numbers are identified with a pair $f = \langle m, e \rangle$ with, a mantissa $m \in M = \{m \in Z / p \in \mathbb{N}, -(10^p - 1) \leq m \leq 10^p - 1\}$, and an exponent $e \in E = \{e \in Z / q \in \mathbb{N}, -q \leq e \leq q\}$.

Abstract values are $f = \langle s, p, em, eM \rangle$ where, $s = +, -, +/-, \bot$ is an abstract sign, p is an integer representing the "number of significant digits" and $[em, eM]$ is the "interval of exponents". For instance $< +, 4, 6, 12 >$ denotes in the concrete model,

$$F' = \{0.1000 * 10^6, 0.1001 * 10^6, \cdots, 0.9999 * 10^{12}\}$$

It is proved to form a complete lattice with a Galois connection with the set of subsets of the concrete model. Abstract operations like *Add*, *Sub*, *Mul*, *Div* are defined. Unfortunately, no interpretation of tests nor of loops is made, thus greatly restricting the precision of the analysis. The analysis is sometimes even weaker than an interval analysis of floating-point numbers, thus much weaker than our analysis.

6.2   CADNA

CADNA implements the CESTAC method [CV88,CV92,PV74,VA85,Vig78], [Vig87,Vig93]. The underlying model is that the round-off errors are of the form $2^{-p}.\alpha_i$ where the α_i are equi-distributed independent random variables on $]-1, 1[$ with uniform law. This law is justified both experimentally and by some theoretical reasons [Knu73]. The perturbation methods goes as follows. At each floating-point operation, we perturbate the round-off towards $+\infty$ or $-\infty$ with the same probability. We execute N times each of the instructions of the program (in practice, $N = 2$ or 3). The mean value "converges" towards the exact mathematical result and the Student test computes a good approximation of the standard deviation of the quasi-Gaussian distribution law of the result.

Thus this method can be used both for improving the computations, and for testing the relevance of a given execution. It is very much used in practice but some bugs are known: its estimates are sometimes too optimistic.There are several reasons for which this may happen [Kah91]. The approximation by a Gaussian law is justified by the central limit theorem but the convergence is very slow on the tail of the distribution (in particular with $N = 2$ or 3). The approximation is very bad on unprobable events (precisely the ones which lead to very costly errors). In order to justify the use of the theorem, we also have to suppose that the round-off errors are random, not correlated, continuously distributed on a small interval. But in general, the errors are only due to a few round-off errors and to singularities (which we might find out by data perturbation but probably not by perturbation of the operations). So errors are not uncorrelated random variables. Also, the distribution of errors is a discrete distribution on floating-point numbers and not on continuous real number. Finally, this is only a "first order approximation": for multiplication and division, second-order terms are not considered, but it might occur that they are not negligible.

7   Conclusion and Future Work

We have presented some ideas about what static analysis can try to do for programs computing with floating-point numbers. Our first concern in the DAEDALUS project is to analyze control-command software (like the Patriot software seen in the introduction) which is not numerically intensive, and for which we think we should have good chances of finding nice solutions. Numeric-intensive software, like scientific codes, are much more complex. Some of them, such as well-conditioned problems, might be amenable to static analysis. More difficult is to consider what can happen for ill-conditioned problems (for example, inverse a matrix with very small determinant). We believe that there is little hope an automatic tool can cope with such problems, but we would like to be shown to be wrong .

In fact, most scientific codes pose new problems to static analyzers. For instance, some codes rely on Monte Carlo methods, or more generally on randomized algorithms. We believe that the static analysis of such algorithms is an interesting prospect, but goes beyond the scope of this paper (see [Mon00,Mon01] for some ideas which could constitute a good basis for future work). What might have to be considered on these codes is that the random generators that are used are only pseudo-random generators. This complexifies again the semantic problem. Also some scientific codes use parallel algorithms which make things even more complex, especially regarding the evaluation order of floating-point operations; they will depend on actual synchronizations between tasks. Our future work will not try to tackle these very subtle problems. The first extension we wish to make is to look at inverse problems i.e. at clever backwards semantics. The aim is to solve the following problem: what precision should we have on the input so that we reach a given precision level on the output. The last point is particularly important in the field of on-board software since the wrong estimate of the precision for the input of a control/command program can be very expensive (for instance, the cost of very precise sensors).

Acknowledgements. Thanks are due to M. Martel, S. Putot and N. Williams for careful proof-reading of this article.

References

[ACFG92] Y. Ameur, P. Cros, J-J. Falcon, and A. Gomez. An application of abstract interpretation to floating-point arithmetic. In *Proceedings of the Workshop on Static Analysis*, 1992.

[Arn92]   A. Arnold. *Systèmes de transitions finis et sémantique des processus communicants*. Masson, 1992.

[Bak75]   G. A. Baker. *Essentials of Padé approximants*. Academic Press, New York, 1975.

[BCD+99] J.-D. Boissonat, F. Cazals, F. Da, O. Devillers, S. Pion, F. Rebufat, M. Teillaud, and M. Yvinec. Programming with CGAL: The example of triangulations. In *Proceedings of the Conference on Computational Geometry (SCG '99)*, pages 421–422, New York, N.Y., June 13–16 1999. ACM Press.

[Bea91]   A. F. Beardon. *Iteration of Rational Functions*. Graduate Texts in Mathematics. Springer-Verlag, 1991.

[BMMM95] J. C. Bajard, D. Michelucci, J. M. Moreau, and J. M. Muller, editors. *Real Numbers and Computers — Les Nombres réels et l'Ordinateur*, 1995.

[Bou90]   F. Bourdoncle. Interprocedural abstract interpretation of block structured languages with nested procedures, aliasing and recursivity. In *PLILP'90*, volume 456 of *LNCS*, pages 307–323. Springer-Verlag, 1990.

[Bou92]   F. Bourdoncle. Abstract interpretation by dynamic partitioning. *Journal of Functional Programming*, 2(4):407–435, 1992.

[Bou93]   F. Bourdoncle. Efficient chaotic iteration strategies with widenings. *Lecture Notes in Computer Science*, 735, 1993.

[CC92a]   P. Cousot and R. Cousot. Abstract interpretation frameworks. *Journal of Logic and Computation*, 2(4):511–547, 1992.

[CC92b]   P. Cousot and R. Cousot. Comparing the Galois connection and widening/narrowing approaches to abstract interpretation, invited paper. In M. Bruynooghe and M. Wirsing, editors, *Proceedings of the International Workshop Programming Language Implementation and Logic Programming, PLILP '92,*, Leuven, Belgium, 13–17 August 1992, Lecture Notes in Computer Science 631, pages 269–295. Springer-Verlag, Berlin, Germany, 1992.

[CC94]   F. Chaitin-Chatelin. Le calcul sur ordinateur à précision finie, théorie et état de l'art. Technical Report TR/PA/94/05, CERFACS, 1994.

[CCF96]   F. Chaitin-Chatelin and V. Frayss. *Lectures on Finite Precision Computations*. SIAM, 1996.

[CCT00]   F. Chaitin-Chatelin and E. Traviesas. Precise, a toolbox for assessing the quality of numerical methods and software. In *16th IMACS World Congress*, 2000.

[CH78]   P. Cousot and N. Halbwachs. Automatic discovery of linear restraints among variables of a program. In *Conference Record of the Fifth Annual ACM SIGPLAN-SIGACT Symposium on Principles of Programming Languages*, pages 84–97, Tucson, Arizona, 1978. ACM Press, New York, NY.

[Che95]   J. M. Chesneaux. *L'Arithmétique Stochastique et le Logiciel CADNA*. Habilitation diriger des recherches, Université Pierre et Marie Curie, Paris, France, November 1995.

[Cle74]   C. W. Clenshaw. Rational approximations for special functions. In D. J. Evans, editor, *Software for Numerical Mathematics*. Academic Press, New York, 1974.

[CV88]   J. M. Chesneaux and J. Vignes. Sur la robustesse de la méthode CESTAC. *Comptes Rendus de l'Académie des Sciences, Paris*, 307(1):855–860, 1988.

[CV92]   J. M. Chesneaux and J. Vignes. Les fondements de l'arithmétique stochastique. *Comptes-Rendus de l'Académie des Sciences, Paris*, 1(315):1435–1440, 1992.

[DM97]   M. Daumas and J. M. Muller, editors. *Qualité des Calculs sur Ordinateur*. Masson, 1997.

[Eda97]   A. Edalat. Domains for Computation in Mathematics, Physics and Exact Real Arithmetic. *Bulletin of Symbolic Logic*, 3(4):401–452, 1997.

[EP97]   A. Edalat and P. J. Potts. Exact real computer arithmetic. Technical report, Department of Computing Technical Report DOC 97/9, Imperial College, 1997.

[ES98]   A. Edalat and P. Snderhauf. A Domain-theoretic Approach to Real Number Computation. *Theoretical Computer Science*, 210:73–98, 1998.

[GGP+01]   E. Goubault, D. Guilbaud, A. Pacalet, B. Starynkévitch, and F. Védrine. A simple abstract interpreter for threat detection and test case generation. In *Proceedings of WAPATV'01 (ICSE'01)*, May 2001.

[GL70]   D. I. Good and R. L. London. Computer interval arithmetic: Definition and proof of correct implementation. *Journal of the Association for Computing Machinery*, 17(4):603–612, October 1970.

[Gol91]   D. Goldberg. What every computer-scientist should know about computer arithmetic. *Computing Surveys*, 1991.

[Gra92]   P. Granger. Improving the results of static analyses of programs by local decreasing iterations. *Lecture Notes in Computer Science*, 652, 1992.

[Gri00]   A. Griewank. *Evaluating Derivatives, Principles and Techniques of Algorithmic Differentiation*. SIAM, 2000.

[HCL+68]   J. F. Hart, E. W. Cheney, C. L. Lawson, H. J. Maehly, C. K. Mesztenyi, J. R. Rice, H. G. Thacher, and C. Witzgall. *Computer Approximations*. Wiley, New York, 1968.

[Hig96]   N. J. Higham. *Accuracy and Stability of Numerical Algorithms*. SIAM, Philadelphia, 1996.

[Kah91]   W. Kahan. The improbability of probabilistic error analyses for numerical computations. Technical report, University of Berkeley, 1991.

[Kah96]   W. Kahan. Lecture notes on the status of IEEE standard 754 for binary floating-point arithmetic. Technical report, Berkeley University, 1996.

[Kar76]   M. Karr. Affine relationships between variables of a program. *Acta Informatica*, (6):133–151, 1976.

[KJ93]   W. Krandick and J. R. Johnson. Efficient multiprecision floating point multiplication with optimal directional rounding. In E. E. Swartzlander, M. J. Irwin, and J. Jullien, editors, *Proceedings of the 11th IEEE Symposium on Computer Arithmetic*, pages 228–233, Windsor, Canada, June 1993. IEEE Computer Society Press, Los Alamitos, CA.

[Kla93]   S. Kla. *Calcul parallèle et en ligne des fonctions arithmétiques*. PhD thesis, Ecole Normale Supérieure de Lyon, 46 Allée d'Italie, 69364 Lyon Cedex 07, France, February 1993.

[KM83]   P. Kornerup and D. W. Matula. Finite-precision rational arithmetic: an arithmetic unit. *IEEE Transactions on Computers*, C-32:378–388, 1983.

[KM85]   P. Kornerup and D. W. Matula. Finite precision lexicographic continued fraction number systems. In *Proceedings of the 7th IEEE Symposium on Computer Arithmetic*, Urbana, USA, 1985. IEEE Computer Society Press, Los Alamitos, CA. Reprinted in E. E. Swartzlander, *Computer Arithmetic*, Vol. 2, IEEE Computer Society Press Tutorial, Los Alamitos, CA, 1990.

[KM88]   P. Kornerup and D. W. Matula. An on-line arithmetic unit for bit-pipelined rational arithmetic. *Journal of Parallel and distributed Computing*, Special Issue on Parallelism in Computer Arithmetic(5), 1988.

[Knu73]   D. Knuth. *The Art of Computer Programming*, volume 2. Addison Wesley, Reading, MA, 1973.

[LMT98]   V. Lefevre, J.M. Muller, and A. Tisserand. Toward correctly rounded transcendentals. *IEEE Transactions on Computers*, 47(11), 1998.

[LN97]   P. Langlois and F. Nativel. Improving automatic reduction of round-off errors. In *IMACS World Congress on Scientific Computation, Modelling and Applied Mathematics*, volume 2, 1997.

[Mar01]   M. Martel. Semantics of floating point operations with error understanding. Technical report, CEA, submitted, May 2001.

[Mon00]   D. Monniaux. Abstract interpretation of probabilistic semantics. In *Seventh International Static Analysis Symposium (SAS'00)*, number 1824 in Lecture Notes in Computer Science. Springer-Verlag, 2000.

[Mon01]   D. Monniaux. An abstract Monte-Carlo method for the analysis of probabilistic programs (extended abstract). In *28th Symposium on Principles of Programming Languages (POPL '01)*. Association for Computer Machinery, 2001.

[Moo79]   R. E. Moore. *Methods and Applications of Interval Analysis*. Society for Industrial and Applied Mathematics, Philadelphia, PA, USA, 1979.

[PE98]   P. J. Potts and A. Edalat. A new representation of exact real numbers. *Electronic Notes in Computer Science*, 6, 1998.

[PEE97]   P. J. Potts, A. Edalat, and H. M. Escardó. Semantics of exact real arithmetic. In *Procs of Logic in Computer Science*. IEEE Computer Society Press, 1997.

[Plo81]   G. Plotkin. A structural approach to operational semantics. Technical Report DAIMI FN-19, Computer Science Department, Aarhus, 1981.

[PV74]   M. La Porte and J. Vignes. Error analysis in computing. In *Information Processing 74*. North-Holland, 1974.

[Reg99]   N. Regal. Petite analyse en nombres flottants. Technical Report DTA/LETI/DEIN/SLA/99-055, CEA, 1999.

[RT73]   J. E. Robertson and K. S. Trivedi. The status of investigations into computer hardware design based on the use of continued fractions. *IEEE Transactions on Computers*, C-22:555–560, 1973.

[Sch83]   C. W. Schelin. Calculator function approximation. *American Mathematical Monthly*, 90(5), May 1983.

[Sco89]   M. Scott. Fast rounding in multiprecision floating-slash arithmetic. *IEEE Transactions on Computers*, 38:1049–1052, 1989.

[Sei83]   R. B. Seidensticker. Continued fractions for high-speed and high-accuracy computer arithmetic. In *Proceedings of the 6th IEEE Symposium on Computer Arithmetic*, Aarhus, Denmark, 1983. IEEE Computer Society Press, Los Alamitos, CA.

[VA85]   J. Vignes and R. Alt. An efficient stochastic method for round-off error analysis. In Miranker Willard and Toupin, editors, *Accurate Scientific Computations, Lecture notes in Computer Science 235*. Springer-Verlag, 1985.

[VACS94] M. Vincius, A. Andrade, J. L. D. Comba, and J. Stolfi. Affine arithmetic. In *INTERVAL'94*, March 1994.

[Vig78]   J. Vignes. New methods for evaluating the validity of mathematical software. *Math. Comp. Simul. IMACS*, 20:227–249, 1978.

[Vig87]   J. Vignes. Contrôle et estimation stochastique des arrondis de calcul. *AFCET Interfaces*, 54:3–10, 1987.

[Vig93]   J. Vignes. A stochastic arithmetic for reliable scientific computation. *Math. Comp. Simul.*, 35:233–261, 1993.

[Vig96]   J. Vignes. A survey of the CESTAC method. In *Proceedings of Real Numbers and Computer Conference*, 1996.

[Vui90]   J. E. Vuillemin. Exact real computer arithmetic with continued fractions. *IEEE Transactions on Computers*, 39(8), 1990.

Estimating the Impact of Scalable Pointer Analysis on Optimization

Manuvir Das[1], Ben Liblit[2], Manuel Fähndrich[1], and Jakob Rehof[1]

[1] Microsoft Research
{manuvir,maf,rehof}@microsoft.com
[2] EECS Department, UC Berkeley
liblit@eecs.berkeley.edu

Abstract. This paper addresses the following question: Do scalable control-flow-insensitive pointer analyses provide the level of precision required to make them useful in compiler optimizations?

We first describe alias frequency, a metric that measures the ability of a pointer analysis to determine that pairs of memory accesses in C programs cannot be aliases. We believe that this kind of information is useful for a variety of optimizations, while remaining independent of a particular optimization. We show that control-flow and context insensitive analyses provide the same answer as the best possible pointer analysis on at least 95% of all statically generated alias queries. In order to understand the potential run-time impact of the remaining 5% queries, we weight the alias queries by dynamic execution counts obtained from profile data. Flow-insensitive pointer analyses are accurate on at least 95% of the weighted alias queries as well.

We then examine whether scalable pointer analyses are inaccurate on the remaining 5% alias queries because they are context-insensitive. To this end, we have developed a new context-sensitive pointer analysis that also serves as a general engine for tracing the flow of values in C programs. To our knowledge, it is the first technique for performing context-sensitive analysis with subtyping that scales to millions of lines of code. We find that the new algorithm does not identify fewer aliases than the context-insensitive analysis.

1   Introduction

Programs written in C typically make widespread use of pointer variables. In order to analyze a program that uses pointers, it is necessary to perform a pointer analysis that computes, at every dereference point in a program, a superset of the set of memory locations that may be accessed by the dereference. These "points-to" sets can be used to perform alias analysis in an optimizing compiler: two memory accesses whose points-to sets do not intersect cannot be aliases. Alias information can be utilized by a variety of optimizations, including but not limited to code scheduling, register allocation, loop unrolling and constant propagation.

Over the years a wide variety of algorithms for pointer analysis have been proposed (including [LR92,And94,EGH94,WL95,Ste96,LH99]). All of these algorithms either do not scale to large programs, or are believed to produce poor

P. Cousot (Ed.): SAS 2001, LNCS 2126, pp. 260–278, 2001.
© Springer-Verlag Berlin Heidelberg 2001

alias information. This is one reason why most optimizing compilers do not perform global pointer analysis, and are therefore forced to make conservative assumptions about potential aliases. In this paper, we argue that scalable pointer analyses do produce precise alias information.

We are interested in determining whether scalable pointer analyses can impact a variety of optimizations. Therefore, we avoid evaluating pointer analyses in the context of a specific optimization and a specific compiler. Instead, we develop a new metric, "alias frequency", that measures the frequency with which a pointer analysis is forced to assert that a pair of statically generated memory accesses in a C program may be aliases. Our experiments show that the alias frequency of scalable pointer analyses (in particular, Das's algorithm [Das00]) is within 5% of the alias frequency of the best possible pointer analysis.

Although this result is extremely encouraging, we must also consider whether the 5% alias queries on which scalable pointer analyses are imprecise may be the very queries that have the greatest impact on a given optimization. If this is so, the code associated with these queries must dominate the run-time of the programs. Then, if we weight the responses to alias queries by dynamic execution counts from profile data, we should expect a large gap in alias frequency between Das's algorithm and the best possible pointer analysis. However, our experiments show that Das's algorithm is within 5% of the best possible pointer analysis in terms of weighted alias frequency as well.

One possible source of the remaining inaccuracy in Das's algorithm is its lack of context-sensitivity. To understand the impact of this limitation, we have developed a new algorithm that is a context-sensitive version of Das's algorithm. Our generalized one level flow (GOLF) algorithm uses the one level flow idea from [Das00] to achieve a limited form of context-sensitivity in addition to subtyping. Our results show no appreciable decrease in alias frequency from context-sensitivity.

GOLF is a general engine for tracing the flow of values in programs with pointers and indirect function calls in a context-sensitive manner. It can be used for applications such as program slicing [Tip95] or escape analysis [Ruf00]. GOLF is the first context-sensitive analysis with subtyping that scales to millions of lines of code. Even though GOLF does not improve alias frequency, it can provide much more precise results than a context-insensitive algorithm if the client of the analysis is itself context-sensitive (see Section 5.2).

In summary, we make the following contributions:

- We present "alias frequency", a new metric for measuring the impact of pointer analysis on optimization.
- We demonstrate that scalable pointer analyses are able to produce precise responses to at least 95% of all alias queries on all of our test programs.
- We show that the addition of context-sensitivity does not improve the alias frequency of scalable pointer analyses.
- We present GOLF, a new flow-insensitive pointer analysis that utilizes a limited amount of context-sensitivity and subtyping. It produces a points-to graph that is linear in the size of the program, in almost linear time.

All points-to sets in the program can be extracted from the graph using CFL-Reachability, in worst-case cubic time.
 – We show that on all of our test programs, GOLF is linear in time and space requirements. We also show that the limited forms of context-sensitivity and subtyping used in GOLF provide the same precision as algorithms with full polymorphism and subtyping. We therefore claim that GOLF is likely to provide the same precision as an algorithm with full polymorphic subtyping.

The rest of the paper is organized as follows: in Section 2, we motivate GOLF through an example. We describe GOLF in Section 3. In Section 4, we present alias frequency. In Section 5, we present our empirical results. We discuss related work in Section 6, and conclude in Section 7.

2   Example

Consider the fragment of a C program with function calls shown below.

```
id(r) { return r; }
p = id_i(&x);
q = id_j(&y);
*p = 3;
```

The goal of a context-sensitive pointer analysis is to avoid confusing the addresses returned from the function *id* to the variables p and q at the two calls to *id*.

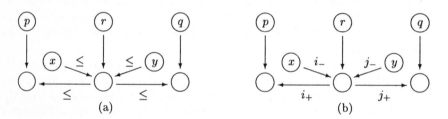

(a)   (b)

The points-to information computed by Das's algorithm is shown in (a) above. The points-to graph shown contains nodes representing memory locations and edges representing pointer relationships. Every node contains a single pointer edge. Thus, the target of the node for p represents the location $*p$. The points-to graph includes special "flow" edges (labeled $\leq$) between nodes. Flow edges are introduced at assignments, one level below (in the points-to graph) the expressions involved in the assignment. In the example program, the implicit assignment from $\&x$ to parameter r induced by the function call introduces a flow edge from the node for x to the pointer target node of r, indicating that the set of symbols represented by $*r$ must include x. The return statement in *id* induces implicit assignments from r to p and from r to q. As a result, the set of symbols represented by $*p$ includes both x and y, even though there is no execution of the program in which the address of y flows to p. As has been pointed out by several authors in previous work [RHS95,RF01], the problem arises because a value flowing in to *id* from one call site (i) is allowed to flow out to a *different* call site (j).

The points-to graph produced by GOLF is shown in (b) above. We label flow edges arising from function calls with identifiers. All edges from a given call site have the same identifier. Edges also have a polarity, indicating whether a value is flowing in to $(-)$ or out from $(+)$ the called function. From this graph, we can see that x need not be included in the set of symbols at $*q$, because the only path from x to $*q$ has an edge labeled i_- followed by an edge labeled j_+. In a "valid" flow path, calls and returns are "matched": an edge labeled i_- may be matched only by an edge labeled i_+.

A valid path in the GOLF graph is one whose sequence of labels forms a string in a context-free language of matched l_- and l_+ labels. It is well known that the presence of valid paths between a pair of nodes can be determined in worst-case cubic time using CFL-Reachability queries [RHS95].

Both Das's algorithm and GOLF achieve scaling partly by limiting the use of flow edges to one level in the points-to graph, while using unification (or, type equality rules) to merge nodes at lower levels. Our experiments show that the restriction of context-sensitivity to one level does not lead to loss of precision compared to full context-sensitivity.

3   GOLF: Generalized One Level Flow

A pointer analysis can be thought of as an abstract computation that models memory locations. Every location τ is associated with an id or set of symbols φ, and holds some contents α (an abstract pointer value) (Figure 1 (b)). A location "points-to" another if the contents of the former is a pointer to the latter. Information about locations can be encoded as a points-to graph, in which nodes represent locations and edges represent points-to relationships.

In Steensgaard's unification-based algorithm [Ste96], the effect of an assignment from y to x is to equate the contents of the locations associated with y and x. This is achieved by unifying (*i.e.*, equating their ids and contents) the locations pointed-to by y and x into one representative location. Das's algorithm extends Steensgaard's algorithm by pushing the effect of assignment processing one level down the chains in the points-to graph (Figure 1). The effect of an assignment from y to x is to introduce a special "flow" edge from the pointed-to location of y to the pointed-to location of x, and to equate *only the contents* of the two pointed-to locations (Figure 1 (a)). Flow edges relate ids of locations: all of the symbols in the id of the source of a flow edge must be included in the id of the target of the edge. Assignment processing is represented declaratively in Figure 1 (b): the type rule says that the program is correctly typed iff the pointed-to locations of y and x have the same contents, and if the id of the pointed-to location of y is a subset of the id of the pointed-to location of x.

GOLF extends Das's algorithm by treating implicit assignments induced by function calls in a special manner, so as to obtain context-sensitive information. The effect of function calls in GOLF is shown in Figure 2. Parameter passing induces flow edges that are labeled by a call site identifier and a polarity (Figure (a)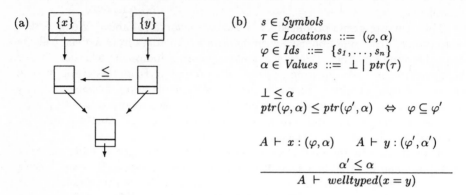

(b) $s \in Symbols$
 $\tau \in Locations ::= (\varphi, \alpha)$
 $\varphi \in Ids ::= \{s_1, \dots, s_n\}$
 $\alpha \in Values ::= \perp \mid ptr(\tau)$

 $\perp \leq \alpha$
 $ptr(\varphi, \alpha) \leq ptr(\varphi', \alpha) \iff \varphi \subseteq \varphi'$

$$\frac{A \vdash x : (\varphi, \alpha) \quad A \vdash y : (\varphi', \alpha') \quad \alpha' \leq \alpha}{A \vdash welltyped(x = y)}$$

Fig. 1. Assignment processing in Das's algorithm. Figure (a) above shows the points-to graph after processing $x = y$. The domains and type rule in figure (b) above provide a declarative specification of assignment processing.

(a)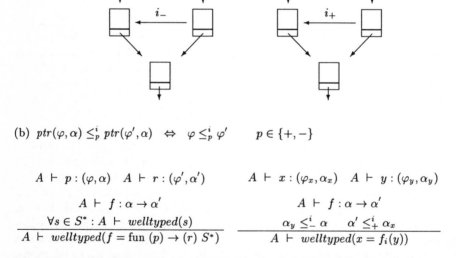

(b) $ptr(\varphi, \alpha) \leq_p^i ptr(\varphi', \alpha) \iff \varphi \leq_p^i \varphi' \qquad p \in \{+, -\}$

$$\frac{A \vdash p : (\varphi, \alpha) \quad A \vdash r : (\varphi', \alpha') \qquad A \vdash x : (\varphi_x, \alpha_x) \quad A \vdash y : (\varphi_y, \alpha_y)}{\begin{array}{cc} A \vdash f : \alpha \to \alpha' & A \vdash f : \alpha \to \alpha' \\ \dfrac{\forall s \in S^* : A \vdash welltyped(s)}{A \vdash welltyped(f = \text{fun } (p) \to (r) \, S^*)} & \dfrac{\alpha_y \leq_-^i \alpha \quad \alpha' \leq_+^i \alpha_x}{A \vdash welltyped(x = f_i(y))} \end{array}}$$

Fig. 2. Function call processing in GOLF. The graph fragments in (a) above represent points-to information after processing $x = f_i(y)$, a call to function f with argument y at call site i. For ease of exposition, we assume that functions are normalized: the statement $f = \text{fun } (p) \to (r) \, S^*$ defines a function f that has a single formal parameter p, an out parameter r that holds the return value, and a statement body S^*. The labeled constraints $\leq_-^i$ and $\leq_+^i$ generated at function calls are similar to instantiation constraints used in polymorphic type inference [Hen93], except that the direction of constraints with negative $(-)$ polarity is reversed to match the direction of flow of values (see [RF01]).

2 (a)). The polarity indicates the direction of flow of values, either into the called function through a formal parameter $(-)$, or out of the function through a return statement $(+)$. Function call processing is represented declaratively through the type rules for function definitions and function calls in Figure 2 (b). Value flow in and out of a called function generates special labeled constraints between the ids of pointed-to locations, while the contents of pointed-to locations are equated. These labeled constraints are similar to subset constraints, except that the labels are used to restrict the ways in which constraints can be composed transitively. As explained in Section 2, we wish to rule out the invalid flow of values that arises when an edge labeled i_-, representing the flow of values into a function at call site i, is followed by an edge labeled j_+, representing the flow of values back to a different call site j.

Valid Flow Paths. The set of valid flow paths is characterized precisely by the grammar shown below, and taken from [RF01]. The sequence of labels encountered along a path of flow edges forms a string. A path is a "valid path" iff its sequence of labels forms a string in the context-free language recognized by non-terminal S:

$$
\begin{aligned}
S &::= P\,N & N &::= M\,N \mid i_-\,N \mid \epsilon \\
P &::= M\,P \mid i_+\,P \mid \epsilon & M &::= i_-\,M\,i_+ \mid M\,M \mid\ \leq\ \mid \epsilon
\end{aligned}
$$

3.1   Declarative Specification

The GOLF algorithm can be viewed as a set of non-standard type inference rules over a simple language of pointer related assignments. The set of rules includes the rules from Figure 2, and the rules from Das's algorithm for handling various kinds of explicit assignment statements, shown below:

$$
\frac{A \vdash x : (\varphi, \alpha) \qquad A \vdash y : (\varphi', \alpha') \qquad \alpha' \leq \alpha}{A \vdash welltyped(x = y)}
$$

$$
\frac{A \vdash x : (\varphi, \alpha) \qquad A \vdash y : \tau \qquad ptr(\tau) \leq \alpha}{A \vdash welltyped(x = \&y)}
$$

$$
\frac{A \vdash x : (\varphi, \alpha) \quad A \vdash y : (\varphi', ptr(\tau)) \qquad \tau = (\varphi'', \alpha'') \qquad \alpha'' \leq \alpha}{A \vdash welltyped(x = *y)}
$$

$$
\frac{A \vdash x : (\varphi', ptr(\tau)) \quad A \vdash y : (\varphi, \alpha) \qquad \tau = (\varphi'', \alpha'') \qquad \alpha \leq \alpha''}{A \vdash welltyped(*x = y)}
$$

3.2   Correctness

We claim that the type rules in Figure 2 and above provide a specification of a correct flow-insensitive but context-sensitive pointer analysis. This follows from the observation that our type rules can be viewed as a restriction of the type system presented by Rehof and Fähndrich in [RF01]. Their type system, which has been shown to be correct, defines an algorithm with full subtyping and polymorphism. The GOLF type rules define an algorithm with one level of subtyping and one level of polymorphism.

There is a formal connection between constraint satisfaction in our type inference rules and valid paths in the GOLF points-to graph. The connection is provided in [RF01].

Global Storage. The goal of GOLF is to identify all valid flow induced by function calls. In C programs, this may include flow because of uses of global variables within functions. It is possible that some flow may occur because of a global variable even though no labeled flow edge is produced in the points-to graph. Reps *et al* have suggested treating globals as extra parameters, but this may lead to a large increase in the size of the points-to graph. Instead, we identify nodes associated with globals (we call these "global storage" nodes) and add self loops on these nodes, labeled with every possible call site and polarity. This conservative approximation ensures that we cannot omit any flow of values through global variables.

A similar problem occurs with indirect accesses through pointer valued parameters. One solution would be to modify our function call rule to add self loops with the given call site label on all nodes below the nodes related by labeled flow edges. Instead, we use the conservative approximation of treating these nodes as global storage nodes.

3.3 Operational Algorithm

Every symbol referenced in the program is associated with a unique location on demand. The program is processed one assignment at a time, including implicit assignments generated by function calls. At every assignment, locations are unified as necessary to satisfy the type equality requirements imposed by the non-standard type inference rules in Figure 2 and Section 3.1. Processing of simple subset constraints and labeled constraints is delayed by introducing flow edges between locations, as shown in Figures 1 and 2. When two locations are unified, flow edges between the locations turn into self loops. Unlabeled ($\leq$) self loops are discarded, but labeled ($\leq_p^i$) self loops are retained in order to capture all valid flow. The GOLF graph could therefore contain more edges than Das's points-to graph. In practice, the increase in edge count is very low.

Once processing of the entire program is complete, points-to sets are produced from the points-to graph. Symbol x must be included in the points-to set at a dereference $*p$ iff there is a valid path from the node associated with x to the node associated with $*p$. Reps *et al* have observed that the presence of such a path can be determined using CFL-Reachability queries [RHS95]. We use single-source queries, one for each symbol in the program, to populate all points-to sets.

Global Storage. We identify and mark global storage nodes in a linear scan of the points-to graph. Instead of adding a linear number of self edges at each global storage node, we account for the effect of the self edges implicitly: if there is a valid path from node u to node v, where v is a global storage node, and there is a valid path from node v to node w, then there must be a valid path from node u to node w. This is because any unmatched labeled edges in the path from u to w through v can be matched by following an appropriate set of self edges at v. In other words, the effect of a global storage node is to introduce transitivity in CFL-Reachability queries. This leads to a modified reachability procedure: node v is reachable from node u iff it is possible to reach from u to v by "stepping" on global storage nodes and using valid paths to "hop" from one global storage node to the next.

3.4 Complexity

The algorithm has two steps: an assignment processing step, which produces a points-to graph with flow edges, and a flow propagation step. The first step has the same complexity as Steensgaard's algorithm. It uses linear space, and has almost linear running-time (in the size of the program). Every implicit assignment causes the addition of a single labeled edge. The number of implicit assignments is linear even in the presence of indirect calls, because there is a single signature for all possible target functions at a call site [Ste96].

The flow step involves a CFL-Reachability query on the graph for each symbol in the program. The worst-case cost of an all-pairs CFL-Reachability query over a graph is cubic in the number of graph nodes [RHS95]. Therefore, the complexity of GOLF is cubic in the size of the program.

3.5 Efficient CFL-Reachability

In this subsection we explain three insights that allow us to efficiently compute points-to sets for large programs.

Memoization. Our first insight is that a simple memoization, borrowed from [Das00], can allow us to amortize the cost of multiple queries by avoiding repeated work. Our experiments show that in every points-to graph, there is a single node (the "blob") that has a large number of outgoing flow edges. In every graph, the blob has an order of magnitude more outgoing edges than any other node. Now consider the set of symbols that have valid paths to the blob. For each such symbol, we would repeat a scan of the subgraph originating from the blob. Instead, we would like to perform the scan from the blob exactly once, cache the result, and share this across all symbols that reach the blob.

We pre-compute the set of nodes reachable from the blob ("frontier nodes"), and the set of symbols that reach the blob. For every symbol that does not reach the blob, we perform a forward scan to dereference nodes, as usual. For a symbol that reaches the blob, we perform a forward scan, but we stop at frontier nodes. Once we have processed all symbols, we append the symbols that reach the blob to the points-to set at every frontier node.

Consider a symbol for which we compose the scan from the blob with the scan from the symbol as described above. Because CFL-Reachability is not transitive, we may be treating more nodes as reachable from the symbol than necessary. However, if the blob is a global storage node, we can compose without loss of precision. The only programs for which the blob is not a global storage node are extremely small, and therefore do not require memoization. On the other hand, there may be some frontier nodes at which the scan from a symbol arrives with less matching requirements for a valid path than the scan from the blob. If we stop the scan at these nodes and compose with the scan from the blob, we may fail to visit some nodes. Therefore, we identify such cases during the scan from the symbol, and continue the scan through the frontier node.

This simple memoization results in dramatic speedup. Our empirical evidence shows that there are many scans that involve the blob, for which we amortize the scan cost. All remaining scans cover very small regions of the graph.

We believe that the existence of the blob is not a coincidence. Rather, it reflects the presence of global variables that are referenced throughout a program. The blob node is an accumulator for large points-to sets. These sets are poor targets for improvement via more precise pointer analysis, because they are unlikely to shrink to very small sets, and because a precise analysis is likely to spend considerable resources tracking global variables. Points-to sets outside the reach of the blob are better targets for more precise analysis.

Global Storage. Our second insight is that we can use the transitive behaviour of global storage nodes to make a single scan more efficient. Global storage nodes serve as points where we can use a divide and conquer strategy to form longer valid paths from shorter valid paths without enforcing matching requirements.

Summary Edges. Our algorithm for a single CFL-Reachability query is based on a demand algorithm outlined by Horwitz *et al* in [HRS95], which improves the efficiency of queries by adding special summary edges to the graph. We have adapted their algorithm to handle nodes that are shared across functions because of unification, and to handle global storage.

4   Alias Frequency

We are interested in estimating the impact of pointer analysis on compiler optimizations, in a manner that is independent of a particular optimizing compiler or optimization. However, previously defined measures of precision for pointer analysis that are independent of a particular optimization, such as average points-to set size and number of singleton points-to sets, provide little indication of the ability of a pointer analysis to enable optimizations by identifying memory accesses as not aliased.

Therefore, we propose "alias frequency", a new metric that estimates the precision of alias information produced by a given pointer analysis.

4.1   Simple Alias Frequency

For a given program, we define *queries* to be a set of alias queries. Each query (e_1, e_2) involves a pair of memory access expressions occuring statically in the program. The alias frequency of a given pointer analysis is the percentage of queries for which the analysis says that e_1 and e_2 may refer to the same memory location in some execution of the program:

$$\text{simple alias frequency} = \frac{\sum_{(e_1,e_2)\in queries} a(e_1,e_2)}{\sum_{(e_1,e_2)\in queries} 1} \times 100$$

$$a(e_1, e_2) = \begin{cases} 1 & \text{if } e_1, e_2 \text{ may be aliases} \\ 0 & \text{otherwise} \end{cases}$$

Alias Queries. An extreme approach to generating alias queries would be to consider all pairs of memory accesses encountered anywhere in the program. This would result in a large number of pairs of accesses from different functions. Most of these pairs are uninteresting, because a typical optimizer will not optimize code across function boundaries. Therefore, we consider only alias queries where both memory access expressions occur in the body of the same function (there may be duplicate pairs). We believe these queries represent most intra-procedural optimizations performed in commonly used C compilers.[1]

Some expressions contain multiple dereference operators. In order to limit the number of queries, we consider only top-level memory accesses from assignment expressions, conditional expressions, and function arguments[2]. We have experimented with different criteria for selecting queries (such as including subexpressions of nested dereferences, and ignoring function arguments), and have found that our results remain consistent.

Categorizing Queries. We categorize memory accesses based on whether they require pointer information to resolve. We define a "symbol-access" recursively: a symbol-access is a variable, a field access operation on a symbol-access, or an array index operation on a symbol-access of array type. Every remaining memory access, including a dereference, an arrow operation, or an array index operation on an object of pointer type, is a "pointer-access". Every alias query relating two symbol-accesses can be answered without pointer analysis. If the two symbol-accesses refer to the same variable, we say they may be aliases:

$$a(s_1, s_2) = \begin{cases} 1 & \text{if } var(s_1) = var(s_2) \\ 0 & \text{otherwise} \end{cases}$$

Measuring a Given Pointer Analysis. Given a pointer analysis that produces a points-to set $pts(e)$ for every expression e (we set $pts(e) = \{var(e)\}$ for a symbol-access e), we can answer queries involving pointer-accesses. Two accesses may be aliases if and only if their points-to sets overlap:

$$a(e_1, e_2) = \begin{cases} 1 & \text{if } pts(e_1) \cap pts(e_2) \neq \emptyset \\ 0 & \text{otherwise} \end{cases}$$

Measuring the Best and Worst Possible Pointer Analysis. We are especially interested in understanding the gap in alias precision between scalable pointer analyses and more precise algorithms. Therefore, we create an artificial lower bound analysis that under-estimates the alias frequency of the best possible safe pointer analysis, by treating every query involving at least one pointer-access

---

[1] Notice that these queries would include aliases between globals and locals referenced in the body of the same function.

[2] Given $**p = x$, we consider $**p$ and x, but not $*p$.

as not aliased. The only exception is when GOLF determines that a pair of accesses refer to the same *single* stack or global symbol. The lower bound analysis treats these pairs as aliases:[3]

$$a(e_1, e_2) = \begin{cases} 1 & \text{if } pts(e_1) = pts(e_2) = \{v\} \\ 0 & \text{otherwise} \end{cases}$$

The lower bound analysis has the property that it is at least as precise as the best possible pointer analysis on every alias query. Therefore, if a given pointer analysis is close in alias frequency to the lower bound analysis, it must be at least as close to any more precise safe pointer analysis.

We also create an artificial upper bound analysis, by treating every query involving at least one pointer-access as aliases. The upper bound analysis indicates whether any form of pointer analysis is necessary for a given program.

Our metric over-estimates the alias frequency of the lower bound analysis, because a pair of accesses of the same variable may not be aliases if the accesses refer to different structure fields. However, we are concerned with the *difference* between a given analysis and the lower bound. Consider pairs of accesses where at least one access is a pointer-access. The lower bound analysis treats such pairs as not aliased, whereas any of our pointer analyses could potentially improve its response to these queries using field distinction. For pairs of symbol-accesses, all of the analyses, including the lower bound analysis, suffer equally. Therefore, our lack of field distinction leads us to conservatively *over-estimate* the precision gap between a given pointer analysis and the lower bound analysis.[4]

4.2   Weighted Alias Frequency

As mentioned in the introduction, we would like to estimate the potential impact on run-time of the alias queries on which a pointer analysis produces a possibly inaccurate response. Therefore, we weight the response $a(e_1, e_2)$ of any analysis to every query by the sum of the dynamic execution counts ($num(e_1) + num(e_2)$, gathered from profile data) of the accesses in the query:

$$\text{weighted alias frequency} = \frac{\sum_{(e_1, e_2) \in queries} a(e_1, e_2) \times (num(e_1) + num(e_2))}{\sum_{(e_1, e_2) \in queries} num(e_1) + num(e_2)} \times 100$$

A small difference between the weighted alias frequency of a given pointer analysis and the lower bound analysis means that a more precise pointer analysis is unlikely to enable additional optimizations that improve run-time significantly.

---

[3] We create dummy symbols, one at each dynamic allocation site, to represent heap storage. The lower bound analysis does not treat accesses of the same heap symbol as aliases, whereas our pointer analyses do.

[4] The same argument applies to accesses of static arrays.

Table 1. Benchmark data. For each program, the table above shows the lines of code, the AST node count, and the running-time (in seconds) of GOLF.

Program	LOC	AST nodes	Time (s)
compress	1,904	2,234	0.05
li	7,602	23,379	0.50
m88ksim	19,412	65,967	0.88
ijpeg	31,215	79,486	1.13
go	29,919	109,134	0.98
perl	26,871	116,490	1.53
vortex	67,211	200,107	4.09
gcc	205,406	604,100	7.17
Word97	2,150,793	5,961,129	133.66

5   Experiments

We have produced a modular implementation of GOLF using the AST Toolkit, which is itself an extension of the Microsoft Visual C++ compiler. Our implementation handles all of the features of C. Details may be found in [Das00]. We implemented GOLF by modifying the rules for parameter passing and return statements in our implementation of Das's algorithm, and by adding a CFL-Reachability engine. Our implementation of Das's algorithm has been tested extensively. Apart from all of the usual testing, we verified the correctness of our implementation of GOLF in two ways. First, we performed reachability queries forward and backward, with and without memoization, and verified that we get the same results in every case. Second, we tested our implementation of CFL-Reachability by treating labeled edges as unlabeled and verifying that we obtain the same points-to sets as with Das's algorithm.

Benchmark Programs. Table 1 shows our benchmark programs, consisting of the integer benchmarks from SPEC95, and a version of Microsoft Word. For each benchmark, we list the total lines of source code (including comments and blank lines), as well as the number of AST nodes (a more accurate measure of program size), and the analysis time (in seconds) for GOLF, averaged over 5 runs. Analysis time includes time to analyze each compilation unit (excluding parse time), time to write out object files, time to read in all of the object files, perform unifications, and compute points-to sets exhaustively at all static dereference points in the program using CFL-Reachability. All of our experiments were conducted on a Dell 610 desktop PC running Windows 2000, with 512MB RAM and a single 800Mhz Intel Pentium III processor.

5.1   Alias Precision of Pointer Analysis

Table 2 shows the simple and weighted alias frequencies of various pointer analyses. We obtained execution counts for computation of weighted alias frequency by instrumenting the benchmarks and running them on their SPEC reference

Table 2. Precision of various pointer analyses. For each benchmark program, the table above shows the simple alias frequency of the lower bound analysis (Lower), GOLF, Das's algorithm (Das00), Steensgaard's algorithm (Ste96), and the upper bound analysis (Upper), and the difference in simple alias frequency between Das00 and Lower (Diff). The same data is also shown for weighted alias frequency. We were not able to obtain dynamic execution counts for Word97.

Program	Simple Alias frequency						Weighted Alias frequency					
	Lower	GOLF	Das00	Ste96	Upper	Diff	Lower	GOLF	Das00	Ste96	Upper	Diff
compress	13.8	14.02	14.02	14.13	32.38	0.22	9.93	9.93	9.93	9.93	28.82	0.0
li	10.17	18.84	18.84	19.53	42.27	8.67	13.10	22.98	22.98	22.99	62.12	9.88
m88ksim	14.97	17.0	17.0	20.44	40.5	2.03	11.53	13.77	13.77	18.67	37.77	2.24
ijpeg	5.93	17.9	17.9	19.14	61.49	11.97	5.55	16.31	16.31	16.31	57.42	10.76
go	7.85	7.87	7.87	7.87	8.35	0.02	9.5	9.73	9.73	9.73	15.53	0.23
perl	9.54	14.45	14.45	14.53	45.17	4.91	3.45	12.56	12.56	12.56	53.87	9.11
vortex	6.12	10.81	10.81	15.71	42.69	4.69	3.7	7.18	7.18	14.51	50.20	3.48
gcc	5.49	11.98	11.98	14.64	50.36	6.49	4.62	9.36	9.36	10.72	51.66	4.74
Word97	6.63	14.45	15.07	20.37	44.21	8.44	-	-	-	-	-	-
Average	8.94	14.15	14.22	16.26	40.82	5.27	7.67	12.73	12.73	14.43	44.67	5.06

inputs.[5] The data shows that all of the scalable pointer analyses are surprisingly close to the lower bound analysis. Das's algorithm does as well as the lower bound analysis on all but 5.2% of the alias queries, on our benchmark programs.

To better understand the loss in precision from scalable pointer analysis, we manually examined a fraction of the queries on which Das's algorithm differs from the lower bound analysis. We found that in almost every case, either the lower bound analysis is unsound, or we could have used straightforward field distinction to resolve the query as not aliased. Therefore, we believe that the gap in alias frequency between scalable pointer analyses and the best possible pointer analysis is in fact *much less* than 5%.

The data in Table 2 also shows that the difference in weighted alias frequency between Das's algorithm and the lower bound analysis is very similar to the difference in simple alias frequency, for every benchmark. We therefore claim that the queries on which Das's algorithm is inaccurate are not likely to provide significant additional opportunity for optimization.

On all of our benchmarks, the differences in weighted alias frequencies between various analyses are very similar to the differences in simple alias frequency between the same analyses. Hence, we argue that simple alias frequency is a useful indicator of precision for implementors of pointer analysis who do not have access to either profile data or optimizing compilers that can consume alias information produced by their analyses.

Das00 vs GOLF. Table 2 shows that the alias frequency of Das's algorithm is not improved by the addition of context-sensitivity for any benchmark other than Word97. This data shows that in practice, scalable pointer analyses do not sacrifice optimization opportunity because of a lack of context-sensitivity.

Ste96. The data also shows that Steensgaard's algorithm is surprisingly close to the lower bound analysis, given the relatively poor precision of the algorithm in

---

[5] The reference input for gcc consists of 56 C source files. We ran gcc on the five largest source files and averaged the execution counts.

terms of points-to set size (see Table 3). We believe that this is largely because the pollution of points-to sets that occurs in Steensgaard's algorithm leads to accumulation of variables across functions, but this pollution does not result in conservative alias relationships between pointer variables from the same function. Also, smaller points-to sets do not imply lower alias frequency, if the smaller sets contain the same subset of common symbols. Finally, points-to set sizes are often artificially inflated by the inclusion of symbols that are out of scope. Table 2 and Table 3 clearly show that traditional measures of precision for pointer analysis do not reflect the ability of the analysis to produce good alias information.

Das00 vs Andersen. Previous work [Das00] has shown that Das's algorithm and Andersen's algorithm [And94] produce almost identical points-to sets. Therefore, their alias frequencies can be expected to be almost identical as well.

Limitations. First, although we measure alias frequency, we are really evaluating pointer analysis. It may be possible to significantly improve the alias frequency of any analysis, including the lower bound analysis, by adding a structure field analysis and/or an array index analysis. Second, our results apply only to C programs; whether they apply to programs written in C++ or Java is an open question. Third, aggressive inter-procedural optimizers may be able to utilize alias information inter-procedurally [Ruf00]. These opportunities are not reflected in our selection of alias queries.

One potential concern with our results may be that scalable pointer analyses appear close to the lower bound analysis because we have swamped the query set with pairs of symbol accesses. We find that on the average, 30% of the queries require some form of pointer information. This large percentage indicates that there is a need for at least some form of pointer analysis in compilers.

As might be expected, we generate a large number of alias queries (10 million queries for Word97). Each query may require reachability on the points-to graph. By using the amortization technique described in Section 3.5, we are able to answer alias queries extremely efficiently. We can answer all queries for Word97 in less than seven minutes.

There may be regions of a program where a more accurate analysis may eliminate aliases. For instance, consider a linked list traversal using previous and current pointers. Our results show that a useful approach may be to first run a scalable pointer analysis, and then apply a more precise shape analysis locally, on a few functions. These functions can be identified using alias frequency.

5.2   Performance and Precision of GOLF

Performance. In the figure below, we chart the running times for GOLF from Table 1. We use the ratio of running-time to program size. The chart shows that this ratio is fairly steady as program size grows, indicating that the analysis scales linearly with program size. GOLF requires roughly twice as much time and as much memory as Das's algorithm. We do not present detailed data on space consumption, which is very low. GOLF requires 20MB for Word97:

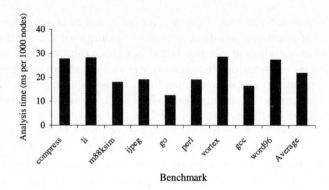

Benchmark

Precision vs Other Scalable Pointer Analyses. Table 3 shows the precision of GOLF measured using traditional metrics. The table shows the average size of points-to sets at dereference points and the number of singleton points-to sets for each benchmark. Following previous work, the size of the points-to set at a dereference point is the number of program symbols, including dummy symbols produced at dynamic allocation sites, in the points-to set of the dereference expression. All three analyses were run with the same settings, using the same implementation. We omit data for points-to sets at indirect call sites, although GOLF can also be used to improve points-to sets for function pointers as well.

Points-to sets with single elements represent opportunites for replacing conditional updates with strong updates. Smaller points-to sets may lead to greater efficiency in subsequent analyses [SH97], as well as less run-time overhead in systems that instrument code [MCE00]. The data shows that GOLF produces more singleton sets than Das's algorithm for several benchmarks. On the whole, our results appear to be consistent with the results of Foster *et al* ([FFA00]), who found little improvement in precision from the addition of polymorphism to a pointer analysis with subtyping. Our benchmark programs are much larger than in [FFA00], and we do see greater improvement on larger programs.

Precision vs Full Polymorphic Subtyping. GOLF approximates a full polymorphic subtyping algorithm by restricting both subtyping and polymorphism to one level in the type structure. Das has already shown that the one level restriction of subtyping does not cause loss in precision [Das00]. The data for the FRD00 and OneLev columns in Table 3 shows that the one level restriction of polymorphism does not cause precision loss either.

It is therefore likely that GOLF extracts most of the precision of an analysis with full polymorphism and subtyping. However, it is still possible that the combination of full polymorphism and full subtyping may eliminate more spurious flow of values than the combination of limited polymorphism and limited subtyping used in GOLF. We were unable to perform a direct comparison, because it has not been possible to scale polymorphic subtyping to large programs.

Context-Sensitive Clients. In order to populate points-to sets, we accumulate all flow of pointer values into a function from its callers. In the example below, the points-to set of l is the same using Das's algorithm or GOLF:

```
void Read(Obj o1, Obj o2) { LockWrap(&o1.lock); LockWrap(&o2.lock); }
```

Table 3. Precision of various pointer analyses. For each benchmark program, the table above shows the average size of points-to sets at static dereference points for Ste96, Das00, GOLF, a polymorphic version of Steensgaard's algorithm (FRD00), and a one level restriction of FRD00 (OneLev). The table also shows the number of dereference points with singleton points-to sets found using each of these algorithms. FRD00 and OneLev cannot be compared directly with the other analyses, because they are based on Rehof's implementation of a polymorphic version of Steensgaard's algorithm [FRD00]. We were not able to use this implementation to analyze Word97.

Program	Average thru-deref size					Singleton sets				
	Ste96	Das00	Golf	FRD00	OneLev	Ste96	Das00	Golf	FRD00	OneLev
compress	2.1	1.22	1.22	2.9	2.9	36	47	47	30	30
li	287.7	185.62	185.62	189.63	194.80	15	39	39	15	15
m88ksim	86.3	3.29	3.27	14.13	15.16	116	638	641	256	251
ijpeg	17.0	13.14	11.78	13.01	14.30	1,671	3,287	3,287	1,802	1,777
go	45.2	14.79	14.79	16.06	16.06	28	28	28	23	23
perl	36.1	22.24	21.90	23.89	23.91	240	1,023	1,155	307	306
vortex	1,064.5	59.86	59.30	57.42	65.70	808	4,855	4,855	4,764	4,764
gcc	245.8	7.96	7.71	90.62	97.17	1,323	6,830	6,896	2,637	2,598
Word97	27,176.3	11,219.5	7,756.6	-	-	11,577	41,904	43,142	-	-

```
void LockWrap(Lock * l) { AcquireLock(l); }
```

However, the labeled edges in GOLF can be used to produce distinct summaries of function behaviour at different call sites. These summaries can be leveraged by a client of GOLF, as long as the client is context-sensitive. For instance, a context-sensitive analysis that tracks lockable objects can use the summaries of `LockWrap` produced by GOLF to conclude that `o1` *must* be locked by the first call to `LockWrap`. Das's algorithm can only say that `o1` *may* be locked by *either* call. We believe that this is the real value of GOLF.

6   Related Work

GOLF. As we mentioned in the introduction, our work on GOLF follows a long line of research on context-sensitive pointer analysis. The most precise algorithms are control-flow-sensitive and context-sensitive [LR92,WL95,EGH94,CRL99]. It is not clear whether any of these algorithms will scale beyond 50,000 lines of code. Previous algorithms for control-flow-insensitive context-sensitive pointer analysis include [LH99,CH00,FRD00]. The first two algorithms follow every edge in the call graph, whether the call graph is pre-computed or constructed on the fly. This may limit their applicability to large programs, which have very large (quadratic sized) call graphs due to indirect calls. On the other hand, [FRD00] appears to scale well, but it does not provide any degree of subtyping, which is important for larger programs.

GOLF is a context-sensitive algorithm with subtyping that scales to large programs. It is an extension of Das's algorithm [Das00]. We apply his one level flow idea to restrict polymorphism without losing precision, and we borrow his caching technique to speed up our flow computation. GOLF can also be viewed as a restriction of Rehof and Fähndrich's general polymorphic subtyping framework in [RF01]. With some modifications to account for unification, globals, and pointers, GOLF can be viewed as a variant of Reps, Horwitz and Sagiv's framework in [RHS95]. GOLF is a scalable instantiation of these two frameworks.

Liang and Harrold have described a mechanism for extracting some context-sensitivity from context-insensitive pointer analyses [LH00]. We believe that their approach could be used to add context-sensitivity to Das's algorithm. It is not clear how GOLF would compare with the resulting analysis.

Ruf [Ruf95] and Foster *et al* [FFA00] have reported empirical investigations of the added precision provided by context-sensitive pointer analysis. Both argue that there is little gain in precision from context-sensitivity. Our results are consistent with theirs, and extend their conclusions to much larger programs. However, we believe that the real value of GOLF is as a context-sensitive value flow analysis that produces polymorphic summaries of function behaviour.

Impact of Flow-Insensitive Pointer Analysis. The issue we have addressed in this paper is the usefulness of control-flow-insensitive pointer analyses in compiler optimizations. Although conventional wisdom says that the lack of flow-sensitivity and structure-field distinction can severely limit the usefulness of scalable pointer analyses, there is no empirical evidence to support this belief. In fact, several studies have produced results that contradict this idea [DMM98,CH00,HP98]. Cheng and Hwu have shown that a context-sensitive pointer analysis with subtyping can enable many optimizations in a compiler [CH00]. Their result inspired us to develop a scalable context-sensitive pointer analysis with subtyping. Hind and Pioli have shown that flow-sensitivity has little impact on the precision of pointer analysis [HP98]. Diwan *et al* have shown that for a particular Java optimization, a flow-insensitive pointer analysis provides all of the precision that can be exploited by an optimizer [DMM98]. Our results are consistent with all of these studies.

We know of no previous work that uses alias frequency to estimate the impact of pointer analysis on compiler optimizations. Diwan *et al* have studied the effect of pointer analysis on a particular Java optimization at several levels, including static points-to information, optimization opportunities enabled, and run-time improvement [DMM98]. Ideally, we would like to repeat their study for every conceivable optimization and every pointer analysis. We propose weighted alias frequency as a practical replacement for such a large set of experimental studies.

One avenue for further improvement in precision that is suggested by our results is to run a scalable analysis globally, and apply more precise analysis locally. Rountev *et al* have proposed this idea in [RRL99]. Our results provide evidence that supports their approach. They use Steensgaard's algorithm as the scalable global analysis. We believe that using GOLF as the global analysis would lead to greater precision. Also, our alias frequency measure can be used in their framework, to identify target functions for more precise analysis.

7   Conclusions

In this paper, we have provided experimental evidence to support the claim that scalable pointer analyses provide precise alias information for C programs. We believe this is a strong argument for the routine use of scalable pointer analysis in optimizing compilers. We have also developed a framework for measuring the impact of pointer analysis on compiler optimizations in a manner that is independent of a particular optimization or optimizing compiler. Finally, we have presented GOLF, the first algorithm that can trace the flow of values in very large C programs, while providing a degree of subtyping and context-sensitivity. We believe that the most useful method for analysis of large programs may be to use a scalable global analysis in conjunction with an expensive local analysis.

Acknowledgements

We would like to thank Tom Reps and Rakesh Ghiya for helpful discussions, and Jim Larus and the anonymous referees for suggestions on the paper.

References

[And94]   L. Andersen. *Program analysis and specialization for the C programming language.* PhD thesis, DIKU, University of Copenhagen, May 1994. DIKU report 94/19.

[CH00]   B. Cheng and W. Hwu. Modular interprocedural pointer analysis using access paths: Design, implementation, and evaluation. In *Proceedings of the ACM SIGPLAN 2000 Conference on Programming Language Design and Implementation,* 2000.

[CRL99]   R. Chatterjee, B. Ryder, and W. Landi. Relevant context inference. In *26th ACM SIGPLAN Symposium on Principles of Programming Languages,* 1999.

[Das00]   M. Das. Unification-based pointer analysis with directional assignments. In *Proceedings of the SIGPLAN 2000 Conference on Programming Language Design and Implementation,* 2000.

[DMM98]   A. Diwan, K. S. McKinley, and J. Eliot B. Moss. Type-based alias analysis. In *Proceedings of the ACM SIGPLAN 98 Conference on Programming Language Design and Implementation,* 1998.

[EGH94]   M. Emami, R. Ghiya, and L. Hendren. Context-sensitive interprocedural points-to analysis in the presence of function pointers. In *Proceedings of the ACM SIGPLAN 94 Conference on Programming Language Design and Implementation,* 1994.

[FFA00]   J. S. Foster, M. Fähndrich, and A. Aiken. Polymorphic versus monomorphic flow-insensitive points-to analysis for C. In *Proceedings of the 7'th International Static Analysis Symposium,* 2000.

[FRD00]   M. Fähndrich, J. Rehof, and M. Das. Scalable context-sensitive flow analysis using instantiation constraints. In *Proceedings of the ACM Conference on Programming Language Design and Implementation,* 2000.

[Hen93]   F. Henglein. Type inference with polymorphic recursion. *ACM Trans. Program. Lang. Syst.,* 15(2):253–289, 1993.

[HP98]   M. Hind and A. Pioli. Assessing the effects of flow-sensitivity on pointer alias analyses. In *Fifth International Static Analysis Symposium, Pisa, Italy,* number 1503 in LNCS, pages 57–81. Springer-Verlag, 1998.

[HRS95]   S. Horwitz, T. Reps, and M. Sagiv. Demand interprocedural dataflow analysis. In *ACM SIGSOFT Symposium on the Foundations of Software Engineering, SIGSOFT Software Engineering Notes 20, 4,* 1995.

[LH99]   D. Liang and M. Harrold. Efficient points-to analysis for whole program analysis. In *Proceedings of the 7th ACM SIGSOFT Symposium on the Foundations of Software Engineering*, 1999.

[LH00]   D. Liang and M. Harrold. Light-weight context recovery for efficient and accurate program analyses. In *Proceedings of the 22nd International Conference on Software Engineering*, June 2000.

[LR92]   W. Landi and B. Ryder. A safe approximate algorithm for interprocedural pointer aliasing. In *Proceedings of the ACM SIGPLAN 92 Conference on Programming Language Design and Implementation*, 1992.

[MCE00]   M. Mock, C. Chambers, and S. J. Eggers. Calpa: A tool for automating selective dynamic compilation. In *In 33rd Annual International Symposium on Microarchitecture, December 2000, (Micro-33), Monterrey, California*, December 2000.

[RF01]   J. Rehof and M. Fähndrich. Type-based flow analysis: From polymorphic subtyping to CFL-Reachability. In *Proceedings of the 28th Annual ACM Symposium on Principles of Programming Languages*, January 2001.

[RHS95]   T. Reps, S. Horwitz, and M. Sagiv. Precise interprocedural dataflow analysis via graph reachability. In *Symposium on Principles of Programming Languages (POPL), San Francisco, California*, 1995.

[RRL99]   A. Rountev, B. Ryder, and W. Landi. Data-flow analysis of program fragments. In *Proceedings of the 7th European Software Engineering Conference and 7th ACM SIGSOFT Symposium on the Foundations of Software Engineering*, 1999.

[Ruf95]   E. Ruf. Context-sensitive alias analysis reconsidered. *Proceedings of the ACM SIGPLAN 95 Conference on Programming Language Design and Implementation*, 1995.

[Ruf00]   E. Ruf. Effective synchronization removal for Java. In *Proceedings of the SIGPLAN 2000 Conference on Programming Language Design and Implementation*, 2000.

[SH97]   M. Shapiro and S. Horwitz. The effects of the precision of pointer analysis. In *LNCS 1302, 4th International Symposium on Static Analysis*. Springer-Verlag, 1997.

[Ste96]   B. Steensgaard. Points-to analysis in almost linear time. In *Conference Record of the 23rd ACM Symposium on Principles of Programming Languages*, 1996.

[Tip95]   F. Tip. A survey of program slicing techniques. *Journal of Programming Languages*, 3(3):121–189, 1995.

[WL95]   R. Wilson and M. Lam. Efficient context-sensitive pointer analysis for C programs. In *Proceedings of the SIGPLAN 95 Conference on Programming Language Design and Implementation*, 1995.

Efficient Computation of Parameterized Pointer Information for Interprocedural Analyses[*]

Donglin Liang and Mary Jean Harrold

Georgia Institute of Technology, Atlanta GA 30332, USA
{dliang,harrold}@cc.gatech.edu

Abstract. This paper presents a modular algorithm that efficiently computes *parameterized* pointer information, in which symbolic names are introduced to identify memory locations whose addresses may be passed into a procedure. Parameterized pointer information can be used by a client program analysis to compute parameterized summary information for a procedure. The client can then instantiate such information at each specific callsite by binding the symbolic names. Compared to *non-parameterized* pointer information, in which memory locations are identified using the same name throughout a program, parameterized pointer information lets the client reduce the spurious information that is propagated across procedure boundaries. Such reduction will improve not only the precision, but also the efficiency of the client. The paper also presents a set of empirical studies. The studies show that (1) the algorithm is efficient; and (2) using parameterized pointer information may significantly improve the precision and efficiency of program analyses.

1 Introduction

Various pointer analyses have been developed to facilitate program analyses of C programs. To support these program analyses, a pointer analysis must associate names with memory locations. A pointer analysis must also provide information that determines the memory locations accessed through pointer dereferences. With this information, a program analysis can first replace the pointer dereferences in a program with the memory locations accessed through such dereferences, and then analyze the program in the usual way [2, 16].

Pointer analysis algorithms can differ in the way in which they assign names to memory locations. Such differences can significantly impact the precision and the efficiency of the program analyses that use the pointer information. Many existing pointer analysis algorithms (e.g., [1, 3, 5, 6, 8, 11, 14, 15, 18, 19]) use the same name to identify a memory location throughout the program. Because a memory location may be accessed throughout the program, its name can appear in several procedures. Therefore, a program analysis that uses this pointer information usually treats such a name as if it were a global variable name.

A few existing pointer analysis algorithms [7, 21] assign different names to a memory location in different procedures. When the address of a memory location

---

[*] Supported by NSF under CCR-9988294, CCR-0096321, and EIA-0196145, by Boeing Aerospace Corporation, and by the State of Georgia under the Yamacraw Mission.

P. Cousot (Ed.): SAS 2001, LNCS 2126, pp. 279–298, 2001.

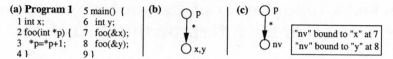

Fig. 1. Program 1 (a), non-parameterized (b) and parameterized (c) points-to graph.

can be passed into a procedure from a callsite, these algorithms use a symbolic name to identify the memory location within the procedure. If the pointer information computed for the procedure is used under different calling contexts, the symbolic name can be used to identify different memory locations. For example, symbolic name nv can be used to identify the memory locations whose addresses are passed into foo() (Figure 1(a)) through p. Under the context of statement 7, nv identifies x. Under the context of statement 8, nv identifies y. The symbolic names used by the algorithms act like reference parameters. Thus, we refer to such symbolic names as *auxiliary parameters*[1], and refer to pointer information containing auxiliary parameters as *parameterized* pointer information.

For supporting program analyses, parameterized pointer information has several advantages over non-parameterized pointer information. First, parameterized pointer information can be used by a program analysis to compute parameterized summary information for a procedure. Such parameterized summary information can be instantiated at a callsite to compute more accurate information about the callsite. For example, using parameterized pointer information, a program analysis reports that nv is modified by foo() (Figure 1). The program analysis then instantiates this information at statement 7 by replacing nv with x, and reports that x is modified by foo() at statement 7. In contrast, using non-parameterized pointer information, the program analysis reports that both x and y may be modified by foo(). The program analysis then uses this information at statement 7 and reports that x and y may be modified by foo() at statement 7. Second, parameterized pointer information for a procedure is more compact than non-parameterized pointer information: in the parameterized pointer information for a procedure, an auxiliary parameter can be used to represent a set of memory locations that require several names to identify in non-parameterized pointer information. Thus, a program analysis creates and propagates less information when using parameterized pointer information.

The major problem with acceptance of existing algorithms that compute parameterized pointer information is that they are not efficient for analyzing large programs. One reason for this inefficiency is that existing algorithms use a flow-sensitive approach, which may not scale to large programs [7, 14, 21]. A second reason for this inefficiency is that existing algorithms may analyze a procedure more than once [7, 21]. This additional analysis increases the expense of the algorithms. Another problem with acceptance of existing algorithms that compute parameterized pointer information is that none of these algorithms have been compared empirically with algorithms that compute non-parameterized pointer information. Thus, it is unknown how much improvement in precision

---

[1] Auxiliary parameters are similar to *symbolic names* [7] or *extended parameters* [21].

and performance can be gained by a program analysis that uses parameterized pointer information instead of non-parameterized pointer information.

This paper presents a modular parameterized pointer analysis algorithm (MoPPA) that efficiently computes points-to graphs for a program. MoPPA follows a three-phase flow-insensitive, context-sensitive pointer analysis framework. MoPPA uses, when possible, auxiliary parameters to identify memory locations whose addresses are passed into a procedure. MoPPA also distinguishes the memory locations that are dynamically allocated in a procedure when the procedure is invoked under different calling contexts.

Compared to other algorithms (e.g., [1, 6, 8, 15, 19]) that are intended to handle large programs, a major benefit of MoPPA is that it provides parameterized pointer information. Another benefit of MoPPA over these algorithms is that MoPPA can distinguish the memory locations dynamically allocated in a procedure under different calling contexts. Therefore, MoPPA may provide more precise pointer information than these algorithms. Compared to existing algorithms that compute parameterized pointer information, a major benefit of MoPPA is its efficiency. MoPPA processes each pointer assignment only once. By storing global pointer information in one global points-to graph, MoPPA propagates, from one procedure to another, only a small amount of information related to parameters. Therefore, MoPPA can efficiently compute the points-to graphs. Another benefit of MoPPA is its modularity—only the information for the procedures within a strongly connected component of the call graph must be in memory simultaneously. Thus, MoPPA may require less memory.

This paper also presents a set of empirical studies. These studies show that, on subjects of up to 100,000 lines of code,

- MoPPA runs in time close to that required by FICS; such time is close to that required by Steensgaard's [19], the most efficient flow-insensitive algorithm.
- Using information provided by MoPPA instead of that provided by FICS or Andersen's algorithm, (a) a program analysis computes on average 12% (maximum 37.9%) fewer flow dependences for a statement in a procedure; (b) a program analysis runs on average 10 (maximum 210 over FICS, maximum 445 over Andersen's) times faster, and computes on average 25% (maximum 57%) fewer transitive interprocedural flow dependences for a statement in a program; and (c) a program slicer runs on average 7 (maximum 72 over FICS, maximum 106 over Andersen's) times faster, and computes on average 12% (maximum 45%) smaller slices.

The studies show that (1) MoPPA is efficient and (2) using parameterized pointer information provided by MoPPA can significantly improve the precision and the efficiency of many program analyses.

The significance of this work is that it provides the first algorithm that efficiently (within one minute) computes parameterized pointer information for programs up to 100,000 lines of code. The work also presents, to the best of our knowledge, the first set of empirical studies that compare the results of program analyses computed using parameterized pointer information with that computed using non-parameterized pointer information. Our studies show that computing parameterized pointer information for large programs is feasible and beneficial.

2   Parameterized Points-to Graphs

This section discusses the points-to graphs constructed by MoPPA and the approach used by MoPPA to assign names to memory locations.

2.1   Points-to Graphs

MoPPA uses points-to graphs to represent pointer information. In a points-to graph, a node represents a set of memory locations whose names are associated with the node. A *field access* edge, labeled with a field name, connects a node representing structures to a node representing a field of the structures. A *points-to* edge, labeled with "*", represents points-to relations. For example, the edge in Figure 1(b) represents that p points to x or y. For efficiency, MoPPA imposes two constraints on a points-to graph: (1) a memory location can be represented by only one node; (2) labels are unique among the edges leaving a node.[2]

MoPPA computes two kinds of points-to graphs. For a program, MoPPA computes a *global* points-to graph that represents the pointer information related to global pointers. For each procedure in the program, MoPPA computes a *procedural* points-to graph that represents the pointer information related to the local pointers in the procedure. The separation of global pointer information from local pointer information lets MoPPA reduce the amount of information that it propagates across procedure boundaries. For example, suppose that at the beginning of main(), global pointer g is forced to point to x. By making this information available in the global points-to graph, MoPPA avoids propagating such information to procedures in which the computation of the pointer information in the procedures does not involve g. When analyzing a program, a program analysis resolves dereferences of global pointers using the global points-to graph.

2.2   Naming Memory Locations

MoPPA identifies memory locations in a procedure using three kinds of names: auxiliary parameter, local, and quasi-global. MoPPA uses an auxiliary parameter, when possible, to identify, in procedure P, a memory location whose address may be passed into P through formal parameters. An auxiliary parameter, as defined in the Introduction, can identify different memory locations under different calling contexts. To support program analyses, MoPPA also provides binding information that maps an auxiliary parameter in P to the names that identify the same memory locations at a callsite to P. For example, MoPPA uses auxiliary parameter nv to identify memory locations for x and y in the points-to graph (Figure 1(c)) for foo() (Figure 1(a)). MoPPA also provides information to map nv to x at statement 7 and to y at statement 8.

MoPPA uses a local name to identify a memory location that cannot be accessed after the procedure returns. A *local name* is a name whose scope includes only one procedure. For example, the memory location for a local variable in procedure P may be identified using a local name whose scope includes only P.

---

[2] Similar constraints are also used in Steensgaard's algorithm [19] and FICS [15].

MoPPA may use a quasi-global name to identify, in a procedure P, the memory location for a global variable or a memory location whose address can be passed into P through global pointers. A *quasi-global name* is a name whose scope may include several procedures, but may not include all procedures in a program. The scope of a quasi-global name ensures that, if a memory location *loc* is identified using a quasi-global name N in P, then *loc* is also identified using N in P's callers. Therefore, MoPPA need not propagate the pointer information for *loc* from P to its callers because such information is stored in the global points-to graph and can be retrieved, using the same name, when the information is needed in P's callers. At most one quasi-global name can be used to identify a memory location in different procedures throughout the program.

Using quasi-global names to improve efficiency is one of the features that distinguish MoPPA from Wilson and Lam's algorithm [21]. In their algorithm, all memory locations, including global variables and those that are accessed through global pointers, are identified using extended parameters (similar to auxiliary parameters) in each procedure. Preliminary studies show that many large programs may use a large number of global pointers. For such programs, propagating information for all global pointers from procedure to procedure may be prohibitively expensive. The studies also show that the values of global pointers do not change often in a program. Therefore, introducing symbolic names to represent the memory locations that are accessed through dereferences of global pointers in each procedure might be unnecessary.

MoPPA uses various rules to determine whether to use an auxiliary parameter, a local name, or a quasi-global name to identify global memory locations (global variables), stack-allocated memory locations (local variables), or heap-allocated memory locations in a procedure. For each global variable g accessed within a procedure P, MoPPA determines whether g is accessed only using its address that is passed into P through formal parameters. If this is the case, MoPPA uses an auxiliary parameter to identify g in P. For example, MoPPA uses auxiliary parameter nv to identify x in foo() in Figure 1(a). However, if g is accessed using its variable name or using an address that is passed into P through global pointers, then MoPPA uses g's variable name as the quasi-global name to identify g in P (e.g., x in main() in Figure 1(a)). This quasi-global name is also used to identify g in P's direct or indirect callers.

For a local variable l that is declared in P, if l cannot be accessed through dereferences of global pointers in the program, MoPPA uses l's variable name as a local name to identify l in P. In any other procedure where l may be accessed, MoPPA uses an auxiliary parameter to identify l. However, if l can be accessed through dereferences of global pointers in the program, MoPPA uses a quasi-global name to identify l in the procedures into which l's address may be passed through global pointers. MoPPA also identifies l using this quasi-global name in the callers to these procedures. In the procedures into which l's address is passed only through formal parameters or dereferences of formal parameters, MoPPA uses an auxiliary parameter to identify l.

Identifying local variables with quasi-global names might cause imprecision in the pointer analysis. A local variable l declared in procedure P can be accessed only in P or in the procedures that P may directly or indirectly call. However, if MoPPA uses a quasi-global name N to identify l in the program, then according to the way in which N's scope is determined, N may appear in procedures that P may never (directly or indirectly) call. Therefore, a program analysis may conclude that l may be accessed in these procedures and compute spurious information. This kind of imprecision can also be introduced by many other existing algorithms (e.g. [1, 8, 19]). One way to reduce such imprecision is to remove, from N's scope, the procedures that P may never (directly or indirectly) call. However, MoPPA does not include this optimization because preliminary studies show that few local variables may be pointed to by global pointers.

MoPPA attempts to distinguish the memory locations allocated on the heap in a procedure P under different calling contexts. Unlike algorithms (e.g., [5]) that distinguish these memory locations by extending their names with call strings, MoPPA makes such distinction only if the distinction may improve the precision of program analyses. Suppose that a statement s in P allocates memory location loc on the heap. If loc's address is not returned to P's callers, then loc can be accessed only within P. MoPPA identifies loc using an *auxiliary local name* whose scope includes only P. If loc's address may be returned to P's callers through the return value or dereferences of formal parameters, but not through global pointers or dereferences of global pointers, MoPPA uses an auxiliary parameter to identify loc in P. MoPPA also creates names, using similar rules, to identify loc in P's callers. Because different names may be created to identify the memory locations returned by P at different callsites, MoPPA can distinguish, in P's callers, the memory locations allocated at s under different calling contexts. However, if loc's address may be returned to P's callers through global pointers or dereferences of global pointers, MoPPA introduces a quasi-global name to identify loc in P and in all callers of P. Therefore, MoPPA does not distinguish memory locations allocated at s under different calling contexts.

For example, let loc be the memory location allocated at statement 14 in Figure 2(a). Because loc is returned to `alloc()`'s callers only through `*f`, MoPPA uses auxiliary parameter `nv2` to identify loc in $G_{\mathtt{alloc()}}$ (Figure 2(d)), the points-to graph for `alloc()`. When loc is returned to `getg()` at statement 10, MoPPA identifies loc using a quasi-global name `gh` because loc may be returned to `getg()`'s callers also through global pointer `g`. When loc is returned to `main()` at statement 3, MoPPA identifies loc using a local name `lh` because loc cannot be returned to `main()`'s callers. Compared to the points-to graphs (Figure 2(e)) constructed by FICS, MoPPA computes more precise pointer information.

In summary, to identify memory locations in the procedures with appropriate names, MoPPA first determines the scope of each quasi-global name N:

- **Rule 1.** If N is the variable name of a global variable and N syntactically appears in a procedure P, then N's scope includes P.
- **Rule 2.** If N identifies a memory location pointed to by another memory location identified by quasi-global name N_1 according to the global points-to graph, and N_1's scope includes P, then N's scope includes P.
- **Rule 3.** If N's scope includes a procedure P, then N's scope includes all the procedures that call P.

MoPPA then determines, for a memory location loc accessed in procedure P, whether there is a quasi-global name for loc whose scope includes P. If so, MoPPA uses this name to identify loc in P.

Otherwise, MoPPA determines whether loc can be accessed before P is invoked or after P returns. If that is the case, MoPPA uses an auxiliary parameter to identify loc in P. Otherwise, MoPPA uses a local name to identify loc in P.

3   Computation of Parameterized Points-to Graphs

This section introduces some definitions and gives an overview of MoPPA.

3.1   Definitions

Memory locations in a program are accessed through *object names*, each of which consists of a variable and a possibly empty sequence of dereferences and field accesses [14].

Object name N_1 is *extended* from object name N_2 if N_1 can be constructed by applying a possibly empty sequence of dereferences and field accesses ω to N_2; we denote N_1 as $\mathcal{E}_\omega\langle N_2\rangle$.

For example, if pointer p points to a **struct** with field a in a C program, then $\mathcal{E}_*\langle p\rangle$ is $*p$ and $\mathcal{E}_{*.a}\langle p\rangle$ is $(*p).a$.

Given an object name N of pointer type, the *points-to node* of N in a points-to graph G is the node
that represents the memory locations that may be pointed to by N. To find the points-to node for N in G, an algorithm first locates or creates, in G, a node n_0 that represents the variable in N. The algorithm then locates or creates a sequence of nodes n_i and edges e_i, $1 \leq i \leq k$, so that $n_0, e_1, n_1, ..., e_k, n_k$ is a path in G, the labels of $e_1, ..., e_{k-1}$ match the sequence of dereferences and field accesses in N, and e_k is a points-to edge. The points-to node of N is n_k.

3.2   Overview of MoPPA

MoPPA computes a global points-to graph G_{glob} for a program and a procedural points-to graph G_P for each procedure P. Let g be a global pointer. If a memory location loc may be pointed to by $\mathcal{E}_\omega\langle g\rangle$ at any point in the program, then a quasi-global name N identifying loc must be associated with the points-to node of $\mathcal{E}_\omega\langle g\rangle$ in G_{glob}. Let v be a local pointer declared in P. If a memory location loc may be pointed to by $\mathcal{E}_\omega\langle v\rangle$ at any point in P under any calling context, then a name N identifying loc must be associated with the points-to node of $\mathcal{E}_\omega\langle v\rangle$ in G_P. Given the points-to graphs, if a memory location loc is identified in P by an auxiliary parameter, then a program analysis can determine the calling contexts under which loc may be accessed by looking at the binding information at the callsite. However, if loc is identified in P by a quasi-global name, a program analysis must assume that loc may be accessed under each calling context.

In addition to the points-to graphs, MoPPA also computes the set of quasi-global names whose scopes may include P according to Rules 1–3 in Section 2. MoPPA uses this information to determine the appropriate name for identifying a memory location in P. To compute this information, MoPPA first collects the global variable names that syntactically appear in P or in procedures directly or indirectly called by P. According to Rules 1 and 3, the scopes of these names

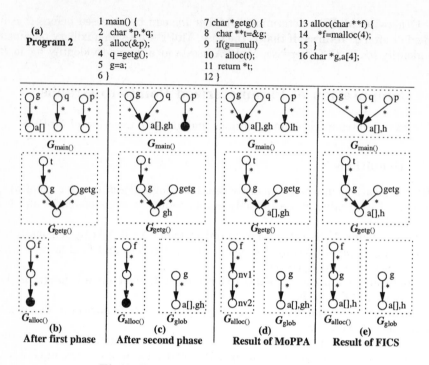

```
(a)              1 main() {            7 char *getg() {        13 alloc(char **f) {
Program 2        2 char *p,*q;         8  char **t=&g;        14  *f=malloc(4);
                 3 alloc(&p);          9  if(g==null)          15 }
                 4 q =getg();          10  alloc(t);           16 char *g,a[4];
                 5 g=a;                11 return *t;
                 6 }                   12 }
```

Fig. 2. Program 2 and its points-to graphs.

include P. MoPPA then searches, beginning at the nodes associated with the global variable names computed for P, for all reachable nodes in G_{glob}. According to Rule 2, the scopes of the names associated with these nodes include P.

MoPPA performs two major tasks in construction of the points-to graphs. The first task detects each pair of object names that may point to common memory locations. MoPPA merges the points-to nodes of these two object names in a points-to graph to ensure that each common memory location pointed to by these two object names is represented by only one node. This merging operation is a variant of the "join" in Steensgaard's algorithm [19]. The second task determines the memory locations represented by each node in the points-to graphs. MoPPA picks appropriate names to identify these memory locations at the node. MoPPA computes the points-to graphs in three phases (Figure 3).

First Phase (Lines 1-8). In the first phase, MoPPA processes each pointer assignment $lhs = rhs$ in each procedure P to build G_P.[3] If rhs is an object name, then MoPPA merges the points-to nodes of lhs and rhs in G_P to capture the fact that lhs and rhs point to the same memory location after this assignment (line 3). If rhs is an address-taking expression "&x", then MoPPA adds variable name x to the points-to node of lhs in G_P to indicate that lhs points to x after the assignment (line 4). If rhs calls a memory allocation function, MoPPA sets

---

[3] MoPPA represents the return value of each function with a variable and treats return statements as assignments (e.g., statement 11 in Figure 2(a) is treated as getg=*t).

a boolean flag HasHeap at the points-to node of *lhs* in G_P (line 5). HasHeap of a node indicates that the node represents a heap-allocated memory location whose name has not yet been determined by MoPPA. In various phases of MoPPA, when two nodes N_1 and N_2 are merged, if HasHeap of N_1 or N_2 is set, then HasHeap of the resulting node is set. Figure 2(b) shows the points-to graphs constructed by MoPPA during this phase for Program 2 in Figure 2(a). Solid nodes in the graphs indicate that HasHeap of these nodes are set.

Second Phase (Lines 9-26). In the second phase, MoPPA processes the callsites in each procedure P to consider the effects, on G_P, of the procedures called by P. Let c be a callsite that calls Q in P. MoPPA first calls BindFromCallee() to search in G_Q for object names $\mathcal{E}_{\omega 1}\langle p \rangle$ and $\mathcal{E}_{\omega 2}\langle q \rangle$ that point to the same node. If p and q are formal parameters bound to a_1 and a_2 respectively at c, then after c is executed, $\mathcal{E}_{\omega 1}\langle a_1 \rangle$ and $\mathcal{E}_{\omega 2}\langle a_2 \rangle$ may point to the same memory location. Thus, BindFromCallee() merges the points-to nodes of $\mathcal{E}_{\omega 1}\langle a_1 \rangle$ and $\mathcal{E}_{\omega 2}\langle a_2 \rangle$ in G_P. If p is a formal parameter bound to a at c and q is a global pointer, then after c is executed, $\mathcal{E}_{\omega 1}\langle a \rangle$ and $\mathcal{E}_{\omega 2}\langle q \rangle$ may point to the same memory location. Thus, BindFromCallee() merges the points-to nodes of $\mathcal{E}_{\omega 1}\langle a \rangle$ and $\mathcal{E}_{\omega 2}\langle q \rangle$ in G_P. For example, when MoPPA processes statement 4 in Figure 2(a), it merges the points-to nodes of q and g in $G_{\text{main}()}$ because getg and g point to the same node in $G_{\text{getg}()}$ (return value getg is treated as a formal parameter in this phase).

MoPPA also determines the memory locations whose addresses may be returned to P at c (lines 14–17). If G_Q shows that a name x is associated with the points-to node of $\mathcal{E}_\omega \langle f \rangle$, in which f is a formal parameter bound to a at c, then, after c is executed, $\mathcal{E}_\omega \langle a \rangle$ may point to x. MoPPA adds x to the points-to node of $\mathcal{E}_\omega \langle a \rangle$ in G_P (line 15). If HasHeap of the points-to node of $\mathcal{E}_\omega \langle f \rangle$ is set, then after c is executed, $\mathcal{E}_\omega \langle a \rangle$ may point to a heap-allocated memory location. Thus, MoPPA sets HasHeap of the points-to node of $\mathcal{E}_\omega \langle a \rangle$ (line 16). For example, when MoPPA processes statement 3 in Figure 2(a), it sets HasHeap of p's points-to node in $G_{\text{main}()}$ because HasHeap of *f's points-to node is set in $G_{\text{alloc}()}$.

In the second phase, MoPPA also constructs the global points-to graph G_{glob} using information in G_P (lines 19–23). MoPPA first calls BindToGlobal() to search in G_P for object names $\mathcal{E}_{\omega 1}\langle g_1 \rangle$ and $\mathcal{E}_{\omega 2}\langle g_2 \rangle$, where g_1 and g_2 are global variables, that point to the same node. BindToGlobal() merges the points-to nodes of $\mathcal{E}_{\omega 1}\langle g_1 \rangle$ and $\mathcal{E}_{\omega 2}\langle g_2 \rangle$ in G_{glob}. MoPPA then determines the memory locations that may be pointed to by object names extended from global pointers (lines 20–23). Let g be a global pointer. If G_P shows that HasHeap of the points-to node of $\mathcal{E}_\omega \langle g \rangle$ is set, then MoPPA creates a new quasi-global name to identify the heap-allocated memory location associated with this node. MoPPA resets HasHeap and adds the new name to the points-to node of $\mathcal{E}_\omega \langle g \rangle$ in G_P (line 21). For example, when MoPPA processes getg() in Figure 2(a) in the second phase, it finds that HasHeap of the points-to node of g is set. Thus, the algorithm creates a name gh, resets HasHeap, and adds gh to the points-to node of g in $G_{\text{getg}()}$. MoPPA also propagates names associated with the points-to node of $\mathcal{E}_\omega \langle g \rangle$ in G_P to the the points-to node of $\mathcal{E}_\omega \langle g \rangle$ in G_{glob}.

In the second phase, MoPPA further computes $GVars[P]$, the set of global variable names that appear syntactically in P or in P's callee (line 26). In this phase, MoPPA processes the procedures in a reverse topological (bottom-up)

Algorithm MoPPA
input $\mathcal{P}$: the program to be analyzed
output   a set of points-to graphs
declare $GVars[P]$: global variable names collected for P
function $\mathcal{A}_c(f)$: return the actual parameter bound to f at c
               $globals(G)$: return the global variable names in G
  begin MoPPA
  1. **foreach** pointer assignment $lhs = rhs$ in each procedure P **do**
  2.   **case** rhs **do**
  3.   object name: merge points-to nodes of lhs and rhs in G_P
  4.   "&x": add x to the points-to node of lhs in G_P
  5.   malloc(): set HasHeap of the points-to node of lhs in G_P
  6.   **endcase**
  7. **endfor**
  8. add global variable names in each procedure P to $GVars[P]$
  9. add all procedures in $\mathcal{P}$ to worklists W_1 and W_2
  10. **while** $W_1 \neq \phi$ **do** /* W_1: sorted in reversed topological order*/
  11.   remove P from the head of W_1
  12.   **foreach** callsite c to Q in P **do**
  13.   BindFromCallee(G_Q,globals(G_Q),G_P,c)
  14.   **foreach** points-to node N of $\mathcal{E}_\omega\langle f\rangle$ in G_Q where f is a formal parameter **do**
  15.   copy names from N to $\mathcal{E}_\omega\langle\mathcal{A}_c(f)\rangle$'s points-to node in G_P
  16.   **if** HasHeap of N is set **then** set HasHeap of $\mathcal{E}_\omega\langle\mathcal{A}_c(f)\rangle$'s points-to node in G_P
  17.   **endfor**
  18.   **endfor**
  19.   BindToGlobal(G_P,globals(G_P),G_{glob})
  20.   **foreach** points-to node N of $\mathcal{E}_\omega\langle g\rangle$ in G_P, g is global **do**
  21.   **if** HasHeap of N is set **then** reset HasHeap of N and add a new name to N
  22.   copy names from N to the points-to node of $\mathcal{E}_\omega\langle g\rangle$ in G_{glob}
  23.   **endfor**
  24.   **if** G_P is updated **then** add P's callers to W_1
  25. **endwhile**
  26. compute $GVars[P]$ for each procedure P using information from P's callees
  27. **foreach** procedure P **do**
  28.   compute the quasi-global names whose scopes include P
  29. **while** $W_2 \neq \phi$ **do**   /* W_2: sorted in topological order */
  30.   remove P from the head of W_2
  31.   **foreach** callsite c to P in P' **do**
  32.   BindFromCaller($G_{P'}$,c,G_P)
  33.   **foreach** name n at the node of $\mathcal{E}_\omega\langle a\rangle$ in $G_{P'}$ and a is an actual bound to f at c **do**
  34.   **if** n is quasi-global name whose scope includes P **then**
  35.   add n to $\mathcal{E}_\omega\langle f\rangle$'s points-to node in G_P
  36.   **elseif** no auxil parameter at $\mathcal{E}_\omega\langle f\rangle$'s node in G_P **and** no auxil parameter to reuse **then**
  37.   create an auxil parameter at $\mathcal{E}_\omega\langle f\rangle$'s points-to node in G_P
  38.   **endif**
  39.   **endfor**
  40.   **endfor**
  41.   BindFromGlobal(G_{glob},globals(G_P),G_P)
  42.   **foreach** name n at $\mathcal{E}_\omega\langle g\rangle$'s node in G_{glob} where g is a global pointer appeared in G_P **do**
  43.   add n to $\mathcal{E}_\omega\langle g\rangle$'s points-to node in G_P
  44.   **foreach** node N whose HasHeap is set in G_P **do**
  45.   reset HasHeap
  46.   **if** no auxiliary parameter associated with N **then** add a new local name to N
  47.   **endfor**
  48.   **if** G_P is updated **then** add P's callees to W_2
  49. **endwhile**
  50. **foreach** callsite c in $\mathcal{P}$ **do** compute binding information at c
  end MoPPA

Fig. 3. MoPPA algorithm.

order on the strongly-connected components of the call graph using a worklist. Figure 2(c) shows the points-to graphs for Program 2 after this phase.

Third Phase (Lines 27–50). In the third phase, MoPPA processes each procedure P to assign appropriate names to identify the memory locations represented by each node in G_P. MoPPA completes this task in four steps. First, MoPPA computes, by using G_{glob} and $GVars[P]$, the set of quasi-global names whose scopes include P (lines 27–28).

Second, MoPPA processes each callsite c that calls P to capture the pointer information introduced by parameter bindings. Let P' be the procedure that contains c. MoPPA first calls BindFromCaller() to search for object names $\mathcal{E}_{\omega 1}\langle a_1 \rangle$ and $\mathcal{E}_{\omega 2}\langle a_2 \rangle$, in which a_1 and a_2 are bound to f_1 and f_2 respectively at c, that point to the same node in $G_{P'}$ (line 32). MoPPA merges the points-to nodes of $\mathcal{E}_{\omega 1}\langle f_1 \rangle$ and $\mathcal{E}_{\omega 2}\langle f_2 \rangle$ in G_P. MoPPA also determines the memory locations that may be pointed to by object names extended from formal parameters (lines 33–39). Let a be an actual parameter that is bound to formal parameter f at c, and n be a name identifying memory location loc in $G_{P'}$. If n is associated with the points-to node of $\mathcal{E}_{\omega}\langle a \rangle$ in $G_{P'}$, then when P is invoked at c, $\mathcal{E}_{\omega}\langle f \rangle$ may point to loc at P's entry. If n is a quasi-global name whose scope includes P, then loc must be identified by n in P. Thus, MoPPA adds n to the points-to node of $\mathcal{E}_{\omega}\langle f \rangle$ in G_P. Otherwise, n is not a quasi-global name or n is a quasi-global name but n's scope does not include P. In this case, loc is identified in P with an auxiliary parameter. MoPPA checks to see whether there is an auxiliary parameter associated with the points-to node of $\mathcal{E}_{\omega}\langle f \rangle$ in G_P. If no auxiliary parameter exists, then MoPPA further checks the k-limiting restriction using the approach described in Subsection 3.4. If MoPPA cannot reuse an existing auxiliary parameter, it creates a new auxiliary parameter and adds this auxiliary parameter to this node. For example, when MoPPA processes statement 10 in Figure 2(a), it finds that actual parameter t may point to g. Because the scope of the quasi-global name for g does not include alloc(), MoPPA introduces auxiliary parameter nv1 to identify this memory location and adds nv1 to the points-to node of f in $G_{\text{alloc}()}$. Note that in the third phase, if two nodes N_1 and N_2 are merged, at most one auxiliary parameter is kept in the resulting node.

Third, MoPPA further determines, by examining G_{glob}, the memory locations that may be represented by nodes in G_P (lines 41–43). Let g_1 and g_2 be global variable names that appear in G_P (i.e., $g_1, g_2 \in$ globals(G_P)). MoPPA calls BindFromGlobal() to search, in G_{glob}, for object names $\mathcal{E}_{\omega 1}\langle g_1 \rangle$ and $\mathcal{E}_{\omega 1}\langle g_1 \rangle$ that point to the same node. BindFromGlobal() merges the points-to nodes of $\mathcal{E}_{\omega 1}\langle g_1 \rangle$ and $\mathcal{E}_{\omega 1}\langle g_1 \rangle$ in G_P. Let g be a global variable name that appears in G_P. If G_{glob} shows that name n is associated with the points-to node of $\mathcal{E}_{\omega}\langle g \rangle$, then MoPPA adds n to the points-to node of $\mathcal{E}_{\omega}\langle g \rangle$ in G_P.

Fourth, MoPPA assigns names for the unnamed heap-allocated memory locations represented by nodes in G_P (lines 44–47). MoPPA examines, in G_P, each node N whose HasHeap is set. If an auxiliary parameter aux is associated with N, then N is pointed to by an object name extended from formal parameters. Therefore, the heap-allocated memory locations associated with N may be returned to P's callers. MoPPA reuses aux to identify these memory locations. However, if no auxiliary parameter is associated with N, then these heap-allocated memory locations are not returned to P's callers. MoPPA creates a new local name to identify these memory locations and adds this name to N. In both cases, MoPPA resets HasHeap of N. For example, MoPPA discovers that, in $G_{\text{alloc}()}$, the points-to graph for alloc() in Figure 2(a), HasHeap of the points-to node of *f is set and an auxiliary parameter nv2 is associated with this node. Therefore, it reuses nv2 to identify the heap-allocated memory

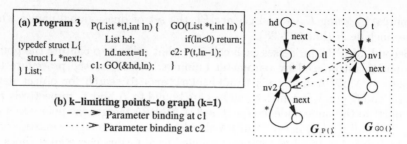

(a) Program 3

```
typedef struct L{
    struct L *next;
} List;
```

```
P(List *tl,int ln) {
    List hd;
    hd.next=tl;
c1: GO(&hd,ln);
}
```

```
GO(List *t,int ln) {
    if(ln<0) return;
c2: P(t,ln−1);
}
```

(b) k–limitting points–to graph (k=1)
- - - ▶ Parameter binding at c1
······▶ Parameter binding at c2

Fig. 4. Example program 3 (a) and its k-limiting points-to graphs (b).

locations represented by this node. In another case, MoPPA discovers that, in $G_{\mathtt{main}()}$, HasHeap of the points-to node of p is set but no auxiliary parameter is associated with this node. Therefore, it creates a local name lh to identify the heap-allocated memory locations represented by this node (Figure 2(d)).

In the third phase, MoPPA processes the procedures in a topological (top-down) order on the strongly-connected components of the call graph using a worklist. After all the points-to graphs stabilize, MoPPA processes each callsite c to compute the binding information between the names in the procedure containing c and the auxiliary parameters in the called procedure (line 50). This step can be done on-demand when the pointer information is used.

Figure 2(d) shows the points-to graphs that MoPPA computes for Program 2. Compared to the points-to graphs (Figure 2(e)) constructed by FICS for this program, MoPPA computes more compact and more precise pointer information.

3.3   Complexity of MoPPA

Let p be the number of procedures in a program $\mathcal{P}$, c be the number of callsites in $\mathcal{P}$, and S be the worst-case actual size of a procedural points-to graph. Without considering the cost of line 8 and lines 26–28, the time complexity of MoPPA is the same as that of FICS, which is $O(N*S*\alpha(N*S,p*S))$ [15], given that α is the inverse Ackermann function, N is $(c+p)$ in the absence of recursion and $(c+p)*S$ in the presence of recursion. The steps taken at lines 8 and 26 are similar to those taken in the modification side-effect analysis. Thus, the time required by these two lines is $O(n^2)$. Line 28 can be done by first mapping the names in $GVars[P]$ to the nodes in G_{glob}, and then searching in G_{glob} beginning at these nodes. Thus, the time required by line 28 is $O(n + S_{glob})$, where S_{glob} is the size G_{glob}. The time complexity of MoPPA is $O(p*(n+S_{glob})+n^2+N*S*\alpha(N*S,p*S))$.

3.4   Handling Recursive Data Structures and Indirect Calls

MoPPA uses a variant of *k-limiting* [13] to handle recursive data structures. The variant limits the number of consecutive *suspicious* nodes—nodes associated with only auxiliary parameters — on a simple path[4] to k (field nodes are not counted). The restriction is checked only when MoPPA processes a recursive

---

[4] A *simple* path does not contain two identical nodes.

call. For example, when MoPPA binds nv2 to G0() at callsite c1 in P() (Figure 4(a)), it attempts to add a new auxiliary parameter in $G_{G0()}$, which would create a simple path with two consecutive suspicious nodes. Thus, when k is 1, MoPPA reuses nv1 and binds nv2 to nv1. Figure 4(b) shows the resulting points-to graphs. Note that because nv2 is supposed to be bound to the memory locations pointed to by nv1.next, in the graph, MoPPA creates a new edge from the node representing nv1.next to the node representing nv1.

MoPPA can use one of the following two solutions to handle programs that contain indirect calls through function pointers. The first solution uses the call graph computed by another algorithm, such as Steensgaard's algorithm. The second solution begins the analysis with a partial call graph, and computes the complete call graph during the analysis. This approach requires iterations between the bottom-up phase and the top-down phase [4], and thus, increases the complexity of MoPPA. To use the second approach, MoPPA keeps an extra *shadow* points-to graph $\widehat{G}_P$ for each procedure P to separate the summary information about P from the pointer information computed for P.[5] In the first phase, MoPPA puts the pointer information into both $\widehat{G}_P$ and G_P. In the second phase, MoPPA uses $\widehat{G}_P$ to update both $\widehat{G}_Q$ and G_Q if P is called by Q, and uses $\widehat{G}_P$ to update G_{glob}. In the third phase, MoPPA uses only the normal points-to graphs for the procedures. At the end of the third phase, MoPPA first examines each indirect call. If MoPPA discovers new callees, it expands the call graph and repeats the second and third phases starting only from the affected procedures. Otherwise, the algorithm computes the binding information and terminates.

4   Empirical Studies

We implemented a prototype of MoPPA using the PROLANGS Analysis Framework (PAF) [10]. Our prototype resolves function pointers using Steensgaard's algorithm. The prototype is parameterized to treat a structure as either an atomic memory location or a collection of fields. In the latter case, the prototype does not account for accesses that require knowledge of the physical layout of a structure. This limitation may affect the safety of the pointer information. However, it should not significantly affect the validity of our studies because (1) this kind of access is rare in programs, and (2) all the algorithms that we compare are implemented in the same way. More sophisticated techniques will be used to handle such accesses in our future work.

We have performed several empirical studies to evaluate the performance of MoPPA and the effectiveness of using the parameterized pointer information provided by MoPPA in program analyses. We compared MoPPA with FICS and Andersen's algorithm. Other studies (e.g., [6, 12, 15, 9]) show that pointer information computed by these two algorithms is very close in precision to many other existing algorithms, including flow-sensitive algorithms. In addition, MoPPA is implemented using the same framework as FICS. Thus, comparison between

---

[5] $\widehat{G}_P$ may be eliminated if MoPPA can determine the procedures that are directly or indirectly called by P.

program	Subject Size			Time(s)	
	LOC	Nodes	Procs	T_M	T_F
dixie	2100	1357	52	0.30	0.19
assem	2510	1993	58	0.67	0.44
smail	3212	2430	59	0.43	0.30
lharc	3235	2539	89	0.51	0.25
simulate	3558	2992	114	0.50	0.27
flex	6902	3762	93	0.89	0.32
rolo	4748	3874	142	0.90	0.54
space	11474	5601	137	1.75	1.36
spim	24322	11352	263	3.43	2.49
mpgplay	17263	11864	135	3.68	2.36
espresso	12864	15351	306	6.01	4.61
moria	25002	20316	482	7.70	3.34
twmc	23922	22167	247	3.92	4.24
nethack	32119	31703	701	48.2	132
povray3†	101033	47254	1216	24.1	8.52

Table 1. Left: Sizes of the subject programs. Right: Time in seconds for MoPPA (T_M) and FICS (T_F).

program	# of heap		# of dependences		
	Mo	FI	Mo	FI	Reduc
dixie	10	7	5.10	6.19	17.7%
assem	17	15	2.68	3.62	25.8%
smail	12	7	2.60	3.20	19.0%
lharc	3	3	2.47	2.52	2.0%
simulate	3	3	2.49	2.58	3.4%
flex	39	7	5.85	6.57	11.0%
rolo	27	10	3.96	4.41	10.3%
space	11	11	2.83	3.03	6.5%
spim	131	17	26.6‡	42.8‡	37.9%
mpgplay	64	58	6.94	6.97	0.4%
espresso	238	111	4.10	4.31	4.8%
moria	1	1	9.17	11.66	21.3%
twmc	144	113	4.26	4.51	5.6%
nethack	17	2	5.00	5.40	7.3%
povray3	147	81	10.01	12.12	17.4%

Table 2. Left: Number of distinguishable names for heap-allocated locations. Right: Average number of flow dependences for a statement.

† Structures in `povray3` are treated as atomtic memory locations.

‡ `spim` contains two large procedures with over 1000 nodes. Without considering these two procedures, the result for MoPPA is 2.83, and the result for FICS is 2.95.

MoPPA and FICS can reveal the extra cost required to perform the sophisticated naming scheme used to obtain parameterized pointer information.

We collected the data for the studies on a Sun Ultra 30 workstation with 640MB of physical memory. Structures in programs other than `povray3` are treated as collections of fields. However, structures in `povray3` are treated as atomic memory locations because our system exhausts available memory otherwise.[6] To capture the pointer information introduced by calls to library functions, the prototype used a set of stubs to simulate these functions.[7]

The left side of Table 1 shows our subject programs. For each program, column *LOC* shows the lines of code (comments included), column *Nodes* shows the number of control flow graph nodes, and column *Procs* shows the number of procedures. These subjects have also been used in other studies [14, 15, 17].

4.1   Study 1

The goal of this study is to evaluate the performance of MoPPA. To investigate the time efficiency of MoPPA, we compared the time to run MoPPA and the time to run FICS on each subject. The right side (T_M, T_F) of Table 1 shows

---

[6] Other studies (e.g., [6, 8, 9]) that report results on large programs also treat structures as atomic memory locations.

[7] Similar stubs have been used in other studies (e.g. [14, 15]).

the comparison. The time shown in the table excludes time to parse and to resolve function pointers for each subject. The table shows that, for our subjects, although MoPPA can be three times slower than FICS, it is still very efficient. This result suggests that MoPPA will scale to large programs as well as FICS. Note that MoPPA is faster than FICS on `twmc` and `nethack` because MoPPA propagates less information from procedure to procedure.

In the study, we also investigated the effectiveness of MoPPA in distinguishing memory locations allocated on the heap by a procedure under different calling contexts. The left side of Table 2 compares the number of distinguishable names for heap-allocated memory locations used by MoPPA(Mo) or by FICS(FI). Two names are distinguishable in a program if, according to the pointer information, the memory locations identified by the names are accessed at different sets of statements. A program analysis may compute more precise information when it uses pointer information consisting of more distinguishable names for heap-allocated memory locations. In FICS, we considered the artificial names that represent heap-allocated memory locations. In MoPPA, we considers the quasi-global names and local names that are created for heap-allocated memory locations. The table shows that, for several programs (e.g. `spim`), MoPPA identifies many more distinguishable names for heap-allocated memory locations than FICS. Thus, a program analysis may compute more precise information when using pointer information provided by MoPPA.

4.2   Study 2

The goal of this study is to evaluate the impact of using pointer information provided by MoPPA and FICS on the computation of flow dependence—one variety of data dependence—within a procedure. A statement s_1 is *flow-dependent* on a statement s_2 if s_1 may use the value set by s_2. Flow dependence can be used in important tasks such as program optimization and data-flow testing.

In this study, we computed the average number of statements on which a statement is flow-dependent. For each callsite, we used its side-effects to compute flow dependences. The right side of table 2 shows the results of this study when the pointer information is provided by MoPPA (Mo) or FICS (FI), and the percentage of spurious flow dependences ($Reduc$) that can be eliminated by using information provided by MoPPA. The table shows that, for several programs (e.g., `moria`), using pointer information provided by MoPPA can significantly ($> 10\%$) reduce the spurious flow dependences, and thus, may significantly improve the precision of program analyses that require data-flow information. Note that, for other programs (e.g., `lharc`) on which the reduction is less significant, using pointer information provided by MoPPA may still improve the precision of program analyses because the spurious information propagated across procedure boundaries may be reduced.

4.3   Study 3

The goal of this study is to evaluate the impact of using pointer information provided by MoPPA or FICS on the precision and the efficiency of program analyses that require transitive interprocedural flow dependence. The study consists of

	Size			Time(s)	
program	Mo	FI	Reduc	Mo	FI
dixie	94.3	139.4	32.3%	0.3	3.2
assem	121.2	174.5	30.6%	0.6	11.7
smail	52.7	123.3	57.3%	0.2	42.1
lharc	64.6	113.7	43.2%	0.3	1.6
simulate	264.4	317.6	16.8%	0.4	2.4
flex	138.0	223.9	38.4%	2.1	4.4
rolo	68.2	95.6	28.6%	0.5	3.1
space†	207	293	29.3%	0.6	71.6
spim†	2107	2269	7.1%	743	22k‡
mpgplay†	2054	2170	5.3%	19.4	23.8
espresso†	2888	3321	13.0%	35.9	6209
moria†	3146	★	–	621	★
twmc†	1152	2387	51.7%	11.4	598
nethack†	2628	★	–	1146	★

	Size			Time(s)	
program	Mo	FI	Reduc	Mo	FI
dixie	612.4	653.3	6.3%	4.2	20.3
assem	640.6	753.0	14.9%	6.0	79.1
smail	675.5	824.7	18.1%	5.6	205
lharc	560.5	697.6	19.6%	6.7	47.4
simulate	1172	1176	0.3%	5.1	18.6
flex†	602	1088	44.6%	16.9	22.9
rolo†	1131	1283	11.8%	19.7	97.4
space†	2249	2504	10.2%	9.5	540
spim†	3434	★	–	3459	★
mpgplay†	3950	4140	4.6%	91.3	127
espresso†	5125	5744	10.8%	187	14k
moria†	★	★	–	★	★
twmc†	12884	12897	0.1%	851	19k
nethack†	★	★	–	★	★

Table 3. Left: Average size of a data slice, Right: Average time in seconds to compute a data slice.

Table 4. Left: Average size of a program slice, Right: Average time in seconds to compute a program slice.

† Data are collected on one slice.

‡ $1k = 1,000$.

★ Data are unavailable: the system does not terminate within the time limit (10 hrs.) or runs out of memory. Data for povray3 are unavailable for the same reason.

two parts. The first part considers the impact on the computation of transitive interprocedural flow dependence. We measured the average number of statements that can transitively affect a specific statement s through flow dependence. For convenience, we refer to this set of statements as the *data slice* with respect to s. We also measured the average time to compute a data slice. These measurements serve as an indicator of the impact of using such pointer information on program analyses that require transitive interprocedural flow dependence.

Table 3 shows these two measurements when the pointer information is provided by MoPPA (Mo) and FICS (FI). The table also shows the reduction in the size of a data slice ($Reduc$) when the pointer information is provided by MoPPA. We obtained the data by running a modified version of our reuse-driven slicer [16]. The table shows that, for many programs we studied (e.g., smail), using pointer information provided by MoPPA can significantly improve the precision and the efficiency of the computation of transitive flow dependence.

The second part of the study considers the impact of using pointer information provided by MoPPA and FICS on program slicing [20], a program analysis that requires transitive flow dependences. We measured the average size of a program slice and the average time to compute such a slice. We obtained the data by running our reuse-driven program slicer on each subject. Table 4 shows the results when the pointer information is provided by MoPPA (Mo) and FICS (FI). The table also shows the reduction in the size of a program slice ($Reduc$) when the pointer information is provided by MoPPA. The results indicate that, for

program	(I) Dependence Size			(II) Data slice† Size			(II) Data slice† Time(s)		(III) Program slice† Size			(III) Program slice† Time(s)	
	Mo	And	Reduc	Mo	And	Reduc	Mo	And	Mo	And	Reduc	Mo	And
space	2.83	3.03	6.5%	207	296	30.1%	0.6	78.8	2249	2504	10.2%	9.5	620
spim	26.6	38.5	31%	2107	2371	11.1%	743	1849	3434	3704	7.3%	3459	5094
mpgplay	6.94	6.96	0.2%	2054	2170	5.3%	19.4	23.6	3950	4120	4.1%	91.3	115
espresso	4.10	4.50	8.9%	2888	3374	14.4%	35.9	16k‡	5125	5732	10.6%	187	20k
moria	9.17	11.6	21%	3146	⋆	–	621	⋆	⋆	⋆	–	⋆	⋆
twmc	4.26	4.49	5.3%	1152	2385	51.7%	11.4	901	12884	12893	0.1%	851	20k
nethack	5.0	5.33	6.1%	2628	⋆	–	1146	⋆	⋆	⋆	–	⋆	⋆

Table 5. Comparing MoPPA (*Mo*) and Andersen's algorithm (*And*): (I) Average number of flow dependences; (II) Size of a data slice and time in seconds to compute such slice; (III) Size of a program slice and time in seconds to compute such slice.

---

†Data are reported for one slice.
‡1*k* = 1,000.
⋆ Data are unavailable: the system does not terminate within the time limit (10 hours) or runs out of memory. Data for **povray3** are unavailable for the same reason.

many our subjects (e.g., `smail`), using pointer information provided by MoPPA can significantly improve the precision and efficiency of program slicing.

By considering the results of both parts of the study, we can conclude that using parameterized pointer information provided by MoPPA may significantly improve the precision and efficiency of many program analyses.

4.4 Study 4

The goal of this study is to compare MoPPA with Andersen's algorithm [1] for supporting program analyses. We repeated Studies 2 and 3 on these two algorithms. Table 5 shows the results. Due to space limitations, we show only programs over 10,000 lines of code. The results closely resemble those presented in Studies 2 and 3. For example, for `space`, when information provided by MoPPA is used, Table 5 shows that a slicer runs 65 times faster and computes 10% smaller slices than using that provided by Andersen's algorithm, whereas Table 4 shows that a slicer runs 56 times faster and computes 10% smaller slices than using that provided by FICS. This similarity is not surprising because other studies [15, 16] show that the information computed by FICS is almost the same as that computed by Andersen's algorithm. The results strengthen our conclusion that using parameterized pointer information provided by MoPPA may significantly improve the precision and efficiency of program analyses.

5   Related Work

Beginning with FICS [15], several flow-insensitive, context-sensitive algorithms [8, 9] that compute one solution for each procedure have been developed. MoPPA extends one of these algorithms by parameterizing the pointer information for each procedure. Similar approaches can be used to extend other algorithms.

Emami et al.'s algorithm [7] and Wilson and Lam's algorithm [21] also compute parameterized pointer information. Emami et al.'s algorithm analyzes a procedure under each specific calling context. The algorithm uses symbolic names to represent local variables that are indirectly accessed but not visible in current procedure. The symbolic names let the algorithm reuse the pointer information computed for a procedure under several calling contexts if the alias configuration for inputs are the same under these calling contexts. Wilson and Lam's algorithm further develops this idea. To increase the opportunity for reuse, the algorithm uses extended parameters to represent global variables and memory locations that can be accessed through dereferences of formal parameters and global pointers in a procedure. In both algorithms, when the alias configuration for inputs of a procedure changes, the procedure must be reanalyzed. MoPPA differs from these two algorithms in that MoPPA analyzes a procedure independently of its calling contexts. Thus, the summary information computed for a procedure can be used for all its calling contexts. The maximum reuse, its flow-insensitivity, and the separation of global information from local information contribute to the efficiency and the scalability of MoPPA.

Other pointer analysis algorithms (e.g., [3, 14]) also use symbolic names to represent memory locations whose addresses are passed into a procedure from calling contexts. However, in these algorithms, because the symbolic names are created before the pointer information at the callsites is computed, two symbolic names may represent the same memory location under a calling context. In the final pointer solution, the symbolic names must be replaced with concrete values. Therefore, these algorithms do not provide parameterized pointer information.

Several other existing pointer analysis algorithms use a modular approach for computing pointer information. One such algorithm is Chatterjee, Ryder, and Landi's *Relevant Context Inference* (RCI) [3]. MoPPA and RCI differ in that, (1) RCI computes non-parameterized pointer information, and (2) RCI computes pointer information using a flow-sensitive approach, and thus, may not scale to large programs. Another modular pointer analysis algorithm is Cheng and Hwu's flow-sensitive algorithm [4], which uses access paths[8] to identify a memory location. One way that MoPPA differs from Cheng and Hwu's algorithm is efficiency. Cheng and Hwu's algorithm must propagate global pointer information from procedure to procedure, and must iterate over pointer assignments and points-to relations using an approach similar to Andersen' algorithm [1]. In contrast, MoPPA reduces the information propagated across procedure boundaries by capturing the global pointer information in a global graph. MoPPA also avoids iteration over pointer assignments and points-to relations by merging points-to nodes using an approach similar to Steensgaard's algorithm [19]. Another way that MoPPA differs from Cheng and Hwu's algorithm is its support for interprocedural program analyses. Access paths used in Cheng and Hwu's algorithm can also identify different memory locations in a procedure under different calling contexts. However, because one memory location may be identified by several access paths, a program analysis using this pointer information may

---

[8] An *access path* is similar to an object name defined in this paper.

propagate more information across procedure boundaries than using the information provided by MoPPA. In addition, mapping an access path from a called procedure to a calling procedure is more expensive than mapping an auxiliary parameter.

Many flow-insensitive algorithms can be described as building points-to graphs or as generating and solving a set of constraints. Both approaches have advantages and disadvantages. Foster, Fahndrich, and Aiken proposed a *polymorphic* flow-insensitive points-to analysis framework that computes pointer information by solving constraints [9]. When the framework uses term constraints, the resulting algorithm is an variant of FICS. The framework differs from MoPPA in that it computes non-parameterized pointer information. Studies show that their current implementation of the framework may not scale to large programs [9].

Some existing pointer analysis algorithms [3, 14] provide *conditional pointer information*, in which a points-to relation may be associated with a condition that specifies the calling contexts under which this relation may hold. Although such conditions may help a program analysis reduce the amount of spurious information propagated across procedure boundaries [17], adding conditions to the points-to relations may increase the complexity of the pointer analysis. Studies show that these algorithms may not scale to large programs [3, 14].

6   Conclusion

This paper presents MoPPA, a modular algorithm that computes parameterized pointer information for C. The paper also presents studies that compare MoPPA with FICS and Andersen's algorithm. The studies show that MoPPA is efficient and that using parameterized pointer information provided by MoPPA can significantly improve the precision and efficiency of program analyses.

Due to space limitations, this paper does not present the details of handling memory accesses using constucts such as `casting` that require knowledge of the physical layout of a structure. Several existing approaches (e.g., [22]) can be incorporated into MoPPA to handle such accesses. Our future work will include investigation of the impact of different approaches on MoPPA. Our future work will also include additional empirical studies on larger programs.

References

1. L. Andersen. Program analysis and specialization for the C programming language. Technical Report 94-19, University of Copenhagen, 1994.
2. D. C. Atkinson and W. G. Griswold. Effective whole-program analysis in the presence of pointers. In *6th International Symposium on the Foundations of Software Engineering*, pages 46–55, Nov. 1998.
3. R. Chatterjee, B. G. Ryder, and W. A. Landi. Relevant context inference. In *26th Symposium on Principles of programming languages*, pages 133–146, Jan. 1999.
4. B. Cheng and W. Hwu. Modular interprocedural pointer analysis using access paths: Design, implementation, and evaluation. In *Conference on Programming Language Design and Implementation*, pages 57–69, June 2000.

5. J.-D. Choi, M. Burke, and P. Carini. Efficient flow-sensitive interprocedural computation of pointer-induced aliases and side effects. In *Symposium on Principles of Programming Languages*, pages 232–245, Jan. 1993.
6. M. Das. Unification-based pointer analysis with directional assignments. In *Conference on Programming Language Design and Implementation*, June 2000.
7. M. Emami, R. Ghiya, and L. J. Hendren. Context-sensitive interprocedural points-to analysis in the presence of function pointers. In *Conference on Programming Language Design and Implementation*, pages 242–256, June 1994.
8. M. Fahndrich, J. Rehof, and M. Das. Scalable context-sensitive flow analysis using instantiation constraints. In *Conference on Programming Language Design and Implementation*, pages 253–263, June 2000.
9. J. S. Foster, M. Fahndrich, and A. Aiken. Polymorphic verus monomorphic flow-insensitive points-to analysis for C. In *Proceedings of 7th International Static Analysis Symposium*, June 2000.
10. P. L. R. Group. PROLANGS Analysis Framework. http://www.prolangs.rutgers.edu/, Rutgers University, 1998.
11. M. Hind, M. Burke, P. Carini, and J.-D. Choi. Interprocedural pointer alias analysis. *ACM Transactions on Programming Languages and Systems*, 21(4):848–894, July 1999.
12. M. Hind and A. Pioli. Which pointer analysis should I use? In *International Symposium on Software Testing and Analysis*, pages 113–123, Aug. 2000.
13. N. Jones and S. Muchnick. Flow analysis and optimization of lisp-like structures. In S. Muchnick and N. Jones, editors, *Program Flow Analysis: Theory and Applications*, pages 102–131. 1979.
14. W. Landi and B. G. Ryder. A safe approximate algorithm for interprocedural pointer aliasing. In *Conference on Programming Language Design and Implementation*, pages 235–248, July 1992.
15. D. Liang and M. J. Harrold. Efficient points-to analysis for whole-program analysis. In *Joint 7th European Software Engineering Conference and 7th ACM Symposium on Foundations of Software Engineering*, pages 199–215, Sept. 1999.
16. D. Liang and M. J. Harrold. Reuse-driven interprocedural slicing in the presence of pointers and recursion. In *International Conference on Software Maintenance*, pages 421–430, Sept. 1999.
17. H. D. Pande, W. A. Landi, and B. G. Ryder. Interprocedural def-use associations for C systems with single level pointers. *IEEE Transactions on Software Engineering*, 20(5):385–403, May 1994.
18. E. Ruf. Context-insensitive alias analysis reconsidered. In *Conference on Programming Language Design and Implementation*, pages 13–23, June 1995.
19. B. Steensgaard. Points-to analysis in almost linear time. In *23rd ACM Symposium on Principles of Programming Languages*, pages 32–41, Jan. 1996.
20. M. Weiser. Program slicing. *IEEE Transactions on Software Engineering*, 10(4):352–357, July 1984.
21. R. P. Wilson and M. S. Lam. Efficient context-sensitive pointer analysis for C programs. In *Conference on Programming Language Design and Implementation*, pages 1–12, June 1995.
22. S. H. Yong, S. Horwitz, and T. Reps. Pointer analysis for programs with structures and casting. *ACM SIGPLAN Notices*, 34(5):91–103, May 1999.

Parametric Optimization of
Open Real-Time Systems

Farn Wang[1]* and Hsu-Chun Yen[2]

[1] Institute of Information Science, Academia Sinica, Taipei, Taiwan, R.O.C.
farn@iis.sinica.edu.tw
[2] Dept. of Electrical Engineering, National Taiwan University, Taipei, Taiwan, R.O.C.
yen@cc.ee.ntu.edu.tw

Abstract. For controllable timed automata, a general parametric optimization framework based on automata-theory is proposed. The framework is general enough to incorporate both the parametric analysis problem and the controller synthesis problem of computer systems. We propose an algorithm for the construction of the characterization of the parameter constraints and controller synthesis, which in turn yields a linear programming solution to parametric optimization.

1 Introduction

As increasing efforts have been devoted to applying CAV techniques to real-world systems, it becomes urgent to design appropriate models and analytical techniques to deal with *parametric optimization* of real-time systems. Many (if not most) of the conventional CAV techniques are only capable of classifying a given system as 'good' or 'bad.' To make things even more complicated, the behavior of many of the real-world systems is often influenced by various engineering constraints, e.g. assumptions on environments in which the systems reside. Suppose the performance of a system is evaluated once with respect to a given constraint setting. Once the constraint changes, traditionally either the evaluation process is restarted, or the performance under the new constraint is calculated using the so-called *extrapolation* technique utilizing results from known system constraints. The former is somewhat time-consuming, whereas the latter suffers from imprecision. In addition, neither technique is appropriate for answering a question like: *find the environment assumptions under which the system performs best*. It is therefore highly desirable to employ an evaluation strategy that is *parametric* in nature. That is, the variations of the engineering constraints are treated as parameters, and the evaluation ends up including such parameters as part of the performance measure.

We demonstrate in this paper a general framework within which parametric optimization is carried out in a *parametric* fashion for real-time systems modeled by *controllable timed automata*. As we shall see later, our framework incorporates both *parametric analysis* and *controller synthesis*, which are two issues that

---

* The work is partially supported by National Science Council, Taiwan, ROC under grant NSC 89-2213-E-001-046.

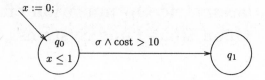

Fig. 1. A Simple Controllable Timed Automaton.

have received increasing attention in the CAV community lately [3–7, 11, 13, 16–18]. Aside from being more general than the problem of parametric analysis or controller synthesis alone, a unique feature of our solution to parametric optimization lies in that we are able to construct a characterization of the parameter constraints and controller synthesis, which in turn yields a linear programming solution to parametric optimization. Such a characterization is valuable both in the construction of a solution controller and in the derivation of the optimal performance. By doing so, re-evaluation of the performance of a system under a new constraint setting is as easy as solving the parameterized inequalities with respect to a new set of parameters. More interestingly, by encapsulating the environment's parameters into our framework of performance evaluation, it becomes feasible to find out the best system performance by solving an optimization version of the parametric inequalities.

Example 1. **A Simple Automaton.** To give the reader a better feel for the issue of parametric optimization of controllable timed automata, consider Figure 1 in which a simple controllable timed automaton is shown. Two operation modes are represented by the ovals in which we have mode names q_0 and q_1, and invariance conditions $x \leq 1$ and *true*, respectively. Between the modes, there is an arc for a transition labeled with a triggering condition (above). The triggering condition contains a special symbol σ which represents the enabling signal from the controller. In this paper, we shall adopt the approach in [6, 7, 13] which assumes that σ is an uninterpreted Boolean function of *regions* [1]. Notice that the automaton is *parametric* in the sense that "cost" is a static parameter for some optional functions of the automaton.

An example specification which we may want to analyze is written in *PCTL* (*Parametric CTL*, defined in Section 2) as follows.

$$\phi \equiv (\text{cost} < 100) \wedge (\theta \geq 1) \wedge (\forall\square_{<\theta}q_0)$$

The formula says that the cost must be less than 100 dollars, parameter θ is greater than or equal to 1, and we want to find out the characterization of θ such that q_0 is true in all computations within θ time units from the initial state. As the transition from q_0 to q_1 is 'controlled' by the environment through the control symbol σ, whether ϕ holds depends not only on the values of the static parameters but also on the control policy imposed on the automaton by the controller (i.e., environment).

Suppose we are given an optimization metric like 'cost $-\theta$.' For the aforementioned 'parametric' timed automaton, specification, and optimization metric, *parametric optimization* in our setting boils down to finding a control policy under which the optimization metric is maximized for a parameterized automaton meeting the specification.

Our framework is capable of analyzing trace-oriented optimization problems of real-time systems. For example, with the same automaton used in figure 1, we may have another specification $\phi' = \text{cost} < 12 \wedge \forall\square(q_0 \rightarrow \forall\lozenge_{\leq\theta}q_1)$, which says that q_1 will eventually be true in time $\leq \theta$ whenever q_0 is true, and an optimization metric $-\theta$. Then the parametric optimization problem asks for the deadline value in all computations, from a q_0 state to a q_1 state, subject to the restriction of ϕ'. Thus it is easy to see that our framework is more general than previous ones like [10].

In example 4 of subsection 3.5 after we have presented our algorithms, we shall present the answers to the parametric optimization problems with these two just-mentioned sets of specifications and optimization metrics.   ‖

Our parametric optimization problem can be thought of as a generalization of both *parametric analysis* ("what parameter settings make a system correct?") [3, 4, 11, 16–18] and *controller synthesis* ("what controller if any induces a correct behavior?") [5–7, 13] of timed automata. For parametric analysis, parameter variables are associated with either temporal operators or timed automata, and problems such as *'Does there exist a valuation of the parameters so that the system meets a given property?'* or *'Is it the case that for all valuations of the parameters the given property always holds for the system?'* are being thought. It has been shown that for parametric timed automata in which parameter variables are allowed to be compared with clocks, the verification problem is in general undecidable [4]. If, however, parameter variables are in existence in the specification (i.e., temporal formulas) only, then the problem becomes decidable [4]. In the context of parametric analysis, Alur *et al.* [3] considered the so-called 'model measuring' problem for *parametric linear time temporal logic* (PLTL). Model measuring is an extension of the standard model checking problem in that the latter only returns 'yes/no' answers, whereas the former provides answers to a number of questions regarding the set of parameter valuations for which the given specification is fulfilled. Emerson and Trefler [11], on the other hand, investigated the model checking problem for *parameterized real-time computation tree logic* (PRTCTL). In [3], PLTL is defined over conventional Kripke structures, whereas in [11], both untimed and (discrete) timed structures are considered for PRTCTL. With respect to dense-time automata, Wang [16] gave a complete characterization of the set of parameter valuations satisfying a specification expressed in *parametric computation tree logic* (PCTL) in terms of a set of linear inequalities. The work of [16] has subsequently been generalized in [17], which shows that parametric analysis remains decidable for the model in which timed automata are augmented by *static parameters* (i.e., nontiming parameters) and temporal formulas are parameterized by both timing and nontiming parameters. In comparison with its predecessors in parametric analysis of timed automata, Wang's algorithm in [17], based upon the technique of dynamic programming, is easier to understand, implement, and analyze.

What makes controller synthesis an important issue is that many interesting real-world systems tend to be *open* in nature, meaning that their behaviors are influenced by the environment. Since the seminal work of Ramadge and Wonham [14], the use of *automata* and *formal languages* to reason about *controllability* of *discrete event dynamic systems* has received much attention in the control community in the past decade. Being recognized as one of the most popular models for representing real-time systems, *timed automata* [2] have naturally become the underlying model for which various *controller synthesis* issues are investigated, aside from a very successful role such a model has played in the *verification* aspects of real-time systems. Consider a dynamic system (modeled by a timed automaton) whose behaviors are to be *controlled* in a certain way so as to meet certain predefined requirements. The *controller synthesis* problem, simply speaking, is to find out whether, for a given system, there is a controller through which the interaction between the system and the controller results in only computations of 'good' behavior. (If such a controller exists, it is also desirable to construct it effectively.) The interested reader is referred to [6] for a *symbolic* approach for controller synthesis. As opposed to providing only yes/no answers in the conventional framework of controller synthesis, a recent article [5] dealt with *quantitative* properties of behaviors for controllable timed automata.

In this paper, we move a step further from previous work [3–7, 11, 13, 16–18] by considering the controller synthesis issue for *parametric timed automata* with respect to system requirements specified by *parametric computation-tree logic (PCTL)* (see [16, 17]). By explicitly allowing static parameters in our model, a richer parametric optimization framework, in comparison with that of [5], is provided. To the best of our knowledge, our work is the first that addresses parametric approach for the optimization of synthesized controller. Unlike the (fixed-point based) backward reachability approach employed in [13] for the controller synthesis problem of timed automata, we generalize the parametric analysis technique devised in [17] to derive, for a given parametric timed automaton A and a PCTL formula ϕ, a complete characterization of the parameter constraint and controller synthesis which is satisfiable if and only if there exists a controller forcing A to meet property ϕ. The characterization contains the information for both controller synthesis and parameter constraint, which enables us to formulate a unified framework in integer linear programming for *parametric optimization* of real-time systems. We feel that our approach is interesting in its own right and may have applications to the analysis of related problems for real-time systems.

The remainder of this paper is organized as follows. Section 2 introduces the model of *statically parametric plants, parametric computation tree logic*, as well as the *parametric optimization problem*. An algorithm, together with an illustrating example, is demonstrated in Section 3 for solving the parametric optimization problem. Section 4 concludes our work.

2 Parametric Optimization Problem

A parametric optimization problem instance in our framework is given as a tuple $\langle A, \phi, \lambda \rangle$ such that A is a controllable timed automaton (statically parametric plant, defined in subsection 2.1) for the description of the system behavior, ϕ is a temporal logic formula for the requirements on the system behaviors, and λ is a linear expression of parameters for the performance measurement. The aim of the problem is to find a valuation (interpretation) of the parameters that maximizes λ and makes A satisfy ϕ under the interpretation for some control strategy. A framework for minimization of λ can be similarly defined by changing the signs of coefficients in λ.

2.1 Statically Parametric Plant (SPP)

An SPP is a timed automaton extended with linear constraints of static parameters and transition controls. In an SPP, people may combine control signals, timing inequalities on clock readings, and linear inequalities of static parameters to write the invariance and transition conditions. Such a combination is called a *state predicate* and is defined formally in the following. Given a set P of basic propositions, a set X of clocks, and a set H of parameter variables, a *state predicate* η of P, X, and H has the following syntax rules.

$$\eta ::= \mathit{false} \mid p \mid x - y \sim c \mid x \sim c \mid \sum a_i \alpha_i \sim c \mid \eta_1 \vee \eta_2 \mid \neg \eta_1$$

where $p \in P$, $x, y \in X$, $a_i, c \in \mathcal{N}$, $\alpha_i \in H$, $\sim \in \{\leq, <, =, \geq, >\}$, and η_1, η_2 are state predicates. Notationally, we let $B(P, X, H)$ be the set of all state predicates on P, X, and H. Note the parameter variables considered in H are static because their values do not change with time in computation of an automaton. A state predicate with only $\sum a_i \alpha_i \sim c$ type literals is called *static*.

Definition 1. (Statically Parametric Plant): A *statically parametric plant* (SPP) is a tuple $(Q, q_0, X, H, \mu, E, \tau, \pi)$ with the following restrictions.
- Q is a finite set of *modes* (operation modes, or control locations).
- $q_0 \in Q$ is the *initial mode*.
- X is a set of clocks with readings in $\mathcal{R}^+$, i.e., the set of nonnegative reals.
- H is a set of parameter variables with values in $\mathcal{N}$, i.e., the set of nonnegative integers.
- μ is a mapping from Q such that for each $q \in Q$, $\mu(q) \in B(\emptyset, X, H)$ is the invariance condition true in q.
- $E \subseteq Q \times Q$ is the set of transitions.
- $\tau : E \mapsto B(\{\sigma\}, X, H)$ is a mapping which defines the transition-triggering conditions. Here σ is a control signal symbol representing the enabling/disabling signal from the controller. Conceptually, σ is an uninterpreted Boolean function of states whose presence on edge e suggests such an edge to be '*controllable*'.
- $\pi : E \mapsto 2^X$ defines the set of clocks to be reset during each transition.   ‖

Figure 1 displays a simple example of an SPP in which $Q = \{q_0, q_1\}$, $X = \{x\}$, $H = \{cost\}$, and σ is the control signal symbol associated with the only transition of the plant. Notice that in this example, the invariance conditions (defined by μ) associated with q_0 and q_1 are $x \leq 1$ and $true$, respectively, although in general, parameter variables are allowed to take part in the invariance conditions. An SPP starts its execution at its initial mode q_0. We shall assume that initially, all clocks read zero. In between mode transitions, all clocks increment their readings at a uniform rate. A transition of an SPP may be fired when the triggering condition of the transition is satisfied. During a transition from modes q_0 to q_1, for each $x \in \pi(q_0, q_1)$, the reading of x is reset. It is worthy of pointing out that in our setting, it is legal to let time elapse even in the presence of an enabled transition. (The reader is encouraged to contrast our model with that of [5] in which transition firings are assumed to be 'urgent.') For instance, in state q_0 with $x = 0.5$ for the SPP depicted in Figure 1, the computation may either stay in q_0 while letting the clock run, or exercise the transition from q_0 to q_1, provided that $cost > 10$ and the controller assigns $true$ to σ. The behavior of an SPP depends not only on the interpretation of the parameter variables, but also on the control policy enforced by the environment during the course of its computation. The interested reader should notice that although the triggering condition hinders on the control signal symbol σ as well as on the static parameter $cost$, they play entirely different roles as far as how they enable or disable the transition is concerned. The values of static parameters are given prior to the execution of the SPP, whereas the control signals are disabled/enabled on a step-by-step basis by the controller as the computation proceeds.

Note that we allow control signals σ to participate in the construction of triggering conditions. This is different from the controller definition in [13] in which at any moment at most one controllable transition can be enabled.

Definition 2. (State): A *state* of SPP $A = (Q, q_0, X, H, \mu, E, \tau, \pi)$ is a pair (q, ν) such that $q \in Q$ and ν is a mapping from X to $\mathcal{R}^+$ (i.e., ν represents the current clock readings). Let U_A be the state set of A.   ‖

Definition 3. (Controller): Given an SPP A, a *controller* χ is a Boolean function $U_A \mapsto \{true, false\}$ which intuitively denotes the action on the control signal (i.e., σ) to enable or disable transitions according to the current states. Since the controller does not depend on the history, it is also a *simple controller*.   ‖
We write $\sigma_\chi(s)$ to denote the truth value of σ at state s under controller χ. (If χ is clear from the context, $\sigma(s)$ is used as a shorthand.) Apparently, it is useless to enable a transition in a mode other than the source mode of the transition. Thus, at a given state (q, ν), it is reasonable to only consider controller χ such that χ disables all the transitions whose source nodes are not in mode q. It should be noted that the same SPP may generate different computations under different controllers and interpretations of its parameter variables.

Definition 4. (Interpretation): An *interpretation* $\mathcal{I}$ for H is a mapping from $\mathcal{N} \cup H$ to $\mathcal{N}$ such that for all $c \in \mathcal{N}$, $\mathcal{I}(c) = c$.   ‖

Definition 5. (Satisfaction of State Predicate): A state (q, ν) satisfies state predicate η under controller χ and interpretation $\mathcal{I}$, written as $(q, \nu) \models^\chi_\mathcal{I} \eta$, iff

- $(q, \nu) \not\models^\chi_\mathcal{I} false$;
- $(q, \nu) \models^\chi_\mathcal{I} \sigma$ iff $\chi((q, \nu))$ (in words, σ is enabled by χ at (q, ν));
- $(q, \nu) \models^\chi_\mathcal{I} x - y \sim c$ iff $\nu(x) - \nu(y) \sim c$;
- $(q, \nu) \models^\chi_\mathcal{I} x \sim c$ iff $\nu(x) \sim c$;
- $(q, \nu) \models^\chi_\mathcal{I} \sum a_i \alpha_i \sim c$ iff $\sum a_i \mathcal{I}(\alpha_i) \sim c$;
- $(q, \nu) \models^\chi_\mathcal{I} \eta_1 \vee \eta_2$ iff $(q, \nu) \models^\chi_\mathcal{I} \eta_1$ or $(q, \nu) \models^\chi_\mathcal{I} \eta_2$; and
- $(q, \nu) \models^\chi_\mathcal{I} \neg \eta_1$ iff $(q, \nu) \not\models^\chi_\mathcal{I} \eta_1$.

If for all χ, we have $(q, \nu) \models^\chi_\mathcal{I} \eta$, then we may write $(q, \nu) \models_\mathcal{I} \eta$. If for all $\mathcal{I}$, we have $(q, \nu) \models_\mathcal{I} \eta$, then we may write $(q, \nu) \models \eta$.   ‖

Definition 6. (Transitions): Given two states $(q, \nu), (q', \nu')$, there is a *mode transition* from ν to ν' in A under controller χ and interpretation $\mathcal{I}$, in symbols $(q, \nu) \rightarrow^\chi_\mathcal{I} (q', \nu')$, iff $(q, q') \in E$, $(q, \nu) \models^\chi_\mathcal{I} \mu(q) \wedge \tau(q, q')$, $(q', \nu') \models^\chi_\mathcal{I} \mu(q')$, $\forall x \in \pi(q, q')(\nu'(x) = 0)$, and $\forall x \notin \pi(q, q')(\nu'(x) = \nu(x))$. In words, for the transition $(q, \nu) \rightarrow (q', \nu')$ along the edge (q, q') to take place under controller χ and interpretation $\mathcal{I}$, it must be the case that the starting and ending invariance conditions (i.e., $\mu(q)$ and $\mu(q')$, respectively) hold in modes q and q', respectively, and the associated triggering condition $\tau(q, q')$ is met as well. Meanwhile, all the clocks specified in $\pi(q, q')$ are reset to zero, while the remaining clock readings remain unchanged. (That is, transition firing is assumed to take place instantaneously.)   ‖

For ease of expression, given a state ν and a $\delta \in \mathcal{R}^+$, we let $(q, \nu) + \delta = (q, \nu + \delta)$ be the state that agrees with (q, ν) in every aspect except for all $x \in X$, $\nu(x) + \delta = (\nu + \delta)(x)$.

Definition 7. ((q, ν)-Run of Controlled and Interpreted SPP): An infinite computation of $A = (Q, q_0, X, H, \mu, E, \tau, \pi)$ starting at state (q, ν) under controller χ and interpretation $\mathcal{I}$ is called a (q, ν)-*run* and is a sequence $((q_1, \nu_1, t_1), (q_2, \nu_2, t_2), \ldots)$ such that

- $q = q_1$ and $\nu = \nu_1$;
- for each $t \in \mathcal{R}^+$, there is an $i \in \mathcal{N}$ such that $t_i \geq t$ (meaning that the run is diverging);
- for each integer $i \geq 1$ and for each real $0 \leq \delta \leq t_{i+1} - t_i$, $(q_i, \nu_i) + \delta \models^\chi_\mathcal{I} \mu(q_i)$ (meaning that the invariance condition $\mu(q_i)$ continuously holds throughout the time interval $[t_i, t_{i+1}]$); and
- for each $i \geq 1$, A goes from (q_i, ν_i) to (q_{i+1}, ν_{i+1}) because of
  - a mode transition, i.e., $t_i = t_{i+1} \wedge (q_i, \nu_i) \rightarrow^\chi_\mathcal{I} (q_{i+1}, \nu_{i+1})$; or
  - time passage, i.e., $t_i < t_{i+1} \wedge (q_i, \nu_i) + t_{i+1} - t_i = (q_{i+1}, \nu_{i+1})$.   ‖

2.2 Parametric Computation-Tree Logic

Parametric Computation Tree Logic (PCTL) is used for specifying the design requirements and is defined with respect to a given SPP. Suppose we are given an SPP $A = (Q, q_0, X, H, \mu, E, \tau, \pi)$. A PCTL formula ϕ for A has the following syntax rules.

$$\phi ::= \eta \mid \phi_1 \vee \phi_2 \mid \neg\phi_1 \mid \exists\phi_1\mathcal{U}_{\sim\theta}\phi_2 \mid \forall\phi_1\mathcal{U}_{\sim\theta}\phi_2$$

Here $\eta \in B(Q, X, H)$, ϕ_1 and ϕ_2 are PCTL formulas, and $\theta \in \mathcal{N} \cup H$. Note that mode names are used as basic propositions for the specification of timely mode changes. $\exists$ means "there exists a computation." $\forall$ means "for all computations." $\phi_1\mathcal{U}_{\sim\theta}\phi_2$ means that along a computation, ϕ_1 is true until ϕ_2 becomes true and ϕ_2 happens with time $\sim \theta$. For example, in a requirement like cost $=$ deadline$+5 \wedge \forall q_0\mathcal{U}_{\leq\text{deadline}}q_1$, parameters "cost" and "deadline" are related and we require that for all computations, q_0 is true until q_1 becomes true in "deadline" time units.

The parameter variable subscripts of modal formulas can also be used as parameter variables in SPP. Also we adopt the following standard shorthands: *true* for $\neg$*false*, $\phi_1 \wedge \phi_2$ for $\neg((\neg\phi_1) \vee (\neg\phi_2))$, $\phi_1 \rightarrow \phi_2$ for $(\neg\phi_1) \vee \phi_2$, $\exists\Diamond_{\sim\theta}\phi_1$ for $\exists$*true* $\mathcal{U}_{\sim\theta}\phi_1$, $\forall\Box_{\sim\theta}\phi_1$ for $\neg\exists\Diamond_{\sim\theta}\neg\phi_1$, $\forall\Diamond_{\sim\theta}\phi_1$ for $\forall$*true* $\mathcal{U}_{\sim\theta}\phi_1$, $\exists\Box_{\sim\theta}\phi_1$ for $\neg\forall\Diamond_{\sim\theta}\neg\phi_1$.

With different controllers and interpretations, a PCTL formula may impose different requirements.

Definition 8. (Satisfaction of PCTL Formulas): We write in notations $(q, \nu) \models_{\mathcal{I}}^{\chi} \phi$ to mean that ϕ is satisfied at state (q, ν) in A under controller χ and interpretation $\mathcal{I}$. The satisfaction relation is defined inductively as follows.

- The base case of $\phi \in B(Q, X, H)$ was previously defined except that $(q, \nu) \models_{\mathcal{I}}^{\chi} q'$ iff $q = q'$;
- $(q, \nu) \models_{\mathcal{I}}^{\chi} \phi_1 \vee \phi_2$ iff either $(q, \nu) \models_{\mathcal{I}}^{\chi} \phi_1$ or $(q, \nu) \models_{\mathcal{I}}^{\chi} \phi_2$
- $(q, \nu) \models_{\mathcal{I}}^{\chi} \neg\phi_1$ iff $(q, \nu) \not\models_{\mathcal{I}}^{\chi} \phi_1$
- $(q, \nu) \models_{\mathcal{I}}^{\chi} (\exists\phi_1\mathcal{U}_{\sim\theta}\phi_2)$ iff there exist a (q, ν)-run $= ((q_1, \nu_1, t_1), (q_2, \nu_2, t_2), \ldots)$ in A, an $i \geq 1$, and a $\delta \in [0, t_{i+1} - t_i]$, s.t.
  - $t_i + \delta \sim t_1 + \mathcal{I}(\theta)$,
  - $(q_i, \nu_i) + \delta \models_{\mathcal{I}}^{\chi} \phi_2$,
  - for all j, δ' s.t. either $(0 \leq j < i) \wedge (\delta' \in [0, t_{j+1} - t_j])$ or $(j = i) \wedge (\delta' \in [0, \delta))$, $(q_j, \nu_j) + \delta' \models_{\mathcal{I}}^{\chi} \phi_1$.

  (In words, there exists a (q, ν)-run along which ϕ_2 eventually holds at some point in time $(\sim t_1 + \mathcal{I}(\theta))$ in the time interval $[t_i, t_{i+1}]$, for some i, and before reaching that point ϕ_1 always holds.)
- $(q, \nu) \models_{\mathcal{I}}^{\chi} (\forall\phi_1\mathcal{U}_{\sim\theta}\phi_2)$ iff for every (q, ν)-run $= ((q_1, \nu_1, t_1), (q_2, \nu_2, t_2), \ldots)$ in A, for some $i \geq 1$ and $\delta \in [0, t_{i+1} - t_i]$,
  - $t_i + \delta \sim t_1 + \mathcal{I}(\theta)$,
  - $(q_i, \nu_i) + \delta \models_{\mathcal{I}}^{\chi} \phi_2$,
  - for all j, δ' s.t. either $(0 \leq j < i) \wedge (\delta' \in [0, t_{j+1} - t_j])$ or $(j = i) \wedge (\delta' \in [0, \delta))$, $(q_j, \nu_j) + \delta' \models_{\mathcal{I}}^{\chi} \phi_1$.

Given an SPP A, a PCTL formula ϕ, a controller χ, and an interpretation $\mathcal{I}$ for H, we say A is a *model* of ϕ under χ and $\mathcal{I}$, written as $A \models_{\mathcal{I}}^{\chi} \phi$, iff $(q_0, \mathbf{0}) \models_{\mathcal{I}}^{\chi} \phi$ where $\mathbf{0}$ is the mapping that maps all clocks to zeros. ‖

2.3 Formal Definition of Problem

A *performance measure* is just a linear expression like $\sum a_i \alpha_i$ where the a_i's are integers (negative or nonnegative) and the α_i's are parameters in H. It represents a metric that the users want to maximize in their system design.

Definition 9. (Parametric Optimization Problem): Given an SPP A, a PCTL formula ϕ, and a performance measure λ ($=\sum a_i \alpha_i$), the *parametric optimization problem* instance for A, ϕ, and λ, denoted as $PO(A, \phi, \lambda)$, is formally defined as the problem of deriving the value $\max\{\sum a_i \mathcal{I}(\alpha_i) \mid \exists \chi (A \models_{\mathcal{I}}^{\chi} \phi)\}$ if it exists. ‖

3 Algorithm

Our algorithm consists of two steps. First, we extend the parametric analysis algorithm for computer systems [17, 18] with controller-choice information. The modified algorithm can then generate a constraint describing the sufficient and necessary condition of a controller (with parameters) for a given $PO(A, \phi, \lambda)$. The second step then uses various techniques in linear algebra to derive the maximum of λ under the constraint.

For the first step, we shall define *controlled region graphs (CR-graphs)* and *controlled path characterization (CP-characterization)* for parametric analysis of controllable timed automata. CR-graphs are like the parametric region graphs introduced in [17, 18]. They are also similar to the region graphs defined in [1] but contain parametric information. A region is a subset of the state space in which all states exhibit the same behavior with respect to the given SPP and PCTL formula.

CP-characterization is derived for each pair of regions in a CR-graph. For each $t \in \mathcal{N}$, it gives a sufficient and necessary condition for the existence of a finite run of t time units from the source region to the destination region. CP-characterization will be useful for the construction of constraints associated with existential path quantifiers ($\exists$).

We need the following three types of integer set manipulations. Given $T_1, T_2 \subseteq \mathcal{N}$,

- $T_1 \cup T_2$ means $\{a \mid a \in T_1 \text{ or } a \in T_2\}$.
- $T_1 + T_2$ means $\{a_1 + a_2 \mid a_1 \in T_1; a_2 \in T_2\}$.
- T_1* means $\{0\} \cup \bigcup_{i \in \mathcal{N}} \sum_{1 \leq j \leq i} T_1$, where $\sum_{1 \leq j \leq i} T_1$ means the addition of i consecutive T_1.

As we shall see later, the notion of *semilinear sets*[1] is crucial in our algorithm of constructing the CP-characterizations. In fact, it will be shown that all integer sets resulting from the above manipulations in our algorithm are semilinear. Semilinear expressions are convenient notations for expressing infinite integer sets constructed regularly. They are also closed under the three manipulations.

---

[1] A semilinear integer set is expressible as the union of a finite number of integer sets like $\{a + b_1 j_1 + \ldots + b_n j_n \mid j_1, \ldots, j_n \in \mathcal{N}\}$ for some $a, b_1, \ldots, b_n \in \mathcal{N}$.

There are also algorithms to compute the manipulation results. Specifically, we know that all semilinear expressions can be represented as the union of a finite number of sets like $a + c*$ (a shorthand for $\{a + c * h \mid h \geq 0\}$). Such a special form is called *periodical normal form (PNF)*. It is not difficult to prove that given operands in PNF, the results of the three manipulations can all be transformed back into PNF[15]. Due to page-limit, we shall skip the details here.

3.1 CR-Graphs

The classic concept of region graphs was originally discussed and used in [1] for verifying dense-time systems. Our CR-graphs are extended from region graphs with constraints on parameter variables. Beside parameter variables, our CR-graphs have an auxiliary clock κ which gets reset to zero once its reading reaches one. The reading of κ is always between 0 and 1, that is, for every state (q, ν), $0 \leq \nu(\kappa) \leq 1$. κ is not used in the user-given SPP and is added when we construct the regions for the convenience of parametric timing analysis. It functions as a ticking indicator for evaluating timed modal formulas of PCTL. ¿From now on, we shall assume that $\kappa \in X$.

The *timing constants* in an SPP A are the integer constants c that appear in conditions such as $x - y \sim c$ and $x \sim c$ in A. The timing constants in a PCTL formula ϕ are the integer constants c that appear in subformulas like $x - y \sim c, x \sim c, \exists \phi_1 \mathcal{U}_{\sim c} \phi_2$, and $\forall \phi_1 \mathcal{U}_{\sim c} \phi_2$. Let $C_{A:\phi}$ be the largest timing constant used in both A and ϕ for the given $PO(A, \phi, \lambda)$.

Given a state (q, ν), $(q, \nu) \models (fr(\kappa) = 0)$ iff $\nu(\kappa)$ is an integer.

Definition 10. (Regions): A *region* of a state (q, ν) for $PO(A, \phi, \lambda)$ is a pair $(q, [\nu])$ such that $[\nu]$, called *clock region* of ν, is the notation for the set of timing inequalities characterizing ν, that is,

$$[\nu] = \left\{ x \sim c \;\middle|\; \begin{array}{l} x \in X; \nu(x) \sim c \\ 0 \leq c \leq C_{A:\phi}; \end{array} \right\} \cup \left\{ x - y \sim c \;\middle|\; \begin{array}{l} x, y \in X; \\ 0 \leq c \leq C_{A:\phi}; \\ \nu(x) - \nu(y) \sim c \end{array} \right\} \cup \{fr(\kappa) = 0\}$$

where c is a non-negative integer. Given a (q, ν), we shall say $(q, \nu) \in (q, [\nu])$. Specifically, $[0]$ is the clock region of mapping 0.   ‖

Our region definition resembles the one in [13]. Interested readers are referred to [1] for an alternative definition of regions based on the notion of *region equivalence*.

Definition 11. (Controlled Region Graph, CR-Graph): The CR-graph for a $PO(A, \phi, \lambda)$ with $A = (Q, q_0, X, H, \mu, E, \tau, \pi)$ is a directed labelled graph $G_{A:\phi} = (V, F)$ such that the vertex set V is the set of all regions and the arc set $F \subseteq V \times V$ consists of the following two types of arcs (v, v') with $v = (q, \Lambda)$ and $v' = (q', \Lambda')$.

- [**mode transitions**] $(v, v') \in F$ iff for all $(q, \nu) \in v$, there are some $\chi, \mathcal{I},$ and $(q', \nu') \in v'$ such that $(q, \nu) \rightarrow^\chi_\mathcal{I} (q', \nu')$.
- [**time passage**] $q = q'$ and for every state $(q, \nu) \in v$, there is a state $(q, \nu') \in v'$ such that

- $(q, \nu) + \delta = (q, \nu')$ for some $\delta \in \mathcal{R}^+$; and
- there is no $\dot{\delta} \in \mathcal{R}^+$, $0 < \dot{\delta} < \delta$, s.t. $(q, \nu) + \dot{\delta}$ is not in v or v' ‖

According to [6, 7, 13], in the controller synthesis problem of timed automata, there is a controller which is a function of states iff there is a controller which is a function of regions. So we shall follow their approach and treat σ simply as a function of regions. We want to derive arc constraints on static parameters and controller choices in CR-graphs so as to construct CP-characterizations. For convenience, given a region $v = (q, \Lambda)$ and a state predicate η, we write $v(\eta)$ for the static state predicate and synthesis decision extracted from η according to the following rules.

- $v(\text{false})$ is false
- $v(\sigma) = \sigma(v)$
- $v(x - y \sim c)$ is true if $x - y \sim c \in \Lambda$; or false otherwise.
- $v(x \sim c)$ is true if $x \sim c \in \Lambda$; or false otherwise.
- $v(\sum a_i \alpha_i \sim c)$ is $\sum a_i \alpha_i \sim c$.
- $v(\eta_1 \vee \eta_2) = v(\eta_1) \vee v(\eta_2)$.
- $v(\neg \eta_1) = \neg(\eta_1)$.

A mode transition arc $(v, v') \in F$ with $v = (q, \Lambda), v' = (q', \Lambda')$ iff (1) $\mu(q) \wedge \tau(q, q')$ is satisfied at all states in v; (2) after the transition, $\mu(q') \wedge \bigwedge_{p \in \pi(q,q')(\Lambda)} p$ is satisfied at all states in v', where $\pi(q, q')(\Lambda)$ is the new clock region identical to Λ except all clocks in $\pi(q, q')$ are reset to zeros. The two conditions can be formulated as follows.

$$xtion(v, v') \equiv \left(\begin{array}{c} v \left(\bigwedge_{p \in \Lambda} p \wedge \mu(q) \wedge \tau(q, q') \right) \\ \wedge v' \left(\bigwedge_{p' \in \Lambda'} p' \wedge \mu(q') \wedge \bigwedge_{p \in \pi(q,q')(\Lambda)} p \right) \end{array} \right)$$

Note that formulas like $\bigwedge_{p \in \Lambda} p \wedge \mu(q) \wedge \tau(q, q')$ extract the truly active part in $\mu(q) \wedge \tau(q, q')$ in region (q, Λ). Then the applications of $v()$ and $v'()$ extract the constraints on static parameters as well as on the control symbol σ, should they exist.

The constraints on time passage arcs hinge on the basic constraints on relations between Λ and Λ' which are free of static parameters. Such constraints can be determined with standard techniques like symbolic weakest precondition calculation [12]. Thus we shall assume the availability of such a procedure $timed(\Lambda, \Lambda')$ which is true iff Λ, Λ' are related in the region time passage relation. Thus a time passage arc $(v, v') \in F$ with $v = (q, \Lambda), v' = (q', \Lambda')$ iff (1) $q = q'$; (2) $timed(\Lambda, \Lambda')$; (3) $\mu(q)$ is satisfied at all states in v, v'. For convenience, we let

$$timed(v, v') \equiv (q = q') \wedge timed(\Lambda, \Lambda') \wedge v \left(\mu(q) \wedge \bigwedge_{p \in \Lambda} p \right) \wedge v' \left(\mu(q') \wedge \bigwedge_{p' \in \Lambda'} p' \right)$$

3.2   CP-Characterization

Given a PCTL formula ϕ_1 and a path $\Gamma = \langle v_1 v_2 \ldots v_m \rangle$ with $v_i = (q_i, \Lambda_i)$, Γ is called a ϕ_1-path iff for some controller χ and some interpretation $\mathcal{I}$, we can embed a valid computation in the path such that along the path, all regions

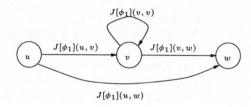

Fig. 2. Central Operation in Uur Kleene's Closure Algorithm.

except the last one satisfies ϕ_1. Likewise, a cycle $\Gamma = \langle v_1 v_2 \ldots v_1 \rangle$ is a ϕ_1-*cycle* if all regions along the cycle satisfy ϕ_1. The ϕ_1-path (cycle) is of t time units long iff along the path (cycle), exactly t arcs have the reading of κ increments from a noninteger to an integer.

To represent CP-characterizations, we shall use pairs like (η, T), where η is a state predicate and T is an integer set. Suppose, for each $v \in V$, the constraint for subformula ϕ_1 satisfied by states in v is notationally $L[\phi_1](v)$. For $v, v' \in V$ and a subformula ϕ_1, the notation for CP-characterization for v, v' is $CP[\phi_1](v, v')$. Conceptually, there is a finite ϕ_1-path $v_1, \ldots, v_m$, with $v_i = (q_i, \Lambda_i)$, of t time units long iff there is a $(\eta, T) \in CP[\phi_1](v_1, v_m)$ such that $t \in T$, the path is a valid computation with respect to η which specifies the satisfiable constraints on parameters and controller-choice, and the controller choice is consistent at the replicated regions in the path.

Now we shall give a procedure for the derivation of the CP-characterization for each pair of regions. The kernel of the procedure is a Kleene's closure computation with an intuitive scheme of vertex-bypassing. Suppose we have three regions u, v and w whose connections in the CR-graph are shown in Figure 2. By bypassing region v, we realize that $CP[\phi_1](u, w)$ should be a minimal superset of $H[\phi_1](u, v, w)$ equal to

$$
\left\{ \left(\eta_1 \wedge \eta_2 \wedge \bigwedge_{(\eta_3, T_3) \in D} \eta_3,\ T_1 + T_2 + \sum_{(\eta_3, T_3) \in D} T_3 * \right) \left| \begin{array}{l} (\eta_1, T_1) \in CP[\phi_1](u, v); \\ (\eta_2, T_2) \in CP[\phi_1](v, w); \\ D \subseteq CP[\phi_1](v, v) \end{array} \right. \right\}
$$

considering all intermediate nodes v. Note that in the calculation of $CP[\phi_1](u, w)$, the time set component T always remains semilinear.

The procedure for computing $CP[\phi_1]()$ is presented in the following.

KClosure$[\phi_1](V, \bar{F})$ /* $\bar{F} \subseteq F$. It is also assumed that for all regions $v \in V$, we know constraint $L[\phi_1](v)$ which makes ϕ_1 satisfied at every state in v. */
{
    For each $(u, w) \notin \bar{F}$, $CP[\phi_1](u, w) := \emptyset$;
    For each $(u, w) \in \bar{F}$ with $u = (q_u, \Lambda_u)$ and $w = (q_w, \Lambda_w)$, do {
        let $\eta := L[\phi_1](u) \wedge (xtion(u, w) \vee timed(u, w))$.
        if $fr(\kappa) \neq 0 \in \Lambda_u$ and $fr(\kappa) = 0 \in \Lambda_w$, $CP[\phi_1](u, w) := \{(\eta, 1)\}$;

else $CP[\phi_1](u, w) := \{(\eta, 0)\}$.
}
For $i := 0$ to $|V|$, do
    Iteratively for each $v \in V$, do
        for each $u, w \in V$, let $CP[\phi_1](u, w) := CP[\phi_1](u, w) \cup H[\phi_1](u, v, w)$;
}

The first two for-loops are for the purpose of setting up the initial values for paths of length one (i.e., directly connected edges). Notice that one unit of time is charged to an edge should κ change from nonzero to zero. One important thing in the design of KClosure[]() is to ensure that the controller always makes consistent decision in each region. This is enforced by the individual controller-choice constraints for each arc along the path. More precisely, if, for example, σ is set to 'true' at some point in time for a region u, and set to 'false' later in the computation for the same region, then both $\sigma(u)$ and $\neg\sigma(u)$ appear (conjunctively) in the predicate characterizing the path, guaranteeing that all satisfiable paths be controller-choice consistent. Lemma 1 establishes the correctness of KClosure[ϕ_1]().

Lemma 1. *Suppose we are given the labeling function $L[\phi_1]()$ for a PCTL formula ϕ_1 on (V, F) and a natural number $t \in \mathcal{N}$. After running algorithm KClosure[ϕ_1](V, F), the following two statements are equivalent.*

1. *there is a $(\eta, T) \in \mathrm{CP}[\phi_1](v, v')$ such that η is satisfiable and $t \in T$;*
2. *there is a computation from a state $(q, \nu) \in v$ to a state in $(q', \nu') \in v'$ under some controller χ and some interpretation $\mathcal{I}$ of t time units such that ϕ_1 is satisfied in all but the last state during the computation.*

Proof Sketch: The forward direction from item 1 to item 2 is easy to prove. The backward direction relies on a proof to show that the choice-consistency constraint (logically i.e., $(\mu(q) \wedge \bigwedge_{p \in \Lambda} p) \wedge \tau(q, q'))$ is sufficient. In the jargon of [13], we need to show that the existence of $C_{A:\phi}$-polyhedral solution controller is a necessary condition for the existence of any solution controller. The proof idea is to transform a non-$C_{A:\phi}$-polyhedral solution controller to a $C_{A:\phi}$-polyhedral one. Then we can prove the new controller also satisfies the same set of modal formulas, as the old one, by structural induction on formulas. $\quad\|$

3.3   Nonzenoness

Zenoness is an undesirable anomaly in real-time computations such that clock readings converge to finite values. Certainly, we do not want such an anomaly sneaks in the constraints derived for the existence of interpretations and controllers. To avoid zenoness, we shall adopt the same approach used in [16]. A state is nonzeno iff from that state on, there is always a computation along which κ gets reset infinitely often. In PCTL, that is $\exists\Box_{\geq 0}\phi_j$ for some $\phi_j \neq false$. This can be expressed as the following constraints on regions.

$$L[\exists\Box_{\geq 0}\phi_j](v) \equiv \bigvee_{u \in V}\left(\left(\bigvee_{(\eta,T)\in CP[\phi_j]((\kappa)v,u)}\eta\right) \wedge \left(\bigvee_{(\eta,T)\in CP[\phi_j](u,u)}(\eta \wedge T > 0)\right)\right)$$

where $\langle\kappa\rangle v$ is the region in a CR-graph that agrees with v in every aspect except that if $\langle\kappa\rangle v = (q,\Lambda)$, then $fr(\kappa) = 0 \in \Lambda$. The constraint essentially says that from $\langle\kappa\rangle v$, we can reach a cycle of nonzero time.

3.4   Labeling Algorithm

Once the CP-characterizations for ϕ_1 have been constructed successfully, we can then turn to the labeling algorithm to calculate the parametric conditions for the modal formulas properly containing ϕ_1. However, there is still one thing which we should define clearly before presenting our labeling algorithm, that is: "How should we derive parameter constraints from things like (η,T) in CP-characterizations?" Suppose, we want to examine if from v to v', there is a run with time $\geq \theta$. To do this, we define semilinear conditions in the form of $T \sim \theta$ with semilinear expressions T in PNF, and the (numerical or variable) parameter θ is calculated according to the following rewriting rules.

- $a + c* \sim \theta \implies a + cj \sim \theta$ where j is a new integer variable never used before.
- $T_1 \cup T_2 \sim \theta \implies (T_1 \sim \theta) \vee (T_2 \sim \theta)$.

Note that since we assume that the operands are in PNF, we do not have to pay attention to the case of $+$ and $*$. Then, the condition that there is a run with time $\geq \theta$ from v to v' can be calculated as $\bigvee_{(\eta,T)\in CP[\phi_1](v,v')}\eta \wedge T \geq \theta$.

In the following, we present the labeling algorithm for $L[\phi](v)$ in the traditional inductive case analysis of formula ϕ.

Label(A, ϕ) {
(1) construct the CR-graph $G_{A:\phi} = (V,F)$;
(2) return $L[\phi]((q_0, [\mathbf{0}]))$;
}

$L[\phi_i](v)$ /* $v = (q, \Lambda)$ */ {
switch(ϕ_i) {
case (*false*), $L[false](v) := false$;

case ($\phi_i = q'$) where $q' \in Q$, $L[q'](v) := true$ if $q = q'$, else $L[q'](v) := false$;

case ($x - y \sim c$ or $x \sim c$), $L[\phi_i](v) := true$ iff $\phi_i \in \Lambda$;

case ($\sum a_i\alpha_i \sim d$), $L[\sum a_i\alpha_i \sim d](v) := \sum a_i\alpha_i \sim d$;

case ($\phi_j \vee \phi_k$), $L[\phi_j \vee \phi_k](v) := L[\phi_j](v) \vee L[\phi_k](v)$;

case ($\neg\eta$), $L[\neg\eta](v) := \neg L[\eta](v)$;

case ($\exists\Box_{\geq 0}\phi_j$), {
  (1) KClosure$[\phi_j](V,F)$;

  (2) $L[\exists\Box_{\geq 0}\phi_j](v) := \bigvee_{u \in V}\left(\begin{array}{l}\left(\bigvee_{(\eta,T)\in CP[\phi_j]((\kappa)v,u)}\eta\right) \\ \wedge\left(\bigvee_{(\eta,T)\in CP[\phi_j](u,u)}(\eta \wedge T > 0)\right)\end{array}\right)$

}

case $(\exists \phi_j \mathcal{U}_{<\theta} \phi_k)$ {

(1) KClosure$[\phi_j](V, F)$;

(2) $L[\exists \phi_j \mathcal{U}_{\leq \theta} \phi_k](v) := \bigvee_{u \in V} \left(\begin{array}{c} L[\phi_k](u) \wedge L[\exists \Box_{\geq 0} true](u) \\ \wedge \bigvee_{(\eta, T) \in CP[\phi_j](\langle \kappa \rangle v, u)} (\eta \wedge T < \theta) \end{array} \right)$

}

case $(\exists \phi_j \mathcal{U}_{\geq \theta} \phi_k, \exists \phi_j \mathcal{U}_{>\theta} \phi_k, \exists \phi_j \mathcal{U}_{<\theta} \phi_k, \exists \phi_j \mathcal{U}_{=\theta} \phi_k)$ can be treated similarly as the last case.

case $(\forall \phi_j \mathcal{U}_{\leq \theta} \phi_k)$, {

(1) KClosure$[\phi_j](V, F)$;

(2) $L[\forall \phi_j \mathcal{U}_{\leq \theta} \phi_k](v) :=$
$$\neg \left(\begin{array}{c} L[\exists (\neg \phi_k) \mathcal{U}_{\leq \theta} \neg (\phi_j \vee \phi_k)](\langle \kappa \rangle v) \\ \vee \bigvee_{\begin{array}{c} u_1 = (q_1, \Lambda_1) \in V, \\ u_2 = (q_2, \Lambda_2) \in V \end{array}} \left(\begin{array}{c} fr(\kappa) = 0 \in \Lambda_1 \wedge fr(\kappa) \neq 0 \in \Lambda_2 \\ \wedge L[\neg \phi_k](u_1) \wedge L[\exists \Box_{\geq 0} true](u_2) \\ \wedge \bigvee_{(\pi, T) \in CP[\neg \phi_k](\langle \kappa \rangle v, u_1)} (\pi \wedge T = \theta) \end{array} \right) \end{array} \right)$$

}

case $(\forall \phi_j \mathcal{U}_{>\theta} \phi_k, \forall \phi_j \mathcal{U}_{\geq \theta} \phi_k, \forall \phi_j \mathcal{U}_{<\theta} \phi_k, \forall \phi_j \mathcal{U}_{=\theta} \phi_k)$ can be treated similarly as the last case.

}

There are two things worthy of mention in the algorithm. First, nonzenoness is properly handled because we require in the algorithm that all computations have a suffix computation satisfying $\exists \Box_{\geq 0}(\ldots)$. Second, the case $\forall \phi_j \mathcal{U}_{\leq \theta} \phi_k$ is handled as the negation of the existence of two types of counter examples. The first counter example type $\exists (\neg \phi_k) \mathcal{U}_{\leq \theta} \neg (\phi_j \vee \phi_k)$ says that ϕ_k is not fulfilled before ϕ_j becomes false in time $\leq \theta$. The rest is for the second counter example type which says that along some computation, ϕ_k is never true in time $\leq \theta$. Note that to characterize the interval which stop right at integer θ, we need constraint $fr(\kappa) = 0 \in \Lambda_1 \wedge fr(\kappa) \neq 0 \in \Lambda_2$.

Example 2. **A Simple CR-Graph.** For the automaton in Figure 1, the associated region graph is shown in Figure 3. To succinctly represent a region, we shall only put down the (true and false) mode names and those indispensable inequalities as a conjunction. All those inequalities which can be deduced from others are omitted. Also for ease of explanation, some of the edges of the region graph are annotated with ↑, ↓, or constraints (over σ and parameters) under which the associated transitions become enabled. An arc (v, v') is annotated with "↑" if $v \not\models fr(\kappa) = 0$ and $v' \models fr(\kappa) = 0$; "↓" if $v \models fr(\kappa) = 0$ and $v' \not\models fr(\kappa) = 0$.

Note that to make a valid characterization, $\theta \geq 1 \wedge \forall \Box_{<\theta} q_0$ must be satisfied. This means that the transition from region v_1 to v_2 must be disabled while the one from v_3 to v_4 must be enabled. In turn, this means that σ must be false at $q \wedge 0 < x < 1$ and true at $q \wedge x = 1$. With the region graph, we can derive relations *xtion*() and *timed*().

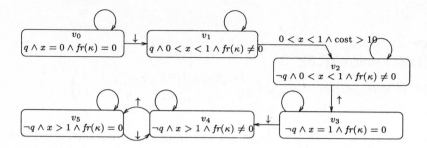

Fig. 3. A Simple Region Graph to Illustrate the Algorithm.

Table 1. Computation of KClosure[]().

$(timed(v_0,v_1),0) \in CP[true](v_0,v_1)$	$(xtion(v_1,v_2),0) \in CP[true](v_1,v_2)$
$(timed(v_1,v_3),1) \in CP[true](v_1,v_3)$	$(timed(v_2,v_4),1) \in CP[true](v_2,v_4)$ (1)
$(xtion(v_3,v_4),0) \in CP[true](v_3,v_4)$	$(timed(v_4,v_5),0) \in CP[true](v_4,v_5)$
$(timed(v_5,v_6),1) \in CP[true](v_5,v_6)$	$(timed(v_6,v_5),0) \in CP[true](v_6,v_5)$

$(true,0) \in CP[true](v_0,v_1)$	$(\sigma(v_1) \wedge cost > 10, 0) \in CP[true](v_1,v_2)$
$(true,1) \in CP[true](v_1,v_3)$	$(true,1) \in CP[true](v_2,v_4)$ (2)
$(\sigma(v_3) \wedge cost > 10, 0) \in CP[true](v_3,v_4)$	$(true,0) \in CP[true](v_4,v_5)$
$(true,1) \in CP[true](v_5,v_6)$	$(true,0) \in CP[true](v_6,v_5)$

$(\sigma(v_1) \wedge cost > 10, 0) \in CP[true](v_0,v_2)$	$(true,1) \in CP[true](v_0,v_3)$
$(\sigma(v_1) \wedge cost > 10, 1) \in CP[true](v_1,v_4)$	$(\sigma(v_3) \wedge cost > 10, 1) \in CP[true](v_1,v_4)$
$(true,1) \in CP[true](v_2,v_5)$	$(\sigma(v_3) \wedge cost > 10, 0) \in CP[true](v_3,v_5)$ (3)
$(true,1) \in CP[true](v_4,v_6)$	$(true,1*) \in CP[true](v_5,v_5)$
$(true,1*) \in CP[true](v_6,v_6)$	

$(\sigma(v_1) \wedge cost > 10, 1) \in CP[true](v_0,v_4)$	$(\sigma(v_3) \wedge cost > 10, 1) \in CP[true](v_0,v_4)$
$(\sigma(v_1) \wedge cost > 10, 1+1*) \in CP[true](v_1,v_5)$	$(\sigma(v_3) \wedge cost > 10, 1+1*) \in CP[true](v_1,v_5)$(4)
$(\sigma(v_3) \wedge cost > 10, 1+1*+1*) \in CP[true](v_3,v_6)$	$(true, 2+1*+1*) \in CP[true](v_2,v_6)$

$\dots$ $\dots$ $\dots$

$timed(v_0,v_1) \equiv true; \; xtion(v_0,v_1) \equiv false; \; timed(v_1,v_2) \equiv false;$

$$xtion(v_1,v_2) \equiv \left(v_1 \begin{pmatrix} q_0 \wedge \neg q_1 \wedge 0 < x < 1 \\ \wedge fr(\kappa) \neq 0 \wedge \sigma \wedge cost > 10 \\ \wedge v_2(\neg q_0 \wedge q_1 \wedge 0 < x < 1 \wedge fr(\kappa) \neq 0) \end{pmatrix} \right) \equiv \sigma(v_1) \wedge cost > 10$$

$timed(v_1,v_3) \equiv true; \; xtion(v_1,v_3) \equiv false; \; timed(v_2,v_4) \equiv true; \; xtion(v_2,v_4) \equiv false;$
$timed(v_3,v_4) \equiv false;$

$$xtion(v_3,v_4) \equiv \left(v_3 \begin{pmatrix} \neg q_0 \wedge q_1 \wedge x = 1 \wedge fr(\kappa) = 0 \\ \wedge \sigma \wedge cost > 10 \\ \wedge v_4(\neg q_0 \wedge q_1 \wedge x = 1 \wedge fr(\kappa) = 0) \end{pmatrix} \right) \equiv \sigma(v_3) \wedge cost > 10$$

$timed(v_4,v_5) \equiv true; \; xtion(v_4,v_5) \equiv false; \; timed(v_5,v_6) \equiv true; \; xtion(v_5,v_6) \equiv false;$
$timed(v_6,v_5) \equiv true; \; xtion(v_6,v_5) \equiv false$

After running algorithm KClosure[q]() on the region graph, we find that the computation of membership relations is that shown in Table 1. In the table, we group the formulas into rows with horizontal lines to make it more readable. The first two rows are set up for length one paths, while the remaining rows are obtained with the transitivity (by-passing) law. In the third row, because of the time 1 self-loops on regions v_5, v_6, we can deduce that $(true, 1*) \in CP[true](v_5, v_5)$, which means that we can cycle through region v_5 for an arbitrary number of times. ‖

In the following discussion, our labeling algorithm is run on a small example to present the idea.

Example 3. **A Test Run of the Labelling Algorithm.** We illustrate our algorithm on the automaton shown in Figure 1 and PCTL specification $\text{cost} < 100 \wedge \theta \geq 1 \wedge \forall \square_{<\theta} q_0$. The region graph is shown in Figure 3. We first have the following derivation.

$$\text{cost} < 100 \wedge \theta \geq 1 \wedge \forall \square_{<\theta} q_0$$
$$\equiv \text{cost} < 100 \wedge \theta \geq 1 \wedge \neg \exists \diamond_{<\theta}((\neg q_0) \wedge \exists \square_{\geq 0} true)$$

According to our labelling algorithm, the characterization formula is

$$L[\text{cost} < 100](\langle \kappa \rangle v_0) \wedge L[\theta \geq 1](\langle \kappa \rangle v_0)$$
$$\wedge \neg \bigvee_{u \in V} \left(L[\neg q_0](u) \wedge L[\exists \square_{\geq 0} true](u) \wedge \bigvee_{(\eta, T) \in CP[true](\langle \kappa \rangle v_0, u)} (\eta \wedge T < \theta) \right)$$

$\neg q_0$ is true only at v_2, v_4, v_5, v_6 and $\exists \square_{\geq 0} true$ is true at all these four regions. Thus we have

$$cost < 100 \wedge \theta \geq 1 \wedge \neg \left(\begin{array}{l} \bigvee_{(\eta, T) \in CP[true](v_0, v_2)} (\eta \wedge \theta > T) \\ \vee \bigvee_{(\eta, T) \in CP[true](v_0, v_4)} (\eta \wedge \theta > T) \\ \vee \bigvee_{(\eta, T) \in CP[true](v_0, v_5)} (\eta \wedge \theta > T) \\ \vee \bigvee_{(\eta, T) \in CP[true](v_0, v_6)} (\eta \wedge \theta > T) \end{array} \right)$$

$$\equiv cost < 100 \wedge \theta \geq 1 \wedge \neg \left(\begin{array}{l} \sigma(v_1) \wedge \text{cost} > 10 \wedge \theta > 0 \\ \vee \sigma(v_1) \wedge \text{cost} > 10 \wedge \theta > 1 \\ \vee \sigma(v_3) \wedge \text{cost} > 10 \wedge \theta > 1 \\ \vee \sigma(v_1) \wedge \text{cost} > 10 \wedge \theta > 1 + 1* \\ \vee \sigma(v_3) \wedge \text{cost} > 10 \wedge \theta > 1 + 1* \\ \vee \sigma(v_1) \wedge \text{cost} > 10 \wedge \theta > 2 + 1 * + 1* \\ \vee \sigma(v_3) \wedge \text{cost} > 10 \wedge \theta > 2 + 1 * + 1* \end{array} \right)$$

$$\equiv cost < 100 \wedge \theta \geq 1 \wedge \neg ((\sigma(v_1) \wedge \text{cost} > 10 \wedge \theta > 0) \vee (\sigma(v_3) \wedge \text{cost} > 10 \wedge \theta > 1))$$
$$\equiv cost < 100 \wedge \theta \geq 1 \wedge (\neg \sigma(v_1) \vee \text{cost} \leq 10 \vee \theta \leq 0) \wedge (\neg \sigma(v_3) \vee \text{cost} \leq 10 \vee \theta \leq 1)$$
$$\equiv cost < 100 \wedge \theta \geq 1 \wedge (\neg \sigma(v_1) \vee \text{cost} \leq 10) \wedge (\neg \sigma(v_3) \vee \text{cost} \leq 10 \vee \theta \leq 1)$$

This formula says that to make the solution existent, the discrete transition must be disabled with either $\sigma(v_1) = false$ or $\text{cost} \leq 10$ at mode q_0 when $0 < x < 1$ is true. Furthermore, according to the last disjunction, if there is going to be a nonzeno computation, then it is necessary that $\sigma(v_3) = true$, $\text{cost} > 10$, and $\theta = 1$. ∥

The following theorem establishes the correctness of our labeling algorithm. The proof parallels that of a similar algorithm presented in [17].

Theorem 1. *Given a* $PO(A, \phi, \lambda)$, *a subformula* ϕ_1, *and* $v = (q, \Lambda)$, *after executing* $L[\phi_1](v)$ *in our labeling algorithm,* $L[\phi_1](v)$ *is satisfiable iff for some* $\mathcal{I}$ *and for some* χ, *for any* $(q, \nu) \in v$, $(q, \nu) \models_{\mathcal{I}}^{\chi} \phi_1$. ∥

3.5 Parametric Optimization Step

Given an SPP $A = (Q, q_0, X, H, \mu, E, \tau, \pi)$ and a PCTL formula ϕ, our labeling algorithm $Label(A, \phi)$ returns predicate $L[\phi]((q_0, [0]))$ (a constraint on parameters and controller choices) in such a way that $L[\phi]((q_0, [0]))$ is satisfiable iff for some interpretation $\mathcal{I}$ and some controller χ, $(q, \mathbf{0}) \models_{\mathcal{I}}^{\chi} \phi$. Then the constraint on parameters and controller choices is fully characterized by $L[\phi]((q_0, [\mathbf{0}]))$. In the following we shall demonstrate how to process $L[\phi]((q_0, [\mathbf{0}]))$ to solve our parametric optimization problem.

Step 1: $L[\phi]((q_0, [\mathbf{0}]))$ can be rearranged into the disjunctive normal form $\Delta_1 \vee \Delta_2 \vee \ldots \vee \Delta_m$, for some m. Each of the conjunctions can be further rearranged to two types of atoms: (type 1) $\sum a_i \alpha_i \sim c$ and (type 2) $\sigma(v)$. Type 2 is for consistency of controller choices. A conjunction is satisfiable iff the subconjunction of its type 1 atoms is satisfiable and the subconjunction of its type 2 atoms is also satisfiable. The satisfiability of conjunctions of type 2 atoms can be solved in the standard BDD or DBM technologies. $L[\phi]((q_0, [\mathbf{0}]))$ remains the same if those conjunctions with unsatisfiable subconjunctions of type 2 atoms are eliminated.

Step 2: Assume that $L[\phi]((q_0, [\mathbf{0}]))$ has no conjunctions with unsatisfiable subconjunctions of type 2 atoms. The constraint on parameters for the existence of any controllers is thus

$$\check{\Delta} = \bigvee_{1 \leq i \leq m; \check{\Delta}_i \text{ is the subconjunction of type 1 atoms of } \Delta_i} \check{\Delta}_i$$

Then the parametric optimization problem can be broken down to m subproblems which ask for the maximum of the objective function on linear inequality systems $\check{\Delta}_i$. Thus, the parametric optimization problem of controllable timed automata is reduced to that of *integer linear programming*, which is reasonably well-studied in the literature, although the size of the linear programming instance is likely to be exponential in the worst case. The answer to our optimization problem is the maximum of the answers to the m subproblems.

Example 4. For the automaton, specification, and optimization metric $(\text{cost} - \theta)$ to maximize in example 1, the optimization metric is $\max(\text{cost} - \theta) = 10 - 0 = 10$ when only zeno computations exist; or $\max(\text{cost} - \theta) = 99 - 1 = 98$ when at least one nonzeno computation exists. Thus the optimization metric is 98 with respect specification *phi* and metric $\text{cost} - \theta$.

After running our algorithm for the second set of specification ϕ' and metric $-\theta$, we find that the optimization metric value $-\theta$ is -1, indicating that 1 is the minimum deadline from a q_0 state to a q_1 state subject to the restriction of ϕ'. Due to page-limit, we leave the details to the readers.   ∥

4 Conclusion

We have investigated the parametric optimization issue of real-time systems modeled by controllable timed automata augmented with static parameters. An algorithm has been proposed for deriving constraints over the static parameters as well as the synthesized controller that would provide an environment in which the system functions correctly. To the best of our knowledge, our work is the first in an attempt to investigate *parametric analysis, controller synthesis* and *parametric optimization* in a unified setting. By giving a complete characterization of the controller as well as the parameter valuations (satisfying a given specification) in terms of a set of linear inequalities, parametric optimization is then carried out in the framework of *integer linear programming*, which is relatively well-studied. The efficiency issue is one thing that has not been addressed much in this work. As region graphs of timed automata, in general, are exponential in size, we expect our algorithm to take exponential time in the worst case. One way to circumvent this inefficiency is to look into the possibility of incorporating the so-called *symbolic techniques*, which have been proven to be useful for controller synthesis (see, e.g., [6]). Analyzing the computational complexity of our algorithm (as well as the problem) and subsequently improving the algorithm (perhaps, based on symbolic approaches) are among our future research of parametric optimization.

References

1. Alur, R., Courcoubetis, C., and Dill, D.L. (1993), Model-Checking in Dense Real-Time, *Information and Computation* **104**, Nr. 1, pp. 2–34.
2. Alur, R. and Dill, D. (1990), Automata for Modeling Real-Time Systems, in *"Automata, Languages and Programming: Proceedings of the 17th ICALP,"* LNCS 443, pp. 332–335, Springer-Verlag, Berlin/New York.
3. Alur, R., Etessami, K., La Torre, S. and Peled, D. (1999), Parametric Temporal Logic for "Model Measuring," in *"Automata, Languages and Programming: Proceedings of the 26th ICALP,"* Springer Verlag.
4. Alur, R., Henzinger, T.A., and Vardi, M.Y. (1993), Parametric Real-Time Reasoning, in *"Proceedings, 25th ACM STOC,"* pp. 592–601.
5. Asarin, E. and Maler, O. (1999), As Soon as Possible: Time Optimal Control for Timed Automata, in F. Vaandrage and J. van Schuppen (Eds.), *Hybrid Systems: Computation and Control*, LNCS 1569, pp. 19-30.
6. Asarin, E., Maler, O., and Pnueli, A. (1995), Symbolic Controller Synthesis for Discrete and Timed Systems, in Antsaklis, P., Kohn, W., Nerode, A., Sastry, S.(eds): *Hybrid Systems II*. LNCS 999,Springer 1995, pp. 1-20
7. Asarin, E., Maler, O., Pnueli, A. and Sifakis, J. (1998), Controller Synthesis for Timed Automata, *Proc. IFAC Symposium on System Structure and Control*, Elsevier, pp. 469-474.
8. Clarke, E. and Emerson, E.A. (1981), Design and Synthesis of Synchronization Skeletons using Branching-Time Temporal Logic, in *"Proceedings, Workshop on Logic of Programs,"* LNCS 131, Springer-Verlag.
9. Clarke, E., Emerson, E.A., and Sistla, A.P. (1986), Automatic Verification of Finite-State Concurrent Systems using Temporal-Logic Specifications, *ACM Trans. Programming, Languages, and Systems*, **8**, Nr. 2, pp. 244–263.
10. Courcoubetis, C. and Yannakakis, M. (1992), Minimum and Maximum Delay Problems in Real-Time Systems. *Formal Methods in System Design* **1**: 385-415, Kluwer Academic Publishers; also in "Proceedings, 3rd CAV," 1991, Springer-Verlag, LNCS 575.
11. Emerson, E. A., and Trefler, R. (1999), Parametric Quantitative Temporal Reasoning, *Proceedings of IEEE-CS Conference on Logic in Computer Science* (LICS), pp. 336–343.

12. T.A. Henzinger, X. Nicollin, J. Sifakis, S. Yovine. Symbolic Model Checking for Real-Time Systems, IEEE LICS 1992.

13. Maler, O. Pnueli, A. and Sifakis, J. (1995), On the Synthesis of Discrete Controllers for Timed Systems. *STACS'95*, LNCS 900, Springer-Verlag.

14. Ramadge, P. and Wonham, W. (1987), Supervisory Control of a Class of Discrete Event Processes, *SIAM J. of Control and Optimization* **25**: 206-230.

15. Wang, F. (1996), Scalable Compositional Reachability Analysis of Real-Time Concurrent Systems. In Proceedings of the 2nd IEEE RTAS (Real-Time Technology and Applications Symposium), Boston, June, 1996.

16. Wang, F. (1996), Parametric Timing Analysis for Real-Time Systems, Information and Computation, Vol. 130, Nr 2, Nov. 1996, Academic Press, ISSN 0890-5401; pp 131-150. Also in *"Proceedings, 10th IEEE Symposium on Logic in Computer Science,"* 1995.

17. Wang, F., Parametric Analysis of Computer Systems, *Formal Methods in System Design*, pp.39-60, 17, 39-60, 2000.

18. Wang, F. and Hsiung, P.-A. (1997), Parametric Analysis of Computer Systems, *AMAST'97*, LNCS 1349.

Embedding Chaos

Natalia Sidorova[1] and Martin Steffen[2]

[1] Department of Mathematics and Computer Science
Eindhoven University of Technology, Den Dolech 2, P.O.Box 513
5612 MB Eindhoven, The Netherlands
n.sidorova@tue.nl

[2] Institut für angewandte Mathematik und Informatik
Christian-Albrechts-Universität
Preußerstraße 1–9, 24105 Kiel, Deutschland
ms@informatik.uni-kiel.de

Abstract. Model checking would answer all finite-state verification problems, if it were not for the notorious state-space explosion problem. A problem of practical importance, which attracted less attention, is to *close* open systems. Standard model checkers cannot handle open systems directly and closing is commonly done by adding an environment process, which in the simplest case behaves *chaotically*. However, for model checking, the way of closing should be well-considered to alleviate the state-space explosion problem. This is especially true in the context of model checking SDL with its asynchronous message-passing communication, since chaotically sending and receiving messages immediately leads to a combinatorial explosion caused by all combinations of messages in the input queues.

In this paper we develop an automatic transformation yielding a closed system. By *embedding* the outside chaos into the system's processes, we avoid the state-space penalty in the input queues mentioned above. To capture the chaotic timing behaviour of the environment, we introduce a non-standard 3-valued timer abstraction. We use *data-flow analysis* to detect instances of chaotic variables and timers and prove the soundness of the transformation, which is based on the result of the analysis.

Keywords: Model checking, open reactive systems, data-flow analysis, SDL.

1 Introduction

Model checking [12] is considered as method of choice in the verification of reactive systems and is increasingly accepted in industry for its push-button appeal. To alleviate the notorious state-space explosion problem, a host of techniques has been invented, e.g., partial-order reduction [21,42] and abstraction [33,12,15], to mention two prominent approaches.

A problem of practical importance, which attracted less attention, is to *close* open systems. Since standard model checkers, e.g., Spin [26], cannot handle open systems, one first has to transform the model into a closed one. This is commonly done by adding an environment process that, in order to be able to infer properties for the concrete system, must exhibit at least all the behaviour of the real environment. The simplest safe abstraction of the environment thus behaves *chaotically*. When done manually, this closing, as simple as it is, is tiresome and error-prone for large systems already due to the

P. Cousot (Ed.): SAS 2001, LNCS 2126, pp. 319–334, 2001.
© Springer-Verlag Berlin Heidelberg 2001

sheer amount of signals. Moreover, for model checking, the way of closing should be well-considered to counter the state-space explosion problem. This is especially true in the context of model checking SDL-programs (*Specification and Description Language*) [38] with its *asynchronous* message-passing communication model. Sending arbitrary message streams to the unbounded input queues will immediately lead to an infinite state space, unless some assumptions restricting the environment behaviour are incorporated in the closing process. Even so, external chaos results in a combinatorial explosion caused by all combinations of messages in the input queues. This way of closing is even more wasteful, since most of the messages are dropped by the receiver due to the discard-feature of SDL-92.

Another problem the closing must address is that the *data* carried with the messages coming from the environment is usually drawn from some infinite data domain. Since furthermore we are dealing with the discrete-time semantics [25,9] of SDL, special care must be taken to ensure that the chaos also shows more behaviour wrt. *timing* issues such as timeouts and time progress.

To solve these three problems, we develop an automatic transformation yielding a closed system. (1) By *embedding* the outside chaos into the system's processes, we avoid the state-space penalty in the input queues mentioned above. (2) We use *data abstraction,* condensing data from outside into a single abstract value $\mathbb{T}$ to deal with the infinity of environmental data. In effect, by embedding the chaos process and abstracting the data, there is no need to ever consider messages from the outside at all. Hence, the transformation removes the corresponding input statements. By removing reception of chaotic data, we nevertheless must take into account the cone of influence of the removed statements, lest we get less behaviour than before. Therefore, we use *data-flow analysis* to detect instances of chaotically influenced variables and timers. (3) To capture the chaotic timing behaviour, we introduce a non-standard 3-valued timer abstraction.

Based on the result of the analysis, the transformation yields a *closed* system $S^{\sharp}$ which shows more behaviour in terms of traces than the original one. For formulas of next-free LTL [37, 32], we thus get the desired property preservation: if $S^{\sharp} \models \varphi$ then $S \models \varphi$.

The remainder of the paper is organized as follows. Section 2 introduces syntax and semantics we use, modelling the communication and timed behaviour of SDL. In Section 3 we present the data-flow algorithm marking variable and timer instances influenced by chaos. Section 4 then develops the transformation and proves its soundness. Finally in Section 5 we conclude with related and future work.

2   Semantics

In this section, we fix syntax and semantics of our analysis. Since we take SDL [38] as source language, our operational model is based on asynchronously communicating state machines (processes) with top-level concurrency. A program *Prog* is given as the parallel composition $\Pi_{i=1}^{n} P_i$ of a finite number of processes. A process P is described by a four-tuple ($Var, Loc, \sigma_{init}, Edg$), where *Var* denotes a finite set of variables, and *Loc* denotes a finite set of *locations* or control states. We assume the sets of variables Var_i of processes P_i in a program $Prog = \Pi_{i=1}^{n} P_i$ to be disjoint. A mapping of variables to values is called a valuation; we denote the set of valuations by

$Val : Var \rightarrow D$. We assume standard data domains such as $\mathbb{N}$, *Bool*, etc., and write D when leaving the data-domain unspecified, and silently assume all expressions to be well-typed. $\Sigma = Loc \times Val$ is the set of states, where a process has one designated initial state $\sigma_{init} = (l_{init}, Val_{init}) \in \Sigma$. An *edge* of the state machine describes a change of configuration resulting from performing an *action* from a set *Act* of actions; the set $Edg \subseteq Loc \times Act \times Loc$ denotes the set of edges.

As actions, we distinguish (1) *input* of a signal s containing a value to be assigned to a local variable, (2) *sending* a signal s together with a value described by an expression to a process P', and (3) *assignments*. In SDL, each transition starts with an input action, hence we assume the inputs to be unguarded, while output and assignment can be *guarded* by a boolean expression g, its guard. The three classes of actions are written as $?s(x)$, $g \triangleright P!s(e)$, and $g \triangleright x := e$, respectively, and we use $\alpha, \alpha' \ldots$ when leaving the class of actions unspecified. For an edge $(l, \alpha, \hat{l}) \in Edg$, we write more suggestively $l \longrightarrow_\alpha \hat{l}$.

Time aspects of a system behaviour are specified by actions dealing with *timers*. Each process has a finite set of timer variables (with typical elements $t, t'_1, \ldots$) which consist of a boolean flag indicating whether the timer is active or not, and a natural number value. A timer can be either *set* to a value, i.e., activated to run for the designated period, or *reset*, i.e., deactivated. Setting and resetting are expressed by guarded actions of the form $g \triangleright set\ t := e$ and $g \triangleright reset\ t$. If a timer expires, i.e., the value of a timer becomes zero, it can cause a *timeout*, upon which the timer is reset. The timeout action is denoted by $g_t \triangleright reset\ t$, where the timer guard g_t expresses the fact that the action can only be taken upon expiration.

As the syntax of a program is given in two levels — state machines and their parallel composition — so is their *semantics*. In SDL's asynchronous communication model, a process receives messages via a single associated input queue. We call a state of a process together with its input queue a *configuration* (σ, q). We write ϵ for the empty queue; $(s, v) :: q$ denotes a queue with message (s, v) (consisting of a signal s and a value v) at the head of the queue, i.e., (s, v) is the message to be input next; likewise the queue $q ::(s, v)$ contains (s, v) most recently entered. The behaviour of a single process is then given by sequences of configurations $(\sigma_{init}, \epsilon) = (\sigma_0, q_0) \rightarrow_\lambda (\sigma_1, q_1) \rightarrow_\lambda \ldots$ starting from the initial one, i.e., the initial state and the empty queue. The step semantics $\rightarrow_\lambda \subseteq \Gamma \times Lab \times \Gamma$ is given as a labelled transition relation between configurations. The labels differentiate between internal τ-steps, "*tick*"-steps, which globally decrease all active timers, and communication steps, either input or output, which are labelled by a triple of process (of destination/origin resp.), signal, and value being transmitted. Depending on location, valuation, the possible next actions, and the content of the input queue, the possible successor configurations are given by the rules of Table 1, where we assume a given set Sig_{ext} of signals exchanged with the environment.

Inputting a value means reading a value belonging to a matching signal from the head of the queue and updating the local valuation accordingly (rule INPUT), where $\eta \in Val$, and $\eta[x \mapsto v]$ stands for the valuation equalling η for all $y \in Var$ except for $x \in Var$, where $\eta[x \mapsto v](x) = v$ holds instead. A specific feature of SDL-92 is captured by rule DISCARD: if the head of the input queue cannot be reacted upon at the current control state, i.e., there is no input action originating from the location treating this signal, then the message is just discarded, leaving control state and valuation unchanged.

Table 1. Step Semantics for Process P.

$$\frac{l \longrightarrow_{?s(x)} \hat{l} \in Edg}{(l, \eta, (s, v) :: q) \to_\tau (\hat{l}, \eta_{[x \mapsto v]}, q)} \text{ INPUT} \qquad \frac{l \longrightarrow_{?s'(x)} \hat{l} \in Edg \Rightarrow s' \neq s}{(l, \eta, (s, \_) :: q) \to_\tau (l, \eta, q)} \text{ DISCARD}$$

$$\frac{l \longrightarrow_{g \triangleright P'!(s,e)} \hat{l} \in Edg \qquad [\![g]\!]_\eta = true \qquad [\![e]\!]_\eta = v}{(l, \eta, q) \to_{P'!(s,v)} (\hat{l}, \eta, q)} \text{ OUTPUT}$$

$$\frac{v \in D}{(l, \eta, q) \to_{P?(s,v)} (l, \eta, q :: (s, v))} \text{ RECEIVE}$$

$$\frac{l \longrightarrow_{g \triangleright x := e} \hat{l} \in Edg \qquad [\![g]\!]_\eta = true \qquad [\![e]\!]_\eta = v}{(l, \eta, q) \to_\tau (\hat{l}, \eta_{[x \mapsto v]}, q)} \text{ ASSIGN}$$

$$\frac{l \longrightarrow_{g \triangleright set\ t := e} \hat{l} \in Edg \qquad [\![g]\!]_\eta = true \qquad [\![e]\!]_\eta = v}{(l, \eta, q) \to_\tau (\hat{l}, \eta_{[t \mapsto on(v)]}, q)} \text{ SET}$$

$$\frac{l \longrightarrow_{g \triangleright reset\ t} \hat{l} \in Edg \qquad [\![g]\!]_\eta = true}{(l, \eta, q) \to_\tau (\hat{l}, \eta_{[t \mapsto off]}, q)} \text{ RESET}$$

$$\frac{l \longrightarrow_{g_t \triangleright reset\ t} \hat{l} \in Edg \qquad [\![t]\!]_\eta = on(0)}{(l, \eta, q) \to_\tau (\hat{l}, \eta_{[t \mapsto off]}, q)} \text{ TIMEOUT}$$

$$\frac{(l \longrightarrow_\alpha \hat{l} \in Edg \Rightarrow \alpha \neq g_t \triangleright reset\ t) \qquad [\![t]\!]_\eta = on(0)}{(l, \eta, q) \to_\tau (l, \eta_{[t \mapsto off]}, q)} \text{ TDISCARD}$$

Unlike input, output is guarded, so sending a message involves evaluating the guard and the expression according to the current valuation (rule OUTPUT). Assignment in ASSIGN works analogously, except that the step is internal. Receiving a message by asynchronous communication simply means putting it into the input queue where in the RECEIVE-rule, P is the identity of the process.

Concerning the temporal behaviour, timers are treated in valuations as variables, distinguishing active and deactivated timer. The *set*-command activates a timer, setting its value to a specified time, *reset* deactivates it; both actions are guarded (cf. rules SET and RESET). A timeout may occur, if an active timer has expired, i.e., reached zero (rule TIMEOUT).

We assume for the non-timer-guards, that at least one of them evaluates to true for each configuration.[1]

The *global* transition semantics for a program $Prog = \Pi_{i=1}^n P_i$ is given by a standard product construction: configurations and initial states are paired, and global transitions synchronize via their common labels. The global step relation $\to_\lambda \subseteq \Gamma \times Lab \times \Gamma$ is given by the rules of Table 2.

---

[1] This assumption corresponds at the SDL source-language level to the natural requirement that each conditional construct must cover all cases, for instance by having at least a default branch: the system should not block because of a non-covered alternative in a case-construct.

Table 2. Parallel Composition.

$$\frac{(\sigma_1, q_1) \to_{P!(s,v)} (\hat{\sigma}_1, \hat{q}_1) \qquad (\sigma_2, q_2) \to_{P?(s,v)} (\hat{\sigma}_2, \hat{q}_2) \qquad s \notin Sig_{ext}}{(\sigma_1, q_1) \times (\sigma_2, q_2) \to_\tau (\hat{\sigma}_1, \hat{q}_1) \times (\hat{\sigma}_2, \hat{q}_2)} \text{ COMM}$$

$$\frac{(\sigma_1, q_1) \to_\lambda (\hat{\sigma}_1, \hat{q}_1) \qquad \lambda = \{\tau, P?(s,v), P!(s,v) \mid s \in Sig_{ext}\}}{(\sigma_1, q_1) \times (\sigma_2, q_2) \to_\lambda (\hat{\sigma}_1, \hat{q}_1) \times (\sigma_2, q_2)} \text{ INTERLEAVE}$$

$$\frac{blocked(l, \eta, q)}{(l, \eta, q) \to_{tick} (l, \eta_{[t \mapsto (t-1)]}, q)} \text{ TICK}$$

Asynchronous communication between the two processes uses a system-internal signal s to exchange a common value v, as given by rule COMM. As far as τ-steps and communication messages using external signals are concerned, each process can proceed on its own by rule INTERLEAVE. Both rules have a symmetric counterpart, which we elide. Time elapses by counting down active timers till zero, which happens in case no untimed actions are possible. In rule TICK, this is expressed by the predicate *blocked* on configurations: $blocked(\gamma)$ holds if no move is possible by the system except either a clock-tick or a reception of a message from the outside, i.e., if $\gamma \to_\lambda$ for some label λ, then $\lambda = tick$ or $\lambda = P?(s,v)$ for some $s \in Sig_{ext}$. In other words, the time-elapsing steps are those with *least priority*. Note in passing that due to the discarding feature, $blocked(\sigma, q)$ implies $q = \epsilon$. The counting down of the timers is written $\eta_{[t \mapsto (t-1)]}$, by which we mean, all currently active timers are decreased by one, i.e., $on(n+1) - 1 = on(n)$, non-active timers are not affected. Note that the operation is undefined for $on(0)$, which is justified by the following lemma.

Lemma 1. *Let S be a system and $(l, \eta, q) \in \Gamma$ a configuration. If $(l, \eta, q) \to_{tick} (l, \eta', q)$, then $[\![t]\!]_\eta \neq on(0)$, for all timers t.*

In SDL, timeouts are often considered as specific timeout *messages* kept in the input queue like any other message, and timer-expiration consequently is seen as adding a timeout-message to the queue. We use an equivalent presentation of this semantics, where timeouts are not put into the input queue, but are modelled more directly by guards. The equivalence of timeouts-by-guards and timeouts-as-messages in the presence of SDL's asynchronous communication model is argued for in [9]. The semantics we use is the one described in [25,9], and is also implemented in *DTSpin* [8,17], a discrete time extension of the *Spin* model checker.

3 Marking Chaotically-Influenced Variable and Timer Instances

In this section, we present a straightforward dataflow analysis marking variable and timer instances that may be influenced by the chaotic environment. The analysis forms the basis of the transformation in Section 4.

The analysis works on a simple *flow graph* representation of the system, where each process is represented by a single flow graph, whose nodes n are associated with the process' actions and the flow relation captures the intra-process data dependencies. Since the structure of the language we consider is rather simple, the flow-graph can be easily obtained by standard techniques.

The analysis works on an abstract representation of the data values, where $\top$ is interpreted as value chaotically influenced by the environment and $\bot$ stands for a non-chaotic value. We write $\eta^\alpha, \eta_1^\alpha, \ldots$ for abstract valuations, i.e., for typical elements from $Val^\alpha = Var \to \{\top, \bot\}$. The abstract values are ordered $\bot \leq \top$, and the order is lifted pointwise to valuations. With this ordering, the set of valuations forms a complete lattice, where we write $\eta_\bot$ for the least element, given as $\eta_\bot(x) = \bot$ for all $x \in Var$, and we denote the least upper bound of $\eta_1^\alpha, \ldots, \eta_n^\alpha$ by $\bigvee_{i=1}^n \eta_i^\alpha$ (or by $\eta_1^\alpha \vee \eta_2^\alpha$ in the binary case).

Each node n of the flow graph has associated an abstract transfer function $f_n :$ $Val^\alpha \to Val^\alpha$. The functions are given in Table 3, where α_n denotes the action associated with the node n. The equations are mostly straightforward, describing the change the abstract valuations depending on the sort of action at the node. The only case deserving mention is the one for $?s(x)$, whose equation captures the inter-process data-flow from a sending to a receiving actions. It is easy to see that the functions f_n are monotone.

Table 3. Transfer Functions/Abstract Effect for Process P.

$$
\begin{aligned}
f(?s(x))\eta^\alpha &= \begin{cases} \eta^\alpha[x \mapsto \top] & s \in Sig_{ext} \\ \eta^\alpha[x \mapsto \bigvee\{[\![e]\!]_{\eta^\alpha} \mid \alpha_{n'} = g \rhd P!s(e) \text{ for some node } n'] & \text{else} \end{cases} \\
f(g \rhd P!s(e))\eta^\alpha &= \eta^\alpha \\
f(g \rhd x := e)\eta^\alpha &= \eta^\alpha[x \mapsto [\![e]\!]_{\eta^\alpha}] \\
f(g \rhd set\ t := e)\eta^\alpha &= \eta^\alpha[t \mapsto on([\![e]\!]_{\eta^\alpha})] \\
f(g \rhd reset\ t)\eta^\alpha &= \eta^\alpha[t \mapsto off] \\
f(g_t \rhd reset\ t)\eta^\alpha &= \eta^\alpha[t \mapsto off]
\end{aligned}
$$

Upon start of the data-flow analysis, at each node, the variables' values are assumed to be defined, i.e., the initial valuation is the least one: $\eta_{init}^\alpha(n) = \eta_\bot$. This choice rests on the assumption that all local variables of each process are properly initialized. We are interested in the least solution to the data-flow problem given by the following constraint set:

$$\eta_{post}^\alpha(n) \geq f_n(\eta_{pre}^\alpha(n)) \tag{1}$$

$$\eta_{pre}^\alpha(n) \geq \bigvee\{\eta_{post}^\alpha(n') \mid (n', n) \text{ in flow relation}\} \tag{2}$$

For each node n of the flow graph, the data-flow problem is specified by two inequations or constraints. The first one relates the abstract valuation η_{pre}^α before entering the node with the valuation η_{post}^α afterwards via the abstract effects of Table 3. The least fixpoint of the constraint set can be solved iteratively in a fairly standard way by

input : the flow-graph of the program
output: $\eta^{\alpha}_{pre}, \eta^{\alpha}_{post}$;

$\eta^{\alpha}(n) = \eta^{\alpha}_{init}(n)$;
$WL = \{n \mid \alpha_n = ?s(x), s \in Sig_{ext}\}$;

repeat
pick $n \in WL$;
let $S = \{n' \in succ(n) \mid f_n(\eta^{\alpha}(n)) \not\leq \eta^{\alpha}(n')\}$
in
for all $n' \in S$: $\eta^{\alpha}(n') := f(\eta^{\alpha}(n))$;
$WL := WL \backslash n \cup S$;
until $WL = \emptyset$;

$\eta^{\alpha}_{pre}(n) = \eta^{\alpha}(n)$;
$\eta^{\alpha}_{post}(n) = f_n(\eta^{\alpha}(n))$

Fig. 1. Worklist Algorithm.

a *worklist algorithm* (see e.g. [29, 24, 35]), where the worklist steers the iterative loop until the least fixpoint is reached. The algorithm for our problem is shown in Fig. 1.

The worklist data-structure WL used in the algorithm is a set of elements, more specifically a set of nodes from the flow-graph, and where we denote by $succ(n)$ the set of successor nodes of n in the flow graph in forward direction. It supports as operation to randomly pick one element from the set (without removing it), and we write $WL\backslash n$ for the worklist without the node n and $\cup$ for set-union on the elements of the worklist. The algorithm starts with the least valuation on all nodes and an initial worklist containing nodes with input from the environment. It enlarges the valuation within the given lattice step by step until it stabilizes, i.e., until the worklist is empty. If adding the abstract effect of one node to the current state enlarges the valuation, i.e., the set S is non-empty, those successor nodes from S are (re-)entered into the list of unfinished one. Since the set of variables in the system is finite, and thus the lattice of abstract valuations, the termination of the algorithm is immediate.

Lemma 2 (Termination). *The algorithm of Figure 1 terminates.*

Proof. Immediate, for set of variables *Var* in the program is finite and hence the lattice $Val^{\alpha} = Var \rightarrow \{\top, \bot\}$ is finite, as well. □

With the worklist as a set-like data structure, the algorithm is free to work off the list in any order. In praxis, more deterministic data-structures and traversal strategies are appropriate, for instance traversing the graph in a breadth-first manner (see [35] for a broader general discussion or various traversal strategies).

After termination the algorithm yields two mappings $\eta^{\alpha}_{pre}, \eta^{\alpha}_{post} : Node \rightarrow Val^{\alpha}$. On a location l, the result of the analysis is given by $\eta^{\alpha}(l) = \bigvee\{\eta^{\alpha}_{post}(\tilde{n}) \mid \tilde{n} = \tilde{l} \longrightarrow_{\alpha} l\}$, also written as η^{α}_l. The definition is justified by the following observation:

Lemma 3. *Given a location l and a node $\hat{n}$ from the flow graph such that $\hat{n} = l \longrightarrow_{\hat{\alpha}} \hat{l}$. Then $\eta^{\alpha}_{pre}(\hat{n}) = \bigvee \{\eta^{\alpha}_{post}(\tilde{n}) \mid \tilde{n} = \tilde{l} \longrightarrow_{\alpha} l\}$.*

4   Closing the System

The analysis marks instances of variables and timers potentially influenced by the chaotic environment. Based on this information, we transform the given system into a closed one, which shows more behaviour than the original. Since for model checking, we cannot live with the infinity of data injected from outside by the chaotic environment, we abstract this infinity into one single abstract value $\top$. For chaotically influenced timer values, we will need a more refined abstraction using 3 different values (cf. Section 4.1). Since the abstract system is still open, we close it in a second step, also implementing the abstract values by concrete ones (cf. Section 4.2). With the chaotic environment embedded into the now closed system, we remove, as optimization for model checking, external signals from the input queues. Special care is taken to properly embed the chaotic behaviour wrt. the timed behaviour.

4.1   Abstracting Data

As mentioned, we extend the data domains each by an additional value $\top$, representing data received from the outside, i.e., we assume now domains such as $\mathbb{N}^{\top} = \mathbb{N} \,\dot{\cup}\, \{\top\}$, $Bool^{\top} = Bool \,\dot{\cup}\, \{\top\}, \dots$, where we do not distinguish notationally the various types of chaotic values. These values $\top$ are considered as the largest values, i.e., we introduce $\leq$ as the smallest reflexive relation with $v \leq \top$ for all elements v (separately for each domain). The strict lifting of a valuation $\eta^{\top}$ to expressions is denoted by $[\![.]\!]_{\eta^{\top}}$, i.e., $[\![e]\!]_{\eta^{\top}} = \top$, if e contains a variable x such that $\eta^{\top}(x) = \top$.

The step semantics is given (as before) by the rules of Tables 1 and 2, except the following differences. $\top$-valued guards behave as evaluating to *true*, i.e., they are replaced by $([\![g]\!]_{\eta^{\top}} = true) \vee ([\![g]\!]_{\eta^{\top}} = \top)$. For the TIMEOUT- and the TDISCARD-rule, the premise concerning the timer remains $[\![t]\!]_{\eta^{\top}} = on(0)$. The RECEIVE-rule is replaced by I-RECEIVEINT and I-RECEIVEEXT for internal and external reception, where the first one equals the old RECEIVE when $s \notin Sig_{ext}$, and the latter postulates $(l, \eta, q) \rightarrow_{P?(s,\top)} (l, \eta, q :: (s, \top))$ when $s \in Sig_{ext}$. To distinguish notationally the original system and its constituents from the intermediate one of this section, we write $P^{\top}$ for an intermediate-level process, $S^{\top}$ for an intermediate level system, etc.

The interpretation of *timer variables* on the extended domain requires special attention. Chaos can influence timers only via the *set*-operation by setting it to a chaotic value in the *on*-state. Therefore, the domain of timer values contains as additional chaotic value $on(\top)$. Since we need the intermediate system to show at least the behaviour of the original one, we must provide proper treatment of the rules involving $on(\top)$, i.e., the TIMEOUT-, the TDISCARD-, and the TICK-rule. As $on(\top)$ stands for any value of active timers, it must cover the cases where timeouts and timer-discards are enabled (because of $on(0)$) as well as disabled (because of $on(n)$ with $n \geq 1$). The second one is necessary, since the enabledness of the tick steps depends on the disabledness of timeouts and timer discards via the blocked-condition.

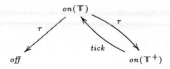

Fig. 2. Timer Abstraction.

To distinguish the two cases, we introduce a refined abstract value $on(\mathbb{T}^+)$ for chaotic timers, representing all *on*-settings larger or equal 1. The non-deterministic choice between the two alternatives — zero and non-zero — is captured by the rules of Table 4. The order on the domain of timer values is given as smallest reflexive order relation such that $on(0) \leq on(\mathbb{T})$ and $on(n) \leq on(\mathbb{T}^+) \leq on(\mathbb{T})$, for all $n \geq 1$. The decreasing operation needed in the TICK-rule is defined in extension to the definition on values from $on(\mathbb{N})$ on $\mathbb{T}^+$ by $on(\mathbb{T}^+) - 1 = on(\mathbb{T})$. Note that the operation is left undefined on $\mathbb{T}$, which is justified by a property analogous to Lemma 1:

Lemma 4. *Let $(l, \eta^{\mathbb{T}}, q^{\mathbb{T}})$ be a configuration of $S^{\mathbb{T}}$. If $(l, \eta^{\mathbb{T}}, q^{\mathbb{T}}) \rightarrow_{tick}$, then $[\![t]\!]_{\eta^{\mathbb{T}}} \notin \{on(\mathbb{T}), on(0)\}$, for all timers t.*

The intermediate system allows to state the soundness of the analysis: whenever a variable at some location contains a $\mathbb{T}$-value, the analysis has marked it by $\mathbb{T}$.

Theorem 5 (Soundness). *Given a system S, its intermediate representation $S^{\mathbb{T}}$, and η^{α} as the result of the analysis. Assume $\gamma_0^{\mathbb{T}} \rightarrow^* \gamma^{\mathbb{T}} = (l, \eta^{\mathbb{T}}, q^{\mathbb{T}})$, where $\gamma_0^{\mathbb{T}}$ is the initial configuration of $S^{\mathbb{T}}$. Then $[\![x]\!]_{\eta^{\mathbb{T}}} = \mathbb{T}$ implies $[\![x]\!]_{\eta_l^{\alpha}} = \mathbb{T}$, and $[\![t]\!]_{\eta^{\mathbb{T}}} \in \{on(\mathbb{T}), on(\mathbb{T}^+)\}$ implies $[\![t]\!]_{\eta_l^{\alpha}} = \mathbb{T}$.*

Next we make explicit the notion of simulation we will use to prove soundness of the abstraction. The new rule I-NONZERO introduces additional τ-steps in the intermediate system not present in the original behaviour. Hence, the simulation definition must honour additional τ-steps of $S^{\mathbb{T}}$ preceding a *tick*-step.

Table 4. Non-determinism for $on(\mathbb{T})$.

$$\frac{[\![t]\!]_{\eta^{\mathbb{T}}} = on(\mathbb{T})}{(l, \eta^{\mathbb{T}}, q^{\mathbb{T}}) \rightarrow_{\tau} (l, \eta^{\mathbb{T}}[t \mapsto on(\mathbb{T}^+)], q^{\mathbb{T}})} \text{ I-NONZERO}$$

$$\frac{l \longrightarrow_{g_t \, \triangleright \, reset \, t} \hat{l} \in Edg \qquad [\![t]\!]_{\eta^{\mathbb{T}}} = on(\mathbb{T})}{(l, \eta^{\mathbb{T}}, q) \rightarrow_{\tau} (l, \eta^{\mathbb{T}}[t \mapsto off], q)} \text{ I-ZERO-TIMEOUT}$$

$$\frac{(l \longrightarrow_{\alpha} \hat{l} \in Edg \Rightarrow \alpha \neq g_t \triangleright reset \, t) \qquad [\![t]\!]_{\eta^{\mathbb{T}}} = on(\mathbb{T})}{(l, \eta^{\mathbb{T}}, q^{\mathbb{T}}) \rightarrow_{\tau} (l, \eta^{\mathbb{T}}[t \mapsto off], q^{\mathbb{T}})} \text{ I-ZERO-TDISCARD}$$

Definition 6 (Simulation). *Given two processes P and P' with sets of configurations Γ and Γ'. Assume further a relation $\leq \,\subseteq\, \Gamma \times \Gamma'$ on configurations and a relation $\leq \,\subseteq\, Lab \times Lab'$ on labels, denoted by the same symbol. A relation $R \subseteq \Gamma \times \Gamma'$ is a simulation if $R \subseteq \,\leq$, and if $(\gamma \; R \; \gamma'$ and $\gamma \to_\lambda \hat{\gamma})$ implies one of the following conditions:*

1. *If $\lambda \neq tick$, then $\gamma' \to_{\lambda'} \hat{\gamma}'$ and $\hat{\gamma} \; R \; \hat{\gamma}'$, for some configuration $\hat{\gamma}'$ and for some label $\lambda' \geq \lambda$.*
2. *If $\lambda = \tau$, then $\hat{\gamma} \; R \; \gamma'$.*
3. *If $\lambda = tick$, then $\gamma' = \gamma'_0 \to_\tau \gamma'_1 \to_\tau \;\ldots\; \to_\tau \gamma'_n \to_{tick} \hat{\gamma}'$ for some $n \geq 0$ such that $\hat{\gamma} \; R \; \hat{\gamma}'$ and $\gamma \; R \; \gamma'_i$ for all γ'_i.*

We write $P \preceq P'$, if there exists a simulation relation R such that $\gamma_{init} \; R \; \gamma'_{init}$ for the initial configurations γ_{init} and γ'_{init} of P resp. P'. The definition of simulation is analogously used for systems.

The simulation definition is given relative to order relations on configurations and on labels. To establish simulation concretely between S and $S^\top$, we define (in abuse of notation) for labels $\leq \,\subseteq\, Lab \times Lab^\top$ as the smallest relation such that $\tau \leq \tau$, and that $v \leq v^\top$ implies $P?(s, v) \leq P?(s, v^\top)$ as well as $P!(s, v) \leq P!(s, v^\top)$. We use the same symbol for the pointwise extension of $\leq$ to compare valuations, states, pairs $(s, v) \leq (s, v^\top)$, queues, and finally configurations.

Lemma 7. *Let S and $S^\top$ as well as $\leq$ be defined as above. Then $S \preceq S^\top$.*

Proof sketch. It is straightforward to check on the rules of Table 1 that for single processes $P \preceq P^\top$. For systems, prove the implication that $P_1 \preceq P_1^\top$ and $P_2 \preceq P_2^\top$ implies $P_1 \parallel P_2 \preceq P_1^\top \parallel P_2^\top$, proceeding similarly by case analysis on the rules of Table 2. There, for the case of TICK, use the fact that $\gamma \leq \gamma^\top$ and $blocked(\gamma)$ implies $\gamma^\top = \gamma_0^\top \to_\tau \gamma_1^\top \to_\tau \;\ldots\; \to_\tau \gamma_n^\top = \hat{\gamma}^\top$ with $blocked(\hat{\gamma}^\top)$ for some $n \geq 0$ and $\hat{\gamma}^\top$, and where furthermore $\gamma \leq \gamma_i^\top$ for all $\gamma_i^\top$. $\qquad\square$

Lemma 8. *Let systems S and $S^\top$ and the relations $\leq$ be defined as above. Then for all formulas φ from next-free LTL, $S \preceq S^\top$ and $S^\top \models \varphi$ implies $S \models \varphi$.*

4.2 Transformation

Based on the result of the analysis, we transform the given system S into an optimized one — we denote it by $S^\sharp$ — which is closed, which does not use the value $\top$, and which is in simulation relation with the original system.

In first approximation, the idea of the transformation is simple: just eliminate actions whose effect, judging from the results of the analysis, cannot be relied on. The transformation is given for each of the syntactic constructs by the rules of Table 5, where we denote a do-nothing statement by *skip*. The set of variables $Var^\sharp$ for $S^\sharp$ equals the original Var, except that for each process P of the system, a fresh timer-variable t_P is added to its local variables, i.e., $Var_P^\sharp = Var_P \,\dot\cup\, \{t_P\}$.

The transformation rules *embed* the chaotic environment's behaviour into a system. We start with the part not interacting with the environment, i.e., the transformation concerning the manipulation of variables and timers. Variable assignments are either left

Table 5. Transformed System.

$$\frac{l \longrightarrow_{g \,\triangleright\, x:=e} \hat{l} \in Edg^{\mathsf{T}} \qquad [\![e]\!]_{\eta_l^\alpha} \neq \mathsf{T} \qquad g^{\sharp} = [\![g]\!]_{\eta_l^\alpha}}{l \longrightarrow_{g^{\sharp} \,\triangleright\, x:=e} \hat{l} \in Edg^{\sharp}} \text{ T-ASSIGN}_1$$

$$\frac{l \longrightarrow_{g \,\triangleright\, x:=e} \hat{l} \in Edg^{\mathsf{T}} \qquad [\![e]\!]_{\eta_l^\alpha} = \mathsf{T} \qquad g^{\sharp} = [\![g]\!]_{\eta_l^\alpha}}{l \longrightarrow_{g^{\sharp} \,\triangleright\, skip} \hat{l} \in Edg^{\sharp}} \text{ T-ASSIGN}_2$$

$$\frac{l \longrightarrow_{?s(x)} \hat{l} \in Edg^{\mathsf{T}} \qquad s \notin Sig_{ext}}{l \longrightarrow_{?s(x)} \hat{l} \in Edg^{\sharp}} \text{ T-INPUT}_1$$

$$\frac{l \longrightarrow_{?s(x)} \hat{l} \in Edg^{\mathsf{T}} \qquad s \in Sig_{ext}}{l \longrightarrow_{gt_P \,\triangleright\, reset\ t_P} \longrightarrow_{set\ t_P:=0} \hat{l} \in Edg^{\sharp}} \text{ T-INPUT}_2$$

$$\frac{}{l \longrightarrow_{gt_P \,\triangleright\, reset\ t_P} \longrightarrow_{set\ t_P:=1} l \in Edg^{\sharp}} \text{ T-NOINPUT}$$

$$\frac{l \longrightarrow_{g \,\triangleright\, P'!(s,e)} \hat{l} \in Edg^{\mathsf{T}} \qquad s \notin Sig_{ext} \qquad g^{\sharp} = [\![g]\!]_{\eta_l^\alpha}}{l \longrightarrow_{g^{\sharp} \,\triangleright\, P'!(s,e)} \hat{l} \in Edg^{\sharp}} \text{ T-OUTPUT}_1$$

$$\frac{l \longrightarrow_{g \,\triangleright\, P'!(s,e)} \hat{l} \in Edg^{\mathsf{T}} \qquad s \in Sig_{ext} \qquad g^{\sharp} = [\![g]\!]_{\eta_l^\alpha}}{l \longrightarrow_{g^{\sharp} \,\triangleright\, skip} \hat{l} \in Edg^{\sharp}} \text{ T-OUTPUT}_2$$

$$\frac{l \longrightarrow_{g \,\triangleright\, set\ t:=e} \hat{l} \in Edg^{\mathsf{T}} \qquad g^{\sharp} = [\![g]\!]_{\eta_l^\alpha} \qquad [\![e]\!]_{\eta_l^\alpha} \neq \mathsf{T}}{l \longrightarrow_{g^{\sharp} \,\triangleright\, set\ t:=e} \hat{l} \in Edg^{\sharp}} \text{ T-SET}_1$$

$$\frac{l \longrightarrow_{g \,\triangleright\, set\ t:=e} \hat{l} \in Edg^{\mathsf{T}} \qquad g^{\sharp} = [\![g]\!]_{\eta_l^\alpha} \qquad [\![e]\!]_{\eta_l^\alpha} = \mathsf{T}}{l \longrightarrow_{g^{\sharp} \,\triangleright\, set\ t:=0} \hat{l} \in Edg^{\sharp}} \text{ T-SET}_2$$

$$\frac{l \longrightarrow_{g \,\triangleright\, reset\ t} \hat{l} \in Edg^{\mathsf{T}} \qquad g^{\sharp} = [\![g]\!]_{\eta_l^\alpha}}{l \longrightarrow_{g^{\sharp} \,\triangleright\, reset\ t} \hat{l} \in Edg^{\sharp}} \text{ T-RESET}$$

$$\frac{l \longrightarrow_{g_t \,\triangleright\, reset\ t} \hat{l} \in Edg^{\mathsf{T}} \qquad g_t^{\sharp} = [\![g_t]\!]_{\eta_l^\alpha}}{l \longrightarrow_{g_t^{\sharp} \,\triangleright\, reset\ t} \hat{l} \in Edg^{\sharp}} \text{ T-TIMEOUT}$$

$$\frac{[\![t]\!]_{\eta_l^\alpha} = \mathsf{T}}{l \longrightarrow_{g_t \,\triangleright\, reset\ t} \longrightarrow_{set\ t:=1} l \in Edg^{\sharp}} \text{ T-NOTIMEOUT}$$

untouched or replaced by *skip*, depending on the result of the analysis concerning the left-hand value of the assignment (rules T-ASSIGN$_1$ and T-ASSIGN$_2$). A non-timer guard g at a location l is replaced by *true*, if $[\![g]\!]_{\eta_l^\alpha} = \mathsf{T}$; if not, the guard stays unchanged for the transformed system. We use $g^{\sharp} = [\![g]\!]_{\eta_l^\alpha}$ as shorthand for this replacement in the rules. For chaotic timers, we represent the abstract values $on(\mathsf{T})$ and $on(\mathsf{T}^+)$ of the intermediate system by the concrete $on(0)$ and $on(1)$, respectively, and directly incorporate the I-NONZERO-step of Table 4 by the transformation rule T-NOTIMEOUT.

For communication statements, we distinguish between signals going to or coming from the environment, and those exchanged within the system. Output to the outside basically is skipped (cf. rules T-OUTPUT$_1$ and T-OUTPUT$_2$). Input from outside is treated similarly. However, just replacing input by unconditionally enabled *skip*-actions would be unsound, because it renders potential *tick*-steps impossible by ignoring the situation when the chaotic environment does *not* send any message. The core of the problem is that with the timed semantics, a chaotic environment not just sends streams of messages, but "chaotically timed" message streams, i.e., with *tick*'s interspersed at arbitrary points.

We embed the chaotic nature of the environment by adding to each process P a new timer variable t_P, used to guard the input from outside.[2] These timers behave in the same manner as the old "chaotic" timers, except that we do not allow the new t_P timers to become deactivated (cf. rules T-INPUT$_2$ and T-NOINPUT). Since for both input and output, the communication statement using an external signal is replaced by a *skip*, the transformation yields a *closed* system.

The relationship between the intermediate and the transformed program will again be based on *simulation* (cf. Definition 6) but with different choices for the order relations on configurations and on labels. Based on the dataflow analysis, the transformation considers certain variable instances as potentially chaotic and unreliable. Hence to compare configurations of $S^\top$ and $S^\sharp$, we have to take η^α into account. So relative to a given analysis η^α, we define the relationship between valuations as follows: $\eta^\alpha \models \eta^\top \leq \eta^\sharp$, iff for all variables $x \in Var$ one of the two conditions hold: $[\![x]\!]_{\eta^\top} = [\![x]\!]_{\eta^\sharp}$ or $[\![x]\!]_{\eta^\alpha} = \top$. Note that nothing is required for the new timer variables t_P.

The set of observable input signals of a process P is defined as

$$Sig^P_{obs} = \{s \in Sig \setminus Sig_{ext} \mid \neg \exists l \longrightarrow_{g \,\triangleright\, P!(s,e)} \hat{l}.\ [\![e]\!]_{\eta^\alpha_l} = \top\}.$$

The observable effect of input and output labels is given by the following equations:

$$\ulcorner P?(s,v)\urcorner = \begin{cases} \tau & \text{if } s \in Sig_{ext} \\ P?(s,v) & \text{if } s \in Sig^P_{obs} \\ P?(s) & \text{else} \end{cases} \qquad \ulcorner P!(s,v)\urcorner = \begin{cases} \tau & \text{if } s \in Sig_{ext} \\ P!(s,v) & \text{if } s \in Sig^P_{obs} \\ P!(s) & \text{else} \end{cases}$$

For *tick*- and τ-labels, $\ulcorner \cdot \urcorner$ acts as identity. With this definition, we choose as order relation on labels $\lambda^\top \leq \lambda^\sharp$ if $\ulcorner \lambda^\top \urcorner = \ulcorner \lambda^\sharp \urcorner$. In accordance with this definition, we set $\leq$ on the input queues of $P^\top$ and $P^\sharp$ inductively as follows: for empty queues $\epsilon \leq \epsilon$. In the induction case $(s, v^\top) :: q^\top \leq q^\sharp$, if $s \in Sig_{ext}$ and $q^\top \leq q^\sharp$. Otherwise, $(s, v^\top) :: q^\top \leq (s, v^\sharp) :: q^\sharp$, if $q^\top \leq q^\sharp$ and furthermore $\ulcorner (s, v^\top) \urcorner = \ulcorner (s, v^\sharp) \urcorner$, where $\ulcorner \cdot \urcorner$ for queue messages is defined in analogy to the definition for labels. This means, when comparing the queues, the *external* messages are ignored for $P^\sharp$, while for the internal messages, the signals must coincide and the value component is compared on the result of the analysis on the potential sending locations. The $\leq$-definitions are extended in the obvious manner to expressions and configurations.

In order to have the transformed system exhibit only more behaviour than the intermediate one, it must be guaranteed that whenever a guarded edge can be taken in $S^\top$,

---

[2] Note that the action $g_{t_P} \triangleright$ *reset* t_P; *set* $t_P := 0$ in rule T-INPUT$_2$ corresponds to the do-nothing step $g_{t_P} \triangleright skip$.

the corresponding guard for $S^\sharp$ likewise evaluates to *true*, where we have to take into account that in the intermediate level, guards with value $\mathbb{T}$ enable the action, as well. This property is an immediate consequence of the construction of the guards $g^\sharp$ in $S^\sharp$.

Lemma 9. *Assume two systems $S^\top$ and $S^\sharp$ and $\eta^\alpha \models (l, \eta^\top) \leq (l, \eta^\sharp)$.*

1. *Let g be a guard of an edge in $S^\top$ originating at location l and $g^\sharp$ its analogue in $S^\sharp$. If $[\![g]\!]_{\eta^\top} \in \{true, \mathbb{T}\}$, then $[\![g^\sharp]\!]_{\eta^\sharp} = true$.*
2. *If $[\![t]\!]_{\eta^\top} \in \{on(0), on(\mathbb{T})\}$, then $[\![t]\!]_{\eta^\sharp} = on(0)$.*

Lemma 10. *Let $\gamma^\top = (l, \eta^\top, q^\top)$ be a configuration of $S^\top$. Then there exists an input-edge starting from l, or an edge guarded by g and where $[\![g]\!]_{\eta^\top} = true$ or $[\![g]\!]_{\eta^\top} = \mathbb{T}$.*

Lemma 11. *Let $\gamma^\top$ and $\gamma^\sharp$ be two configurations of $S^\top$ and $S^\sharp$, such that $\eta^\alpha \models \gamma^\top \leq \gamma^\sharp$. If blocked$(\gamma^\top)$, then $\gamma^\sharp = \gamma_0^\sharp \to_\tau \gamma_1^\sharp \to_\tau \ldots \to_\tau \gamma_n^\sharp = \hat{\gamma}^\sharp$ for some configurations $\gamma_i^\sharp$ and some $n \geq 0$ such that $\gamma^\top \leq \gamma_i^\sharp$ for all i, and blocked$(\hat{\gamma}^\sharp)$.*

Lemma 12. *Let $S^\top$ and $S^\sharp$ as well as $\leq$ be defined as above. Then $S^\top \preceq S^\sharp$.*

Proof sketch. With the help of Lemma 9, it is straightforward to check on the rules of Tables 1 and 4 together with the transformation rules, that for single processes $P^\top \preceq P^\sharp$. For systems, prove the implication that $P_1^\top \preceq P_1^\sharp$ and $P_2^\top \preceq P_2^\sharp$ implies $P_1^\top \,\|\, P_2^\top \preceq P_1^\sharp \,\|\, P_2^\sharp$, proceeding similarly by case analysis on the rules of Table 2. There, for the case of TICK, use Lemma 11.   □

Having established simulation between the two levels, we can proceed to the relationship we are really interested in, namely: the transformed systems must be a safe abstraction as far as the logic is concerned. Being in simulation relation guarantees preservation of LTL-properties as long as variables influenced by chaos are not mentioned. Therefore, we define as set of observable variables $Var_{obs} = \{x \mid \neg \exists l \in Loc. \, [\![x]\!]_{\eta_l^\alpha} = \top\}$. Note that the additional timer variables t_P are unobservable.

Lemma 13. *Let the relations $\leq$ and Var_{obs} be defined as above. Then for all formulas φ from next-free LTL, $S^\top \preceq S^\sharp$ and $S^\sharp \models \varphi$ implies $S^\top \models \varphi$.*

This brings us to the paper's final result: as immediate consequence of the above development, we obtain the desired property preservation:

Corollary 14. *Let S, $S^\sharp$, and Var_{obs} be defined as before, and φ a next-free LTL-formula mentioning only variables from Var_{obs}. Then $S^\sharp$ is closed and $S^\sharp \models \varphi$ implies $S \models \varphi$.*

5   Conclusion

In this paper, we apply dataflow analysis to transform an open system into a closed, safe abstraction, well-suited for model checking. The method of embedding chaos has been successfully applied in the context of the Vires project (*V*erifying *I*ndustrial *Re*active *S*ystems) [43]. To cope with the complexity of the project's verification case study, an industrial wireless ATM medium-access layer protocol (Mascara) [16, 44], we followed a compositional approach, which immediately incurred the problem of closing the modules [39, 40].

Related Work. Closing open (sub-)systems is common for software *testing*. In this field, a work close to ours in spirit and techniques is the one of [14]. It describes a dataflow algorithm to close program fragments given in the C-language with the most general environment and at the same time eliminating the external interface. The algorithm is incorporated into the *VeriSoft* tool. Similar to the work presented here, they assume an asynchronous communicating model, but do not consider *timed* systems and their abstraction. Similarly, [20] consider partial (i.e., open) systems which are transformed into closed ones. To enhance the precision of the abstraction, their approach allows to close the system by an external environment more specific than the most general, chaotic one, where the closing environment can be built to conform to given assumptions, which they call filtering [18]. As in our work, they use LTL as temporal logic and Spin as model checker, but the environment is modelled separately and is not embedded into the system.

A more fundamental approach to model checking open systems, also called reactive modules [5], is known as *module* checking [31][30]. Instead of transforming the system into a closed one, the underlying computational model is generalized to distinguish between transitions under control of the module and those driven by the environment. MOCHA [7] is a model checker for reactive modules, which uses alternating-time temporal logic [6] as specification language.

Slicing, a well-known program analysis technique, resembles the analysis described in this paper, in that it is a data-flow analysis computing — in forward or backward direction — parts of the program that may depend on the certain points of interest (cf. for a survey [41]). The analysis of Section 3 computes in a forward manner the cone of influence of all points of the system influenced from the outside. The usefulness of slicing for model checking is explored in [34], where slicing is used to speed up model checking and simulation for programs in Promela, Spin's input language. However, the program transformation in [34] is not intended to preserve program properties in general. Likewise in the context of LTL model checking, [19] use slicing to cut away irrelevant program fragments but the transformation yields a safe, property-preserving abstraction and potentially a smaller state space.

Future Work. While chaos is useful as the most abstract approximation of the environment, one often can verify properties of a component only under assumptions or restrictions on the environment behaviour. For future work we plan to generalize the framework to embed also environments given by timed LTL-formulas. For timers, a more concrete behaviour than just using random expiration periods could be automatically extracted from the sub-components by data-flow techniques, leading to more refined timer abstraction.

References

1. *Electronic Proceedings of the Fourth International SPIN Workshop, Paris, France,* Nov. 1998.
2. ACM. *First Annual Symposium on Principles of Programming Languages (POPL) (Boston, MA),* January 1973.
3. ACM. *Twelfth Annual Symposium on Principles of Programming Languages (POPL),* January 1985.

4. R. Alur, editor. *CAV '96, Proceedings of the 8th International Conference on Computer-Aided Verification, New Brunswick, NJ*, volume 1102 of *Lecture Notes in Computer Science*, 1996.

5. R. Alur and T. A. Henzinger. Reactive modules. In LICS'96 [28], pages 207–218.

6. R. Alur, T. A. Henzinger, and O. Kupferman. Alternating-time temporal logic. In *Proceedings of the IEEE Symposium on Foundations of Computer Science, Florida*, Oct. 1997.

7. R. Alur, T. A. Henzinger, F. Mang, S. Qadeer, S. K. Rajamani, and S. Tasiran. Mocha: Modularity in model checking. In Hu and Vardi [27], pages 521–525.

8. D. Bošnački and D. Dams. Integrating real time into Spin: A prototype implementation. In Budkowski et al. [11].

9. D. Bošnački, D. Dams, L. Holenderski, and N. Sidorova. Verifying SDL in Spin. In Graf and Schwartzbach [22].

10. E. Brinksma, editor. *International Workshop on Protocol Specification, Testing and Verification IX*. North-Holland, 1989. IFIP TC-6 International Workshop.

11. S. Budkowski, A. Cavalli, and E. Najm, editors. *Proceedings of Formal Description Techniques and Protocol Specification, Testing, and Verification (FORTE/PSTV'98)*. Kluwer Academic Publishers, 1998.

12. E. Clarke, O. Grumberg, and D. Long. Model checking and abstraction. *ACM Transactions on Programming Languages and Systems*, 16(5):1512–1542, 1994. A preliminary version appeared in the Proceedings of POPL 92.

13. E. M. Clarke and R. P. Kurshan, editors. *Computer Aided Verification 1990*, volume 531 of *Lecture Notes in Computer Science*. Springer-Verlag, 1991.

14. C. Colby, P. Godefroid, and L. J. Jagadeesan. Automatically closing of open reactive systems. In *Proceedings of 1998 ACM SIGPLAN Conference on Programming Language Design and Implementation*. ACM Press, 1998.

15. D. Dams, R. Gerth, and O. Grumberg. Abstract interpretation of reactive systems: Abstraction preserving $\forall$CTL*,$\exists$CTL*, and CTL*. In Olderog [36].

16. I. Dravapoulos, N. Pronios, A. Andristou, I. Piveropoulos, N. Passas, D. Skyrianoglou, G. Awater, J. Kruys, N. Nikaein, A. Enout, S. Decrauzat, T. Kaltenschnee, T. Schumann, J. Meierhofer, S. Thömel, and J. Mikkonen. *The Magic WAND, Deliverable 3D5, Wireless ATM MAC, Final Report*, Aug. 1998.

17. Discrete-time Spin. http://win.tue.nl/~dragan/DTSpin.html, 2000.

18. M. Dwyer and D. Schmidt. Limiting state explosion with filter-based refinement. In *Proceedings of the 1st Internaltional Workshop in Verification, Abstract Interpretation, and Model Checking*, Oct. 1997.

19. M. B. Dwyer and J. Hatcliff. Slicing software for model construction. In *Proceedings of the ACM SIGPLAN Workshop on Partial Evaluation and Semantics-Based Program Manipulation (PEPM'99)*, Jan. 1999.

20. M. B. Dwyer and C. S. Pasareanu. Filter-based model checking of partial systems. In *Proceedings of the 6th ACM SIGSOFT Symposium on the Foundations of Software Engineering (SIGSOFT '98)*, pages 189–202, 1998.

21. P. Godefroid. Using partial orders to improve automatic verification methods. In Clarke and Kurshan [13], pages 176–449. an extended Version appeared in ACM/AMS DIMACS Series, volume 3, pages 321–340, 1991.

22. S. Graf and M. Schwartzbach, editors. *Proceedings of the Sixth International Conference on Tools and Algorithms for the Construction and Analysis of Systems (TACAS 2000)*, volume 1785 of *Lecture Notes in Computer Science*. Springer-Verlag, 2000.

23. O. Grumberg, editor. *CAV '97, Proceedings of the 9th International Conference on Computer-Aided Verification, Haifa. Israel*, volume 1254 of *Lecture Notes in Computer Science*. Springer, June 1997.

24. M. S. Hecht. *Flow Analysis of Programs*. North-Holland, 1977.

25. G. Holzmann and J. Patti. Validating SDL specifications: an experiment. In Brinksma [10], pages 317–326. IFIP TC-6 International Workshop.

26. G. J. Holzmann. *Design and Validation of Computer Protocols*. Prentice Hall, 1991.

27. A. J. Hu and M. Y. Vardi, editors. *Computer-Aided Verification, CAV '98, 10th International Conference, Vancouver, BC, Canada, Proceedings*, volume 1427 of *Lecture Notes in Computer Science*. Springer-Verlag, 1998.

28. IEEE. *Eleventh Annual Symposium on Logic in Computer Science (LICS) (New Brunswick, New Jersey)*. Computer Society Press, July 1996.

29. G. Kildall. A unified approach to global program optimization. In *Proceedings of POPL '73* [2], pages 194–206.

30. O. Kupferman and M. Y. Vardi. Module checking revisited. In Grumberg [23].

31. O. Kupferman, M. Y. Vardi, and P. Wolper. Module checking. In Alur [4], pages 75–86.

32. O. Lichtenstein and A. Pnueli. Checking that finite state concurrent programs satisfy their linear specification. In *Twelfth Annual Symposium on Principles of Programming Languages (POPL) (New Orleans, LA)* [3], pages 97–107.

33. D. Long. *Model Checking, Abstraction and Compositional Verification*. PhD thesis, Carnegie Mellon University, 1993.

34. L. I. Millet and T. Teitelbaum. Slicing promela and its application to model checking, simulation, and protocol understanding. In *Electronic Proceedings of the Fourth International SPIN Workshop, Paris, France* [1].

35. F. Nielson, H.-R. Nielson, and C. Hankin. *Principles of Program Analysis*. Springer-Verlag, 1999.

36. E.-R. Olderog, editor. *Working Conference on Programming Concepts, Methods and Calculi, San Miniato, Italy*. IFIP, North-Holland, June 1994.

37. A. Pnueli. The temporal logic of programs. In *Proceeding of the 18th Annual Symposium on Foundations of Computer Science*, pages 45–57, 1977.

38. Specification and Description Language SDL, blue book. CCITT Recommendation Z.100, 1992.

39. N. Sidorova and M. Steffen. Verification of a wireless ATM medium-access protocol. In *Proceedings of the 7th Asia-Pacific Software Engineering Conference (APSEC 2000), 5.–8. December 2000, Singapore*, pages 84–91. IEEE Computer Society, 2000. A preliminary and longer version appeared as Universität Kiel technical report TR-ST-00-3.

40. N. Sidorova and M. Steffen. Verifying large SDL-specifications using model checking. Feb. 2001. To appear in the LNCS-proceedings of the 10th SDL-Forum 2001 "Meeting UML".

41. F. Tip. A survey of program slicing techniques. *Journal of Programming Languages*, 3(3):121–189, 1995.

42. A. Valmari. A stubborn attack on state explosion. *Formal Methods in System Design*, 1992. Earlier version in the proceeding of CAV '90 Lecture Notes in Computer Science 531, Springer-Verlag 1991, pp. 156–165 and in Computer-Aided Verification '90, DIMACS Series in Discrete Mathematics and Theoretical Computer Science Vol. 3, AMS & ACM 1991, pp. 25–41.

43. Verifying industial reactive systems (VIRES), Esprit long-term research project LTR-23498. http://radon.ics.ele.tue.nl/~vires/, 1998-2000.

44. A wireless ATM network demonstrator (WAND), ACTS project AC085. http://www.tik.ee.ethz.ch/~wand/, 1998.

Analyzing Fair Parametric Extended Automata

Ahmed Bouajjani[2], Aurore Collomb-Annichini[1],
Yassine Lakhnech[1], and Mihaela Sighireanu[2]

[1] VERIMAG, Centre Equation, 2 av. de Vignate, 38610 Gières, France
Aurore.Annichini@imag.fr, Yassine.Lakhnech@imag.fr
[2] LIAFA, University of Paris 7, 2 place Jussieu, 75251 Paris cedex 5, France
abou@liafa.jussieu.fr, sighirea@liafa.jussieu.fr

Abstract. We address the problem of verifying safety and liveness properties for infinite-state systems, using symbolic reachability analysis. The models we consider are *fair parametric extended automata*, i.e., counter automata with parametric guards, supplied with fairness conditions on their transitions. In previous work, we shown that symbolic reachability analysis using acceleration techniques can be used to generate finite abstractions (symbolic graphs) of the original infinite-state model. In this paper, we show that this analysis can be also used to introduce fairness conditions on the generated abstract model allowing to model-check liveness properties. We show first how to translate faithfully the fairness conditions of the infinite-state original model to conditions on the generated finite symbolic graph. Then, we show that we can also synthesize automatically new fairness conditions allowing to eliminate infinite paths in the symbolic graph which do not correspond to valid behaviours in the original model. These infinite paths correspond to abstractions of boundedly iterable (nested) loops. We show techniques allowing to decide this bounded iterability for a class of components in the symbolic graph. We illustrate the application of these techniques to nontrivial examples.

1 Introduction

Symbolic reachability analysis is a powerful paradigm used in the verification of infinite-state systems, such as extended automata, communicating automata through unbounded queues, parameterized systems, etc. It consists in using finite structures to represent infinite sets of configurations, and iterative exploration procedures to compute (a finite representation of) the set of all reachable configurations, or an upper approximation of this set. To help termination, and in some cases to force it, these procedures are often enhanced by acceleration techniques which allow to compute in one step the effect of sequences of transitions instead of one single transition in the system. Typically, an acceleration step corresponds to the computation of (an upper approximation of) the set of reachable configurations by iterating an arbitrary number of times some sequence of transitions (a circuit in the control graph of the system). For instance, starting from an initial value $x = 0$, the iteration of a transition which increments the variable x by 2 leads to the set of configurations $\{0, 2, 4, \ldots\}$ which can be represented by the constraint $x = 2n$, with $n \geq 0$. Acceleration techniques allow to compute

P. Cousot (Ed.): SAS 2001, LNCS 2126, pp. 335–355, 2001.

this finite representation in one step instead of computing the infinite sequence of approximations $\{0\}, \{0, 2\}, \{0, 2, 4\}, \ldots$

The construction of the set of reachable configurations allows to check (on-the-fly) safety properties. More interestingly, this construction can also be used to generate finite abstractions of the analyzed model on which standard finite model-checking procedures can be applied. Indeed, given any finite partition of the set of configurations, it is possible to construct a finite symbolic graph (the quotient graph according to this partition) which simulates the original system. In general, the exploration procedures used to generate the reachability set produce a finite symbolic graph, when they terminate. The nodes of this graph are symbolic configurations (sets of configurations) and the edges correspond to the application of transitions of the system or acceleration steps (meta-transitions). Since the symbolic graph simulates the analyzed system, if it satisfies a property then the original system also satisfies it (we suppose here that properties involve only universal path quantification, e.g., linear-time properties).

In previous works, we have shown that this approach can be applied to verify fully automatically safety properties of infinite-state models such as communicating automata with unbounded queues [1], and parametric extended automata (automata with clocks and counters) [5]. However, while very successful in the case of safety properties, this approach fails in general when applied to the verification of liveness properties. This is due to the fact that, almost always, liveness properties only hold under fairness conditions saying that infinite iterations of certain transitions are not allowed. Therefore, the question we address is, given an infinite-state model with fairness conditions, how to introduce automatically fairness conditions on the finite abstract model generated by means of symbolic reachability analysis, in order to be able to model-check liveness properties.

In fact, the fairness conditions that must be introduced on the symbolic graph are of two sorts. First, the original infinite-state model may have fairness conditions expressed on its transitions (in its infinite configuration graph). These conditions must be translated faithfully on the transitions of the finite abstract model (symbolic configuration graph). Moreover, additional fairness conditions must be inferred since it is often the case that the finite abstract model has loops that do not correspond to a possible infinite execution path in the original model. For instance, consider a transition θ which increments a variable x by 2 if $x \leq M$, where M is a positive integer parameter. The set of reachable configurations from the initial value $x = 0$, after executing θ at least once is:

$$x = 2(n + 1) \wedge n \geq 0 \wedge 2n \leq M$$

Our exploration procedure (with acceleration) will compute this set. It will also produce a symbolic configuration graph having a loop on the set given above since this set is closed under the application of θ. However, it is clear that the iteration of θ is bounded due to the guard $x \leq M$. The problem is to infer automatically this fact and to express it as a fairness constraint on the symbolic graph. This problem can be more general than the one illustrated by this example and may concern a whole component of the symbolic graph, corresponding to nested loops and not only to a simple one. However, this problem is clearly as hard as deciding termination of programs (halting problem of Turing machines) and cannot be solved automatically in general.

The question of extending symbolic reachability techniques in order to generate finite abstractions with fairness conditions can be addressed in a similar manner for several kinds of infinite-state models. To illustrate our approach, we consider in this paper only numerical models which are *fair parametric extended automata*, i.e., automata with integer counters that can be reset, incremented, and compared against parameters. The fairness conditions are expressed on the transitions of the model under constraints on the source configurations of these transitions. Constraints on these source configurations are expressed using predicates on the variables of the system.

We show that our reachability analysis procedures and the acceleration techniques we developed in [5] can be exploited and adapted in order to deal with fairness conditions.

First, we show how the translation of fairness conditions from the original model to the abstract one can be done using symbolic reachability analysis. The idea is simple and consists in considering an extended model with additional boolean variables corresponding to the predicates involved in the fairness conditions. This forces our symbolic analysis procedure to split the abstract model according to these predicates. This makes easy the translation of the fairness conditions on the transitions of the so obtained symbolic graph, and ensures the soundness of this translation.

Then, we consider the harder problem of inferring new fairness conditions corresponding to bounded iterability of loops, and more generally to bounded iterability of some kinds of connected components (nested loops). The main intuitive idea we develop is that, to perform an acceleration step, our techniques are based on an analysis of the transitions in order to compute the effect of their iterations. From this analysis, we can actually extract informations about the bounded/unbounded iterability of these transitions. If we consider again the example mentioned above, we can determine automatically that the transition θ adds to x the value 2 each time it is executed. Then, from this fact, we first infer that, after executing $n + 1$ times the transition θ starting from $x = 0$, we get the value $x = 2(n + 1)$, and we know also that $2n < M$ should be true since the guard must be satisfied. This is basically what our acceleration techniques do in order to compute the set of reachable configurations. Now, it is also possible to infer from the fact above that θ can only be iterated a finite number of times. This can be done by deciding whether there exists an n such that the obtained value after n iterations of θ (i.e., $0 + 2n$) falsifies the guard, that is, an n such that $2n > M$. This is obviously true (in this example), which allows to infer the boundedness of the loop. We show that this basic idea allows to decide the bounded iterability of any elementary circuit in the symbolic graph. Moreover, we show that this result can be extended to some classes of nested loops (connected components), by showing that the analysis of the iterability of these components can be reduced to the analysis of simple loops.

The same approach can also be applied to timed models (with real-valued clocks) under some restrictions, essentially time-determinism (transitions in the analyzed loops must take fixed time values which may be parameterized).

We show that our techniques can be applied to many nontrivial examples. In particular, we consider a parametric timed model of the Bounded Retransmission Protocol (with unbounded counters and clocks, parametric values of the number of retransmissions, and of the timeouts), and show that our techniques generate automatically a finite abstraction of the system and fairness constraints which allow to model-check the liveness properties of the protocol, in addition to its safety properties. Other examples are considered to illustrate the case where the ability to analyze nested loops is needed.

Related Work: There exist many work on the symbolic reachability analysis of infinite-state systems using acceleration techniques [8, 7, 9, 3, 2, 5]. These works consider mainly the case of safety properties. In [10, 18], techniques for automatic verification of liveness properties are proposed in the framework of regular model checking, for the particular case of length preserving transformations on sequences, e.g., actions of parameterized networks of processes connected sequentially. In [6], techniques for translating fairness conditions from a concrete to a finite abstract model, as well as a procedure for computing safe fairness conditions on the abstract model are proposed in the particular case of parameterized sequential networks of processes.

There exist many works on proving liveness properties, and in particular the termination of programs [14, 16]. These works do not propose fully automatic techniques, but are based on a general proof principle which consists in finding a ranking function on configurations which decreases along each execution path according to a suitable well-founded ordering. Few recent works try to automatize this principle and propose heuristics for the generation of such ranking functions in some restricted cases [12, 11]. These works reason about the structure of the original model, whereas our techniques are applied on the structure of the symbolic graph generated by the reachability analysis. This fact actually is important. Indeed, in our symbolic graph, according to our acceleration techniques, loops in the original model are unfolded until we find sequences of transitions that have a periodic effect. This unfolding helps for the computation of the effect of iterated transitions but also in the reasoning about the boundedness of these iterations. It turns out that our techniques are powerful enough to deal with complex cases for which, if we reason directly on the original model, it is necessary to define a ranking function which decreases according to a lexicographic ordering on the variables, which is hard to guess automatically.

Outline: In Section 2, we give some basic definitions and introduce the kind of constraints and operations used in our models. In Section 3, we introduce the model of fair parametric extended automata and its semantics. In Section 4, we recall from [5] the symbolic structures, the reachability algorithm, and the extrapolation techniques. In Section 5, we show how the concrete fairness conditions may be translated into fairness constraints at the abstract level. In Section 6, we present the conditions needed and the methods used in order to synthesize fairness conditions for simple loops of the symbolic graph. In Section 7, we show how the results for simple loops can be extended to nested loops.

2   Preliminaries

Let $\mathcal{X}$ be a set of variables and let x range over $\mathcal{X}$. The set of *arithmetical terms* over $\mathcal{X}$, denoted $AT(\mathcal{X})$, is defined by the grammar:

$$t ::= 0 \mid 1 \mid x \mid t - t \mid t + t \mid t * t$$

The set of *first-order arithmetical formulas* over $\mathcal{X}$, denoted $FO(\mathcal{X})$, is defined by the grammar:

$$\phi ::= t \leq t \mid \neg\phi \mid \phi \vee \phi \mid \exists x. \ \phi \mid Is\_int(t)$$

Formulas are interpreted over the set of reals. The predicate Is_int expresses the fact that a term has an integer value. The fragment of $FO(\mathcal{X})$ of formulas without the Is_int predicate is called the *first-order arithmetics of reals* and denoted $RFO(\mathcal{X})$. The fragment of $FO(\mathcal{X})$ of formulas without multiplication ($*$) is called the *linear arithmetics* and is denoted $LFO(\mathcal{X})$. It is well-known that the problem of satisfiability in $FO(\mathcal{X})$ is undecidable, whereas it is decidable for both fragments $RFO(\mathcal{X})$ and $LFO(\mathcal{X})$.

Let $\mathcal{P}$ be a set of *parameters*. Parameters can be seen as variables that are not modified by the system (they keep their initial values all the time). Then, a *simple parametric constraint* is a conjunction of formulas of the form $x \prec t$ or $x - y \prec t$, where $x, y \in \mathcal{X}$, $\prec \in \{<, \leq\}$, and $t \in AT(\mathcal{P})$. We denote by $SC(\mathcal{X}, \mathcal{P})$ the set of simple parametric constraints.

We consider *simple operations* on variables corresponding to sets of special kinds of assignments. We allow assignments of variables that are either of the form $x := y + t$ or of the form $x := t$, where $x, y \in \mathcal{X}$ are variables (x and y may be the same variable), and $t \in AT(\mathcal{P})$.

Let $\boldsymbol{x} = (x_1, x_2, \ldots, x_n)$ be the vector of all variables under consideration. Simple operations correspond to assignements of the form $\boldsymbol{x} := A\boldsymbol{x} + \boldsymbol{b}$ where $\boldsymbol{b}$ is a n-dim vector of terms, and A is a $n \times n$ $\{0,1\}$-matrix such that each row has at most one non-zero (1) value. Let us call *simple matrices* such $n \times n$ $\{0,1\}$-matrices.

3   Fair Parametric Extended Automata

We consider in our work models which are automata supplied with integer counters and real valued clocks. Counters and clocks can be reset using simple operations, and they can tested using simple parametric constraints (they can be compared to parameters in these constraints). Moreover, we consider fairness conditions on the transitions of these models. To simplify the presentation, we focus here on the case where only counters are considered. A Parametric Extended Automaton (PEA) is a tuple $\mathcal{T} = (Q, X, P, \delta)$ where:

- Q is a finite set of *control states*,
- X is a finite set of *counters* ranging over the set positive integers $\mathbb{N}$,
- P is a finite set of *parameters* ranging over positive integers,

- δ is a finite set of *guarded actions* of the form $(q_1, g(X, P), sop, q_2)$ where $q_1, q_2 \in Q$, $g(X, P) \in SC(X, P)$ is a *guard*, and sop is a simple operation over X.

A configuration of $\mathcal{T}$ is a triplet $\gamma = \langle q, \mu, \pi \rangle$ where q is a control state, μ and π are respectively valuations of the counters and parameters. For each guarded action $\tau = (q_1, g, sop, q_2) \in \delta$ we define a transition relation between configurations: $\langle q_1, \mu_1, \pi_1 \rangle \rightarrow_\tau \langle q_2, \mu_2, \pi_2 \rangle$ iff $\pi_1 = \pi_2$, $g(\mu_1, \pi_1)$ is true, and $\mu_2 = sop(\mu_1)$. Then, a *computation sequence* is a sequence $\gamma_0 \tau_0 \gamma_1 \tau_1 \gamma_2 \ldots$ such that, for every $i \geq 0$, $\gamma_i \rightarrow_{\tau_i} \gamma_{i+1}$, and either it is infinite, or it is finite but maximal (cannot be prolonged).

We introduce *constrained fairness* conditions on PEAs expressed on their transitions. Let a *constrained action* be a pair $\langle \tau, f(X, P) \rangle$ where τ is a guarded action and $f(X, P) \in FO(X, P)$ is a formula expressing a constraint on the sources of τ. A Fair PEA is a tuple $(Q, X, P, \delta, \mathcal{W}, \mathcal{B})$, where (Q, X, P, δ) is a PEA, $\mathcal{W}$ and $\mathcal{B}$ are respectively set and set of sets of constrained actions.

The set $\mathcal{W}$ (called justice set) allows to express *weak fairness* conditions saying that whenever an action is permanently enabled, it must be executed sometime in the future (hence, it will be executed infinitely often). The set $\mathcal{B}$ (called boundedness set) allows to express *bounded iterability* conditions saying that, for each $U \in \mathcal{B}$, if *all actions* in U are taken infinitely often, then it must also be the case for some action *not* in U. Formally, using the notations $\exists^\omega$ for "there exists infinitely many", and $T(U)$ for the set of transitions appearing in U, a computation sequence $\sigma = \gamma_0 \tau_0 \gamma_1 \tau_1 \gamma_2 \ldots$ is *fair* iff:

- $\forall \langle \tau, f \rangle \in \mathcal{W}. \forall i \geq 0$, if $\forall j \geq i.\ \gamma_j \models f$ and $\exists \gamma.\ \gamma_j \rightarrow_\tau \gamma$ then $\exists k \geq i.\ \tau_k = \tau$,
- $\forall U \in \mathcal{B}$, if $\forall \langle \tau, f \rangle \in U. \exists^\omega j.\ (\tau_j = \tau$ and $\gamma_j \models f)$, then $\exists \tau' \notin T(U). \exists^\omega k.\ \tau_k = \tau'$.

The following example shows how constrained fairness conditions can be used to express non trivial fairness conditions.

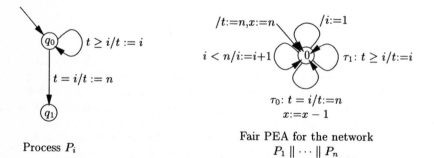

Process P_i

Fair PEA for the network
$P_1 \| \cdots \| P_n$

Fig. 1. Example for Constrained Fairness.

Example 1. Consider the parameterized network $P_1 \parallel \cdots \parallel P_n$ where each process P_i is described in Figure 1. At control state q_0, the processes are competing for getting a resource. Process P_i has the resource when $t = i$ and it moves to control state q_1 when it does not need the resource anymore. A process of smaller index can, however, preempt a process of bigger index number. It is natural to assume that a process that has the resource and is never preempted, eventually reaches control state q_1.

We are interested in verifying that eventually all processes reach q_1, under the assumption that all transitions are weak fair. The parameterized system can be modeled by a fair parametric extended automaton as shown in Figure 1. In this automaton, x counts the processes in control state q_0. The property we want then to check is whether eventually $x = 0$, i.e. $\Diamond x = 0$.

Clearly this property is not satisfied, if we do not assume any fairness on the transition τ_0 decrementing x. Assuming that this transition is weakly fair is, however, too strong because if we remove the guard $t \geq i$ in P_i, the system $P_1 \parallel \cdots \parallel P_n$ will not satisfy the property of interest but still the fair extended automaton does. In fact, what we would like to express is: if the value of t remains always unchanged, then eventually a transition decrementing x is taken. To express this property we add a variable to (for t old) to the abstract system, and add the assignment $to := t$ to the transition τ_1. Then, the constrained weak fairness condition $(\tau_0, to = t)$ expresses the property we want.

4   Symbolic Reachability Analysis

We present now the main principles of the symbolic reachability analysis techniques developed in [5]. For a PEA $\mathcal{T}$, these techniques build (when they terminate) a symbolic reachability graph $SG(\mathcal{T}) = (V, E)$ where V is a finite set of structures representing (infinite) sets of configurations of $\mathcal{T}$ and $E \subseteq V \times V$ is a finite set of transitions between structures in V, corresponding to transitions of $\mathcal{T}$. The fairness conditions are defined similarly to Fair PEA. The constrained edges of the symbolic graph are pairs $\langle e, b \rangle$ with $e \in E$ and b is a boolean expression (in $SC(\mathcal{X}, \mathcal{P})$) on the source configuration of e. A Fair $SG(\mathcal{T})$ is a tuple $(V, E, \mathcal{W}_{SG}, \mathcal{B}_{SG})$ where $\mathcal{W}_{SG}$ (the justice set) is a set of constrained edges and $\mathcal{B}_{SG}$ (the boundedness set) is a set of sets of constrained edges.

4.1   Symbolic Representation Structures

In order to represent sets of configurations of PEAs, we use *Constrained Parametric Difference Bound Matrices*, introduced in [5], which is an extension of the Difference Bound Matrices (DBM) [13] used for the representation of reachability sets of (non parametric) timed automata [4].

Definition 1. *Let $\mathcal{T} = (Q, X, P, \delta)$ be a PEA, let $X = \{x_1, ..., x_n\}$ be the set of counters of the PEA $\mathcal{T}$, and let x_0 be an additional counter whose value is always equal to 0. A parametric difference bound matrix (PDBM) which represents a set of configurations over X is a $(n + 1) \times (n + 1)$ matrix M of elements* *in* $AT(P) \times \{<, \leq\}$. *Each entry of* M, $M[i, j] = (t, \prec)$ *encodes the constraint* $x_i - x_j \prec t$. *Given a valuation* π *of parameters, the semantics of* M *is defined by* $[\![M]\!]_\pi = [\![\wedge_{ij} M(i, j)]\!]_\pi$.

A constrained PDBM, *is a pair* $S = (M, \phi)$ *where* M *is a PDBM and* ϕ *is a constraint in* $FO(P)$. *Given a valuation* π *of parameters, the semantics of* (M, ϕ) *is defined by* $[\![(M, \phi)]\!] = \{(\mu, \pi) \mid \mu \in [\![M]\!]_\pi, \pi \in [\![\phi]\!]\}$.

The extrapolation procedure [5] used to help termination of the reachability analysis introduces new parameters, called *iteration parameters*. These parameters correspond to numbers of iterations of control loops. Let N be the set of these new parameters. The definition of constrained PDBM is extended to represent sets of configurations represented by means of variables in N.

Definition 2. *An* open PDBM *is a PDBM which elements are terms in* $AT(P\cup N) \times \{<, \leq\}$. *An* open constrained PDBM *is a constrained PDBM* (M, ϕ) *where* M *is a open PDBM and* ϕ *is a constraint in* $FO(P \cup N)$.

The semantics of open PDBM and open constrained PDBM are defined similarly, by considering also valuations ν of iteration parameters in N. Given an open PDBM M (resp. constrained PDBM $S = (M, \phi)$), we denote by $Iter(M)$ (resp. $Iter(S)$) the set of iteration variables appearing in M (resp. in M or ϕ).

Definition 3. *A* symbolic configuration Γ *is a pair* (q, S) *where* $q \in Q$ *is a control state, and* S *is a constrained PDBM. A symbolic configuration* $\Gamma = (q, S)$ *includes* $\Gamma' = (q', S')$ *(notation* $\Gamma \supseteq \Gamma'$*) if* $q = q'$ *and* $[\![S]\!] \supseteq [\![S']\!]$.

[5] shows how the standard operations on DBM (transformation into a canonical form, intersection, and inclusion test) can be lifted to (open) constrained PDBM. We have implemented in C++ a package providing data structures and operations for manipulating (open) constrained PDBM over integer or real variables. This package is distributed with the tool TREX[1].

The operations on (open) constrained PDBM manipulate arithmetical terms in $AT(P)$ and boolean formulas over comparisons of the form $t \prec t'$, with $t, t' \in AT(P)$ and $\prec \in \{<, \leq\}$. We have implemented in TREX a package allowing to represent in a compact way these terms and formulas, using arithmetical and logical simplification rules (symmetry of arithmetical operations, factorization, properties of boolean connectives, etc.). Our representation also includes information about the nature of terms (real/integer, linear/non-linear) and formulas (in $LFO(X, P)$ or $RFO(X, P)$). This allows to invoke the suitable decision procedures: OMEGA [17] in the integer linear case, or REDUCE [15] otherwise.

4.2   Building Symbolic Reachability Graphs

Let $\mathcal{T}$ be a PEA. The procedure proposed in [5] computes, given an initial symbolic configuration Γ_0, the symbolic reachability graph $SG(\mathcal{T})$ representing the set $post^*(\Gamma_0)$. For that, starting from Γ_0, the transitions of $\mathcal{T}$ are applied,

---

[1] http://www.liafa.jussieu.fr/~sighirea/trex and
  http://www-verimag.imag.fr/~annichin/trex

when possible, to build new vertices in $SG(\mathcal{T})$. For a transition τ of $\mathcal{T}$ and a symbolic configuration Γ, we denote by $post_\tau(\Gamma)$ the vertex computed by applying τ to Γ. The new vertices of $SG(\mathcal{T})$ are treated according to a depth-first traversal. The construction stops when each new generated vertex is covered by (included in) some already computed vertex.

During this construction, an *extrapolation* technique is used to help termination. The extrapolation technique defined in [5] is based on guessing automatically the effect of iterating an arbitrary number of times a control loop (cycle in the control graph of $\mathcal{T}$) starting from a given symbolic configuration, and checking that this guess is exact (does not introduce non reachable configurations). We present below the main idea of the extrapolation technique.

Let θ be a control loop in $\mathcal{T}$, i.e., a path $\tau_0 \dots \tau_k$ with $\forall i \in \{0, \dots, k\}, \tau_i = (q_i, g_i, sop_i, q_i')$, such that $q = q_0 = q_k'$ and $\forall i \in \{0, \dots, k-1\}, q_i' = q_{i+1}$. Let $\Gamma = (q, S = (M, \phi))$ be a symbolic configuration. We note by $post_\theta(\Gamma)$ the computation $(post_{\tau_k} \circ \dots \circ post_{\tau_0})(\Gamma)$. Suppose that we have computed $S_1 = (M_1, \phi_1)$ and $S_2 = (M_2, \phi_2)$ such that $(q, S_1) = post_\theta(q, S)$ and $(q, S_2) = post_\theta(q, S_1)$. Let $\Delta = M_1 - M$ and $\Delta' = M_2 - M_1$. If for all values of parameters $\Delta = \Delta'$, we may guess that the symbolic configuration obtained after n iterations of θ is $post_\theta^n(q, S) = (q, S_n = (M + n * \Delta, \phi \wedge n \geq 0))$. To check the exactness of this guess, we have to check that for all $n \geq 0$, the application of θ on (q, S_n) has an effect of adding Δ, provided the guards in θ are satisfied. This corresponds to the induction step for the proof of exactness. If the extrapolation can be applied, $post_\theta^n(q, S_n)$ is added to the set of vertices V in $SG(\mathcal{T})$, and the transition $((q, S_1), post_\theta^n(q, S_n))$ to the set of edges E.

5   Translation of Fairness Constraints

We explain how one can adapt the symbolic reachability analysis presented in Section 4 to take into account concrete fairness conditions. To do so, consider a set of constrained actions $\langle \tau_i, f_i \rangle$, for $i = 1, \dots, n$. We associate to each predicate f_i a boolean variable b_i. Then, we extend the symbolic configurations Γ to $\langle \Gamma, \nu \rangle$, where ν is a valuation of the b_i's such that if $\nu(b_i)$ is true (*resp.* false), then there is concrete configuration in Γ that satisfies (*resp.* falsifies) f_i. Notice that the same symbolic configuration Γ may be extended to many extended configurations. Now, we have to lift the predicate transformers $post_\tau$ and $post_\theta$ to extended configurations. Let us first deal with the simple case of $post_\tau$. We then define $post_\tau^f$ as the function that takes an extended configuration $\langle \Gamma, \nu \rangle$ as argument and yields a set $post_\tau^f(\langle \Gamma, \nu \rangle)$ of extended configurations as result. The set $post_\tau^f(\langle \Gamma, \nu \rangle)$ is such that the following conditions are satisfied:

1. If $\langle \Gamma', \nu' \rangle \in post_\tau^f(\langle \Gamma, \nu \rangle)$, then $post_\tau(\Gamma) = \Gamma'$,
2. if $\langle \Gamma', \nu' \rangle \notin post_\tau^f(\langle \Gamma, \nu \rangle)$, then there is no configuration in Γ that evaluates $(f_1, \cdots, f_n)$ to ν'.

Now, the symbolic reachability graph contains an edge labeled by τ from $\langle \Gamma, \nu \rangle$ to all extended configurations in $post_\tau^f(\langle \Gamma, \nu \rangle)$. The definition of $post_\theta^f$ is similar except that in the symbolic reachability graph we will also have edges connecting all configurations in $post^f_\theta(\langle\Gamma, \nu\rangle)$.

Now, we can explain how to translate the concrete fairness conditions to fairness conditions on the symbolic reachability graph. Thus, assume that $\langle\tau, f\rangle$ is in the set $\mathcal{W}$ of constrained weak fairness conditions. Then, when verifying a property on the symbolic reachability graph, we only need to consider paths that contain infinitely many τ-edges, if from some point on they only contain extended configurations where the boolean associated to f evaluates to *true*. In other words, we will have that $\mathcal{W}_{SG}$ contains the constrained edge $\langle e_\tau, b_f\rangle$, where e_τ stands for the edges labeled by τ and b_f is the boolean associated to f. Similarly, for a set $U = \{\langle\tau_i, f_i\rangle \mid 1 \leq i \leq n\} \in \mathcal{B}$ expressing a boundedness condition, we will have that $\{\langle e_{\tau_i}, \vee^n_{i=1} b_i\rangle \mid 1 \leq i \leq n\} \in \mathcal{B}_{SG}$.

6   Synthesis of Fairness Constraints for Elementary Loops

We explain how boundedness conditions can be synthesized for the loops of the symbolic graph which do not correspond to any legal infinite computation in the original fair PEA.

Let consider the simplest case of a self-loop θ (i.e., a loop with only one transitions). To show that θ is finitely (*boundedly*) iterable, the idea is to show that for all configurations γ_0 belonging to the initial symbolic configuration, all executions paths resulting from iterating θ stop. Now, suppose that given an arbitrary number $n \geq 0$, we can compute the configuration $\theta^n(\gamma_0)$ obtained after n iterations of θ starting from γ_0 Then, deciding that θ is boundedly iterable can be reduced to decide if for all initial configurations γ_0, there exists an $n \geq 0$ such that the configuration $\theta^n(\gamma_0)$ does not satisfy the guard of θ.

We will show that, under some conditions, the analysis of complex connected components of the symbolic graph may be reduced to the above idea for analysis of self-loops. For this, we proceed by induction on the complexity of connected component to be analyzed, C. The simpler case are elementary circuits, for which we define the *degree of complexity*, $degree(C) = 1$. For a non-elementary connected component, its degree is defined inductively by $degree(C) = max_{C' \in C}(degree(C')) + 1$ for all C' connected (strict) subcomponent of C. In this section we consider elementary circuits.

6.1   Computation of the Effect

Let $\theta = \Gamma_0\tau_0\Gamma_1\tau_1\Gamma_2...\tau_{k-1}\Gamma_k$ be a computation sequence of the symbolic graph such that θ is an elementary circuit, i.e., $\Gamma_0 \supseteq \Gamma_k$ and $\forall 0 \leq i < j < k. \ \Gamma_i \not\supseteq \Gamma_j$.

Let $\tau = (q_1, g(X, P), sop, q_2)$ be a transition, and let sop correspond to the assignement $x := A_\tau x + b_\tau$ of the counters (including x_0) where A_τ is $(n+1) \times (n+1)$ simple matrix, and b_τ is a $(n+1)$-vector of terms in $AT(\mathcal{P})$.

We can lift operations on vectors of counters to operations on PDBMs in the following manner. First, we transform the vector b_τ into a $(n+1) \times (n+1)$ matrix of terms B_τ defined by: $\forall 0 \leq i, j \leq n. \ B_\tau[i, j] = b_\tau(i) - b_\tau(j)$. Then, applying the assignement $x := A_\tau x + b_\tau$ on a set of configurations described by a PDBM M leads to a PDBM $M' = A_\tau * M * A_\tau^T + B_\tau$ where A_τ^T is the transposed matrix of A_τ.

In this way, the effect of a transition of the symbolic graph on a PDBM is given by a pair of matrices $(A, B) \in A \times B$, where A is the class of simple matrices, and B is defined by:

$$B = \{B \mid \forall 0 \leq i, j \leq n. \quad B[i,j] \in AT(P \cup N) \wedge B[i,j] = -B[j,i] \wedge \\ \forall 0 \leq k \leq n. \quad B[i,k] + B[k,j] = B[i,j]\}$$

Matrices in A and B have nice properties. Indeed, A is closed under multiplication of matrices, and B is closed under addition and closed under multiplication with matrices in A. Notice that, matrices in B represent parameterized configurations of counters (they encode single vectors of terms). We define the mapping $cf : B \to (AT(P \cup N))^{n+1}$, which maps each matrix in B to the corresponding parameterized configuration for counters.

Using these properties of sets A and B, it is easy to show that the effect of a sequence of transitions $\tau_0 \tau_1 ...$ on a PDBM is also given by a pair of matrices $(A, B) \in A \times B$. Consequently, starting with a PDBM $M_0 \in \Gamma_0$ and iterating one time θ gives a new PDBM $\theta(M_0) = A_\theta * M_0 * A_\theta^T + B_\theta$ where the pair $(A_\theta, B_\theta) \in A \times B$ cumulates the effect of the sequence of transitions composing θ. The following proposition states the conditions under which $\theta^n(M_0)$ can be computed.

Proposition 1. *Let* $\theta = \Gamma_0 \tau_0 \Gamma_1 \tau_1 \Gamma_2 ... \tau_{k-1} \Gamma_k$ *be an elementary circuit in a symbolic graph such that* $\Gamma_0 = (q_0, (M_0, \phi_0))$ *and the effect of the sequence of transitions* $\tau_0, ..., \tau_{k-1}$ *is given by matrices* (A_θ, B_θ). *If the following PDBM* $\Delta_\theta = A_\theta * M_0 * A_\theta^T + B_\theta - M_0$ *satisfies the conditions:*

- SC_1: $A_\theta * \Delta_\theta * A_\theta^T = \Delta_\theta$ *and*
- SC_2: Δ_θ *is a closed parameterized configuration for counters, i.e.,* $\Delta_\theta \in B$ *and is closed (i.e., does not contain variables in* N)

then, $\forall x_0 \in [\![M_0, \phi_0]\!]. \ \forall n \geq 0. \quad \theta^n(x_0) = x_0 + n * cf(\Delta_\theta)$.

Both conditions SC_1 and SC_2 correspond to conjunctions of equalities between arithmetical expressions over integers. These formulas are decidable in the linear case, i.e., for LFO formulas. Condition SC_1 is similar to the first condition for exactness of extrapolation (see Section 4). Condition SC_2 means that the effect of each iteration is *deterministic*, that is, each iteration of θ has the effect of adding the same (parametric) value defined by Δ_θ.

Example 2. We apply Proposition 1 for the extended automaton on Figure 2 (a), which symbolic graph contains only one self-loop $\theta = \Gamma_0 \ t_1 \ \Gamma_0$. For this circuit $A_\theta = I$ and $B_\theta = \begin{pmatrix} 0 & 2 \\ -2 & 0 \end{pmatrix} \in B$. For all M_0, $\Delta_\theta = A_\theta * M_0 * A_\theta^T + B_\theta - M_0 = B_\theta$ which satisfies trivially the conditions SC_1 and SC_2. By Proposition 1 we have $\theta^n(x_0) = x_0 + n * (0, -2)$, since $cf(\Delta_\theta) = (0, -2)$.

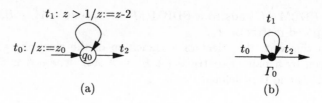

Fig. 2. A Simple Parameterized Extended Automaton (a) and Its Symbolic Graph (b).

Remark 1. The computation presented above can be extended to the case of Parameterized Timed Automata for time-deterministic circuits. Since the evolution of clock variables is given not only by the operations on transitions, but also by the guards and the invariants, the computation of the effect of loops should take into account these elements. However, the computation of Δ_θ is already done during the symbolic reachability algorithm for extrapolation. We have to test in addition that Δ_θ satisfies condition SC_2.

6.2   Synthesis of Fairness Constraints

We say that an elementary circuit θ is *boundedly iterable* in the configuration Γ_0 if there is an integer $n \geq 0$ such that $\theta^n(\Gamma_0) = \emptyset$.

By Proposition 1, we know that for every parametric configuration $x_0 \in \Gamma_0$, $\theta^n(x_0) = x_0 + n * cf(\Delta_\theta)$. Let us denote by $\tau_{[0,i-1]}$ the sequence of transitions $\tau_0...\tau_{i-1}$, for any $i \in \{0, ..., k-1\}$, and by $\tau_{[0,i-1]}(x)$ the effect of the sequence of transitions $\tau_0...\tau_{i-1}$ on x (if $i = 0$, we consider that no transition is applied). Then, we have:

Proposition 2. *Let θ be an elementary circuit such that Δ_θ satisfies SC_1 and SC_2. Then θ is boundedly iterable iff $\forall x_0 \in \Gamma_0. \exists n \geq 0. \exists i \in \{0, ..., k - 1\}. \tau_{[0,i-1]}(x_0 + n * cf(\Delta_\theta)) \not\models guard(\tau_i)$.*

The formula given by Proposition 2 have an equivalent form in terms of operations on PDBM:

$$\forall P \forall N \forall X_0. \quad \phi_0(P, N) \wedge M_0(P, N, X_0) \implies$$
$$\exists n \geq 0. \quad \vee_{i=0}^{k-1} \tau_{[0,i-1]}(M_0 + n * \Delta_\theta) \cap guard(\tau_i) = \emptyset$$

The validity of this formula is decidable in the linear case, since all variables are integers. If the formula above is valid, we synthesize a boundedness constraint $T(\theta) \in \mathcal{B}_{SG}$ for the set $T(\theta) = \{\tau_0, ..., \tau_{k-1}\}$ of transitions in θ.

From the test given in Proposition 2, we can build a formula $\phi_i^{\theta, \Gamma_0}(x, n)$ giving the condition under which after iterating n times θ on the configuration $x \in \Gamma_0$, the execution stops at the transition τ_i:

$$\phi_i^{\theta, \Gamma_0}(x_0, n) = \tau_{[0,i-1]}(x_0 + n * cf(\Delta_\theta)) \not\models guard(\tau_i)$$

which is easy to translate in terms of operations on PDBM.

Example 3. We consider here an example which is inspired from the model of the Bounded Retransmission Protocol. It is a system with two clocks c_1 and c_2 and a counter x (see Figure 3 (a)). Intuitively, c_1 represents the clock of a

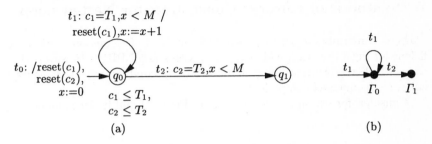

Fig. 3. An Elementary Circuit of BRP.

sender and c_2 the clock of a receiver. These clocks are compared with parametric bounds T_1 and T_2 supposed to be real values. The counter x counts the number of times the loop $q_0 t_1 q_0$ is performed. The transition t_1 corresponds in BRP to a retransmission action by the sender. The number of these retransmissions is bounded by M which is an integer parameter. The question is whether the state q_1 (considered as a bad state) is reachable. Roughly speaking, this corresponds to a property of synchronization between the sender and the receiver in BRP: the timeout of the receiver should not expire before the sender has finished all its retransmissions.

The symbolic graph generated for this example is given on Figure 3 (b), where $\Gamma_0 = (q_0, S_0)$ and $\Gamma_1 = (q_1, S_1)$ with

$$S_0 \equiv (M_0 = (0 \le c_1 \le T_1 \wedge (n+1) * T_1 \le c_2 \le (n+2) * T_1 \wedge,$$
$$c_1 - c_2 = (n+1) * T_1 \wedge x = n+1)$$
$$\phi_0 = (0 \le n \wedge 0 \le T_1 \wedge (n+2) * T_1 \le T_2 \wedge n < M))$$
$$S_1 \equiv (M_1 = (0 \le c_1 \le T_1 \wedge T_2 \le c_2 \wedge c_1 - c_2 = (n+1) * T_1 \wedge x = n+1),$$
$$\phi_1 = (0 \le n \wedge 0 \le T_1 \wedge (n+1) * T_1 \le T_2 \le (n+2) * T_1 \wedge n+1 < M))$$

The presence of the unfair loop in Γ_0, $\theta = \Gamma_0 t_1 \Gamma_0$, fails the verification of the reachability property for q_1. By analyzing θ, we find that Δ_θ (on both clocks and counters) is a parameterized configuration and $\Delta_\theta(c_1) = 0$, $\Delta_\theta(c_2) = T_1$, $\Delta_\theta(c_2 - c_1) = T_1$, and $\Delta_\theta(x) = 1$. By Proposition 2 we have that θ is boundedly iterable iff the formula:

$$\forall T_1, T_2, c_1, c_2. \ \forall M, x, n. \ \ \phi_0 \wedge M_0 \implies \exists n' \ge 0. \ x + n' \ge M$$

After the elimination of real variables (T_1, T_2, c_1, c_2), we obtain the following linear formula on integer variables:

$$\forall M, x, n. \ \ 0 \le n \wedge n < M \wedge x = n+1 \implies \exists n' \ge 0. \ x + n' \ge M$$

which is clearly valid. Hence, we can generate a boundedness condition for this loop, saying that if t_1 is taken infinitely often, then transitions different from t_1, including t_2, are also taken infinitely often.

7   Synthesis of Fairness Constraints for Nested Loops

Fairness constraints generation based on analysis of elementary circuits is sufficient for dealing with a wide class of systems (e.g., BRP). However, there are cases which require reasoning about arbitrary combination of elementary circuits, i.e., connected components.

Consider, for example, the program of Figure 4 and its PEA model.

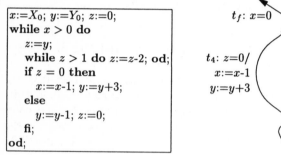
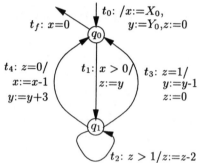

Fig. 4. Example of Nested Loops.

The approaches [12, 11] based on ranking functions will fail to prove the termination of this program. Indeed, the ranking functions synthesized for the innermost and the outermost **while** statements cannot be ordered according to a lexicographic order using the structure of the program: the behaviour of the inner depends on the value of y computed in the outermost loop, which behaviour depends of the value of z computed in the innermost loop. In our approach, the reachability algorithm applied on the extended automaton of Figure 4 generates the symbolic graph given on Figure 5 and Table 1. In this graph, we represent by dotted transitions a sequence of transitions. For example, configuration Γ_1 is reached from Γ_0 by executing the sequence t_0, t_1. The symbolic graph has several self-loops build from transition t_2. Using the method presented in Section 6, we can infer that these loops are boundedly iterable, which means that the innermost **while** statement always stops. The connected components starting in Γ_0' and Γ_0'' correspond to the outermost **while** statement for respectively odd and even values of the parameter Y_0. Indeed, from the initial configuration Γ_0, we unfold one time the outermost **while** statement. After executing the sequence $t_0 t_1 t_2 t_2^*$ (the parameter n_0 is introduced by iterating t_2 in Γ_2), we have two cases depending on which transition (t_3 or t_4) is chosen in configuration Γ_2. If transition t_3 is chosen, we deduce that Y_0 is odd (see constraint

ϕ_0' in Table 1). By unfolding once more the outermost **while** statement (i.e., the sequence $t_1t_2t_2^*t_4$), we generate a configuration which differs from Γ_0 by the vector ($x_0 = 0, x = -1, y = 2, z = 0$). After two more unfoldings, the outermost **while** produces the same effect. The extrapolation technique generates the configuration Γ_0' and the connected component $t_1t_2t_2^*t_3t_1t_2t_2^*t_4$ starting in Γ_0'. The effect of each of the components starting in Γ_0' and Γ_0'' is to add

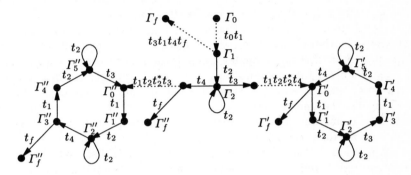

Fig. 5. Symbolic Graph for the Example of Nested Loops.

Table 1. Main Symbolic Configurations for Graph on Figure 5.

conf.	ctrl. state	PDBM			constraint
		x	y	z	
Γ_0	q_0	X_0	Y_0	0	$\phi_0 \equiv X_0, Y_0 \geq 0$
Γ_0'	q_0	$X_0\text{-}n_1'\text{-}1$	$Y_0+2n_1'+2$	0	$\phi_0' \equiv Y_0 = 2n_0+3, X_0, Y_0, n_1', n_0 \geq 0$
Γ_1'	q_1	$X_0\text{-}n_1'\text{-}1$	$Y_0+2n_1'+2$	$Y_0+2n_1'+2$	ϕ_0'
Γ_2'	q_1	$X_0\text{-}n_1'\text{-}1$	$Y_0+2n_1'+2$	$Y_0+2n_1'\text{-}2n_2'$	$\phi_0', n_2' \geq 0$
Γ_3'	q_0	$X_0\text{-}n_1'\text{-}1$	$Y_0+2n_1'+1$	0	ϕ_0'
Γ_4'	q_1	$X_0\text{-}n_1'\text{-}1$	$Y_0+2n_1'+1$	$Y_0+2n_1'+1$	ϕ_0'
Γ_5'	q_1	$X_0\text{-}n_1'\text{-}1$	$Y_0+2n_1'+1$	$Y_0+2n_1'\text{-}2n_3'\text{-}1$	$\phi_0', n_3' \geq 0$
Γ_0''	q_0	$X_0\text{-}n_1''\text{-}1$	$Y_0+2n_1''+2$	0	$\phi_0'' \equiv Y_0 = 2n_0, X_0, Y_0, n_1'', n_0 \geq 0$
Γ_1''	q_1	$X_0\text{-}n_1''\text{-}1$	$Y_0+2n_1''+2$	$Y_0+2n_1''+2$	ϕ_0''
Γ_2''	q_1	$X_0\text{-}n_1''\text{-}1$	$Y_0+2n_1''+2$	$Y_0+2n_1''\text{-}2n_2''$	$\phi_0'', n_2'' \geq 0$
Γ_3''	q_0	$X_0\text{-}n_1''\text{-}2$	$Y_0+2n_1''+5$	0	ϕ_0''
Γ_4''	q_1	$X_0\text{-}n_1''\text{-}2$	$Y_0+2n_1''+5$	$Y_0+2n_1''+5$	ϕ_0''
Γ_5''	q_1	$X_0\text{-}n_1''\text{-}2$	$Y_0+2n_1''+5$	$Y_0+2n_1''\text{-}2n_3''+3$	$\phi_0'', n_3'' \geq 0$

the vector $cf(\Delta) = (0, -1, 2, 0)$, which satisfies the conditions SC_1 and SC_2 of Proposition 1. This is due to the fact that the effect of innermost loops is reset by the transitions t_3 and t_4. However, these components are not elementary circuits. Then, we need to generalize the techniques given in Section 6 in order to deal with a whole connected component. We show hereafter that, under some conditions, reasoning about connected components can be reduced to reasoning about elementary circuits.

7.1 Computation of the Effect

Case 1. Consider the (simpler) case of a connected component C having a unique elementary circuit θ containing the initial configuration of C, $\Gamma_0 = (q_0, (M_0, \phi_0))$. The connected subcomponents of C different from θ may share zero or more symbolic configurations with θ (see first part of Figure 6).

We build from C a connected component C_θ having the same degree and execution paths that C, but where the connected subcomponents different from θ share with θ at most one symbolic configuration. For this, let $\theta = \Gamma_0\tau_0\Gamma_1\tau_1\Gamma_2$ $...\tau_{k-1}\Gamma_0$. We order the configurations of θ according to the transition relation, i.e., $\Gamma_0 \prec \Gamma_1 \prec \Gamma_2... \prec \Gamma_{k-1}$. Since θ is the unique elementary circuit in C containing Γ_0, the unique path relating Γ_i to Γ_j with $i < j$ is contained in θ. Let Γ_i be a configuration of θ shared with a subcomponent of C. We note by $CC(\Gamma_i)$ the maximal connected subcomponent of C not including θ, such that Γ_i is the minimal (in sense of $\prec$) configuration of $CC(\Gamma_i)$ shared with θ. Then, C_θ is build from θ and, for each configuration Γ_i of θ, we put a copy of $CC(\Gamma_i)$ such that the only configuration shared with θ is Γ_i.

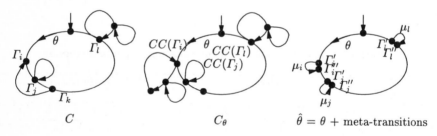

$$C \qquad\qquad C_\theta \qquad\qquad \hat\theta = \theta + \text{meta-transitions}$$

Fig. 6. Building $\hat\theta$ for C.

By construction, it follows that execution paths of C and C_θ are equal. This means that if C_θ is boundedly iterable, C is also boundedly iterable. The result of iterating one time C on a configuration x is defined by $C(x) = \{x' \mid \exists n_1...n_{k-1} \geq 0.\ \ x' = (\tau_{k-1} \circ CC(\Gamma_{k_1})^{n_{k-1}} \circ ... \circ CC(\Gamma_1)^{n_1} \circ \tau_0)(x)\}$. Clearly, this set has cardinality ≥ 1, since the iteration parameters introduce non-deterministic behaviours. In order to be able to compute this set, we need to introduce additional conditions ensuring that applying C gives always the same result, i.e., its effect is deterministic.

Suppose that it is possible to compute for each subcomponent $CC(\Gamma_i)$ of C_θ the effect $\Delta_{CC(\Gamma_i)}$ satisfying the conditions of Proposition 1. Then, we can replace the subcomponent $CC(\Gamma_i)$ by a meta-transition μ_i, which operation is $x' := x + n * cf(\Delta_{CC(\Gamma_i)})$ with $n \geq 0$ (a new, unused $n \in N$ for each meta-transition). The meta-transition μ_i is introduced by splitting Γ_i in two: Γ_i' and Γ_i'', the source resp. the target of μ_i.

In this way, we obtain an elementary circuit, called $\hat{\theta}$, which is built with transitions from θ and with meta-transitions involving iteration parameters $n \in N$. The result of Proposition 1 can be applied to this circuit and we obtain that:

Proposition 3. *If $\Delta_{\hat{\theta}} = A_{\hat{\theta}} * M_0 * A_{\hat{\theta}}^T + B_{\hat{\theta}} - M_0$ satisfies conditions SC_1 and SC_2, then $\forall x_0 \in [\![M_0, \phi_0]\!] \forall n \geq 0.\ C^n(x_0) = x_0 + n * cf(\Delta_{\hat{\theta}})$.*

We recall that condition SC_2 asks that $\Delta_{\hat{\theta}}$ is a configuration and it does not contain iteration parameters, so the set $C(x)$ has cardinality 1. This is possible if the circuit θ contains transitions with reset operations such that the effect of meta-transitions is canceled.

Example 4. Consider the connected component C' containing Γ_0' in the symbolic graph given on Figure 4 (b). It corresponds to an odd initial value for Y_0 and has only one elementary circuit θ' containing Γ_0'. The elementary loops in Γ_2' and Γ_5' can be reduced to meta-transitions. Moreover, the effect computed using $\hat{\theta}'$ is a configuration with $\Delta_{C'}(x) = -1$, $\Delta_{C'}(y) = 2$, and $\Delta_{C'}(z) = 0$. By Proposition 3, we have that $\forall x_0 \in \Gamma_0 \forall n \geq 0.\ C'^n(x_0) = x_0 + n * cf(\Delta_{C'})$. The same computation may be done for connected component corresponding to even values of Y_0.

Remark 2. In some cases, we can deal with the presence of iteration parameters in $\Delta_{\hat{\theta}}$. The simpler case is when all operations in C cumulate values in counters, i.e., all assignments have the form $x := x + t$ (there are no reset operations). Indeed, in absence of reset operations, the (meta-)transitions in $\hat{\theta}$ cumulate their results, and the effect of the circuit is given by: $C^n(x) = x + \Sigma_{1 \leq i < \infty} n_i * cf(\Delta_i)$, where $\Delta_i \in B$ are build from terms of assignments in (meta-)transitions.

Case 2. Consider a connected component C having several elementary circuits including its initial configuration $\Gamma_0 = (q_0, (M_0, \phi_0))$. Let $\Theta(C)$ be the set of these elementary circuits. In order to analyze C, we build from C a connected component $\tilde{C}$ having the same degree and execution paths that C, but where each connected subcomponent including Γ_0 contains only one elementary circuit of $\Theta(C)$. Moreover, each pair of such subcomponents shares only Γ_0 (see Figure 7). For this, let θ_i be an elementary circuit in $\Theta(C)$. With θ_i, we consider all maximal connected subcomponents sharing states with θ_i and without another elementary circuit in $\Theta(C)$. This will form the maximal connected subcomponent of C built around θ_i. We note by $CC(\theta_i)$ this subcomponent and by $EC(C)$ the set of all these subcomponents, $EC(C) = \{CC(\theta_i) \mid \theta_i \in \Theta(C)\}$. Then, $\tilde{C}$ is build from $EC(C)$ by splitting states such that the only state shared by each pair of subcomponents $CC(\theta_i)$ is the initial configuration Γ_0.

It is easy to show that C and $\tilde{C}$ have the same execution paths. This means that if $\tilde{C}$ is boundedly iterable, C is also boundedly iterable. The paths build by iterating one time C on x are given by $C(x) = \cup_{\theta_i \in \Theta(C)} (\cup_{j \neq i} CC(\theta_j))^* CC(\theta_i)$.

Now, if we consider separately each subcomponent $CC(\theta_i)$ of $\tilde{C}$, we can use Proposition 3 to compute its effect, and to reduce it to a meta-transition. In the best case, where all the subcomponents $CC(\theta_i)$ may be reduced to a meta-transition, we can compute, for each $\theta_i \in \Theta(C)$ the effect of $(\cup_{j \neq i} CC(\theta_j))^*$

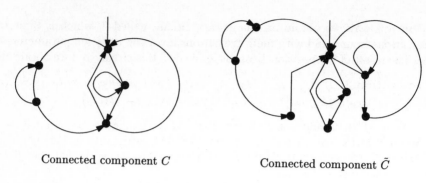

Connected component C　　　　　Connected component $\tilde{C}$

Fig. 7. Building $\tilde{C}$.

$CC(\theta_i)$, noted $\Delta_{CC+(\theta_i)}$. Then, iterating C an arbitrary number of times n increments x by a parameterized configuration chosen non-deterministically in the set $\{n_1 * \Delta_{CC+(\theta_1)}, \ldots, n_l * \Delta_{CC+(\theta_l)} \mid n_1 \geq 0, \ldots, n_l \geq 0\}$. To be able to characterize C^n, we require that all these values be equal.

Theorem 1. *Let C be a connected component with $degree(C) \geq 1$, and $\Gamma_0 = (q_0, (M_0, \phi_0))$ its initial configuration. If C satisfies the following two conditions:*

- *Each strict subcomponent of C can be reduced to a meta-transitions.*
- *For all elementary circuit θ_j containing the initial state of C, the effect $\Delta_{CC(\theta_j)}$ satisfies conditions SC_1 and SC_2 and are all equal to a closed parameterized configuration Δ_C.*

Then, $\forall x_0 \in [\![M_0, \phi_0]\!] \forall n \geq 0$. $C^n(x_0) = x_0 + n * cf(\Delta_C)$.

Proof. If it exists only one elementary circuit including Γ_0, the result follows from Proposition 3. If C contains more than one elementary circuits including Γ_0, we compute its effect using $\tilde{C}$ build like above. The execution of $\tilde{C}$ is given by $\Sigma_i (\cup_{j \neq i} CC(\theta_j))^* CC(\theta_i)$, i.e., the sum of executions including at least an elementary circuit. By hypothesis, we can compute $\Delta_{CC(\theta_j)}$. Moreover, we have that all $\Delta_{CC+(\theta_j)}$ satisfies SC_1, SC_2, and are equal to Δ_C. Then, using the definition of the execution of $\tilde{C}$, it follows that for any number of iterations n of $\tilde{C}$, iterations executed in any order, $\tilde{C}^n(\Gamma_0) = \Gamma_0 + n * \Delta_C$. Since C and $\tilde{C}$ have the same execution paths and Δ_C represents a parameterized configuration (and not a zone), the result follows.

7.2　Synthesis of Fairness Constraints

We say that a connected component C is *boundedly iterable* in the configuration Γ_0 if there is an integer $n \geq 0$ such that $C^n(\Gamma_0) = \emptyset$.

We show now how fairness constraints can be synthesized if C satisfies the hypothesis of Theorem 1. The idea is to synthesize a formula for C expressing the fact that all execution paths of C stop. By Theorem 1, we know that for every parametric configuration $x_0 \in \Gamma_0$, $C^n(x_0) = x_0 + n * cf(\Delta_C)$. Moreover, we can built from C the component $\tilde{C}$ (see 7.1), which has the same execution paths like C and disjoint connected subcomponents in $EC(C)$. For each connected subcomponent of $EC(C)$, let $\theta = \Gamma_0\tau_0\Gamma_1...\Gamma_{k-1}\tau_{k-1}\Gamma_0$ (in $\Theta(C)$) be its elementary circuit including the initial configuration of C. Following the method described in Section 6, we build from θ and the meta-transitions μ_i ($0 \leq i < k$) corresponding to the connected component $CC(\Gamma_j)$, the elementary circuit $\hat{\theta} = \Gamma_0'\mu_0\Gamma_0''\tau_0\Gamma_1'...\Gamma_{k-1}'\mu_{k-1}\Gamma_{k-1}''\tau_{k-1}\Gamma_0'$. We denote by $\hat{\theta}_{[0,j-1]}$ the sequence $\mu_0\tau_0...\mu_{j-1}\tau_{j-1}\mu_j$. Since all subcomponents of C may be reduced to meta-transitions, we can construct for each subcomponent $CC(\Gamma_j)$ the formula $\phi_l^{CC(\Gamma_j),\Gamma_j}(x,n)$ which gives the condition under which after iterating n times $CC(\Gamma_j)$ on the configuration $x \in \Gamma_j$, the execution of $CC(\Gamma_j)$ stops at its l-th configuration.

We show that we can construct from these formulas another formula $\phi_j^{\hat{\theta},\Gamma_0}(x,n)$ saying that after iterating n times $\hat{\theta}$ on the configuration $x \in \Gamma_0$, the execution of $\hat{\theta}$ stops at its j-th configuration ($0 \leq j \leq k-1$). This formula is the disjunction of three formula expressing all the possible cases in which the execution may stop in configuration Γ_j.

Case 1. None of edges outgoing from Γ_j and remaining in $CC(\theta_i)$ can be taken:

$$\phi_{j,(1)}^{\hat{\theta},\Gamma_0}(x,n) = \exists m_0,...,m_j \geq 0. \bigwedge_{\tau:\Gamma_j \to_\tau \Gamma, \Gamma \in CC(\theta)} \hat{\theta}_{[0,j-1]}(x + n * cf(\Delta_C)) \not\models guard(\tau)$$

The integer variables $m_0,...,m_j$ are iteration parameters used in the meta-transitions of the sequence $\hat{\theta}_{[0,j-1]}$. We can quantify existentially all these variables due to the determinism of the symbolic graph.

Case 2. The execution stops into the connected subcomponent $CC(\Gamma_j)$, but not in the first configuration of this component, i.e., Γ_j:

$$\phi_{j,(2)}^{\hat{\theta},\Gamma_0}(x,n) = \exists m_0,...,m_j, m \geq 0. \bigvee_{l \neq 0} \phi_l^{CC(\Gamma_j),\Gamma_j}(\hat{\theta}_{[0,j-1]}(x + n * cf(\Delta_C)), m)$$

Case 3. The execution of $CC(\Gamma_j)$ does not terminate, which means that the hypothesis of infinitely often execution of *all* transitions in C is not satisfied:

$$\phi_{j,(3)}^{\hat{\theta},\Gamma_0}(x,n) = \exists m_0,...,m_j \geq 0. \forall m \geq 0. \neg\phi^{CC(\Gamma_j),\Gamma_j}(\hat{\theta}_{[0,j-1]}(x + n * cf(\Delta_C)), m)$$

Proposition 4. *Let $CC(\theta)$ be a connected component having a unique elementary circuit θ such that we can compute its effect $\Delta_{CC(\theta)}$. Then $CC(\theta)$ is boundedly iterable iff $\forall P \forall N \forall x_0. \Gamma_0(x_0, P, N) \Longrightarrow \exists n \geq 0. \bigvee_{j \in \{0,...,k-1\}} \phi_j^{\hat{\theta},\Gamma_0}(x_0, n)$.*

It is easy to show that the test given above can be translated into a test using operations on PDBM. The formula obtained is decidable in the linear case.

The criterion to test bounded iterability of C is obtained by the conjunction of all the formula obtained for each component in $EC(C)$. If this criterion is valid, we can synthesize the boundedness constraint $T(C) \in \mathcal{B}_{SG}$ for the set $T(C)$ of transitions in C.

Example of Nested Loops (cont.) Let consider the symbolic graph given on Figure 5. Let C' be the connected component starting in Γ_0', which corresponds to an odd initial value for Y_0. Let θ' be the elementary circuit of C' containing Γ_0'. The effect of C' may be computed since the elementary loops in Γ_2' and Γ_5' can be reduced to meta-transitions. Moreover, the effect of C' is constant and equal to $cf(\Delta_{C'}) = (0, -1, 2, 0)$ (see the beginning of this section). Then, the Proposition 4 can be applied. The formulas built for cases **2** and **3** above are trivially false, since all the connected sub-components of C' stop. For case **1**, the formulas built for the configurations other than Γ_0' and Γ_3' (i.e., for $j = 0, 3$) are also trivially false, since it is always possible to take a transition in C' from these configurations. For both configurations Γ_0' and Γ_3', we obtain the formula following involving the guard of the transition t_1:

$$\phi_{0,(1)}^{\theta',\Gamma_0'}(x, y, z, n) \equiv (x_0, x, y, z) + n * cf(\Delta_{C'}) \not\models guard(t_1) \equiv x - n \le 0$$

By Proposition 4 we have that C' is boundedly iterable iff the formula $\forall X_0, Y_0 \forall n_1' \forall x, y, z.\ \Gamma_0' \implies \exists n \ge 0.\ x - n \le 0$ is valid. Since in Γ_0' we have that $x = X_0 - n_1' - 1$, this formula is valid because for all values of X_0 and n_1' it always exists an integer $n \ge 0$ such that $X_0 - n_1' - 1 - n \le 0$. So, the boundedness condition $T(C') \in \mathcal{B}_{SG}$ is generated. The same analysis can be done for the component starting in Γ_0''.

8   Conclusion

We have presented a method for verifying safety and liveness properties for fair parameterized extended automata (PEA). Our method is based on symbolic reachability analysis using powerful symbolic representation structures and extrapolation techniques. We have mainly developed techniques allowing to determine whether a component (i.e., a loop and some kind of nested loops) in the symbolic graph is boundedly iterable, i.e., corresponds to the abstraction of a terminating component of the original model. Our techniques can deal with complex systems that cannot be analyzed by the existing automatic techniques, e.g., those based on synthesis of ranking functions [12, 11]. In particular, we have shown how our techniques can be used to analyze automatically a parameterized version of BRP protocol.

References

1. P. Abdulla, A. Annichini, and A. Bouajjani. Symbolic verification of lossy channel systems: Application to the bounded retransmission protocol. In *Proceedings of 5th TACAS*, volume 1579 of *LNCS*. Springer Verlag, 1999.
2. P. Abdulla, A. Bouajjani, B. Jonsson, and M. Nilsson. Handling global conditions in parametrized system verification. In *Proceedings of 11th CAV*, volume 1633 of *LNCS*. Springer Verlag, 1999.
3. P.A. Abdulla, A. Bouajjani, and B. Jonsson. On-the-fly analysis of systems with unbounded, lossy, FIFO channels. In *Proceedings of the 10th CAV*, volume 1427 of *LNCS*, pages 305–317. Springer Verlag, 1998.

4. R. Alur and D.L. Dill. A theory of timed automata. *Theoretical Computer Science*, 126:183–235, 1994.

5. A. Annichini, E. Asarin, and A. Bouajjani. Symbolic techniques for parametric reasoning about counter and clock systems. In E.A. Emerson and A.P. Sistla, editors, *Proceedings of the 12th CAV*, volume 1855 of *LNCS*, pages 419–434. Springer Verlag, July 2000.

6. K. Baukus, Y. Lakhnech, and K. Stahl. Verifying universal properties of parameterized networks. In *Proceedings of FTRTFT*, 2000.

7. B. Boigelot, P. Godefroid, B. Willems, and P. Wolper. The power of qdds. In *Proceedings of SAS'97*, volume 1302 of *LNCS*. Springer Verlag, 1997.

8. B. Boigelot and P. Wolper. Symbolic verification with periodic sets. In *Proceedings of the 6th CAV*, volume 818 of *LNCS*. Springer Verlag, 1994.

9. A. Bouajjani and P. Habermehl. Symbolic reachability analysis of fifo-channel systems with nonregular sets of configurations. In *Proceedings of ICALP'97*, LNCS. Springer Verlag, 1997.

10. A. Bouajjani, B. Jonsson, M. Nilsson, and T. Touili. Regular model checking. In E.A. Emerson and A.P. Sistla, editors, *Proceedings of the 12th CAV*, volume 1855 of *LNCS*, pages 403–418, July 2000.

11. M. Colon and H. Sipma. Synthesis of linear ranking functions. In *Proceedings of TACAS'01*, 2001.

12. D. Dams, R. Gerth, and O. Grumberg. A heuristic for the automatic generation of ranking functions. In *Proceedings of WAVe*, pages 1–8, 2000.

13. D. Dill. Timing assumptions and verification of finite-state concurrent systems. In J. Sifakis, editor, *Proceedings of the 1st CAV*, volume 407 of *LNCS*, pages 197–212. Springer Verlag, 1989.

14. R.W. Floyd. Assigning meanings to programs. In *In. Proc. Symp. on Appl. Math. 19*, pages 19–32. American Mathematical Society, 1967.

15. A.C. Hearn. *REDUCE — User's and Contributed Packages Manual*. Codemist Ltd., February 1999. version 3.7.

16. Z. Manna and A. Pnueli. Completing the temporal picture. *Theoretical Computer Science*, 83(1):97–130, 1991.

17. Omega Team. *The Omega Library*, November 1996. version 1.1.0.

18. A. Pnueli and E. Shahar. Liveness and acceleration in parametrized verification. In *Proceedings of the 12th CAV*, volume 1855. Springer Verlag, 2000.

Incompleteness, Counterexamples, and Refinements in Abstract Model-Checking

Roberto Giacobazzi[1] and Elisa Quintarelli[1,2]

[1] Dip. di Informatica, Università di Verona
Strada Le Grazie 15, 37134 Verona (Italy)
[2] Dip. di Elettronica e Informazione, Politecnico di Milano
Piazza Leonardo da Vinci, 20133 Milano (Italy)
{giaco,quintare}@sci.univr.it

Abstract. In this paper we study the relation between the lack of completeness in abstract interpretation of model-checking and the structure of the counterexamples produced by a model-checker. We consider two dual forms of completeness of an abstract interpretation: Forward and backward completeness. They correspond respectively to the standard γ/α completeness of an abstract interpretation and can be related with each other by adjunction. We give a constructive characterization of Clarke et al.'s spurious counterexamples in terms of both forward and backward completeness of the underlying abstract interpretation. This result allows us to understand the structure of the counterexamples that can be removed by systematically refining abstract domains to achieve completeness with respect to a given operation. We apply our result to improve static program analysis by refining the model-checking of an abstract interpretation.
Keywords: Completeness, Model-checking, Verification, Abstract Interpretation, Domain Refinement, Program Analysis.

1 Introduction

Many authors recognized in the possibility of modifying abstract models by modifying abstractions a great potential for improving abstract model-checking in precision and reducing complexity (e.g. see Section 9 in [10]), but few applications of these techniques are known in the field of model-checking. In this paper we observe that there exists a strong connection between the standard notion of complete abstract interpretation [6, 7, 14] and the corresponding one for abstract model-checking [10, 2], and we show how the latter one can be achieved by minimally modifying abstract domains.

Completeness in abstract interpretation corresponds to require that no loss of precision is introduced by approximating a semantic function computed on abstract objects with respect to approximating the same computation on concrete objects. Therefore, no loss of precision is accumulated in abstract computations by approximating concrete input objects. This property comes directly from the original definition of Galois-connection based abstract interpretations [6, 7]: If

P. Cousot (Ed.): SAS 2001, LNCS 2126, pp. 356–373, 2001.

α and γ is a pair of adjoint functions in a Galois connection specifying an abstract interpretation, and $\mathcal{O}$ and $\mathcal{O}^\sharp$ are respectively the concrete and abstract operations, we say that the abstract interpretation is complete if $\alpha \circ \mathcal{O} = \mathcal{O}^\sharp \circ \alpha$. Recently, Giacobazzi et al. [14] observed that completeness for an abstract interpretation, i.e., abstract domains and abstract operations, only depends upon the structure of the underlying abstract domains and, in particular, that it is always possible to make any abstract domain A complete with respect to a concrete function $\mathcal{O}$ by minimally extending or even reducing A. This process is known as the *complete shell/core* of A. This means that a systematic domain transformer can be introduced to improve precision of domains with respect to a given function by letting the new domains be complete with respect to this function.

The Problem

The idea of abstract (state-)model-checking is that of verifying temporal properties against an approximated model which is systematically derived from the concrete semantics of the system we want to analyze. This is always achieved by approximating the information contained in its states. Since the pioneering work on model-checking and abstraction by Clarke et al. [3], a number of works have applied this idea to reduce the phenomenon of "state explosion" (e.g. [8, 10, 17]). Indeed, verifying a temporal logic formula against a model is in general a hard problem (PSPACE complete for CTL*) [1, 11, 16]. The problem of refining abstract model checking is precisely that of improving precision in temporal logic verification by refining a state partition (called in [3] an abstraction) that turns out to provide a too rough abstract model for verifying a given temporal property of interest. Roughly speaking, by refining the abstraction in abstract model-checking we gain precision, namely the refined model becomes more selective (being closer to the concrete model) than the abstract one. Moreover, the size of the new refined abstract model has to be kept as small as possible in order to avoid to re-introduce the "state explosion" phenomenon. Formulated in this way, this is indeed precisely a domain refinement problem: Improve abstractions (viz. enhance domains) in such a way that the new abstraction contains the least amount of information that is needed to achieve a given precision degree [12, 13]. It is not an easy task to apply the standard abstract domain refinement theory ([7, 12, 13]) to abstract model-checking refinement. This because of two reasons: (1) Even though any state partition can be associated with a Galois connection, the reverse does not hold in general. Therefore it is not always immediate to associate a refined state partition with a refined abstract domain (or equivalently Galois connection) as the latter may not correspond to a state partition. (2) We need to express the meaning of improving precision in abstract model-checking by refining domains. This has to be related with the structure of the formulas that are verified in the new refined model. We solve both these problems in the context of abstract domain refinements to achieve complete abstract model checking.

Main Results

In abstract model-checking soundness means that when a property is true in the abstract model it will also be true in the concrete one. However, the approximation may not be complete in the sense of model-checking, i.e., if the property of interest is false in the abstract model, the counterexample produced by the model-checker may be the result of some particular traces in the approximated model, which are not present in the concrete one, i.e., which do not correspond to any concrete computation. In [2] this phenomenon has been isolated, and these counterexamples have been called *spurious*. We consider spurious counterexamples as a measure for the achieved precision in systematically refining abstract model-checking by standard domain transformers. We first introduce the notions of *backward* and *forward completeness* for an abstract interpretation. While backward completeness corresponds precisely to the standard notion of completeness for an abstract interpretation [7, 14], forward completeness is less well-known and it corresponds to what is sometimes called "exactness" of an abstract interpretation (e.g. [4]). We show that forward and backward completeness are dual notions, and that, as well as for backward completeness, also forward completeness can be achieved by minimally refining abstract domains. Then we observe that any abstract domain refinement induces a refined state partition which in turn reduces the amount of spurious counterexamples in the refined abstract model. Finally we show that the counterexample-guided abstraction refinement by Clarke et al. [2] corresponds precisely to iteratively compute the backward (forward)-complete shell of the corresponding abstraction with respect to the forward (backward) state transition function. This provides a purely algebraic characterization of spurious counterexamples in terms of standard abstract interpretation theory. Moreover, this result allows us to characterize the structure of spurious counterexamples that can be removed by refining a domain to achieve completeness with respect to an arbitrary function, therefore including most domain refinements known in the literature. Our results are applied in the systematic refinement of data-flow analysis as the model-checking of abstract interpretations, as formulated in [20].

Related Works

The body of research on the connection among model-checking, abstract interpretation and data-flow analysis is huge, even though this field still represents a major challenge in formal methods. In particular the problem of completeness in abstract model-checking has been studied by a number of authors both theoretically and from the point of view of improving model-checking algorithms. In [2] the authors proposed an automatic refinement technique which uses information obtained from erroneous counterexamples produced by a model-checker. They introduced the notion of spurious counterexample and gave an algorithm based on the inverse image of the forward transition function to refine the abstraction. However, the authors did not consider the classical notions of abstract interpretation in order to improve the precision of the approximated models.

In our work we prove that this algorithm can be formulated as an instance of the more general problem of making an abstraction complete in the standard sense of abstract interpretation. In [9] Cousot and Cousot introduced a novel general temporal language, inspired by Kozen's μ-calculus, which includes most standard specification languages such as CTL and CTL* as special cases. The authors proved that the classical state-based model-checking of this language is an abstract interpretation of its trace-based semantics, which turns out to be incomplete. More recently Ranzato [19] found the complete shell according to [14] of Cousot's state-based model-checking abstraction. This construction has been applied to the whole specification language introduced in [9], proving that there exists no complete abstraction which includes the state-model-checking and it is strictly more abstract than the trace-based model-checking. This proves that it is impossible for state-model-checking to achieve completeness with respect to trace-model-checking, without including the traces them self. In [5] the authors introduced a new concept of completeness, called *partial completeness*, for problems which are intended to check abstract fix-points for specifications. A checking algorithm is partially complete when in case of termination the answer is exact. This notion can be directly applied in model-checking problems, where one is interested in partially complete abstractions, i.e., approximations of a given model which always yield an affirmative answer when the specification is correct (i.e. it holds in the original model) and the algorithm does terminate. This notion of completeness seems different from the one considered in this paper, but further research is needed to better understand the relation between these two notions of completeness.

Structure of the Paper

The paper is organized as follows: In Sections 2 and 3 we recall first the main notions concerning temporal logic and model checking, and then the standard theory of Galois-connection based abstract interpretation. The main results of the paper are in Section 4, Section 5, and Section 6. In Section 4 we introduce forward and backward completeness of an abstract interpretation and we study the relation between these two notions and a constructive method to minimally modify domains in order to achieve either forward or backward completeness. In Section 5 we introduce abstract model checking refinement by domain transformers and in Section 6 we characterize the precision of a refined abstract model in terms of Clarke's spurious counterexamples. Finally, in Section 7 we give a model-checking perspective of the problem of complete data-flow analysis. Section 8 concludes with future works.

2 Temporal Logic and Model-Checking

In the following we consider a fragment ∀CTL* of the branching time temporal logic CTL* [3, 11]: The formulas of ∀CTL* do not contain existential quantifiers. Of course, all the results apply to the universal fragment of the weaker language CTL, as well. In $\forall$CTL* universal properties are expressed through the path quantifier $\forall$ ("for all futures") that quantifies over (infinite) execution sequences. The temporal operators G (**G**enerally, always), F (**F**inally, sometime) X (ne**X**t time), and U (**U**ntil) express properties of a single execution sequence. These operators, as well as other syntactic possibilities, can be freely nested in a formula. Given a set $Prop$ of propositions, the set Lit of *literals* is defined as $Lit = Prop \cup \{\neg q \mid q \in Prop\} \cup \{\text{true}, \text{false}\}$. *State formulas* ϕ and *Path formulas* ψ are inductively defined by the following grammar, where $p \in Lit$:

State formulas: $\phi ::= p \mid \phi \wedge \phi \mid \phi \vee \phi \mid \forall\psi$

Path formulas: $\psi ::= \phi \mid \psi \wedge \psi \mid \psi \vee \psi \mid G\psi \mid F\psi \mid X\psi \mid U(\psi, \psi)$

Observe that negation is allowed only for literals. Therefore, the results that allow us to write the existential modal operator using universal formulas do not hold here. Observe also that F is superfluous because $F\psi = U(\text{true}, \psi)$.

A *transition system* is a pair $\langle \Sigma, R \rangle$ consisting of a set Σ of *states* and a *transition relation* $R \subseteq \Sigma \times \Sigma$ that is assumed to be total. A *Kripke structure* is a tuple $\mathbb{M} = \langle \Sigma, R, I, \| \cdot \| \rangle$ where $\langle \Sigma, R \rangle$ is a transition system, $I \subseteq \Sigma$ is the set of *initial states*, and $\| \cdot \| : Lit \longrightarrow \wp(\Sigma)$ is the *interpretation function* such that $\| p \| = \{ s \in \Sigma \mid s \models p \}$. For $\forall$CTL* the notion of *satisfaction* of a state formula ϕ by a state s ($s \models \phi$) is as usual [10]. If $\mathbb{M} = \langle \Sigma, R, I, \| \circ \| \rangle$ is a Kripke structure, we say that $\mathbb{M} \models \varphi$ if and only if $\forall s \in I : s \models \varphi$. Given a temporal formula φ the satisfiability problem for φ is that of checking if there exists a Kripke structure $\mathbb{M}$ such that $\mathbb{M} \models \varphi$. In the case of CTL* (hence of $\forall$CTL*) this problem is decidable [11]. For verification purposes the following problem is known as the *(global) model-checking problem (MCP)*: given $\mathbb{M} = \langle \Sigma, R, I, \| \circ \| \rangle$ and a formula φ, check if $\mathbb{M} \models \varphi$.

3 Abstract Interpretation

In the following $\langle C, \leq, \vee, \wedge, \top, \bot \rangle$ denotes a complete lattice C, with ordering $\leq$, *lub* $\vee$, *glb* $\wedge$, greatest element (top) $\top$, and least element (bottom) $\bot$. The downward closure of $S \subseteq C$ is defined as $\downarrow S \overset{\text{def}}{=} \{x \in C \mid \exists y \in S. \ x \leq y\}$. $\downarrow x$ is a shorthand for $\downarrow \{x\}$, while the upward closure $\uparrow$ is dually defined. The notation $C \cong D$ denotes that C and D are isomorphic possibly ordered structures. Recall that a function $f \in C \to D$ is (Scott-)continuous if f preserves *lub*'s of (nonempty) chains iff f preserves *lub*'s of directed subsets. In the following we consider Galois connection based abstract interpretation [6]. A pair of functions $f : A \to B$ and $g : B \to A$ forms an *adjunction* if

$$\forall x \in A. \forall y \in B. \ f(x) \leq_B y \Leftrightarrow x \leq_A g(y).$$

f (resp. g) is the *left- (right-)adjoint* to g (f) and it is an additive (co-additive) function, i.e., f preserves *lub*'s (*glb*'s) of all subsets of A (empty-set included). Additive and co-additive functions f admit respectively right and left adjoint: $f^+ \overset{\text{def}}{=} \lambda x. \ \bigvee \{ y \mid f(y) \leq x \}$ and $f^- \overset{\text{def}}{=} \lambda x. \ \bigwedge \{ y \mid x \leq f(y) \}$ respectively.

Remember that $(f^+)^- = (f^-)^+ = f$. A *Galois connection* (GC for short) is an adjunction between posets, and it is denoted (A, f, B, f^+). In GC-based abstract interpretation the concrete and abstract domains, C and A, are often assumed to be complete lattices and are related by abstraction $\alpha : C \to A$ and concretization $\gamma : A \to C$ maps forming a GC (C, α, A, γ). If in addition $\forall a \in A.\ \alpha(\gamma(a)) = a$, then we call (C, α, A, γ) a Galois insertion (GI) of A in C. When (C, α, A, γ) is a GI then each value of the abstract domain A is useful in representing C, because all the elements of A represent distinct members of C, being γ 1-1. Any GC may be lifted to a GI by identifying in an equivalence class those values of the abstract domain with the same concretization. This process is known as *reduction* of the abstract domain. An *upper closure operator* on a poset C is an operator $\rho : C \to C$ which is monotone, idempotent, and extensive ($\forall x \in C.\ x \leq \rho(x)$). Lower closures are dually defined. The set of all upper (lower) closure operators on C is denoted by $uco(C)$ ($lco(C)$). Each closure is uniquely determined by the set of its fix-points $\rho(C)$. A fundamental property of closure operators is that if C is a complete lattice then both $\langle uco(C), \sqsubseteq, \sqcup, \sqcap, \lambda x.\top, \lambda x.x \rangle$ ordered point-wise, and $\langle \rho(C), \leq, \vee_\rho, \wedge, \top, \rho(\bot) \rangle$ with $\vee_\rho X = \rho(\vee X)$, are complete lattices. It is well known since [7] that abstract domains can be equivalently specified either as Galois insertions or as (sets of fix-points of) upper closures on the concrete domain. In particular $X \subseteq C$ is the set of fix-points of an upper closure ρ on C iff X is a *Moore-family* of C, i.e., $X = \mathcal{M}(X) \stackrel{\text{def}}{=} \{\wedge S \mid S \subseteq X\}$ — where $\wedge \varnothing = \top \in \mathcal{M}(X)$, iff X is isomorphic to an abstract domain A in a GI (C, α, A, γ), i.e. $A \cong \rho(C)$ with $\iota : \rho(C) \to A$ and $\iota^{-1} : A \to \rho(C)$ being the isomorphism, and $(C, \iota \circ \rho, A, \iota^{-1})$ is the GI, i.e. $\rho = \gamma \circ \alpha$. Therefore $uco(C)$ is isomorphic to the so called *lattice of abstract interpretations* of C [7]. For any $X \subseteq C$, $\mathcal{M}(X)$ is called the *Moore-closure* of X in C, i.e., $\mathcal{M}(X)$ is the least (w.r.t. set-inclusion) subset of C which contains X and it is a Moore-family of C. In this case $A \sqsubseteq B$ iff $B \subseteq A$ as Moore families of C, iff A is more concrete than B. In the following we will find particularly convenient to identify closure operators (and therefore abstract domains) with their sets of fix-points, possibly by using as notation capital Latin letters.

4   Backward and Forward Completeness

In abstract interpretation there are two equivalent ways to express the soundness of an abstraction [6]. Let C be a complete lattice, $f : C \to C$, (C, α, A, γ) be a Galois insertion, and $f^\sharp : A \to A$. Then (C, α, A, γ) and $f^\sharp$ provide a sound abstraction of f if $\alpha \circ f \leq f^\sharp \circ \alpha$, or equivalently (by adjunction) if $f \circ \gamma \leq \gamma \circ f^\sharp$. While these two definitions of soundness are equivalent, they are not equivalent when equality is required. In the first case $\alpha \circ f = f^\sharp \circ \alpha$ means that no loss of precision is accumulated by approximating the input arguments of a given semantic function; while $f \circ \gamma = \gamma \circ f^\sharp$ means that no loss of precision is accumulated by approximating the result of computations on abstract objects. These two notions represent therefore two different forms of completeness: The first is related with input arguments of a computation, while the second is related with its output.

We distinguish here between these two forms of completeness: The first is called *backward* ($\mathcal{B}$) and the second is called *forward* ($\mathcal{F}$) completeness. The reason for these names will be clear later in the paper.

Definition 1. *Let C be a complete lattice, $f : C \to C$, (C, α, A, γ) be a Galois insertion, and $f^\sharp : A \to A$.*

- *(C, α, A, γ) and $f^\sharp$ are $\mathcal{B}$-complete for f if $\alpha \circ f = f^\sharp \circ \alpha$.*
- *(C, α, A, γ) and $f^\sharp$ are $\mathcal{F}$-complete for f if $f \circ \gamma = \gamma \circ f^\sharp$.*

$\mathcal{B}$-completeness (see [14]) corresponds to ask that the approximate function $f^\sharp$ perfectly mimics the concrete function f, when the latter is approximated in A, viz. both are compared in the abstract domain A. Conversely, $\mathcal{F}$-completeness corresponds to ask that $f^\sharp$ perfectly mimics the function f applied to the same abstract arguments, viz. they are both compared in the concrete domain C. The following proposition extends a result in [14] about $\mathcal{B}$-completeness to $\mathcal{F}$-completeness. In this case there exists an either $\mathcal{B}$ or $\mathcal{F}$ complete abstract function $f^\sharp$ in an abstract domain A iff the best correct approximation $\alpha \circ f \circ \gamma$ of f is respectively either $\mathcal{B}$ or $\mathcal{F}$ complete. This means that, as well as for $\mathcal{B}$-completeness [14], also $\mathcal{F}$-completeness is a property of abstract domains, namely a property of the GI (C, α, A, γ).

Proposition 1. *Let C be a complete lattice, $f : C \to C$, and (C, α, A, γ) be a Galois insertion. There exists $f^\sharp : A \to A$ such that (C, α, A, γ) and $f^\sharp$ are $\mathcal{B}$-complete ($\mathcal{F}$-complete) for f iff $\alpha \circ f = \alpha \circ f \circ \gamma \circ \alpha$ ($f \circ \gamma = \gamma \circ \alpha \circ f \circ \gamma$).*

Therefore, we can define when a domain (closure operator) is $\mathcal{B}/\mathcal{F}$-complete for a semantic function as follows.

Definition 2. *Let C be a complete lattice and $\rho \in uco(C)$ be an abstract domain. ρ is $\mathcal{B}$($\mathcal{F}$)-complete for f if $\rho \circ f = \rho \circ f \circ \rho$ ($f \circ \rho = \rho \circ f \circ \rho$).*

While $\mathcal{B}$-completeness is well known in abstract interpretation and it corresponds to the standard notion of completeness [18, 14], the notion of forward completeness is less known. $\mathcal{B}$-completeness means that the domain ρ is expressive enough such that no loss of precision is accumulated by abstracting in ρ the arguments of a function f. Conversely, $\mathcal{F}$-completeness means that no loss of precision is accumulated by approximating the result of the function f computed in ρ. This justifies the choice of the backward and forward names above. In the following we denote by $\mathcal{F}(C, f) \stackrel{\text{def}}{=} \{ \rho \mid f \circ \rho = \rho \circ f \circ \rho \}$ and $\mathcal{B}(C, f) \stackrel{\text{def}}{=} \{ \rho \mid \rho \circ f = \rho \circ f \circ \rho \}$ respectively the set of $\mathcal{F}$ and $\mathcal{B}$ complete abstractions of C for f. It is worth noting that in general $\mathcal{F}(C, f) \not\subseteq \mathcal{B}(C, f)$ and $\mathcal{F}(C, f) \not\subseteq \mathcal{B}(C, f)$, namely they are incomparable notions.

Example 1. Let $Sign^+$ be the domain in Fig. 1 which is an abstraction of $\langle \wp(\mathbb{Z}), \subseteq \rangle$ for the analysis of integer variables and $sq : \wp(\mathbb{Z}) \to \wp(\mathbb{Z})$ be the square operation defined as follows: $sq(X) = \{ x^2 \mid x \in X \}$ for $X \in \wp(\mathbb{Z})$. Let $\rho \in uco(\wp(\mathbb{Z}))$ be the closure operator associated with $Sign^+$, i.e. $\rho = \gamma \circ \alpha$, where the abstraction and concretization maps are the most obvious ones. The best correct approximation of sq in $Sign^+$ is $sq^\sharp : Sign^+ \to Sign^+$ such that $sq^\sharp(X) = \rho(sq(X))$, with $X \in Sign^+$. It is easy to see that the upper-closure operators $\rho_a = \{\mathbb{Z}, [0, +\infty], [0, 10]\}$ and $\rho_b = \{\mathbb{Z}, [0, 2], [0]\}$, respect the following facts: $\rho_a = \{\mathbb{Z}, [0, +\infty], [0, 10]\} \in \mathcal{F}(Sign^+, sq^\sharp)$ but $\rho_a = \{\mathbb{Z}, [0, +\infty], [0, 10]\} \notin \mathcal{B}(Sign^+, sq^\sharp)$ (for example, $\rho_a(sq^\sharp(\rho_a([0]))) = [0, +\infty]$ but $\rho_a(sq^\sharp([0])) = [0, 10]$) and $\rho_b = \{\mathbb{Z}, [0, 2], [0]\} \in \mathcal{B}(Sign^+, sq^\sharp)$ but $\rho_b = \{\mathbb{Z}, [0, 2], [0]\} \notin \mathcal{F}(Sign^+, sq^\sharp)$ (e.g. $\rho_b(sq^\sharp(\rho_b([0, 2]))) = \mathbb{Z}$ but $sq^\sharp(\rho_b([0, 2])) = [0, 10]$). The arrows in Fig. 1 show the non fix-points results of $sq^\sharp$.

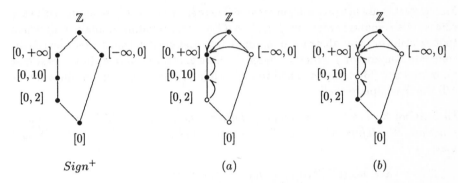

Fig. 1. The Abstract Domain $Sign^+$ and Two Abstractions.

Clearly, when an abstract domain ρ is both $\mathcal{B}$ and $\mathcal{F}$ complete for f, then ρ is a morphism, i.e., $\rho \circ f = f \circ \rho$, namely $\mathcal{F}(C, f) \cap \mathcal{B}(C, f) = \{\rho \mid \rho \circ f = f \circ \rho\}$. Note that in the Example 1, $\{\mathbb{Z}, [0, +\infty], [-\infty, 0], [0]\} \in \mathcal{F}(Sign^\sharp, sq^\sharp) \cap \mathcal{B}(Sign^\sharp, sq^\sharp)$.

The following result is the main result in [14] and it is the basis for a constructive characterization of the complete shell of an abstract domain, viz. the least (most abstract) domain which is $\mathcal{B}$-complete and includes a given domain. This result constructively characterizes the structure of $\mathcal{B}$-complete abstract domains for continuous functions. Recall that, if $f : C \to C$ is a unary function, then $f^{-1}(y) = \{x \mid f(x) = y\}$.

Theorem 1 ([14]). *Let $f : C \to C$ be continuous and $\rho \in uco(C)$. Then ρ is $\mathcal{B}$-complete for f iff $\bigcup_{y \in \rho(C)} max(f^{-1}(\downarrow y)) \subseteq \rho(C)$.*

It is easy to see in Example 1 that ρ_a is not $\mathcal{B}$-complete because it does not include the maximal inverse image of $sq^\sharp$ (see Fig. 1), namely the point $[0, 2]$.

An analogous, but simpler to prove, result can be stated for $\mathcal{F}$-completeness. In this case, we can characterize $\mathcal{F}$-complete domains for merely monotone operators.

Theorem 2. *Let $f : C \to C$ be monotone and $\rho \in uco(C)$. ρ is $\mathcal{F}$-complete for f iff $\forall x \in \rho(C). f(x) \in \rho(C)$.*

Therefore, while $\mathcal{B}$-complete domains are closed under (maximal) inverse image of the function f, $\mathcal{F}$-complete domains are closed under direct image of f. It is easy to see in Example 1 that ρ_b is not $\mathcal{F}$-complete because it does not include the direct image of $sq^\sharp$ (see Fig. 1), namely the points $[0, 10]$ and $[0, +\infty]$. Both Theorem 1 and 2 together specify a strong relation between $\mathcal{B}$ and $\mathcal{F}$ completeness, which can be specified in terms of adjunction when f admits a right adjoint f^+.

Corollary 1. *Let C be a complete lattice and $f : C \to C$ be an additive function. Then $\mathcal{B}(\wp(S), f) = \mathcal{F}(\wp(S), f^+)$.*

Moreover it is always possible, in view of Theorem 1 and 2, to associate with each continuous semantic function $f : C \to C$ a corresponding domain refinement that transforms any abstract domain A into the closest (most abstract) $\mathcal{B}/\mathcal{F}$-complete domain for f which includes (is more concrete than) A. In the first case we obtain the ($\mathcal{B}$-)complete shell in [14], while in the second we obtain what we call the $\mathcal{F}$-complete shell.

Definition 3. *Let C be a complete lattice and $f : C \to C$ be a continuous function. We define $\mathcal{R}_f^{\mathcal{B}} : uco(C) \to uco(C)$ and $\mathcal{R}_f^{\mathcal{F}} : uco(C) \to uco(C)$ such that:*

- $\mathcal{R}_f^{\mathcal{B}} = \lambda X \in uco(C).\ \mathcal{M}(\bigcup_{y \in X} max(f^{-1}(\downarrow y)))$;
- $\mathcal{R}_f^{\mathcal{F}} = \lambda X \in uco(C).\ \mathcal{M}(f(X))$.

It is immediate to prove that both $\mathcal{R}_f^{\mathcal{B}}$ and $\mathcal{R}_f^{\mathcal{F}}$ are monotone operators on $uco(C)$. The following result, which follows by Theorem 1 and 2, characterizes in a unique domain-equational form the $\mathcal{B}/\mathcal{F}$-complete shell of abstract domains for a continuous function $f : C \to C$.

Theorem 3. *Let $f : C \to C$ be a continuous function and $A \in uco(C)$ be an abstract domain. Let $\ell \in \{\mathcal{B}, \mathcal{F}\}$:*

$$X \text{ is } \ell\text{-complete for } f \text{ and } X \sqsubseteq A \text{ iff } X = A \sqcap \mathcal{R}_f^\ell(X);$$

Therefore, the greatest (viz, most abstract) domain which includes A and which is ℓ-complete for f is $\mathcal{S}_f^\ell(A) = gfp(\lambda X.\ A \sqcap \mathcal{R}_f^\ell(X))$. This domain is called the ℓ-*complete shell* of A with respect to f. Note that, as proved for the $\mathcal{B}$-complete shell in [14], $\mathcal{R}_f^\ell$ above is a co-additive operator on the lattice of abstract interpretations $uco(C)$, and that $\lambda X.\ \mathcal{S}_f^\ell(X)$ is a monotone, idempotent, and reductive operator on $uco(C)$, i.e. $\mathcal{S}_f^\ell \in lco(uco(C))$.

5   Refining State Partitions vs Refining Domains

In this section we study how to systematically refine abstract model-checking, namely we consider functions of type $\wp(\Sigma) \to \wp(\Sigma)$ with Σ being the set of states in a transition system $\langle \Sigma, R \rangle$. The following definition introduces the notion of abstract Kripke structure according to Dams et al. [10].

Definition 4. *Let* $\mathbb{M} = \langle \Sigma, I, R, \| \circ \| \rangle$ *be a Kripke Structure and* $(\wp(\Sigma), \alpha, A, \gamma)$ *be a GI. The corresponding abstract Kripke Structure* $\mathbb{M}^{\sharp} = \langle A, I^{\sharp}, R^{\sharp}, \| \circ \|^{\sharp} \rangle$ *is defined as follows:*

- $a \in I^{\sharp}$ *iff* $\exists d \in I.\ \alpha(\{d\}) = a$;
- $R^{\exists\exists} \stackrel{def}{=} \{ (X, Y) \mid \exists_{x \in X} \exists_{y \in Y}.\ R(x, y) \}$;
- $R^{\sharp}(a_1, a_2)$ *iff* $a_2 \in \{ \alpha(Y) \mid Y \in min \{ Y' \mid R^{\exists\exists}(\gamma(a_1), Y') \} \}$;
- $\| p \|^{\sharp} \stackrel{def}{=} \{ a \in A \mid \gamma(a) \subseteq \| p \| \}$.

Note that for any $a \in A$, the minimal sets Y' such that $R^{\exists\exists}(\gamma(a), Y')$ are all singletons.

In the following we consider abstract domains as specified by a GI, or equivalently by a closure operator on $\wp(\Sigma)$, where Σ is the set of states of a transition system $\langle \Sigma, R \rangle$. This is apparently in contrast with the original (standard) definition of abstract model-checking by Clarke et al. [3]. In this latter case the abstraction is specified by a surjection function, called *state partition*, $h : \Sigma \to S$ on a given set S of *abstract states*. Notice that any surjection $h : \Sigma \to S$ induces an equivalence relation $\equiv$ on the set of states Σ in the following way: Let $a, b \in \Sigma$, then $a \equiv b$ iff $h(a) = h(b)$. Given a surjection $h : \Sigma \to S$ we can immediately derive a GI in the following way: $(\wp(\Sigma), \alpha_h, \wp(S), \gamma_h)$, where $\alpha_h(X) \stackrel{def}{=} \{ h(x) \mid x \in X \}$ is the abstraction function and $\gamma_h(Y) \stackrel{def}{=} \{ x \mid h(x) \in Y \}$ is the concretization function. Note that the GI is defined by considering $\wp(S)$ instead of S, because it is not assumed that the set of abstract states S is partial ordered.

The main problem with this approach and abstract domain refinement is that, in general, if $f : \wp(\Sigma) \to \wp(\Sigma)$ is some predicate transformer on the transition system $\langle \Sigma, R \rangle$, then the refined domain $\mathcal{S}_f^{\ell}(\gamma_h \circ \alpha_h) \in uco(\wp(\Sigma))$, with $\ell \in \{\mathcal{F}, \mathcal{B}\}$, may not be of the form $\wp(S)$ for some set of abstract states S. In particular $\mathcal{S}_f^{\ell}(\gamma_h \circ \alpha_h)$ may not be a Boolean algebra, and therefore the powerset of some set. Because we abstract state-model-checking, it is sufficient to observe how the refined domain abstracts each single state. Indeed, any abstract domain refinement induces a domain surjection in the following way: Let $\widehat{S} \cong \{ \mathcal{S}_f^{\ell}(\gamma_h \circ \alpha_h)(\{x\}) \mid x \in \Sigma \}$, then the function $\widehat{h} \stackrel{def}{=} \lambda x \in \Sigma.\ \mathcal{S}_f^{\ell}(\gamma_h \circ \alpha_h)(\{x\})$ is a surjection from Σ into $\widehat{S}$ such that: $|S| \leq |\widehat{S}|$ and $(\wp(\Sigma), \alpha_{\widehat{h}}, \wp(\widehat{S}), \gamma_{\widehat{h}})$ is a GI. This corresponds to improve the partition induced by h into a finer partition of the concrete states as induced by $\widehat{h}$. This improvement is obtained by considering a new set of abstract states each one consisting of the (unique) best possible abstraction of each concrete state according to the refined closure $\mathcal{S}_f^{\ell}(\gamma_h \circ \alpha_h)$.

Proposition 2. *Let* $h : \Sigma \to S$ *be a state partition and* $(\wp(\Sigma), \alpha_h, \wp(S), \gamma_h)$ *be the corresponding GI. If* $\mathcal{S} : uco(\wp(\Sigma)) \to uco(\wp(\Sigma))$ *is a domain refinement, i.e. a monotone function such that* $\forall X \in uco(\wp(\Sigma)).\ \mathcal{S}(X) \sqsubseteq X$, *then the function* $h_{\mathcal{S}} : \Sigma \to \{ \mathcal{S}(\gamma_h \circ \alpha_h)(\{x\}) \mid x \in \Sigma \}$ *such that* $h_{\mathcal{S}} = \lambda x.\ \mathcal{S}(\gamma_h \circ \alpha_h)(\{x\})$ *is a refinement of the state partition* h.

Therefore, the standard theory of abstract domain refinement (see [13]) can be fully applied directly to refine any abstract (state-)model-checking problem. In this latter case, a refined state partition function can be systematically derived from the refined abstract domain as described in Proposition 2.

Example 2. Consider the transition system $\langle [0,9], R \rangle$ where the transition relation R is shown on the left in Fig. 2 with continuous lines. Consider the state partition function $h(x) = x \bmod 4$. Following Definition 4, this induces an abstract Kripke structure associated with the GI $(\wp([0,9]), \alpha_h, \wp(\{a,b,c,d\}), \gamma_h)$ as depicted in Fig. 2 with empty boxes and dashed lines. Let $f : \wp([0,9]) \to \wp([0,9])$ be such that $f(X) = \{3\}$. The forward complete shell of $\gamma_h \circ \alpha_h$ is $gfp(\lambda X. \; \gamma_h \circ \alpha_h \sqcap \mathcal{R}_f^{\mathcal{F}}(X)) = \mathcal{R}_f^{\mathcal{F}}(\gamma_h \circ \alpha_h)$, and it is immediate to observe that it induces a new state partition function $\widehat{h}$ such that

$$\widehat{h}(x) = \begin{cases} x & \text{if } x = 3,7 \\ h(x) & \text{otherwise} \end{cases}$$

The GI $(\wp([0,9]), \alpha_h, \wp(\{a,b,c,d\}), \gamma_h)$ is not $\mathcal{F}$-complete for f, e.g. if $\rho_h = \gamma_h \circ \alpha_h$ then $f(\rho_h(\{2,6\})) = \{3\}$ but $\rho_h(f(\rho_h(\{2,6\}))) = \{3,7\}$. In this case, in order to obtain the complete shell of ρ_h we have to add the abstract state $\{3\}$ to the abstract domain. This leads to a partition of the abstract state $\{3,7\}$ into two more concrete states: $\{3\}$ which is introduced by adding the forward image of f, and $\{7\}$ which is a new state (actually, it is a renaming of the state $\{3,7\}$) corresponding to the (unique) best possible approximation in $\mathcal{R}_f^{\mathcal{F}}(\gamma_h \circ \alpha_h)$ of the concrete state 7. This induces a refined abstract Kripke structure associated with the refined GI $(\wp([0,9]), \alpha_{\widehat{h}}, \wp(\{a,b,c,d,e\}), \gamma_{\widehat{h}})$, as shown on the right in Fig. 2.

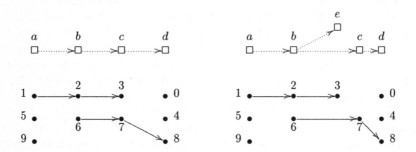

Fig. 2. An Abstract Kripke Structure and Its Refinement.

6   Completeness and Counterexamples

We are in the position to apply forward or backward completeness abstract domain refinement to abstract (state-)model-checking problems. In this section we relate the abstract domain refinement for both backward and forward completeness with the presence of suitable counterexamples in abstract model-checking.

A *path* in a Kripke Structure $\mathbb{M} = \langle \Sigma, I, R, \| \circ \| \rangle$ is an infinite sequence in $\mathbb{N} \to \Sigma$, denoted $\pi = s_0, s_1, \ldots$, such that $s_0 \in I$ and for every $i \in \mathbb{N}$, $R(s_i, s_{i+1})$ holds. Traditionally, a terminating execution has a final state which is repeated forever. With π_i we denote i-th state in the path, i.e., s_i. Given a Galois insertion $(\wp(\Sigma), \alpha, A, \gamma)$ and concrete and abstract paths π and $\pi^\sharp$ respectively, we denote by $\alpha(\pi)$ the sequence $\alpha(\pi_0), \alpha(\pi_1), \ldots$ and by $\gamma(\pi^\sharp)$ the set $\{ \pi \mid \alpha(\pi) = \pi^\sharp \}$. Given a path π and a state $x \in \Sigma$, $x \in \pi$ iff $\exists i \in \mathbb{N}$ such that $x = \pi_i$. The forward predicate transformer associated with R is $post[R] : \wp(\Sigma) \to \wp(\Sigma)$, which is defined as $post[R](X) = \{ s \in \Sigma \mid R(x, s) \wedge x \in X \}$. Dually, we can define the backward predicate transformer associated with R as $\widetilde{pre}[R] : \wp(\Sigma) \to \wp(\Sigma)$, which is defined as $\widetilde{pre}[R](X) = \{ s \in \Sigma \mid \forall x \in \Sigma.\ R(s, x) \Rightarrow x \in X \}$. The following is a well known fact about forward and backward predicate transformers (e.g. [15]).

Proposition 3. $(\wp(\Sigma), post[R], \wp(\Sigma), \widetilde{pre}[R])$ *is a Galois connection.*

Let us consider a domain refinement which is specified as the $\mathcal{F}/\mathcal{B}$-complete shell with respect to a continuous function $f : \wp(\Sigma) \to \wp(\Sigma)$ as given in Theorem 1. Let $R_f \subseteq \Sigma \times \Sigma$ be the relation associated with f, i.e. such that $R_f(x, y) \Leftrightarrow y \in f(\{x\})$. It is immediate to observe that $f = post[R_f]$.

Proposition 4. *Let* $f : \wp(\Sigma) \to \wp(\Sigma)$ *be additive. Then we have*

$$\mathcal{B}(\wp(\Sigma), f) = \mathcal{B}(\wp(\Sigma), post[R_f]) = \mathcal{F}(\wp(\Sigma), f^+) = \mathcal{F}(\wp(\Sigma), \widetilde{pre}[R_f]).$$

Traditionally, a model-checker is used to determine whether a temporal formula holds in a model. If the answer is negative, i.e., the model does not possess the property specified by the formula, then the model checker generates a counterexample. Let $\mathcal{S} : uco(C) \to uco(C)$ be an abstract domain refinement, i.e., a monotone operator such that $\mathcal{S}(X) \sqsubseteq X$ for any abstract domain $X \in uco(C)$ [13]. It is immediate to observe that $\mathcal{S}$ reduces the number of counterexamples that might be generated by the model-checker. Recall that, given a Kripke structure $\mathbb{M} = \langle \Sigma, I, R, \| \circ \| \rangle$ and a formula $\varphi \in \forall \text{CTL}^*$, $\mathbb{M} \not\models \varphi$ iff $\exists s \in I.\ s \not\models \varphi$, iff there exists a path starting at I which does not satisfy φ. This because $\forall \text{CTL}^*$ can only express formulas that describe behaviors that should hold on *all paths* from the initial states. Hence, if A is an abstract domain and $\mathbb{M}^A$ and $\mathbb{M}^{\mathcal{S}(A)}$ are respectively the abstract and refined Kripke structures associated with A and $\mathcal{S}(A)$, then we have that:

$$\{ \varphi \mid \mathbb{M}^A \not\models \varphi \} \supseteq \{ \varphi \mid \mathbb{M}^{\mathcal{S}(A)} \not\models \varphi \}.$$

It is therefore natural to consider counterexamples as a measure of the achieved precision in abstract model-checking when the abstract domain is refined. However, not all counterexamples are admissible, because an abstract counterexample might not be valid in the concrete model. Clarke's et al. [2] introduced the notion of *spurious counterexample* in order to model this situation[1].

---

[1] Note that we consider path counterexamples only. Clarke's et al. [2] consider instead *loop* counterexamples, which reduce to paths by means of loop unfolding.

Definition 5. *Let $(\wp(\Sigma), \alpha, S^\sharp, \gamma)$ be a GI. Consider the concrete and abstract Kripke structures $\langle \Sigma, I, R, \| \circ \| \rangle$ and $\langle S^\sharp, I^\sharp, R^\sharp, \| \circ \|^\sharp \rangle$ and $\varphi \in \forall CTL^* \cap LTL$. An abstract path $\pi^\sharp$ is a spurious counterexample if $\pi_0^\sharp \not\models \varphi$ and $\gamma(\pi^\sharp) = \varnothing$.*

The following theorem relates spurious counterexamples with backward and forward completeness with respect to $post[R]$ and $\widetilde{pre}[R]$ respectively. The idea is that if a counterexample is spurious for an abstraction ρ, then there exists a concrete state x for which ρ fails to be forward complete for $post[R]$ in x. The proof relies upon the fact that for spurious counterexamples $\pi^\sharp$, $\gamma(\pi^\sharp) = \varnothing$ and therefore there exists a concrete state x from which there is no forward transition into an abstract state, while there is a forward transition from $\rho(\{x\})$. This clearly violates completeness for $post[R]$.

Theorem 4. *Let $(\wp(\Sigma), \alpha, S^\sharp, \gamma)$ be a GI and $\rho = \gamma \circ \alpha$. Let $\varphi \in \forall CTL^*$ and $\pi^\sharp$ be a counterexample. If $\pi^\sharp$ is spurious then there exists $i \in \mathbb{N}$ such that $\forall x \in \gamma(\pi_i^\sharp)$ reachable from the states in I, i.e., $\gamma(\pi_0^\sharp) \cap I$, it holds that:*

$$\rho(post[R](\rho(\{x\}))) \neq \rho(post[R](\{x\})).$$

In particular, by Theorem 4, if $\pi^\sharp$ is spurious then there exists $\pi \in \gamma(\pi^\sharp)$ and $x \in \pi$ such that $\rho(post[R](\rho(\{x\}))) \neq \rho(post[R](\{x\}))$, or equivalently, by Proposition 4, there exists $x \in \pi$ such that $\rho(\widetilde{pre}[R](\rho(\{x\}))) \neq \widetilde{pre}[R](\rho(\{x\}))$.

The complete shell abstract domain refinement can therefore be used to systematically refine abstract model-checking in order to eliminate spurious counterexamples. In particular, the machinery developed in [2] to eliminate spurious counterexamples in abstract Kripke structures can be formally reduced to the complete shell refinement operation introduced in [14]. The following example, taken from [2], shows this phenomenon.

Example 3. Consider a program with a variable whose values range in the following interval $D = [1, 12]$ and which is represented by a transition system with states $\Sigma = \{1, \cdots, 12\}$, initial states $I = \{1, 2, 3, 7, 8, 10, 11\}$ and transition relation:

$$R = \left\{ \begin{array}{c} \langle 1, 4 \rangle, \langle 2, 5 \rangle, \langle 3, 6 \rangle, \langle 4, 9 \rangle, \langle 5, 9 \rangle, \langle 6, 6 \rangle, \langle 7, 12 \rangle, \\ \langle 8, 8 \rangle, \langle 9, 9 \rangle, \langle 10, 10 \rangle, \langle 11, 11 \rangle, \langle 12, 12 \rangle \end{array} \right\}$$

Let $S^\sharp$ be the set of four abstract states $S^\sharp = \{\hat{1}, \hat{2}, \hat{3}, \hat{4}\}$, corresponding to the equivalence classes of concrete states $\{1, 2, 3\}$, $\{4, 5, 6\}$, $\{7, 8, 9\}$, and $\{10, 11, 12\}$. Suppose that a model-checker gives an abstract counterexample $\pi^\sharp = \hat{1}, \hat{2}, \hat{3}, \hat{4}$. It is easy to see that $\pi^\sharp$ is spurious, in fact, this abstract trace does not correspond to any concrete trace in the transition system. By Theorem 4 we can note that $\gamma(\hat{3}) = \{7, 8, 9\}$, moreover only the concrete state 9 of this set is reachable from initial states in I, but it does not have any transition into a different concrete state. Therefore 9 does not have a transition to a state which is abstracted by $\hat{4}$.

Note that, if there exists $\pi \in \gamma(\pi^\sharp)$ and $x \in \pi$ such that $\rho(post[R](\{x\})) \neq \rho(post[R](\rho(\{x\})))$ then this may not imply that $\pi^\sharp$ is spurious. Consider for instance the abstract path $\pi^{\sharp} = \widehat{1}, \widehat{2}, \widehat{3}$ of Example 3. It is easy to check that $\rho(post[R](\rho(\{6\}))) = [4,9]$, whereas $\rho(post[R](\{6\})) = [4,6]$, but $\pi^{\sharp}$ corresponds to the concrete paths $1, 4, 9$ and $1, 5, 9$. Therefore, the complete shell refinement may induce a too strong refinement in the domain with respect to what is strictly necessary to remove spurious counterexamples, as shown in the following example. This phenomenon can be controlled by checking, at each iterate in the *gfp*-computation of the complete shell, the presence of spurious counterexamples.

Example 4. Consider the transition system in Example 3. Let $(\wp([1,12]), \alpha, A, \gamma)$ be the corresponding GI, with $A = \wp(\{[1,3], [4,6], [7,9], [10,12]\})$. By Theorem 1 and Proposition 4, the $\mathcal{B}$-complete shell $gfp(\lambda X.\ \gamma \circ \alpha \sqcap \mathcal{R}^{\mathcal{B}}_{post[R]}(X))$ is obtained as the limit of the sequence of abstract domains $\{A^i\}_{i \in \mathbb{N}}$ defined as follows:

$$A^i = \begin{cases} A & \text{if } i = 0 \\ \mathcal{M}(\widetilde{pre}[R](A^{i-1}) \cup A) & \text{otherwise} \end{cases}$$

This sequence of abstract domains converges in three steps to the fix-point. Each abstract domain A^i induces a refined partition according to Proposition 2 in the following way:

Domains		Refined partition
A^0	$\longrightarrow$	$\{[1,3], [4,6], [7,9], [10,12]\}$
A^1	$\longrightarrow$	$\{[1,3], [4,5], [6,6], [7,7], [8,9], [10,12]\}$
A^2	$\longrightarrow$	$\{[1,2], [3,3], [4,5], [6,6], [7,7], [8,9], [10,12]\}$ (fix-point)

Consider the partition induced by A^1. The new abstract states $\{4,5\}$ and $\{7\}$ are introduced by computing the maximal inverse image of $post[R]$ in the states $\{10, 11, 12\}$ and $\{7, 8, 9\}$, whereas the states $\{6\}$ and $\{8, 9\}$ are added to obtain a partition of $\wp([1, 12])$. Now consider the partition induced by A^2. The new abstract states $\{3\}$ and $\{1, 2\}$ are introduced by computing respectively the inverse image of $post[R]$ in the states $\{6\}$ and $\{4, 5\}$ of A^1.

It is worth noting that the partition induced by A^1 is sufficient to remove any spurious counterexample. Therefore the refinement process can be stopped after the first iteration. This condition can be verified by checking counterexamples at each iterates in the fix-point computation.

7 Complete Data-Flow Analysis: A Different Perspective

In this section we sketch, by means of a simple example, how we can design sound and complete data-flow analysis algorithms as complete model-checking of abstract interpretations. Once again, completeness is achieved by removing spurious counterexamples.

The idea of data-flow analysis as model-checking goes back to Steffen's pioneering work [22]. More recently Schmidt [20, 21] showed that data-flow analysis problems can be formulated as model-checking problems of a *trace-based abstract interpretation* of operational semantics. Intuitively, the concrete semantics of a program is a tree whose paths represent execution traces and whose nodes display the program's changing states. The abstract interpretation of the semantics of a program is also a computation tree, but whose nodes contain the abstraction of information contained in concrete states. To be useful, a program abstract computation tree must safely simulate the concrete computation tree that it represents. Thus any property that holds in an abstract tree must also hold for all the corresponding concrete trees. However, the dual notion of completeness does not hold in general, namely the properties that do not hold in the abstract may not be counterexamples for the concrete.

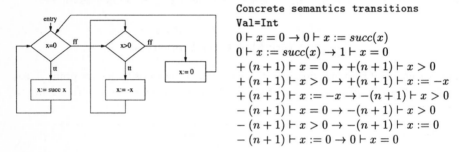

Concrete semantics transitions
Val=Int

$$0 \vdash x = 0 \rightarrow 0 \vdash x := succ(x)$$
$$0 \vdash x := succ(x) \rightarrow 1 \vdash x = 0$$
$$+ (n+1) \vdash x = 0 \rightarrow +(n+1) \vdash x > 0$$
$$+ (n+1) \vdash x > 0 \rightarrow +(n+1) \vdash x := -x$$
$$+ (n+1) \vdash x := -x \rightarrow -(n+1) \vdash x > 0$$
$$- (n+1) \vdash x = 0 \rightarrow -(n+1) \vdash x > 0$$
$$- (n+1) \vdash x > 0 \rightarrow -(n+1) \vdash x := 0$$
$$- (n+1) \vdash x := 0 \rightarrow 0 \vdash x = 0$$

Fig. 3. Flowchart and Concrete Interpretation.

Let us consider the flowchart program depicted in Fig. 3. Its concrete semantics is expressed as a set of transition rules between program states. A program state is an element of $Val \times ProgramPoint$ and is written as $n \vdash p$, where n is the value of the variable x at program point p. Note that in this example the concrete computation tree is an infinite execution trace.

The fundamental idea in Schmidt's trace-based abstract interpretation [20, 21] is to replace an execution trace of the program by transition rules that use abstract values instead of run-time values. The result is an *abstract computation tree*, where multiple possible executions traces are presented by a non-deterministic branching in the abstract tree.

In the example above we consider a program analysis which detects whether x is zero or not. This corresponds to replace the concrete domain $Val = Int$ by $AbsVal = \{0, \neq 0\}$ and by rewriting the state transition rules accordingly. More in detail, we consider a function $\beta : Val \rightarrow AbsVal$, which maps concrete values to their most precise abstractions. For the example, in Fig. 3, we have $\beta(0) = 0$ and $\beta(\pm(n + 1)) = \neq 0$. Moreover, the following *homomorphism property* is necessary in order to let the abstract transitions correctly simulate the concrete ones: if $(v \vdash p) \rightarrow (v' \vdash p')$ is a concrete transition, then there must exist an abstract transition, $(\beta(v) \vdash p) \rightarrow (a' \vdash p')$, such that $\beta(v') \leq a'$, where $\leq$ is the approximation order between abstract values. The resulting abstract semantics transitions are shown in Fig. 4:

```
Abstract semantics transitions          Refined Abstract semantics transitions
0 ⊢ x = 0 → 0 ⊢ x := succ(x)            0 ⊢ x = 0 → 0 ⊢ x := succ(x)
0 ⊢ x := succ(x) →≠ 0 ⊢ x = 0           0 ⊢ x := succ(x) → + ⊢ x = 0
≠ 0 ⊢ x = 0 →≠ 0 ⊢ x > 0                + ⊢ x = 0 → + ⊢ x > 0
≠ 0 ⊢ x > 0 →≠ 0 ⊢ x := −x              + ⊢ x > 0 → + ⊢ x := −x
≠ 0 ⊢ x > 0 →≠ 0 ⊢ x := 0               + ⊢ x := −x → − ⊢ x > 0
≠ 0 ⊢ x := −x →≠ 0 ⊢ x > 0              − ⊢ x = 0 → − ⊢ x > 0
≠ 0 ⊢ x := 0 → 0 ⊢ x = 0                − ⊢ x > 0 → − ⊢ x := 0
                                        − ⊢ x := 0 → 0 ⊢ x := 0
```

Fig. 4. Abstract Interpretation of Flowchart.

Consider the safety CTL formula $\varphi = \forall G \forall F(x = 0)$ specifying that *for each program state in any trace it is possible to reach a program state where the value of the variable x is* 0. It is easy to check that the abstract tree does not satisfy this property because there exists an infinite trace $\neq 0 \vdash x = 0 \rightarrow \neq 0 \vdash x > 0 \rightarrow \neq 0 \vdash x := -x \rightarrow \neq 0 \vdash x > 0 \rightarrow \ldots$ that invalidates the specification. In this case, the abstraction is too rough because this is an infinite abstract trace that does not correspond to any concrete trace, i.e., we have found a spurious counterexample for φ.

In order to find a sound and complete trace based abstract interpretation, we have to refine the abstraction. By applying the backward complete shell refinement for $post[R]$, with R being the transition relation specified above, we obtain a refined model which includes the abstract values $\{0, +, -, \neq 0\}$. In this case, the abstraction function is such that $\beta(0) = 0$, $\beta(+(n+1)) = +$ and $\beta(-(n+1)) = -$. The resulting refined abstract semantics transitions, according to Definition 4, are shown in Fig. 4. It is easy to check that the refined abstract tree now satisfies the property φ.

8   Conclusions

In this work we have studied the impact of the notions of forward and backward completeness in abstract interpretation based model-checking. Our results allows us to apply standard abstract interpretation theory to refine abstract models when they result too rough for verifying temporal properties of interest. We have proved that the precision of the abstract model-checking problem for a Kripke structure $\mathbb{M} = \langle \Sigma, I, R, \| \circ \| \rangle$ is strictly connected to the precision of the underlying abstract domain, and that spurious counterexamples can be removed by considering the complete shell of the abstract domain with respect to the $post[R]$ predicate transformer.

It is particularly interesting to study what kind of counterexamples that can be removed when the refinement is computed with respect to an arbitrary function f, possibly different from $post[R]$. In this case our results allows us to formally derive the structure of those counterexamples that can be removed by an arbitrary domain refinement operation, provided that this operation can be encoded as a complete shell, namely it corresponds to the complete shell refinement $\mathcal{S}_f^{\mathcal{B}}$ with respect to a given function f. It is easy to see that if $\mathbb{M}^A$ is an abstract Kripke structure associated with an abstract domain A and a concrete transition system $\langle \Sigma, R \rangle$, the refinement operation $\mathcal{S}_f^{\mathcal{B}}$ returns a refined Kripke structure $\mathbb{M}^{\mathcal{S}_f^{\mathcal{B}}(A)}$ according to Proposition 2 which, for a given formula φ, removes all the counterexamples that corresponds to the traces in a modified (simplified) transition system $\langle \Sigma, R \wedge R_f \rangle$. This new transition system includes only those transitions that satisfy both the original relation R and the relation associated with f. The consequences of this observation in static program analysis by abstract model checking are under investigation.

Acknowledgments

The interest in applying the constructive characterization of completeness in [14] to Clarke's spurious counterexamples came to our attention in a discussion we had with Andreas Podelsky during a breakfast at Place de la Sorbonne, Paris, in July 2000. We wish to thank Andreas for having pointed to us the work of Clarke, Francesco Ranzato, and the anonymous referees for their helpful comments. Part of this work was carried out while the authors were visiting the Laboratoire d'Informatique, École Polytechnique, Palaiseau, France. This work has been supported by the Italian MURST project: *"Certificazione automatica di programmi mediante interpretazione astratta"*.

References

1. E. M. Clarke, E. A. Emerson, and A. P. Sistla. Automatic verification of finite-state concurrent system using temporal logic specification. *ACM Trans. Program. Lang. Syst.*, 8(2):244–263, 1986.
2. E. M. Clarke, O. Grumberg, S. Jha, Y. Lu, and H. Veith. Counterexample-guided abstraction refinement. In *Proc. of the 12th Internat. Conf. on Computer Aided Verification (CAV '00)*, volume 1855 of *Lecture Notes in Computer Science*, pages 154–169. Springer-Verlag, Berlin, 2000.
3. E. M. Clarke, O. Grumberg, and D. E. Long. Model checking and abstraction. *ACM Trans. Program. Lang. Syst.*, 16(5):1512–1542, 1994.
4. P. Cousot. Types as abstract interpretations (Invited Paper). In *Conference Record of the 24th ACM Symp. on Principles of Programming Languages (POPL '97)*, pages 316–331. ACM Press, New York, 1997.
5. P. Cousot. Partial completeness of abstract fixpoint checking, invited paper. In *Proceedings of the Fourth International Symposium on Abstraction, Reformulations and Approximation, SARA '2000, Lecture Notes in Artificial Intelligence 1864*, pages 1–25, Horseshoe Bay, Texas, USA, 26–29 July 2000. Springer-Verlag, Berlin, Germany.

6. P. Cousot and R. Cousot. Abstract interpretation: A unified lattice model for static analysis of programs by construction or approximation of fixpoints. In *Conference Record of the 4th ACM Symp. on Principles of Programming Languages* (*POPL '77*), pages 238–252. ACM Press, New York, 1977.

7. P. Cousot and R. Cousot. Systematic design of program analysis frameworks. In *Conference Record of the 6th ACM Symp. on Principles of Programming Languages* (*POPL '79*), pages 269–282. ACM Press, New York, 1979.

8. P. Cousot and R. Cousot. Refining model checking by abstract interpretation. *Automated Software Engineering*, 6(1):69–95, 1999.

9. P. Cousot and R. Cousot. Temporal abstract interpretation. In *Conference Record of the Twentyseventh Annual ACM SIGPLAN-SIGACT Symposium on Principles of Programming Languages*, pages 12–25, Boston, Mass., January 2000. ACM Press, New York, NY.

10. D. Dams, R. Gerth, and O. Grumberg. Abstract interpretation of reactive systems. *ACM Trans. Program. Lang. Syst.*, 19(2):253–291, 1997.

11. E. A. Emerson. Temporal and modal logic. In J. van Leeuwen, editor, *Handbook of Theoretical Computer Science*, volume B: Formal Models and Semantics. Elsevier, Amsterdam and The MIT Press, Cambridge, Mass., 1990.

12. G. Filé, R. Giacobazzi, and F. Ranzato. A unifying view of abstract domain design. *ACM Comput. Surv.*, 28(2):333–336, 1996.

13. R. Giacobazzi and F. Ranzato. Refining and compressing abstract domains. In P. Degano, R. Gorrieri, and A. Marchetti-Spaccamela, editors, *Proc. of the 24th Internat. Colloq. on Automata, Languages and Programming* (*ICALP '97*), volume 1256 of *Lecture Notes in Computer Science*, pages 771–781. Springer-Verlag, Berlin, 1997.

14. R. Giacobazzi, F. Ranzato, and F. Scozzari. Making abstract interpretation complete. *Journal of the ACM*, 47(2):361–416, March 2000.

15. C. Loiseaux, S. Graf, J. Sifakis, A. Bouajjani, and S. Bensalem. Property preserving abstractions for the verification of concurrent systems. *Formal Methods Syst. Des.*, 6:1–36, 1995.

16. Z. Manna and A. Pnueli. *The Temporal Logic of Reactive and Concurrent Systems*. Springer-Verlag, Berlin, 1992.

17. M. Müller-Olm, D. Schmidt, and B. Steffen. Model-checking. A tutorial introduction. In G. Filé, editor, *Proceedings of the International Static Analysis Symposium* (*SAS '99*), volume 1694 of *Lecture Notes in Computer Science*, pages 330–354. Springer-Verlag, Berlin, 1999.

18. A. Mycroft. Completeness and predicate-based abstract interpretation. In *Proc. of the ACM Symp. on Partial Evaluation and Program Manipulation* (*PEPM '93*), pages 179–185. ACM Press, New York, 1993.

19. F. Ranzato. On the completeness of model checking. In *Proc. of European Symposium on Programming* (*ESOP '01*), Lecture Notes in Computer Science. Springer-Verlag, Berlin, 2001.

20. D. A. Schmidt. Data flow analysis is model checking of abstract interpretation. In *Proceedings of the 25th ACM SIGPLAN-SIGACT symposium on Principles of programming languages* (*POPL '98*), pages 38–48. ACM Press, New York, 1998.

21. D. A. Schmidt. Trace-based abstract interpretation of operational semantics. *Lisp and Symbolic Computation*, 10(3):237–271, 1998.

22. B. Steffen. Data flow analysis as model checking. In A. Meyer, editor, *Proc. of Theoretical aspects of computer software* (*TACS '91*), volume 526 of *Lecture Notes in Computer Science*, pages 346–364. Springer-Verlag, Berlin, 1991.

Language-Based Security:
What's Needed and Why

Fred Schneider

Computer Science Department, Cornell University
fbs@cs.cornell.edu

Abstract. Language-based security leverages program analysis and program rewriting in enforcing security policies. The approach promises efficient enforcement of fine-grained access-control policies, and it seems to require a trusted computing base of only modest size. This talk discusses progress and prospects for the area. Traditional security problems viewed through the lens of programming language research invites novel uses of various well understood results from the area. It also provides reason to revisit assumptions and research directions that have been driving forces in languages research.

P. Cousot (Ed.): SAS 2001, LNCS 2126, pp. 374–374, 2001.
© Springer-Verlag Berlin Heidelberg 2001

A Behavioral Module System for the Pi-Calculus

Sriram K. Rajamani and Jakob Rehof

Microsoft Research
{sriram,rehof}@microsoft.com

Abstract. Distributed message-passing based asynchronous systems are becoming increasingly important. Such systems are notoriously hard to design and test. A promising approach to help programmers design such programs is to provide a *behavioral type system* that checks for behavioral properties such as deadlock freedom using a combination of type inference and model checking. The fundamental challenge in making a behavioral type system work for realistic concurrent programs is state explosion. This paper develops the theory to design a *behavioral module system* that permits decomposing the type checking problem, saving exponential cost in the analysis. Unlike module systems for sequential programming languages, a behavioral specification for a module typically assumes that the module operates in an appropriate concurrent context. We identify assume-guarantee reasoning as a fundamental principle in designing such a module system.

Concretely, we propose a behavioral module system for π-calculus programs. Types are CCS processes that correctly approximate the behavior of programs, and by applying model checking techniques to process types one can check many interesting program properties, including deadlock-freedom and communication progress. We show that modularity can be achieved in our type system by applying circular assume-guarantee reasoning principles whose soundness requires an induction over time. We state and prove an assume-guarantee rule for CCS. Our module system integrates this assume-guarantee rule into our behavioral type system.

1 Introduction

Several computing systems are built today in a distributed wide-area setting, using an asynchronous message-passing programming model. These programs are notoriously hard to design and test, due to inherent difficulties in dealing with concurrency. Better programming languages and programming tools for building such programs are becoming increasingly important.

In hardware and protocol design, there has been success in modeling different agents as communicating finite state machines, and using model checking to explore the interactions between the agents. However, agents in concurrent software tend to have more complicated communication structure than their counterparts in hardware. Indirect references and dynamic creation of new objects play a prominent role in interactions between software agents. For instance, one agent can create a new object and send the object's reference to a second agent. Following this, both agents can read or change the object's contents. Such

P. Cousot (Ed.): SAS 2001, LNCS 2126, pp. 375–394, 2001.

interactions are typically hard to model using communicating finite state machines. The π-calculus provides a simple way to model such interactions. The combination of fresh name generation and channel passing allows faithful modeling of several complicated communication patterns between software agents. However, in spite of its simple semantics, it is hard to automatically analyze π-calculus programs for checking behavioral properties. Recently, there has been considerable interest in designing so called *behavioral type systems* for statically checking important behavioral properties such as deadlock freedom and communication progress for π-calculus programs. Behavioral type systems use type inference to extract behavioral abstractions of the program, called *behavioral types*, and use model checking to explore the state space of these behavioral types. The fundamental obstacle in making a behavioral type system scale is the exponential state space explosion in model checking. The only hope for dealing with state explosion on realistic programs is to partition the type checking and model checking problems to operate on pieces of the program, thereby saving exponential amount of analysis time. We develop the theory required to design a *behavioral module system*, which makes such partitioning possible.

Our work is inspired by the behavioral type systems proposed by Igarashi and Kobayashi [11]. Here, types are CCS-like processes that correctly approximate the behavior of π-calculus programs, and types are inferred from programs. A model checker is used as a subroutine inside the typechecker for checking interesting program properties, including deadlock-freedom and communication progress. In this paper, we propose to incorporate *assume-guarantee* reasoning [17,1,3] to enable modular type checking in such a system. Assume-guarantee reasoning allows the programmer to state behavioral abstractions of a module that hold only in contexts where the module will actually be used.

Since our types are CCS processes, we need an assume-guarantee rule that works for CCS. All known assume-guarantee rules require the process calculus to have a nonblocking semantics. Since CCS processes can block, previous assume-guarantee results are not directly applicable. This paper has three technical contributions:

- We state and prove an assume-guarantee rule for CCS.
- We propose a behavioral type system for π-calculus in which types are CCS processes. Our type system is a variant of Igarashi and Kobayashi's type system, and it includes name restriction in the process types.
- We show that name restriction in CCS allows for a natural integration of our assume-guarantee rule into the behavioral type system.

There are significant technical hurdles in designing a behavioral module system for a concurrent programming language. Module systems for sequential programming languages such as ML allow the user to specify abstractions of modules using type signatures. Module systems tactfully combine analysis and user annotation to partition type checking. A type signature of a module in ML is typically independent of the sequential context where the module is used. However, it is often impossible to state useful behavioral abstractions of a module that hold in all concurrent contexts. This phenomenon is well known in the specification and verification of reactive systems [17,1,3]. Thus, we need to allow the user

$$S = \mu\alpha.(x?.m!.a?.\alpha + a?.(m!)^*)$$
$$U_s = \mu\gamma.(x!.\gamma)$$
$$Sender = \nu x.(S \mid U_s)$$
$$\hat{Sender} = \mu\alpha.(m!.a?.\alpha)$$

$$R = \mu\beta.(m?.(y!.a!.\beta + m?.(a!)^*))$$
$$U_r = \mu\delta.(y?.\delta)$$
$$Receiver = \nu y.(R \mid U_r)$$
$$\hat{Receiver} = \mu\beta.(m?.a!.\beta)$$

$$System = \nu m, a.(Sender \mid Receiver)$$

Fig. 1. A Sender and Receiver in CCS.

to state behavioral abstractions of a module that hold only in contexts where the module will actually be used. The resulting module system needs to reason about a module using behavioral abstractions of its environments. For instance, if we have two concurrent modules P and Q with behavioral specifications P' and Q', then we assume Q' as the environment for establishing that P' is a correct abstraction of P. Similarly, we assume P' as the environment for establishing that Q' is a correct abstraction of Q. Since behavioral abstractions are used circularly to reason about each other, the soundness of the reasoning needs to be established. Such circular proof rules are called assume-guarantee(A-G) rules, and their soundness requires an induction over time. We identify assume-guarantee reasoning as a fundamental principle in designing a behavioral module system.

The remainder of the paper is organized as follows. Section 2 contains two examples illustrating various aspects of our module system. In Section 3 we state and prove an assume-guarantee rule for CCS. In Section 4 we propose a behavioral module system for π-calculus. In Section 5 we discuss related work, and Section 6 concludes the paper.

2   Examples

We show two examples, one to illustrate the assume-guarantee rule and one to illustrate our type system. We follow the syntax for CCS and π-calculus from [16].

Figure 1 shows a *Sender* process sending messages to a *Receiver* process. The *Sender* and *Receiver* communicate through a message channel m and an acknowledgement channel a, that are known apriori to both processes. *Sender* comprises of process S that does the actual communication, and a local user process U_s which is consulted before every message transmission. *Receiver* comprises of process R that does the actual communication, and a local user process U_r which is consulted after every message reception. Suppose we want to check a safety property of *System* such as deadlock freedom, specified by a temporal-logic formula ψ. One way to do this is to explore the state space of *System* using a model checker. In order to alleviate state explosion, it is useful to write abstractions of the components of the system, and run the model checker on each component separately. If the user writes abstract specifications $\hat{Sender}$ and $\hat{Receiver}$ for the sender and receiver respectively, one could attempt using the following compositional proof rule to avoid exploring the state space of $System$.

$$
\frac{
\begin{array}{l}
Sender \subseteq \hat{Sender} \\
Receiver \subseteq \hat{Receiver} \\
(\eta m, a)(\hat{Sender} \mid \hat{Receiver}) \models \psi
\end{array}
}{
(\eta m, a)(Sender \mid Receiver) \models \psi
} \quad \text{[COMP]}
$$

The restriction operator η in $(\eta m, a)(\hat{Sender} \mid \hat{Receiver})$ prevents the environment from interacting with $Sender$ and $Receiver$ through the channels m and a. For present purposes, it can be taken to be the same as the name restriction operator of [16] for CCS.[1]

The obligation $Sender \subseteq \hat{Sender}$ requires that every behavior of $Sender$ is a possible behavior of $\hat{Sender}$. Note that the interaction between the component processes S and U_s has been abstracted away in the specification $\hat{Sender}$. Thus, the state space of $\hat{Sender}$ is smaller than that of $Sender$. However, the problem with [COMP] is that, in fact, $Sender \nsubseteq \hat{Sender}$, since $Sender$ can be sending arbitrary messages if acknowledgements arrive at unexpected times, whereas $\hat{Sender}$ ignores spurious acknowledgements. Also, $Receiver \nsubseteq \hat{Receiver}$ for similar reasons. Since these obligations do not hold, the rule [COMP] cannot be used to prove that $System$ does not deadlock.

The abstract process $\hat{Sender}$ is a correct abstraction of $Sender$ only in an appropriate environment. Similarly, abstract process $\hat{Receiver}$ is a correct abstraction of $Receiver$ only in an appropriate environment. The assume-guarantee proof rule shown below, allows the $Sender$ and $Receiver$ to be analyzed in composition with their abstract environments:

$$
\frac{
\begin{array}{l}
(\eta m, a)(Sender \mid \hat{Receiver}) \subseteq \hat{Sender} \\
(\eta m, a)(\hat{Sender} \mid Receiver) \subseteq \hat{Receiver} \\
(\eta m, a)(\hat{Sender} \mid \hat{Receiver}) \models \psi
\end{array}
}{
(\eta m, a)(Sender \mid Receiver) \models \psi
} \quad \text{[AG]}
$$

Note that the obligations of the [AG] rule require the $Sender$ to conform with $\hat{Sender}$ only in the environment provided by $\hat{Receiver}$. Similarly $Receiver$ is required to conform with $\hat{Receiver}$ only in the environment provided by $\hat{Sender}$. Thus, a model checker can discharge the obligations of the [AG] rule and prove deadlock freedom of $System$ without having to explore the entire state space of $System$ directly. The soundness of such a proof rule requires certain side conditions expressing progress, and is established using an induction over time. In Section 3 we state such side conditions and prove this rule for CCS.

Now suppose that the $Sender$ is part of a vendor on the world wide web and the $Receiver$ is part of a customer. A common situation is the customer first goes

---

[1] The reason we use the notation η is technical and will be explained later.

$$S(m, a) = \mu\alpha.(x?.m!.a?.\alpha + a?.(m!)^*)$$
$$U_s = \mu\gamma.(x!.\gamma)$$
$$Sender(m, a) = \nu x.(S(m, a) \mid U_s)$$

$$\tau_{S(m,a)} = \mu\alpha.(x?.m!.a?.\alpha + a?.(m!)^*)$$
$$\tau_{U_s} = \mu\gamma.(x!.\gamma)$$
$$\tau_{Sender(m,a)} = \nu x.(\tau_{S(m,a)} \mid \tau_{U_s})$$

$$\hat{\tau}_{Sender(m,a)} = \mu\alpha.(m!.a?.\alpha)$$

$$R(m, a) = \mu\beta.(m?.(y!.a!.\beta + m?.(a!)^*))$$
$$U_r = \mu\delta.(y?.\delta)$$
$$Receiver(m, a) = \nu y.(R(m, a) \mid U_r)$$

$$\tau_{R(m,a)} = \mu\beta.(m?.(y!.a!.\beta + m?.(a!)^*))$$
$$\tau_{U_r} = \mu\delta.(y?.\delta)$$
$$\tau_{Receiver(m,a)} = \nu y.(\tau_{R(m,a)} \mid \tau_{U_r})$$

$$\hat{\tau}_{Receiver(m,a)} = \mu\beta.(m?.a!.\beta)$$

$$Vendor(m, a) = www![m, a].Sender(m, a)$$
$$Customer = www?[m, a].Receiver(m, a)$$
$$System$$
$$= \nu www.((\nu msg, ack. Vendor(msg, ack))$$
$$\mid Customer)$$

$$\tau_{Vendor(m,a)} = www![(m, a)\tau_{Receiver(m,a)}].$$
$$(\tau_{Sender(m,a)} \mid \tau_{Receiver(m,a)})$$
$$\tau_{Customer} = www?[(m, a)\tau_{Receiver(m,a)}].$$
$$\tau_{Receiver(m,a)} \uparrow \{m, a\}$$

Fig. 2. An Sender-Reciver System in π-Calculus and Its Process Types.

to the vendor's website and after authentication gets fresh channels (these could be fresh URLs) over which the transaction actually happens. Such an interaction can be modeled using the channel name generation and channel passing capabilities of the π-calculus. Figure 2 shows a model of the above scenario in the π-calculus. If we want to check that the vendor process *Vendor* and customer process *Customer* do not deadlock, we need to be able to handle channel passing in our analysis. A promising approach is to first use a type-system to construct first-order approximations of the processes called process-types, and use model checking on the process-types. In Section 4 we build a type-system inspired by the work of Igarashi and Kobayashi to abstract π-calculus processes using CCS processes as process types. The right side of Figure 2 shows the process types generated by the type-system for each π-calculus process on the left. A model checker is used as a subroutine inside the type-checker. In our type system, it turns out that the model checker is asked to check:

$$(\eta msg, ack)(\tau_{Sender(msg,ack)} \mid \tau_{Receiver(msg,ack)}) \models \psi$$

Here $\tau_{Sender(msg,ack)}$ is the process type for the $Sender(msg, ack)$ process and $\tau_{Receiver(msg,ack)}$ is the process type for the $Receiver(msg, ack)$ process. These process types are identical to the *Sender* and *Receiver* processes from Figure 1. The notation $z![\tau].P$ is used for the type of a process which sends a channel along z and continues as P, where τ is a type describing the interactions that could possibly happen on the sent channel. If the user writes behavioral type specifications $\hat{\tau}_{Sender(msg,ack)}$ and $\hat{\tau}_{Receiver(msg,ack)}$ at the module interfaces for $Sender(msg,ack)$ and $Receiver(msg,ack)$ we can use our assume-guarantee rule to mitigate the state-explosion that happens inside the type-checker.

Figure 3 shows a staged-server system [13] with two stages. This example was inspired from a web-crawler example in [14]. *StageA* receives inputs from

$Sem = \mu\beta.(acquire!.release?.\beta)$

$StageA = A?[x].acquire?.(\nu y)B?[y].y?.x!$

$StageB = \mu\alpha.(B?[y].y!.release!.\alpha)$

$System = (*StageA) \mid StageB^k \mid Sem^k$

$\tau_{Sem} = \mu\beta.(acquire!.release?.\beta)$

τ_{StageA}
$\quad = A?[(x)x!].acquire?.(\nu y)B?[(y)y!].(y? \mid y!)$

$\tau_{StageB} = \mu\alpha.(B?[(y)y!].release!.\alpha)$

$\tau_{System} = (*\tau_{StageA}) \mid \tau_{StageB}^k \mid \tau_{Sem}^k$

Fig. 3. A Staged-Server in π-Calculus and Its Process Types.

the user and then passes each request to $StageB$. When $StageB$ responds to the request, the response is first received by $StageA$ and then passed on to the user. The system comprises of an unbounded number of copies of $StageA$ and k copies of $StageB$. For the purpose of resource control, k copies of a semaphore process Sem are used to control access to the k copies of $StageB$. Name generation is used to model matching the requests with appropriate responses. With every request, $StageA$ generates a new channel y, sends y to $StageB$, and waits for a response on channel y. The right hand side of Figure 3 shows the process types generated by our type system. The channel passing from $StageA$ to $StageB$ has been approximated in the process types. Note that $StageA$ sends a new channel y to $StageB$. Upon receiving the channel y, $StageB$ does $y!$. The type τ_{StageA} does not send any channels to $StageB$. The effect of $StageB$ doing $y!$ is statically transferred inside the description of τ_{StageA} by the type system.

The process $System$ satisfies the following property: whenever $StageA$ wants to send a message to $StageB$ after successfully acquiring the semaphore (by executing $acquire?$), then the send $B![y]$ never blocks. Even though τ_{System} is an infinite state system, due to unbounded number copies of τ_{StageA}, we can check this property on τ_{System} by using a model checker with counting abstraction similar to [12].

3   Assume-Guarantee Rule for CCS

In this section we give syntax and semantics of CCS processes, and we define trace containment for such processes. The main result of the section is Theorem 1, which gives an assume-guarantee rule for CCS.

3.1   Syntax and Semantics of CCS Processes

The syntax of CCS processes P is given by the following definition.

$$P ::= \alpha \mid \mathbf{0} \mid \Sigma_i G_i \mid P \mid Q \mid \mu\alpha.P \mid (\nu x)P$$

$$G ::= x!^t.P \mid x?^t.P$$

The structural preorder $\preceq$ is the least reflexive and transitive relation closed under the following rules, together with renaming and reordering of bound variables and reordering of terms in a summation. The notation $P \equiv Q$ abbreviates $P \preceq Q$ and $Q \preceq P$. The set of free names of P is denoted $\mathrm{fn}(P)$.

$$P \mid 0 \equiv P \qquad P \mid Q \equiv Q \mid P \qquad P \mid (Q \mid R) \equiv (P \mid Q) \mid R$$

$$(\nu x)0 \equiv 0 \qquad \mu\alpha.P \equiv P[\mu\alpha.P/\alpha]$$

$$\frac{x \notin \mathrm{fn}(P)}{P \mid (\nu x)Q \preceq (\nu x)(P \mid Q)} \qquad \frac{P \preceq P' \quad Q \preceq Q'}{P \mid Q \preceq P' \mid Q'}$$

Figure 4: Structural Preorder

$$P \xrightarrow{\epsilon} P \qquad [\text{EPS}]$$

$$(\ldots + x!^{t_1}.P + \ldots) \mid (\ldots + x?^{t_2}.Q + \ldots) \xrightarrow{x^{t_1,t_2}} P \mid Q \qquad [\text{REACT}]$$

$$(\ldots + x!^t.P + \ldots) \xrightarrow{x^t} P \qquad [\text{O-COMM}]$$

$$(\ldots + x?^t.P + \ldots) \xrightarrow{x^t} P \qquad [\text{I-COMM}]$$

$$\frac{P \xrightarrow{x^{t_1,t_2}} P'}{(\nu x)P \xrightarrow{\tau^{t_1,t_2}} (\nu x)P'} \quad [\text{TAU}] \qquad \frac{P \xrightarrow{\ell} P' \quad x \notin \ell}{(\nu x)P \xrightarrow{\ell} (\nu x)P'} \quad [\text{RES}]$$

$$\frac{P \preceq P' \quad P' \xrightarrow{\ell} Q' \quad Q' \preceq Q}{P \xrightarrow{\ell} Q} \quad [\text{S-CONG}] \qquad \frac{P \xrightarrow{\ell} P'}{P \mid Q \xrightarrow{\ell} P' \mid Q} \quad [\text{PAR}]$$

Eta rules

$$\frac{P \xrightarrow{x^{t_1,t_2}} P'}{(\eta x)P \xrightarrow{x^{t_1,t_2}} (\eta x)P'} \quad [\text{ETA1}] \qquad \frac{P \xrightarrow{\ell} P' \quad x \notin \ell}{(\eta x)P \xrightarrow{\ell} (\eta x)P'} \quad [\text{ETA2}]$$

In the rules above, ℓ ranges over actions of the form $x!^t, x?^t, x!^{t_1,t_2}, x?^{t_1,t_2}$ or τ^{t_1,t_2}.

Figure 5: Labeled Reduction on CCS Processes

We write $*P$ as an abbreviation for $\mu\alpha.(P \mid \alpha)$, P^* as an abbreviation for $\mu\alpha.(P.\alpha)$, and P^k as an abbreviation for k copies of process P in parallel. Throughout this section, P,Q, P' and Q' range over CCS processes.

We augment the usual syntax of CCS with tags on send and receive operations. Actions in CCS are of the form $x!^t, x?^t, x!^{t_1,t_2}, x?^{t_1,t_2}, \tau^{t_1,t_2}$ or ϵ. The actions $x!^t$ and $x?^t$ denote commitments and actions $x!^{t_1,t_2}, x?^{t_1,t_2}$ denote reactions. Note that commitments have a single tag and reactions have two tags. The action τ^{t_1,t_2} denotes the invisible or silent reaction, and action ϵ denotes the null action.

Figure 5 defines the labeled reduction relation on processes. As indicated by rule S-CONG in Figure 5, reduction is modulo structural congruence, defined in Figure 4. Note that in addition to the usual rules for the restriction operator ν we have rules ETA1 and ETA2 for the restriction operator η. This operator is the same as ν, only with different observability properties: The expression $(\eta\overline{x})P$ is simply meta-notation for a ν-abstraction whose interactions can be observed. This notation is needed to state our assume-guarantee rule.

Sometimes it is insignificant if an action is a send or receive. In such cases, we drop the ? and ! symbol from the action for brevity. Let Act be the set of all actions of the form $x^{t_1,t_2}, x^t, \tau^{t_1,t_2}$ or ϵ. We use $\omega, \omega_1, \omega_2, \ldots$ to range over finite sequences of actions, and we write $\omega_{[i]}$ to denote the i'th element of ω. If P is a CCS process with

$$P \xrightarrow{\omega_{[0]}} P_1 \xrightarrow{\omega_{[1]}} P_2 \xrightarrow{\omega_{[2]}} \ldots P_{n-1} \xrightarrow{\omega_{[n-1]}} P_n$$

then $\omega = \omega_{[0]}\omega_{[1]}\omega_{[2]} \ldots \omega_{[n-1]}$ is a *trace* of P. In such cases, we lift reductions to sequences of actions and write $P \xrightarrow{\omega} P_n$. The set of all traces of P is denoted $\text{Tr}(P)$. We let $\text{Act}(\omega)$ denote the set of actions occurring in the trace ω, and we define for a process P the set of actions $\text{Act}(P) = \bigcup_{\omega \in \text{Tr}(P)} \text{Act}(\omega)$.

We will assume that, for any set of processes under consideration, tags are used only once, *i.e.*, no tag occurs twice in the processes. We let $\text{T}(P)$ denote the set of tags occurring in P.

Let $\omega = \omega_{[0]}\omega_{[1]} \ldots \omega_{[n]}$ be a trace in $\text{Tr}((\eta\overline{x})(P \mid Q))$, $\omega_{[i]} \in \text{Act}$. For an element $\omega_{[i]}$ in ω we will now define the *projection of $\omega_{[i]}$ onto P*, denoted $(\omega_{[i]})_P$, as follows. The definition is by cases over the form of $\omega_{[i]} \in \text{Act}$:

$$(x^{t_1,t_2})_P = \begin{cases} x^{t_1,t_2} & \text{if } t_1 \in \text{T}(P) \text{ and } t_2 \in \text{T}(P) \\ x^{t_1} & \text{if } t_1 \in \text{T}(P) \text{ and } t_2 \notin \text{T}(P) \\ x^{t_2} & \text{if } t_1 \notin \text{T}(P) \text{ and } t_2 \in \text{T}(P) \\ \epsilon & \text{if } t_1 \notin \text{T}(P) \text{ and } t_2 \notin \text{T}(P) \end{cases}$$

$$(\tau^{t_1,t_2})_P = \begin{cases} \tau^{t_1,t_2} & \text{if } t \in \text{T}(P) \text{ and } t_2 \in \text{T}(P) \\ \epsilon & \text{if } t_1 \notin \text{T}(P) \text{ or } t_2 \notin \text{T}(P) \end{cases}$$

$$(x^t)_P = \begin{cases} x^t & \text{if } t \in \text{T}(P) \\ \epsilon & \text{if } t \notin \text{T}(P) \end{cases}$$

$$(\epsilon)_P = \epsilon$$

The projection $(\omega_{[i]})_Q$ is defined analogously. If $\omega = \omega_{[0]}\omega_{[1]}\omega_{[2]} \ldots \omega_{[n-1]}$ is a trace of $P \mid Q$, then we define the *projection of ω onto P*, denoted ω_P, to be given by

$$(\omega_P)_{[i]} = (\omega_{[i]})_P \text{ for } i = 0 \ldots n - 1$$

and the projection of ω onto Q, denoted ω_Q, is defined analogously.

We need an operation to combine traces. Let $\oplus$ be the partial function on $\mathsf{Act} \times \mathsf{Act}$, given by $x^t \oplus x^{t'} = x^{t,t'}$ and $\ell \oplus \epsilon = \epsilon \oplus \ell = \ell$ for all $\ell \in \mathsf{Act}$. For traces ω_1 and ω_2 of equal length we define $\omega_1 \oplus \omega_2$ by setting $(\omega_1 \oplus \omega_2)_{[i]} = (\omega_1)_{[i]} \oplus (\omega_2)_{[i]}$. We consider traces *modulo* ϵ, that is, any number of occurrences of ϵ can be tacitly inserted or removed from a trace (hence any trace has some representative of any given length greater than some smallest length). Finally, if $\bar{x}$ is a list of channel names, we define the relation

$$\bar{x} \vdash \ell \sim \ell'$$

to hold if and only if $\ell \oplus \ell'$ is well defined and both of the following conditions are satisfied for all $x \in \bar{x}$:

  - if ℓ is of the form x^t, then $\ell' \neq \epsilon$
  - if ℓ' is of the form x^t, then $\ell \neq \epsilon$

We lift the relation to traces of equal length n, by defining $\bar{x} \vdash \omega_1 \sim \omega_2$ to hold if and only if for all $i = 0 \ldots n - 1$ we have $\bar{x} \vdash (\omega_1)_{[i]} \sim (\omega_2)_{[i]}$.

Lemma 1. *Assume that $\mathsf{Act}(\omega) \subseteq \mathsf{Act}(A) \cup \mathsf{Act}(B)$. Then we have: $\omega \in \mathsf{Tr}(A \mid B)$ if and only if $\omega_A \oplus \omega_B$ is well defined and $\omega_A \in \mathsf{Tr}(A)$ and $\omega_B \in \mathsf{Tr}(B)$ and $\omega = \omega_A \oplus \omega_B$.*

Lemma 2. *Assume that $\mathsf{Act}(\omega) \subseteq \mathsf{Act}(A) \cup \mathsf{Act}(B)$. Then we have: $\omega \in \mathsf{Tr}((\eta\bar{x})(A \mid B))$ if and only if $\bar{x} \vdash \omega_A \sim \omega_B$ and $\omega_A \in \mathsf{Tr}(A)$ and $\omega_B \in \mathsf{Tr}(B)$ and $\omega = \omega_A \oplus \omega_B$.*

Note that Lemma 2 coincides with Lemma 1 if $\bar{x}$ is empty.

3.2   Trace Containment

For a trace ω, let ω^τ denote the trace that arises from ω by eliding all τ actions. Also, let ω° denote the sequence that arises from ω by replacing all actions of the form x^{t_1, t_2} or x^t with x. For a trace ω, we define the *norm* of ω, denoted $\mathsf{N}(\omega)$, to be the sequence $(\omega^\tau)^\circ$. We write $\omega =_{\mathsf{N}} \omega'$ as an abbreviation for $\mathsf{N}(\omega) = \mathsf{N}(\omega')$.

We say that a process I is *trace contained in* process S with respect to process P, written $I \subseteq_P S$, if and only if $I \equiv (\eta\bar{x})(P \mid Q)$ and for every $\omega \in \mathsf{Tr}(I)$ there exists $\omega' \in \mathsf{Tr}(S)$ such that $\omega' =_{\mathsf{N}} \omega_P$. We abbreviate $I \subseteq_I S$ as $I \subseteq S$.

Let x be a channel name in $\bar{x}$. We say that x is a *non-blocking* channel of process P in the process $(\eta\bar{x})(P \mid Q)$ if and only if whenever the following conditions hold:

1. $P \xrightarrow{\omega_1} P'$
2. $Q \xrightarrow{\omega_2} Q'$

3. $\bar{x} \vdash \omega_1 \sim \omega_2$
4. $P' \equiv (\ldots + a^{t_1}.P'' + \ldots)$

then we have

$$Q' \xrightarrow{\tau^*} (\ldots + \bar{a}^{t_2}.Q'' + \ldots)$$

where τ^* is some sequence of τ actions, $a = x?$ and $\bar{a} = x!$, or $a = x!$ and $\bar{a} = x?$ for some x.

3.3   Assume-Guarantee Rule

Given an implementation I and specification S, suppose we want to check if $I \subseteq S$. Suppose further that $I = (\nu\bar{x})(P \mid Q)$ is a composition of two processes P and Q that interact over a set of channels $\bar{x}$, and that the specification $S = (\nu\bar{x})(P' \mid Q')$ is structurally similar to the implementation I. Then Theorem 1 gives a way of checking if $I \subseteq S$ without exploring the entire state space of I directly.

Theorem 1. *(Assume-Guarantee) For any processes P, Q, P', Q' suppose*

A1. $(\eta\bar{x})(P \mid Q') \subseteq_P P'$
A2. $(\eta\bar{x})(P' \mid Q) \subseteq_Q Q'$
A3. *Every channel x in $\bar{x}$ is either non-blocking for P in $(\eta\bar{x})(P \mid Q')$ or non-blocking for Q in $(\eta\bar{x})(P' \mid Q)$.*

Then we have

$$(\eta\bar{x})(P \mid Q) \subseteq (\eta\bar{x})(P' \mid Q')$$

Before proving the theorem we state a few lemmas. In the following, we will sometimes use process superscripts on traces, as in ω^P. This is a naming convention intended as a help to remind the reader that ω^P is in $\mathsf{Tr}(P)$.

Lemma 3. *If $\bar{x} \vdash \omega_1 \sim \omega_2$ and $\omega_1 =_N \omega_1'$, then $\bar{x} \vdash \omega_1' \sim \omega_2$.*

Lemma 4. *If $\omega_1 \oplus \omega_2$ is well defined and $\omega_1 =_N \omega_1'$, then $\omega_1' \oplus \omega_2$ is well defined and $\omega_1 \oplus \omega_2 =_N \omega_1' \oplus \omega_2$.*

Lemma 5. *Suppose that*

1. $\omega \in \mathsf{Tr}((\eta\bar{x})(P \mid Q))$
2. $\omega^{P'} \in \mathsf{Tr}(P')$ with $\omega^{P'} =_N \omega_P$
3. $(\eta\bar{x})(P' \mid Q) \subseteq_Q Q'$

Then there exists $\omega^{Q'} \in \mathsf{Tr}(Q')$ such that $\omega^{Q'} =_N \omega_Q$.

For natural numbers k, we can talk about *trace containment up to k*, denoted $\subseteq_P^k$, by defining $(\eta\bar{x})(P \mid Q) \subseteq_P^k P'$ if and only if for all traces $\omega \in \mathsf{Tr}((\eta\bar{x})(P \mid Q))$ of length at most k, there exists $\omega' \in \mathsf{Tr}(P')$ with $\omega' =_N \omega_P$.

Lemma 6. *Suppose, for any k, that*

1. $(\eta\overline{x})(P \mid Q) \subseteq_P^k P'$
2. $(\eta\overline{x})(P \mid Q) \subseteq_Q^k Q'$

Then $(\eta\overline{x})(P \mid Q) \subseteq^k (\eta\overline{x})(P' \mid Q')$.

Lemma 7. *Let* $\omega \in Tr((\eta\overline{x})(P \mid Q))$ *and let* $\omega^{P\mid Q'} \in Tr((\eta\overline{x})(P \mid Q'))$ *such that*

1. $(\eta\overline{x})(P \mid Q') \subseteq_P P'$
2. $\omega_P =_N (\omega^{P\mid\overline{Q'}})_P$
3. $\omega^{P\mid Q'}.\tilde{\omega} \in Tr((\eta\overline{x})(P \mid Q'))$

Then there exists $\omega^{P'} \in Tr(P')$ *such that* $\omega^{P'} =_N \omega_P.(\tilde{\omega})_P$.

Lemma 8. *(Context Substitution)*
Assume

$$(\eta\overline{x})(P \mid Q) \xrightarrow{\omega} (\eta\overline{x})(P_k \mid Q_k)$$

and $\omega^{P\mid Q'} \in Tr((\eta\overline{x})(P \mid Q'))$ *with* $\omega =_N \omega^{P\mid Q'}$ *and* $\omega_P = (\omega^{P\mid Q'})_P$. *Then*

$$(\eta\overline{x})(P \mid Q') \xrightarrow{\omega^{P\mid Q'}} (\eta\overline{x})(P_k \mid Q'_k)$$

for some Q'_k.

We are now ready to prove Theorem 1.

Proof. Assuming A1, A2 and A3 we prove by induction on the length of traces in $Tr((\eta\overline{x})(P \mid Q))$ the stronger conclusion

B1. $(\eta\overline{x})(P \mid Q) \subseteq (\eta\overline{x})(P' \mid Q')$ and
B2. $(\eta\overline{x})(P \mid Q) \subseteq_P P'$ and
B3. $(\eta\overline{x})(P \mid Q) \subseteq_Q Q'$.

Let $\omega = \omega_0\omega_1 \ldots \omega_{k-1}\omega_k \ldots \omega_n$ be an arbitrary trace in $Tr((\eta\overline{x})(P \mid Q))$. Let $\omega_{\leq i}$ denote the prefix $\omega_0\omega_1 \ldots \omega_i$, for $0 \leq i \leq n$. We assume the induction hypothesis holds for $\omega_{\leq k}$ and prove it for $\omega_{\leq(k+1)}$.
We first establish the following:

C1. $\omega_{\leq i} \in Tr((\eta\overline{x})(P \mid Q))$ for all $0 \leq i \leq n$.
C2. $\exists\omega_k^{P'\mid Q} \in Tr((\eta\overline{x})(P' \mid Q))$. $\omega_{\leq k} =_N \omega_k^{P'\mid Q} \wedge (\omega_{\leq k})_Q = (\omega_k^{P'\mid Q})_Q$.
C3. $\exists\omega_k^{P\mid Q'} \in Tr((\eta\overline{x})(P \mid Q'))$. $\omega_{\leq k} =_N \omega_k^{P\mid Q'} \wedge (\omega_{\leq k})_P = (\omega_k^{P\mid Q'})_P$.

C1 follows by the assumptions and the definition of $\omega_{\leq i}$. To prove C2, we first observe that, because $\omega_{\leq k} \in Tr((\eta\overline{x})(P \mid Q))$, Lemma 2 shows that $(\omega_{\leq k})_P \in Tr(P)$ and $(\omega_{\leq k})_Q \in Tr(Q)$ and

$$\overline{x} \vdash (\omega_{\leq k})_P \sim (\omega_{\leq k})_Q \tag{1}$$

By induction hypothesis (B2) applied to $\omega_{\leq k}$ we get

$$\exists\omega_k^{P'} \in Tr(P'). (\omega_{\leq k})_P =_N \omega_k^{P'} \tag{2}$$

Now, choose $\omega_k^{P'}$ according to (2). By (1), (2) and Lemma 3 we have

$$\bar{x} \vdash \omega_k^{P'} \sim (\omega_{\leq k})_Q \tag{3}$$

Define $\omega_k^{P'|Q}$ by setting

$$\omega_k^{P'|Q} = \omega_k^{P'} \oplus (\omega_{\leq k})_Q$$

Then $\omega_k^{P'|Q}$ is well defined and in $\mathsf{Tr}((\eta\bar{x})(P' \mid Q))$ by (3) and Lemma 2. Because (by (2)) we have $\omega_k^{P'} =_\mathsf{N} (\omega_{\leq k})_P$, it follows from Lemma 4 that

$$\omega_k^{P'} \oplus (\omega_{\leq k})_Q =_\mathsf{N} (\omega_{\leq k})_P \oplus (\omega_{\leq k})_Q$$

which shows that

$$\omega_k^{P'|Q} =_\mathsf{N} \omega_{\leq k} \tag{4}$$

Furthermore, it follows from the definition of $\omega_k^{P'|Q}$ that

$$(\omega_{\leq k})_Q = (\omega_k^{P'|Q})_Q \tag{5}$$

It follows from (4) and (5) that $\omega_k^{P'|Q}$ is a witness of C2. This concludes the proof of C2. The claim C3 is proven by a symmetric argument, using induction hypothesis (B3).

We now proceed to prove B1, B2 and B3 for the inductive case $k+1$ by a case analysis on the form of ω_{k+1}. For space reasons we prove only one representative case. The full proof can be found in the technical report [20].

– **Case 1.** ω_{k+1} is an interaction x^{t_1,t_2}, for $x \in \bar{x}$: WLOG let $t_1 \in \mathsf{T}(P)$, $t_2 \in \mathsf{T}(Q)$, and let x be non-blocking for P in $(\eta\bar{x})(P \mid Q')$.
  We know from C3 that, for some $\omega_k^{P|Q'} \in \mathsf{Tr}((\eta\bar{x})(P \mid Q'))$ we have

$$\omega_{\leq k} =_\mathsf{N} \omega_k^{P|Q'} \text{ and } (\omega_{\leq k})_P = (\omega_k^{P|Q'})_P \tag{6}$$

By our assumptions, $\omega_{k+1} = x^{t_1,t_2}$, so that P can make the commitment x^{t_1} in step ω_{k+1}. Hence, we have

$$(\eta\bar{x})(P \mid Q) \xrightarrow{\omega_{\leq k}} (\eta\bar{x})(P_k \mid Q_k) \xrightarrow{x^{t_1,t_2}} (\eta\bar{x})(P_{k+1} \mid Q_{k+1})$$

with $P_k \xrightarrow{x^{t_1}} P_{k+1}$, for some $P_k, Q_k, P_{k+1}, Q_{k+1}$. By (6) together with Lemma 8 we can conclude that

$$(\eta\bar{x})(P \mid Q') \xrightarrow{\omega_k^{P|Q'}} (\eta\bar{x})(P_k \mid Q_k')$$

for some Q_k'. Because x is non-blocking for P in $(\eta\bar{x})(P \mid Q')$, it follows that

$$Q_k' \xrightarrow{\tau^*} Q'' \xrightarrow{x^{t_3}} Q_{k+1}'$$

for some sequence of τ-actions τ^* and some t_3, Q'', Q'_{k+1}. Putting the previous results together, we can conclude that

$$(\eta\overline{x})(P \mid Q') \xrightarrow{\omega_k^{P|Q'}}$$
$$(\eta\overline{x})(P_k \mid Q'_k) \xrightarrow{\tau^*}$$
$$(\eta\overline{x})(P_k \mid Q'') \xrightarrow{x^{t_1,t_3}}$$
$$(\eta\overline{x})(P_{k+1} \mid Q_{k+1})$$

Hence, we have

$$\omega_k^{P|Q'}.\tau^*.x^{t_1,t_3} \in \mathsf{Tr}((\eta\overline{x})(P \mid Q')) \tag{7}$$

By (6), (7) and assumption A1, Lemma 7 is applicable (taking $\tilde{\omega} = \tau^*.x^{t_1,t_2}$), and we get that there exists $\omega^{P'} \in \mathsf{Tr}(P')$ such that

$$\omega^{P'} =_{\mathsf{N}} (\omega_{\leq k})_P.(\tau^*.x^{t_1,t_3})_P =_{\mathsf{N}} (\omega_{\leq k})_P.x^{t_1} = (\omega_{\leq k+1})_P$$

Hence, we have

$$\omega^{P'} =_{\mathsf{N}} (\omega_{\leq k+1})_P \tag{8}$$

thereby showing B2 for the inductive step $k + 1$, as witnessed by $\omega^{P'}$ in (8). Since $\omega_{\leq k+1} \in \mathsf{Tr}((\eta\overline{x})(P \mid Q))$, it follows from (8) together with A2 via Lemma 5 that there exists $\omega^{Q'} \in \mathsf{Tr}(Q')$ with $\omega^{Q'} =_{\mathsf{N}} (\omega_{\leq k+1})_Q$. This shows B3 for the inductive step $k + 1$. Lemma 6 applied to B2 and B3 for $k + 1$ then yields B1 for the step $k + 1$.
- **Remaining cases.** See technical report [20].

$\square$

A model checker can discharge obligations A1, A2 and A3 and reach the desired conclusion. Note that

$$(\eta\overline{x})(P \mid Q) \subseteq (\eta\overline{x})(P' \mid Q') \quad \Rightarrow \quad (\nu\overline{x})(P \mid Q) \subseteq (\nu\overline{x})(P' \mid Q')$$

Thus, η is just a meta-process notation that lets us state the obligations A1, A2 and A3, all of which require observing the interactions on channels in $\overline{x}$. We note that model checking CCS is undecidable in general. However model checking is decidable for certain fragments of CCS such as the finite control fragment, which disallows μ recursion inside parallel composition, and the ν free fragment. In order to model check an arbitrary CCS process one could first construct an abstraction that falls in such a decidable fragment and then model check the abstraction.

Theorem 1 generalizes to the case of any finite parallel composition $\prod_i P_i$. Since the proof method is the same as shown in the proof of Theorem 1, we confine ourselves to recording

Theorem 2. *(Assume-Guarantee) Let $\xi_i = P'_1 \mid \ldots \mid P'_{i-1} \mid P'_{i+1} \mid \ldots \mid P'_n$, for $i = 1 \ldots n$. Then the following inference rule is sound*

$$\frac{\forall i.\ (\eta\overline{x})(P_i \mid \xi_i) \subseteq_{P_i} P'_i}{(\eta\overline{x})\prod_i P_i \subseteq (\eta\overline{x})\prod_i P'_i}(*)$$

In the reduction rules below, the structural preorder $\preceq$ is as defined in Figure 4 with the additional rule $*P \preceq *P \mid P$.

Syntax

$$P ::= \mathbf{0} \quad \mid \quad \Sigma_i G_i \quad \mid \quad P \mid Q \quad \mid \quad *P \quad \mid \quad (\nu x)P$$

$$G ::= x!^t[\overline{y}].P \quad \mid \quad x?^t[\overline{y}].P$$

Semantics

$$(\ldots + x!^t[\overline{z}].P + \ldots) \mid (\ldots + x?^{t'}[\overline{y}].Q + \ldots) \xrightarrow{x^{t,t'}} P \mid [\overline{z}/\overline{y}]Q \quad [\text{R-COM}]$$

$$\frac{P \xrightarrow{\ell} P'}{P \mid Q \xrightarrow{\ell} P' \mid Q} \quad [\text{R-PAR}] \qquad \frac{P \preceq P' \quad P' \xrightarrow{\ell} Q' \quad Q' \preceq Q}{P \xrightarrow{\ell} Q} \quad [\text{R-SP-CONG}]$$

$$\frac{P \xrightarrow{x^{t_1,t_2}} P'}{(\nu x)P \xrightarrow{\tau^{t_1,t_2}} (\nu x)P'} \quad [\text{R-NEW1}] \qquad \frac{P \xrightarrow{\ell} P' \quad x \notin \ell}{(\nu x)P \xrightarrow{\ell} (\nu x)P'} \quad [\text{R-NEW2}]$$

Figure 6: Syntax and Semantics of π Calculus

$$\mathbf{0} \rhd \mathbf{0} \quad [\text{T-ZERO}] \qquad \frac{\gamma_i \rhd G_i \text{ for } i = 1 \ldots n}{\gamma_1 + \ldots + \gamma_n \rhd G_1 + \ldots + G_n} \quad [\text{T-CHOICE}]$$

$$\frac{\Gamma_1 \rhd P_1 \quad \Gamma_2 \rhd P_2}{\Gamma_1 \mid \Gamma_2 \rhd P_1 \mid P_2} \quad [\text{T-PAR}] \qquad \frac{\Gamma_1 \rhd P}{x!^t[(\overline{y})\Gamma_2].(\Gamma_1 \mid [\overline{z}/\overline{y}]\Gamma_2) \rhd x!^t[\overline{z}].P} \quad [\text{T-OUT}]$$

$$\frac{\Gamma \rhd P}{*\Gamma \rhd *P} \quad [\text{T-REP}] \qquad \frac{\Gamma \rhd P}{x?^t[(\overline{y})(\Gamma \uparrow_{\nu - \overline{y}})].(\Gamma \uparrow_{\overline{y}}) \rhd x?^t[\overline{y}].P} \quad [\text{T-IN}]$$

$$\frac{\Gamma \rhd P \quad \Gamma \leq \Gamma'}{\Gamma' \rhd P} \quad [\text{T-SUB}] \qquad \frac{\Gamma \rhd P \quad WF(\Gamma \uparrow_{\nu - \overline{x}})}{(\nu \overline{x})\Gamma \rhd (\nu \overline{x})P} \quad [\text{T-NEW}]$$

Figure 7: Typing Rules

provided that the side-condition $(*)$ *is satisfied:*

$$(*) \begin{cases} \forall x \in \overline{x}. \; \forall i, j. \\ \textit{either } x \textit{ non-blocking for } P_i \textit{ in } (\eta\overline{x})(P_i \mid \xi_i) \\ \textit{or } x \textit{ non-blocking for } P_j \textit{ in } (\eta\overline{x})(P_j \mid \xi_j) \end{cases}$$

4 A Behavioral Module System for π-Calculus

The syntax and semantics of the π calculus is shown in Figure 6. We use abstract processes Γ for types and type environments. A type judgment in this system is of the form $\Gamma \rhd P$, meaning that the abstract process Γ is a correct abstraction of the concrete π calculus process P. In the sequel, we will refer to abstract processes Γ as *process types*. Throughout the remainder of this section, P, P_i and P' range over π-calculus processes.

Our type system is a variant of the system presented by Igarashi and Kobayashi [11], with the primary difference being that our process types are exactly CCS. The process types of Igarashi and Kobayashi form a subcalculus of CCS, because they do not include the name restriction operator, ν. The inclusion of name restriction enables us to type processes more precisely. Consider the following example process $P = (\nu cd)P'$ where P' is the process

$$\begin{pmatrix} c?.d!+ \\ c!.d! \end{pmatrix} \mid (\nu x)\begin{pmatrix} x!^{t_1} \mid x?^{t_2}.c!^{t_4} \mid \\ x?^{t_3}.c?^{t_5} \end{pmatrix} \mid (d?^{t_6})$$

The type of P' in the Igarashi-Kobayashi type system is the process type Γ given by

$$\begin{pmatrix} c?.d!+ \\ c!.d! \end{pmatrix} \mid \begin{pmatrix} t_1 \mid t_2.c!^{t_4} \mid \\ t_3.c?^{t_5} \end{pmatrix} \mid \begin{pmatrix} d?^{t_6} \end{pmatrix}$$

In this type, the restriction $(\nu x)\dots$ has been elided, and all occurrences of x are replaced by tags t_1, t_2, t_3, with $t.\Gamma'$ reducing to Γ'. This is an abstraction of name restriction, and it introduces an overapproximation of the concrete semantics. In this case, the type Γ contains an execution where the receive $d?^{t_6}$ blocks for ever, which arises when reductions on t_2 and t_3 are followed by a reaction between $c!^{t_4}$ and $c?^{t_5}$. However, in process P all executions result in a successful interaction on channel d. In contrast, since our process types contain name restriction, the process type of P is identical to P in our system.

The process types in our type system are defined by the following syntax:

$$\begin{aligned}
\tau \text{ (tuple types)} \quad &::= (x_1, x_2, \dots, x_n)\Gamma \\
\Gamma \text{ (process types)} &::= \mathbf{0} \mid \alpha \mid \gamma_1 + \dots + \gamma_n \mid (\Gamma_1 \mid \Gamma_2) \mid \mu\alpha.\Gamma \mid (\nu x)\Gamma \\
\gamma \quad\quad &::= x!^{\mathbf{t}}[\tau].\Gamma \mid x?^{\mathbf{t}}[\tau].\Gamma
\end{aligned}$$

This language is equivalent to CCS, with typed channels. Channel types do not influence reduction semantics of process types. However, they are used by the type system to model higher-order message passing in π calculus. The reduction semantics of process types is given by Figure 5. For given process type Γ, each tag t uniquely determines an occurrence of either $x!^t[\tau]$ or $x?^t[\tau]$. In the context of Γ let $\mathcal{T}(t)$ denote the type τ thus associated with t. We abbreviate $x!^t[0]$ as $x!^t$.

The typing rules of our type system are shown in Figure 7. The type system includes subtyping in rule [T-SUB]. Our subtyping relation $\leq$ is *weak simulation* [16], defined as $\Gamma_1 \leq \Gamma_2$ if and only if for all action sequences ω, whenever $\Gamma_1 \xrightarrow{\omega} \Gamma_1'$, then there exists ω' and Γ_2' such that $\Gamma_2 \xrightarrow{\omega'} \Gamma_2'$ with $\omega =_\mathsf{N} \omega'$ and $\Gamma_1' \leq \Gamma_2'$. This definition of $\leq$ satisfies the axioms for a *proper subtyping relation* as defined by Igarashi and Kobayashi [11]. The rule for name restriction [T-NEW] and the rule for input [T-IN] use the *anonymization operator* $\Gamma \uparrow_S$, where S is a set of channel names. The formula $\Box\psi$ in rule [T-NEW] refers to an invariant, such as deadlock freedom. In order to define the anonymization operator, we first define the *type elimination operator* $\Gamma \backslash_S$, where S is a set of channel names, and it is defined by

$$0\backslash_S = 0$$
$$\alpha\backslash_S = \alpha$$
$$(x?^t[\tau].\Gamma)\backslash_S = \begin{cases} x?^t[\tau].(\Gamma\backslash_S) & \text{if } x \notin S \\ x?^t.(\Gamma\backslash_S) & \text{otherwise} \end{cases}$$
$$(x!^t[\tau].\Gamma)\backslash_S = \begin{cases} (x!^t[\tau].\Gamma)\backslash_S & \text{if } x \notin S \\ x!^t.(\Gamma\backslash_S) & \text{otherwise} \end{cases}$$
$$(\gamma_1 + \cdots \gamma_n)\backslash_S = (\gamma_1\backslash_S) + \cdots + (\gamma_n\backslash_S)$$
$$(\gamma_1 \mid \gamma_n)\backslash_S = (\gamma_1\backslash_S) \mid (\gamma_n\backslash_S)$$
$$(\gamma_1 \& \gamma_n)\backslash_S = (\gamma_1\backslash_S)\&(\gamma_n\backslash_S)$$
$$(\mu\alpha.\Gamma)\backslash_S = \mu\alpha.(\Gamma\backslash_S)$$
$$((\nu\overline{x})\Gamma)\backslash_S = (\nu\overline{x})(\Gamma\backslash_{S-\overline{x}})$$

Note that the type elimination operator leaves ν-bound names intact. For any set of channels S, let $\mathcal{G}(S)$ be the most general environment on channels S defined by:

$$\mathcal{G}(S) = \mu\alpha.(\sum_{x \in S}(x! + x?)).\alpha$$

The *anonymization operator* $\Gamma \uparrow_S$ is defined as: [2]

$$\Gamma \uparrow_S = (\nu S).(\Gamma\backslash_S \mid \mathcal{G}(S))$$

The rule [T-NEW] uses the predicate $WF(\Gamma)$ which is defined to hold if and only if for all traces $\omega = \omega_0\omega_1 \ldots \omega_n \in \text{Tr}(\nu V.\Gamma)$, for all $0 \le i \le n$, if $\omega_i = \tau^{t_1, t_2}$ then $\mathcal{T}(t_1) \ge \mathcal{T}(t_2)$.

The rule [T-NEW] is parameterized on the formula $\Box\psi$. The formula expresses a safety property on the channels $\overline{x}$. For example, it could express the invariant about deadlock freedom on channels in $\overline{x}$. Discharging this assumption will require CCS-model checking of the process type $(\eta\overline{x})\Gamma \uparrow_{\nu-\overline{x}}$.

We now state a subject reduction theorem, similar to the one in [11]. A proof of the theorem can be found in the technical report [20].

Theorem 3 (Subject Reduction). *If $\Gamma \triangleright P$ and $P \xrightarrow{\ell} P'$ with $WF(\Gamma)$, then there exists Γ' such that $\Gamma \xrightarrow{\ell} \Gamma'$ and $\Gamma' \triangleright P'$.*

Type checking in our type system requires a model checking step to discharge the assumption

$$(\eta\overline{x})\Gamma \uparrow_{\nu-\overline{x}} \models \Box\psi \tag{9}$$

in the rule [T-NEW]. Since our types are CCS processes, Theorem 1 applies. We can therefore alleviate the state space explosion in the model checker using user

---

[2] This definition is equivalent to the definition provided by Igarashi and Kobayashi. Our definition allows refining $\mathcal{G}(S)$ using flow computation, in order to improve precision.

specified types. More precisely, Theorem 1 shows that the following inference rule is sound for discharging the assumption (9) when Γ is a composition $\Gamma = \Gamma_1 \mid \Gamma_2$:

$$(\eta\overline{x})(\Gamma_1' \mid \Gamma_2') \models \Box\psi$$

$$(\eta\overline{x})(\Gamma_1 \mid \Gamma_2') \subseteq_{\Gamma_1} \Gamma_1'$$

$$\frac{(\eta\overline{x})(\Gamma_1' \mid \Gamma_2) \subseteq_{\Gamma_2} \Gamma_2'}{(\eta\overline{x})(\Gamma_1 \mid \Gamma_2) \models \Box\psi} \quad [\text{AG}]$$

provided that every channel x in $\overline{x}$ is either non-blocking for Γ_1 in $(\eta\overline{x})(\Gamma_1 \mid \Gamma_2')$ or non-blocking for Γ_2 in $(\eta\overline{x})(\Gamma_1' \mid \Gamma_2)$.

The behavioral types Γ_1' and Γ_2' are user-specified types, analogous to user-specified type signatures in a type system such as ML. In order to apply the [AG] rule, a model checker is needed to discharge the assumptions of the rule and its side-condition. However, the types Γ_1' and Γ_2' are typically more abstract than Γ_1 and Γ_2 and consequently, the state spaces of Γ_1' and Γ_2' could be much smaller than the state spaces of Γ_1 and Γ_2. Thus, using the [AG] rule helps us avoid exploring the state-space of $\Gamma_1 \mid \Gamma_2$, thereby alleviating state explosion. Indeed, if the program subjected to type checking is well modularized, this may save an exponential amount of work.

5   Related Work

Several behavioral type systems have been proposed recently in which types are process-like structures, including [18, 22, 19, 21, 11]. Also, other analyses have been proposed to check behavioral properties of concurrent programs, including [8, 9, 7].

Our work was foremostly inspired by the generic type system of Igarashi and Kobayashi [11]. While Igarashi and Kobayashi use a ν-free fragment of CCS for their process types, our type system uses the entire CCS. In particular, the presence of hiding in the form of name restriction in the process types improves precision, and opens up several opportunities for modular type checking by exploiting hiding. We use an assume-guarantee principle to discharge the safety check at name restriction (rule [T-NEW]) in a modular way. Using this technique, we can exploit abstract behavioral specifications. The use of this principle in the context of behavioral type systems appears to be new.

Model checking CCS processes is undecidable in general. However, decidable fragments of CCS have been identified by either disallowing parallel composition under recursion or by disallowing name restriction [4]. Tools have been built to perform bisimulation checking, refinement and model checking of such decidable fragments of CCS [5].

Assume-guarantee rules that allow apparently circular assumptions about operating contexts can be traced back to [17, 1, 2]. Recent work has used such techniques to model check large hardware circuits [3, 15, 6, 10]. However, all these rules require a nonblocking assumption on the process calculus, and are not directly applicable for model checking CCS. Our assume-guarantee rule for CCS requires progress as a side condition that needs to be checked using the model checker, and, to the best of our knowledge, our soundness result for assume-guarantee reasoning in CCS is new.

6   Conclusion

Checking behavioral properties of concurrent, message-passing programs is an important and difficult problem in todays distributed programming environment. The major obstacle for doing this in practice is the state-explosion problem inherent in model checking. Previous work in model checking strongly suggests that solving this problem requires abstraction and modular methods, so that one can check a large system by checking parts of the system and combine the results.

In sequential languages such as ML, module systems have proven to be very successful for providing both abstraction and modularity. However, the sequential notion of a module system cannot be directly applied to checking behavioral types of concurrent programs, because it is much harder to define what a module boundary means in concurrent contexts. In particular, few interesting properties of concurrent programs are satisfied independent of their intended context of use. Hence, it appears that new principles of modularity are needed for behavioral type systems.

In this paper, we have proposed that assume-guarantee reasoning is a key principle for modular behavioral type checking. Using the assume-guarantee principle, the behavior of a module is precisely guaranteed only under assumptions about its concurrent context. If we want to combine two modules, they can be checked under apparently circular assumptions on each others behavioral "signatures" (circularity is resolved by an induction over time). If programs are well modularized, this principle can lead to an exponential speed up of type checking. Furthermore, this principle suggests ways in which users can provide abstract behavioral specifications at module boundaries.

CCS processes have been proposed as behavioral types for π calculus programs. In order to enable assume-guarantee reasoning for a general class of behavioral type systems, we have proven the assume-guarantee principle sound for CCS with respect to trace containment. To the best of our knowledge, this result is new for CCS. Prior assume-guarantee results require non-blocking semantics on the process calculus and hence cannot be directly applied to CCS. We have shown how this result can be integrated into a particular type system for the π calculus, thereby enabling modular behavioral type checking for message-passing programs. Hiding in the form of name restriction permits writing modular programs in the π calculus. Our type system exploits hiding to decompose the type checking problem.

Much work remains to be done to apply our results to a realistic programming language. In addition to handling the variety of constructs in a realistic language, we need to provide a natural way for the programmer to write behavioral specifications. A realistic system will require a combination of automation (type inference and model checking) and user-annotations (behavioral specifications), and it must allow important programming idioms to type.

Acknowledgements

We thank Greg Meredith for several interesting discussions on behavioral type systems, and on the π-calculus. We also would like to thank Andreas Podelski for comments on this paper.

References

1. M. Abadi and L. Lamport. Composing specifications. *ACM Transactions on Programming Languages and Systems*, 15(1):73–132, 1993.
2. M. Abadi and L. Lamport. Conjoining specifications. *ACM Transactions on Programming Languages and Systems*, 17(3):507–534, 1995.
3. R. Alur and T. A. Henzinger. Reactive modules. In *LICS'96: Logic in Computer Science*, pages 207–218. IEEE Computer Society Press, 1996.
4. S. Christensen, Y. Hirshfeld, and F. Moller. Decidable subsets of CCS. *The Computer Journal*, 37(4):233–242, 1994.
5. R. J. Cleaveland, J. Parrow, and B. Steffen. The Concurrency Workbench: a semantics-based tool for the verification of finite-state systems. *ACM Transactions on Programming Languages and Systems*, 15(1):36–72, 1993.
6. A. Eiriksson. The formal design of 1M-gate ASICs. In *FMCAD'98: Formal Methods in Computer-Aided Design*, LNCS 1522, pages 49–63. Springer-Verlag, 1998.
7. J. Feret. Confidentiality analysis of mobile systems. In *SAS'00: Static Analysis Symposium*, LNCS 1824, pages 135–154. Springer-Verlag, 2000.
8. C. Flanagan and M. Abadi. Types for safe locking. In *ESOP'99: European Symposium on Programming*, LNCS 1576, pages 91–108. Springer-Verlag, 1999.
9. C. Flanagan and S. N. Freund. Type-based race detection for Java. In *PLDI 00: Programming Language Design and Implementation*, pages 219–232. ACM, 2000.
10. T. A. Henzinger, X. Liu, S. Qadeer, and S. K. Rajamani. Formal specification and verification of a dataflow processor array. In *ICCAD'99:Computer-Aided Design*, pages 494–499. IEEE Computer Society Press, 1999.
11. A. Igarashi and N. Kobayashi. A generic type system for the Pi-calculus. In *POPL'01: Principles of Programming Languages*, pages 128–141. ACM, 2001.
12. R. M. Karp and R. E. Miller. Parallel program schemata. *Journal of Computer and System Sciences*, 3:147–195, 1969.
13. J. R. Larus and M. Parkes. Using cohort scheduling to enhance server performance. Technical Report MSR-TR-2001-39, Microsoft Research, 2001.
14. L. McDowell. Tappan: The asynchronous programming language specification and analysis system. Summer-Intern Project Report, Microsoft Research, 2000.
15. K. L. McMillan. A compositional rule for hardware design refinement. In *CAV'97: Computer-Aided Verification*, LNCS 1254, pages 24–35. Springer-Verlag, 1997.
16. R. Milner. *Communicating and Mobile Systems: the π-Calculus*. Cambridge University Press, 1999.
17. J. Misra and K. M. Chandy. Proofs of networks of processes. *IEEE Transactions on Software Engineering*, SE-7(4):417–426, 1981.

18. H. R. Nielson and F. Nielson. Higher-order concurrent programs with finite communication topology. In *POPL'94: Principles of Programming Languages*, pages 84–97. ACM, 1994.
19. F. Puntigam and C. Peter. Changeable interfaces and promised messages for concurrent components. In *SAC'99: Symposium on Applied Computing*, pages 141–145. ACM, 1999.
20. S. K. Rajamani and J. Rehof. A behavioral module system for the Pi-calculus. Technical report, Microsoft Research, 2001.
21. A. Ravara and V. Vasconcelos. Typing non-uniform concurrent objects. In *CONCUR'00: Concurrency Theory*, LNCS 1877, pages 474–488. Springer-Verlag, 2000.
22. N. Yoshida. Graph types for monadic mobile processes. In *FSTTCS: Software Technology and Theoretical Computer Science*, LNCS 1180, pages 371–387. Springer-Verlag, 1996.

An Abstract Interpretation Framework for Analysing Mobile Ambients

Francesca Levi and Sergio Maffeis

Dipartimento di Informatica, Università di Pisa
Corso Italia 40, I-56100 Pisa, Italy
{levifran,maffeis}@di.unipi.it

Abstract. We introduce an abstract interpretation framework for Mobile Ambients, based on a new fixed-point semantics. Then, we derive within this setting two analyses computing a safe approximation of a property about the run-time topological structure of processes which is relevant to security.

1 Introduction

Mobile Ambients (MA) [5] has recently emerged as a core programming language for the Web, and at the same time as a model for reasoning about properties of mobile processes. MA is based on the notion of *ambient*. An ambient is a bounded place, where multi-threaded computation takes place; roughly speaking, it generalizes both the idea of agent and the idea of location. Each ambient has a *name*, a collection of *local processes* and a collection of *subambients*. Ambients are organized in a tree, which can be dynamically modified, according to three basic capabilities: $\text{in} \, n$ allows an ambient to enter into an ambient n ($m[\text{in} \, n. \, P_1 \mid P_2] \mid n[Q] \mapsto n[m[P_1 \mid P_2] \mid Q]$); $\text{out} \, n$ allows an ambient to exit from an ambient n ($n[m[\text{out} \, n. \, P_1 \mid P_2] \mid Q] \mapsto m[P_1 \mid P_2] \mid n[Q]$); $\text{open} \, n$ allows to destroy the boundary of an ambient n ($\text{open} \, n. \, P \mid n[Q] \mapsto P \mid Q$).

Several static techniques, such as Type Systems [10,3,2,4,8,1] and Control Flow Analysis (CFA) [12–14,9], have been devised to study and establish various security properties of MA, based on notions of classification and information flow. Although these approaches are strictly related and compute safe approximations of similar properties concerning the run-time topological structure of processes, their formulation as "ad hoc" syntax-directed systems makes it difficult to formally compare them.

We follow here the approach to program analysis of *abstract interpretation* [7,6]. The main idea of abstract interpretation is that program analyses effectively compute an approximation of the program semantics so that the specification of program analyses should be formally derivable from the specification of the semantics. The typical approach suggested by abstract interpretation consists of: replacing the concrete domain of computation with an abstract domain modelling the property we are interested in; establishing a relation between the concrete and the abstract domain which formalizes safeness and precision of approximations; deriving, in a systematic way, an approximate safe semantics over

P. Cousot (Ed.): SAS 2001, LNCS 2126, pp. 395–411, 2001.
© Springer-Verlag Berlin Heidelberg 2001

the abstract domain. We refer the reader to Appendix A for more details on the abstract interpretation theory. One of the most important and critical steps for applying abstract interpretation consists in the choice of the concrete semantics one should start from. The standard reduction semantics of MA [5] is not adequate to abstraction, because it heavily relies on the syntax and uses structural rules and structural congruence to bring the participants of a potential reaction into contiguous positions. In order to overcome the above problems, we propose a new semantics for MA (equivalent to the standard reduction semantics) based on the simple observation that an MA process is essentially a tree of ambients, each one containing a set of active processes controlling its movements. Then we obtain, by stepwise approximation of the semantics, two analyses computing a safe approximation of the following (run-time) information: for any ambient which ambients and capabilities may be contained inside. This information has been fruitfully used to establish security properties, such as secrecy [9], and to validate a firewall protocol [12].

Because of space limitations we omit the presentation of the standard reduction semantics of MA [5] and the comparison with our normal semantics which can be found in the extended version of the paper [11]). The normal semantics is presented in Section 3, and the two derived abstractions in Sections 4 and 5.

2   Mobile Ambients

We enhance the standard syntax for the *Mobile Ambients* calculus without communication, adding labels to capabilities, restrictions and ambients, and partitioning the set of names.

Let $\mathcal{L}$ be a set of labels (ranged over by $\ell, \ell', \ldots$) and let $\mathcal{L}_I = \{\ell_i \mid \ell \in \mathcal{L}, i \in I\}$ be the corresponding set of indexed labels (ranged over by $\lambda, \mu, \gamma, \ldots$). Let $\mathcal{N}$ (ranged over by $n, m, h, k, \ldots$) and let $\widehat{\mathcal{N}}$ (ranged over by $\widehat{n}, \widehat{m}, \widehat{h}, \widehat{k}, \ldots$) be sets of *names*, such that $\mathcal{N} \cap \widehat{\mathcal{N}} = \emptyset$. Moreover, let $\widehat{\mathcal{N}}_I = \{\widehat{n}_i \mid \widehat{n} \in \widehat{\mathcal{N}}, i \in I\}$ be the set of indexed names derived from $\widehat{\mathcal{N}}$. To have a more compact notation we may use $n, m, h, k, \ldots$ also for generic elements of $\widehat{\mathcal{N}}_I$, when the meaning is clear from the context.

Definition 2.1 (Processes). *Processes over indexed labels $\mathcal{L}_I$ and names $\mathcal{N} \cup \widehat{\mathcal{N}}_I$ are built according to the following syntax:*

$M,N ::=$	*(capabilities)*	$P,Q ::=$	*(processes)*
$\mathsf{in}\, n$	*enter n*	0	*inactivity*
$\mathsf{out}\, n$	*exit n*	$(\nu n_\lambda)\, P$	*restriction*
$\mathsf{open}\, n$	*open n*	$P \mid Q$	*parallel composition*
		$!P$	*replication*
		$n_\lambda[P]$	*ambient*
		$M_\lambda . P$	*prefix*

Standard syntactical conventions are used: trailing zeros are omitted, and parallel composition has the least syntactic precedence. We refer to the usual notions of names, free names, and bound names of a process P as $n(P)$, $fn(P)$, $bn(P)$.

We present some basic concepts, which are necessary to define the semantics and the abstractions. A *substitution* of names and indexed names is a function $\eta : \mathcal{N} \cup \widehat{\mathcal{N}}_I \to \mathcal{N} \cup \widehat{\mathcal{N}}_I$. Standard notation $P[m/n]$ and $P\eta$ is used for the application of a substitution to a process. As far as it concerns indexed labels, we denote by $\Lambda(P)$ the set of labels occurring in P. A *renaming* of indexed labels is a function $\rho : \mathcal{L}_I \to \mathcal{L}_I$. Standard notation $P[\lambda/\mu]$ and $P\rho$ is used for the application of a renaming to a process.

Indexed names $\widehat{\mathcal{N}}_I$ are used to replace bound names with fresh names. To that purpose we assume two injective functions $H_\mathcal{L} : \mathcal{L} \to \widehat{\mathcal{N}}$ and $H_{\mathcal{L}_I} : \mathcal{L}_I \to \widehat{\mathcal{N}}_I$ such that $H_{\mathcal{L}_I}(\ell_i) = \hat{n}_i$ if $H_\mathcal{L}(\ell) = \hat{n}$. We also adopt a notion of equivalence over processes. We define the renaming and substitution of indexes, induced by an injective function $\iota : I \to I$, as $\rho_\iota : \mathcal{L}_I \to \mathcal{L}_I$ and $\eta_\iota : \widehat{\mathcal{N}}_I \to \widehat{\mathcal{N}}_I$, such that $\rho_\iota(\ell_i) = \ell_{\iota(i)}$ and $\eta_\iota(\hat{n}_i) = \hat{n}_{\iota(i)}$. We say that P and Q are *equivalent up to renaming and substitution of indexes* $(P \sim Q)$ if $P\rho_\iota\eta_\iota = Q$, for a renaming ρ_ι and a substitution η_ι induced by some ι.

Moreover, we say that a process P is *active* if $P = M_\lambda. Q$ or $P = !Q$. In the following we use $\mathcal{P}$ and $\mathcal{AP}$ respectively for the set of processes and for the subset of active processes. Furthermore, we use $\mathcal{A}$ (ranged over by $a,b,c,\ldots$) for the set of labelled names n_λ, such that $n \in \mathcal{N} \cup \widehat{\mathcal{N}}_I$ and $\lambda \in \mathcal{L}_I$, augmented with a distinct symbol @.

Remark 2.2. It is worth mentioning that the idea of annotating processes is typical of Flow Logic [15], where labels are introduced to keep distinct multiple occurrences of the same object and to handle α-conversion. In our approach indexed labels and names are similarly used both in the normal semantics and in the abstract interpretation. In particular, indexes are meaningless as far as it concerns the normal semantics and the second abstraction. Instead, they are necessary to define the first abstraction (see Example 4.9 and Example 4.10 of Section 4).

3 The Normal Semantics

The normal semantics is based on the intuitive interpretation of a process as a tree of ambients, each one containing a set of active processes. We use a set, called a *topology*, to represent the tree of ambients, and a set, called a *configuration*, to represent the active processes contained in each ambient.

For instance a process $a[\text{in } k_\mu. \text{in } m_\gamma \mid \text{out } m_\nu. d[0] \mid b[0]] \mid c[!\text{in } m_\lambda]$ (where $a, b, c, d \in \mathcal{A}$ are labelled ambients) is represented by

$$(\{\ _a^@, \ _c^@, \ _b^a\}, \{\ ^a\text{in } k_\mu. \text{in } m_\gamma, \ ^a\text{out } m_\nu. d[0], \ ^c!\text{in } m_\lambda\}).$$

The topology contains $_b^a$ because b is a son of a, and contains $_a^@$ and $_c^@$ because a and c are sons the outermost ambient @. The configuration contains

$^c!\mathrm{in}\, m_\lambda$ because the active process $!\mathrm{in}\, m_\lambda$ is executable inside c. Moreover, it contains $^a\mathrm{in}\, k_\mu.\,\mathrm{in}\, m_\gamma$ and $^a\mathrm{out}\, m_\nu.\, d[0]$ because both the active processes $\mathrm{in}\, k_\mu.\,\mathrm{in}\, m_\gamma$ and $\mathrm{out}\, m_\nu.\, d[0]$ are executable inside a.

In this representation restriction is handled in a particular way. For instance a process $(\nu n_\lambda)\,(n_\gamma[\mathrm{in}\, m_\mu])$ is represented by $(\{\, _{(\hat{n}_i)_\gamma}{}^@\},\{\, ^{(\hat{n}_i)_\gamma}\mathrm{in}\, m_\mu\})$, where $\hat{n}_i \in \widehat{\mathcal{N}}_I$ is the fresh name provided by the indexed label attached to restriction, namely $H_{\mathcal{L}_I}(\lambda) = \hat{n}_i$.

Notice that, since in this representation the constructs of restriction, parallel composition and ambient are implicitly represented, the standard structural rules and structural congruence (including α-conversion) of the reduction semantics are no longer necessary.

States. Formally, a state is a pair which consists of a topology and a configuration: the topology is a standard representation of a tree via a set of pairs (son, father) and the configuration is simply a set of pairs associating each active process to its enclosing ambient.

Definition 3.1 (States). *A state S is a pair (T, C) where*

1. $T \in \wp(\mathcal{A} \times \mathcal{A})$ *such that, if $(a,b),(a,c) \in T$ then $b = c$ (topology);*
2. $C \in \wp(\mathcal{A} \times \mathcal{AP})$ *(configuration).*

We extend to states in the obvious way the notions of labels, renaming, substitution, equivalence up to renaming and substitution of indexes $\sim$. Moreover, we use $\mathcal{S}$ for the set of states.

Normalization Function. In order to derive the initial state from a process and to handle the processes, which became executable after a step, we introduce a normalization function $\delta : (\mathcal{A} \times \mathcal{P}) \to \mathcal{S}$. Intuitively, $\delta(a, P)$ gives the state representing process P assuming that P is contained in ambient a. Thus, the initial state corresponding to a process P is $\delta(@, P)$.

DRes	$\delta\,^a(\nu n_\lambda)\, P =$	$\delta\ ^a P[H_{\mathcal{L}_I}(\lambda)/n]$
DAmb	$\delta\,^a b[P]$ $=$	$\delta\,^b P\ \cup\ (\{\, _b^a\}, \emptyset)$
DZero	$\delta\,^a 0$ $=$	$(\emptyset,\ \emptyset)$
DPar	$\delta\,^a P \mid Q$ $=$	$\delta\,^a P\ \cup\ \delta\,^a Q$
DBang	$\delta\,^a !P$ $=$	$(\emptyset, \{^a!P\})$
DPref	$\delta\,^a N_\lambda.\, P$ $=$	$(\emptyset, \{^a N_\lambda.P\})$

Table 1. The Normalization Function δ

The normalization function δ is shown in Tab. 1 (where $\delta\ ^a P$ stands for $\delta(a, P)$). Rule **DRes** eliminates the restriction by replacing the bound name n

with the fresh name $H_{\mathcal{L}_I}(\lambda)$ provided by the indexed label λ. Rule **DAmb** adds ambient b to the topology as son of the enclosing ambient a and normalises the process contained in b. Rule **DPar** gathers the processes and the topologies built in each of its two branches. The last rules simply add the active process to the configuration.

Transitions. Transitions are obtained by the rules of Tab. 2 which realize the unfolding of recursion, the movement in and out of ambients, and the opening of ambients. The rules use the normalization function to handle the continuations. Moreover, they use a function $new : \mathcal{P} \to \mathcal{P}$, such that $new(P) = Q$, where $Q = P\rho_\iota$ for some fresh renaming of indexes ρ_ι. In the following, $T[\ _b{}^a/\ _d{}^c]$ denotes the replacement in the topology of every pair $_d{}^c$ with $_b{}^a$. Analogously for configurations.

Bang $\dfrac{^a!P \in C}{(T,C) \mapsto \delta\ ^a new(P)\ \cup\ (T,C)}$

In $\dfrac{c =\ ^a\mathrm{in}\, m_\gamma.\, P \in C \qquad _a{}^b,\ _{m_\mu}{}^b \in T \qquad a \neq m_\mu}{(T,C) \mapsto \delta\ ^a P\ \cup\ ((T \setminus \{\ _a{}^b\}) \cup \{\ _{a^{m_\mu}}{}^b\}, C \setminus \{c\})}$

Out $\dfrac{c =\ ^a\mathrm{out}\, m_\gamma.\, P \in C \qquad _a{}^{m_\mu},\ _{m_\mu}{}^b \in T \qquad a \neq m_\mu}{(T,C) \mapsto \delta\ ^a P\ \cup\ ((T \setminus \{\ _a{}^{m_\mu}\}) \cup \{\ _a{}^b\}, C \setminus \{c\})}$

Open $\dfrac{c =\ ^a\mathrm{open}\, m_\gamma.\, P \in C \qquad _{m_\mu}{}^a \in T \qquad a \neq m_\mu}{(T,C) \mapsto \delta\ ^a P\ \cup\ ((T \setminus \{\ _{m_\mu}{}^a\})[\ _b{}^a/\ _b{}^{m_\mu}], (C \setminus \{c\})[^a Q_\beta/{}^{m_\mu}Q_\beta])}$

Table 2. Transitions $\mapsto$

Rule **Bang** creates a fresh copy (equivalent up to renaming of indexes) of the process under replication. The last three rules correspond to the usual reduction rules of movements and opening (shown in the Introduction). Rule **In** verifies that the capability in m is enabled by checking if there exists a parallel ambient named m. Then, it modifies both the topology and the configuration accordingly: (i) it updates the father of a, (ii) it removes the executed capability and adds its (normalized) continuation. **Out** acts in an analogous way. Rule **Open** also extends the state by adding the set of processes and subambients acquired by a from the destroyed ambient m.

The Collecting Semantics. We can now define the core of the abstract interpretation framework, the *collecting semantics*. In order to have a correct semantics we have to consider only processes and states which satisfy some restrictions on indexed names and labels ensuring that multiple occurrences of the same process or of ambients with the same name are keep distinct.

Definition 3.2 (Well-Labelled). *A process P is* well-labelled *if: (i) for each $\hat{n}_i \in n(P)$, such that $\hat{n}_i = H_{\mathcal{L}_I}(\ell_i)$, $\ell_i \notin \Lambda(P)$; (ii) the (indexed) labels used in capabilities, ambients and restrictions are distinct one from each other. A state $S = (T, C)$ is* well-labelled *if condition (i) holds (for P replaced by S) and for each $^a P \in C$, P is well-labelled.*

In the following we assume that both $\mathcal{P}$ and $\mathcal{S}$ range only over well-labelled processes and states.

The domain is the power-set of well-labelled states up to renaming and substitution of indexes. We use $[S]$ for equivalences classes of states with respect to $\sim$. We assume that $\subseteq$ and $\cup$ over states are defined component-wise.

Definition 3.3. *The* concrete domain *is $\langle \wp(\mathcal{S}_{/\sim}), \subseteq \rangle$.*

The concrete semantics is defined in a standard way as the least fixed-point of a continuous operator.

Definition 3.4 (Collecting Semantics). *Let $X \in \wp(\mathcal{S}_{/\sim})$ and let $P \in \mathcal{P}$ a process. We define $\mathfrak{S}_{Coll}[\![P]\!] = \mathit{lfp}\ \Psi([\delta\ ^@P])$ where $\Psi(X) = \bigcup_{[S] \in X} \{[S'] \mid S \to S'\}$.*

Examples. The following example better explain the reason to consider well-labelled processes only.

Example 3.5. Labels have to be distinct to guarantee that the translation function δ does not lose different instances of the same process or of ambients with the same name. For instance, for $P = \mathrm{in}\, m_\lambda \mid \mathrm{in}\, m_\lambda$ we would have $\delta(\ ^@P) = (\emptyset,\ ^@\mathrm{in}\, m_\lambda)$. The remaining condition concerning the free names of $\widehat{\mathcal{N}}_I$ is necessary for a correct treatment of restrictions. For instance, for $Q = (\nu n_\lambda)\, (n_\gamma[0]) \mid (\hat{n}_i)_\mu[0]$, where $H_{\mathcal{L}_I}(\lambda) = \hat{n}_i$, we would have $\delta(\ ^@Q) = (\{\ _{(\hat{n}_i)_\mu}{}^@,\ _{(\hat{n}_i)_\gamma}{}^@ \}, \emptyset)$. Even if the two ambients are keep distinct by labels μ and γ, this is not correct because they share the same name $\hat{n}_i$.

The following example stresses an important aspect concerning indexed labels and names: replication produces processes equivalent up to renaming and substitution of indexes.

Example 3.6. Consider the following process $Q = n_{\ell_1}[\mathrm{in}\, n_{\ell'_1}]$. We have $\mathfrak{S}_{Coll}[\![!Q]\!] = X$, such that X is the minimal set of states (up to renaming and substitution of indexes) where

1. $(\emptyset,\ ^@!Q) \in X$, and for each $(T, C) \in X$, $^@!Q \in C$;
2. for each $k \in N$ there exists $S = (T, C) \in X$ such that $\Lambda(S) \subseteq \bigcup_{j \in \{1, k\}} \{\ell_j, \ell'_j\}$ and $fn(S) = \{n\}$, and for each $j \in \{1, k\}$ either $_{n_{\ell_j}}{}^@ \in T$ and $^{n_{\ell_j}}\mathrm{in}\, n_{\ell'_j} \in C$ or $_{n_{\ell_j}}{}^{n_{\ell_h}} \in T$, with $h \neq j$, and $^{n_{\ell_j}}\mathrm{in}\, n_{\ell'_j} \notin C$.

The idea is that every unfolding of recursion produces a new copy of ambient n labelled by ℓ_j for a fresh index j. Any ambient n_{ℓ_j} may enter inside any other n_{ℓ_h} provided that $h \neq j$.

4   A First Abstraction

We devise a first abstraction aimed at capturing the following property: for each ambient, which ambients and capabilities can be contained inside. We obtain a safe and computable approximation of the property above by combining two basic abstractions.

We begin by considering abstract states where the topology is a hierarchy of ambients, possibly not a tree, and where the configuration contains also the father of the enclosing ambient of any active process. For example, a state $S = (\{ {}_a^@, {}_b^@ \}, {}^a \text{in} k_\mu. \text{in} m_\gamma)$ is abstracted to $S^\diamond = (\{ {}_a^@, {}_b^@ \}, {}^a \text{in} k_\mu. \text{in} m_\gamma)$. The abstract state is equivalent to the concrete one with a minor modification: every active process is annotated by a *partial topology*, that is by the father of the enclosing ambient. For instance, we have ${}^a \text{in} k_\mu. \text{in} m_\gamma$, because $\text{in} k_\mu. \text{in} m_\gamma$ is an active process of ambient a, whenever a is contained in @.

To understand the relevance of the partial topology it is necessary to look at the abstraction of a set of states. Consider a state $S' = (\{ {}_a^b, {}_b^@ \}, {}^a \text{in} m_\gamma)$ which is abstracted to $S'^\diamond = (\{ {}_a^b, {}_b^@ \}, {}^a \text{in} m_\gamma)$. The set $\{S, S'\}$ is abstracted to the unique abstract state which is the union:

$$(\{ {}_a^b, {}_b^@, {}_a^@ \}, \{ {}^a \text{in} m_\gamma, \quad {}^a \text{in} k_\mu. \text{in} m_\gamma \}).$$

Obviously the obtained abstract topology is not a tree. For instance we have both ${}_a^b$ and ${}_a^@$. In this case the partial topology allows us to distinguish between the possibly multiple fathers of an ambient. For instance, it says that process $\text{in} k_\mu. \text{in} m_\gamma$ is executable when a is inside @, while $\text{in} m_\gamma$ is executable when a is inside b.

This abstraction is of course not enough to achieve a computable semantics, in that we may have infinite processes equivalent up to renaming of indexes (see Example 3.6). Hence, we abstract also indexes by keeping only the following information concerning labels: whether there is *at most* one occurrence or *any number* of occurrences.

For example, consider the states

$$S = ({}_{n_\lambda}^@, {}^{n_\lambda} \text{open} m_\mu) \text{ and } S' = ({}_{n_\lambda}^@, \{ {}^{n_\lambda} \text{open} m_\mu, {}^{n_\lambda} \text{open} m_\gamma \})$$

where $\lambda = \ell_1'$, $\mu = \ell_1$ and $\gamma = \ell_2$. The abstraction gives the following $S^\diamond$ and $S'^\diamond$

$$S^\diamond = ({}_{n_\lambda}^@, {}^{n_\lambda} \text{open} m_{\ell_1}) \text{ and } S'^\diamond = ({}_{n_\lambda}^@, {}^{n_\lambda} \text{open} m_{\ell_\omega}).$$

Capability $\text{open} m$ in state S is abstracted to $\text{open} m_{\ell_1}$, and the two copies of $\text{open} m$ in state S' are abstracted $\text{open} m_{\ell_\omega}$. The label ℓ_ω (with multiplicity ω) represents any number of occurrences of the corresponding object equivalent up to renaming of indexes, while a label ℓ_1 (with multiplicity one) represents at most one occurrence of the corresponding object.

Abstract Domain. Abstract labels are $\mathcal{L}^\diamond = \{ \ell_1, \ell_\omega \mid \ell \in \mathcal{L} \}$ (ranged over by $\lambda^\diamond, \mu^\diamond, \gamma^\diamond, \ldots$). Abstract names are $\mathcal{N} \cup \widehat{\mathcal{N}}$ (ranged over by $n^\diamond, m^\diamond, k^\diamond, h^\diamond, \ldots$).

Analogously, we use $\mathcal{A}^\circ$ (ranged over by $a^\circ, b^\circ, c^\circ, \ldots$) for the set of abstract labelled names $n^\circ{}_{\lambda^\circ}$, augmented with the distinct symbol @. The relation between names and labels has to be modified accordingly. We define $H_{\mathcal{L}^\circ} : \mathcal{L}^\circ \to \widehat{\mathcal{N}}$ such that $H_{\mathcal{L}^\circ}(\ell_1) = H_{\mathcal{L}^\circ}(\ell_\omega) = H_{\mathcal{L}}(\ell)$.

Abstract processes are built according to the syntax of Def. 2.1 over names $\mathcal{N} \cup \widehat{\mathcal{N}}$ and labels $\mathcal{L}^\circ$. In the following we use $\mathcal{P}^\circ$ and $\mathcal{AP}^\circ$ for the set of abstract processes and active abstract processes.

Definition 4.1 (Abstract States). *An* abstract state S° *is a pair* (T°, C°) *where*

1. $T^\circ \in \wp(\mathcal{A}^\circ \times \mathcal{A}^\circ)$ *(abstract topology);*
2. $C^\circ \in \wp((\mathcal{A}^\circ \times \mathcal{A}^\circ) \times \mathcal{AP}^\circ)$ *(abstract configuration).*

All the previously defined notions on states and processes are adapted to abstract states and processes in the expected way. Only the notion of well-labelling requires some care.

Definition 4.2 (Well-Labelled). *An abstract process P° is well-labelled if :*
(i) for each $\hat{n} \in n(P^\circ)$, such that $\hat{n} = H_{\mathcal{L}^\circ}(\lambda^\circ)$, $\lambda^\circ \notin \Lambda(P^\circ)$; (ii) $\ell_1 \in \Lambda(P^\circ)$ implies $\ell_\omega \notin \Lambda(P^\circ)$ (and vice-versa); (iii) there is at most one occurrence of any label ℓ_1. An abstract state $S^\circ = (C^\circ, T^\circ)$ is well-labelled if conditions (i) and (ii) hold (with P° replaced by S°), and for each ${}^a_{} P^\circ \in C^\circ$, P° is well-labelled.

In the following, we consider only well-labelled abstract states and processes denoted by $\mathcal{S}^\circ$ and $\mathcal{P}^\circ$, respectively.

We consider an ordering over abstract states which reflects the intuition that ℓ_1 is more precise than ℓ_ω. Therefore, let $\subseteq^\circ$ be the minimal ordering over $\mathcal{S}^\circ$, such that $S^\circ \subseteq S'^\circ$ implies $S^\circ \subseteq^\circ S'^\circ$, and such that $S^\circ \subseteq^\circ S^\circ[\ell_\omega/\ell_1]$. As usual we use $\cup^\circ$ as the least upper bound w.r.t. $\subseteq^\circ$. Notice that for $\lambda = \ell_1$ and $\gamma = \ell_\omega$

$$({}_{n_\lambda}{}^{b^\circ}, \ {}^{b^\circ}_{n_\lambda} P^\circ) \cup^\circ ({}_{n_\gamma}{}^{b^\circ}, \ {}^{b^\circ}_{n_\gamma} P^\circ) = ({}_{n_\gamma}{}^{b^\circ}, \ {}^{b^\circ}_{n_\gamma} P^\circ).$$

Definition 4.3. *The* abstract domain *is* $\langle \mathcal{S}^\circ, \subseteq^\circ \rangle$.

To simplify the notation in the following we may omit the over-script $-^\circ$ for any syntactic category, when the meaning is clear from the context.

The Galois Connection. We present now the relation between the concrete and the abstract domain establishing a standard Galois connection (see Appendix A). A state is abstracted, as explained at the beginning of the section, by introducing the partial topology in processes, by replacing indexed labels $\mathcal{L}_I$ by labels with multiplicity $\mathcal{L}^\circ$ and by modifying names $\widehat{\mathcal{N}}_I$ accordingly. A set of states is abstracted to the abstract state containing the abstraction of each element.

Let $S \in \mathcal{S}$ be a state. We define $\rho_S^\circ : \mathcal{L}_I \to \mathcal{L}^\circ$ such that $\rho_S^\circ(\ell_i) = \ell_\omega$, if $\ell_i, \ell_j \in \Lambda(S)$ with $i \neq j$, and $\rho_S^\circ(\ell_i) = \ell_1$ otherwise. Moreover, we define $\eta_S^\circ : \widehat{\mathcal{N}}_I \to \widehat{\mathcal{N}}$ such that $\eta_S^\circ(\hat{n}_i) = \hat{n}$.

Definition 4.4. *Let* $X \in \wp(\mathcal{S}/_\sim)$, $(T, C) \in \mathcal{S}$ *and* $S^\circ \in \mathcal{S}^\circ$. *We define* $\alpha :$ $\wp(\mathcal{S}/_\sim) \to \mathcal{S}^\circ$ *and* $\gamma : \mathcal{S}^\circ \to \wp(\mathcal{S}/_\sim)$ *as follows*

1. $\alpha((T, C)) = (T, C^\circ)\rho_S^\circ\eta_S^\circ$, *where* $C^\circ = \{\ _a^b P \mid \ _a^b \in T,\ ^a P \in C\}$.
2. $\alpha(X) = \bigcup_{[S] \in X}^\circ \alpha([S])$, *where* $\alpha([S]) = \bigcup_{S' \in [S]}^\circ \alpha(S')$;
3. $\gamma(S^\circ) = \bigcup\{[S] \mid \alpha([S]) \subseteq^\circ S^\circ\}$.

Lemma 4.5 (Galois Insertion). *The pair of functions* (α, γ) *forms a Galois insertion between* $\langle \wp(\mathcal{S}/_\sim), \subseteq \rangle$ *and* $\langle \mathcal{S}^\circ, \subseteq^\circ \rangle$.

Abstract Semantics. The abstract normalization function $\delta^\circ : (\mathcal{A}^\circ \times \mathcal{A}^\circ) \times \mathcal{P}^\circ \to \mathcal{S}^\circ$, shown in Tab 3, is the obvious adaptation of δ to the abstract domain, where $\cup^\circ$ is used instead of $\cup$ to properly handle labels with multiplicity.

$$\delta^\circ \ _a^b (\nu n_\lambda) P = \delta^\circ \ _a^b P[H_{\mathcal{L}^\circ}(\lambda)/n]$$
$$\delta^\circ \ _a^b c[P] \quad = \delta^\circ \ _c^a P \cup^\circ (\{\ _c^a\}, \emptyset)$$
$$\delta^\circ \ _a^b 0 \quad = (\emptyset,\ \emptyset)$$
$$\delta^\circ \ _a^b P \mid Q \quad = \delta^\circ \ _a^b P \cup^\circ \delta^\circ \ _a^b Q$$
$$\delta^\circ \ _a^b !P \quad = (\emptyset, \{\ _a^b !P\})$$
$$\delta^\circ \ _a^b M_\lambda. P \quad = (\emptyset, \{\ _a^b M_\lambda. P\})$$

Table 3. The Normalization Function δ°

The abstract transitions are obtained by the rules of Tab. 4. The rules use a function $new_\omega : \mathcal{P}^{\circ'} \to \mathcal{P}^\circ$, such that $new_\omega(P) = P\rho$ for the renaming ρ, where $\rho(\ell_1) = \ell_\omega$ for any $\ell_1 \in \Lambda(P)$. We also use

$$C \setminus^\circ \{\ _a^b M_{\lambda^\circ}. P\} = \begin{cases} C \text{ if } \lambda^\circ = \ell_\omega \\ \\ (C \setminus\ _a^b M_{\lambda^\circ}. P) \text{ if } \lambda^\circ = \ell_1 \end{cases}$$

The rules are similar to the ones of Tab. 2. We explain the relevant differences only. The rule for the unfolding of replication creates a copy of the replicated process where every label has multiplicity ω, instead of creating a fresh copy (equivalent up to renaming of indexes). Consider the rule corresponding to the execution of a capability in m. First, it verifies that the capability is executable by looking if there exist an ambient named m, which is contained in the father b of a. Then, it extends both the topology and the configuration accordingly: (i) it adds the new father m_{μ° to a, (ii) it adds both the normalized continuation and the parallel processes to the set of processes executable when a is contained in m_{μ°. The other rules are adapted in an analogous way. Notice that in the rule for opening also the processes executable in any ambient c, when this is contained in the destroyed ambient, have to be updated.

It is important to stress that both the partial topology and the multiplicity of labels are fruitfully exploited. Consider for instance the rule corresponding to the execution of a capability $in\,m$. The father b of a, recorded in the partial topology, is used both to establish the enabling of $in\,m$ and to find out which processes are executable inside a in parallel with $in\,m.\,P$. The movement of an ambient named m inside itself is permitted only if the multiplicity of m is ω. Moreover, a capability $in\,m$ with multiplicity one can be exercised only once, and so is not executable in the new father m_{μ° of a. By contrast, a capability $in\,m$ with multiplicity ω is still executable in the new father m_{μ° of a, as the other parallel processes.

$$\frac{ {}_a^b!P \in C }{ (T,C) \mapsto^\circ \delta \circ\ {}_a^b new_\omega(P)\ \cup^\circ (T,C) }$$

$$\frac{ c =\ {}_a^b\, in\, m_{\lambda^\circ}.\, P \in C \qquad {}_a^b,\ {}_{m_{\mu^\circ}}{}^b \in T \qquad (a = m_{\ell'_1} \Rightarrow \ell'_1 \neq \mu^\circ) }{ (T,C) \mapsto^\circ \delta\circ\ {}_a^{m_{\mu^\circ}} P\ \cup^\circ (T \cup^\circ \{\ {}_a^{m_{\mu^\circ}}\},\, C \cup^\circ (C\backslash^\circ\{c\})[\ {}_a^{m_{\mu^\circ}} Q/\ {}_a^b Q]) }$$

$$\frac{ c =\ {}_a^{m_{\mu^\circ}}\, out\, m_{\lambda^\circ}.\, P \in C \qquad {}_a^{m_{\mu^\circ}} \in T \qquad (a = m_{\ell'_1} \Rightarrow \ell'_1 \neq \mu^\circ) }{ (T,C) \mapsto^\circ \underset{\{b|\ {}_{m_{\mu^\circ}}{}^b \in T\}}{\cup^\circ} \left(\delta\circ\ {}_a^b P\ \cup^\circ (T \cup^\circ \{\ {}_a^b\},\, C \cup^\circ (C\backslash^\circ\{c\})[\ {}_a^b Q/\ {}_a^{m_{\mu^\circ}} Q]) \right) }$$

$$\frac{ {}_a^b\, open\, m_{\lambda^\circ}.\, P \in C \qquad {}_{m_{\mu^\circ}}{}^a \in T \qquad (a = m_{\ell'_1} \Rightarrow \ell'_1 \neq \mu^\circ) }{ (T,C) \mapsto^\circ \delta\circ\ {}_a^b P\ \cup^\circ (T \cup^\circ T[c^a/c^{m_\mu}],\, C \cup^\circ C[\ {}_a^b Q/\ {}_{m_\mu}^a Q][\ {}_c^a Q'/\ {}_c^{m_\mu} Q']) }$$

Table 4. Abstract Transitions $\mapsto^\circ$

Definition 4.6 (The Abstract Collecting Semantics). *Let* $S^\circ \in \mathcal{S}^\circ$ *and let* $P \in \mathcal{P}$. *We define* $\mathfrak{S}_{Coll^\circ}[\![P]\!] = lfp\ \Psi^\circ(\{\alpha([\delta\ ^@P])\ \})$ *where* $\Psi^\circ(S^\circ) = \bigcup^\circ S'^\circ$ *such that* $S^\circ \mapsto^\circ S'^\circ$.

The abstract collecting semantics is a safe approximation of the concrete one and so is an upper approximation of the property we are interested in. Safeness is stated in classical abstract interpretation style (see Appendix A).

Theorem 4.7 (Safeness). *Let* $S \in \mathcal{S}$ *and* $P \in \mathcal{P}$. *We have* $\alpha(\Psi(S)) \subseteq^\circ \Psi^\circ(\alpha(S))$ *and* $\alpha(\mathfrak{S}_{Coll}[\![P]\!]) \subseteq^\circ \mathfrak{S}_{Coll^\circ}[\![P]\!]$.

Examples. We present some examples to summarize the more interesting aspects of the abstraction. The following example shows the advantages obtained by combining together multiplicity and partial topology.

Example 4.8. Consider the process $P = n_\lambda[\text{in}\, k_\epsilon. \,\text{in}\, m_\nu \mid m_\gamma[0]] \mid k_\mu[\text{open}\, n_\beta]$, where labels $\{\epsilon, \mu, \nu, \lambda, \beta, \gamma\}$ are distinct also up to renaming of indexes. We have, $\mathfrak{S}_{Coll}[\![P]\!] = \{S_0, S_1, S_2\}$ such that

$$S_0 = (\{\, n_\lambda{}^@, \; m_\gamma{}^{n_\lambda}, \; k_\mu{}^@ \}, \{\, {}^{n_\lambda}\text{in}\, k_\epsilon. \,\text{in}\, m_\nu, \; {}^{k_\mu}\text{open}\, n_\beta \})$$

$$S_1 = (\{\, n_\lambda{}^{k_\mu}, \; m_\gamma{}^{n_\lambda}, \; k_\mu{}^@ \}, \{\, {}^{n_\lambda}\text{in}\, m_\nu, \; {}^{k_\mu}\text{open}\, n_\beta \})$$

$$S_2 = (\{\, m_\gamma{}^{k_\mu}, \; k_\mu{}^@ \}, \; {}^{k_\mu}\text{in}\, m_\nu).$$

Notice that capability $\text{in}\, m$ is not exercised inside n because, m is not a sibling of n when it is executable. Moreover, k acquires by opening n only ambient m and capability $\text{in}\, m$. We have $\alpha(\{S_0, S_1, S_3\}) = (T^\diamond, C^\diamond)$, where (to improve readability we use $\{\epsilon, \mu, \nu, \lambda, \beta, \gamma\}$ for the corresponding abstract labels with multiplicity one)

$$T^\diamond = \{\, n_\lambda{}^@, \; m_\gamma{}^{n_\lambda}, \; k_\mu{}^@, \; n_\lambda{}^{k_\mu}, \; m_\gamma{}^{k_\mu} \}$$

$$C^\diamond = \{\, {}^{n_\lambda{}^@}\text{in}\, k_\epsilon. \,\text{in}\, m_\nu, \; {}^{k_\mu{}^@}\text{open}\, n_\beta, \; {}^{k_\mu{}^@}\text{in}\, m_\nu, \; {}^{n_\lambda{}^{k_\mu}}\text{in}\, m_\nu \}).$$

Let us compare the abstraction of the collecting semantics to the abstract collecting semantics. We have $\mathfrak{S}_{Coll^\diamond}[\![P]\!] = (T^\diamond \cup \{\, n_\lambda{}^{m_\gamma} \}, C^\diamond)$. The abstract semantics is safe but not exact, i.e. $\alpha(\mathfrak{S}_{Coll}[\![P]\!]) \subset^\diamond \mathfrak{S}_{Coll^\diamond}[\![P]\!]$. The labels with multiplicity and the partial topology are essential to have no loss of information in the configuration. Since $\text{in}\, k_\epsilon$ has multiplicity one, it is no longer executable after the movement of n in k. Therefore, $\text{in}\, m_\nu$ is the only process which is contained in n when n is inside k, and which is acquired by k, when opening n.

The subtle point is that, in the abstract semantics, n moves inside m. In fact, we have that $\text{in}\, m$ is executable, when n is inside k, and that k may contain ambient m. The abstract semantics cannot capture that k effectively contains ambient m only after the dissolution of n.

The following examples better explain the role of indexes in the abstraction. As we have discussed any labelling of a process P respecting the requirements of Definition 3.2 is enough to have a correct normal semantics of P. However, the choice of labels has dramatic consequences on the precision of the abstraction. Indeed, a typical schema to annotate processes is to keep all labels distinct also up to renaming of indexes so that only the copies produced by replication are identified by the abstraction.

Example 4.9. Consider the processes

$$P_1 = n_{\ell_1}[\text{in}\, k_\mu] \mid n_{\ell_2}[\text{in}\, m_\gamma] \mid m_\lambda[0]$$

$$P_2 = n_\beta[\text{in}\, k_\mu] \mid n_\epsilon[\text{in}\, m_\gamma] \mid m_\lambda[0]$$

where $\{\mu, \gamma, \lambda, \beta, \epsilon\}$ are distinct also up to renaming of indexes. We have

$$\mathfrak{S}_{Coll}[\![P_1]\!] = (\{\ n_{\ell_1}{}^@,\ n_{\ell_2}{}^@,\ m_\lambda{}^@,\ n_{\ell_2}{}^{m_\lambda}\}, \{\ ^{n_{\ell_1}} \text{in}\, k_\mu,\ ^{n_{\ell_2}} \text{in}\, m_\gamma\})$$

$$\mathfrak{S}_{Coll}[\![P_2]\!] = (\{\ n_\beta{}^@,\ n_\epsilon{}^@,\ m_\lambda{}^@,\ n_\epsilon{}^{m_\lambda}\}, \{\ ^{n_\beta} \text{in}\, k_\mu,\ ^{n_\epsilon} \text{in}\, m_\gamma\}).$$

The collecting semantics of P_1 and P_2 are equivalent up to renaming of labels. In the abstract semantics we have (for readability we use $\{\mu, \gamma, \lambda, \beta, \epsilon\}$ for the corresponding labels with multiplicity one)

$$\mathfrak{S}_{Coll^\circ}[\![P_1]\!] = (\{\ n_{\ell_\omega}{}^@,\ m_\lambda{}^@,\ n_{\ell_\omega}{}^{m_\lambda}\}, \{\ ^{n_{\ell_\omega}}{}^{\circ} \text{in}\, k_\mu,\ ^{n_{\ell_\omega}}{}^{\circ} \text{in}\, m_\gamma\})$$

$$\mathfrak{S}_{Coll^\circ}[\![P_2]\!] = (\{\ n_\beta{}^@,\ n_\epsilon{}^@,\ m_\lambda{}^@,\ n_\epsilon{}^{m_\lambda}\}, \{\ ^{n_\beta}{}^{\circ} \text{in}\, k_\mu,\ ^{n_\epsilon}{}^{\circ} \text{in}\, m_\gamma\}).$$

Due to a different choice of labels the two copies of ambient n are identified by the abstract semantics of P_1, while they are keep distinct by the abstract semantics of P_2.

Example 4.10. Consider the process $Q = n_\lambda[\text{in}\, n_\gamma]$ of Example 3.6, where $\lambda = \ell_1$ and $\gamma = \ell'_1$. We have for $\mu = \ell_\omega$ and $\epsilon = \ell'_\omega$,

$$\mathfrak{S}_{Coll^\circ}[\![Q]\!] = (\ n_\lambda{}^@,\ ^{n_\lambda}{}^{\circ} \text{in}\, n_\gamma)$$

$$\mathfrak{S}_{Coll^\circ}[\![!Q]\!] = (\{\ n_\mu{}^@,\ n_\mu{}^{n_\mu}\}, \{\ ^{n_\mu}{}^{\circ} \text{in}\, n_\epsilon,\ ^{n_\mu}{}^{n_\mu} \text{in}\, n_\epsilon,\ ^@ !Q\}).$$

The labels with multiplicity allows us to distinguish process $!Q$ from process Q. In the abstract semantics of Q the label of n is ℓ_1, which forbids the movement of n inside itself. Oppositely, in the abstract semantics of $!Q$ the unfolding of recursion produces a label ℓ_ω for n, which forces this movement. This result for $!Q$ is necessary to have a safe approximation of the concrete semantics, where the unfolding of replication produces multiple copies of n, which may interact with each other (see Example 3.6). In this example, the abstract semantics is exact, namely $\mathfrak{S}_{Coll^\circ}[\![Q]\!] = \alpha(\mathfrak{S}_{Coll}[\![Q]\!])$ and $\mathfrak{S}_{Coll^\circ}[\![!Q]\!] = \alpha(\mathfrak{S}_{Coll}[\![!Q]\!])$.

5   A Second Abstraction

On top of the previous abstraction, we define a new coarser abstraction, aimed at computing more efficiently a safe approximation of the same property. The abstraction is obtained by simply dropping multiplicity from labels and partial topologies from processes. For example, consider the states shown at the beginning of Section 4, where $\lambda = \ell'_1$, $\mu = \ell_1$ and $\gamma = \ell_2$:

$$S = (\ n_\lambda{}^@,\ ^{n_\lambda} \text{open}\, m_\mu) \text{ and } S' = (\ n_\lambda{}^@, \{\ ^{n_\lambda} \text{open}\, m_\mu,\ ^{n_\lambda} \text{open}\, m_\gamma\}).$$

In the new abstraction S° and S'° are represented by the same abstract state $(\ n_{\ell'}{}^@,\ ^{n_{\ell'}} \text{open}\, m_\ell)$, because the ability to distinguish one occurrence from multiple occurrences has been lost.

Abstract Domain. Abstract labels are $\mathcal{L}$ and abstract names are $\mathcal{N} \cup \widehat{\mathcal{N}}$. Thus, the relation between names and labels is given by function $H_{\mathcal{L}} : \mathcal{L} \to \widehat{\mathcal{N}}$ (see Section 2). We use $\mathcal{A}^\circ$ (ranged over by $a^\circ, b^\circ, c^\circ \ldots$) for the set of abstract labelled names n_ℓ, such that $n \in \mathcal{N} \cup \widehat{\mathcal{N}}$ and $\ell \in \mathcal{L}$, augmented with the distinct symbol @. Abstract processes are built according to the syntax of Def. 2.1 over names $\mathcal{N} \cup \widehat{\mathcal{N}}$ and labels $\mathcal{L}$. We use $\mathcal{P}^\circ$ and $\mathcal{AP}^\circ$ for the set of abstract and active abstract processes.

Definition 5.1 (Abstract States). *An abstract state S° is a pair (T°, C°) where*

1. *$T^\circ \in \wp(\mathcal{A}^\circ \times \mathcal{A}^\circ)$ (abstract configuration);*
2. *$C^\circ \in \wp(\mathcal{A}^\circ \times \mathcal{AP}^\circ)$ (abstract configuration).*

All the previously defined notions on states and processes are adapted to abstract states and processes in the expected way. We use $\mathcal{S}^\circ$ for the set of abstract states.

The abstract domain is given by abstract states ordered by inclusion (we assume $\subseteq$ and $\cup$ defined component-wise).

Definition 5.2. *The abstract domain is $\langle \mathcal{S}^\circ, \subseteq \rangle$.*

In the following we may omit the over-script $-^\circ$ for any syntactic category, when the meaning is clear from the context.

The Galois Connection. We present now the relation between the abstract domain of Def 4.3 and the new abstract domain establishing, as before, a Galois connection (see appendix A).

An abstract state is abstracted, as explained at the beginning of the section, by dropping the multiplicity from labels and the partial topology from processes. To this purpose, we use a renaming $\rho^\circ : \mathcal{L}^\circ \to \mathcal{L}$, such that $\rho^\circ(\ell_1) = \rho^\circ(\ell_\omega) = \ell$.

Definition 5.3. *Let $(T^\circ, C^\circ), S^\circ \in \mathcal{S}^\circ$, and $S^\circ \in \mathcal{S}^\circ$. We define $\alpha^\circ : \mathcal{S}^\circ \to \mathcal{S}^\circ$ and $\gamma^\circ : \mathcal{S}^\circ \to \mathcal{S}^\circ$ as follows*

1. *$\alpha^\circ((T^\circ, C^\circ)) = (T^\circ, \{\ ^a P \mid\ ^{b}_{a} P \in C^\circ\})\rho^\circ$;*
2. *$\gamma^\circ(S^\circ) = \bigcup^\circ \{S^\circ \mid \alpha^\circ(S^\circ) \subseteq S^\circ\}$.*

Lemma 5.4 (Galois Insertion). *The pair of functions $(\alpha^\circ, \gamma^\circ)$ forms a Galois insertion between $\langle \mathcal{S}^\circ, \subseteq^\circ \rangle$ and $\langle \mathcal{S}^\circ, \subseteq \rangle$.*

Abstract Semantics. The abstract normalization function $\delta^\circ : \mathcal{A}^\circ \times \mathcal{P}^\circ \to \mathcal{S}^\circ$ is equal to the concrete one (shown in Tab 1) with ℓ in place λ and $H_{\mathcal{L}}$ in place of $H_{\mathcal{L}_I}$. The abstract transitions are obtained by the rules of Tab. 5. The unfolding of replication simply creates a copy of the replicated process without modifying the labels. The rules for movements and opening are similar to the corresponding rules of the abstract semantics (see Tab. 4) restricted to multiplicity ω. There is only one difference: the topology is used instead of the partial topology. For instance, a capability in m is executed inside an ambient a, if a and an ambient named m have a common father in the topology.

$$\frac{^a!P \in C}{(T,C) \mapsto^\circ \delta^\circ \, ^aP \, \cup \, (T,C)}$$

$$\frac{^a\mathbf{in}\,m_\ell.\,P \in C \qquad {}^b_a,\, m_{\ell'}{}^b \in T}{(T,C) \mapsto^\circ \delta^\circ \, ^aP \, \cup \, (T \cup \{\, _a{}^m\ell' \,\}, C)}$$

$$\frac{^a\mathbf{out}\,m_\ell.\,P \in C \qquad {}_a{}^m\ell' \in T}{(T,C) \mapsto^\circ \delta^\circ \, ^aP \, \cup \, (T \, \cup \, T[\, _a{}^b/\, m_{\ell'}{}^b], C)}$$

$$\frac{^a\mathbf{open}\,m_\ell.\,P \in C \qquad m_{\ell'}{}^a \in T}{(T,C) \mapsto^\circ \delta^\circ \, ^aP \, \cup \, (T \, \cup \, T[\, _b{}^a/\, _b{}^m\ell'], C \, \cup \, C[\, ^aQ/\, ^m\ell' Q])}$$

Table 5. Abstract Transitions $\mapsto^\circ$

Definition 5.5 (The Abstract Collecting Semantics). *Let* $S^\circ \in \mathcal{S}^\circ$ *and let* $P \in \mathcal{P}$. *We define* $\mathfrak{S}_{Coll^\circ}[\![P]\!] = lfp\,\Psi^\circ(\{\alpha^\circ(\alpha([\delta \,^@P]))\,\})$ *where* $\Psi^\circ(S^\circ) = \bigcup S'^\circ$ *such that* $S^\circ \mapsto^\circ S'^\circ$.

The new abstract collecting semantics is a safe approximation of the abstract collecting semantics of Def. 4.6.

Theorem 5.6 (Safeness). *Let* $S^\circ \in \mathcal{S}^\circ$ *and* $P \in \mathcal{P}$. *We have* $\alpha^\circ(\Psi^\circ(S^\circ)) \subseteq \Psi^\circ(\alpha^\circ(S^\circ))$ *and* $\alpha^\circ(\mathfrak{S}_{Coll^\circ}[\![P]\!]) \subseteq \mathfrak{S}_{Coll^\circ}[\![P]\!]$.

It is a well-known results of abstract interpretation that Galois insertions are closed under composition. Therefore, Theorem 5.6 implies that the new abstract collecting semantics is a safe approximation of the concrete one[1].

Examples. There are several interesting examples showing the differences with the abstraction of Section 4. For instance this abstraction doesn't distinguish between one or more than one occurrence. Thus, the processes Q and $!Q$ of Example 4.10 are identified. Another loss of information is due to the removal of the partial topology, as the following example explains.

Example 5.7. Consider the process $P = P_1 \mid P_2 \mid P_3$, where $P_1 = !n_\lambda[\mathbf{in}\,m_\mu.\,\mathbf{in}\,k_\nu]$, $P_2 = !m_\beta[0]$ and $P_3 = !k_\gamma[0]$. We assume that labels $\{\lambda, \mu, \nu, \beta, \gamma\}$ are distinct also up to renaming of indexes. In the first abstraction we have (for readability we use $\{\lambda, \mu, \nu, \beta, \gamma\}$ for the corresponding abstract labels with multiplicity ω), $\mathfrak{S}_{Coll^\circ}[\![P]\!] = (T^\circ, C^\circ)$ where

$$T^\circ = \{\, _{n_\lambda}{}^@,\, _{k_\gamma}{}^@,\, _{m_\beta}{}^@,\, _{n_\lambda}{}^{m_\beta} \}$$

$$C^\circ = \{\, _{n_\lambda}{}^@\,\mathbf{in}\,m_\mu.\,\mathbf{in}\,k_\nu,\, _{n_\lambda}{}^{m_\beta}\,\mathbf{in}\,m_\mu.\,\mathbf{in}\,k_\nu,\, _{n_\lambda}{}^{m_\beta}\,\mathbf{in}\,k_\nu,\, ^@P_1,\, ^@P_2,\, ^@P_3 \}.$$

---
[1] $\alpha^\circ(\alpha(\mathfrak{S}_{Coll}[\![P]\!])) \subseteq \mathfrak{S}_{Coll^\circ}[\![P]\!]$.

Capability in k is not executed inside n, because it becomes executable only after the execution of in m, and k cannot be contained in m.

In the new abstraction we have (for readability we use $\{\lambda, \mu, \nu, \beta, \gamma\}$ for the corresponding abstract labels without indexes),

$$\mathfrak{S}_{Coll^\circ}\llbracket P \rrbracket = (T^\circ \cup \{ {_{n_\lambda}}^{k_\gamma} \}, \{ {^{n_\lambda}} \text{in} \, m_\mu. \, \text{in} \, k_\nu, \, {^{n_\lambda}} \text{in} \, k_\nu, \, {^@}P_1, \, {^@}P_2, \, {^@}P_3 \}).$$

Now in k is executed, because n and k have @ as a common father. The abstract semantics cannot capture that in k becomes executable inside n only after the movement inside m.

6 Conclusions

The main contribution of the paper is the definition of an abstract interpretation framework for MA, based on the normal semantics. The normal semantics uses an explicit representation of the topological structure of processes, in terms of topology and configuration, which is more viable for abstraction than the standard reduction semantics. We have shown two safe abstractions establishing a property concerning the run-time topological structure of processes: the proposed abstract semantics are effectively program analyzers. By restricting the attention to a process P of size n, in the first case the topology of the greatest state contains at most $O(n^2)$ elements and the configuration at most $O(n^3)$ elements. Hence, the iterations before reaching the fixed-point are at most $O(n^3)$. Any iteration has complexity $O(n^4)$, because it requires to check at most $O(n)$ conditions for any element of the configuration. Similarly, in the second case we have at most $O(n^2)$ iterations, where any iteration has complexity $O(n^3)$. Therefore, it is not difficult to devise a naive implementation of the first analysis in $O(n^7)$ and of the second one in $O(n^5)$ by using standard algorithms.

There are several CFA [12,13,9], in Flow Logics style, which compute safe approximations of the same property. More in detail, the analysis of [12] could be obtained in our framework from the abstract transition rules of Tab. 5, by weakening the conditions to be checked for the execution of the continuations of capabilities. Our second analysis is therefore more precise than the one of [12], which can be implemented in $O(n^3)$ using more sophisticated techniques [16]. The CFA of [13] is a very powerful exponential counting analysis that refines the approach of [12] essentially by using multiplicity and by considering sets of abstract states rather than abstract states. The relation between the two analyses is demonstrated by a formal comparison in abstract interpretation style. We could obtain this analysis by removing the partial topology from the domain of our first analysis and by a standard "lift" to the power-set. Our first analysis combines together the idea of multiplicity from [13] and in some sense the idea of using contextual information like the partial topology from the CFA of [9] for Safe Ambients [10]. The integration of these two aspects allows us to have a simple polynomial analysis collecting non-trivial information. For instance as shown by Example 4.8 of Section 4 the analysis is able to capture that capabilities with multiplicity one can be used only once although it does not employ sets of abstract states as in [13].

In our opinion the semantic-based abstract interpretation approach demonstrates several advantages over the "ad-hoc" syntax-based approaches. We have shown that existing analyses and new analyses can be specified in a common framework, where the analyses have a simpler formulation, are related to a formal definition of the property we want to approximate, and are safe and directly compared in terms of precision by construction. The obtained analyses (in particular the one of [12]) are more precise without affecting the complexity from an algorithmic point of view. Moreover, we believe that within this framework new analyses could be derived by simply modifying the abstract domain of properties according to standard abstract interpretation techniques.

This work is part of a project aimed at studying the relationship among abstract interpretation, CFA and types. We intend, as a short term goal, to specify also the types of MA [5, 2] within the proposed abstract interpretation framework. We believe that the formalization of CFA[2] and types in a common setting would allow us to finally compare their expressive power, integrate them, understand the pros and cons of each approach, and possibly for which class of properties one method is more adequate than another.

References

1. M. Bugliesi and G. Castagna *Secure Safe Ambients*. Proceedings of POPL '01, pages 222-235. ACM Press 2001.
2. L. Cardelli, G. Ghelli and A. Gordon *Mobility types for mobile ambients*. Proceedings of ICALP' 99, LNCS 1644, pages 230-239. Springer-Verlag, 1999.
3. L. Cardelli and A. Gordon *Types for mobile ambients*. Proceedings of 26th ACM Principles of Programming Languages (POPL' 99), pages 79-92. ACM Press, 1999.
4. L. Cardelli and G. Ghelli and A. Gordon. *Ambient Groups and Mobility Types*. Proceedings of IFIP TCS 2000, LNCS 1872, pages 333-347. Springer-Verlag, 2000.
5. L. Cardelli and A. Gordon. *Mobile Ambients* Proceedings of FoSSaCS' 98, LNCS 1378, pages 140-155. Springer-Verlag, 1998.
6. P. Cousot and R. Cousot, *Systematic Design of Program Analysis Frameworks*, Proceedings of POPL '79, pages 269–282, ACM Press, 1979.
7. P. Cousot and R. Cousot, *Abstract Interpretation: a unified lattice model for static analysis of programs by construction or approximation of fix-points*, Proceedings of POPL '77, pages 238–252, ACM Press, 1977.
8. M. Dezani-Ciancaglini and I. Salvo *Security Types for Mobile Safe Ambients*. Proceedings of ASIAN'00, LNCS 1961, pages 215-236, Springer-Verlag, 2000.
9. P. Degano and F. Levi and C. Bodei *Safe Ambients: Control Flow Analysis and Security*. Proceedings of ASIAN'00, LNCS 1961, pages 199-214, Springer-Verlag, 2000.
10. F. Levi and D. Sangiorgi *Controlling Interference in Ambients*. Proceedings of the 27th ACM Principles of Programming Languages (POPL' 00), pages 352-364. ACM Press, 2000.

---

[2] Notice that the proposed analyses could be extended to the full language with communication.

11. F. Levi and S. Maffeis *An Abstract Interpretation Framework for Analysing Mobile Ambients (Extended Version)*.
    Available at http://www.di.unipi.it/~levifran/papers.html.
12. F. Nielson, H.R. Nielson, R.R. Hansen and J.G. Jensen *Validating firewalls in mobile ambients*. Proceedings of CONCUR' 99, LNCS 1664, pages 463-477. Springer-Verlag, 1999.
13. R. R. Hansen and J. G. Jensen and F. Nielson and H. R.Nielson *Abstract Interpretation of Mobile Ambients* Proceedings of SAS'99, LNCS 1694, pages 135-148, Springer-Verlag, 1999.
14. H. R. Nielson and F. Nielson *Shape Analysis for Mobile Ambients* Proceedings of POPL' 00, pages 135-148, ACM Press, 2000.
15. F. Nielson and H. R. Nielson and C. Hankin *Principles of Program Analysis*, Springer,1999.
16. F. Nielson and H. Seidl, *Control-Flow Analysis in Cubic Time*, To appear in Proc. of ESOP'01.

A   Some Background on Abstract Interpretation

We briefly recall the basic concepts of abstract interpretation. The main idea is that of establishing a formal relationship, using Galois connections, between the concrete domain $\langle C, \leq \rangle$ of computation and a simpler abstract domain $\langle A, \leq^\alpha \rangle$ modelling the property we want to approximate. The ordering $\leq^\alpha$ is intended to model precision so that $a \leq^\alpha a'$ means that a' is a safe approximation of a.

Definition A.1 (Galois Connection). *Let (α, γ) be a pair of functions, such that $\alpha : C \to A$ (abstraction) and $\gamma : A \to C$ (concretization). The pair (α, γ) is a Galois connection iff $\forall c \in C, \forall a \in A, \alpha(c) \leq^\alpha a \Leftrightarrow c \leq \gamma(a)$. If also $\alpha(\gamma(a)) = a$, then (α, γ) is called a Galois insertion.*

Given a semantics S, computed as the least fixed-point of a semantic function F over the concrete domain, $\alpha(S)$ gives the exact abstract property corresponding to S. Therefore, safeness of an approximate semantics S^α over the abstract domain is guaranteed by the simple condition $\alpha(S) \leq^\alpha S^\alpha$. One of the main results is that a safe approximate semantics S^α can be computed as the least fixed-point of an abstract semantic function F^α as stated by the following theorem.

Theorem A.2 (Safeness). *Let (α, γ) be a Galois connection between $\langle C, \leq \rangle$ and $\langle A, \leq^\alpha \rangle$. Moreover, let $F : C \to C$ and $F^\alpha : A \to A$ be monotonic functions. If $\alpha(F(c)) \leq^\alpha F^\alpha(\alpha(c))$, for each $c \in C$, then $\alpha(lfp\ F) \leq^\alpha lfp\ F^\alpha$.*

Abstract Interpretation-Based Static Analysis of Mobile Ambients*

Jérôme Feret

Département d'Informatique de l'École Normale Supérieure
ENS-DI, 45, rue d'Ulm, 75230 PARIS cedex 5, France
jerome.feret@ens.fr
http://www.di.ens.fr/~feret

Abstract. We use Abstract Interpretation to automatically prove safety properties of mobile ambients with name communications. We introduce a non-standard semantics in order to distinguish different recursive instances of agents. This allows us to specify explicitly both the link between agents and the ambient names they have declared, and the link between agents and the ambients they have activated.

Then we derive from this non-standard semantics an abstract semantics which focuses on interactions between agents. This abstract semantics describes non uniformly which agents can be launched in which ambients and which ambient names can be communicated to which agents. Such a description is required to prove security properties such as non-interference or confinement for instance.

1 Introduction

The development of large scale communicating distributed systems imposes the design of both good models for mobile computation and well-fitted methods for analyzing properties of mobile systems. Mobility has quite a broad meaning. In the π-calculus [16], mobility is implicitly described by name passing: agents communicate channel names. This dynamically changes the communication topology between agents. In mobile ambients [4], mobility is explicit: ambients are bounded places and agents give them the capability to move inside other ambients taking their content with them. The connections between these two models are not well known yet. Anyway, we know that the asynchronous π-calculus can be encoded into the ambient calculus [2, p:5]. Security properties of mobile systems are usually described either by simulation relations (such as non-interference [15]) or by some constrains over their control flow (such as confinement or level of secrecy [12]). Nevertheless, existing analyses often describe a set of configurations which lead to a leak of security, then prove that such configurations can never occur. This second step requires both control flow and system shape approximation.

In previous works, we have proposed a control flow analysis [9], and an occurrence counting analysis [10] for π-calculus specified mobile systems. We propose

---

* This work was supported by the RTD project IST-1999-20527 "DAEDALUS" of the European FP5 programme.

P. Cousot (Ed.): SAS 2001, LNCS 2126, pp. 412–430, 2001.

to extend our framework with explicit mobility. In this paper we restrict our study to the analysis of the control flow of a mobile ambient, just considering name communications (instead of capability path communications). Our analysis consists in tagging each agent by an unambiguous marker which encodes the history of the replications that have led to its creation. Then, we label all the objects (ambients and ambient names) with the marker of the agent which has created them. We abstract for each agent both the set of the ambients it can be spawned in, and the set of the ambient names which can be communicated to it. We capture algebraic properties on the involved markers too.

We claim that distinguishing the objects created by the recursive instances of an agent is crucial when analyzing mobile systems. The main difference between a mobile system and a system written in CCS is that recursive instances of agents can interfere via the objects they have themselves declared. Nevertheless, this aspect of mobility is ignored by most of the analyses proposed in literature, which either identify recursive instances of agents [17, 11, 18] or prevent the recursive declaration of ambient names [3]. Ambient groups [1] use dependent types to prevent names of a fresh group from ever being received outside the initial scope of this group. In addition, our analysis also handles the algebraic properties of the markers. This allows us to describe the interaction between recursive instances of agents, whereas [1] can only prove that ambient names are confined inside the recursive instance of the agent which has created it.

The semantics for mobile ambients is given in Sect. 2. The non-standard semantics is introduced in Sect. 3. The abstract interpretation framework is reminded in Sect. 4. Eventually we design a generic abstraction of the interactions between agents in Sect. 5 and give three examples of analyses in Sect. 6.

2   Mobile Ambients

Mobile ambients [4] are a model of mobile computation. It describes a set of *agents* which are distributed throughout hierarchically organized domains called *ambients*. Agents interact inside ambients which makes the ambients move, taking with them their content. We consider a lazy version of mobile ambients in that replications are performed only when necessary. For the sake of simplicity, we restrict ourselves to name communications: just names and not capability paths can be communicated. Let $\mathcal{N}$ be a countable set of ambient names and Lbl a countable set of labels. We give in Fig. 1 the standard semantics of the mobile ambients. We locate each syntactic component of the system by placing distinct labels of Lbl.

Example 1. We model a system S which describes a *client-server* protocol. To make things clearer, public (or global) names are written in roman, all the other names are written in *italic* and we abstract away many computational aspects. A resource creates recursively an unbounded number of clients. Each client is represented by a packet $p[]$ which contains an ambient named "request". This ambient contains the client's query $\langle q \rangle$. At first, each packet enters the "server" ambient and then activates a pilot ambient "duplicate" which communicates the packet name to the server. This communication creates a recursive instance of an ambient named "instance" which will process the packet. The "instance"

$$n \in \mathcal{N} \quad \text{(ambient name)}$$
$$l \in Lbl \quad \text{(label)}$$

$$M ::= in^l\ n \quad \text{(can enter } n)$$
$$-\ out^l\ n \quad \text{(can exit } n)$$
$$-\ open^l\ n \quad \text{(can open } n)$$
$$-\ !open^l\ n \quad \text{(can duplicate itself}$$
$$\text{before opening } n)$$

$$P, Q \ ::= \ (\nu\ n)P \quad \text{(restriction)}$$
$$-\ \mathbf{0} \quad \text{(inactivity)}$$
$$-\ P \mid Q \quad \text{(composition)}$$
$$-\ n^l[P] \quad \text{(ambient)}$$
$$-\ M.P \quad \text{(capability action)}$$
$$-\ io.P \quad \text{(input/output action)}$$

$$io ::= (n)^l.P \quad \text{(input action)}$$
$$-\ !(n)^l.P \quad \text{(input action}$$
$$\text{with replication)}$$
$$-\ \langle n \rangle^l \quad \text{(async output action)}$$

Input action and restriction are the only name binders, in $(n)^l.P$, $!(n)^l.P$ and $(\nu\ n)P$, occurrences n in P are bound. Usual rules about scopes, substitution and α-conversion apply. We denote by $\mathcal{FN}(P)$ (resp. $\mathcal{BN}(P)$) the set of the free (resp. bound) names of P.

(a) Syntax.

$$P \equiv Q \qquad \text{if } P \sim_\alpha Q \qquad (\alpha\text{-conversion})$$
$$P \mid Q \equiv Q \mid P \qquad \text{(Commutativity)}$$
$$(P \mid Q) \mid R \equiv P \mid (Q \mid R) \qquad \text{(Associativity)}$$
$$P \mid \mathbf{0} \equiv P \qquad \text{(Zero par)}$$
$$(\nu\ n)\mathbf{0} \equiv \mathbf{0} \qquad \text{(Zero Res)}$$
$$(\nu\ n)(\nu\ m)P \equiv (\nu\ m)(\nu\ n)P \qquad \text{(Swapping)}$$
$$(\nu\ n)(P \mid Q) \equiv P \mid ((\nu\ n)Q) \text{ if } n \notin \mathcal{FN}(P) \qquad \text{(Extrusion Par)}$$
$$(\nu\ n)(m^l[P]) \equiv m^l[(\nu\ n)P] \quad \text{if } n \neq m \qquad \text{(Extrusion Amb)}$$

(b) Congruence relation.

$$n^i[in^k\ m.P \mid Q] \mid m^j[R] \xrightarrow{in(i,j,k)} m^j[n^i[P \mid Q] \mid R]$$
$$m^i[n^j[out^k\ m.P \mid Q] \mid R] \xrightarrow{out(i,j,k)} n^j[P \mid Q] \mid m^i[R]$$
$$open^i\ n.P \mid n^j[Q] \xrightarrow{open(i,j)} P \mid Q$$
$$!open^i\ n.P \mid n^j[Q] \xrightarrow{open(i,j)} P \mid Q \mid !open^i\ n.P$$
$$(n)^i.P \mid \langle m \rangle \xrightarrow{com(i,j)} P[n \leftarrow m]$$
$$!(n)^i.P \mid \langle m \rangle \xrightarrow{com(i,j)} P[n \leftarrow m] \mid !(n)^i.P$$

$$\frac{P \xrightarrow{\lambda} Q}{n^i[P] \xrightarrow{\lambda} n^i[Q]} \qquad \frac{P \xrightarrow{\lambda} Q}{P \mid R \xrightarrow{\lambda} Q \mid R} \qquad \frac{P' \equiv P,\ P \xrightarrow{\lambda} Q,\ Q \equiv Q'}{P' \xrightarrow{\lambda} Q'}$$

(c) Reduction relation.

Fig. 1. Standard Semantics.

ambient enters the packet, reads the request and sends it back inside an ambient named "answer". At last, the packet exits the "server" ambient.

S is defined as follows:

$\nu\mathbf{Pub} := (\nu\ request)(\nu\ make)(\nu\ server)(\nu\ duplicate)(\nu\ instance)(\nu\ answer),$
$\mathbf{C}_1 := request^{13}[\langle q\rangle^{14}],\ \mathbf{C}_2 := open^{15}instance,$
$\mathbf{C}_3 := in^{16}server.duplicate^{17}[out^{18}p.\langle p\rangle^{19}],$
$\mathbf{C} := (\nu\ q)(\nu\ p)p^{12}[\mathbf{C}_1\ |\ \mathbf{C}_2\ |\ \mathbf{C}_3]\ |\ \langle make\rangle^{20},$
$\mathbf{I}_1 := answer^8[\langle rep\rangle^9],\ \mathbf{I}_2 := out^{10}server,\ \mathbf{I} := in^5k.open^6request.(rep)^7(\mathbf{I}_1\ |\ \mathbf{I}_2),$
$\mathbf{S}_1 := !open^2duplicate,\ \mathbf{S}_2 := !(k)^3.instance^4[\mathbf{I}],\ \mathbf{S} := server^1[\mathbf{S}_1\ |\ \mathbf{S}_2],$
$S := (\nu\mathbf{Pub})(\mathbf{S}\ |\ !(x)^{11}.\mathbf{C}\ |\ \langle make\rangle^{21}).$

The following computation sequence describes the behaviour of the system:

$(\nu\mathbf{Pub})(\mathbf{S}\ |\ !(\underline{x})^{11}.C\ |\ \langle\underline{make}\rangle^{21})$

$\longrightarrow (\nu\mathbf{Pub})\left(\begin{array}{l}!(x)^{11}.C\ |\ \langle make\rangle^{20}|\ \underline{server}^1[\mathbf{S}_1\ |\ \mathbf{S}_2]\ |\\ (\nu\ q_1)(\nu\ p_1)p_1{}^{12}\left[\begin{array}{l}request^{13}[\langle q_1\rangle^{14}]\ |\ \mathbf{C}_2\ |\\ in^{16}\underline{server}.duplicate^{17}[out^{18}p_1.\langle p_1\rangle^{19}]\end{array}\right]\end{array}\right)$

$\longrightarrow (\nu\mathbf{Pub})(\nu\ q_1)(\nu\ p_1)$
$\left(\left(!(x)^{11}.C\ |\ \langle make\rangle^{20}|\ server^1\left[\mathbf{S}_1\ |\ \mathbf{S}_2\ |\ \underline{p}_1{}^{12}\left[\begin{array}{l}request^{13}[\langle q_1\rangle^{14}]\ |\ \mathbf{C}_2\ |\\ duplicate^{17}[out^{18}\underline{p}_1.\langle p_1\rangle^{19}]\end{array}\right]\right]\right)\right)$

$\longrightarrow (\nu\mathbf{Pub})(\nu\ q_1)(\nu\ p_1)$
$\left(\left(!(x)^{11}.C\ |\ \langle make\rangle^{20}|\ server^1\left[\begin{array}{l}!\underline{open}^2duplicate\ |\ \mathbf{S}_2\ |\ \underline{duplicate}^{17}[\langle p_1\rangle^{19}]\ |\\ p_1{}^{12}[\underline{request}^{13}[\langle q_1\rangle^{14}]\ |\ \mathbf{C}_2]\end{array}\right]\right)\right)$

$\longrightarrow (\nu\mathbf{Pub})(\nu\ q_1)(\nu\ p_1)$
$\left(\left(!(x)^{11}.C\ |\ \langle make\rangle^{20}|\ server^1\left[\begin{array}{l}\mathbf{S}_1\ |\ !(\underline{k})^3.instance^4[\mathbf{I}]\ |\ \langle\underline{p}_1\rangle^{19}|\\ p_1{}^{12}[request^{13}[\langle q_1\rangle^{14}]\ |\ \mathbf{C}_2]\end{array}\right]\right)\right)$

$\longrightarrow (\nu\mathbf{Pub})(\nu\ q_1)(\nu\ p_1)$
$\left(\left(!(x)^{11}.C\ |\ \langle make\rangle^{20}|\ server^1\left[\begin{array}{l}\mathbf{S}_1\ |\ \mathbf{S}_2\ |\ \underline{p}_1{}^{12}[request^{13}[\langle q_1\rangle^{14}]\ |\ \mathbf{C}_2]\ |\\ instance^4[in^5\underline{p}_1.open^6request.(rep)^7(\mathbf{I}_1|\mathbf{I}_2)]\end{array}\right]\right)\right)$

$\longrightarrow (\nu\mathbf{Pub})(\nu\ q_1)(\nu\ p_1)$
$\left(\left(!(x)^{11}.C|\ \langle make\rangle^{20}|\ server^1\left[\begin{array}{l}\mathbf{S}_1\ |\ \mathbf{S}_2\ |\\ p_1{}^{12}\left[\begin{array}{l}request^{13}[\langle q_1\rangle^{14}]\ |\ open^{15}\underline{instance}\ |\\ \underline{instance}^4[open^6request.(rep)^7(\mathbf{I}_1|\mathbf{I}_2)]\end{array}\right]\end{array}\right]\right)\right)$

$\longrightarrow (\nu\mathbf{Pub})(\nu\ q_1)(\nu\ p_1)$
$\left(\left(!(x)^{11}.C\ |\ \langle make\rangle^{20}|\ server^1\left[\mathbf{S}_1\ |\ \mathbf{S}_2\ |\ p_1{}^{12}\left[\begin{array}{l}request^{13}[\langle\underline{q}_1\rangle^{14}]\ |\\ open^6\underline{request}.(rep)^7(\mathbf{I}_1\ |\ \mathbf{I}_2)\end{array}\right]\right]\right)\right)$

$\longrightarrow^*(\nu\mathbf{Pub})(\nu\ q_1)(\nu\ p_1)$
$(!(x)^{11}.C\ |\ \langle make\rangle^{20}|\ \underline{server}^1[\mathbf{S}_1\ |\ \mathbf{S}_2\ |\ p_1{}^{12}[answer^8[\langle q_1\rangle^9]\ |\ out^{10}\underline{server}]])$

$\longrightarrow (\nu\mathbf{Pub})(\nu\ q_1)(\nu\ p_1)$
$(!(x)^{11}.C\ |\ \langle make\rangle^{20}|\ server^1[\mathbf{S}_1\ |\ \mathbf{S}_2]\ |\ p_1{}^{12}[answer^8[\langle q_1\rangle^9]])$

$\longrightarrow^*(\nu\mathbf{Pub})(\nu\ q_1)(\nu\ p_1)(\nu\ q_2)(\nu\ p_2)(!(x)^{11}.C\ |\ \langle make\rangle^{20}|\ server^1[\mathbf{S}_1\ |\ \mathbf{S}_2]|$
$\qquad\qquad\qquad p_1{}^{12}[answer^8[\langle q_1\rangle^9]]\ |\ p_2{}^{12}[answer^8[\langle q_2\rangle^9]])$ $\qquad\square$

3   Non-standard Semantics

The non-standard semantics is a refined one with explicit substitution. It restores the link between the recursive instances of agents and the objects they have created (i.e. the names they have declared and the ambients they have activated). Following $D\pi$ [13] style, we describe a mobile system with a set of agents tagged with a location marker. Furthermore, the embedding structure of the ambients imposes a description of the hierarchical tree of the administrative domains (or ambients). This is given by a set of activated ambients[1] (seen as locations) tagged with location markers specifying the surrounding ambient. We assume that a system is run inside a top level ambient which has no location. The link between agents and the ambient names they have declared is made explicit by tagging each agent by an unambiguous history marker allocated at its creation. Then, each new ambient name is tagged with the history marker of the agent which has declared it. Thus, we restore the link between agents and the ambients they have activated by tagging each activated ambient with the history marker of the agent which has activated it.

Let S be a closed mobile system in the ambient calculus. We assume without any loss of generality that two name binders ($\nu\, n$ or (n)) are never used to bind the same ambient name. *History markers* are binary trees the node of which are labeled with elements of Lbl^2 and the leaves of which are not labeled. The tree having a node labeled λ, a left sibling t_1 and a right one t_2 is denoted by $N(\lambda, t_1, t_2)$. We denote by Id the set of the history markers. *Ambient names* are described by a pair (n, id) where n specifies which action ($\nu\, n$) has created it while id is the history marker of the agents which has declared this name. *Activated ambients* are identified by a pair (i, id) where i is the label of the ambient constructor which has activated the ambient while id is the history marker of its activator[2]. The top level ambient is represented by the pair $(\text{top}, \varepsilon)$ (we assume that top $\in Lbl$ has not been used for labeling S yet). *Location markers* are pairs (i, id), too. A location marker refers to the ambient where a process is spawned.

A *non-standard configuration* [20,9] is a set of thread instances, where a thread instance is a tuple composed by a syntactic component, a history marker, a location marker and an environment. The syntactic component is either a syntactic copy of an agent of S or an activated ambient denoted by $n^i[\bullet]$. The history marker is unambiguously allocated at the thread creation. The location marker indicates where the thread is run. The environment specifies the origin of the free syntactic ambient names of the syntactic component.

Example 2. We give here the non-standard configuration reached after completing two sessions of our server[3]:

---

[1] Also called privileged ambients in [4].

[2] An ambient cannot be identified by its ambient name because two distinct activated ambients can have the same name [4, p:12].

[3] We do not figure the origin of public names.

$$
\begin{cases}
(\mathrm{server}^1[\bullet], \varepsilon, (\mathrm{top}, \varepsilon), \emptyset) \\
(\mathrm{answer}^8[\bullet], id_0', (12, id_0), \emptyset) \\
(\mathrm{answer}^8[\bullet], id_1', (12, id_1), \emptyset) \\
(p^{12}[\bullet], id_0, (\mathrm{top}, \varepsilon), [p \mapsto (p, id_0)]) \\
(p^{12}[\bullet], id_1, (\mathrm{top}, \varepsilon), [p \mapsto (p, id_1)]) \\
(!(x)^{11}.\mathbf{C}, \varepsilon, (\mathrm{top}, \varepsilon), \emptyset) \\
(\langle \mathrm{make} \rangle^{20}, id_1, (\mathrm{top}, \varepsilon), \emptyset) \\
(\mathbf{S}_1, \varepsilon, (1, \varepsilon), \emptyset) \\
(\mathbf{S}_2, \varepsilon, (1, \varepsilon), \emptyset) \\
(\langle rep \rangle^9, id_0', (8, id_0'), [rep \mapsto (q, id_0)]) \\
(\langle rep \rangle^9, id_1', (8, id_1'), [rep \mapsto (q, id_1)])
\end{cases}
$$

where:

$$
\begin{cases}
id_0 = N((11, 21), \varepsilon, \varepsilon) \\
id_1 = N((11, 20), \varepsilon, id_0) \\
id_0' = N((3, 19), \varepsilon, id_0) \\
id_1' = N((3, 19), \varepsilon, id_1)
\end{cases}
$$

The top five instances represent the hierachic structure of nested ambients, the others describe the agent distribution. Location markers allow in reconstructing the following ambient:

$$
(\nu \, \overline{n}) \quad {}^{(\mathrm{top}, \varepsilon)}\left[
\begin{array}{l}
!(x)^{(11, \varepsilon)}.\mathbf{C} \mid \langle \mathrm{make} \rangle^{(20, id_1)} \mid \mathrm{server}^{(1, \varepsilon)}[\mathbf{S}_1 \mid \mathbf{S}_2] \mid \\
(p, id_0)^{(12, id_0)}[\mathrm{answer}^{(8, id_0')}[\langle (q, id_0) \rangle^{(9, id_0')}]] \mid \\
(p, id_1)^{(12, id_1)}[\mathrm{answer}^{(8, id_1')}[\langle (q, id_1) \rangle^{(9, id_1')}]]
\end{array}
\right]
$$

in where ambients, ambient names and agents are stamped with their own makers. Thanks to name markers, we avoid conflict between ambient names. So we can extrude their declaration inside the top level ambient. In this way, the shortcut $(\nu \overline{n})$ denotes the declaration of all the ambient names of the configuration. It appears explicitly that, in each packet, both the name of the packet and that contained in the "answer" ambient embedded in the packet have been declared by the same recursive instance of the resource $!(x).\mathbf{C}$. This means that the answer of a query is sent to the good client. □

The non-standard semantics is given in Fig. 3 by both an initial non-standard configuration and a reduction relation. Their definitions use the extraction function β defined in Fig. 2. Given a continuation P, an history marker id, a location marker loc and an environment E, $\beta(P, id, loc, E)$ gives the set of all the thread instances that must be spawned to simulate the computation of the process $E(P)$ identified with the marker id, in the ambient denoted by loc. It especially deals with new ambient name declaration and new ambient activation.

We informally describe the non-standard semantics. For the sake of the brevity, we only detail the non-standard *in* migration rule. *in* migration rule involves two distinct ambients λ, μ and an agent ψ. They are respectively denoted by three configurations $(n^i[\bullet], id_1, loc_1, E_1)$, $(m^j[\bullet], id_2, loc_2, E_2)$ and $(in^k o.P, id_3, loc_3, E_3)$. The *in* migration rule is enabled if and only if the two ambients are located in the same ambient (this gives the constrain $loc_1 = loc_2$), the agent is located in the first ambient (this gives $loc_3 = (i, id_1)$) and the agent capability can interact with the name of the second ambient (this is encoded by the constrain $E_2(m) = E_3(o)$). The result of such a migration is that the first

$$\beta(n^i[P], id, loc, E) = \beta(P, id, (i, id), E) \cup \{(n^i[\bullet], id, loc, [n \mapsto E(n)])\}$$
$$\beta(P \mid Q, id, loc, E) = \beta(P, id, loc, E) \cup \beta(Q, id, loc, E)$$
$$\beta((\nu\, n)P, id, loc, E) = \beta(P, id, loc, (E[n \mapsto (n, id)]))$$
$$\beta(M.P, id, loc, E) = \{(M.P, id, loc, E_{|\mathcal{FN}(M.P)})\}$$
$$\beta(io.P, id, loc, E) = \{(io.P, id, loc, E_{|\mathcal{FN}(io.P)})\}$$
$$\beta(0, id, loc, E) = \emptyset$$

Fig. 2. Extraction Function.

ambient moves inside the second one (its location is just replaced by (j, id_2)). All it content is taken with it (this does change neither their location markers, nor their environments), but the agent ψ is executed and its continuation is spawned inside the first ambient (ψ is replaced by $\beta(P, id_3, loc_3, E_{3|\mathcal{FN}(P)})$). The *out* migration is simulated in the same way. The ambient dissolution is a bit much complex since all the locations of the dissolved ambient content are changed. We shall notice that each time a resource is fetched a new history marker is deterministically allocated: it is given by $N((i, j), id_i, id_j)$ where i is the label of the resource, id_i is the history marker of the resource, j is the label of the thread which enforces the resource fetching and id_j is the history marker of this thread. We do not need a congruence relation because our set-based representation of configurations makes structural congruence rules useless and the use of history markers avoids conflicts between ambient names.

Standard and non-standard semantics are strongly bisimilar. The proof relies on that non-standard computations cannot yield conflicts between history markers. Moreover, in accordance to the following proposition, we can simplify the shape of the history markers without losing the consistency of our semantics.

$$\phi_1 : \begin{cases} Id & \to & (Lbl^2)^\star \\ N(a, b, c) & \mapsto & a.\phi_2(N(c)) \\ \varepsilon & \mapsto & \varepsilon \end{cases} \qquad \phi_2 : \begin{cases} Id & \to & Lbl^\star \\ N((i, j), b, c) & \mapsto & j.\phi_2(N(c)) \\ \varepsilon & \mapsto & \varepsilon \end{cases}$$

Proposition 1. *Let ϕ be ϕ_1 or ϕ_2 and $C_0 \longrightarrow \ldots \longrightarrow C_n$ be a non-standard computation sequence, where $C_0 = C_0(S)$. For all $i, j \in [\![0, n]\!]$, $(p, id, loc, E) \in C_i$ and $(p', id', loc', E') \in C_j$, such that $\phi(id) = \phi(id')$ then $id = id'$.*

Such simplifications allow us to reduce the cost of our analysis, but also lead to a loss of accuracy, since they merge information related to distinct computation sequences of the system.

4   Abstract Interpretation Framework

We denote by $\mathcal{C}$ the set of all possible non-standard configurations and by Σ the set of transition labels. We are actually interested in the set $Coll(S)$ of all the configurations a system may take during a finite sequence of computation steps. This is given by its collecting semantics [5] and can be expressed as the least fix point of a $\cup$-complete endomorphism $\mathbb{F}$ on the complete lattice $\wp(\Sigma^\star \times \mathcal{C})$ defined as follows:

$$\mathbb{F}(X) = \{(\varepsilon, \beta(S))\} \cup \left\{ (u.\lambda, C') \,\middle|\, \exists C \in \mathcal{C},\ (u, C) \in X \text{ and } C \xrightarrow{\lambda} C' \right\}$$

$$C_0(S) = \beta(S, \varepsilon, (\text{top}, \varepsilon), \emptyset).$$

(a) Initial configuration.

If C is a non-standard configuration,
if there are λ, μ, ψ in C, $(\lambda \neq \mu)$
with $\lambda = \left(n^i[\bullet], id_1, loc_1, E_1\right)$, $\mu = \left(m^j[\bullet], id_2, loc_2, E_2\right)$ and $\psi = \left(in^k o.P, id_3, loc_3, E_3\right)$,
such that $loc_1 = loc_2$, $loc_3 = (i, id_1)$ and $E_2(m) = E_3(o)$
then $C \overset{in(i,j,k)}{\longrightarrow} (C \setminus \{\lambda, \psi\}) \cup \left(n^i[\bullet], id_1, (j, id_2), E_1\right) \cup \beta\left(P, id_3, loc_3, E_{3|\mathcal{FN}(P)}\right).$

If C is a non-standard configuration,
if there are λ, μ, ψ in C,
with $\lambda = \left(m^i[\bullet], id_1, loc_1, E_1\right)$, $\mu = \left(n^j[\bullet], id_2, loc_2, E_2\right)$ and $\psi = \left(out^k o.P, id_3, loc_3, E_3\right)$,
such that $loc_2 = (i, id_1)$, $loc_3 = (j, id_2)$ and $E_1(m) = E_3(o)$
then $C \overset{out(i,j,k)}{\longrightarrow} (C \setminus \{\mu, \psi\}) \cup \left(n^j[\bullet], id_2, loc_1, E_2\right) \cup \beta\left(P, id_3, loc_3, E_{3|\mathcal{FN}(P)}\right).$

If C is a non-standard configuration,
if there are λ, μ in C, with $\lambda = \left(open^i m.P, id_1, loc_1, E_1\right)$ and $\mu = \left(n^j[\bullet], id_2, loc_2, E_2\right)$,
such that $loc_1 = loc_2$ and $E_1(m) = E_2(n)$.
then $C \overset{open(i,j)}{\longrightarrow} (C \setminus (\{\lambda, \mu\} \cup A)) \cup \beta\left(P, id_1, loc_1, E_{1|\mathcal{FN}(P)}\right) \cup A'$
where $\begin{cases} A = \{(a, id, loc, E) \in C \mid loc = (j, id_2)\} \\ A' = \{(a, id, loc_2, E) \mid (a, id, (j, id_2), E) \in C\}. \end{cases}$

If C is a non-standard configuration,
if there are λ, μ in C, with $\lambda = \left(!open^i m.P, id_1, loc_1, E_1\right)$ and $\mu = \left(n^j[\bullet], id_2, loc_2, E_2\right)$,
such that $loc_1 = loc_2$ and $E_1(m) = E_2(n)$,
then $C \overset{open(i,j)}{\longrightarrow} (C \setminus (\{\mu\} \cup A)) \cup \beta\left(P, N((i,j), id_1, id_2), loc_1, E_{1|\mathcal{FN}(P)}\right) \cup A'$
where $\begin{cases} A = \{(a, id, loc, E) \in C \mid loc = (j, id_2)\} \\ A' = \{(a, id, loc_2, E) \mid (a, id, (j, id_2)), E) \in C\}. \end{cases}$

(b) Move rules.

If C is a non-standard configuration,
if there are λ, μ in C, with $\lambda = ((n)^i.P, id_1, loc_1, E_1)$ and $\mu = (\langle m \rangle^j, id_2, loc_2.E_2)$,
such that $loc_1 = loc_2$,
then $C \overset{com(i,j)}{\longrightarrow} (C \setminus \{\lambda, \mu\}) \cup \beta(P, id_1, loc_1, E_1[n \mapsto E_2(m)]_{|\mathcal{FN}(P)}).$

If C is a non-standard configuration,
if there are λ, μ in C, with $\lambda = (!(n)^i.P, id_1, loc_1, E_1)$ and $\mu = (\langle m \rangle^j, id_2, loc_2.E_2)$,
such that $loc_1 = loc_2$,
then $C \overset{com(i,j)}{\longrightarrow} (C \setminus \{\mu\}) \cup \beta(P, N((i,j), id_1, id_2), loc_1, E_1[n \mapsto E_2(m)]_{|\mathcal{FN}(P)}).$

(c) Communication rules.

Fig. 3. Non-standard Semantics.

This least fix-point is usually not decidable, so we use the Abstract Interpretation framework [6] to compute a sound – but not necessary complete approximation of it. More precisely, we use the relaxed version of Abstract Interpretation [7], in where, among others, the abstract domain is not supposed to be complete under lowest upper bound; furthermore, no abstraction function is required.

Definition 1. *An abstraction is a tuple* $(C^\sharp, \sqsubseteq^\sharp, \bigsqcup^\sharp, \bot^\sharp, \gamma, C_0^\sharp, \leadsto, \nabla)$ *such that*

1. $(C^\sharp, \sqsubseteq^\sharp)$ *is a pre-order;*
2. $\bigsqcup^\sharp : \wp_{finite}(C^\sharp) \to C^\sharp$ *such that* $\forall A^\sharp \in \wp_{finite}(C^\sharp)$, $\forall a^\sharp \in A^\sharp$, $a^\sharp \sqsubseteq^\sharp \bigsqcup^\sharp(A^\sharp)$;
3. $\bot^\sharp \in C^\sharp$ *satisfies* $\forall a^\sharp \in C^\sharp$, $\bot^\sharp \sqsubseteq^\sharp a^\sharp$;
4. $\gamma : C^\sharp \to \wp(\Sigma^\star \times C)$ *is a monotonic map which satisfies* $\gamma(\bot^\sharp) = \emptyset$;
5. $C_0^\sharp \in C^\sharp$ *is such that* $(\varepsilon, C_0(S)) \in \gamma(C_0^\sharp)$;
6. $\leadsto \in \wp(C^\sharp \times \Sigma \times C^\sharp)$ *is an abstract deterministic labeled transition relation over* $C^\sharp$ *such that :* $\forall C^\sharp \in C^\sharp$, $\forall (u, C) \in \gamma(C^\sharp)$, $\forall \lambda \in \Sigma$, $\forall \overline{C} \in C$,

$$C \xrightarrow{\lambda} \overline{C} \implies \exists \overline{C}^\sharp \in C^\sharp, \ (C^\sharp \overset{\lambda}{\leadsto} \overline{C}^\sharp \text{ and } (u.\lambda, \overline{C}) \in \gamma(\overline{C}^\sharp));$$

7. $\nabla : C^\sharp \times C^\sharp \to C^\sharp$ *is a widening operator which satisfies:*
   - $\forall C_1^\sharp, C_2^\sharp \in C^\sharp$, $C_1^\sharp \sqsubseteq^\sharp C_1^\sharp \nabla C_2^\sharp$ *and* $C_2^\sharp \sqsubseteq C_1^\sharp \nabla C_2^\sharp$,
   - $\forall (C_n^\sharp)_{n \in \mathbb{N}} \in (C^\sharp)^{\mathbb{N}}$, *the sequence* $(C_n^\nabla)_{n \in \mathbb{N}}$ *defined as*

$$\begin{cases} C_0^\nabla &= C_0^\sharp \\ C_{n+1}^\nabla &= C_n^\nabla \nabla C_{n+1}^\sharp \end{cases}$$

is ultimately stationary.

$C^\sharp$ is an abstract domain. It captures the properties we are interested in, and abstracts away many other properties. The pre-order $\sqsubseteq^\sharp$ describes the amount of information which is known about the properties we approximate. We use only a pre-order to allow some concrete properties to be described by several unrelated abstract elements. $\bigsqcup^\sharp$ is used to gather the information described by several abstract elements, for the sake of generality, it does not necessarily compute the lowest upper bound of a finite set of abstract elements which may not even exist. $\bot^\sharp$ describes the empty set, it provides the basis for our abstract iteration. γ is a concretization function which maps each abstract property to the set of the concrete elements which satisfy this property. $C_0^\sharp$ is an abstract element which describes the properties satisfied by the initial configuration of the system. $\leadsto$ is used for mimicking the concrete transition system in the abstract domain and ∇ is used to ensure the convergence of the analysis.

In accordance with Def. 1.6, the abstract counterpart $\mathbb{F}^\sharp$ to $\mathbb{F}$, defined as:

$$\mathbb{F}^\sharp(X^\sharp) = \bigsqcup^\sharp \left\{ \overline{C}^\sharp \mid \exists \lambda \in \Sigma, \ C^\sharp \in X^\sharp, \ C^\sharp \overset{\lambda}{\leadsto} \overline{C}^\sharp \right\} \cup \{C_0^\sharp; X^\sharp\}$$

satisfies the soundness condition $\forall C^\sharp \in C^\sharp$, $\mathbb{F} \circ \gamma(C^\sharp) \subseteq \gamma \circ \mathbb{F}^\sharp(C^\sharp)$. Using Kleene's theorem, we obtain the soundness of our analysis:

Theorem 1. $lfp_{\emptyset}\mathbb{F} \subseteq \bigcup_{n \in \mathbb{N}} \left[\gamma \circ \mathbb{F}^{\sharp n}\right](\bot^{\sharp}).$

Following [5], we compute a sound and decidable approximation of our abstract semantics by using the widening operator ∇:

Theorem 2. *The abstract iteration [7, 8] of* $\mathbb{F}^{\sharp}$ *defined as follows:*

$$
\begin{cases}
\mathbb{F}_0^{\nabla} = \bot^{\sharp} \\
\mathbb{F}_{n+1}^{\nabla} = \begin{cases} \mathbb{F}_n^{\nabla} & \text{if } \mathbb{F}^{\sharp}(\mathbb{F}_n^{\nabla}) \sqsubseteq \mathbb{F}_n^{\nabla} \\ \mathbb{F}_n^{\nabla} \nabla \mathbb{F}^{\sharp}(\mathbb{F}_n^{\nabla}) & \text{otherwise} \end{cases}
\end{cases}
$$

is ultimately stationary and its limit $\mathbb{F}^{\nabla}$ *satisfies* $Coll(\mathcal{S}) \subseteq \gamma(\mathbb{F}^{\nabla}).$

Remark 1. We claim that this framework is highly extensible: given two abstractions $(\mathcal{C}_1^{\sharp}, \sqsubseteq_1^{\sharp}, \bigsqcup_1^{\sharp}, \bot_1^{\sharp}, \gamma_1, C_{0_1}^{\sharp}, \rightsquigarrow_1, \nabla_1)$ and $(\mathcal{C}_2^{\sharp}, \sqsubseteq_2^{\sharp}, \bigsqcup_2^{\sharp}, \bot_2^{\sharp}, \gamma_2, C_{0_2}^{\sharp}, \rightsquigarrow_2, \nabla_2)$ and a reduction operator[4] $\rho : \mathcal{C}_1^{\sharp} \times \mathcal{C}_2^{\sharp}$ which satisfies:

$$\forall a^{\sharp} \in \mathcal{C}_1^{\sharp} \times \mathcal{C}_2^{\sharp}, \ \gamma_1(a_1^{\sharp}) \cap \gamma_2(a_2^{\sharp}) \subseteq \gamma_1(b_1^{\sharp}) \cap \gamma_2(b_2^{\sharp}), \ \text{denoting } \rho(a^{\sharp}) \text{ by } (b_1^{\sharp}, b_2^{\sharp}).$$

The following tuple $(\mathcal{C}^{\sharp}, \sqsubseteq^{\sharp}, \bigsqcup^{\sharp}, \bot^{\sharp}, \gamma, C_0^{\sharp}, \rightsquigarrow, \nabla)$ where

- $\mathcal{C}^{\sharp} = \mathcal{C}_1^{\sharp} \times \mathcal{C}_2^{\sharp};$
- $\sqsubseteq^{\sharp}, \bigsqcup^{\sharp}, \bot^{\sharp}$ and ∇ are defined pair-wise;
- $\gamma : \begin{cases} \mathcal{C}^{\sharp} \to \wp(\Sigma^{\star} \times \mathcal{C}) \\ (a_1^{\sharp}, a_2^{\sharp}) \mapsto \gamma_1(a_1^{\sharp}) \cap \gamma_2(a_2^{\sharp}); \end{cases}$
- $C_0^{\sharp}(\mathcal{S}) = \rho(C_{0_1}^{\sharp}, C_{0_2}^{\sharp});$
- $\rightsquigarrow$ is defined by:
  $a \rightsquigarrow d$ if and only if denoting $\rho(a)$ by $(b_1^{\sharp}, b_2^{\sharp})$, there exists $c_1^{\sharp} \in \mathcal{C}_1^{\sharp}, c_2^{\sharp} \in \mathcal{C}_2^{\sharp}$ such that $b_1^{\sharp} \rightsquigarrow_1 c_1^{\sharp}, b_2^{\sharp} \rightsquigarrow_2 c_2^{\sharp}, d = \rho(c_1^{\sharp}, c_2^{\sharp}).$

is also an abstraction.

5 Control Flow Analysis

We propose to describe all the potential interactions between all the agents of a given mobile ambient. For that purpose we will compute for each thread an approximation of both the set of the ambients it can be immediately located in and the set of the ambient names which can be communicated to this thread. We want a non-uniform description of this. This means that we will compare the history marker of each thread with the marker of its location and with the markers of the ambient names it is communicated to.

The main difficulty is to synthesize such comparisons throughout computation steps. We use the history marker of each thread as a pivot to synthesize the comparison between the other markers (location markers and markers of the ambient names) of this thread. Furthermore we use synchronization conditions on

---

[4] ρ allow simplifying the properties obtained in the two abstractions.

ambient names and on locations of the agents in establishing a comparison between the history markers of all the involved threads. Our main strategy is easy: we first gather all the information we have about the pairs of markers (this means we will abstract sets of tuples of markers). Then synchronization conditions give equality relationships between tuple components. If equality relationships are satisfiable, the abstract computation step is enabled and we compute, for each new thread, the comparison between its history marker and its other markers.

For each $n \in \mathbb{N}$, we introduce an abstract pre-order $(Id_n^\sharp, \sqsubseteq_n)$ to represent sets of n-uples of history markers. Thus, each $Id_n^\sharp$ is related to $\wp(Id^n)$ by a monotonic concretization function γ_n. We introduce a few abstract primitives to handle these domains: a representation of the empty set $\bot_n^\sharp$, a representation of the initial identifier $\varepsilon^\sharp$, an abstract union $\bigsqcup_n$, an associative abstract concatenation $\bullet^\sharp$ to gather the abstraction of tuple sets, an abstract join $assert$ to enforce synchronization conditions, an abstract projection Π and an abstract push operator $push$ which is used to calculate the abstraction of the set of the new markers when fetching a resource. These primitives shall satisfy the following properties:

- $\gamma_n(\bot_n^\sharp) = \emptyset$;
- $\varepsilon \in \gamma_1(\varepsilon^\sharp)$;
- $\forall A \in \wp_{finite}(Id_n^\sharp)$, $\bigsqcup_n(A) \in Id_n^\sharp$ and $\forall a^\sharp \in A$, $a^\sharp \sqsubseteq_n \bigsqcup_n(A)$;
- $\forall a \in Id_n^\sharp$, $b \in Id_m^\sharp$, $(a \bullet^\sharp b) \in Id_{n+m}^\sharp$ and
$$\left\{ (id_i)_{i \in [[1;n+m]]} \,\middle|\, \begin{matrix} (id_i)_{i \in [[1;n]]} \in \gamma_n(a^\sharp), \\ (id_{i+n})_{i \in [[1;m]]} \in \gamma_m(b^\sharp) \end{matrix} \right\} \subseteq \gamma_{n+m}(a \bullet^\sharp b);$$
- $\forall a^\sharp \in Id_n^\sharp$, $\forall A \in \wp([[1;n]]^2)$, $assert(A, a^\sharp) \in Id_n^\sharp$ and
$\{(id_i)_{i \in [[1;n]]} \mid (id_i) \in \gamma_n(a^\sharp), \forall (k,l) \in A, \, id_k = id_l\} \in \gamma_n(assert(A, a^\sharp))$;
- $\forall a^\sharp \in Id_n^\sharp$, $\forall p \in \mathbb{N}$, $\forall (s_k)_{k \in [[1;p]]} \in [[1;n]]^{[[1;p]]}$ such that (s_k) is a one to one sequence, $\Pi_{(s_k)}(a^\sharp) \in Id_p^\sharp$ and
$\{(id_{s_k})_{k \in [[1;p]]} \mid (id_i)_{i \in [[1;n]]} \in \gamma_n(a^\sharp)\} \subseteq \gamma_p(\Pi_{(s_k)}(a^\sharp))$;
- $\forall a^\sharp \in Id_3^\sharp$, $push_{(i,j)}(a^\sharp) \in Id_2^\sharp$ and
$\{(N((i,j), id_1, id_2), id_3) \mid (id_1, id_2, id_3) \in \gamma_3(a^\sharp)\} \subseteq \gamma_2(push_{(i,j)}(a^\sharp))$.

Moreover we define the operator $dpush \in \mathcal{F}(Id_1^\sharp, Id_2^\sharp)$ by:

$$\forall a \in Id_1^\sharp, \quad dpush(a) = assert(\{(1,2)\}, a \bullet^\sharp a).$$

$dpush$ satisfies the following property:

$$\forall a \in Id_1^\sharp, \quad \{(id, id) \mid id \in \gamma_1(a)\} \subseteq \gamma_2(dpush(a)).$$

We denote by $\mathcal{P}$ the set of all the syntactic components of $\mathcal{S}$. We describe the set of ambients in which threads can be launched by associating with each pair $(P, i) \in (\mathcal{P} \times Lbl)$ a description of the set of the marker pairs (id_P, id_i) such that an instance of P may be stamped with both the history marker id_P and the location marker (i, id_i). In addition, we describe the set of the ambient names which can be communicated to a thread by relating each triplet $(P, m, n) \in (\mathcal{P} \times \mathcal{BN}(\mathcal{S}) \times \mathcal{BN}(\mathcal{S}))$ to a description of the set of the marker pairs (id_P, id_n) such that an instance of the P may be stamped with the marker id_P whereas the syntactic name m of P is bound to the ambient name (n, id_n). In this way, our abstraction $(\mathcal{C}^\sharp, \sqsubseteq^\sharp, \bigsqcup^\sharp, \bot^\sharp, \gamma, C_0^\sharp, \rightsquigarrow, \nabla)$ is defined as follows:

- $\mathcal{C}^{\sharp} = \mathcal{F}(\mathcal{P} \times Lbl, Id_2^{\sharp}) \times \mathcal{F}(\mathcal{P} \times \mathcal{BN}(\mathcal{S}) \times \mathcal{BN}(\mathcal{S}), Id_2^{\sharp})$
- $\sqsubseteq^{\sharp}, \bigsqcup^{\sharp}, \nabla$ are defined component-wise then pair-wise.
- $\bot^{\sharp}$ is given by the pair of functions which relate any elements to $\bot_2^{\sharp}$;
- $\gamma((f, g))$ is given by the set of the configurations C which satisfy:

$$(P, id, (i, id_i), E) \in C \Longrightarrow \begin{cases} (id, id_i) \in \gamma_2(f(P, i)) \text{ and} \\ E(m) = (n, id_n) \Longrightarrow (id, id_n) \in \gamma_2(g(P, m, n)). \end{cases}$$

- $C_0^{\sharp}$ and $\rightsquigarrow$ are given in Figs. 5-7.

Abstract transition rules just mimic the non-standard ones, therefore they are quite complicated because non-standard transition rules handle several synchronizations between markers. Their definition uses an abstract extraction function $\beta^{\sharp}$ defined in Fig. 4.

- $\beta^{\sharp}(n^i[P], id^{\sharp}, loc^{\sharp}, E^{\sharp}) = (a[(n^i[\bullet], j) \mapsto loc^{\sharp}(j)], b[(n^i[\bullet], n, m) \mapsto E^{\sharp}(n, m)])$
  where $(a, b) = \beta^{\sharp}(P, id^{\sharp}, [i \mapsto dpush(id^{\sharp})], E^{\sharp})$;
- $\beta^{\sharp}(P \mid Q, id^{\sharp}, loc^{\sharp}, E^{\sharp}) = \bigsqcup^{\sharp}\{\beta^{\sharp}(P, id^{\sharp}, loc^{\sharp}, E^{\sharp}); \beta^{\sharp}(Q, id^{\sharp}, loc^{\sharp}, E^{\sharp})\};$
- $\beta^{\sharp}((\nu \, n)P, id^{\sharp}, loc^{\sharp}, E^{\sharp}) = \beta^{\sharp}((\nu \, n)P, id^{\sharp}, loc^{\sharp}, E^{\sharp}[(n, n) \mapsto dpush(id^{\sharp})]);$
- $\beta^{\sharp}(M.P, id^{\sharp}, loc^{\sharp}, E^{\sharp}) = (a, b)$
  where $\begin{cases} a = [(M.P, i) \mapsto loc^{\sharp}(i)] \\ b = [(M.P, m, n) \mapsto E^{\sharp}(m, n) \text{ if } m \in \mathcal{FN}(M.P)]; \end{cases}$
- $\beta^{\sharp}(io.P, id^{\sharp}, loc^{\sharp}, E^{\sharp}) = (a, b)$
  where $\begin{cases} a = [(io.P, i) \mapsto loc^{\sharp}(i)] \\ b = [(io.P, m, o) \mapsto E^{\sharp}(m, o) \text{ if } m \in \mathcal{FN}(io.P)]; \end{cases}$
- $\beta^{\sharp}(0, id^{\sharp}, loc^{\sharp}, E^{\sharp}) = \bot^{\sharp}.$

Fig. 4. Abstract Extraction Function.

$\beta^{\sharp}$ is an abstract counterpart to β. It calculates all the interactions obtained by spawning a continuation in an abstract location: given $P \in \mathcal{P}$, $id^{\sharp} \in Id_1^{\sharp}$, $loc^{\sharp} \in \mathcal{F}(Lbl, Id_2^{\sharp})$ and $E^{\sharp} \in \mathcal{F}(\mathcal{BN}(\mathcal{S}) \times \mathcal{BN}(\mathcal{S}), Id_2^{\sharp})$, $\beta^{\sharp}(P, id^{\sharp}, loc^{\sharp}, E^{\sharp})$ gives a pair $(a, b) \in \mathcal{C}^{\sharp}$ which describes all the interactions obtained by spawning a syntactic component P identified by a marker described by $id^{\sharp}$, in a location described by $loc^{\sharp}$ and with an environment described by $E^{\sharp}$, as expressed by the following proposition:

Proposition 2. $\beta(P, id, (i, id_i), E) \in \gamma(\beta^{\sharp}(P, id^{\sharp}, loc^{\sharp}, E^{\sharp}))$, $\forall i \in Lbl, id, id_i \in Id$ with $id \in \gamma_1(id^{\sharp})$, $(id, id_i) \in \gamma_2(loc^{\sharp}(i))$ and $\forall E \in \mathcal{F}(\mathcal{FN}(P), (\mathcal{BN}(\mathcal{S}) \times Id))$ such that $\forall m, n \in \mathcal{BN}(\mathcal{S})$, $\forall id_n \in Id$, $[E(m) = (n, id_n) \Rightarrow (id, id_n) \in \gamma_2(E^{\sharp}(m, n))].$

We now give some intuition about the abstract transition rules. For the sake of the brevity, we focus on the *in* migration abstract rule. The three syntactic components λ, μ and ψ denote the three threads involved in the non-standard *in* migration rule. We check for each pair (l_λ, n_m) whether there can be a configuration containing instances of λ, μ and ψ, such that both instances of λ and μ are surrounded by an instance of an ambient labeled with l_λ, ψ is located in the

$$C_0^\sharp = \beta^\sharp(\mathcal{S}, \varepsilon^\sharp, [\text{top} \mapsto dpush(\varepsilon^\sharp)], \emptyset)$$

Fig. 5. Abstract Initial Configuration.

Let $(f,g) \in \mathcal{C}^\sharp$, if there are $\lambda = n^i[\bullet]$, $\mu = m^j[\bullet]$, $\psi = in^k o.P$,
if $\bigsqcup_{10}\{A(l_\lambda, n_m) \mid l_\lambda \in Lbl,\ n_m \in \mathcal{BN}(\mathcal{S})\} \neq \perp_{10}^\sharp$,
then $(f,g) \overset{in(i,j,k)}{\rightsquigarrow} \bigsqcup^\sharp\{(f',g); \beta^\sharp(P, id^\sharp, loc^\sharp, E^\sharp)\}$ where

- $A(l_\lambda, n_m) = assert(sync, f(\lambda, l_\lambda) \bullet^\sharp f(\mu, l_\lambda) \bullet^\sharp f(\psi, i) \bullet^\sharp g(\mu, m, n_m) \bullet^\sharp g(\psi, o, n_m))$,
- $sync = \{(2,4); (1,6); (8,10); (3,7); (5,9)\}$,
- $f' = f[(\lambda, j) \mapsto \bigsqcup_2(\{f(\lambda, j)\} \cup \{\Pi_{(1,3)}(A(l_\lambda, n_m)) \mid l_\lambda \in Lbl,\ n_m \in \mathcal{BN}(\mathcal{S})\})]$,
- $id^\sharp = \bigsqcup_1\{\Pi_{(5)}(A(l_\lambda, n_m)) \mid l_\lambda \in Lbl, n_m \in \mathcal{BN}(\mathcal{S})\}$,
- $loc^\sharp = [i \mapsto \bigsqcup_2\{\Pi_{(5,6)}(A(l_\lambda, n_m)) \mid l_\lambda \in Lbl, n_m \in \mathcal{BN}(\mathcal{S})\}]$,
- $E^\sharp = [(q,r) \mapsto \Pi_{(1,2)}(assert(\{(1,3)\}, (g(\phi, q, r) \bullet^\sharp id^\sharp))), \forall(q,r) \in \mathcal{BN}(\mathcal{S})^2]$.

Let $(f,g) \in \mathcal{C}^\sharp$, if there are $\lambda = m^i[\bullet]$, $\mu = n^j[\bullet]$, $\psi = out^k o.P$,
if $\bigsqcup_{10}\{A(l_\lambda, n_m) \mid l_\lambda \in Lbl,\ n_m \in \mathcal{BN}(\mathcal{S})\} \neq \perp_{10}^\sharp$,
then $(f,g) \overset{out(i,j,k)}{\rightsquigarrow} \bigsqcup^\sharp\{(f',g); \beta^\sharp(P, id^\sharp, loc^\sharp, E^\sharp)\}$ where

- $A(l_\lambda, n_m) = assert(sync, f(\lambda, l_\lambda) \bullet^\sharp f(\mu, i) \bullet^\sharp f(\psi, j) \bullet^\sharp g(\lambda, m, n_m) \bullet^\sharp g(\psi, o, n_m))$,
- $sync = \{(1,4); (1,7); (3,6); (5,9); (8,10)\}$,
- $f' = f[(\mu, l_\lambda) \mapsto \bigsqcup_2(\{f(\mu, l_\lambda)\} \cup \{\Pi_{(3,2)}(A(l_\lambda, n_m)) \mid n_m \in \mathcal{BN}(\mathcal{S})\})]$,
- $id^\sharp = \bigsqcup_1(\{\Pi_{(5)}(A(l_\lambda, n_m)) \mid l_\lambda \in Lbl, n_m \in \mathcal{BN}(\mathcal{S})\})$,
- $loc^\sharp = [i \mapsto \bigsqcup_2(\{\Pi_{(5,6)}(A(l_\lambda, n_m)) \mid l_\lambda \in Lbl, n_m \in \mathcal{BN}(\mathcal{S})\})]$,
- $E^\sharp = [(q,r) \mapsto \Pi_{(1,2)}(assert(\{(1,3)\}, (g(\phi, q, r) \bullet^\sharp id^\sharp))), \forall(q,r) \in \mathcal{BN}(\mathcal{S})^2]$.

Let $(f,g) \in \mathcal{C}^\sharp$, if there are $\lambda = open^i m.P$, $\mu = n^j[\bullet]$,
if $\bigsqcup_8\{A(l_\lambda, n_m) \mid l_\lambda \in Lbl,\ n_m \in \mathcal{BN}(\mathcal{S})\} \neq \perp_8^\sharp$,
then $(f,g) \overset{open(i,j)}{\rightsquigarrow} \bigsqcup^\sharp\{(f',g); \beta^\sharp(P, id^\sharp, loc^\sharp, E^\sharp)\}$ where

- $A(l_\lambda, n_m) = assert(sync, f(\lambda, l_\lambda) \bullet^\sharp f(\mu, l_\lambda) \bullet^\sharp g(\lambda, m, n_m) \bullet^\sharp g(\mu, o, n_m))$,
- $sync = \{(1,5); (2,4); (3,7); (6,8)\}$,
- $f' = f[(\psi, l_\lambda) \mapsto \bigsqcup_2(\{f(\psi, l_\lambda)\} \cup \{B(\psi, l_\lambda, n_m) \mid n_m \in \mathcal{BN}(\mathcal{S})\}), \forall \psi \in \mathcal{P}]$,
  where $B(\psi, l_\lambda, n_m) = \Pi_{(9,2)}(assert(\{(3,10)\}, A(l_\lambda, n_m) \bullet^\sharp f(\psi, j)))$,
- $id^\sharp = \bigsqcup_1\{\Pi_{(1)}(A(l_\lambda, n_m)) \mid l_\lambda \in Lbl,\ n_m \in \mathcal{BN}(\mathcal{S})\}$,
- $loc^\sharp = [l_\lambda \mapsto \bigsqcup_2\{\Pi_{(1,2)}(A(l_\lambda, n_m)) \mid n_m \in \mathcal{BN}(\mathcal{S})\}, \forall l_\lambda \in Lbl]$,
- $E^\sharp = [(q,r) \mapsto \Pi_{(1,2)}(assert(\{(1,3)\}, (g(\lambda, q, r) \bullet^\sharp id^\sharp))), \forall(q,r) \in \mathcal{BN}(\mathcal{S})^2]$.

Let $(f,g) \in \mathcal{C}^\sharp$, if there are $\lambda = !open^i m.P$, $\mu = n^j[\bullet]$,
if $\bigsqcup_8\{A(l_\lambda, n_m) \mid l_\lambda \in Lbl,\ n_m \in \mathcal{BN}(\mathcal{S})\} \neq \perp_8^\sharp$,
then $(f,g) \overset{open(i,j)}{\rightsquigarrow} \bigsqcup^\sharp\{(f',g); \beta^\sharp(P, id^\sharp, loc^\sharp, E^\sharp)\}$ where

- $A(l_\lambda, n_m) = assert(sync, f(\lambda, l_\lambda) \bullet^\sharp f(\mu, l_\lambda) \bullet^\sharp g(\lambda, m, n_m) \bullet^\sharp g(\mu, o, n_m))$,
- $sync = \{(1,5); (2,4); (3,7); (6,8)\}$,
- $f' = f[(\psi, l_\lambda) \mapsto \bigsqcup_2(\{f(\psi, l_\lambda)\} \cup \{I(\psi, l_\lambda, n_m) \mid n_m \in \mathcal{BN}(\mathcal{S})\}), \forall \psi \in \mathcal{P}]$
  where $I(\psi, l_\lambda, n_m) = \Pi_{(9,2)}(assert(\{(3,10)\}, A(l_\lambda, n_m) \bullet^\sharp f(\psi, j)))$,
- $id^\sharp = \bigsqcup_1\{\Pi_{(1)}(loc^\sharp(l_\lambda)) \mid \forall l_\lambda \in Lbl\}$,
- $loc^\sharp = [l_\lambda \mapsto push_{(i,j)}(\bigsqcup_3\{\Pi_{(1,3,2)}(A(l_\lambda, n_m)) \mid n_m \in \mathcal{BN}(\mathcal{S})\}), \forall l_\lambda \in Lbl]$,
- $E^\sharp = [(q,r) \mapsto push_{(i,j)}\bigsqcup_3\{I(q, r, l_\lambda, n_m) \mid l_\lambda \in Lbl,\ n_m \in Lbl\}, \forall(q,r) \in \mathcal{BN}(\mathcal{S})^2]$
  where $I(q, r, l_\lambda, n_m) = \Pi_{(1,3,10)}(assert(\{(1,9)\}, A(l_\lambda, n_m) \bullet^\sharp g(\lambda, q, r)))$.

Fig. 6. Abstract Move Rules.

Let $(f, g) \in \mathcal{C}^{\sharp}$, if there are $\lambda = (n)^i.P$, $\mu = \langle m \rangle^j$ two sub-processes of $\mathcal{S}$, if $\bigsqcup_4 \{A(l_\lambda) \mid l_\lambda \in Lbl\} \neq \perp_4^{\sharp}$,

then $(f, g) \overset{com(i,j)}{\rightsquigarrow} \bigsqcup^{\sharp} \{(f, g); \beta^{\sharp}(P, id^{\sharp}, loc^{\sharp}, E^{\sharp})\}$ where

- $A(l_\lambda) = assert(\{(2, 4)\}, f(\lambda, l_\lambda) \bullet^{\sharp} f(\mu, l_\lambda))$
- $id^{\sharp} = \bigsqcup_1 (\{\Pi_{(1)}(A(l_\lambda)) \mid \forall l_\lambda \in Lbl\})$,
- $loc^{\sharp} = [l_\lambda \mapsto \Pi_{(1,2)}(A(l_\lambda)), \forall l_\lambda \in Lbl]$,
- $E^{\sharp} = [(q, r) \mapsto \bigsqcup_2 \{I(q, r, l_\lambda) \mid l_\lambda \in Lbl\}, \forall (q, r) \in \mathcal{BN}(\mathcal{S})^2]$

where $I(q, r, l_\lambda) = \begin{cases} \Pi_{(1,6)}(assert(\{(3, 5)\}, A(l_\lambda) \bullet^{\sharp} g(\mu, m, r))) & \text{if } q = n \\ \Pi_{(1,6)}(assert(\{(1, 5)\}, A(l_\lambda) \bullet^{\sharp} g(\lambda, q, r))) & \text{otherwise} \end{cases}$

Let $(f, g) \in \mathcal{C}^{\sharp}$, if there are $\lambda =\,!(n)^i.P$, $\mu = \langle m \rangle^j$ two sub-processes of $\mathcal{S}$, if $\bigsqcup_4 \{A(l_\lambda) \mid l_\lambda \in Lbl\} \neq \perp_4^{\sharp}$,

then $(f, g) \overset{com(i,j)}{\rightsquigarrow} \bigsqcup^{\sharp} \{(f, g); \beta^{\sharp}(P, id^{\sharp}, loc^{\sharp}, E^{\sharp})\}$ where

- $A(l_\lambda) = assert(\{(2, 4)\}, f(\lambda, l_\lambda) \bullet^{\sharp} f(\mu, l_\lambda))$,
- $id^{\sharp} = \bigsqcup_1 \{\Pi_{(1)}(loc^{\sharp}(l_\lambda)) \mid l_\lambda \in Lbl\}$,
- $loc^{\sharp} = [l_\lambda \mapsto push_{(i,j)}(\Pi_{(1,3,2)}(A(l_\lambda))), \forall l_\lambda \in Lbl]$,
- $E^{\sharp} = [(q, r) \mapsto \bigsqcup_2 \{I(q, r, l_\lambda) \mid l_\lambda \in Lbl\} \forall (q, r) \in \mathcal{BN}(\mathcal{S})^2]$ where

$I(q, r, l_\lambda) = \begin{cases} push_{(i,j)}(\Pi_{(1,3,6)}(assert(\{(3, 5)\}, A(l_\lambda) \bullet^{\sharp} g(\mu, m, r)))) & \text{if } q = n \\ push_{(i,j)}(\Pi_{(1,3,6)}(assert(\{(1, 5)\}, A(l_\lambda) \bullet^{\sharp} g(\lambda, q, r)))) & \text{otherwise} \end{cases}$

Fig. 7. Abstract Communication Rules.

instance of λ and both the ambient name of the instance μ and the name the capability of ψ work on are linked to an ambient name created by an instance of the action $(\nu\, n_m)$. We then compute $A(l_\lambda, n_m)$ which is a description of the relation between the involved markers: we first gather the descriptions of all the involved marker pair abstractions: the first three marker pair abstractions describe the location of λ, μ and ψ while the two last marker pair abstractions describe the linkage of the syntactic ambient names m in λ and o in ψ; we then take into account synchronization conditions between the components of these abstract tuples: the third and the seventh (resp. the fifth and the ninth) components shall be equal since they both denote the thread marker associated to μ (resp. ψ); the synchronization between the second and the fourth components denotes that λ and μ must be located in the same instance of the ambient labeled l_λ; the one between the first and the sixth denotes that ψ must be located in the good instance of the ambient λ and the one between the eight and the tenth enforces the equality between the ambient name of μ and the name the capability of ψ works on. We then extract from $A(l_\lambda, n_m)$ an approximation of the interactions which may be created by performing the *in* migration rule on this redex: the instance of λ can move inside the one of μ, keeping the same history marker (given by the first component of the abstract tuples), but its location marker is then the history marker of the instance of μ (given by the third component). We are left to spawn the continuation of ψ, all its markers remain unchanged. The other abstract rules follow the same schema.

6   Abstract Domain

Various domains can be used to instantiate the family of parametric domains $(Id_n)_{n\in\mathbb{N}}$, depending on the expected complexity and accuracy. We propose three particular instantiations. The first one abstracts away the information about markers. The result is an uniform control flow analysis. The second one only keeps the equality relationships among markers, and gives an analysis which presents strong connections with group creation [1]. The third one allows for the algebraic comparison of markers which is, to the best of our knowledge, out of the range of analyses presented in literature.

6.1   Uniform Control Flow Analysis

An uniform analysis can be obtained by instantiating all the elements of the family $(Id_n^\sharp)_{n\in\mathbb{N}}$ with the lattice $(\{\bot, \top\}, \sqsubseteq)$. $\{\bot, \top\}$ is related to $\wp(Id^n)$ by the following concretization function γ_n defined by $\gamma_n(\bot) = \emptyset$ and $\gamma_n(\top) = Id^n$.

The abstract primitives are then defined as follows:

- $\varepsilon^\sharp = \top$;

- $\forall A \in \wp(\{\bot; \top\})$, $\bigsqcup_n(A) = \begin{cases} \bot & \text{if } \top \notin A \\ \top & \text{otherwise}; \end{cases}$

- $\forall a, b \in \{\bot, \top\}$, $(a \bullet^\sharp b) = \begin{cases} \bot & \text{if } a = \bot \text{ or } b = \bot \\ \top & \text{if } a = \top \text{ and } b = \top; \end{cases}$

- $\forall a \in \{\bot, \top\}$, $assert(A, a) = a$, $\Pi_X(a) = a$ and $push_{(i,j)}(a) = a$.

The resulting analysis is always at least as precise as [17], but takes into account unreachable code.

6.2   Confinement

We now focus on the equality relationships between markers. This allows us to analyze whether an ambient name can only be communicated to the recursive instance which has created it, and whether a thread is always surrounded by an ambient activated by the recursive instance which have spawned it.

We define $Id_n^\sharp$ as the lifted set $\mathcal{G}_n \cup \bot_n$ of all the non-oriented graph having vertices in $[|1; n|]$. The transitive closure of a graph $(\mathcal{G}, \curvearrowright)$ is denoted by $(\mathcal{G}, \curvearrowright^*)$. The pre-order, the concretization function and the abstract primitives are defined on $\mathcal{G}_n$ as follows, and they can be easily lifted to $\mathcal{G}_n \cup \bot_n$:

- $\forall \curvearrowright_1, \curvearrowright_2 \in \wp([|1; n|]^2)$, $([|1; n|], \curvearrowright_1) \sqsubseteq_n ([|1; n|], \curvearrowright_2) \iff \curvearrowright_2 \subseteq \curvearrowright_1$;
- $\forall([|1; n|], \curvearrowright) \in \mathcal{G}_n$, $\gamma_n(([|1; n|], \curvearrowright)) = \{(id_i)_{i\in[|1;n|]} \mid k \curvearrowright l \implies id_k = id_l\}$;
- $\varepsilon^\sharp = (\{1\}, \emptyset)$;
- $\forall A \in \wp(\mathcal{G}_n)$, $\bigsqcup_n(A) = ([|1; n|]; \curvearrowright_\cup)$
  where $i \curvearrowright_\cup j \stackrel{\Delta}{\iff} \forall([|1; n|], \curvearrowright) \in A, i \curvearrowright^* j$;
- $\forall a = ([|1; n|], \curvearrowright_a) \in \mathcal{G}_n, b = ([|1; m|], \curvearrowright_b) \in \mathcal{G}_m$, $(a \bullet^\sharp b) = ([|1; n + m|], \curvearrowright_\bullet)$
  where $i \curvearrowright_\bullet j \stackrel{\Delta}{\iff} \begin{cases} i \curvearrowright_a j \text{ if } i, j \in [|1; n|] \\ (i - n) \curvearrowright_b (j - n) \text{ if } i, j \in [|n + 1; n + m|]; \end{cases}$

- $\forall([|1;n|],\curvearrowright)\in\mathcal{G}_n,\ A\in\wp([|1;n|]^2),\ assert(A,([|1;n|],\curvearrowright))=([|1;n|],A\cup\curvearrowright);$
- $\forall a=([|1;n|],\curvearrowright_a)\in\mathcal{G}_n,\ \Pi_{(s_k)_{k\in[|1;p|]}}(a)=([|1;p|],\curvearrowright_\Pi)$

where $i\curvearrowright_\Pi j \overset{\Delta}{\Longleftrightarrow} i,j\in[|1;p|],\ s_i\curvearrowright_a^* s_j;$
- $\forall a\in\mathcal{G}_3,\ push_{(i,j)}(a)=([|1;2|],\emptyset).$

As in [1] this analysis can only prove that an ambient name is confined inside the scope of the recursive instance which has declared it. It is unable to prove that a name which first exits this scope can then only be sent back to the recursive instance which had created it.

6.3   Non-uniform Analysis with Algebraic Comparisons

We now abstract algebraic comparisons between markers. Following Prop. 1, we only abstract the right comb of each tree. We then use the reduced-product of two abstractions. Our first abstraction consists in abstracting component-wise the shape of the history markers associated to threads, their locations, and their ambient names. We use a regular description of sets of trees: we introduce Id_n^{Reg} as the set of all the n-uples of regular automata over the alphabet Lbl^2. Id_n^{Reg} is related to $\wp(Id^n)$ by the following concretization function:

$$\gamma_n((A_i)_{i\in[|1;n|]})=\{(id_i)_{i\in[|1;n|]}\mid \forall i\in[|1;n|],\ \phi_1(id_i)\in\mathcal{L}(A_i)\}$$

- $\varepsilon^\sharp$ is an automaton which only recognizes the word ε;
- $\bigsqcup_n$ applies component-wise the classical finite union of regular automata;
- $\bullet^\sharp$ (resp. Π) is the classical concatenation (resp. projection) of tuples;
- $assert(\{(a,b)\}\cup A,Q)_i=\begin{cases}(assert(A,Q))_i & \text{if } i\notin\{a;b\}\\ (assert(A,Q))_a\cap(assert(A,Q))_b & \text{otherwise}\end{cases}$
- since there can be infinite increasing sequences of regular languages, we need a widening operator ∇. It is sufficient to construct a widening operator for regular automata and to apply it component-wise. Given $\delta\in\mathbb{N}^*$, a convenient choice for $A_1\nabla A_2$ consists in quotienting the set of the states of the automaton $A_1\cup A_2$ by the relation $\sim_\delta$ that identifies the states of an automaton which have the same δ-depth residues[5]. The higher δ is, the more accurate and expensive the analysis is.

Our second abstraction captures non-uniform comparisons between the number of occurrences of each pattern inside sets of marker pairs. For each $n\in\mathbb{N}$, we introduce the set $\mathcal{V}_n$ of distinct variables $\{x_i^\lambda\mid i\in[|1;n|],\ \lambda\in Lbl^2\}$. The abstract domain $\wp(\mathbb{N}^{\mathcal{V}_n})$ is related to $\wp(Id^n)$ by the monotonic map γ_n:

$$\gamma_n(A)=\{(id_i)_{i\in[|1;n|]}\mid \exists(n_t)_{t\in\mathcal{V}_n}\in A,\ \forall x_i^\lambda\in\mathcal{V}_n,\ n_{x_i^\lambda}=|\phi_1(id_i)|_\lambda\}.$$

$\wp(Id^n)$ is then related to the complete lattice of the affine equality systems on the set of variables $\mathcal{V}_n$, denoted by Id_n^{rel}. This domain is described with its lattice operations in [14]. We describe the remaining abstract primitives as follows:

---

[5] The δ-depth residue set of a state q in a labeled transition system $(\mathcal{Q},\Sigma,\rightarrow)$ is defined as $\{u\in\Sigma^*\mid|u|\leqslant\delta\text{ and }\exists q'\in\mathcal{Q}\ q\overset{u}{\rightarrow}q'\}.$

- $\varepsilon^\sharp$ is given by the system $\{x_1^\lambda = 0, \forall \lambda \in Lbl^2;$
- given $K \in Id_n^{rel}$ and $K' \in Id_m^{rel}$, we obtain the abstract concatenation of K and K', by renaming each variable x_i^λ to x_{i+n}^λ in K', and gathering all the constrains of the two systems;
- $assert(\{i_1 = j_1; ...; i_p = j_p\}, K)$ corresponds to inserting all the constrains of the form $x_{i_k}^\lambda = x_{j_k}^\lambda$, $\forall k \in [|1; p|]$, $\lambda \in Lbl^2$ in K;
- $\Pi_{(i_1,...,i_p)}(K)$ corresponds to collect all the constrains involving just the variables $\{x_{i_k}^\lambda\}$ and then renaming each variable $x_{i_k}^\lambda$ into the variable x_k^λ;
- $push_{(i,j)}(K)$ is obtained by replacing in each constrains each occurrence of the variable $x_2^{(i,j)}$ by the expression $x_2^{(i,j)} - 1$ and then applying the abstract projection $\Pi_{(2,3)}$.

Example 3. We run the third analysis on the system of Example 1, we denote the result by (f, g). We succeed in proving that an ambient name created by the binder $(\nu\ q)$ can only be communicated either to the agent $\langle q \rangle^{14}$ in a "request" ambient surrounded by an p ambient, or to the agent $\langle rep \rangle^9$ in a "answer" ambient surrounded by an p ambient. In the second case, we also capture these properties:

$$\begin{cases} \gamma_2(g(\langle rep \rangle^9, rep, q)) = \{(3.19).(11, 20)^n.(11, 21), (11, 20)^n(11, 21)\} \\ \gamma_2(f(\langle rep \rangle^9, 8)) = \{(3.19).(11, 20)^n.(11, 21), (3.19).(11, 20)^n.(11, 21)\} \\ \gamma_2(f(\text{answer}^8[\bullet], 12)) = \{(3.19).(11, 20)^n.(11, 21), (11, 20)^n.(11, 21)\} \\ \gamma_2(g(p^{12}[\bullet], p, p) = \{(11, 20)^n.(11, 21), (11, 20)^n.(11, 21)\}, \end{cases}$$

this proves that the ambient name communicated inside the "query" ambient and the name of the packet which surrounds this "query" ambient have been both declared by the same recursive instance of the client resource.   □

Remark 2. Our confinement analysis is not an abstraction of our non-uniform analysis, because two distinct markers may be recognized by the same automaton while containing the same occurrence number of each pattern (i.e having the same Parikh vector [19]). The equality of the Parikh vector implies the equality of markers if they are recognized by an automaton only composed of an acyclic path between an initial and a final state and without embedded cycle, and such that the set of the Parikh vectors of the cycles of this automaton are linearly independent. Nevertheless, we may use the reduced product of both our confinement analysis and our non-uniform control flow analysis to solve this problem.

6.4   About the Complexity of Our Analyses

We shortly describe the time complexity of our analyses. In the following table, the first line denotes the redex detection and information propagation, the second line denotes the cost of performing an abstract operation and the third one denotes the maximum iteration number.

	0-CFA	confinement	ω-CFA
scan	$t.n^2.i_p$	$t.n^2.i_p$	$t.n^2.i_p$
domain complexity	1	1	σ^3
height of the abstract iteration	i	i	$i.\sigma^\delta$
time-complexity	$i.t.n^2.i_p$	$i.t.n^2.i_p$	$i.t.n^2.\sigma^{\delta+3}.i_p$

where N is the system length; t is the number of the distinct transition labels which occur during the analysis: t is cubic in the worst case, but is only quasi-linear in practice; n is the sum of the number of name binders and the number of ambient activators: it is linear in N; i is the number of interactions between the agents of the system: in practice i is quasi-quadratic in N, but is cubic in the worst case; i_p is a bound to the number of the interactions with Q, for any fixed process Q: i_p is quadratic in worst case in N, but is quasi-linear in practice; σ is the number of pattern occurring in markers: it is either linear or quadratic in N, depending on the choice for the history markers (Cf. Prop. 1); $\delta \in \mathbb{N}^*$ is chosen as a parameter of our abstraction.

Both effective transitions and effective interactions are detected during our iteration. This allows us to speed up the analysis, the cost of which only depends on the number of both effective transition kinds and effective interactions.

7 Conclusion and Perspectives

We have described a parametric framework for automatically inferring a description of the interferences between recursive instances of the agents of a mobile ambient in a polynomial time. Our framework also applies when extending the model with mobility control [15] or higher order communication. As in the π-calculus [9], we would like to extend this framework to analyze the behaviour of an open system executed in a hostile context.

This framework is highly extensible and is very likely to be enriched by an occurrence counting analysis. Analyses in literature [11, 18] are not polynomial, but we are working on a polynomial one inspired by [10]. Our long-range forecast is to use the low-level properties we compute to synthesize high-level properties which may be expressed in a modal logic as suggested in [3].

Acknowledgments. We deeply thank anonymous referees for their significant comments on an early version of this paper. We wish also to thank Patrick and Radhia Cousot, Arnaud Venet, Antoine Miné and Francesco Logozzo, for their comments and discussions.

References

1. L. Cardelli, G. Ghelli, and A. D. Gordon. Ambient groups and mobility types. In *Proc. TCS'00*, LNCS, pages 333–347. Springer, 2000.
2. L. Cardelli and A. D. Gordon. Types for mobile ambients. In *Proc. POPL'99*, pages 79–92. ACM, 1999.
3. L. Cardelli and A. D. Gordon. Anytime, anywhere: Modal logics for mobile ambients. In *Proc. POPL'00*, pages 365–377. ACM Press, 2000.
4. Luca Cardelli and A. D. Gordon. Mobile ambients. *Theoretical Computer Science*, 240(1):177–213, June 2000.
5. P. Cousot. Semantic foundations of program analysis. In S.S. Muchnick and N.D. Jones, editors, *Program Flow Analysis: Theory and Applications*, chapter 10, pages 303–342. Prentice-Hall, Inc., Englewood Cliffs, 1981.
6. P. Cousot and R. Cousot. Abstract interpretation: a unified lattice model for static analysis of programs by construction or approximation of fixpoints. In *Proc. POPL'77*, pages 238–252, Los Angeles, California, U.S.A., 1977.
7. P. Cousot and R. Cousot. Abstract interpretation frameworks. *Journal of logic and computation*, 2(4):511–547, 1992.
8. P. Cousot and R. Cousot. Comparing the Galois connection and widening-narrowing approaches to abstract interpretation. In *Proc. PLILP'92*, LNCS, pages 269–295. Springer, 1992.
9. J. Feret. Confidentiality analysis of mobile systems. In *Proc. SAS'00*, LNCS, pages 135–154. Springer, 2000.
10. J. Feret. Occurrence counting analysis for the pi-calculus. *Electronic Notes in Theoretical Computer Science*, 39(2), 2001.
11. R. R. Hansen, J. G. Jensen, F. Nielson, and H. Riis Nielson. Abstract interpretation of mobile ambients. In *Proc. SAS'99*, LNCS, pages 134–148. Springer, 1999.
12. M. Hennessy and J. Riely. Resource access control in systems of mobile agents. In *Proc. HLCL'98*, ENTCS. Elsevier, 1998.
13. M. Hennessy and J. Riely. A typed language for distributed mobile processes. In *Proc. POPL'98*. ACM Press, 1998.
14. M. Karr. Affine relationships among variables of a program. *Acta Informatica*, pages 133–151, 1976.
15. F. Levi and D. Sangiorgi. Controlling interference in ambients. In *Proc. POPL'00*, pages 352–364. ACM Press, 2000.
16. R. Milner, J. Parrow, and D. Walker. A calculus of mobile processes. *Information and Computation*, pages 1–77, 1992.
17. F. Nielson, H. Riis Nielson, R. R. Hansen, and J. G. Jensen. Validating firewalls in mobile ambients. In *Proc. CONCUR'99*, LNCS, pages 463–477. Springer, 1999.
18. H. Riis Nielson and F. Nielson. Shape analysis for mobile ambients. In *Proc. POPL'00*, pages 142–154. ACM Press, 2000.
19. R. J. Parikh. On context-free languages. *Journal of the ACM*, 13:570–581, 1966.
20. A. Venet. Automatic determination of communication topologies in mobile systems. In *Proc. SAS'98*, LNCS, pages 152–167. Springer, 1998.

Static Analysis and Software Assurance

David Wagner

EECS Computer Science Division
University of California, Berkeley
Berkeley, CA 94720-1776, USA
daw@cs.berkeley.edu
http://www.cs.berkeley.edu/~daw/

Abstract. In the past decade, explosive growth in computer networks has brought security issues to the forefront. One of the greatest challenges in computer security today is the software assurance problem: How do we deal with the fact that our most trusted software, even our security software itself, is often buggy?

In this talk, I will discuss how static analysis can help with the software assurance problem. I will describe some recent experience with static analysis tools for vulnerability detection. I will also survey a number of open problems in the field and suggest a few promising directions for future research.

P. Cousot (Ed.): SAS 2001, LNCS 2126, pp. 431–431, 2001.

A Type and Effect Analysis
of Security Protocols

Andrew D. Gordon[1] and Alan Jeffrey[2]

[1] Microsoft Research
[2] DePaul University

Abstract. We propose a new method to check authenticity properties of cryptographic protocols. First, code up the protocol in the spi-calculus of Abadi and Gordon. Second, specify authenticity properties by annotating the code with correspondence assertions in the style of Woo and Lam. Third, figure out types for the keys, nonces, and messages of the protocol. Fourth, check that the spi-calculus code is well-typed according to a novel type and effect system. Our main theorem guarantees that any well-typed protocol is robustly safe, that is, its correspondence assertions are true in the presence of any opponent expressible in spi. It is feasible to apply this method by hand to several well-known cryptographic protocols. It requires little human effort per protocol, puts no bound on the size of the opponent, and requires no state space enumeration. Moreover, the types for protocol data provide some intuitive explanation of how the protocol works. Our method has led us to the independent rediscovery of flaws in existing protocols and to the design of improved protocols. My talk will describe our method and give some simple examples. Papers describing the method in detail appear elsewhere [1, 2].

References

1. A.D. Gordon and A. Jeffrey. Authenticity by typing for security protocols. In *14th IEEE Computer Security Foundations Workshop*. IEEE Computer Society Press, 2001. To appear.
2. A.D. Gordon and A. Jeffrey. Typing correspondence assertions for communication protocols. In *Mathematical Foundations of Programming Semantics 17*, Electronic Notes in Theoretical Computer Science. Elsevier, 2001. To appear.

P. Cousot (Ed.): SAS 2001, LNCS 2126, pp. 432–432, 2001.

Abstracting Cryptographic Protocols
by Prolog Rules

Bruno Blanchet

INRIA Rocquencourt
B.P. 105, 78153 Le Chesnay Cedex, France
Bruno.Blanchet@inria.fr

Abstract. Most current cryptographic protocol verifiers meet the state space explosion problem, and have to limit the number of executions of the considered protocol during the verification. To solve these problems, we introduce an abstract representation of cryptographic protocols, based on Prolog rules, and use it to verify secrecy properties of protocols.

1 Introduction

This short summary is a reference for the author's invited talk for SAS'01. It presents a new technique for verifying cryptographic protocols, that is described in detail in [5]. The design of cryptographic protocols is difficult and error-prone. This can be illustrated by attacks found in existing protocols [1, 4, 8, 13]. It is therefore important to have automatic tools to verify these protocols. Many different techniques have been used in this area: model-checking [13], rewriting [9], theorem proving [15], typing [2], abstract interpretation [6, 11, 14] (more references can be found in [5]). One of the most widely used techniques is model-checking, but it meets two important problems:

- A first problem is the state space explosion: even for small specifications of protocols, the number of states to explore during verification is very large. Then, the verification of complex protocols becomes impossible.
- Most model-checking tools limit the number of the runs of the protocol, to ensure the termination of the verification process. Indeed, at each run, the protocol creates new values. For an unbounded number of runs, an unbounded number of new values would be needed, and the number of states would be infinite. However, limiting the number of runs of the protocol has serious consequences: an attack that appears with more runs will remain undiscovered. This is a problem for the certification of protocols, and manual proofs have to be done to show that the result obtained for a small number of runs extends to an unbounded number.

These problems have already been tackled by previous works: [17] avoids the state space explosion by using the Strand Space Model, but still sometimes limits the number of runs of the protocol to guarantee termination. [7, 16] do

P. Cousot (Ed.): SAS 2001, LNCS 2126, pp. 433–436, 2001.
© Springer-Verlag Berlin Heidelberg 2001

not limit the number of runs of the protocol, by recycling the new values created at each run. However, they limit the number of *parallel* runs of protocols.

We introduce an abstract representation of cryptographic protocols, based on Horn clauses (the basis of Prolog), that solves these problems by performing well-chosen approximations that preserve attacks. This representation yields a more efficient analysis than [14], by representing rules that generate the knowledge of the attacker, instead of representing this knowledge by tree automata. It is also more precise than [6], since our analysis is relational, and it distinguishes values created at the same point of the protocol in different sessions.

2   Representation of Cryptographic Protocols

We assume that the protocol is executed in the presence of an attacker that can listen to messages, compute, and send messages.

In our representation, messages are represented by terms. For instance, the term $\mathsf{pencrypt}(c_0, \mathsf{pk}(sk))$ represents the encryption of c_0 under the public key $\mathsf{pk}(sk)$, corresponding to the secret key sk. The facts are of the form $\mathsf{attacker}(M)$ meaning that the attacker may have the term M. Our abstract representation of the protocol consists of inference rules of the knowledge of the attacker. For example, the rule:

$$\mathsf{attacker}(\mathsf{pencrypt}(m, \mathsf{pk}(sk))) \wedge \mathsf{attacker}(sk) \rightarrow \mathsf{attacker}(m)$$

means that the attacker can decrypt a message when it has the secret key: if the attacker has the encrypted message $\mathsf{pencrypt}(m, \mathsf{pk}(sk))$ and the secret key sk, it can obtain the cleartext m.

We also represent the actions of the agents involved in the protocol as inference rules of the knowledge of the attacker. Indeed, if the agent A has received the messages $M_1, \ldots, M_n$, and sends the message M, we consider that the attacker has relayed the messages $M_1, \ldots, M_n$ and intercepts A's reply M. This yields the rule:

$$\mathsf{attacker}(M_1) \wedge \ldots \wedge \mathsf{attacker}(M_n) \rightarrow \mathsf{attacker}(M).$$

If the attacker has the messages $M_1, \ldots, M_n$, it can send them to A, simulating the beginning of a protocol run, and obtain the reply M.

Using these principles, we can abstract a cryptographic protocol by a set of Horn clauses. This representation is obviously an abstraction of the multi-set rewriting representation [9]: the number of times a message appears is ignored, to remember only that it has appeared. It is also an abstraction of the linear logic representation of [10]. Moreover, we have built an automatic translator from the applied pi calculus [3] (restricted to certain equational theories) to our representation. Our representation is more abstract than most usual ones:

- The messages are not organized into separate runs. For instance, the ith step of the protocol can be repeated several times when the previous steps have been executed only once. More generally, a step of the protocol can be repeated any number of times as soon as the previous steps have been executed at least once.

- Moreover, the freshness of nonces is modeled by considering fresh values as functions of the messages previously received by the creator of the value. Therefore, the fresh values are considered as different if and only if the previous messages are different. The same nonces are reused in several sessions of the protocol, when the previous messages are the same. Therefore, we can have a finite space even when considering an infinite number of sessions.

These approximations are keys to an efficient verification of the protocols, and enable us not to limit the number of executions of the considered protocol.

3   Verifying Secrecy Properties

We use our representation to verify secrecy properties of protocols: if the fact attacker(M) cannot be derived from the rules representing the protocol, then the adversary cannot have M, and the term M remains secret. This is exactly the kind of information that usual Prolog systems compute. However, they do not terminate on the rules representing a protocol, so we have designed, proved correct, and implemented an efficient algorithm to handle this particular situation. This algorithm is fully detailed in [5].

The experimental results show that many examples of protocols of the literature, including Skeme [12], can be analyzed by our tool with very small resources: from less than 0.1 s for simple protocols to 23 s for the main mode of Skeme, and less than 2 Mb of memory.

References

[1] Martín Abadi. Explicit Communication Revisited: Two New Attacks on Authentication Protocols. *IEEE Transactions on Software Engineering*, 23(3):185–186, March 1997.

[2] Martín Abadi. Secrecy by typing in security protocols. In *Theoretical Aspects of Computer Software*, volume 1281 of *Lecture Notes on Computer Science*, pages 611–638. Springer Verlag, 1997.

[3] Martín Abadi and Cédric Fournet. Mobile Values, News Names, and Secure Communication. In *28th Annual ACM SIGPLAN-SIGACT Symposium on Principles of Programming Languages (POPL '01)*, pages 104–115, London, United Kingdom, January 2001. ACM Press.

[4] Martín Abadi and Roger Needham. Prudent engineering practice for cryptographic protocols. *IEEE Transactions on Software Engineering*, 22(1):6–15, January 1996.

[5] Bruno Blanchet. An Efficient Cryptographic Protocol Verifier Based on Prolog Rules. In *14th IEEE Computer Security Foundations Workshop (CSFW-14)*, Cape Breton, Canada, June 2001.

[6] Chiara Bodei. *Security Issues in Process Calculi*. PhD thesis, Università di Pisa, January 2000.

[7] Philippa Broadfoot, Gavin Lowe, and Bill Roscoe. Automating Data Independence. In *6th European Symposium on Research in Computer Security (ES-ORICS 2000)*, volume 1895 of *Lecture Notes on Computer Science*, pages 175–190, Toulouse, France, October 2000. Springer Verlag.

[8] Michael Burrows, Martín Abadi, and Roger Needham. A Logic of Authentication. *Proceedings of the Royal Society of London A*, 426:233–271, 1989. A preliminary version appeared as Digital Equipment Corporation Systems Research Center report No. 39, February 1989.

[9] Grit Denker, Jose Meseguer, and Carolyn Talcott. Protocol Specification and Analysis in Maude. In N. Heintze and J. Wing, editors, *Proc. of Workshop on Formal Methods and Security Protocols*, Indianapolis, Indiana, 25 June 1998.

[10] N. A. Durgin, P. D. Lincoln, J. C. Mitchell, and A. Scedrov. Undecidability of bounded security protocols. In *Workshop on Formal Methods and Security Protocols (FMSP'99)*, Trento, Italy, 5 July 1999.

[11] Jean Goubault-Larrecq. A Method for Automatic Cryptographic Protocol Verification (Extended Abstract), invited paper. In *Fifth International Workshop on Formal Methods for Parallel Programming: Theory and Applications (FMPPTA'2000)*, Cancún, Mexique, May 2000. Springer-Verlag.

[12] Hugo Krawczyk. SKEME: A Versatile Secure Key Exchange Mechanism for Internet. In *Proceedings of the Internet Society Symposium on Network and Distributed Systems Security*, February 1996. Available at http://bilbo.isu.edu/sndss/sndss96.html.

[13] Gavin Lowe. Breaking and Fixing the Needham-Schroeder Public-Key Protocol using FDR. In *Tools and Algorithms for the Construction and Analysis of Systems*, volume 1055 of *Lecture Notes on Computer Science*, pages 147–166. Springer Verlag, 1996.

[14] David Monniaux. Abstracting Cryptographic Protocols with Tree Automata. In *Static Analysis Symposium (SAS'99)*, volume 1694 of *Lecture Notes on Computer Science*, pages 149–163. Springer Verlag, September 1999.

[15] Larry C. Paulson. The Inductive Approach to Verifying Cryptographic Protocols. *Journal of Computer Security*, 6(1–2):85–128, 1998.

[16] A.W. Roscoe and P.J. Broadfoot. Proving Security Protocols with Model Checkers by Data Independence Techniques. *Journal of Computer Security*, 7(2, 3):147–190, 1999.

[17] Dawn Xiaodong Song. Athena: a New Efficient Automatic Checker for Security Protocol Analysis. In *Proc. of 12th IEEE Computer Security Foundation Workshop (CSFW-12)*, Mordano, Italy, June 1999.

Security-Typed Languages
and Distributed Computation

Andrew Myers

Computer Science Department
Cornell University
andru@cs.cornell.edu
http://www.cs.cornell.edu/andru/

Abstract. Recently there has been considerable interest in programming languages that encode security policies in type declarations. Type-checking is used to determine whether a program enforces these policies. This approach enjoys many of the benefits of static type-checking, but is particularly of interest because it can enforce information flow properties such as noninterference, for which purely dynamic mechanisms are ineffective.

Enforcing information flow properties for distributed systems adds a new challenges: mutual distrust among the principals, and untrusted hosts. Our new approach, *secure program partitioning*, automatically rewrites a program into communicating subprograms that run securely on the set of available hosts yet collectively implement the original program. This fine-grained rewriting is based on the security types in the original program and the trust relationships among principals and hosts in the system. Computation in the original program is written in a single-host style, yet the resulting distributed system can satisfy the strong confidentiality and integrity properties specified by the program.

P. Cousot (Ed.): SAS 2001, LNCS 2126, pp. 437–437, 2001.

Author Index

Lecture Notes in Computer Science

For information about Vols. 1–2013
please contact your bookseller or Springer-Verlag

Vol. 2055: M. Margenstern, Y. Rogozhin (Eds.), Machines, Computations, and Universality. Proceedings, 2001. VIII, 321 pages. 2001.

Vol. 2056: E. Stroulia, S. Matwin (Eds.), Advances in Artificial Intelligence. Proceedings, 2001. XII, 366 pages. 2001. (Subseries LNAI).

Vol. 2057: M. Dwyer (Ed.), Model Checking Software. Proceedings, 2001. X, 313 pages. 2001.

Vol. 2059: C. Arcelli, L.P. Cordella, G. Sanniti di Baja (Eds.), Visual Form 2001. Proceedings, 2001. XIV, 799 pages. 2001.

Vol. 2060: T. Böhme, H. Unger (Eds.), Innovative Internet Computing Systems. Proceedings, 2001. VIII, 183 pages. 2001.

Vol. 2062: A. Nareyek, Constraint-Based Agents. XIV, 178 pages. 2001. (Subseries LNAI).

Vol. 2064: J. Blanck, V. Brattka, P. Hertling (Eds.), Computability and Complexity in Analysis. Proceedings, 2000. VIII, 395 pages. 2001.

Vol. 2065: H. Balster, B. de Brock, S. Conrad (Eds.), Database Schema Evolution and Meta-Modeling. Proceedings, 2000. X, 245 pages. 2001.

Vol. 2066: O. Gascuel, M.-F. Sagot (Eds.), Computational Biology. Proceedings, 2000. X, 165 pages. 2001.

Vol. 2068: K.R. Dittrich, A. Geppert, M.C. Norrie (Eds.), Advanced Information Systems Engineering. Proceedings, 2001. XII, 484 pages. 2001.

Vol. 2070: L. Monostori, J. Váncza, M. Ali (Eds.), Engineering of Intelligent Systems. Proceedings, 2001. XVIII, 951 pages. 2001. (Subseries LNAI).

Vol. 2071: R. Harper (Ed.), Types in Compilation. Proceedings, 2000. IX, 207 pages. 2001.

Vol. 2072: J. Lindskov Knudsen (Ed.), ECOOP 2001 – Object-Oriented Programming. Proceedings, 2001. XIII, 429 pages. 2001.

Vol. 2073: V.N. Alexandrov, J.J. Dongarra, B.A. Juliano, R.S. Renner, C.J.K. Tan (Eds.), Computational Science – ICCS 2001. Part I. Proceedings, 2001. XXVIII, 1306 pages. 2001.

Vol. 2074: V.N. Alexandrov, J.J. Dongarra, B.A. Juliano, R.S. Renner, C.J.K. Tan (Eds.), Computational Science – ICCS 2001. Part II. Proceedings, 2001. XXVIII, 1076 pages. 2001.

Vol. 2075: J.-M. Colom, M. Koutny (Eds.), Applications and Theory of Petri Nets 2001. Proceedings, 2001. XII, 403 pages. 2001.

Vol. 2076: F. Orejas, P.G. Spirakis, J. van Leeuwen (Eds.), Automata, Languages and Programming. Proceedings, 2001. XIV, 1083 pages. 2001.

Vol. 2077: V. Ambriola (Ed.), Software Process Technology. Proceedings, 2001. VIII, 247 pages. 2001.

Vol. 2078: R. Reed, J. Reed (Eds.), SDL 2001: Meeting UML. Proceedings, 2001. XI, 439 pages. 2001.

Vol. 2081: K. Aardal, B. Gerards (Eds.), Integer Programming and Combinatorial Optimization. Proceedings, 2001. XI, 423 pages. 2001.

Vol. 2082: M.F. Insana, R.M. Leahy (Eds.), Information Processing in Medical Imaging. Proceedings, 2001. XVI, 537 pages. 2001.

Vol. 2083: R. Goré, A. Leitsch, T. Nipkow (Eds.), Automated Reasoning. Proceedings, 2001. XV, 708 pages. 2001. (Subseries LNAI).

Vol. 2084: J. Mira, A. Prieto (Eds.), Connectionist Models of Neurons, Learning Processes, and Artificial Intelligence. Proceedings, 2001. Part I. XXVII, 836 pages. 2001.

Vol. 2085: J. Mira, A. Prieto (Eds.), Bio-Inspired Applications of Connectionism. Proceedings, 2001. Part II. XXVII, 848 pages. 2001.

Vol. 2086: M. Luck, V. Mařík, O. Stěpánková, R. Trappl (Eds.), Multi-Agent Systems and Applications. Proceedings, 2001. X, 437 pages. 2001. (Subseries LNAI).

Vol. 2089: A. Amir, G.M. Landau (Eds.), Combinatorial Pattern Matching. Proceedings, 2001. VIII, 273 pages. 2001.

Vol. 2091: J. Bigun, F. Smeraldi (Eds.), Audio- and Video-Based Biometric Person Authentication. Proceedings, 2001. XIII, 374 pages. 2001.

Vol. 2092: L. Wolf, D. Hutchison, R. Steinmetz (Eds.), Quality of Service – IWQoS 2001. Proceedings, 2001. XII, 435 pages. 2001.

Vol. 2093: P. Lorenz (Ed.), Networking – ICN 2001. Proceedings, 2001. Part I. XXV, 843 pages. 2001.

Vol. 2094: P. Lorenz (Ed.), Networking – ICN 2001. Proceedings, 2001. Part II. XXV, 899 pages. 2001.

Vol. 2095: B. Schiele, G. Sagerer (Eds.), Computer Vision Systems. Proceedings, 2001. X, 313 pages. 2001.

Vol. 2096: J. Kittler, F. Roli (Eds.), Multiple Classifier Systems. Proceedings, 2001. XII, 456 pages. 2001.

Vol. 2097: B. Read (Ed.), Advances in Databases. Proceedings, 2001. X, 219 pages. 2001.

Vol. 2098: J. Akiyama, M. Kano, M. Urabe (Eds.), Discrete and Computational Geometry. Proceedings, 2000. XI, 381 pages. 2001.

Vol. 2099: P. de Groote, G. Morrill, C. Retoré (Eds.), Logical Aspects of Computational Linguistics. Proceedings, 2001. VIII, 311 pages. 2001. (Subseries LNAI).

Vol. 2105: W. Kim, T.-W. Ling, Y-J. Lee, S.-S. Park (Eds.), The Human Society and the Internet. Proceedings, 2001. XVI, 470 pages. 2001.

Vol. 2106: M. Kerckhove (Ed.), Scale-Space and Morphology in Computer Vision. Proceedings, 2001. XI, 435 pages. 2001.

Vol. 2110: B. Hertzberger, A. Hoekstra, R. Williams (Eds.), High-Performance Computing and Networking. Proceedings, 2001. XVII, 733 pages. 2001.

Vol. 2118: X.S. Wang, G. Yu, H. Lu (Eds.), Advances in Web-Age Information Management. Proceedings, 2001. XV, 418 pages. 2001.

Vol. 2119: V. Varadharajan, Y. Mu (Eds.), Information Security and Privacy. Proceedings, 2001. XI, 522 pages. 2001.

Vol. 2121: C.S. Jensen, M. Schneider, B. Seeger, V.J. Tsotras (Eds.), Advances in Spatial and Temporal Databases. Proceedings, 2001. XI, 543 pages. 2001.

Vol. 2126: P. Cousot (Ed.), Static Analysis. Proceedings, 2001. XI, 439 pages. 2001.